PENGUIN BOOKS

DAMNED WHORES AND GOD'S POLICE

Anne Summers was born in Deniliquin, New South Wales, in 1945. She grew up in Adelaide where she attended Cabra Convent and the University of Adelaide before moving to Sydney, where she became active in the women's movement and began her writing career. In 1975, after the publication of this book, she joined the *National Times* as a feature writer and in 1976 won a Walkley award for a series of articles on NSW prisons. In 1978 she became a Fellow at the World Press Institute in St Paul, Minnesota, and in 1979 was appointed political correspondent for the *Australian Financial Review*. During her five years in the Canberra Press Gallery she was also Canberra correspondent for the *Far Eastern Economic Review* and Australian correspondent for *Le Monde*. In 1983 she was appointed to head the Office of the Status of Women in the Prime Minister's Department. In 1986 she rejoined the *Australian Financial Review* as United States editor in New York, and was also the North American manager for John Fairfax Ltd. From 1987 to 1989 she was editor-in-chief of *Ms.* magazine and co-owner of Matilda Publications, Inc., which owned *Ms.* and *Sassy* magazines. After several years as editor-at-large of *Ms.* she returned to Australia in June 1992 as a political consultant to Prime Minister Paul Keating, a position she held until just after the 1993 elections. She is presently editor of *Good Weekend* magazine. In 1989 she was made an Officer of the Order of Australia for services to the media and to women. She is also the author of *Gamble for Power* (1983) and, with Margaret Bettison, *Her Story: Australian Women in Print 1788–1975* (1980).

ANNE SUMMERS

Damned Whores

AND

God's

Police

PENGUIN BOOKS

Penguin Books Australia Ltd
487 Maroondah Highway, PO Box 257
Ringwood, Victoria 3134, Australia
Penguin Books Ltd
Harmondsworth, Middlesex, England
Viking Penguin, A Division of Penguin Books USA Inc
375 Hudson Street, New York, New York 10014, USA
Penguin Books Canada Limited
10 Alcorn Avenue, Toronto, Ontario, Canada M4V 3B2
Penguin Books (NZ) Ltd
182–190 Wairau Road, Auckland 10, New Zealand

First published 1975 by Allen Lane, A Division of Penguin Books Ltd
First published in paperback 1975 (Penguin)
This (revised) edition published by Penguin Books Australia Ltd 1994

1 3 5 7 9 10 8 6 4 2

Produced by McPhee Gribble
56 Claremont Street, South Yarra, Victoria 3141, Australia
A division of Penguin Books Australia Ltd

Typeset in Plantin
Printed in Australia by Australian Print Group

National Library of Australia
Cataloguing-in-Publication data:
Summers, Anne, 1945–
Damned whores and God's police.
Updated ed.
Includes index.
ISBN 0 14 023187 0.
1. Women – Australia – History. 2. Women's rights – Australia.
I. Title.
305.420994

CONTENTS

To my mother

When this book was first published the reviews ranged from luke-warm to unremittingly hostile but it quickly found an audience of women, and men, who were receptive to what was then a new way of looking at ourselves and our country. I was also pleased to learn that although it was published only in Australia and New Zealand the book managed to find its way into the hands of feminists around the world. I received enthusiastic letters from women in Canada, the United States, England, South Africa and Nigeria. I was sorry it was never published in either Britain or the United States, despite vigorous efforts on my part, but it is good to know that books have a way of finding their way around the world despite the decisions of international publishing houses.

This book would probably never have been written had it not been for the efforts of the late Professor Henry Mayer who let me into his post-graduate programme in the University of Sydney's Government Department even though he knew I had a contract with Penguin Books, who gave my draft chapters attention worthy of a thesis and then, when the book was finally published, insisted I honour my undertaking to submit it for examination for a post-graduate degree. It took several years of negotiating our way around the labyrinthine university regulations to obtain agreement that, despite its most irregular title, I could submit for examination the published book – rather than have it re-typed and bound into the usual thesis format. I happened to be in Southern Africa, on assignment for the *Australian Financial Review* for whom I worked by 1979, when I received a telegramme from Henry informing me that I had been awarded a PhD for the book. He had only one request: that he not have to attend the graduation ceremony. We both stayed away, but I want to place on record here my immense debt to this extraordinary man who, sadly, died in 1991.

Most of the new material I have added to this book was written in New York City. Working on an Australian book from that distance was not easy, and it would have been impossible without the unstinting help of a great many friends, former colleagues and kind strangers who responded to urgent faxes seeking information. I would like to thank the people in the following government offices who helped by sending much of the documentation I required: the Office of the Status of Women, the office of the Sex Discrimination Commissioner, the Affirmative Action Agency and the Equal Pay Unit in the Department of Industrial Relations; I am especially grateful to Sue Binney, Kay Daniels, Liz Harvey, Mary Murnane, Angela Nordlinger, Lyndall Ryan, Gavin Souter and, most of all, Chris Ronalds, who collected and sent over reams of material and found a wonderful researcher, Jane Ellis, who did some last-minute checking. We tried hard to produce an error-free book; if we failed, the responsibility is mine.

I also want to thank those people in New York who stood by me while I rushed to finish these new chapters: Pat and Richard Cantor for generously giving me their apartment to work in while they were being initiated into the delights of Down Under; Anne Banks, Cate Breslin, Jane Ciabattari, Grace Lichtenstein, Robin Reisig and Marilyn Webb who invited me into their writers' group and have been a great source of encouragement and friendship; Molly Haskell and Martha Lear for allowing me access to the Upper West Side Writers' Studio, that haven of industry and solitude where it was impossible not to write; Clare O'Brien for reading more drafts than should have been necessary; and, above all, Chip Rolley for his unwavering support at all times.

What none of us knew in May 1992 as I rushed to meet my deadline was that I would have to set aside this work for almost a year because of an irresistible invitation from Prime Minister Paul Keating to return to Australia as a consultant in his office on women's issues. This invitation provided me with the opportunity to put my money where my mouth was, so to speak, and give advice on implementing many of the policies women had long advocated. My return to Canberra, and to women's policy issues, was especially helpful for this project as it enabled me to bring myself up-to-date on the reality, as distinct from the theory, of how these issues were developing. Altogether it was a rare and extremely enjoyable opportunity to work at a high political level with a man who, despite a prior reputation of having little interest in women's issues, proved to be extraordinarily responsive and willing to instigate big political reforms. His election promises to women in the 1993 campaign were the most comprehensive ever made by an Australian political leader and once they are implemented Australian women will truly be able to say that much of the agenda we drew up twenty years ago has been accomplished.

Sydney
April 1993

[T]he damned whores the moment that the[y] got below fel a fighting amonst one a nother and Capt Meridith order the Sergt. not to part them but to let them fight it out . . .

– LT RALPH CLARK of the First Fleet,
The Journals and Letters of Lt Ralph Clark 1787–1792

If Her Majesty's Government be really desirous of seeing a well-conducted community spring up in these Colonies, the social wants of the people must be considered. If the paternal Government wish to entitle itself to that honoured appellation, it must look to the materials it may send as a nucleus for the formation of a good and great people. For all the clergy you can despatch, all the schoolmasters you can appoint, all the churches you can build, and all the books you can export, will never do much good, without what a gentleman in that Colony very appropriately called 'God's police' – wives and little children – good and virtuous women.

– CAROLINE CHISHOLM,
Emigration and Transportation Relatively Considered, 1847

INTRODUCTION TO
THE NEW EDITION

Much has changed in the twenty years since I first began writing this book. Australia itself has altered in important ways; we are a more diverse and tolerant nation than we used to be. Women's lives are different, and for the most part better; we have more choices, and more opportunities. Men's lives, as a result, have changed too. But what can be said about the nature and, especially, the quality of these changes? To attempt to answer that question is both enticing and intimidating. How can twenty years of struggle and set-back, trial and triumph be encapsulated in a few pages? How can we possibly assess and measure what has occurred, when we have witnessed and been part of nothing less than a revolution in the lives of women and men? How can we make sense of it all?

I believe that to address these questions adequately, a new book is needed and I hope that someone, somewhere, right now is hatching another 'big book', a sweeping feminist perspective on contemporary Australia, because we need another interpretation, a new perspective. I am happy to update my account, where it is now factually inaccurate, and to provide a perspective on some of the important changes of the past two decades, but we need new voices and new visions.

So much has changed since 1975, International Women's Year, when this book first appeared. Parts of the book now seem antiquated and perhaps even irrelevant. For instance, the description in Chapter Five of the social security system and its impact on women no longer stands because of the many important (and continuing) changes to that system over the past two decades. Some of the book's descriptions of contemporary culture, and even of the women's movement, now seem quaint and outmoded. Much of the language we use today to describe everyday exploitation or abuse of women did not even exist then. The term sexual harassment had yet to be coined; we had not begun to speak of domestic violence although we were becoming depressingly aware of how widespread what we referred to as wife-bashing was; what I clumsily called petty rape is now more accurately known as date rape or acquaintance rape. We had only just begun to grapple with barriers to employment opportunities such as sex discrimination and we had yet to discover the glass ceiling. The women's movement is now twenty-five years old and is very different from the inchoate, youthful movement of the early 1970s. We now have our own story to tell, our history of what we thought and felt, and what we have achieved during a quarter century of struggle. So there is a great deal to examine, to reflect on and to make judgements about.

Despite all this, I felt the existing chapters offer a perspective on the period in which they were written and should stand. If we constantly rewrite history to fit how we see things now, we forget how things used to be and, equally important to future scholars, how we used to see them. So the core of the book remains intact but I have added to it a new beginning and a new end. I decided not to add to the historical chapters, tempting though it was to re-enter the seemingly never-ending debate about the virtues or otherwise of the convict women. Since my efforts to rescue these women from the condescending moralism of previous (and mostly male) historians, a veritable industry seems to have built itself around the fate and fortunes of the somewhat less than 25,000 women who came to this country as convicts. A few of the more recent writers, Portia Robinson being a prime example, have sought to discount my account on ideological grounds. She attacks my interpretation as a guileless acceptance of the judgement of contemporary authorities that the convict women were whores (totally missing my point about the imposed sexual slavery that was de facto British policy at the time), and tries to tether to a few flimsy biographical sketches the unsustainable notion that most women in early Australia were virtuous wives and mothers.[1] But most have endorsed my premise and either, as in the case of Robert Hughes[2] added even more graphic documentation than I was able to muster from the secondary sources I mostly used or, as with Marian Aveling[3], dispensed with my feminist preoccupation with the status of women in favour of a gender analysis of the power of the state.

While deciding not to engage with any of these theses, I am nevertheless obliged to correct an error which was brought to my attention by Robert Hughes some twelve years after this book was first published. Hughes pointed out that Lt Ralph Clark was on Norfolk Island on 3 June 1790 – the day the *Lady Juliana* sailed into Sydney Harbour – and could not, therefore, have made the famous remark about 'not more of those damned whores' on the day I said he did. I acknowledge this error, and having been unable to retrace the archival steps that led me to the quote in the first place, decided to replace it with another from Ralph Clark. His journals, having now been published, leave the reader in no doubt that he continually referred to the female convicts as damned whores.

This new Introduction updates the picture I presented in 1975, providing something of a measure of how much change has taken place while also canvassing some of the things we still need to do. I begin with a few personal thoughts on how to achieve lasting change developed as a result of working in government and in the media, both here in Australia and in the United States. The various jobs I have held inside these powerful institutions have given me the opportunity to test, often in a very direct and hands-on fashion, the question of how we expand women's opportunities, and how governments and the media contribute – or impede – this process.

The rest of this Introduction largely follows the chronological sequence of the first half of the book, and I have used the chapter titles as sub-headings to make it easier to refer back and forth. I have also introduced some new subjects, such as women in politics, which I did not deal with before, and have included random observations where relevant. I have replaced the previous last chapter, Prospects for Liberation, which was a rather muddled attempt to look into the future, with a new section titled Letter to the Next Generation. Here, I tell the story of the women's movement in Australia since the early 1970s and try to give young women today an understanding of their legacy. This book was always a passionate perspective on women in Australia's past and present. I hope it remains so.

THE PERSONAL IS STILL POLITICAL

While I was working on the first edition of this book, trying to apportion my time between long hours of solitary library research and the exhilarating activism of the early women's movement, my perspective was very much that of the community organizer. Like most of my contemporaries in the movement, I viewed the media with suspicion, especially as it seemed so hostile to our cause, and we regarded government mainly as a source of funds in return for which we felt we were expected to prune our radicalism to fit existing policies. I would never have guessed back then that I would spend the next sixteen years moving between government and the media.

What I would once have been quick to label as selling out has in fact been a fascinating voyage of discovery and insight. I have had four major work experiences since 1975: writing for Australian newspapers, first the *National Times* and later the *Australian Financial Review* in Canberra and then in New York; running the Office of the Status of Women in the first Hawke Government; working with the United States women's movement, and the New York-based magazine industry, as Editor-in-Chief of *Ms.* magazine; and, most recently, working as a political consultant in the office of Prime Minister Paul Keating. Each has helped shape my views on how women can achieve genuine and lasting change. I have come to understand the real power of government and of media, as distinct from how these are often imagined from the outside. These continuing encounters with reality, some of them involving the challenge of how actually to design and put into effect policies long advocated by the women's movement, quickly rid me of my youthful utopianism. I became, instead, a fervent pragmatist, committed to the notion that political change is usually incremental and that we must grab every bit we can whenever the opportunity strikes and not, as I would have argued twenty years ago, hold out for that perfection which, in politics as in life, almost never ever arrives.

INSIDE THE MEDIA

The newspaper world I entered in late 1975, a few weeks after the publication of this book, while not being exclusively male was certainly very male-dominated. Not only were all the editors and most of the high-ranking staff men, but a male culture pervaded the workplace. A great deal of business was conducted in the pub across the road from the office, and to hold down a job in journalism in those days the ability to drink was almost as important as being able to write. Nevertheless there was a genuine and quite pressing interest in 'the story' of the changes that were happening in women's lives, especially on the part of the editor of the *National Times*, the first paper I worked on. In fact, the very first story I wrote when I joined the staff was a two-page account of what happens to women and their children once they leave women's refuges and strike out on their own. It was comforting to be able to learn the craft of journalism by writing about so familiar a subject.

But the media's coverage of the revolution in women's lives has been sporadic and patchy and very often coloured by ridicule, prejudice or even hostility. It is difficult to think of many – indeed any – other issues or subjects where the coverage could be so subjective and so unfriendly. Even though there are now greater numbers of women in journalism, few have made it to the very top or to positions where they can influence the tone and content of what is presented. Many sections of newspapers are still written from a male vantage-point and seem to assume a male readership, or the headlines put on stories give that impression. Women are still routinely described in newspapers by the colour of their hair or their maternal status (and sometimes both) – 'a young blonde mother of two was rescued today' – whereas men tend to be described by their occupations alone. Stories about so-called women's issues, such as child-care, are not seen as hard news warranting serious attention. When Prime Minister Keating included major changes to child-care policy in an economic statement during the 1993 election campaign, some reporters attacked him for confusing major issues with supposedly soft items. These reporters – and they included several women – seemed unaware of the extent to which their reaction reflected unfair and outmoded assumptions about what is news. (Not to mention what is of obvious importance to a nation's economic and social future.)

The media are not comfortable covering the story of the profound changes that continue to take place in the relations between women and men because they are themselves part of the story. It is ironic, to say the least, that while many major papers continue to treat this story less than fairly in their news and feature pages, their management is embroiled in battles with reporters over maternity leave, child-care, job-sharing and other contemporary work and family issues. But you would never know this from reading the papers. Part of the reason for this apparent double-standard is the code of professional conduct which requires journalists to quarantine their own opinions and, by extension, their personal lives, from what they are writing about. Some journalists manage this so successfully the reader would never suspect they were as busy juggling jobs, children and personal interests as most modern parents these days are. But I can also sympathise with the dilemma this presents to journalists and their editors.

A reporter who wears her heart on her sleeve (as distinct from a columnist who is paid to air opinions), or otherwise burdens readers with her personal problems may soon find herself out of a job. Such an approach is likely to polarise readers into those who agree and those who don't, and thus diminish the reporter's credibility as an objective witness, and to reduce the number of sources who judge it worth their while to provide information to someone whose mind is already made up.

Of course life is more complicated than that, and over time both readers and sources are likely to get at least a feel for the views of particular reporters but I found during my time as a reporter that it was important to maintain some form of cordon sanitaire between my personal views and my professional conduct. Sometimes this meant maintaining a frosty civility towards politicians I knew to be incorrigible sexual harassers, and otherwise engaging with all manner of creeps and low-life. I took the view that the short-term, one-on-one approach to change was energy misdirected. I was a reporter not a crusader, and the best I could do to improve opportunities for women in journalism – and elsewhere – was to conform to the highest professional standards of conduct, as women in the industry before me had done, thus helping pave the way for future generations of women to get jobs in journalism. This need not mean totally suppressing private views or desisting from political activity. Unlike in the United States where during the early 1990s newspapers forbade their staff from participating in the huge pro-choice marches in Washington, Australian editors recognise the distinctions between private and professional opinions and actions.

This whole debate is relevant to what I view as the naive notion, long advocated by certain strands of feminism, that the only way to make the media less sexist and more female-friendly is to have more women journalists, editors, producers and so on. While it is certainly to be hoped that a critical mass of women in the media would alter the predominantly male ethos which still prevails in most places, this by itself would not necessarily produce the kind of changes feminists crave. Just look at the traditional women's magazines which are run and staffed by women but where issues affecting women, such as child-care, seldom get an airing! Nor can we assume that women in management positions in the media will behave all that differently from men in such jobs. It can be argued that getting the job requires individuals to be socialized in corporate conduct of a kind that is gender-blind, and therefore what needs to be changed is the corporate culture. It also seems to me to be placing an unfair burden on the few women who do make it to top jobs in the media to require that, in addition to the stresses and strains of the job itself, they are expected to be activists and advocates on behalf of their sex. Of course, we should shun the old Queen Bee syndrome, whereby women who made it kicked away the ladder, ensuring no other woman could come close and compete for a share of what used to be a stingy stipend of glory for our gender. But we should take care to ensure women are not set up to fail in their chosen profession because we have saddled them with unreasonable expectations of the power of an individual to alter decades of doing things a certain way.

The kind of change we should strive for is that which permanently alters the priorities and perceptions about what is important in our society; for that to happen, the media should reflect a broader world than they tend to do at present. There are some small signs that the need for change is starting to be recognised. At least some of the issues are getting a regular run in columns such as 'A Woman's Place' by Sue Neales which in 1992 began to appear weekly in the *Age*, joining the ranks of the longer-running columns 'Corporate Woman' in the *Australian Financial Review* and Adele Horin's 'My Generation' in the *Sydney Morning Herald*. Perhaps the real breakthrough will be when men become writers of such columns, but it is important that the columns at least are there. A decade ago, when I wrote for the *Financial Review*, they did not exist and there was rarely a spot in the paper where I could raise such issues. Unless I could legitimately find a news angle – and the Fraser years in Canberra seldom produced women-related news except in the form of budget cuts for, say, women's refuge funding – there was rarely a hook for such stories. There are a few more hooks today, and a lot more women working in journalism, but the culture of the news media has responded more sluggishly than the society it supposedly reflects.

HEADING THE OFFICE OF THE STATUS OF WOMEN

My experience of working for government as a feminist bureaucrat or femocrat[4], as they are called, drew me into that very seductive world of helping theories evolve into government policies; it was to be a time of activity and accomplishment where one could feel pride in the fact that we were making actual, measurable progress. When I went there in 1983, the Office of the Status of Women had recently been returned from the bureaucratic outhouse to which the Fraser Government had consigned it to the power and prestige of the Prime Minister's Department. This not only honoured a campaign commitment by Bob Hawke but was a potent acknowledgment of the increased political power of women. Labor front-bencher and the party's most senior woman, then Senator Susan Ryan, had worked assiduously since the mid-1970s to improve Labor's standing with women, arguing to her colleagues that the party needed women's votes if it were to regain office. She developed policies designed to appeal to women, including the very basic commitment to take their views and needs seriously by politically upgrading the women's policy advice office, and in 1983 for the first time women and men voted Labor in about equal numbers.

The Office was charged with helping the government deliver on its election promises, especially the undertaking to introduce sex discrimination and affirmative action legislation, but we were also given the brief of monitoring what all government departments were doing so we could identify, and try to head off, any measures likely to have a detrimental impact on women. This latter role cast us as something akin to the God's Police of the bureaucracy, and made us very unpopular as we poked around other people's policies and wrote comments on their Cabinet submissions. I soon learned the immense power of the Prime Minister in the Australian political system.

Without the strong support Bob Hawke gave us in that role, we would have been isolated and impotent. But with his blessing, reinforced from time to time with a telling phrase or sentence in an important speech, the Office became a powerhouse of enterprise and activity. We worked with big business, the trade union movement and the higher education sector to pilot programmes which were later enshrined in affirmative action laws; we became involved in tax reform; we got more women appointed to boards and authorities; we got a commitment to increase the number of child-care places. A powerful symbol of Hawke's support came in 1985 when for the first time in Australian political history a prime minister introduced a piece of legislation: the affirmative action bill.[5] Some of the work we did was invisible to those outside government, for example, heading off potential disasters such as the abolition or reduction of certain programmes proposed at Budget time each year with monotonous regularity by the Department of Finance. In such cases, success meant that a particular thing did *not* happen but it was hardly the kind of victory that could be trumpeted from the rooftops. Indeed, much of what we did had to be kept secret until such time as the government had reached a decision and was ready to make an announcement. These facts of bureaucratic life were almost impossible to explain to our sisters in the women's movement, many of whom expected us to be always available and accountable – to them.

In fact, there were constant mutterings from many in the women's movement who were suspicious of the 'sisters in suits' – beige suits were a trademark of femocrats in the early 1980s! – and who feared that femocrats would water down the policies they'd put on the political agenda. The tension between those inside the bureaucracy and the activists outside is in many ways necessary and even beneficial, keeping the femocrats honest and the activists in touch with what is politically possible. It may not always seem this way, especially when the tension spills over into outright hostility – as happens from time to time – but femocrats, unlike almost any other bureaucrats except perhaps for Aboriginal bureaucrats and those of some ethnic origins, are in an unenviable position. They tend to be seen within the bureaucracy as infiltrators whose primary loyalty is to an outside constituency – as missionaries, rather than as professional public servants – while the constituents characterize them as part of the government – as mandarins, in fact – and as driven by goals of careerism and self-preservation. Getting the balance right, so as to be credible and therefore effective with one's departmental and government masters, while not losing touch with women in the community, is extremely difficult and personally wearing. Most femocrats retire after a few years suffering from burn-out, the task of balancing their competing worlds in the end too big a personal price to pay.

While at the Office I became a member of an OECD Working Party on the Role of Women and the Economy and at the two meetings in Paris I attended had the opportunity to meet with women doing comparable jobs in other countries. It was here that I learned that Australia had become an inadvertent pioneer on status of women policies. The Working Party included women from Japan, Germany, Canada, France and the United States and they were astonished, and envious, to learn about Australia's achievements. They were generally impressed by Australia's high-level political commitment to women's issues, and they were especially taken with the Women's Budget Statement, a Budget document in which all government departments have to report annually on how their policies and programmes affected women. This of course was the Reagan era in the United States, a time when policy for women was going backwards. In fact, while Australia was adopting a professional approach to the issue – appointing femocrats and listening to their advice – Ronald Reagan nominated his daughter to lead the American delegation to the 1985 United Nations World Conference of Women in Nairobi.

The responsiveness of the Australian political system, and especially of Labor leaders, to the political clout of women was again apparent to me in 1992 when I returned to Canberra to act as a consultant on women's issues to Prime Minister Paul Keating. Unlike American political leaders who tend to react to their lack of popularity with women voters either by ignoring the problem, or with utter cynicism (by initiating advertising campaigns designed to scare or seduce women), Australian leaders are much more prepared to woo votes with policies. Like Hawke, Keating showed himself willing to heed professional advice and to act on issues of which he had no particular prior knowledge or interest. Keating took an additional step, authorizing use of the very democratic tool of market research to seek the views of the women of 'middle Australia', women not usually reached by government – or able to put their views to a prime minister.[6] As a result, he was armed with concrete information about what women actually thought was deficient in existing government policies – the perceived failure to provide adequate and affordable child-care, the need for special women's health measures and the wrenching plea to stop violence against women. Keating outlined his policy responses to these subjects in speeches and in grabs on the nightly news, communicating directly to people, including women, rather than through slick advertising. He was prepared to be bold in his approach and to take quantum leaps in areas such as child-care. In less than a year he transformed himself from a politician women had tended to distrust to a leader able to respond appropriately to a diverse range of groups of Australian people, among them women. And unlike the United States, or possibly any other country apart from Iceland and Norway, both of which have progressive records on women's issues, Keating – and Australia – demonstrated once again that good policies make excellent politics.

EDITING *MS.* MAGAZINE

The more than two years I spent as Editor-in-Chief of *Ms.* magazine gave me an unparallelled vantage point from which to assess the workings and accomplishments of the American women's movement. I went into the job taking for granted, as I am sure most Australians would, that America represented the pinnacle of the achievements of second-wave feminism. I very quickly learned how wrong this assumption was. Many of the entitlements Australian women take for granted, such as federally-funded child-care, mandated (if unpaid) maternity leave or the existence of women's policy advisers at every level of government, simply did not exist in the United States. Even more surprising, but seemingly related, was the low number of women holding elected office, especially in federal politics.

In 1988, my first full year at *Ms.* and a United States presidential election year, there were only twenty-five women in the entire United States Congress, a mere 4.7 per cent.[7] I made political coverage a top priority of the magazine; in the United States women register and vote in greater numbers than men, and we published figures which showed that in the previous election, in 1986, women's voting patterns had delivered the margin of victory to a significant proportion of the winning contenders.[8] So it seemed self-evident to me that, as in Australia, women's votes would be solicited and that a relatively large circulation (550,000), mainstream feminist magazine which for the first time was treating electoral politics seriously would be in for some serious wooing by candidates. Not so, as it turned out. The major party candidates were courteous, they answered our monthly questions on policy issues, but they evidently felt there was no advantage, and perhaps some disadvantage, in getting too close to *Ms.* magazine. The biggest surprise was the calculated contempt shown to us by Democratic contender Michael Dukakis who had agreed to pose along with his senior campaign staff, many of whom including his campaign manager were women, for the cover of our October 1988 issue. Right at the last minute, after our photographic team had already flown to Boston, Dukakis cancelled. 'Scheduling difficulties', was the official explanation. Cold feet was the truth.

I was amazed at the seeming impotence of the women's movement, their inability to influence or even be part of the campaign debate, and the fact that politicians could so easily disregard them. Ultimately I became convinced that at least part of the responsibility for the movement's political frailty lies with the movement itself, especially the national leadership, which has no political strategy whatsoever and seems incapable of putting together a pragmatic plan to force the political system to deliver to American women the social and economic equity long promised by the movement's rhetoric. It can perhaps be postulated that the Reagan–Bush era is responsible for the movement's failure, that twelve years of feminist-unfriendly administrations in Washington left the movement battle-scarred and exhausted. If that is the case, that exhaustion appears to be near-terminal as the advent of the feminist-friendly Clinton administration had not in the first six months of the new regime produced anything remotely resembling the kind of partnership Australian feminists have managed to forge with government. (Letter to the Next Generation, the final chapter in this new edition explores this theme more fully.) Indeed, early in 1993 there seemed almost to be an air of hostility towards President Clinton, and a strange ambivalence by many feminists towards Hillary, his high-profile and policy-active wife.

Instead of the joy, and appreciation, one might have expected from feminists during his first few weeks in office as Clinton reversed one after another of Reagan and Bush's restrictive abortion measures, there were complaints and even outright opposition from women's movement leaders, who claimed the changes did not go far enough. After more than a decade of fighting to preserve abortion rights, the National Organization for Women astonishingly opposed Clinton's proposed Freedom of Choice Act, a measure which would give the right to abortion a federal legislative base and remove it from the vagaries of judicial review. Their opposition stemmed from the view that it was not sufficient to keep abortion legal; the proposed law should make abortion easily accessible by forbidding states to impose any restrictions, such as the need for parental consent for minors.[9] American feminist leaders will not settle for anything less than purist perfection and, as a result, they mostly end up with nothing. Rather than entrench even a few basic rights which can be built on and expanded later (as Australian feminists did with the *Sex Discrimination Act 1984*), women's movement leaders – as distinct from their frustrated and apparently impotent membership – would rather fight than win. This is what happened with the Equal Rights Amendment in 1982 when the refusal of feminist leaders to compromise on substance or tactics left American women without a constitutional guarantee of equality.

Why is this the case? Why has the movement which brought the world the second wave of feminism proved incapable of delivering the political agenda it originally mapped out? Movement leaders have a tendency to defensively blame the media, blame the politicians, blame anybody in fact rather than engage in the kind of self-reflection that might provide some answers. Movement leaders will protest that the powers that be are afraid of the F-word – feminism – when in fact the movement has its own F-word problems: the movement is too dominated by fame, factionalism and fuzzy-thinking to provide American women with the representation they are entitled to – and so badly need.

The American women's movement is no different from American society in general in its obsession with fame and celebrity. The movement has its own celebrities, and the famous American feminists are very famous indeed – women like Gloria Steinem, Betty Friedan, Kate Millett, Susan Brownmiller and Bella Abzug are known to millions of people across the globe. This phenomenon does not exist in the women's movement anywhere else in the world, and certainly not in Australia, where a much greater egalitarianism prevails. Nor have other national movements surrendered much of their political agenda to the fads of the famous. For, far from being able or willing to resist this national fetish, American feminism has become so dependent upon celebrities that it has had serious consequences for the movement's credibility and effectiveness.

The women's movement uses famous people to raise money, to make political statements and to march in the front row of political demonstrations. The rationale is that the presence of a Jane Fonda, a Glenn Close, a Whoopi Goldberg or a Cybill Shepherd will attract the media and result both in better coverage of the event or the issue, and a greater chance of ordinary people paying attention. In practice it means that a tremendous amount of effort goes into persuading famous people, especially movie stars, to lend public support to women's movement causes and activities. This gives American feminist events a very different character to those in Australia. I attended the star-studded dinner in Washington D.C. the night before the massive pro-choice abortion march in April 1989, and was struck by how elitist and alien it was. The movie stars did some mingling at the post-dinner reception (naturally, you had to pay extra for the privilege of such propinquity), and each celebrity immediately attracted a cluster of starstruck women who pushed past bodyguards to have their brief encounter with fame. The next morning the stars – wearing their Distinguished Guest sashes – were closeted in a special VIP tent until the march began.

The sight of feminists fawning over movie stars is something to behold, especially if the particular star's recent roles have not exactly been ones feminists would want to review favourably. (Glenn Close, star of *Fatal Attraction*, provided a case in point at the time of the march.) But this is usually overlooked if the star is willing to lend her celebrity to a pro-feminist statement or event. The presence of fame seems to blunt the critical faculties of the non-famous who will simper and gush and otherwise demean themselves. The inequalities involved are more extreme than those between women and men; indeed if any woman grovelled towards her husband or boyfriend the way some feminists kowtow towards the rich and famous, we would feel we hadn't progressed very far.

American feminism's dependence on fame, and the famous, seriously weakens the women's movement. Time and energy that could be applied to political struggle, lobbying politicians to get legislation passed for instance, are diverted to selecting, seducing and then servicing the celebrities (don't think these people stop being temperamental just because they are donating their services to a worthy cause). But perhaps even more important, it means the movement has surrendered control of its political agenda. In a sense, the women's movement has become captive to the ideological whims of the celebrities who, in turn, usually only have strong (public, at least) feelings about issues involving personal lifestyle choices such as abortion. It is almost unheard of to have famous names lending their support on economic issues – they are too complicated, too difficult – and maybe this is why these subjects are so neglected by American feminism. Yet it is issues like equal pay and job opportunities that affect the daily lives of most women and are of more immediate, urgent and continuing relevance than the more fashionable subjects Hollywood stars feel strongly about.

No political movement is free of factionalism, and the women's movement is no exception, but only the American women's movement would conduct so many of its fights, and especially the feuds between famous feminists, in the media. This of course does nothing to improve the impression of unity amongst feminists, and thus weakens the movement as a whole.

The most famous feminist feud, between Gloria Steinem and Betty Friedan, author of the 1963 classic *The Feminine Mystique*, seems to have started in 1970 when Steinem formed the Women's Action Alliance in seeming competition with Friedan's brainchild, the National Organization for Women.[10] Two years later, Friedan reacted to the founding of *Ms.* magazine by issuing a press release stating that Gloria Steinem 'was ripping off the [women's] movement for private profit' and that 'no one should mistake her for a leader'. Steinem retaliated by telling a reporter: 'If I have a lot of problems about my being a leader of the women's movement, I'm sure *she* has even more about me being a leader of the women's movement'.[11] The willingness of both parties to perpetuate, and escalate, their hostility via the media would horrify most Australian feminists who would see it as unsisterly to publicly denounce one another in this fashion.[12] Nor would Australian feminists publicly trash other women for having the temerity to offer alternative views of reality, especially of feminism, as American feminists do, seemingly without hesitation. In 1991 Steinem described *Washington Post* journalist Sally Quinn as a water bug (a creature Australians know as a cockroach) for an article which questioned the political achievements of the women's movement. As Editor of *Ms.* magazine, Robin Morgan used her letter to readers, to describe, in mid-1993, (the admittedly controversial) author Camille Paglia as 'a publicity-obsessed, intellectually bereft, rather pathetic person trying to revive the lie that women want to be raped'.[13] Comments of this kind might be made in private by Australian feminists, but it is difficult to think of a single example of them occurring in print – let alone in a supposedly feminist journal.

This fractiousness among individuals repeats itself in organizational animosity. The major women's groups find it difficult to agree on a broad, common agenda and are surprisingly fuzzy in their thinking about issues and strategy. It should not seem a dauntingly difficult task to identify the three or four key issues that, once won, could transform the lives of millions of American women. Such a battle plan would command respect from women and from legislators, and might oblige candidates for office to become more responsive to the political demands of the women's movement. But the sad reality is that during the Reagan–Bush years abortion rights was virtually the only issue on which movement leaders could find common ground – and even then there were plenty of disagreements about tactics. The frenetic political activity around abortion rights in the late 1980s and early 1990s actually helped disguise the extent of disagreement within the movement. Most grassroots members of the major organizations are probably unaware of it. Yet the movement's inability to organize around a broad-based agenda, and to link it to a tough-minded electoral strategy, has meant American women have endured a decade where nothing new was accomplished, and some entitlements (federally-funded abortions for poor women, for instance) were taken away. The Reagan–Bush years were not good for American women, but they were even worse for the American women's movement because it lost its perspective – and its nerve. The movement has always had a tendency to dwell on single-issues, especially those of a personal or cultural nature, at the expense of the economic issues. The movement spent the 1980s preoccupied with abortion, pornography, sexual abuse (especially of children, including present-day adult 'survivors') and, after the Clarence Thomas–Anita Hill Senate hearings[14], sexual harassment. While these are all important subjects, for most women, job protection, pay equity and affordable child-care loom larger as day-to-day imperatives. For the women's movement to do justice to American women, it needs to be out there fighting on a broader front, forcing the political system to deliver economic justice to women so that they have real choices about their lives. The woman who can't afford to leave a violent husband because she has only a low-paying job is probably not going to be overly impressed to see Jane Fonda in the front line of an abortion rights march. For no number of famous faces could hide the fact that the American women's movement entered the 1990s without a strategy for improving the lives of American women. The contrast with the Australian movement, which has a clear and articulated agenda, could not be greater.

TWO DECADES OF CHANGE

The way we talk now about women, and about women and men, is very different from twenty years ago. Even when the words are the same, their meaning has evolved. When I wrote the Introduction to the first edition of this book, I fumbled for a definition of feminism. As a movement, we were still working our way through the differences between radical feminist, socialist feminist and women's liberationist – to name just the major groups then – and our definitions were long and convoluted. The sheer simplicity of the notion that feminism is merely 'advocacy of equal rights and opportunities for women, especially the extension of their activities in social and political life', as the *Macquarie Dictionary* puts it, was just not available then.[15] Dictionaries produced since the arrival of the women's movement reflect the fact that feminism has entered everyday language.

We might still debate shades of meaning, or complain about being misrepresented in the media or elsewhere, but we are doing this from an entirely different vantage point now. Back in 1975 when we were still groping for the words that described who we were and what we wanted, we were still trying to make the case. We were tentative, pleading for legitimacy, wanting to be taken seriously and our language was less certain than it is today.

We also had trouble differentiating clearly between sexism and male chauvinism and the terms were often used interchangeably, and usually vituperatively. We had yet to grasp the distinction between sex, or gender, as an organizing principle of social relations, usually to the disadvantage of women, and the aggressive advocacy by individual men of the continuance of this system. Today the dictionary deals matter of factly with concepts we were just beginning to understand and define. Sexist is an adjective describing 'an attitude which stereotypes a person according to gender or sexual preference, rather than judging on individual merits', states the *Macquarie Dictionary*. Its other adjectival meaning encompasses 'pertaining to sexual exploitation or discrimination, esp. in advertising, language, job opportunities, etc.', while as a noun, it describes 'a person who displays sexist attitudes'. What could be more simple!

We had yet to start using the term gender. We described the world as being determined by differences, and inequalities, in sex and, while the distinction is perhaps a semantic one, I believe that once we began to use the more neutral term gender more people could understand, and agree with us. The colloquial association of sex with sexual activity made it a word some people, including many women, just could not bring themselves to say. Incredible as this might sound today, major newspapers were only just permitting words like pregnant and virgin to appear in their pages.[16] When Germaine Greer's classic work *The Female Eunuch* was published in 1970 I was surprised to discover that its salty language presented some difficulties for many women who were otherwise eagerly receptive to its message. I first realized this when I spoke at a seminar on Greer's book held in Sydney in the early 1970s and met a middle-aged woman who confessed that she had covered the book in brown paper and hidden it amongst her shoes because her husband had forbidden her to read it!

Ten years later, Australia's landmark anti-discrimination legislation, the *Sex Discrimination Act 1984*, may have had a less difficult time making its way through Parliament had its very title not been seen as so inflammatory.[17] Hysterical critics of the Bill claimed it would do everything from 'denigrate marriage' to 'force [women] into a gender-free, unisex society, in which women are locked into the paid labour-force for their entire lifetimes just like men (except for brief periods of maternity leave)'.[18] Such fanatical opponents would doubtless have used everything in their ideological armory against the legislation whatever it was called. After all, the more neutrally titled Equal Rights Amendment (ERA) in the United States met equally illogical opposition and, in the end, failed to be ratified. But the name of the Australian legislation provided its critics with additional fodder, something they were quick to try to exploit; fortunately they failed but only because the newly elected Labor government had a strong public commitment to ensuring the legislation passed. The 1984 debate remains the longest in the history of the Australian Parliament and the eventual vote in the House of Representatives saw several members of the Coalition cross the floor against their colleagues who opposed the Bill. Eight years later, when Prime Minister Keating introduced significant amendments to the Act, the heat had gone out of the debate. There was no dissent, and the Opposition supported the measures designed to toughen up the legislation.

It also seemed necessary in the mid-1970s to devote a lot of time to talking about the family, a term I then used in quotation marks to indicate that I was referring to an ideological construct rather than a social norm. It was not easy at the time to document what was true then, and is even more the case today, and that is that an increasing number of Australians do not live within traditional nuclear families. Yet the political rhetoric of the time proceeded from the assumption that most people did live within this traditional structure or if they didn't, they should. Not only was this kind of hectoring unfair to single parents, divorced or single people and the many other groupings of people who did not conform to this traditional pattern, but it was also flying in the face of what was actually happening in our society. Today, even conservative politicians acknowledge (if with regret) the diversity of living arrangements and we can now use the word family to encompass a wide range of blood and other relationships.

But in the early 1970s the research material simply did not exist. The Commission on Human Relationships had yet to complete its work of investigating the reality of contemporary Australians' lives. The Australian Institute of Family Studies had not yet been established and the census figures were frustratingly uninformative on such matters.[19] Since the 1986 census statistics on families have improved and there is now more accurate information available on how people actually live. In that year 42.8 per cent of families comprised married parents with dependent children (a decrease of 5 per cent since 1982)[20], which means that more than half the population was living in family or household arrangements other than this.

When this book was written it seemed important to try to have something to say on the relationship between sex oppression and capitalism; not even the most ardent Marxist would probably bother to do so today and I certainly have lost interest in this once-pressing subject. There is these days a vigorous debate amongst many Australian feminists about how theoretically to accommodate the relationship between feminism and the state, a debate which has generated some useful and informative books.[21] But, as I noted in the personal section at the beginning of this Introduction, my own interests these days are not in the realm of theory and I have not engaged in this debate.

In 1975 we could not really speak of a specific women's agenda. We had a list of demands, we were evolving a coherent analysis of why and how women had been excluded from most areas of public life but we were still camped on the fringes of politics. Today we are far less marginal and, in some areas at least, we can claim to be part of the mainstream. The responsiveness of political parties and governments in this country, particularly the federal government, has been very significant. Even before the term gender gap in voting had been coined, party officials had identified, and exploited, this phenomenon to their advantage. The Liberal Party since its inception had given women a guaranteed place in the party structure and part of its electoral strategy was to appeal, through family oriented policies, to women voters who, until the late 1970s, tended to vote more conservatively than men. The most spectacular example of this occurred in 1978 when Malcolm Fraser introduced family allowances, a special (at the time, non-income tested) payment to women based on the number of children they had. (The payment combined the former child-endowment allowance and the child tax rebate and was a daring step because it took a tax advantage from the husband and converted it into a direct payment to the wife/mother.) The Labor Party had been a trade-union dominated party until the late 1960s and was not especially appealing to many women, but once Gough Whitlam became leader in the mid-1960s and especially after he became prime minister in 1972, he set out to attract women voters. By the mid-1980s the ALP had instigated affirmative action policies within its ranks to ensure women were represented in party structures, although it has yet to take similar action to improve the representation of women in Parliament. Labor differed from the Liberals in that it had no qualms about taking up feminist issues and so began what has remained a strong alliance between the women's movement and the ALP. As Lyndall Ryan describes it, 'the pragmatic face of feminism found a space in the political agenda that had not previously existed'.[22]

During the Labor governments of the 1980s and continuing into the 1990s, women's issues became an explicit part of the government agenda, and feminists were brought into the bureaucracy to give advice and implement policy. In 1983, early in the first Hawke Government, Australia ratified the United Nations Convention on the Elimination of All Forms of Discrimination Against Women (CEDAW), which gave it a constitutional ability (under the foreign affairs power) to legislate against sex discrimination, and which also exposed the nation to international scrutiny of its policies and practices towards women. This was a potent acknowledgement of the government's willingness to legislate and otherwise act to improve the status of women, and during the rest of that decade a large number of initiatives followed. These ranged from announcing a five-year National Agenda for Women, to increased funding for child-care and women's refuges, to legislation to promote equal opportunity for women in the work-force.

The 1993 election campaign saw further evidence of Labor's willingness to embrace a feminist agenda – in stark contrast to the Coalition parties whose stance ranged from policy paralysis to, in the case of child-care, policy plagiarism. During the campaign Paul Keating undertook to accommodate two long-standing feminist policy demands: to make work-related child-care available to all who needed it by the end of the decade (in addition to making care more affordable to middle-income families by the payment of a cash rebate to reduce the cost of child-care), and to 'cash out' the dependent spouse tax rebate into a direct payment, to be called the Home Child Care Allowance, for mothers at home with children. He made other promises too: to set up a new service for women and children escaping domestic violence in rural and remote areas; to give a significant funding boost to women's organizations, and to provide funds to the Australian Institute of Judicial Administration 'to develop courses for magistrates and judges to help them identify prejudices that might impact on their judicial conduct towards women'.[23] Responding to these promises, the previously sceptical feminist writer Dale Spender enthused: 'Paul Keating got it right when he launched his women's policy. Apart from the fact that the entire female population benefitted from being taken seriously, the "promises" that produced the greatest buzz were the ones that cost the least but made the right noises about access and equity. End gender bias in the law. Send judges back to school, the Prime Minister declared to the enthusiastic gathering. [Justices] Elizabeth Evatt and Deirdre O'Connor were named as models for the day. And every woman – from the sex worker to the middle-class divorcee and the wealthy victim of domestic violence – got the message. The law which has been made by men over the centuries could well start to respect women's experience. Equity, access, a fair deal. It's a motivating force for women.'[24] When Labor won its historic victory in 1993, women were widely acknowledged to have contributed to the win and, indeed, the exit polls on election day indicated that, at least in some age groups, for the first time in Australian electoral history, more women than men voted Labor.[25]

In looking at the changes in Australia of the past twenty years, we also have to take into account the vast economic and political upheavals which have reverberated around the world. The beginning of the 1990s saw the end of Communism in Eastern Europe, and the Soviet Union collapsed into a confused constellation of independent states, changes which brought mixed blessings for the women of these beleaguered nations. Under Communism, women had had little choice about participating in the economy and the consequent double burden of paid jobs and housework weighed more heavily on them than on their sisters in Western countries. The services sector failed to provide, or adequately distribute consumer goods, especially food. Women had to spend long hours after their day in the office or factory queuing for whatever food was available, after which they would return home to put whatever they could on the table. The labour-saving devices which make life considerably easier for so many people in the West were rarely available. Contraceptives were hard to get, making abortion, usually performed under nightmarish and unsafe medical conditions, the only option for controlling fertility. But women did enjoy better government-provided support than is usual in many Western countries, services which were being withdrawn in the name of efficiency and reform as these countries struggled to introduce market economies. As well as losing their child-care and family leave, many women also lost their jobs as work-forces were slashed and places of employment closed. Some of the newly elected leaders, equating women's participation in public life with Communism rather than with human progress, removed provisions which guaranteed women political representation, while others argued that it was more democratic for women to stay home and become full-time housewives.

Two major recessions affecting most of the industrialized world, one at the beginning of each decade since this book was published, have altered the face of employment. The experience of women in the work-force, especially in the most affected industries, may have to be reassessed in the light of this. In some industries, finance being just one example, women were beginning to gain a foothold, or to move through the ranks into management, when economic adversity forced layoffs or hiring freezes, with the most recently hired or promoted being the most vulnerable. The recession of the early 1990s, coming as it did after almost a decade of profligate corporate behaviour which leveraged future earnings with unprecedented levels of debt the economy is no longer able to sustain, may produce grim and permanent changes to our ability to provide jobs. We are having to accustom ourselves to uncertainty, and to lower our expectations about the inevitability of progress. These changes affect everyone, but they may have a greater impact on those women whose attachment to the work-force is most recent, or who do not possess the skills and flexibility to adjust to what is happening.

In other words, we have experienced two decades of change, some of it turbulent and unsettling. Our private worlds have altered as we reached to realize our full potential as women and as human beings, and as we struggled to achieve equality within our relationships; our nation has had to adjust in response to our claims for full citizenship and for recognition of our special needs as women; and our larger world, planet Earth, to which we are more intimately connected than ever before because of modern communications technology, has reverberated under the shock of wars, massacres, famine, ecological disasters and political revolution.

The remainder of this introduction specifically addresses claims or arguments made in the first edition, updating or amplifying where necessary.

STILL A SEXIST CULTURE?

It is too soon to sound the death-knell of sexism as an organizing principle of Australian culture and society; we still stereotype people according to their gender and we still fail to acknowledge fully the contribution women have made to the evolution of Australian culture. Nevertheless, it is no longer legitimate to complain, as it was in 1975, that women artists are invisible and neglected. One of the most exciting and energizing aspects of cultural life in Australia in the past two decades has been the emergence of so many talented and creative women – and the rediscovery and retrospective homage paid to women who had been 'manhandled' by history.

Undoubtedly women's greatest successes have been in the field of writing. Works of fiction and non-fiction by and about women now abound and are routinely included on school and university reading lists where once students were presented with reading lists that seemed only to include male authors. Today there are thriving sub-categories like detective fiction and collections of essays. In the non-fiction field, it has become almost commonplace for women's activities and women's history to be the subject of scholarly works and to take their place within the archives of our national intellectual heritage. The popular Writers' Week of the Adelaide Festival of Arts which was once an almost all male affair, now routinely has several women on its organizing committee and women are prominent amongst invitees and audience – although this was not achieved without a fight.[26] It would be a scandal nowadays if women's works were overlooked when the prestigious literary prizes are handed out each year. And while some women contend that Australian women are still less likely to be published and to be reviewed than men, this is not the impression I have.[27]

In other areas of the arts, there is less cause for congratulations. Women are no longer invisible or excluded from most fields but they are a long way from achieving parity in terms of representation and, especially, income. An Australia Council study on women in the arts conducted in 1983 found that across all artforms women were disadvantaged compared to men and that the difficulties women artists experienced were very similar to those suffered by women in the labour force at large.[28] Other studies have shown women musicians to be especially disadvantaged, getting fewer jobs and earning considerably less than men, while in the visual arts, where women are actually in the majority, they nevertheless are more likely to work part-time and to earn less.[29]

A pilot study of women in the visual and performing arts in Western Australia in 1991 concluded that women's opportunities varied with the artform – with theatre providing better opportunities than music but not as good as dance – and that smaller, more commercially attuned galleries and theatres provided better opportunities for women artists than the larger funded bodies which supposedly had EEO programmes.[30] Similarly, women's opportunities are more limited in film and television as was eloquently attested to by speaker after speaker at a one-day conference on the subject sponsored by Women in Film and Television in Sydney in September 1992.

What is different today, however, is that women's participation in the arts is an issue, just as the depiction of women in the media and in various artforms is also hotly debated. It is no longer necessary to make the case that women artists are entitled to practise and to receive support; in fact women artists now receive project and fellowship support from the government at a level equivalent to their male counterparts, and almost half the members of the Australia Council's Boards and Committees are women.[31] So with women no longer being overlooked for funding, the question today is how to make institutions and companies more responsive to women practitioners, including the recognition that many women have special needs or responsibilities – such as having to care for children – which are usually more likely to impinge on their participation than on men's. This entire debate has had some interesting and unanticipated consequences, the principal one perhaps being the demystification of the artist in society as the language of work-place reform, equal employment opportunity and financial equity is applied to people who perhaps were once seen as untouched by such mundane concerns.

MANZONE COUNTRY REVISITED

While Australian culture is not the thoroughly masculine construct that prevailed in the mid-1970s, it is still true in the early 1990s that women's views and presence are under-represented. We are still coming to terms as a society and as a nation with how to reconcile our various parts into a fair and coherent whole. The debate includes such issues as Aboriginal reconciliation, multiculturalism, reconciling work and family responsibilities (as part of the larger question of achieving balance between the work we do and the leisure we need), and how to conduct ourselves as a largely European nation on the cusp of Asia. It does not yet adequately address what should perhaps be the most fundamental question of all: achieving reconciliation between women and men.

Although this is something we all discuss constantly – it is referred to in books and in the media, and is a new and permanent thread through our lives – we have not yet learned how to make it part of the national debate about who we are. This is not likely to happen until more women become more involved in all aspects of national life, from politics to religion, from business to the arts. Until then, despite the significant changes which have occurred, women will still tend to be portrayed as the other, as a separate group, somewhat on the periphery of our society. As I noted earlier in this chapter, the media in this country (as elsewhere) have barely begun to report and comment fairly and adequately on this revolution within our society, and within our families. Often the subject is treated as remote and even alien, as if the writer were dealing with a foreign war rather than day-to-day domestic reality. Women themselves are fed up with this and want nothing more than to be integrated into every aspect of life, wanting at the same time to ensure their special needs, usually arising from being mothers, are not overlooked. It is no coincidence that during the launch of the National Agenda for Women during the 1993 election campaign, the loudest cheers from the mostly female audience came when Prime Minister Keating said he had announced his sweeping new child-care policies as part of his national economic statement, *Investing in the Nation*, the previous day 'rather than the very tempting option of "saving them up" for today, because I think it is time that child-care was included amongst our mainstream economic issues . . . the time is long past, as far as I am concerned, where child-care was tagged as "a women's issue" or a "welfare issue" . . .'[32]

The portrayal of women in many areas of the media, and in advertising, continues to be a source of outrage not just to feminists but to women in all walks of life who feel their dignity assailed or their sense of justice offended by stereotypes or sexually degrading imagery. Despite this their protests seemingly have little impact. Why? Such images evidently work, with women as well as men, or presumably they would not continue to be used. Or are advertisers and media proprietors uncaring, or oblivious to the reactions of women? It is difficult to see such practices continuing if they suddenly were to carry a commercial penalty and it may well be that women's best weapon is an economic one: the refusal to purchase products, including media products, that use offensive images of women.

Twenty years ago, women's magazines were under fire for failing to acknowledge the changes that were starting to occur in women's lives. In the chapter entitled Suburban Neurotics? I characterized the major traditional magazines as recognizing only women's family and domestic roles. Today, those magazines are very different – but no more realistic. They have largely abandoned their traditional women's service functions of advice on health and other family matters, and have evolved into a rather bizarre mixture of royalty, celebrity and the occult! They now peddle escapism on a grand scale with psychics, tarot card readers and clairvoyants providing pages of advice while the front of the magazines are crammed with gossip, scandal and the latest exploits of princesses and movie stars. Nowadays there's barely room for the recipes. It is a strange evolution and one that probably reflects the extraordinary concentration of media ownership in Australia rather than any particularly astute reading of the wishes of the readers. After all, now that the three major traditional magazines all offer women essentially the same editorial fare, where is the choice anyway?

Only the magazines directed at younger women, *Cleo*, *Cosmopolitan*, *New Woman* and the teenage bible *Dolly*, offer anything like a realistic depiction of the actual lives of their readers and the issues and problems they have to contend with. These magazines do address subjects like sex, self-esteem, sexual harassment and the multitude of day-to-day hassles in any young woman's life, and in this respect they are at least continuing to conform to the notion of women's service which was the editorial rationalization for what we used to criticize in the past. Today, those traditions have been abandoned by the magazines which used to cater for older women and they have simply become entertainment vehicles, primarily there to provide escape or distraction to readers whose real lives they now never bother to write about.

In 1988 it would have been unthinkable for the Australian bicentenary celebrations to have ignored the contribution of women, and there was a special women's programme with funds set aside to achieve this. The bicentennial book-publishing programme included specially commissioned works by and about women. Yet, since then, the neglect of women in our history and culture has been identified by a parliamentary committee as a major impediment to women achieving full equality. The 1992 report, *Half Way to Equal* (also known as the Lavarch Report after its chairman, Labor MP and, since the 1993 elections, Attorney-General Michael Lavarch) was the result of a bipartisan inquiry into equal status and equal opportunity for women in Australia. Among its many recommendations were proposals that 'public museums and institutions . . . be encouraged . . . to include adequate depictions of women's history; and [that] the Government investigate the possibility of funding a National Women's Place which would fully acknowledge women's contribution to Australian society and provide ongoing support and recognition of women's contribution'.[33] The report also argued that the Australian honours system needed to be more responsive to women's accomplishments especially in the voluntary sector. Women presently are awarded about

24 per cent of all honours, but of the highest ranking awards – the Companion and the Officer of the Order of Australia – all but a tiny fraction go to men.

Clearly, there is still a long way to go before our culture adequately reflects women's aspirations and contributions. Most societal institutions have been slow to respond to the massive changes that have occurred in women's lives, leaving many women feeling frustrated and impatient, wondering why it is they have to continue to wait for the acknowledgement and recognition that seems so obvious and so just.

THE SPORTING WIFE

Sport remains a national obsession in Australia and although men are twice as likely as women to play sport, women's sport is no longer the poor relation it was two decades ago. Women's teams receive media coverage when once they were ignored and championships in sports like netball (which is played by more people, all of them women, than any other sport) are now shown live on television. Nevertheless, discrimination against women in sports is still rampant and was a major subject of investigation by the Lavarch Committee which found cause for complaint in virtually every area of sports participation and administration. The Lavarch Report concluded there was inequality in prize money, in sponsorship, in funding and, despite some improvements, in media coverage of women's sports.[34] The report also noted that very few women have used the Sex Discrimination Act to complain about unequal treatment in sport, but this may change as the Sex Discrimination Commissioner has since issued guidelines on how to use the Act in relation to sport.[35] Women's participation in sports, and the status of women's sports, like women and the arts, women in politics, women in virtually every area of Australian life, is at last an issue for public debate and remedy. To this extent, there is progress even if there is still a long way to go.

THE RAVAGED SELF

There is no doubt that most women in Australia today are pleased with the changes in their lives, with their increased opportunities, with the greater freedom they enjoy compared with their mothers, and with the independence that participation in the work-force provides. Research conducted in mid-1992 for the Office of the Status of Women amongst average-income women around Australia produced remarkably consistent findings: 'Women and their status in Australian society are perceived to have undergone a major and dramatic transformation. The changes and gains made can be described as both "revolutionary" and "evolutionary". The women of "middle Australia" generally recognise these changes and tend to embrace their new roles in a positive manner'.[36] The women also acknowledged that enormous pressure and stress had accompanied the positive changes; they felt they had to succeed as wives, as mothers and in the workplace. They were generally impatient for the men in their lives to catch up to the new realities, and to do their fair share of household and other necessary tasks, and they were also angry that so many workplaces were still condescending or hostile towards women. But there was near unanimity that they did not want to turn back the clock: women valued their choices and their new-found financial independence too much.

So what does this mean for women's sense of self? Are the conflicts and contradictions involved in being female today less corrosive than a generation ago? I believe they are, since women have much greater choice than then, but it is also true that new pressures and constraints have arisen and some of these may be at least as destructive in their own way as the old ones. The stress and constant tiredness that besets so many working mothers is too high a price to pay for increased choice, and women rightly resent it. Other women feel the pressure to be Superwomen: able to effortlessly combine being a career woman with being the proud mother of perfect children with being a responsive and exciting lover, a gourmet cook and still have some personal space.

For the most part, women have been the shock absorbers of change, the ones who have made all the adjustments, taken on all the extra work, including that tiresome, and tiring, work of managing the emotional lives of their families. In short, women are doing more of everything and they are getting impatient about the unfairness of it all. Market research conducted in 1992 by the *Bulletin* on how Australians feel about themselves and their country, especially on social issues produced, among other things, the following conclusion:

Australian married and de facto couples consistently agree that a wide range of household chores and family decisions should be shared fairly equally regardless of gender. Yet this is not the reality. Women are being shortchanged, and they are angry about the inequality which persists in their lives. Women tend to initiate family break-ups in Australia – often to the bewilderment of their male partners, who fail to perceive the tension over the gap between ideal and reality in family life.[37]

It is perhaps because of these pressures that women's use of drugs, including cigarettes and alcohol, has increased over the past two decades. Women still have a greater reliance on pain-killers, tranquillizers and sleeping tablets than do men, and the 'dependency gap' seems not to be narrowing. In the early 1970s women's consumption of these substances accounted for two-thirds of total usage (see Table on p. 151). Ten years later, according to the 1989–90 National Health Survey, women were 50 per cent more likely to use these drugs than men; while the proportion of both men and women using such medications had increased slightly since the early 1980s, women's greater dependence remains marked.[38]

Many young women are confronting a different set of pressures from those their mothers experienced. They are growing up in a distressingly confusing world to which they are reacting in almost inexplicably self-destructive ways. There seems to be an alarming epidemic of eating disorders amongst teenage girls and while conventional wisdom ascribes its causes to low self-esteem there is really very little understanding about why it has become such a problem. Naomi Wolf's *The Beauty Myth*, for instance, contends that this self-hatred and obsession with body weight amongst young women coincided with the rise of the women's movement[39] but she does not draw an obvious, albeit unpalatable, conclusion that this may have been a reaction to the repudiation of beauty and physical attractiveness by many 1970s feminists. Were these young women repulsed by their mothers' and older sisters' nonchalance towards weight, body hair, make-up and clothes? What new notions of femininity are infecting the psyches of these young girls, and why are they so insidious? Why do they find the world so difficult just when it seems to be providing them with chances not available to any previous generation of women? Is it the pressure of being pioneers and the lack of a path to follow, or is it a deep-seated ontological fear that they – and we – are dealing with nothing less than a profound change in what it means to be a woman? Who wants to carry that burden? Older women can argue that it is preferable to what went before, but young women have no experience of what went before and can hardly be expected to incorporate that in to how they view themselves and their place in the world. We should acknowledge that young women are having a hard time today, and that older generations really haven't a clue as to why this is or what to do about it. The greater propensity for young girls today to take up smoking (just when many of their mothers are finally winning the battle to quit) is perhaps further evidence of the pressure they are under. These are issues that need urgent investigation and redress if young women are to reap the bounties their futures should hold for them.

It is perhaps ironic that it is middle-aged and older women who are more content today. Many of the women whose unfulfilled or frustrated lives were part of the inspiration for this chapter in the first edition are today more able to pursue their dreams. Although as a society we still place a premium on youth, and tend to attach a stigma to ageing, this is starting to change. Women themselves were not slow to recognise the opportunities presented by living longer: the post-menopausal freedom facing a woman in her fifties who is still healthy, able to work and with perhaps thirty more years to live. As the large baby-boom generation – that which also produced the women's movement in Australia, if not in the United States – begins to age, self-interest will see it dictate further major social and political changes. Age discrimination will figure prominently on the political agenda as baby-boomers resist being forced to retire from the work-place. Health issues, especially those affecting middle-aged women, are already starting to attract debate.

Many of those same second wave feminist writers who helped women understand who we were and what we wanted two decades ago are now beginning to address issues affecting older women. A world which valued women only for their child-bearing abilities accorded women little status or power once those years were over; this state of affairs is, needless to say, totally unacceptable to the pioneers of the women's movement who are themselves now middle-aged or older. Betty Friedan published a major work on ageing, *The Fountain of Age*, in late 1993, and Germaine Greer has tackled what once was seen as the stigmatised subject of menopause.[40] Just as twenty years ago women had to tackle the patronising and often discriminatory attitudes of doctors, especially obstetricians and gynaecologists, today women are having to contend with a medical profession that treats menopause as a psychological disorder. Women are now insisting that the real physical problems accompanying menopause be taken seriously. In the past many doctors tended to dismiss such symptoms as hot flushes and night sweats as inevitable and natural and therefore not requiring treatment. Today, medical advice seems to promise relief, in the form of hormone replacement therapy (HRT), but we still do not know at what future health risk and very little research appears to be being done.

Women's health generally is grossly neglected yet it is central to our sense of self which in turn is critical for our well-being. There has never been a serious study of women's health in this country although during the 1993 federal election campaign then Health Minister Brian Howe undertook to commission a longitudinal study of women's health so that we might improve our understanding of the different physical stages of women's lives and the long-term impact of drugs like oral contraceptives and HRT.

There are many issues in women's health that seem not to have changed much in two decades, while others seem more urgent today. We have gone backwards when it comes to choices about contraception, with new techniques such as implants still in their early stages of acceptability (and the long-term risks still unknown). Several of the conctraceptives in long-term use, such as some of the IUDs, have now been proven to have caused infertility and other problems. The contraceptive pill is still problematic, as I argued in 1975, and is not always advised for women over thirty-five, especially those who are obese or who smoke. The increase in sexually transmitted diseases has made the condom prevalent again as a prophylaxis but it was never especially reliable in preventing pregnancy.

A whole movement has arisen to champion women's rights in child-birth, something which did not exist in the mid-1970s when parturition was more likely to be organized around the time-tables and other needs of the delivering doctor. The rights of mothers are now a cause, with a growing literature of its own, able to bring informed debate to the many issues involved in child-birth. Had such a movement been active when this book was being researched, I may have been less inclined to arrive at the sweeping advocacy of Caesareans over natural child-birth which, on the evidence of the mail I have received over the years, was the most controversial assertion I managed to make in the entire work. Today, I leave such subjects to those who are more qualified to debate them; they are too specialized for someone who is neither a mother nor a health practitioner to take on.

Increasingly all of us have to deal with diseases such as cancer, especially breast and cervical cancer, which seem more prevalent today, although we don't know why (another compelling reason for specialised research on women's health), and a great deal of effort over the past decade has gone into encouraging women to monitor their health to try and detect early signs of such diseases. At the same time, many women are becoming more combative about health issues. Inspired to a large extent by AIDS activists who have adopted militant tactics with drug companies and government agencies to fight for less costly drugs and increased funds for AIDS research, many women are pursuing the issue of breast cancer with tenacity. They point out that the annual death toll from breast cancer far exceeds that from AIDS yet breast cancer lags far behind AIDS when it comes to attracting research funds and political support. Women, especially many who are surviving breast cancer, are determined to change this; their activism is a welcome sign that the political agenda for reforms affecting women continues to broaden and be responsive to newly perceived needs.

Women in Australia have been less prone to AIDS than men but many are nevertheless at risk and most people who are not in long-term monogamous relationships have had to adjust their sexual practices to avoid exposure to diseases which are spread by sexual activity. There seems to have been an alarming rise in infertility amongst women in their twenties and thirties, much of it apparently due to the spread of sexually transmitted diseases such as chlamydia. This in turn has led to a greatly increased demand for in vitro fertilization and other medical techniques which can help women to conceive. The whole issue has been a controversial subject amongst some feminists who argue against the cost and commercialisation of such services as well as the physical and emotional burden they impose on women. Other approaches such as surrogacy are condemned outright as exploitation of the female host's body. At the same time, few of the feminists who argue this have done much to discourage the cruel and untrue but still prevalent view that women are somehow incomplete, and certainly unfulfilled, if they have not borne a child. It is a cruel hoax on women to tell them they are feminine failures if they are infertile and at the same time condemn the technologies and practices which offer the possibility of redress.

THE POVERTY OF DEPENDENCE

The original argument of this chapter was that women were economically deprived both in the work-force and by the welfare system. The most reliable means for a woman to protect herself against poverty was through marriage, giving her access to her husband's income which was deemed to be greater than any income she could generate for herself. Today this is less likely to be the case. Women's earnings relative to men's have improved significantly, single women are generally able to achieve financial self-sufficiency and are not forced into marriage for economic reasons, and the welfare system now delivers more effectively – and for the most part more generously in real terms – than was the case in the early 1970s. At the same time, women as a group still earn less than men, are more reliant on the social security system, have less access to non-pension retirement income, may spend periods of their lives without remuneration doing voluntary or domestic work, and many women today still find themselves barely able to survive economically.

Previously I identified elderly women on pensions as the poorest group; today the proportion of elderly women reliant on the pension has declined from 80 per cent in 1981 to 66 per cent in 1991 (although the decline in men receiving the age pension has been even greater, from 74 to 50 per cent).[41] The decline is due to the introduction in 1983 of an income test on pensions for people aged over seventy and, since 1985, an assets test on all pensions as well as improved superannuation coverage – all of which have served to leave in the welfare net people of modest or no means at all beyond the pension. Today we would have to add to those most likely to be poor sole parents, 80 per cent of whom are women, and more than half of whom have no income other than social security benefits.[42] In 1991 those on benefits numbered 252,104 with 431,884 children.[43] A number of government initiatives have sought to improve the financial standing of single parents: the Child Support Agency has improved the extent and the amount collected from non-custodial parents, schemes like the Jobs, Education and Training (JET) programme encourage them to rejoin the work-force and, it is argued, extension of the right to retain fringe benefits for the first twelve (instead of the current six) months of employment would counteract the present work-force disincentive effects of the Sole Parents Pension.

In addition to being financially deprived, single mothers, especially young ones, still encounter immense discrimination and the charge that they are breeding machines, having babies to attract welfare payments. Social attitudes have changed, however; we no longer refer, negatively, to unmarried mothers or call their children illegitimate. As around 40 per cent of all marriages end in divorce, the majority of sole parents with children are likely to have been married at some stage. What is striking is the economic consequences of divorce for women, as compared to men. Women initiate 60 per cent of all divorces but do so without being necessarily aware of the likely financial impact of the breakup. Research by the Australian Institute of Family Studies into what happens to people after divorce found both partners suffered from the collapse of their domestic economy, but that women suffered the most – and for longer. Men have usually recovered and attained a higher standard of living within three years of separation, while women suffer a 'severe drop' which is likely only to be repaired if she can find a new partner.[44] But woe betide the sole parent who is discovered to be in a casual relationship with a man while she is in receipt of a pension; whether or not that man contributes to the household finances, if he spends two or more nights with the sole parent her pension is liable to be terminated.

The income support system is exempt from the operation of the Sex Discrimination Act, with the result that some forms of discrimination against women persist. While it could be argued that women here benefitted from such discriminatory practices as the earlier retirement age (and hence earlier eligibility for the age pension – although in the 1993 Budget the government announced plans to phase in over two decades an equal retiring age for women), and that the Sole Parents Pension enables single mothers to have a degree of financial independence they might not otherwise enjoy, other practices have the opposite effect. One example of this is the continuing practice of treating the family as the income unit when it comes to social security, in contrast to the taxation system where the individual is the unit. The result is that women are excluded from eligibility from certain benefits, such as unemployment benefits, if their husband has more than a token income, forcing them to become financially dependent. For women accustomed to the independence of their own income, such dependency is not especially welcome. (The reverse also applies, with men unable to claim benefits if their wives are earning, but in practice it is usually women who are disadvantaged by this policy.) Although women comprised 35.9 per cent of people unemployed for twenty-six weeks or less[45], only 25 per cent of recipients of unemployment benefits in 1991 were women.[46] Budgetary constraints are always cited as the reason for governments being unable to treat married people as individuals under the social security system, but until this can be achieved women will not achieve full economic independence. The dependent spouse rebate, available to tax-payers who have a non-earning spouse (invariably a wife) has long been attacked by women's groups for its perpetuation of the concept of dependency and for its implied insult to women in the work-force, who receive no tax recognition of the cost of working.

WOMEN, WORK AND WAGES

The surest way for women to ensure their economic independence is through employment with adequate remuneration. Even though women have moved from being 29 per cent of the work-force in 1966 to 42 per cent in 1990, and an average of 52 per cent of all women are in paid employment, their opportunities have not blossomed in a corresponding fashion. The many spectacular instances of women doing new or different jobs ('the first woman mechanic!', 'the first woman judge!', etc.) should not blind us to the fact that for the vast majority of women workers, their employment patterns are predictable and unaltering. The work-force remains segregated by gender with 54.5 per cent of women employed as clerks, salespersons or personal service workers. In contrast, the two largest male occupations – tradesperson and labourer – account for 40.3 per cent of total male employment.[47] Women work overwhelmingly in just four industries; fully 75.3 per cent of employed women in 1991 worked in community services; wholesale or retail trade; finance, property and business services; or recreation, personal and other services.[48] Men's work-force experience is somewhat more diverse: around 59 per cent of men work in the top four male employment industries.

Women continue to earn less than men. Women's full-time average weekly earnings in August 1991 were 85 per cent of men's, with the ratio dropping to 67 per cent if junior and part-time earnings are also included.[49] Although the concept of equal pay for work of equal value was mandated by the then Conciliation and Arbitration Commission in 1972, it has remained an elusive goal for most employed women. There are several reasons: the continuing gender segregation of the work-place, with women and men doing different work which is remunerated differently; the failure of the union movement to bring forward cases to establish the 'equal value' of varying skills; the broken employment patterns of most women due to child-bearing and family responsibilities, and their inability to work as much overtime as men; women's greater propensity to take part-time or casual jobs; and the fact that women are less likely to belong to strong unions capable of negotiating pay equity for them. Women are also less likely than men to receive over-award payments and, where they do, to receive comparable amounts.[50]

Even women in managerial jobs earn less than their male counterparts, with women in the private sector earning only 72 per cent of men's salaries, being, therefore, even worse off than public sector women managers, who at least made 87 per cent of male salaries.[51] But compared with other countries, there has at least been measurable improvement in the gender pay gap since the 1970s. In some categories of earnings women make 93 per cent of men's wages, a statistic which in 1992 earned Australia high praise from the International Labour Organisation. In the United States, by contrast, women's average earnings remain at 70 per cent of men's; the gender pay gap has not narrowed there as it has in Australia and many European countries[52], and few nations can point to a continuing commitment on the part of their national governments to the goal of pay equity. The Australian government established an Equal Pay Unit within the Department of Industrial Relations in 1990 with a mandate to provide advice to the government, and to increase community awareness of pay equity issues. The early information papers produced by this Unit were impressive, and while a bureaucratic body of this kind cannot move markets, or otherwise intervene to improve women's pay, its brief to provide material for government submissions to industrial tribunals should ensure that, at least while Labor remains in power, the government will keep the issue of pay equity within its focus.

The longer-term remedy to ensuring women receive equal pay is to provide equal access to education and skills-training so that they enter the labour market equipped to compete for more skilled, and thus higher-paying, jobs. Progress here seems slow, in part because it takes years to acquire an education and then build up employment experience, but it does appear that the numbers of women developing such skills is expanding. For instance, since 1987 more women than men have been enrolling in higher education and by 1990 women accounted for 53 per cent of all student enrolments.[53]

Women students still opt overwhelmingly for the traditional fields of study of education and arts, and are thus not diversifying their opportunities sufficiently, but even here there is some movement. Fifty per cent of women students in 1990 chose education or arts but that was better than the early 1980s when 70 per cent did. More women are now studying business, science and health and even engineering (where women are now around 10 per cent of all students) and women are more than 50 per cent of law students. Despite these gains we are still not at the point where women feel confident they can embark on any field of university study. The same is true of technical and further education. Although women made up around 45 per cent of all TAFE students in 1989, there were few areas of study where men and women students were equally distributed (in fact, applied science was the only area). Most women were taking business studies, personnel services, industrial services or general studies, while the largest single bloc of male students, almost a quarter of total enrolments, had headed straight for engineering.

While the federal government, via the Department of Employment, Education and Training's Gender Access and Equity Plan, has a nominal commitment to raising the educational and skill levels of girls and women, it does not appear to be an important national priority. Yet the upgrading of the skills-base of the present and future work-force *is* at least implicitly recognized as a necessary step for Australia to take in order to regain international competitiveness. It should not be difficult for the two goals to be combined under a structural adjustment strategy. A 1991 OECD report on women's role in the economies of member countries noted that 'gender segregation creates a major labour market rigidity (and) . . . is also a source of labour market inequalities' both of which were bad for women, and bad for the economy.[54] The report argued for 'a new perspective on women as economic actors', and directly challenged 'the traditional assumption that equity and efficiency are mutually exclusive outcomes'.[55]

This is important new thinking, and the kind of perspective that ought to be adopted by the Australian government. I find it extraordinary that, thirty years after women began moving into the paid work-force in massive numbers, it is still necessary to make the case that improving women's skills and opportunities is not a welfare programme but, rather, represents an investment in both the individual (whose life will be enhanced as a result) and our society (which should benefit from adding to the nation's bank of talent). At the same time, many of the skills women do possess are often undervalued or not remunerated by employers because they are perceived as natural female competencies or domestic tasks that are usually performed free in the home or elsewhere. Women often acquire skills while outside the paid work-force through participation in community organizations and in managing the home but, a government report on the subject showed, '. . . women themselves rarely recognise these skills because they are not acquired within the paid work-force. Yet many women develop technical, management, finance, interpersonal and organizational expertise which is transferable into paid work situations'.[56] Nor has sufficient financial recognition been accorded to the additional skills women in traditional occupations such as nursing or secretarial work have had to acquire as a result of changing technologies in these fields.[57] Secretaries and nurses are now required to be able to understand and operate sophisticated computers and other machines, and to continually upgrade these skills to keep pace with changes in these technologies, but there has not been a commensurate increase in their salaries.

LEGAL PROTECTIONS

The Sex Discrimination Act became law in 1984. 'Thousands of women' since then, according to Quentin Bryce, federal Sex Discrimination Commissioner from 1987–1992, 'have used the Act to seek a remedy when they suffer discrimination. Many women have spoken of the symbolic significance of the Act, of how it stands as a source of courage and support to them when they are treated unfairly . . .'[58] Gauging the effectiveness of the legislation after even a decade of operation is not easy. One measure is the numbers of people who have complained under the Act. Their number is not large, but it is growing and, perhaps not surprisingly, a majority have been women. In 1990–91 803 people, 728 of them women, complained, compared with 440 in 1987–88.[59] But it may also be the case that the mere existence of the legislation goes a long way towards accomplishing its primary goals, which are 'to eliminate, so far as is possible, discrimination against persons on the ground of sex, marital status or pregnancy . . . to eliminate . . . sexual harassment in the workplace and in educational institutions; and to promote recognition and acceptance within the community of the principle of the equality of men and women'.[60] This seemed to be the sentiment of a great many of the submissions to the Lavarch Inquiry in 1991–92. 'The feeling conveyed by the submissions is that generally speaking many of the more blatant examples of discrimination are no longer in evidence,' the inquiry's discussion paper stated. 'For example, advertisements for employment are no longer categorised under sex; women can join most clubs, and educational institutions take care in applying admission criteria that women are not directly discriminated against.'[61]

The Lavarch Report included a comprehensive review of both the sex discrimination and affirmative action legislation and concluded: 'While there is still need for further education of [sic] the implications of the legislation, successes to date suggest that it is time aspects of the current Acts be amended to reflect the more sophisticated level of public understanding [of gender-based discrimination].'[62]

The report went on to recommend a detailed series of changes, virtually all of which the Government later said it was prepared to accept.[63] The most significant were the extension of the Sex Discrimination Act to include industrial awards and to cover dismissal on the grounds of family responsibilities, the strengthening of the sexual harassment provisions, and a new power enabling determinations of the Human Rights and Equal Opportunity Commission (where the Sex Discrimination Commissioner is located) to be enforceable by the Federal Court. The government also agreed to amend the *Affirmative Action (Equal Employment Opportunity for Women) Act 1986* to cover voluntary organisations employing more than 100 people (in addition to the private sector companies and educational institutions already covered), and to adopt a policy of contract compliance to ensure that all recipients of government contracts and industry assistance comply with their obligations under the affirmative action law.

The willingness of the federal government to improve and strengthen these laws is heartening because as our understanding of discrimination increases, or as new forms of inequality are identified, different responses may be called for. As well, the philosophical issues underpinning the legislation continue to be debated. Some of these issues, such as the adequacy of the present definition of 'indirect discrimination', and the vulnerability of the clause allowing 'special measures' to promote women's equality are too technical to be canvassed in detail here.[64] What is relevant for the purposes of this discussion is the political will involved, the extent to which governments recognize the importance of these discrimination issues and the equal opportunity measures designed to counter them, and are prepared to respond when change is deemed necessary. On the record to date, it must be said the political will is present; what is required is perhaps somewhat more aggressive application of these laws and, in the case of affirmative action, greater attention to the quality of the compliance now that most companies covered are fulfilling their obligations to submit annual reports on the steps they are taking to improve opportunities for their female employees. The Affirmative Action Agency took the view in the early years of the legislation that its priority was to achieve maximum compliance, that is ensure that all institutions covered by the legislation submit their annual reports. Having achieved that, the next step is to begin evaluating the contents of those reports with a view to encouraging employers to accelerate the pace of change.[65]

The mere existence of anti-discrimination laws has led to the opening up of new areas of employment to women, with perhaps the most spectacular example being the military. There are some people, including many women, who do not feel that such change represents progress; in fact there is a curious symmetry of thinking on this subject between old-fashioned traditionalists and new-fashioned feminists. The former hold to stereotyped notions about women's place which they see as being in the home rather than in the trenches, while the latter hold dear the stereotyped notion that women, being intrinsically peace-loving, belong everywhere *but* the military. Neither view takes into account the desires of thousands of young Australian women who want to join the armed forces and who until very recently were prevented from occupying more than a handful of available jobs. Some of these young women are taken with the idea of being soldiers, or pilots or naval cadets, but most are attracted to the military because it provides them with an income while they acquire skills training they could not otherwise obtain. Indeed much of the feminist criticism of women in the military is made by women who have the privilege of a university or other higher education but who apparently have trouble identifying with the trade or technical education aspirations of young women from a different stratum of society.

When the Sex Discrimination Act first became law, the Australian Defence Forces (ADF) had successfully sought an exemption enabling it to preclude women from positions defined as combat or combat-related. In order to comply with the legislation, the ADF was obliged to review each and every designation in the three armed services and determine whether it was combat, combat-related or whether they could risk having women perform the task. As head of the Office of the Status of Women at the time, I chaired the interdepartmental committee which was given the responsibility for this review, and was astonished at the resistance to opening up *any* positions to women displayed by the military members of the committee. We fought tooth and nail for more than a year but still only succeeded in having 16,300 positions – or around 25 per cent of all ADF positions – declared able to be filled by women.[66] These figures made the situation look better for women than in fact was the case, however, since despite a 16 per cent increase in the number of women Defence Force personnel in the first two years of the operation of the Act, by mid-1986 women comprised only 7.9 per cent of the ADF. This was less than the de facto quotas that had been in effect before the Sex Discrimination Act.[67]

In May 1990, the government decided to open up combat-related, but not combat, positions to women. This decision was prompted partly by principle, the desire to extend opportunities to women, and partly by pragmatism: reviews had revealed a majority of service-women to be dissatisfied at being denied promotion because they were excluded by law from gaining the pre-requisite experience.[68] If the military wished to attract and retain talented women, it was going to have to address this anomaly, went the argument within the government.[69] It seems likely that the military didn't care one way or another, but the government insisted on progress so that by May 1991, women comprised 12.1 per cent of the ADF.[70] In late 1992, Gordon Bilney, then the Minister for Defence, Science and Personnel, announced that some combat positions were to be opened, enabling women to fly combat aircraft and to serve on submarines. Areas of combat involving direct physical contact with the enemy would remain restricted, the Minister said, arguing that service-women themselves agreed they should not engage in hand-to-hand combat.[71] As a result of the decision 99 per cent of Navy and RAAF positions are now open to women, and over 80 per cent of Army positions (the lower percentage in the Army reflects the higher number of combat positions potentially involving direct combat).

The presence of so many women in the work-force has meant that new codes of conduct between women and men have become necessary. It has become essential to draw up rules about peer relationships and the unacceptability of old-style male predatory sexual behaviour in the work-place. It has also become necessary to develop new language, particularly the term sexual harassment, to describe such behaviour. It has been depressingly apparent for more than a decade now that many men have resorted to harassment to try to deter women from entering occupations or industries in the past dominated by men. Many women pioneering jobs in such non-traditional areas as the police force, the fire brigade or the water board have had to endure treatment from their male colleagues which was demeaning, insulting, humiliating and often cruel. It is also now against the law but the incidence has, if anything, increased. A 1992 report on sexual harassment in the New South Wales public service found harassment of women to be highest in the police force with 40 per cent of women officers reporting having been subjected to such treatment.[72] But what is cause for even greater concern in the early 1990s is the apparent spread of such harassment to areas such as schools and white-collar work-places where women have long had a presence and were presumed to have been accepted by their male colleagues. The sharp increase in this sign of resentment against women – even young girls at school – is a nasty and alarming warning that our surge towards true equality still faces many obstacles.

Complaints about sexual harassment constituted the largest category of complaints under the Sex Discrimination Act in the early 1990s, and it was an area nominated by the Lavarch Report as requiring a significant strengthening in the Act. Those recommendations were accepted and in 1992 the government extended the Act to cover harassment by students against each other or against teachers, and harassment by landlords or other providers of goods and services. It also repealed the provision that required victims to have been disadvantaged by the harassment (for example to have lost one's job over it), in addition to having been humiliated, offended or intimidated and for any of these to have been a reasonable response to the behaviour in question.

There is no doubt that women's participation in all areas of society will never be on terms of true equality while sexual harassment persists. While it is true that some women have been found to have engaged in sexual harassment of men, it is predominantly men who are the perpetrators of such behaviour. But it is unacceptable behaviour whoever initiates it – as was recognised by the Australian Defence Force which in early 1992 issued an instruction to its members on inappropriate sexual behaviour. Initially this was intended to deal mainly with sexual harassment between members of the opposite sex, but it was extended to include unwelcome approaches to members of the same sex, and became an important part of the justification for the government's decision in late 1992 to end the ban on gay men and lesbians serving openly in the military. Sexual behaviour of any kind is not appropriate in any work-place and one of the challenges facing women and men alike as the labour-force becomes more and more integrated is to develop ways of working side-by-side in a co-operative, harmonious and non-intimidating manner. This should not be as difficult as it so far seems to have been, but experience suggests we have a long way to go yet before the right level of professional conduct is achieved.

Nor has the presence of so many women in the work-force yet made a marked impact on the way work is structured. The work-place is still mostly organized around employment patterns developed earlier this century when the work-force was overwhelmingly male (with the assumption that each male worker had a domestic support system in the form of a wife), and women have been expected to fit themselves into this pattern and try to reconcile it with their family responsibilities as best they can. Society in general, and employers in particular, have been slow to respond to the human and family needs of people at work. We talk about working mothers but never about working fathers, although increasingly men are almost as likely as women to take time off work for child-related reasons. A study of workers with family responsibilities conducted by the Australian Institute of Family Studies in 1992 found that 71 per cent of mothers and 64 per cent of fathers had taken an average of nine days off work to care for children in the previous twelve months, and that while mothers were more likely to stay home to look after sick children, mothers and fathers were equally likely to stay home during school holidays, to attend school events or take children to medical or dental appointments.[73]

But it is women who bear most of the burden – the double burden, as it is so aptly called – of domestic responsibilities on top of the hours they spend in the work-place. A survey of how Australians spend their time, conducted by the Australian Bureau of Statistics in 1987, shows that regardless of income, education, age, social background or employment status women do twice as much unpaid work – most of it household work – as men.[74] While men now do more domestic work (shopping, cooking, cleaning, laundry and so on) than they did in the early 1970s, they still manage to find a great deal more time for leisure activities than women do. It is not surprising, then, that many employed women, especially those with young children, find that constant tiredness and feelings of stress are the counterpoint to the economic and other rewards of having a job. How women actually cope with this work-load was described with sardonic humour by *Sydney Morning Herald* columnist Adele Horin in mid-1992:

all over Australia, mothers with young children work miracles each morning by getting to the office, the factory or the shop by nine o'clock, or even 7.30. If the country were being run with the efficiency these women bring to their early morning labours, Australia would be an economic tiger, not a sheep. They've worked for two to three hours, these unsung heroes of the labour force, by the time the rest of the office walks in. They've hung out a load of washing in the dawn light. They've covered school books and breastfed babies; cajoled sleepy children out of bed and force-fed them breakfast. They've dealt with tantrums and sock fetishes, toddlers who insist on dressing themselves and children who won't get dressed. They've cleaned up kitchens, bathrooms and bedrooms, and finally themselves before flying out the door, entreating their brood to follow. They've dropped their charges at schools, kindergartens and child-care centres, negotiated the peak hour, hunted for all-day parking spaces, caught buses, taxis in emergencies, and hit the desk or counter at opening time. Every time I hear politicians exhort Australians to work harder, I think of this female underground toiling invisibly in the gray dawn in order to get to work on time.[75]

Women with young children constitute the fastest-growing section of the labour-force; in 1983 48 per cent of women with children aged under twelve were in the work-force, by 1991 that figure had increased to 63 per cent.[76] The revolution in the work-place will not be complete until we find ways to share domestic work more equitably, and to reorganize the work-place (especially hours of work) in ways that are more compatible with the family and personal needs of employees, especially women.

Since the mid-1980s the federal government has recognized this as an issue requiring legal, financial and educational intervention. Child-care, that most basic support service for working parents, and an issue described by Lyndall Ryan as 'the litmus test of the State's response to women's issues'[77], has greatly expanded since the early 1980s. Federally subsidized child-care places increased from 46,000 in 1983 to 168,000 in 1991[78] and during the 1993 federal election campaign Prime Minister Keating undertook to meet total work-related demand for child-care by 2001, a promise which also included meeting 84 per cent of demand by 1997. With this pledge, the government finally acknowledged that it has a responsibility to support the family needs of working parents, an attitude that ranks Australian governments (Labor governments, at any rate) amongst the most progressive in the world on such issues. Similarly, the government has ratified the International Labour Organization's Convention No. 156, thereby making it an aim of national policy to 'enable workers with family responsibilities, who are employed or wish to be employed, to do so without discrimination and, as far as possible, without conflict between their employment and their family responsibilities'. This obliges the government to amend, or introduce, laws to facilitate the implementation of the Convention and to provide information to the community on how its objectives can be met. In January 1993, Australia again scored a world first when amendments to the Sex Discrimination Act became operative which outlawed discrimination on the grounds of family responsibilities.

Most employers are still in the dark ages when it comes to responding to the family needs of their work-force but there are some signs that, at least with large companies, change is beginning. The Affirmative Action Agency each year recognizes company initiatives with a series of awards. Among those so honoured in 1991 were programmes introduced by IBM to assist female employees with family responsibilities and another to assist women with management potential to undertake training, and a child-care feasibility study amongst its employees by Nissan Australia.[79] More companies need to follow these examples. Other social institutions also need to recognize the new reality of women's increased and permanent participation in the work-force. For example, school hours are totally incompatible with most people's hours of employment; they seem to be still arranged around the assumption that women are full-time housewives and mothers able to be home in mid-afternoon when children get out of school. This means parents have to scramble to make arrangements for the care of children after school, while at government level funding is diverted from child-care to after-school programmes, which, if schools were used more imaginatively, would probably not be needed. School holidays are an additional burden for adults and force the need to make special arrangements on parents whose own holidays do not occur so frequently.

Most places of business likewise have hours which create organizational nightmares for working women. While in some cities shopping hours have been extended to evenings and weekends, banks, post offices, motor vehicles registration and driver's license offices are usually only open during business hours, and rarely at weekends, thus failing to recognize the new reality of women's work. When the demand is made for flexible hours, job sharing and similar arrangements, they are often portrayed as benefits for women, to make juggling home and work easier, but it should not just be women who have to make the adjustments.

Working women, especially those who are middle-aged, are increasingly having to deal with caring for elderly parents – often at a time when their own children are still dependent. Women in this so-called sandwich generation face what can be an extremely demanding and stressful responsibility when added to a full-time job, particularly when a parent or child is ill. In the past, it would have been women who carried most of this burden, who were working daughters as well as working mothers, but recent Australian research suggests that today men are just as likely as women to take time off from work to attend the needs of a parent or parent-in-law.[80] Both government policy and a population which is living longer mean caring for ageing parents is going to become a major issue for more and more working people. Government policy on the aged encourages community rather than residential care which, in practice, means families care for their own. We can expect the need to take time off from work for this purpose to increase, and for it to become yet another issue employers need to take into account when addressing the family responsibilities of their employees.

The trade union movement has become more responsive to women workers and their needs, aided in part by the rise to prominence of credible and influential women unionists like Anna Booth in the Textiles, Clothing and Footwear Union and Jennie George who in 1991 became the first woman Assistant Secretary of the Australian Council of Trade Unions. The ACTU aims for women to be 50 per cent of its executive by the year 2000, and during the 1993 federal election it devoted funds and staff power to a special campaign directed at working women. At a time when union membership overall is declining, trade union leaders like Bill Kelty, Secretary of the ACTU, have astutely decided to target women, the fastest growing segment of the labour-force, in an effort to boost numbers. To achieve this goal it has been necessary to champion policies, such as child-care, which women will find attractive and which were not previously on the union movement's agenda, and to initiate industrial campaigns, such as those for supplementary payments and the Minimum Rates Adjustment process, which have led to increased earnings for low paid women workers. While some sections of the union movement remain oblivious to the needs of women in the work-force, the willingness of the ACTU and some of the more progressive unions to address these issues is a welcome change.

A COLONIZED SEX

A major premise of this book was that women have been subjugated by physical force as well as by the social pressure of the exhortative stereotypes. There is no question that such violence continues today, has seemingly increased and appears to be a direct response on the part of some men to their relative loss of power as women's opportunities have improved. This is a grim conclusion but many women consider that there is a direct connection, as the market research report 'The Women's View' prepared for the Office of the Status of Women in 1992 attests. Many of the women interviewed for the report saw recent increases in violence against women as 'a direct result of the changes in their status in society. Violence is virtually seen as the price paid by women for their new found freedom and independence'.[81] This profoundly depressing conclusion was repeated by woman after woman in the research focus groups:

'Violence has increased . . . it's resentment and confusion about male roles . . . so they are attacking . . . maybe men need to be taught more to bring their feelings out . . . a lot of men can't talk, so they attack, they use the physical . . . years ago, you had a boyfriend and he protected you, now you have equality, you fight.'

Brisbane woman, aged 40–55

'The bad side of all this is the violence . . . the power thing of rape; there is more violence now and it's very threatening at the moment . . . it's all about power . . . the men are trying to get some of that power back and rape is more about power than sex . . . they need to hurt someone, to show authority and this is threatening us more and more.'

Mackay woman, aged 25–39

The perceptions of these women that violence against women has increased appears to be right. There is no doubt that reporting of violence has increased. For instance, police figures show that the incidence of reported rapes in the early 1990s was more than three times that of twenty years earlier (5.63 per 100,000 population in 1973–74 to 18.28 in 1990–91).[82] Does this mean that more rapes are being committed or merely that women are more likely to report assaults than in the past? Have women responded positively to years of feminist argument that victims of such crimes have nothing to be ashamed of, and that changes to the law have made pressing charges less of an ordeal than in the past? We cannot be sure, especially in the absence of a thorough (and long-overdue) national investigation into violence against women. But it does seem that both propositions are true. Women *are* more likely to report crimes of violence – and are also more likely to disclose past episodes of sexual violence such as incest or other forms of child sexual abuse. But it also appears that violence against women has risen, perhaps quite dramatically.

We also know that women are most likely to suffer violence at the hands of men they know. A 1985 study of sexual assault conducted by the New South Wales Bureau of Crime Statistics and Research found that only 20 per cent of incidents which were reported to police involved assault by a person totally unknown to the complainant at the time.[83] A similar conclusion was reached by the Sexual Assault Referral Centre at Queen Elizabeth Hospital in Adelaide: '. . . it is our clear impression that most violent sexual assaults occasioning severe physical injury occur in the context of marital or de facto relationships in which violence of all sorts has been a common feature. Such sexual assaults are least likely to be proceeded with through the courts by the victim'.[84] Few cases may be prosecuted but at least the law now enables prosecution to take place. In 1976 South Australia became the first State to make marital rape a crime and by 1989 when Queensland finally followed suit, all States had revoked the ancient English legal principle that 'by their mutual matrimonial consent and contract the wife hath given up herself on this kind unto her husband, which she cannot retract'.

In early 1993 when remarks by a South Australian Supreme Court judge to the jury in a rape in marriage case the previous year became public they caused a national uproar. The reaction became an instructive example of current attitudes towards violence against women. The judge, Justice Derek Bollen, had told the jury: 'There is, of course, nothing wrong with a husband faced with his wife's refusal to engage in intercourse, in attempting in an acceptable way, to persuade her to change her mind, and that may involve a measure of rougher than usual handling.'[85] These remarks were denounced by women and men from across the political spectrum and in editorials and letters from readers in virtually every newspaper in the country. There were calls for the Judge to be sacked. The media led the discussion of the need for judges to be educated on gender issues, and for the method of selecting judges to be changed so that more women could sit on the bench. Typical of the comment his words evoked was the following, from an editorial in the *Examiner* in Launceston:

'Justice Bollen's statement accepts that force and the fear that come from it are legitimate tactics which husbands can employ with their wives. All of those involved in the fight against domestic violence will despair at the judge's comments and the damage they have done. Recent surveys of young Australian males found that an alarmingly high number regard some level of domestic violence as acceptable. It is an attitude that will take a long time to overcome, especially with comments like those made by Justice Bollen.'[86]

The outcry was instructive because it was something of a barometer both of how much has changed – and what has not. The man charged apparently thought he could abuse his wife with impunity – but his wife had the courage eventually to leave him and the law now enabled her to take him to court. The Judge reflected archaic attitudes when he appeared to favour the accused and, in another part of his summing up seemed more concerned that innocent men escape false rape charges than raped women receive justice – but he was roundly condemned by public figures, women's groups and newspapers around the country. The outrage would have been even greater, in my opinion, had the details of the charges been made public. The 'rougher than usual handling' remarks might suggest some slapping around of the wife by the husband; they hardly seemed to describe forced anal intercourse, forced oral intercourse, forced vaginal intercourse and the forcible insertion of a bottle into the wife's vagina – events which took place, not in a single night but repeatedly over a two year period.[87]

It must become an urgent national task to tackle the alarming incidence of domestic violence. Some welcome changes to the law and to police procedure have meant that the abusing man can be taken into custody without his victim having to lodge a complaint; and orders requiring abusive men to stay away from home are more easily obtained. Police and women's groups have worked, often together, to try to overcome the attitude so prevalent in the past that such violence is 'only a domestic' and thus does not warrant police intervention. But these measures seem to have done little to reduce the toll, and in some ways may even have led to more violence as men with orders out against them have hunted down their wives – and sometimes their children as well – and killed them.

To eliminate this violence, governments and community groups need to approach it in the same systematic, long-term way as they have addressed issues like smoking and drink-driving. Not only do sufficient funds have to be set aside to ensure that the right kind of persuasive publicity campaign can be mounted for as long as is needed to convince men that this behaviour is reprehensible and wrong, but subsidiary preventive and follow-up strategies are needed. We have to foster the attitude that violence in the home is shameful and unmanly; and we also need to break the circle of violence that so often sees people perpetuate behaviour which they witnessed or themselves suffered when they were young and vulnerable. At the same time, individuals and communities can try to work with known offenders and develop tactics to address such problems. One example of this approach is the anti-grog councils established by Aboriginal women in several Northern Territory communities, to reduce consumption of alcohol, a factor in much of the violence in those communities and elsewhere.

WOMEN IN POLITICS

It has become very apparent over the past two decades that for the kind of broad-based and comprehensive change that we still need to occur, women must be involved in making laws and implementing policy. There is now little disagreement that women should be represented at all levels of elective office and this is starting to happen. From 1979–1990, the percentage of women in State parliaments increased from 4.8 per cent to 11 per cent, and in federal parliament from 3.2 per cent to 12.5 per cent.[88] The 1993 federal elections saw a decrease of one in the number of women in federal parliament as although three additional women won House of Representatives seats, four fewer women senators were returned. Since the mid-1970s women have seemed assured of at least one seat in the federal Cabinet[89], with Senator Margaret Guilfoyle holding senior jobs in the Fraser Government, and Senator Susan Ryan and after her, Ros Kelly, appointed to the Hawke Cabinet. Kelly remained a member of Paul Keating's first two Cabinets. Joan Child became the first woman to be Speaker of the House of Representatives, and Anne Levy occupied a similar spot in the South Australian Upper House. Women ministers were no longer the exception in State governments, and even where present in token numbers, at least they were finally there. In 1990, Carmen Lawrence in Western Australia and Joan Kirner in Victoria became Australia's first women State Premiers, thus opening the way for women to hold leadership positions at all levels of government.[90] In 1992 Rosemary Follett became Chief Minister of the ACT, the first woman to be elected to this position. South Australia continued its tradition of innovation when then Premier John Bannon appointed Dame Roma Mitchell as the nation's first woman governor, a move that was later emulated by Queensland's Labor Premier Wayne Goss who in 1992 made Leneen Forde the State's governor.

Local government proved to be an even more receptive ground for women, with 19.57 per cent of positions Australia-wide in 1992 being held by women.[91] In some parts of the country, the Northern Territory for instance, women's representation in local government was as high as 30 per cent. It became no longer unusual for a woman to be elected mayor, even of a large city. Brisbane and Melbourne led the way with Sallyanne Atkinson and Winsome McCaughey. It is perhaps not surprising that women can achieve a higher level of political representation closer to home where presumably the demands of juggling family and work in addition to politics at least does not require the additional stress of large amounts of travel.

Yet there is still something unsatisfying about this record. Even in public life, women have tended to be stereotyped, given portfolio responsibility for areas like education or welfare and, of course, women's issues, all of which are deemed more suitable than the more robust (or masculine) portfolios of treasury, transport or defence. There have been some exceptions: Margaret Guilfoyle was Minister for Finance for a while and Ros Kelly at the time of writing was in charge of sport and environmental issues, and of course there were the State premiers who presided over the entire range of government responsibility. But then finance could be seen as the good housekeeping of government, and environment as Mum keeping the backyard clean; it has been difficult for women in public life to transcend the stereotypes of their sex, especially as to defy or renounce them too precipitously could mean being seen as unfeminine and perhaps be electorally dangerous.

The women premiers had the sour satisfaction of being told they were only given the jobs because they were female, that they were a much-needed, highly visible and thus handily symbolic contrast to their inept or corrupt male predecessors. In fact, whole new political theories developed around the appointments of Lawrence and Kirner. 'At a time of crisis, it was not a strong man that was wanted,' said Rod Cameron, managing director of the Sydney-based market research firm ANOP and political pollster for the ALP during the 1980s. 'Strong men had made the mess. It was an honest woman with the appearance of down-to-earth common sense who was chosen to clean it up.'[92] Cameron predicted the future 'feminisation of politics' as voters rejected in their leaders brute strength and ockerism in favour of 'intelligence, common sense, honesty and creativity – an unusual combination of virtues more likely to be found among women than men'.

This kind of argument has its dangers for it encourages the belief that *any* woman politician is going to be an improvement over just about any man, and this simply is not the case. Rather than try and make the spurious case that women are ethically superior, we should be recognizing and extolling the diversity of women's talents and interests. Rather than try to argue that the characteristics that make some women good mothers will necessarily make any woman a superior politician, we should acknowledge that some women are dishonest and unscrupulous (just as plenty of men are sensitive and creative). Women politicians are, after all, politicians as well as being women and in order to win office and stay there, often decide it is necessary to do things which go against this stereotype. We must have the maturity to acknowledge this so that we can start to become much more tough-minded in our approach to our political representation. It is not enough merely to elect more women to parliament; we have to ensure enough of those women have sufficient talent and energy to qualify them to become ministers and, ultimately, prime ministers. The larger the pool, one would hope, the greater the likelihood we can be proud of our women politicians – not simply because they are there, but because they are good.

DAMNED WHORES AND GOD'S POLICE

The contention that women are ethically superior has strong appeal, particularly to many feminists. It provides the intellectual foundation, for instance, for the American feminist Carol Gilligan's best-selling book *In A Different Voice* which argues that women represent a higher order of morality than men.[93] This book articulates the assumptions underlying the general proposition that 'the world would be a better place if run by women' and its many associated beliefs, such as the notion that girls' presence in classrooms serves to moderate the behaviour of rambunctious schoolboys. Such thinking is in direct conflict with the earlier feminist intellectual premise that most, if not all, behavioural differences between women and men were the result of environmental factors, especially sex-role conditioning and its concomitant exhortation to girls to act like ladies, set their sights lower than their brothers and in general confine their behaviour and their ambitions.

What kind of feminism is it that now seeks not only to give legitimacy to sex-based differences, but to reverse the previous hierarchy, which ascribed superiority to men's physical and intellectual prowess, and replace it with women's supposed ethical and emotional strengths? Is this just a late-20th century version of the God's Police stereotype, or is it a genuine breakthrough in our thinking about the qualities contemporary society now has the greatest need for? I am unable to see it as anything other than regressive. This is exactly what Caroline Chisholm contended – that 'good and virtuous women' were the much needed civilizing agents in a rough and ready colonial society – and, the major argument of this book, she thereby provided the ideological underpinnings for more than a century of domestic servitude by Australian women. It is hardly progress for us to argue that women in public life should be political housewives, cleaning up after the men. Of course a strong case can be made for the need for these qualities and virtues ascribed to women to become the governing principles of our society, but why perpetuate the surely sexist notion that these qualities are gender innate? Why not encourage their nurturance in men, just as we have fostered in women the belief that no ambition is now beyond them?

The stereotypes which twenty years ago could be depicted as the organizing principles of Australian life still exist but they have lost their potency. Or it seemed they had. Certainly the good girl/bad girl polarity is virtually extinct; these days all girls want to be bad if bad means making choices about their lives and refusing to follow paths preordained by previous generations. The most visible single symbol of the bad girl in the bad old days was the so-called unmarried mother and her illegitimate child; as already pointed out such language is now thankfully obsolete along with the attitude that makes moral judgements about women on the basis of their sexual behaviour. A further barometer of changed attitudes is the outcry that occurs when, from time to time and most recently in Melbourne in 1991, a judge opines that rape is a less serious offence if committed on a prostitute. The judicial assumption in such cases is misdirected in two respects: that a person who earns their living from sexual acts has abrogated the right to withdraw consent, and that rape is a sexual act rather than an act of violence. Once, these assumptions would never have been challenged. Today, it is almost routine to do so.

So while we can argue that the stereotypes are still there, submerged in the national consciousness, they are not as coercive as they once were. Today women can surmount them or ignore them; certainly women can exist beyond these parameters – which was exactly what the women's movement, and feminism, in the early 1970s set out to do. What a cruel irony it would be if feminism in the 1990s were to succeed in reimposing a stereotype, one that so chillingly resembles Caroline Chisholm's model woman, and justifying it in the name of human progress. Once we espouse model behaviour we logically create categories of deviance from it. We see this already in the shrill moralism surrounding the new imperative of political correctness in thought and deed: the condemnations of those who are deemed not to be 'PC' are as tyrannical (and often as arbitrary) as the denouncements of damned whores used to be.

NOTES

1. See Portia Robinson, *The Hatch and Brood of Time: A study of the first generation of native-born white Australians 1788–1828*, Oxford University Press, Melbourne, 1985, especially the chapter 'I Am Not for Marrying'.

2. See Robert Hughes, *The Fatal Shore: A History of the Transportation of Convicts to Australia 1788–1868*, Collins, London, 1987.

3. For instance, Marian Aveling, 'Bending the Bars: Convict Women and the State', in Kay Saunders and Raymond Evans (eds), *Gender Relations in Australia: Domination and Negotiation*, Harcourt Brace Jovanovich, Sydney, 1992.

4. For an appreciation of this uniquely Australian contribution to the practice (if not the theory) of the relationship between feminism and the state, see Sophie Watson, (ed.), *Playing the State: Australian Feminist Interventions*, Allen & Unwin, Sydney, 1990, who casts a British eye over the phenomenon of the the femocrat, and Hester Eisenstein, *Gender Shock: Practising Feminism on Two Continents*, Allen & Unwin, Sydney, 1991, for an American perspective. Eisenstein also has a chapter on femocrats in the Watson collection. Both Watson and Eisenstein, each of whom found themselves in Australia in the early 1980s, were simultaneously shocked and impressed to encounter femocrats. Watson describes coming from an impoverished university in Margaret Thatcher's England to 'a foreign and somewhat dazzling world' – Canberra. 'The feminists I met exchanged coded gossip about their ministers' plans for the following day, about the policies they were trying to "get up", about the million-dollar budget they had won for women's research, about the interstate meeting they were flying to tomorrow. I was baffled. What relationship did these women have to the academic or community-based feminisms with which I was familiar? What kind of feminism did they espouse? Why did everyone wear designer frocks and smart Italian shoes to work?' Watson, ibid., p. 4.

5. This precedent was followed up in 1992 when Paul Keating, then Prime Minister, introduced amendments to the *Sex Discrimination Act 1984* in the House of Representatives.

6. The research and its findings are referred to in more detail later in this chapter, and were described by Prime Minister Paul Keating in a speech launching the National Agenda for Women on 10 February 1993.

7. Following the 1992 congressional elections accompanying the presidential elections which saw Bill Clinton elected, and which occurred in what was widely dubbed 'the year of the woman', the numbers increased to 52 (5 senators and 47 members of the House of Representatives) but American women are still a far smaller proportion of elected federal

representatives than is the case in Australia where women made up 12.5 per cent of the federal parliament.

8. See 'Special Report: How women will elect the next President', *Ms.*, April 1988, pp. 75–79.

9. 'The Borking of Bill', *New Republic*, 17 May, 1993, p. 7.

10. See Marcia Cohen, *The Sisterhood: The Inside Story of the Women's Movement and the Leaders Who Made It Happen*, Fawcett Columbine, New York, 1989, pp.310–311.

11. ibid. p. 336–37.

12. See, for instance, the anthologies edited by Robin Morgan: *Sisterhood Is Powerful*, Vintage, New York, 1970, and *Sisterhood is Global*, Anchor Books, New York, 1984.

13. 'On the Road', *Ms.*, May/June 1993, p.1.

14. In 1991 during a Senate Judiciary Committee confirmation hearing to review the suitability of Clarence Thomas to be appointed to the United States Supreme Court, allegations were brought forth that he had many years before sexually harassed Anita Hill, another lawyer and a colleague at the Equal Opportunity Commission where they both worked at the time. Professor Hill's and Mr Thomas's testimony to the committee – where she outlined the allegations and he staunchly denied them – were televised live in the United States and gave the issue of sexual harassment an instant national profile.

15. *The Macquarie Dictionary*, 1988 edition. The dictionary that sat by my side as I wrote this book, *The Concise Oxford Dictionary*, 1964, offered 'advocacy, extended recognition, of the claims of women' but no hint as to what those claims might be. Today it is standard for dictionaries to have a more precise definition. For instance *Webster's New Collegiate Dictionary*, 1987, puts it this way: '**1.** the theory of the political, economic and social equality of the sexes. **2.** organized activity on behalf of women's rights and interests'.

16. I am indebted for this information to Gavin Souter, author of the two authoritative and prize-winning volumes of history of the media company John Fairfax Ltd. See *Company of Heralds: A century and a half of Australian publishing by John Fairfax Limited and its predecessors 1831–1981*, Melbourne University Press, Melbourne, 1981, and *Heralds and Angels: The House of Fairfax 1841–1990*, Melbourne University Press, Melbourne, 1991.

17. Chris Ronalds, the Sydney feminist barrister who drafted the legislation, noted in an article that the legislation 'unfortunately became known as "the Sex Bill".' See Chris Ronalds, 'Government Action Against Employment Discrimination' in Watson, op. cit., p. 108.

18. Cited in Chris Ronalds, *Affirmative Action and Sex Discrimination*, Pluto Press, Sydney. Updated 2nd edn, 1991, pp. 16–17.

19. The Australian Institute of Family Studies was established by the federal government in 1980 with a brief to conduct research on the factors affecting marital and family stability. While the reasons for setting up the institute were obviously ideological, reflecting the political views of the Fraser government, it has taken a distinctly broad approach to its mandate to work 'with the object of promoting the protection of the family as the natural and fundamental group unit in society' and in fact studies all kinds of family situations.

20. Reported in *Family Matters* (Australian Institute of Family Studies Newsletter), No. 20, April 1988, p. 37.

21.   See, for instance, Sophie Watson, op. cit., Marian Sawer, *Sisters in Suits: Women and public policy in Australia*, Allen & Unwin, Sydney, 1990; Anna Yeatman, *Bureaucrats, Technocrats, Femocrats*, Allen & Unwin, Sydney, 1990.

22.   Lyndall Ryan 'Feminism and the Federal Bureaucracy', in Watson, op. cit. p. 73.

23.   'National Agenda for Women', speech by the Prime Minister, the Hon. P. J. Keating MP, Bankstown Town Hall, Sydney, 10 February 1993.

24.   'Next time, ask a woman', Dale Spender, *Sydney Morning Herald*, 16 March 1993.

25.   According to Channel 9/AGB McNair Federal Election Exit Poll data 54 per cent of women aged 25–39 voted Labor compared to 46 per cent of men in the same age group.

26.   See Sophie Watson, 'Feminist Cultural Production: the Tampax Mafia, an Interview with Chris Westwood of the Belvoir Street Theatre', Watson, op. cit. p. 225–26.

27.   See Dale Spender, *The Writing or the Sex? or, why you don't have to read women's writing to know it's no good*, Pergamon Press, New York, 1989, for an example of this complaint.

28.   Cited in Victoria Rogers, Cora V. Baldock and Denise Mulligan, 'What Difference Does It Make? Women in the visual and performing arts in Western Australia'. Draft of a report commissioned by the Australia Council and the WA Department for the Arts, January 1993, p. 20.

29.   ibid. p. 23.

30.   ibid.

31.   'National Agenda for Women: Implementation Report', prepared by the Office of the Status of Women, Canberra, September 1992, p. 125.

32.   National Agenda for Women, speech.

33.   *Half Way to Equal*, Report of the Inquiry into Equal Opportunity and Equal Status for Women in Australia by the House of Representatives Standing Committee on Legal and Constitutional Affairs, April 1992, p. 177.

34.   ibid. pp. 107–49.

35.   *Women, Sport and Sex Discrimination: Guidelines on the Provisions of the Sex Discrimination Act 1984*, Human Rights and Equal Opportunity Commission, Sydney, August 1992.

36.   'The Women's View: Market research study on women's perceptions of themselves and government programs and policies', conducted for the Office of the Status of Women by Consumer Contact, July–August 1992, p. 25.

37.   Ben Sandilands, 'The heartland speaks. What we want, what we fear', report of first Australian Social Monitor survey conducted by AMR: Quantum, *Bulletin*, 28 July 1992, pp. 40–4.

38.   'Women's Budget Statement 1991–92', AGPS 1991–92 Budget Related Paper No. 5, Canberra, 1991, pp. 408–9. It is salient that OSW includes such drug reliance in its measuring of equality; it is included in general health and is one of 14 Gender Equality Indicators regularly monitored by the office. Others include women's work-force participation, access to child-care, earnings, access to superannuation, life expectancy, and so on.

39. Naomi Wolf, *The Beauty Myth: How Images of Beauty Are Used Against Women*, William Morrow, New York, 1991, p. 185.

40. Germaine Greer, *The Change: Women, Ageing and the Menopause*, Hamish Hamilton, London, 1991.

41. 'National Agenda for Women: Implementation Report', 1992, p. 220.

42. *Half Way to Equal*, op. cit., p. 90.

43. 'Women's Budget Statement 1991–92', p. 296.

44. Sheila Browne, 'The Great Divide. How women lose out after divorce', *Sydney Morning Herald*, 18 February 1993.

45. ibid. p. 174.

46. ibid.

47. 'Women's Budget Statement 1991–92', p. 174.

48. ibid.

49. 'Equal Pay: A background paper', Department of Industrial Relations, Canberra, n.d. (c. 1991), p. 7.

50. See *Just Rewards: A Report of the Inquiry into Sex Discrimination in Overaward Payments*, AGPS, Canberra, 1992.

51. ibid.

52. Peter Passell, 'Women's Work: The Pay Paradox', *New York Times*, 25 March 1992.

53. These figures, and those applying to TAFE enrolments, come from 'Women's Budget Statement 1991–92', op. cit., pp. 154–63. It should be noted that the rapid rate in the increase of female enrolments in higher education since 1985 has been due in part to the gradual transfer of nurse education from hospitals to institutions of higher education and of course the vast majority of nurses still are women, but even when these students are excluded from the calculations women make up more than 50 per cent of enrolments.

54. *Shaping Structural Change: The Role of Women*, report by a high-level group of experts to the Secretary-General, Organisation for Economic Cooperation and Development, Paris, 1991, p. 14.

55. ibid. p. 7.

56. Eva Cox and Helen Leonard, *From Ummm . . . to Aha! Recognising Women's Skills*, a research project seeking to record how women perceive and value the skills they develop in unpaid community work, conducted under the Women's Research and Employment Initiatives Program, Department of Employment, Education and Training, AGPS, Canberra, May 1991 p. 5.

57. *Shaping Structural Change*, op. cit., p. 19.

58. Quentin Bryce, 'Unfinished Business', The Pamela Denoon Lecture, International Women's Day 1992, Canberra, 9 March 1992.

59. 'Sex Discrimination Legislation: A Discussion Paper', prepared for the House of Representatives Standing Committee on Legal and Constitutional Affairs, for the Inquiry into Equal Opportunity and Equal Status for Australian Women, January 1992, p. 11; *Annual Report 1990/91* Human Rights and Equal Opportunity Commission, Canberra, AGPS, 1991, p. 183.

60. Cited in 'Sex Discrimination Legislation', ibid., p. 4.

61. ibid. p. 15.

62. *Half Way to Equal,* op. cit., p. 259.

63. Speech by the Prime Minister, the Hon. P. J. Keating MP to the Inaugural Forum of the Coalition of Australian Participating Organisations of Women (CAPOW!), Canberra, 19 September 1992.

64. See *Half Way to Equal,* op. cit., pp. 211–80 for an informed discussion of some of these issues; see also Ronalds, *Affirmative Action,* op. cit.

65. See Affirmative Action Agency, *Quality and Commitment: The Next Steps,* The Final Report of the Effectiveness Review of the *Affirmative Action (Equal Employment Opportunity for Women) Act 1986,* AGPS, Canberra, December 1992.

66. There were many ironies to my chairing this committee, as this was not an issue that I had given much thought to before having this job foisted on me and I had mixed feelings about how big a priority I should make it. My militancy on the issue increased in direct proportion to the amount of resistance I encountered from the armed forces; the military men on the committee insisted on coming to meetings in full military regalia and delighted in being obtuse and obstinent every inch of the way. For me, the ironies involved reached their delicious zenith when I found myself one day shouting at these khaki-clad gentlemen, arguing for the right of women to be cooks in the Army. (They had argued that cooking for troops was combat-related and thus had to be excluded!)

67. 'Women's Budget Program 1986–87: An Assessment of the Impact on Women of the 1986–87 Budget', Canberra, AGPS, 1986, p. 62; the quotas in effect before the enactment of the Act were 10 per cent maximum for the Air Force and Navy, and 5-6 per cent for the Army. See Elizabeth Harvey, 'From Camp Follower to Commander: Women in the Australian Defence Force', *South Australian Labor Herald,* Summer 1991.

68. Harvey, ibid. The author was on the staff of the Minister for Defence, Science and Personnel at the time of the decision.

69. ibid.

70. 'Women's Budget Statement 1991–92', op. cit., p. 142.

71. 'Women to serve in subs and fighters', press release by the Minister for Defence, Science and Personnel, Gordon Bilney MP, 18 December 1992.

72. Reported in the *Sunday Telegraph,* 6 September 1993. After the police force, the highest levels of harassment occurred in the NSW Art Gallery, the ambulance service, the fire brigade and the Maritime Services Board.

73. Audrey Vanden Heuvel, *When Roles Overlap: Workers with Family Responsibilities,* Australian Institute of Family Studies for the Work and Family Unit, Department of Industrial Relations, Canberra, 1993, p. v.

74. Selected findings from 'Juggling Time: How Australians Use Family Time', Canberra, Office of the Status of Women, 1991, p. 5.

75. Adele Horin, 'Dawn breaks on a modern miracle', *Sydney Morning Herald,* 25 August 1992.

76. 'Women's Budget Statement 1991–92', op. cit., p. 221.

77. Ryan, in Watson, op. cit., p. 77.

78. 'Women's Budget Statement 1991–92', op. cit., p. 221.

79. 'The Triple A List', Affirmative Action Agency, Initiatives recognised by the 1991 Portfolio Affirmative Action Awards, Sydney, 1991.

80. Vanden Heuvel, op. cit., p. 49.

81. *The Women's View*, op. cit., p. 49.

82. Compiled from police department annual reports. Note that definitions of rape vary from State to State, and have changed over time, so the figures are indicative of an apparent trend rather than strictly comparable.

83. Cited in National Committee on Violence, *Violence: Directions for Australia*, Australian Institute of Criminology, Canberra, 1990, p. 30.

84. ibid. p. 30.

85. Reported in *Australian*, 11 January 1993.

86. *Examiner*, 14 January 1993.

87. The charges and Justice Bollen's original instructions to the jury are contained in *Director of Public Prosecutions Reference no. of 199 pursuant to section 350(1a) and section 351 of the Criminal Law Consolidation Act 1935*, the reference to the Full Court which Justice Bollen signed on 4 January 1993.

88. Office of the Status of Women, Department of the Prime Minister and Cabinet, 'National Agenda for Women Mid-Term Implementation Report on the 1988–92 Five Year Action Plans', August 1990, p. 87.

89. Dame Enid Lyons, the first woman elected to the House of Representatives (in 1943) was a member of federal cabinet from 1949 to 1951 although she was not a minister, but it was not until 1966 that Senator Annabel Rankin became the first woman minister.

90. Unfortunately, both premiers were defeated in their subsequent elections, Kirner in 1992 and Lawrence in early 1993. Kirner resigned the leadership in March 1993; at the time of writing Lawrence was Leader of the Opposition in Western Australia.

91. *Half Way to Equal*, p. 164.

92. Rod Cameron, 'Feminisation – the Major Emerging Trend Underlying Future Mass Audience Response', address to the 11th National Convention of the Public Relations Institute of Australia. 19 October 1990.

93. Carol Gilligan, *In a Different Voice*, Harvard University Press, Cambridge, Massa., 1982.

INTRODUCTION

This is a book about Australia. More particularly, it is about women and the ideology of sexism which has governed so much of our lives – an ideology which has determined and limited the extent to which women have been really able to participate in Australian society.

The first white person recorded as being born in Australia was a woman. Her name was Rebekah Small and she was born on 22 September 1788. However, for those who would attach symbolic importance to this, and possibly speculate that women were to occupy a pre-eminent place in the new colony, it is not the fact of being first-born but rather her name which is significant. Her surname could be seen as a presage of the status which women in this country could expect, while the first name assigned to her (in prophetic prescience by Mary Parker Small, her convict mother?) was symbolic of the likely prospects for women in a society that was both sexist and patriarchal. According to the Biblical scholar Lockyer, Rebekah has the following meaning:

Rebekah is another name with an animal connection. Although not belonging to any animal in particular, it has reference to animals of a limited class and in a peculiar condition. The name means a 'tie rope for animals' or 'a noose in such a rope'. Its root is found in a noun meaning a 'hitching place' or 'stall' and is connected with a 'tied-up calf or lamb', a young animal peculiarly choice and fat. Applied to a female, the figure suggests her beauty by means of which men are shared and bound. Thus another meaning of Rebekah is that of 'captivating'.[1]

The life of Rebekah Small is distinguished from those of most women in convict Australia in that it has been recorded. We know that in 1806 she married Francis Oakes, a missionary, and that she had fourteen children, most of whom she outlived. She died in 1883. Such records survive to give us fragmentary details of the lives of a number of individual women and this is all we have from which to glean some idea of what life in early Australia was like for most women. Our knowledge is, therefore, scanty and inadequate and so our comprehension of the social forces and ideas which determined their lives – and which still persist today – is very hazy.

The intention of this book is to begin the process of reversing this lack of comprehension. In what follows I suggest a framework within which to explore the experiences of women in Australia's past and present, and I put forward an argument which tries to make intelligible what I see as the crucial determinants of women's lives today. In my view, we cannot begin to understand the position of women today simply by amassing statistics on how many women are in the work- force, how they fare within the education system, how many are married, how many children they have, and so on. By doing that we might assemble an elaborate composite of information, but this Statistical Woman would be an artificial construct which would provide no insight into the experiential dimension of women's current position in Australian society, and would be of limited value even for outlining the many variants and complexities of those areas of women's lives which are open to more objective scrutiny. Such an approach would give a shallow and static picture, whereas I am concerned to try and illuminate not merely the heterogeneity existing within the common experience of being female in Australia today, but also the changes which have occurred since this country was first colonized. I do not think we can begin to understand women's position in Australia today, nor men's attitudes to women, without at least a cursory consideration of those past events and ideas which cast shadows on the present. Nor do I think that a comprehensive picture of women's expectations and experiences can be gained by confining one's inquiry to narrowly defined conventional academic disciplines. This book is neither history nor sociology although it draws on techniques and materials from both disciplines. It also explores other areas such as literature, psychology and medicine. In style it is both 'academic' and 'journalistic'. It employs extensive documentation when necessary, on the one hand; and expansive speculation or description culled from experience and observation on the other. As such, this book does not fit easily into any existing categories of works which analyse either Australian society or the position of women therein. Accordingly, I want to explain in some detail what I have attempted to do, and what some of my major premises are.

Since most books about Australia totally ignore women, or at best give them the token consideration of a single section or chapter, there was no possibility of my following any of the conventions established in that field. Virtually all writers about Australian society and history use the terms 'Australian' and 'male' synonymously and so anyone who wishes to write about women has to seek guidance and precedents from other areas. There does exist quite a large body of writing about women in Australia. (There is virtually nothing written about *men* in Australia but, given the assumptions of most writers about Australia, this would be quite superfluous.) Until very recently, when the emergence of the new feminism gave rise to a preoccupation with experiential writing, there had been three ways of writing about women. I felt that Australian society and history needed to be subjected to re-analysis in the light of many of the insights and assumptions of the new feminism and so a book simply about my own experiences would not have met this need. But neither did I consider any of the previous ways of writing about women to be capable of accommodating what I felt needed to be done. In order to illustrate this I will briefly describe each of these methods and what I consider to be their limitations.

The first method can be called the feminist* approach. Generally it isolates a group of female activists, or concentrates on a single campaign – such as the struggle for suffrage – which has involved several groups and it writes about them *in vacuo*. Such writings about feminists are invaluable for recording and evaluating feminist activities of past and present but they are, by definition, concerned only with politically conscious, active women and not with *all* women. Often the campaigns of feminists herald social changes which will ultimately affect larger numbers of women, and their activities can therefore be treated as indices of the changing nature of women's position. Many of the memoirs of individual feminists contain informative accounts of women in other areas, for example, exploitation of women in factories, or the inequality of women before the law, and thus provide some intelligence of the position of the submerged, inarticulate majority of women. But if we want a more detailed explication and understanding of the experiences of that majority, as distinct from the feminist minority, we cannot concentrate on the activists.

The second method of writing about women comprises those ubiquitous accounts of individual women, those biographies which are generally narrative rather than analytical. Their subjects are usually selected for their notoriety, for their unusually diligent pursuit of social reform, because they pioneered a career or activity new to their sex, or because they happened to be attached by family or

* The term *feminist* is often misunderstood, especially as its meaning has shifted in common usage in recent years: it will be defined more fully later in this Introduction.

marriage to a famous man. A good biography can afford a microcosmic view of a larger society and can be of general as well as of particular interest. But most writing in this category does not attain this distinction; with most biographers of women there is an obsessive tendency to reproduce detailed minutiae from the subject's family life and to treat whatever it was that secured her fame with indulgence and sentimentality. Such writing tells us very little about the female subject and even less about her female contemporaries.

The third method is the token fragment approach. Here a general (that is, mainly concerned with men) account of a particular social phenomenon or historical occurrence will include a cursory account of the activities of what is considered to be an important group of women. In practice this approach is generally a throwaway although it is potentially the most valuable for it treats the activities of women in a social context while the other two methods isolate women and can tend to treat them as objects outside the usual processes of society. But seldom do practitioners of this method develop its potential: they treat the activities of women as peripheral without ever asking why this is so, or even *if* it is so.

Past Australian writing about women has fallen exactly into this pattern. We have quite a large body of feminist literature, mainly accounts of the suffrage movements and of individuals prominent in these movements. There is also a considerable amount of institutional feminist writing: the activities of bodies such as the Women's Christian Temperance Union or the Women's Services Guild have been the subject of numerous books, articles and pamphlets. The (usually female) thesis writer who searches for material for her history of women's suffrage or some similar topic will be pleasantly surprised to find that her subjects wrote voluminously and have left ample testimonies of their activities. She is surprised because she has been assured by her supervisor that 'nothing has been written about women'. Such ignorance merely highlights the major deficiency of the feminist method at present: in Australia especially, such writing has not been absorbed into any intellectual tradition of teaching or writing. Each new generation of researchers has had to begin afresh for there are no definitive works surveying the field to date or compiling and assessing the debates. Until such works begin to be written, forcing awareness of the existence of this rich lode of literature, feminist writing will continue to collect dust on the shelves of libraries and remain unread and unabsorbed into any tradition.

This has been the fate of Norman MacKenzie's *Women in Australia*

(Melbourne, 1962).* Although not strictly speaking a feminist book it must be included in this category because it deals only with restricted groups of women. It is concerned with women who are politically active (although not only as feminists), with women in the workforce and with women in education. MacKenzie made some attempt to relate his conclusions about women to various Australian social and historical phenomena, but his lack of overall theoretical perspective as well as his neglect of non-organized women meant that his book has remained outside the mainstream of Australian social criticism. His work is an example of the limitations of the feminist approach: because it isolates women it can be ignored by those with the social or political power to alleviate at least some of the things that the book was trying to draw attention to.

Biographies of women suffer a mixed fate. Scholarly works like Margaret Kiddle's *Caroline Chisholm* (Melbourne, 1950) are read by fairly select groups and are occasionally referred to by historians of the period but they too generally fail to be integrated into any tradition because the subject of their research is too often relegated to a footnote in the more general studies. There is a double standard of writing and criticism operating here which has ensured that a vicious circle exists: biographies about women are seldom taken seriously, certainly not in the way that a political biography of a male politician or some other prominent man is, and hence biographers of women have tended to internalize both *this* and the fact that women are trivialized and not taken seriously within Australia anyway. The result has been a plethora of chatty, discursive books about Australian women which have concentrated almost totally on their subjects' domestic affairs and which have reinforced the practice of not taking biographies of women seriously.

Some academic works concerned with the lives of famous and infamous women are absorbed into a kind of folklore. Here the distinctions between legend and fact become blurred and, in any case, the subjects of these biographies exist as eccentrics or heroines, both categories which ensure that they are removed from serious consideration as individuals who could be seen as providing some insights into the general situation of women of their age. There are also a number of short biographical works on famous women such as Mary Gilmore which have been specially written as school texts; they are most likely to be used in literature courses, providing 'back-

---

* A revised edition of this book has recently appeared. See S. Encel, N. MacKenzie and M. Tebbutt, *Women and Society*, Cheshire, Melbourne, 1974.

ground' biographical and historical material. Again, there is no way in which any of these biographies are permitted to become part of a general consciousness about women's position in Australian society.

The third method – the token fragment – is by no means common in this country. A search of the indexes of book after book of Australian history reveals no mention of either women or the family. There are exceptions, of course. Russel Ward's *The Australian Legend* (Melbourne, 1958) is one, and any book concerned with Australia prior to 1850 can hardly avoid at least mentioning female convicts and immigrants, but even in these works there is usually only a paragraph or two or, at the very most, a chapter. Moreover, the bias – in many cases amounting to outright misogyny – against treating women as historical subjects worthy of detailed analysis, has meant that these fragments remain as unintegrated ephemera and are seldom related to the major theories about the evolution of Australian civilization. Some of these biases, as they emerge in particular works or arguments, will be explored in more detail throughout this book.

The net result of all this has been that there exists a profound ignorance about the roles which women have played in our history and also of the ways in which women have been suppressed and prevented from moving outside those roles. I hope to begin eroding some of that ignorance with my insistence on the importance of understanding the historical processes by which women's current situation has evolved; unless we have some comprehension of the sources of that situation and the functions the oppression of women has fulfilled for Australian society then our chances for evolving political strategies for the liberation of women will be remote.

Contemporary sociological writing has also contributed to both misunderstanding and neglect of the position of women in Australia. In sociology the tendency to isolate one aspect of women's social existence and develop theories about that alone is fairly pronounced. There are, for instance, a great many articles and sub-theories about 'women in the workforce' but it is rare to find one which does more than outline the participation rates of women, enquire into the reasons for married women working and perhaps make some general comments about women's concentration in low-status and unequally paid jobs. Occasionally some historical perspective will be included but seldom is the analysis related to those tendencies in the Australian economy and society which have precipitated the increased participation of married women workers. In general, however, sociologists are far more likely than historians to include some consideration of women's activities in their general analysis of society. But they are often guilty of the same form of sexist scholarship as the general historian: that of interpolating, rather than integrating, a particular facet of women's many roles into their overall schema. Their sexism consists of treating women as a homogeneous object-group, not recognizing their varieties of aspiration and experience; and of fragmenting whole individuals into a series of objectified roles which are based on sex stereotypes.

The term 'role' when applied to women's activities has become a non-historical objectification. It is often used descriptively rather than analytically and has acquired an amorphous blanket quality: it is employed to describe everything that women do, but it actually tells us nothing. Even those writers who acknowledge that some changes have occurred in its content in the past 200 years still assume some fundamental universal content such as child rearing. Few writers in Australia have subjected this content to historical analysis and so discovered that this particular function has undergone quite marked changes even in the past eighty years. Since the entry of married women into the paid workforce has assumed such social importance in the past decade it has become fashionable to speak of women's two 'roles': home and work. Used loosely, as it often is, this dual terminology suggests a dual existence rather than a single life characterized by several, possibly contradictory, social demands and expectations.

A similarly uncritical use of the term 'the family' has added to the propensity to reduce the discussion of women's activities to simple schema whose content is assumed rather than actually described and analysed. Such a term implies the existence of a universal institution – or at least one that is common to all societies – whose variations at present and in the past are totally overlooked. It is questionable whether it is possible to speak of 'the Australian family of 1975' let alone use this term to describe the varieties of familial groupings and relationships which have existed among Europeans in this country since 1788. The term assumes a norm, at present the heterosexual 'nuclear' family of conjugal couple and two or three children. Yet there are an enormous number of exceptions to this norm: people who live in a vast range of non-kinship household arrangements or with kin who extend beyond the 'nuclear' norm; and these are not accommodated by the insistence that we can treat this country as a society in which 'the family' is the pre-eminent form of social organization. Such a sweeping generalization excludes from consideration and hence from awareness of their special needs or problems single people, unmarried heterosexual couples, homosexuals, single-parent families, childless couples, migrant families with several generations coexisting in one household, one-sex or mixed-sex communes, and people living in institutions such as prisons, orphanages, children's homes, convents or seminaries. If all of the people living in these extra-'nuclear' family relationships were added up they would probably outnumber those who live according to the norm and so the norm is of dubious value even for describing how the majority of Australians live. It is also evident from the great variety of situations described above that the situation of women is going to differ markedly according to how they live: how then can we speak of women's 'role' in 'the family'? If sociologists do this – without acknowledging that this blanket phrase is in reality one that can only be applied to a proportion (and possibly a quite small proportion) of the female population – then their findings and theories are going to be of very limited value. They are going to exclude enormous numbers of women and yet appear to be oblivious of having excluded them. They will continue to propagate the fiction that all women live in situations defined by traditional sex roles without exploring the processes by which some women follow these while others reject them.

For the reasons outlined above I found I could not follow the established conventions of Australian historical or sociological writing. I see the need to move beyond merely accepting the premise that people's lives are to a large extent governed by sex roles and to start investigating the extent of this control and the influence it has had in shaping Australian society. Both women and men are socialized into sex-role behaviour but what follows concentrates mainly on women and on the social forces which affect women. These of course include men, and sex-role behaviour in men, for it is impossible to talk about women's lives without also talking about men. Within a society where men occupy all positions of power in government, law, the churches, and the civil service, women as a group are powerless and that powerlessness needs to be explored. Women in Australia *are* powerless but we still do not understand exactly how or why. In 1958 Kathleen Fitzpatrick said that women 'have a legal right to do almost anything, but they are in fact hedged in with invisible barriers which keep them, as it were, on the outer of our national life.'[2] This assessment is still true seventeen years later but so far no one has tried to delineate these 'invisible barriers' with any clarity or precision. This is what I have attempted to do.

Broadly my argument is that women in Australia are forced to eke out a precarious psychic and physical existence within a society which has denied them cultural potency and economic independence and hence has prevented women from being able to construct their own identities or from having more than a very restricted choice about what they can do with their lives. Although basic sexist assumptions about women and men were transported from England with the First Fleet, social and economic conditions in the first fifty years of colonization of this country gave rise to an indigenous variety of the ideology of sexism. A particularly rigid dualistic notion of women's function in colonial society was embodied in two stereotypes. They have been both descriptive and prescriptive, at the one time both adumbrating a function for women and exhorting them to conform to it, and also maintaining that they actually represented what women were. Each is a sex-role stereotype which exaggerates the characteristics of the basic dualistic notion that women are either good or evil: this judgement is based on whether or not women conform to the wife/mother roles prescribed by the bourgeois family.

Prior to 1840 when the majority of the population in colonial Australia did not live in this kind of family structure, and women were viewed primarily as objects of sexual gratification, the 'Damned Whore' stereotype was predominant. Female convicts and female immigrants were expected to be, and were treated as, whores, and this label was applied indiscriminately to virtually all women in the colony. During the 1840s and 1850s the bourgeois family was propagated as the most suitable form of social organization for the new nation and the 'God's Police' stereotype assumed ascendancy. Its general prescription was that women as wives of men and mothers of children were entrusted with the moral guardianship of society, that they were expected to curb restlessness and rebelliousness in men and instil virtues of civic submission in children. Both these functions were to be exercised primarily through family relationships but during the past century the sphere of this function has expanded. Women have been permitted some participation in social or political affairs, so long as they confined that participation to performing this moral policing. While this kind of role has been the lot of women in most Western societies, in Australia it has acquired an almost evangelical cast and many of its particularities have given it a unique form. It is perhaps no coincidence that in 1915 Australia was the first country to appoint women police:

They (the first women police) did little in the way of tracking down criminals. Their work consisted mainly in patrolling dance halls, parks, beaches and other places where young people congregate, on the lookout for girls under age. They also watched railway stations, bus terminals and wharves. They developed a flair for detecting girls who were trying to appear over eighteen, or who had run away from home.[3]

The God's Police stereotype has also included the redemptive idea that women could and should police other women.

These stereotypes are the product of a society in which sex is viewed as a major means of categorizing people and assigning their social functions. The justificatory ideology – sexism – has been a major component of Australia's social structure and an exploration of sexism is one of the principle concerns of this book. Although the ideology and practice of sexism will be discussed continually throughout this book it is necessary to say a little about it now for it is often misunderstood. Sexism

refers to a division made between people on genital/sexual grounds which goes beyond the simple biological classification and into the area of suppositions about personality, ability, equality etc. It is about a series of alleged differences extrapolated from one basic biological difference . . . it seems to me to be sexist to say that women are 'naturally' emotional, men are 'naturally' rational, even though it may be true and non-sexist to say that because of sexist expectations in our society men and women may be more inclined in either of these directions.[4]

Sexism is a sex/political means of identifying and then dividing people. Often it is confused with 'male chauvinism' and used as a synonymous term. Sexism does *not* mean male dominance – although the political system of male dominance, patriarchy, is the usual form of sexism in this era. Men occupy dominant positions in all important political, economic and cultural institutions and are able to control the lives of some other men and all women. This is not a necessary corollary of sexism: a matriarchy or a gynarchy would also be sexist. It is always necessary to look at the power structure which upholds and reinforces a sex distinction and to see who benefits from it.

In practice sexism, like racism, is almost always discriminatory. Such a division of society could not be maintained unless one group had the power to enforce it, and that it chooses to enforce it generally means that considerable benefits derive to members of the powerful group from the division. The discrimination of racism is usually quite patent even though the economic reasons for race discrimination are always glossed over with ideologies which supposedly rationalize the imputed inferiority of the oppressed race.

Two distinct but overlapping processes coincide in perpetuating such oppression. The ruling group constructs an ideology to justify the validity of its own political, economic and cultural practices and then universalizes it, that is, decrees that it ought to be subscribed to by all people, even those outside the ruling group. It then labels as inferior, and not deserving of its own status, those who do not conform to its dictates. At the same time it refuses to recognize, or to give equal status to, the culture of the oppressed group. This is where the differences matter. It is not possible for the two (or three or however many) groups to coexist with equal power and status. The ruling group protects its power, and continues to reinforce its convictions of its own superiority, by denying the other group access to that power or status. And this power is maintained partly by convincing the other group that its own culture is worthless. Such power can only be maintained while the ruling group controls the major economic resources of society and is thus in a position to enforce the subordination of the other group which must accede to the ruling group's ideology in order to exist.

In Australia the overall control system is that of a capitalist economy and the ruling group is the class which controls the means of production. It is composed entirely of white men. Its ideology justifies its own class, race and sex position in order to perpetuate the capitalist system and it maintains its class, race and sex superiority through the political, economic and cultural institutions of society. Both race and sex ideologies were transported from England with the capitalist system but they have been maintained in Australia with a distinct and explicable fervour. The ideology of racism was used to justify the invasion of the continent and the dispossession of the original inhabitants of their land. The ideology of sexism has served several varying purposes in Australia's economic development and these are explored at some length in the second part of this book.

These mediating ideologies of racism and sexism are generally overlooked, or paid insufficient attention, by Marxists who concentrate entirely on class relations and class ideology. But it seems likely that for two large groups in Australia, women and Aborigines, class ideology is relevant only in a very generalized sense and its relevance is mediated through the more specific ideologies of race and sex. Members of these groups have a primary self-identification as women or as Blacks, which precedes class identification. Both groups are specifically oppressed through the use which society makes or has made of their sex or race, uses which may not always be directly related to the maintenance of the capitalist system. Those theories of capitalism which underrate the importance of these mediating ideologies are neglecting vital areas of subversion and revolt.

The class struggle has only limited relevance to people who are largely outside it even when they are conscious of being exploited. For that exploitation is a function of their sex or race. *That* is the consciousness they already have or that which they are more likely to arrive at. Having attained that consciousness they are then in a better position to be aware of the wider system of control which perpetuates their specific oppression. But the ideologies of sex and race are powerful and pervasive. They are continually reinforced at every level of society. The manner in which they are upheld even by those who are themselves oppressed and exploited is a measure of the intricate nexus of repression which occurs within capitalism and which prevents the massed opposition to capitalism of all oppressed groups. The working class, as defined by Marxists, is exploited within the capitalist system but its members are preponderantly white men, and they uphold the values of both sexism and racism. And they benefit considerably from upholding them: they protect their jobs by keeping Australia white and they preserve their own little domain of personal power and sustenance by living in bourgeois families. Similarly women and Aborigines apply racist and sexist values to each other – and to themselves. Thus the exploration of the ubiquitousness of these mediating ideologies is important not only as a necessary task in itself but for gaining an understanding of the ways in which their perpetuation prevents revolt against the larger system.

I will concentrate on sexism and I want to stress that to concentrate simply on its most blatant discriminatory manifestations tends to obscure its pervasiveness and hence its power. To point to such things as wife-bashing, the refusal to give women the right to abortion or to allow them equal wages with men, is indeed to illustrate patriarchal power in a sexist society. But such examples are not necessary consequences of sexism and concentrating on them tends to disguise the more subtle and intricate textures which are the basis of sexism and which lead to these extreme discriminations. It is possible to envisage a benevolent patriarchy or one which wanted to alter the present content of one or both sex roles. In such a system women could have equal legal rights and access to the cultural, economic and political institutions of society. But unless that society had also abandoned a sexual division of labour in every area of existence, most especially in family relationships, then it would still be sexist. A reversal of the current division, whereby men were housekeepers and women went out to work, would be sexist – and it would not be long before such a society generated its specific ideological justification for this particular form of ascribing social functions. Men and women sharing roles which are currently performed by one sex only would only be non-sexist in so far as all assumptions and expectations about what men (or women) should 'normally' do disappeared. But to see sexism as only manifested in the work (in families and outside) that people do is to neglect the vast array of cultural assumptions, prejudices, myths, fears and other ideologies which shore up this ideology and which are embodied in practically every institution, ritual and pastime in this country.

I will give just a few examples. The Christian Church is based absolutely on sexist assumptions which have been given the authority of divine law: the male God with a saviour son borne by a woman (there is no need for gods to be born in the way mortals are) has imposed a basic pattern of male spiritual and political power contrasted with women's purely reproductive function. Introduction rituals in Australia dictate that men shake hands with each other when meeting for the first time – women do not shake each other by the hand and they choose whether or not to extend their hand to men. A national pastime – drinking – has distinct rules, rights and conventions for each sex.

Sexism is a system of oppression within capitalism and, like the larger system, it is neither static nor uniform in its manifestations. 'Oppression', writes Sheila Rowbotham,

is not an abstract moral condition but a social and historical experience. Its forms and expressions change as the mode of production and the relationships between men and women, men and men, women and women, change in society. Thus, while it is true that women were subordinated to men before capitalism and that this has affected the position of women in capitalist society, it is also true that the context of oppression we fight against now is specific to a society in which the capacity of human beings to create is appropriated by privately owned capital and in which things produced are exchanged as commodities.[5]

The various permutations which have occurred in the oppression of women in Australia are traced in Part Two.

Oppression can be explored and evaluated by outlining the many dimensions of the structure, for example, of relations between the sexes, and its supporting ideology and by attempting to assess the extent to which the less powerful group complies with its situation of powerlessness. Both measures are necessary if we are to understand the nature of that oppression and the means by which it changes. Sexism differs from other systems of oppression because of the close relations between women and men. Women's oppression is often not seen or felt as such because, unlike most other political systems, many members of the two groups are bound to each other by ties of mutual affection. The ideology of 'the family' prescribes that the sexes love each other and such love, and the institution on which it is based, often disguise the existence, or the extent, of women's oppression. A further difference in women's oppression also stems from this close relationship: the women who are most compliant with sexist norms are awarded certain compensations. These are culturally determined, and in Australia the main compensation has been to give the maternal role a revered status. This status is largely a sham since it is superficial and is by no means an adequate compensation for the demands of the role. But most women have accepted it for it has enabled them to attach value to an activity which is unique to their sex and thereby to wear the role with pride.

For most of Australian history this compensatory status has been sufficient to quell whatever restlessness many women must have felt. It has only been during periods when the demands of motherhood have been completely out of tune with other social forces that revolt has occurred. Mostly this has taken the form of a demand to alter the content of the role or else to increase its status in recognition of an expansion of the role which has already occurred. But occasionally it has been a revolt against the role itself and it is these occasions which really threaten to undermine sexism. Such a revolt can be named *feminism*.

Feminism has to be distinguished from *female consciousness*. Female consciousness describes the first situation: it entails a heightened awareness amongst women of their sex roles. But it is awareness coupled with acceptance of sexism. Women with female consciousness wish to preserve their roles as wives and mothers and the special and separate status they carry. Such female consciousness can often lead to militant action if women feel that their effective performance of those roles is being threatened. Women have formed Housewives' Associations and Consumer Protection Groups and have been active in resident action groups and other community activities in attempts to prevent encroachments on what they cherish as their unique contribution to society. This female consciousness is active acceptance of female roles and differs from the more passive acceptance which characterizes most women who comply with sexist norms.

Feminism is more difficult to define since its meaning has altered in recent years. At the turn of the century feminism meant support for women's rights. The rights sought were defined differently in different countries and in Australia were rather circumscribed. The early feminists here sought to extend the area of women's participation in society but, as Chapter Eleven argues, they did not seriously wish to challenge the sexist *status quo*. Since the rise of the Women's Liberation Movement in the late 1960s feminism has been radicalized to mean rejection of sexism and sex roles, and what radical feminists seek today is the freedom to decide what to do with their lives without the determining mantle of sex limiting or impeding their opportunities. The older form of feminism has also resurged with large numbers of women demanding an expansion of existing sex roles.

Whether this new wave of feminism will be able to alter significantly the sexist *status quo* remains to be seen. The radical feminists have correctly identified the sexist division of societies as the major way in which women are oppressed but this recognition needs to be coupled both with a comprehensive understanding of the complex and subtle ways in which sexism permeates every facet of social and economic organization, and with a revolutionary strategy for undermining it. I see this work as contributing to the first requirement: this book assumes a critical stance towards sexism and concentrates on important events, issues and ideas in the development of sexism in Australia.

This book has taken almost four years to research and write. During that time I have changed my ideas, not only about the book's subject matter but also about how it should be written. When I began, I was very concerned to present an extensively documented case for my contentions and although I felt unfettered by the traditional boundaries of academic research, I was nevertheless still convinced of the need to adhere to its conventions of scholarship. I have recently felt increasingly that this is not so necessary, especially when it can often lead to omitting important insights and observations simply because they cannot be incorporated within an academic framework. Thus, the chapters written most recently diverge considerably from the patterns I established with those I wrote first. This will be evident to the reader. But since I see my work as reflecting my ideas at any given time, I saw no need to rewrite these earlier chapters to give the book a uniformity of style or method.

What follows is the result of four years of thinking and writing and engagement in numerous political activities. The latter, especially, have profoundly influenced me. I have been involved in three major political activities in the last three years: the establishing of *Refractory Girl*, a women's studies journal which was begun in December 1972;

the squatting movement in Victoria Street, Kings Cross, as part of a protest against the tearing down of inner-city low rent housing areas to be replaced by high-rise speculative office or hotel developments; and the setting up of Elsie Women's Refuge in Glebe in March 1974. Each of these involvements has been the result of convictions I have had about the economic and cultural needs of disadvantaged groups in our society, the majority of whom in each case have been women. But my ideas have been altered to some extent as a result of these practical involvements. I see the constant interaction of ideas and action as being necessary to my self-development and my struggle against oppression in the various forms it takes in Australian society. I hope that this book will provide ideas and incentive to others who are similarly engaged in such struggles.

Notes

1. Dr Herbert Lockyer, R.S.L., *The Women of the Bible*, Pickering and Inglis, London, 1967, pp. 134–5.
2. Professor Kathleen Fitzpatrick, during presentation of the Victorian Women Graduates' Association Memorial Screen, *Melbourne University Gazette*, *1958*, p. 9.
3. H. A. Lindsay, 'The World's First Policewoman', *Quadrant*, March 1959, p. 76.
4. Article by Kay, in *Liberaction* (Newsletter of Hobart Women's Action Group), Nos 21–22, January–February 1974.
5. Sheila Rowbotham, *Woman's Consciousness, Man's World*, Penguin Books, 1973, p. xiii.

PART ONE

THE NEXUS
OF OPPRESSION

Within a supposedly free and independent Australia women are a colonized sex. They are denied freedom of movement, control of their bodies, economic independence and cultural potency. This oppressed state derives from the status of 'the family' in Australia and the responsibilities assigned to women within that institution.

CHAPTER ONE

A SEXIST CULTURE

The very concept of a 'female' culture is a bewildering and problematic one. Once we have extended our idea of culture beyond the conventional conception of it as a deposit of intellectual and artistic artefacts, we can see that women can legitimately claim a 'culture' of our own – an experience of living which is, in some respects, characterized by wholeness where the male culture is not, which has always been an important ingredient of human life, and which has never been acknowledged in any intellectual tradition. On the other hand, the female condition has never been a self-determined state, so there is nothing we can lay claim to as our own.

EILEEN HALEY, 'Crossing the Sexual Frontier',
Refractory Girl, No. 1, Summer 1972/73

The experiences of women in Australia are closely tied to family life. More so than with men, the lives of most women are defined by their family relationships and these relationships, and the conventions and prescriptions they give rise to, need to be explored if we wish to try and understand the position of women in this country. Family relationships differ for individual women and are governed by objective factors such as class and race, and by various subjective forces. However the convention amongst social scientists and other analysts has been to obscure varieties of family relationships under an embracing institutionalized label: 'the family'. This label disguises differences between individuals and between the sexes in their experiences and perceptions of family relationships. Yet it is probably the illusion of uniformity produced by this label which has enabled 'the family' to assume its paramount place in the assembly of revered Australian institutions and has ensured that it receives at least a perfunctory reference in every piece of writing about contemporary Australian culture. Donald Horne, for instance, writes, 'The "home" occupies as central a position in Australian life as land in a peasant community except that it is disposable after death; there can be an equally strong sense of family, except that as children become adult the family group dissolves, the children go their own way.'[1] An almost identical view is presented by Craig McGregor: 'Australians are a very family-minded people. The family forms a very tight social unit and its members often count for more than close friends even after the original family circle has broken up and its younger members have set up homes of their own.'[2]

This ostensible family-centredness is so taken for granted that no commentator feels obliged to do more than pay token homage to its existence. Rarely has a writer about Australian mores attempted to probe behind this shared assumption, to investigate the actual shape and texture of the image, to spell out just what this fact, if indeed it is a fact, implies for the cultural life of the nation.

This is largely because, for men, family life is part of an assumed background. It is just one stopping place in their landscape of experience. Rarely are a man's familial roles the sole motivating fact of his existence and even if many men at times feel, like Paula's husband in Elizabeth Harrower's *The Long Prospect*, that 'A man was just a machine to make money'[3], to keep his wife and family well-heeled, they still have their socially approved escape routes. Sport, the pub and clubs, and a variety of other pursuits enable men to find at least temporary relief from the irritations, the tensions and the petty trivialities of domestic life.

For most women, things are very different. It is paramount that we know a woman's marital and maternal status, and whatever else she may aspire to or have already achieved will be assessed against this basic barometer. To be a Mother of Two would seem to be a more important status for an Australian woman than any other conceivable accolade, and if a woman does chance to succeed in other spheres but has not distinguished herself in the maternal stakes, or at least expressed a desire to, her deservedness and even her psychological stability are likely to be called into question.[4] This insistence on evaluating women in terms of their familial roles is certainly maintained by most Australian writers and commentators, but in doing so, they are simply reflecting what is a constant reality for most women. Childhood socialization directs a woman's ambitions into narrowly circumscribed marital goals and girls learn early that success in this sphere is necessary to achieve womanhood and that any other goals they may harbour must be tailored to accommodate this primary end.

Successive generations of women, it will be argued later, have collaborated in perpetuating this existential straitjacket but these women have been victims of circumstances which provided them with a fixed choice. Denied economic independence, unable to control their fertility adequately, and always aware of the reprobation which awaits the rebel, none but a handful of Australian women has had the opportunity to do any more than submit to living out their lives as dutiful wives and bountiful mothers; and having no alternatives and wanting some share of human happiness, they have accepted and enjoyed this as best they could.

The major impediment to female rebellion, and that which keeps women physically and psychologically bound to their family-centred roles has been the absence of any cultural tradition which approved of women being anything else. At every level of what we call culture, the dominant ideas and the forms in which expression is given to them have been devised by men and have reflected what they considered to be worthy of identification and perpetuation. This has been the case in that body of organized expression we generally call 'the Arts', in the theories and interpretations marshalled by intellectuals to describe what they see as distinctive features of our way of life, in the recreational activities of ordinary Australians, and in the ideas and actions that govern everyday life. And so it is somewhat ironic to realize that those people who have written about Australian culture – and in recent years they have, without exception, been men – have not attempted to examine in any way the implications of what they have all identified as the family-centredness of Australian life. The one exception has been Ronald Conway who tries to examine our history and current social mores in terms of a Jungian psycho-historical framework. He identifies dominant ethics prevailing at particular periods and categorizes them according to whether what he sees as 'male' ('patrist') or 'female' ('matrist') qualities determined ideas and events.[5] This leads him to consider family life and sexual mores in some detail and he is thus forced to consider the role of women in Australian society. No other recent book has thought it necessary to do this and the result has been constantly reiterated analyses of those areas of Australian life which involve the public activities of men. This has meant not only that women have been omitted from consideration, but that the qualities and attributes of Australian society identified as important have been ones which were germane to male interests and ambitions. This has thus ensured that there was no possible way in which women could, within these frameworks, be considered. It has been a closed shop: Australian society has been written about by men as if it consisted only of men.

Where women *have* participated in Australian culture it has had to be with due acquiesence to a game whose rules were drawn up without their consent. They have had to conform to what men assured them was important. Occasionally a few brave women have been especially refractory, have defied the prevailing orthodoxies and have struck out where their hearts and minds drove them. They went unrewarded, and they were often labelled eccentric because they could not be accommodated within the current mode. For at no level in our culture is there a rallying point, a legitimating tradition or even a socially valued metaphor which begins to explore, much less fully articulates, the experiences of women. Such a tradition would necessarily be distinct from the present dominant male one, at least until men began to recognize and to cherish the validity of female experiences in the way women have had to value men's expressions of *their* experiences. Such recognition might pave the way to a reunion, to a genuine reciprocity, to a mutual awareness that human experience is varied and perverse, not merely along lines of age or class or nation, but also along lines of sex. At present we are light years away from this dissolution of sex differences and sexism is as powerful a national cleavage as any of these other acknowledged divisive forces.

The system of dualism in Western philosophy as a method of organizing ideas has produced numerous theories attempting to describe and validate separate and opposing sexual characteristics. The distinctions of mind/body, good/evil, Logos/Eros have all at times been utilized in the spurious quest to give male supremacy a philosophical justification. By defining woman as separate and as radically different (not just in biological capacity but, as theorists as diverse as Nietzsche and Jung have argued, in essence from man) the realities of power and exploitation and cultural apartheid have been obscured or even justified. The bludgeoning of the female psyche by Western philosophy and by religious and cultural myths and shibboleths has been exposed in numerous books[6]; but it has not been widely recognized in this country where it seems that divisions between people based on sex are amongst the foundations of our culture.

For the purposes of this discussion four 'levels' of culture will be identified and examined throughout the next four chapters. These levels are distilled for descriptive and analytical purposes only and are not to be seen as purporting to present a new interpretative framework for analysing Australian culture; *that* can be left to the social scientists. My present concern is simply to illustrate the original contention that women are denied an explicit and socially valued place in what is generally identified as our culture; and to trace some of the consequences of this.

The first 'level', the organized body of expression called 'the Arts' and here including literature, painting and music, obviously contains its own hierarchies of artistic ambition and critical acclaim but it would take an entire book to plough through the 'popular' and 'high' levels of each area. My argument will have to rest on a selection of works and themes. The major points to be made are in any case independent of current fashions because I am arguing that there has existed throughout Australian history a systematic omission of women from what have been judged the highest achievements in any field. This disbarment has been of two kinds. First, a rigid physical exclusion. Women have not been completely denied the opportunity to become practitioners of any art form although, as will be described later, it is doubly difficult for a woman artist simply to practise her art, let alone have the leisure and the freedom from domestic responsibilities to enable her to aspire to excellence. What has occurred has been a more subtle and more damaging form of ostracism. Female art forms have simply been adjudged to occupy a distinct universe, one which is apart from and inferior to the male, which is unselfconsciously upheld as the universal model. This cultural apartheid has, like its political form, achieved the predictable result of ensuring that men forgot that it existed: women who conformed to its boundaries were usually ignored and the only time a woman achieved notice – and generally it was better called notoriety – was when she tried to crash through the barriers into the male world.

The second form of exclusion has been that of critical neglect. Since the majority of critics are men, they have not considered that they have any obligation to inquire as to what is going on on the other side of the cultural fence. Or, when the male critics have ventured over, they have applied the same norms which pertain in the male art world and have found either that women did not measure up (not suspecting that women artists might be trying for something different) or they have been scornful or patronizing. In a recent review of a first novel by a woman, a *Sydney Morning Herald* reviewer wrote, 'I will no doubt be condemned for suggesting that this excellent but to me somewhat intense novel is a woman's book: but I must add by way of penance that it is very intelligent . . .'[7] Such a view assumes, not merely that there are two kinds of literature, one for men and one for women, but that the former is intrinsically superior and if the latter exhibits any qualities usually attributed to the male model, this is an occasion for surprise. It ignores the differing aspirations of male and female artists, aspirations that are connected with their differing experiences of the world.

When a man delineates the dimensions and the excruciating complexities of his existential situation, he situates these within the experiences which have shaped his consciousness. This is considered a proper and commendable thing to do. But the experiences which bring similar realizations to women are very different. They necessarily revolve around the expectations of domestic responsibility and maternal fulfilment which women are socialized to desire and to find satisfying. Yet to write about these experiences is judged to be trivial, to make the work of no interest to men and, even if the work is considered to be 'intelligent' – how insidious a put-down, implying that such a quality is rare in women's writing – it is still primarily a 'women's book'. The message to men is clear: you'll find this boring, stay well clear. It is rather like attacking the Blacks for being dirty while conveniently forgetting that we have neglected to provide them with bathrooms, or even with running water. If women's experience of the world is so different from men's, how else can they be true to themselves except by writing about it? Male critics, and those women who court their favour[8], cling to an ethnocentric view of reality which erects its own standards, in this case those devised by and for men for their creations, as the only possible standards by which to evaluate a work.

These judgements apply especially to literature, the one art form in Australia to which the contribution of women has been, in quantitative terms, as great as that of men. For this reason and also because literature even more than painting is the major source of powerful cultural symbols – characters and decisive experiences – which have an enduring and often a determining effect on the image a country has of itself, this discussion of the first 'level' of culture will confine itself to literature.

There were two major themes of what we can term 'colonial literature'. First was the evolving of the Australian Man of the Bush, that brash, rugged, sardonic individual (despite his dependence on his mates) who has been the hero of countless sagas from Clancy of the Overflow, through Ned Kelly to the various characters who inhabit the pages of Steele Rudd, Joseph Furphy and Henry Lawson. He might be a swaggie, a stockman or even a city larrikin; later he was a member of the AIF, an urban worker or an itinerant rural wanderer, but he always possessed at least some of those characteristics which a swarm of men writers detected in themselves or in the males they observed and which they were anxious to transpose into a living legend. Probably more written words have been devoted to creating, and then to analysing and extolling, this composite Australian male than to any other single facet of Australian life.

The second theme, which set itself up in opposition to the crude nationalism of the first, was that of the pristine intellectual, again always a male, who was revulsed by the barbarism of colonial, especially rural or small-town colonial mores. His cultural affinities were invariably with England although he was strongly drawn to the physical immediacy of the Australian continent, a land which fascinated him and gripped his imagination while it stultified his intellect, and as a result he suffered from what Martin Boyd has labelled 'geographic schizophrenia' and was destined to wander relentlessly between the two countries, a spiritual exile in search of an ineluctable and remote fulfilment. Richard Mahony is of course the prototype for this second theme although the men of the Langton family in Martin Boyd's quartet[9] pursue the theme and add to it the further dimension of how it persisted through several generations of the one family.

The women writers who contributed to the first theme were incapable of pursuing it in its pure form. Those women who wrote about the bush, or who identified in some way with the nationalistic tradition of realism – Barbara Baynton, Miles Franklin, Katharine Susannah Prichard, Mary Gilmore, Henrietta Drake-Brockman – concentrated either on the women of the bush (and their lives were very different) or were forced in order to be true to their own experiences, to draw a wider canvas and to write about whole settlements or communities. Those who chose to write about women were forced into a thematic corner for the women of the bush were not able to be individuals; they could not rival the attributes of their men. They were copers, responding to settings that most of them had neither chosen nor enjoyed, and as such their stories were chronicles of reaction. The staple themes of the bush wife were those of coping with natural hazards, such as fire, snakes or drought – all potent with Freudian imagery and insinuation – with threats from hostile Aborigines or rapacious swaggies or with sheer psychological phenomena, such as enervating loneliness, or ill-defined fear. Women in the bush could be strong characters but they were not allowed, in the literature as in life, to rival their husband's monopolization of the national characteristics. If a woman wanted to write about an individual woman she had to be somehow separated from the norm; she had, for instance, as in Prichard's *Coonardoo*, to be black. Nor was it easy for a woman writer who wanted to try and depict with some honesty and understanding what life in the bush looked like from the furnace-like kitchen or the unattended child-bed. Apart from the intrinsic difficulties of women writing in a tradition that was largely male-initiated and defined, petty rivalries insinuated their way into a field which could only accommodate a certain number of writers.

Mary Gilmore claims that Henry Lawson came to her and pre-emptorarily told her that both of them could not continue to write as their work was too similar. He told her that since she had been trained as a teacher she could go back to that whereas he was dependent on writing for a living. She told him:

'I won't write any more in that line again at all.' Of course, that was my natural line. I was born in the bush and I knew it and all the things, you know, that I was telling him I would have written for myself. And then, of course, when I had said I'd give up, he said 'I don't want you to give up,' he said, 'I'll give up!' Of course I was terrified. 'Oh no!' I said, 'you can't, you mustn't.' I said, 'You know, Henry, you can use strong language that I can't use, and the things can be more natural and true to life,' so he agreed to that, and so I drew back and I never did any more of that kind of writing.[10]

But she continued to provide him with material, including the story which has earned him a place in our literary archives as having a rare understanding of the plight of women in the bush, *The Drover's Wife*. The story which Lawson wrote was the story of Mary Gilmore's mother and she was the little six-year-old girl who watched the baby in the story and it was her brother who said to their mother, 'Mama, when I'm grown up I'm not going away building, I'll stay home and take care of you.'[11] Lawson turned this into slightly rougher speech and the story became his.

Mary Gilmore is regarded by many people who knew her personally, or who have researched some of her claims, to be notoriously untruthful and to have engaged in self-aggrandizement by insisting on credit for actions or influences for which she could not possibly have been responsible. So this claim may either be totally untrue or else wildly exaggerated. But rather than just dismiss Gilmore as a crazy woman or an inveterate liar, it is necessary in the context of my argument to ask *why* she seemed compelled to act in this fashion. She was already acquiring a reputation of her own as a writer and so this apparent need to engage in a vicarious form of fame-seeking is difficult to understand. She must have been bedevilled by the insecurity of lacking confidence in her own abilities and perhaps hoped that associations such as that with Henry Lawson would enhance her own success. It is noteworthy that the people she selected for this purpose were almost always male writers.

Mary Gilmore's seemingly inexplicable actions are perhaps an excellent illustration of the endemic insecurities of women writers who seek recognition for their work. Because they have no tradition of their own to identify with – and which could legitimate their achievements – they are forced to try to identify with standards devised by men. This entails self-abnegation and leads to a form of schizophrenic insecurity. I later discuss how Henry Handel Richardson resolved this dilemma. Perhaps Mary Gilmore tried to gain recognition and respect from the definers of the male tradition by claiming that some of its notable contributions were in fact inspired by her, thereby insisting that she was entitled to some share of the accolades these men writers received.

The other women writers of this turn-of-the-century period, those who did not care to participate in the nation-building literary frenzy, concentrated on chronicling social life in the cities or else clambered into sheer fantasy. Ada Cambridge became a perspicacious observer of the manners of Melbourne middle-class society and applied a gentle wit and a mild irony to its pretensions and hypocrisies. Rosa Campbell-Praed discarded any pretensions to critical accolades and created superb if implausible heroines who dashed all over the country, achieving extraordinary feats though usually ending up with a suitable male companion. A revealing feature of her writings was her proclivity for having her female characters dispense with weak, cowardly or uninteresting men and take up, legally or otherwise, with more exciting characters. She had a marvellous, if unconventional, romantic strain, one that was definitely at odds with the current literary tradition even though it generally used its settings and even some of its themes. Neither she nor Cambridge nor any of the bevy of women who wrote novels at this time are remembered by any but literary historians or they are rediscovered every generation or so by the curious woman who, searching for some reference point for her own restlessness, digs into the past.

The novels of these women were not great works, but they are as competent as those of Boldrewood, Rudd, Louis Stone and many other men whose works are still read. These women and their works have not been absorbed into the tradition for the tradition was a rigid one, preoccupied with men's lives, searching for epochal dimensions and thereby forced to turn to the vast remoteness of the outback, a location which as we have seen offered little scope for women. There was no alternative tradition to which women could contribute and they were evidently unable, or did not see the need, to try and create a workable alternative for themselves.

Those women who wanted recognition of their literary creations had to crash through from the domestic dramas or the romantic escapades of their contemporaries into the universe of men; once there they were accepted only inasmuch as they conformed to the standards and preoccupations these men had defined. Their situation was therefore precarious and almost invariably dishonest, for by conforming to men's ideals they were denying something in themselves. They were sublimating their own needs and their own experiences while vicariously contributing to those of men. Occasionally they would be true to themselves and, as in Mary Gilmore's poem 'Mother', some of their real feelings would be permitted to emerge but too much of this was condemned as self-indulgent. So they invariably circumscribed themselves to avoid being classed, crucified and condemned as women writers for the common judgement of *their* literary products was resoundingly denigratory. According to the *Bulletin* at the time, ' . . . feminine literature consists largely of that inane drivel of monthly journals, in which fifth-rate writers gush in pages of weltering stupidity about coroneted heroes, noblemen of impossible elegance, and demi-gods from the Upper House of the British Legislature.'[12]

That writers who were female felt this kind of sexist criticism to impede their creative efforts was demonstrated by the delineator of the second colonial literary tradition, Henry Handel Richardson. She is the classic example of a woman being forced to deny self in order to pursue her craft unimpeded. She was determined to conceal her sex until her reputation was established, a task which took four novels and twenty-one years. In using a male pseudonym, Ethel Richardson was acquiring a basic form of self-protection which a great many women writers, including the Bronte sisters, George Eliot and George Sand, felt compelled to have. But while these masquerades gave women the freedom to write as they wished, their maintenance often entailed the price of psychic schizophrenia or even loss of fixed identity. This was Richardson's tragedy for by the time she was writing, the novel was concerned with psychological explorations. Her novels were in many respects autobiographical but in order to write about herself and still conceal her female identity she was obliged to assume a male persona and thereby move into a limbo of self-assigned androgyny in which honest self-exploration was virtually impossible.[13] Androgynous self-identification is nowadays advocated by some people as a means of negating sexist categorization and

Virginia Woolf argued in 1928 that the great creative mind was necessarily androgynous[14] but neither argument can accommodate the dilemma of Richardson.

Denial of one's sex is not equatable with having the profound insight necessary to be able to portray characters of either sex. There is a range of universal human emotions, responses and yearnings which both sexes experience but these are mediated by the usual cultural situation of each sex which has a determining influence on the actual experience. So long as social differentiation between the sexes remains, a writer who denies this, for self or for created characters, is in danger of overlooking decisive areas of human activity. Shakespeare, as Woolf suggests, may have had an androgynous mind but it was not necessary for him to repudiate his male identity. Richardson's masquerade was forced upon her by the common practice of critics applying sexist and demeaning judgements to the writings of women. She was a fugitive from discriminatory treatment and sought to solve the resulting problems for her work by writing about women as a man. She did this so skilfully in the novel about her schooldays, *The Getting of Wisdom*, that no one suspected that the young Laura Rambowtham was a self-portrait. But once out of the realm of reminiscence her difficulties became manifold and were reflected in her major work, *The Fortunes of Richard Mahony*. She was obliged to transpose her own cultural and psychic alienation onto Mahony, a man, and as convention demanded, to portray him as married to a rather prosaic Australian wife. The critical result was inescapable: Mary Mahony became equated with the pedestrian Australian culture which impeded Richard Mahony's soaring imagination and Richardson was responsible for, if not creating, then at least providing a powerful reinforcement to the idea that women as wives are impediments to male self-realization. Since Australian society has not permitted women to be anything else, this literary creation became yet another of the cultural deadweights denying women individuality and self-determination.

In striving for her own independence but failing to realize that such a battle cannot be a solitary one if real gains are to be made, Richardson achieved success within the male literary world; but it was a tawdry victory for it contained within it the denial of the intrinsic merit of female creativity. Richardson played the game by the male rules, denying herself the opportunity to explore her own specifically female experiences and thereby perpetuating the prejudice that women's experiences are unworthy material for a national literary tradition.

Although Australian literature has undergone several innovations since the colonial period there has been no alteration in the pattern of excluding women. The definitive trends have all been totally preoccupied with male experiences, and where women have been included as subjects their presence has always been to serve some symbolic or ideological purpose. They may be props, or sounding boards for the central male characters, or they reappear, with the monotonous regularity of the weekly wash, as stereotyped and passive suburban housewives. Those later writers whose style is a Nietzschean rejection of the democratic realism of colonial literature all tend to, equate women with life itself and, making heavy use of the symbolic possibilities of the womb and its mysterious cycles and life-nurturing potentialities, invest in their female characters a capacity for trans-porting men, through sexual intercourse, out' of the pedestrian realms of everyday life into a timeless and spirit-rejuvenating territory. This means of evading having to cope with women as unique and diverse individuals, reducing them instead to a sexist conglomerate, has been used by Patrick White and A. D. Hope, the two 'grand old men' of Australian letters. In his study of sex and nature in modern poetry, John Docker argues that for Hope, woman, a universal category, is an object or process for the artist-male to explore, and that she is used by Hope as an ideological end for himself.[15]

White uses women in a similar way. In *The Vivisector* two of the female characters, the prostitute Nance Lightfoot and Hero Pavloussi, the artist-hero's Greek mistress, are depicted as the embodiments of 'life'. White employs the dualistic device of dividing life and, in this case, women into two opposing categories. Good and evil are personified into two characters, in very much the same way as, this book argues, Australian women have been subjugated by stereotyped cultural impositions. But White also uses women in the way Richardson used Mary Mahony, to represent suburban stultification. In his play *A Season at Sarsaparilla* White has the three housewives speaking identical lines simultaneously, implying that women at least in their housewife roles can be reduced to a composite configuration which allows them no means of individual expression. Their husbands on the other hand, dreary as they might be, at least retain a semblance of individuality even if it is only by virtue of their having different jobs. The models presented by this literature, White and Hope being examples of an almost ubiquitous tendency in twentieth century post-realist writing, offer no hope to women. They are presented with the alternatives of trying to be Nature incarnate to enable their jaded lovers to reach back into a pretechnological past, and thus of living at a level of pure biological capacity; or of submitting to aimless anonymity as housewife slaves. *The Aunt's Story* is a cautionary tale for women who are disinclined to follow either route: exiled to a joyless Gehenna of unfulfilled sexual fantasy and frustration, the single woman who has no bodily contact with men is an amputated anthropoid, lacking that penetration by the penis which will complete her humanity.

A similar preoccupation with stereotyped females, and their use for the working out of male dilemmas appears in the writings of younger men, showing that *their* revolt against the old men is one of form rather than substance. Although he shows a little more sympathy for the psychic deadlock resulting from female socialization, Frank Moorhouse retains much of the methodology of the Nietzscheans: he implants in his female characters those qualities which he wants to contrast with those possessed by the male protagonist. These are usually mysticism, or other forms of irrationality, sexual prudery or simple lack of imagination and innovation in social relations. The same themes recur in Moorhouse as were seen in all our literature except that here they are, by virtue of the modernity of the settings and situations and the pretensions of some of the characters, seemingly in discontinuity with what went before.

At a time when Australian playwrights are subjecting the institution of mateship to some trenchant criticism, Moorhouse is affirming a variety of male comradeship which, while it possesses a self-awareness and is more intellectually based than the digger variety, is nevertheless posed as an alternative to the threatening ubiquitousness of women. In *The Girl who met Simone de Beauvoir in Paris*[16] three beleaguered males sit around and pun about a retreat into buggery to escape the aggressive retribution of two feminist women. Moorhouse depicts a variety of women who are individualistic, non-conformers or otherwise set apart from the female stereotype but their presence serves to make the conflict-resolution or ironic self-parody of the hero more impressive: the women still function as props around which the central concerns, which invariably involve only male self-preservation, are explored.

Ray Lawler's *The Summer of the Seventeenth Doll* began what has become a central concern with Australian male writers of plays: a critical examination of mateship. Plays like *The Back-room Boys*, *White with Wire Wheels*, *Rooted* and *Don's Party* have all explored the fragility of the bonds which men still affirm as precious and indissoluble, and a secondary concern with all of these works has been the detrimental effect on relations between the sexes that

retention of the myth has. Olive, in *The Doll* is portrayed as a hopelessly romantic irrational female who is content to sublimate her
desire for children in almost idolatrous attachment to the gaudy
kewpie dolls which Roo brings her from Queensland each year;
she rejects the security of marriage in order to retain an idealized
attachment to the independent male who renews his masculinity
afresh each year by his seven-month confrontation with nature in
the cane-fields. Olive sees her role as being to sustain Roo's illusions
about his masculinity especially as he gets older and is challenged by
younger men; Roo compliantly accepts, even demands, this role.
He does not 'womanize' while up North, unlike his philandering
mate, Barney, because his identity is secured by Olive's idealized
devotion. But their relationship is glass-brittle; the fantasized life
of the lay-off season cannot endure into old age and declining physical
strength. Roo expects Olive to provide the traditional female qualities
of succour and emotional protection when he meets his existential
crisis. But all he can offer her is marriage, something she had had
to reject seventeen years before in order to play out his attenuated
summer games. When she rejects *his* rejection of her seventeen years
of self-sacrifice he deserts her, the rifts between Roo and Barney
healed by a mutual hostility towards women. Lawler allows the
women in his play only the slightest range of possible lifestyles and
identities. His work is an affirmation of the retreat into male solidarity
being possible even if, as Barney says, ultimately they will be both
'left in the cold'. Lawler does not dare even suggest what will happen
to Olive, left to sink hopelessly among the smithereens of the
seventeenth doll.

Drama perhaps even more than literature is able to create characters
whose quintessential representation of a contemporary issue or
dilemma secures their absorption into a culture, so that subsequently
the mere mention of the name of that character becomes a kind of
shorthand for referring to a particular situation or set of personal
problems. Jimmy Porter in John Osborne's *Look Back in Anger* is
such a character and so were several of Ibsen's creations.

In recent Australian drama Alf and Hughie Cook in *The One Day
of the Year* have come to symbolize the clash between the values
of the old Australian 'digger' mentality and those of the newly
educated post-war rising middle class, a battle typically fought out
between two males, father and son. No such enduring female character
has emerged from contemporary Australian drama; those women
who do appear serve dramatic functions in relation to the main
conflict which is always between the men. Jan Castle, the girl from

the North Shore in Seymour's play, is the agent for the brutal attack on the brash cockiness of the working-class Australian and is portrayed as a snob and a bitch, but we are given no insight into *her* conflicts, into what attracted her to Hughie the working-class boy at university. She is a shallow, virtually faceless persona, a stereotype which serves a useful dramatic function but which offers no comment on the problems of a girl trying to escape *her* family and the particular demands of her social class. Similarly the wives in David Williamson's play *Don's Party* serve mainly as props to the central male characters. Certainly Williamson has gone beyond Seymour; his female characters are two-dimensional and we are given some notion of *their* failed aspirations and their present self-hatred and despair. Part of the point of the play is to delineate the extent to which the fragile egos of Don and his 'mate' have been cossetted and sustained by their long-suffering wives, the bearers of the brunt of the illusions and self-deceptions of their husbands; but the audience's sympathies are directed towards the men.

The consequences of this are two-fold. Firstly, there have been no noteworthy or memorable female characters created who exist outside, or who challenge the God's Police stereotype* of Australian womanhood. It is surprising that no playwright has utilized the rich dramatic possibilities of the alternative stereotype. We would still be dealing in cultural constructs rather than real people but the possibility of variety from the claustrophobia of a single option might open the way to further change. The reason the Whore stereotype has been neglected seems to confirm my thesis about male writers: the women usually depicted by this stereotype are independent, self-assertive creatures who do not need men and would therefore be poor material for a man needing a character against which to contrast his own dilemmas. And so Australian women are not presented with a viable alternative to the stereotype. Nor is there even a reasonably complex working out in any of the recent Australian plays which have been seen by mass audiences round the country of the demands, conflicts and disappointments of what it is like to try and live in accordance with that stereotype. Secondly, the result has been that there are virtually no rewarding parts for Australian actresses in indigenous drama. A newspaper interview with actresses from the Melbourne Pram Factory gave voice to their discontent in this respect: 'Their complaints centre round the scarcity of parts for women in many plays currently being written. A quick glance over recent APG

* See Introduction p. 67

programmes reveals three major productions without a single female part: Oakley's *Beware of Imitations*, and *The Feet of Daniel Mannix;* and Jack Hibberd's *A Stretch of the Imagination*.'[17]

The single exception to this would seem to be the character of Sally Banner created by Dorothy Hewett in *The Chapel Perilous*. Hewett has said of her work:

What I think I succeed in is writing some big roles for women. These brilliant young men playwrights of ours haven't done that yet. I guess it's the frustrated actress in me – I'm writing roles I'd love to play. But all the actresses tell me my women's roles are terrific. Well, we have to know how women think – and that's what I'm trying to get across on stage.[18]

In *The Chapel Perilous*, Hewett has created a superb female character, one who does express the varying demands made upon a woman as she grows up and struggles against society's proscriptions and its terrible retribution when she transgresses the boundaries within which women are supposed to reside contentedly. Sally Banner is no quiescent and compliant little girl. At school she tells a school mate, 'I want to feel everything. To tell everything, to walk naked . . .'[19] Later after she has defied the world, abandoned her husband and her child, joined the Communist Party and been betrayed by her lover – for whom she forsook everything – she tells the same woman,

. . . I could never accept annihilation. The shadow of it lay over everything I did. My whole life has been a struggle to be identified with someone, something, anything that gave me even a brief sense of my own immortality. And yet I've always known, even when I struggled hardest, that annihilation was the end of it. Even when – no, especially when – I was wild with joy because I thought I'd found, even for a moment that immortal otherness at last.[20]

Inevitably Sally Banner fails, and in the conventional way. She becomes annihilated and absorbed by the tentacles of fame and fortune, and she curbs her anarchic instincts and, old age advancing, begins to conform to a subsidiary stereotype, that of the Famous Woman, winner of an OBE and donor of a stained glass window to her old school chapel. Shortly before her capitulation to the forces which defeat her she voices her own epitaph: ' . . . I had a tremendous world in my head and more than three-quarters of it will be buried with me.'[21]

What words from the mouth of an Australian woman! Here is a mere woman voicing an anguish which, from reading the books and plays of the last few decades, we would have thought was confined to men. For perhaps the first time in our literature a woman has been permitted to express universal problems and not have them sound incongruous or pretentious.

Sally Banner is some thirty years later providing substance to balance that lop-sided world that so disturbed Christina Stead's Teresa Hawkins when she could find no written recognition of her internal turmoil: 'At each thing she read, she thought, yes, it's true, or no, it's false, and persevered with satisfaction and joy, illuminated because her world existed and was recognized by men. But why no women? She found nothing in the few works of women she could find that was what they must have felt.'[22] It would be consoling to think that at last the tide was turning, that it was being recognized that women's lives and ideas are as complicated, as disillusioning and as unresolved as men's, and that *The Chapel Perilous* was simply the first wave of a new, integrated literature. But it was performed for two short seasons, seen by perhaps a few hundred people. It has had none of the delirious success of *The One Day of the Year* or *Don's Party*, and has been noticed only by the devoted followers of new drama. Few of the women for whom it would be so rewarding have even heard of it and it is probably a sad truth that it will go the way of its few predecessors.

For there *have* been works, written by women, which have at least tried to portray an alternative existence to the cosy wife/mother stereotype, or which have probed the discontent which so often accompanies the living out of this supposed ideal existence. But, remarkably, none of these books is known beyond small circles of searchers who, over several generations, have sought and clung to whatever books they could find which spoke to them in a language which approached their own needs and conflicts and which depicted situations or quests which resembled theirs. Several processes have operated to censor the reading of generations of women for whom these books might have held out a small glimmer of hope that their alienation from the expectations of a crushing and suffocating society was not unique, and that therefore there was some possibility of transcending it.

Some of these books have been misinterpreted. Christina Stead was probably the first Australian woman in the post-realism era to begin to challenge the literary stereotype. Her books, principally *For Love Alone* and *Seven Poor Men of Sydney*, both of which are set in Sydney, were for years ignored by those who preside over syllabuses of Australian Literature courses at universities, just as the fact that she chose to live in England was deemed sufficient reason for not considering her an Australian writer. This fate was not extended to writers like Patrick White, Martin Boyd or George Johnston who similarly sought exile in climes more conducive to the requirements of their art.[23] Stead's virtues are now beginning to be recognized and her books are being re-issued in Australia and being read at universities, but there has been no critical recognition of one of her major contributions to Australian literature: her characterization of women. Her prose style and poetic descriptions have received accolades but her depiction of the turmoils experienced by young women growing up in a repressive Australian culture have gone unremarked upon except by those feminist teachers who usually in adult education classes – outside these definitive university walls where status and standards are determined – have tried to redress the balance.

There have also been works by writers who while being acknowledged for their other books have found that those which concentrate on the fortunes of a beleaguered woman are steadfastly ignored. Kylie Tennant is a good example. She is well known for books such as *The Battlers, Foveaux* and *Tell Morning This*, all of which are powerful chronicles of communities, which contain perceptive portraits of women but where these are not the central concern of the novel. By contrast her *Ride on Stranger* is somehow omitted from the list of her credentials; it figures in the bibliographies but it is seldom read or discussed. This book was published in 1943, three years before the first English-language translation of Camus's *L'Etranger* (*The Outsider*) appeared. Its central character can be seen as forming a connecting link between Teresa Hawkins and Sally Banner. Shannon Hicks is an unwanted child subject to ridicule for being called by her mother's maiden name, jeered at by schoolteachers for wanting to be a lawyer ('Why, there is only one thing for girls to do, and that is to grow up to be good wives and mothers. Isn't that so?').[24] Doomed to wander relentlessly through a variety of social and political situations, never fully accepted because her rejection of the traditional female destiny made her an alien and enigmatic figure, she is a rare female creation in Australian literature. Yet only one critic (a woman) has even recognized her:

I have written at this length on Shannon because there has been, among Australian reviewers and critics, a curious reluctance to believe in her, or to accept her. In America she was immediately acknowledged as interesting and significant, but it is hard not to form the impression, reading H. M. Green and T. Inglis Moore, the *Bulletin* reviewer, and others, that

Australians in their understanding of feminine psychology have not caught up with Ibsen, let alone anything more modern; nor have they recognized that Shannon, as Stranger, is that figure, more typical than any other of our age, who stands outside society and whose solutions as presented in literature, have been among the main themes of serious writing in our time.[25]

Literary critics have no trouble identifying, and either decrying or ignoring, the standard feminist who pops up in so many Australian novels. She appears in varying guises in the work of Miles Franklin and Dymphna Cusack and in Kylie Tennant's other novels: a women, usually unmarried, who is staunchly sceptical about men's pretensions and is scornful of a male-constructed and male-run world. She is however usually a transparent figure, whose main function seems to be to provide propagandist light-relief to the complexities of the other characters. Her continual appearance has not helped the creation of a clear tradition within our literature of writing seriously about women, of examining the many facets of their lives with the same inquiring concern which is applied to men and to male psychology. Because she has been an underdeveloped character it has been too easy for the critics to pose her as the only alternative to current modes in men's writing and to sneer at the possibility of a serious examination of women by a woman writer. Creations like Shannon Hicks are conveniently forgotten.[26]

There are some quite remarkable parallels between the career of Shannon Hicks and Emily Lawrence, the main female character in Elizabeth Harrower's *The Long Prospect*. This book belongs to a third category in the processes by which these books about women have been suppressed. All of Harrower's novels have been denied critical attention in Australia. The only article ever, to my knowledge, to have appeared about her work claimed that she

. . . is a writer of remarkable stature in the current sense. Along with Patrick White, albeit of slighter range and power than Australia's dominating literary genius, she stands head and shoulders above the current pack of sociological realists in the national novel . . . Barry Humphries may satirize the surface absurdities of the Australian norm; but Elizabeth Harrower has seen deep into the destructive core.[27]

Emily Lawrence in *The Long Prospect*, like Shannon Hicks and, incidentally, like Louisa Lawson and countless other Australian women whose names have never been recorded, suffers the pain and intellectual frustration of being denied books by the Philistines in whose charge she has been placed. Within a general Australian anti-intellectualism, women who harbour longings for a stimulating world between hard-covers suffer more because such abstract ardour is patently incompatible with the concrete demands of being a wife and mother. Intellectual women, that is to say women who translate their intelligence into carefully formulated opinions or Utopian longings, have been and remain objects to terrify men, even intellectual men (for *their* claim to merit is then not unique) and are automatically exiled from an easy friendship with other women. It is not easy to guess why literary representations of such women should prove similarly terrifying but this has been, apparently, the reason for their neglect.

Elizabeth Harrower must possess a very special strength and conviction to be able to continue to write her splendid books about women for a world which mostly fails even to acknowledge their existence.[28] Other women have lacked her tenacity and when their offerings have been ignored have disappeared. There has been a string of works by young women who have never published again.[29] A similar descent into anonymity also occurs with many young male writers and one cannot ever be certain of the reasons for a writer's failure to publish a second book but it is certainly the case that where there is no encouragement to pursue what is probably the hardest and loneliest of crafts, only the most stalwart and determined will persist.

There are particular difficulties for any woman who tries to combine being wife and mother with writing. She will have more domestic responsibilities and therefore less sheer *time* than the husband/father who writes. Good serious writing requires solitude and tranquillity. Many a male writer has a wife or mistress or some devoted person to cosset him, feed him, protect him from the telephone and other jangling intrusions of the outside world, to listen to his ideas (and often suggest many of them), type manuscripts and correct spelling, to soothe away despair and self-doubt, to convince him of the worth of his project. In short, to create and maintain the environment in which writing can be done. The traditional two-line acknowledgement: 'To my wife, without whom etc. . . . ' is a nauseatingly jejune recompense which disguises what is often the absolute truth, as would rapidly become apparent if the slaves upon whose supportive psyches these books are written were to withdraw their services. The wives of writers contribute more than is ever acknowledged to the getting out of a book.

Similarly, the conflicts and double-binds of the mother/wife/writer are ignored by all but the overburdened women themselves. Gwen Harwood's poem 'Burning Sappho' describes the frustration, anger and, finally, fury at the never-ending demands made by children, visitors and husband each time the poet/housewife takes up her pen to write.[30] Charmian Clift recounted how her work suffered because of her other duties:

I knew by this time [1946] I was a writer and of course George [Johnston, her husband] encouraged me very much indeed. At this point I should have taken wings and started to fly but at this point also, of course, I was involved in having children, and for many years I had this dual thing, the frustrations that are inevitable with any creative person being tied and bound and at the same time struggling, beating one's head against a wall to do what one wants to do. I think those are terribly difficult years for any young woman and for a young woman who wants to write or paint or anything else, even more so.[31]

But on top of the demands of motherhood, a woman is also a wife, and especially if her husband is involved in his own creative work, has other demands placed upon her. Clift remarks that her collaboration with Johnston in several novels was actually

a phony collaboration because I was beyond the stage where I could collaborate any longer. I wanted to do my own work in my own way. In any case, I didn't have time because I was the one who had to learn the Greek and I was our interpreter and I was our cook, and I had this awful problem on my hands of two small children who were lost and bewildered and lonely in a foreign country, and it took about a year to adjust all that. Then I found that I was going to have another baby, and this plunged me back into a long long tunnel which I thought I'd just got clear of.[32]

When Clift's work is compared to Johnston's, it is always regarded as being slighter. Should we then take into account what it was that prevented her from attaining the heights that she herself probably aimed for but, because she put others and their needs before her own, could not reach? Those women writers who have been most prolific and most successful have always had the physical assistance of their husbands or of secretaries who did their typing and answered their telephones and generally played the kind of protective role which we are inclined to associate with being a wife. Both Kylie Tennant and Henry Handel Richardson have had substantial help from their husbands in getting their books out and this must be seen as a factor in their success. Writers who are childless or who have not married are in an easier position in that less of their time will have to be spent in tending to other people's needs. But it is a monstrous expectation which decrees that a woman should have to eschew some of the things she wants in order to have the others. Why should a woman have to sacrifice marriage and children, if these are what she desires, so that she may be a successful writer, while men need not make such a choice? The battle against physical or psychological disabilities is seen as semi-heroic when it occurs in a man. Scott Fitzgerald was pitied because of his wife's diagnosed insanity: no wonder he took to drink people said sympathetically. The New South Wales Government awarded Henry Lawson a literary pension while tacitly acknowledging that his alcoholism would prevent him from ever writing again. Allowances and concessions are made in such cases. They are made to the person if not to the art. It is recognized that the art is debilitated by these circumstances. What then of the woman for whom a comparable debilitation is virtually the premise of her existence? How can she be accommodated in a world which almost by definition requires a supportive individual and culture?

The kind of criticism mounted in this section has begun to penetrate the consciousness of a number of men writers and some are beginning to make attempts to move away from using women as stereotyped props. These efforts constitute a change but it would be a mistake to conclude that a rash of Coralie Lansdownes is all that is needed. What is happening at present is the creation of a new stereotype, that of the 'liberated woman'. The difference is that this stereotyped character is the main, or a central, figure rather than a prop but she remains a stereotype nevertheless. As such she is a projection of men's fantasies, expectations or fears rather than a representation of a real person. Whether or not many men will be able to move away from merely updating their stereotypes and acquire the necessary insight and empathy to be able to create female characters who crystallize the dilemmas of women today remains to be seen. But more importantly, until women writing about themselves is acknowledged as being as worthy an endeavour as either men writing about men or men writing about women, and men begin not only to read such writing but *to treat it seriously*, then an important part of my argument has not been met.

This does not yet appear to be happening. In the last few months (late 1974) a spate of new books by young Australian writers has been published and they have been extensively promoted by the Literature Board of the Australian Council for the Arts. They have included three good works of fiction by women – Vicki Viidikas,

Suzanne Holly Jones and Christine Townend. But while they have been given virtually the same amount of publicity as the men's books they have not received equal attention from the book review pages of newspapers nor have any of them been treated as seriously *as literature* as the books of Robert Adamson and Bruce Hanford, Michael Wilding, Peter Carey and others. The physical exclusion and critical neglect of women from Australian literature will persist until those things which impede women writers are recognized. Even if they are acknowledged their erosion will not follow automatically, but this could be the beginnings of the process of redressing the solid male balance of this level of Australian culture.

NOTES

1. Donald Horne, *The Lucky Country*, Penguin Books, 1965, p. 30.

2. Craig McGregor, *Profile of Australia*, Penguin Books, 1968, p. 351.

3. Elizabeth Harrower, *The Long Prospect*, Sun Books, Melbourne, 1966, p. 196.

4. Both Germaine Greer and Elizabeth Reid, adviser to the Prime Minister on women's affairs, have been subjected to this kind of public speculation, the former because of her outspokenness on female sexuality, the latter because she revealed in a press interview that her daughter was cared for by her estranged husband. Both women have been viciously attacked, mainly by other women, in the correspondence columns of daily newspapers, in letters which have questioned the right of these women to even claim identification with the female sex. One letter signed by (Mrs) Elizabeth Foss which appeared in the *Sydney Morning Herald*, 16 April 1973, said: 'I realized quite early on that it would be too much to hope that Mr Whitlam would choose a "normal sort of woman" more in tune with what women in this country really want to say, and was disillusioned that once more we have a neo-academic talking for us. Miss Reid is not talking for me now and probably never will. Will someone happily married, who has reared a family through thick and thin, please stand up and be counted.'

5. Ronald Conway, *The Great Australian Stupor*, Sun Books, Melbourne, 1971.

6. For instance, Eva Figes, *Patriarchal Attitudes*, Faber and Faber, London, 1970; Kate Millett, *Sexual Politics*, Rupert Hart Davis, London, 1971; H. R. Hays, *The Dangerous Sex*, Methuen, London, 1966.

7. Maslyn Williams, 'Dilemmas of Liberation', *Sydney Morning Herald*, 5 May 1973 (review of Jay Gilbert, *Boy Peace*).

8. In another review Thelma Forshaw forsook any sympathy for the double-bind in which women find themselves when she wrote, 'As a man wrote *Madame Bovary*

(and *Anna Karenina,* twice mentioned in Nell Dunn's novel), so I expect only a man will have the deep insight, detachment and large compassion to write the tragic novel of the twentieth century woman who is being devalued in her deepest being during her enforced transition into some other sex.' *Sydney Morning Herald,* 31 July 1971 (review of Nina Bawden, *The Birds on the Trees* and Nell Dunn, *The Incurable*).

9.   Martin Boyd, *The Cardboard Crown,* 1952; *A Difficult Young Man,* 1955; *Outbreak of Love,* 1957; *When Blackbirds Sing,* 1962. (These are now published by Lansdowne Press, Melbourne.)

10.   Hazel de Berg, taped interview with Dame Mary Gilmore. Tape No. 84. I wish to thank Ms de Berg for her kind permission to quote from this interview.

11.   ibid.

12.   The *Bulletin,* 9 March 1889.

13.   For a more detailed exposition of this argument, one which is enhanced by supporting textual material, see Anne Summers, 'The Self Denied: Australian Women Writers, their image of women', *Refractory Girl,* No. 2, Autumn 1973, pp. 4–11.

14.   Virginia Woolf, *A Room of One's Own,* Penguin Books, 1965, pp. 102–3.

15.   John Docker, 'Sex and Nature in Modern Poetry', *Arena,* No. 22, 1970, pp. 20 and 23.

16.   Frank Moorhouse, *The Americans, Baby,* Angus & Robertson, Sydney, 1972.

17.   Helen Garner, 'Where's women in the worlds men create?' The *Digger,* 10–24 March 1973, p. 9.

18.   Kevon Kemp, 'Dorothy Hewett writes the roles she would love to play', The *National Times,* 4–9 September 1972.

19.   Dorothy Hewett, *The Chapel Perilous,* Currency Press, Sydney, 1972, p. 18.

20.   ibid., p. 84.

21.   ibid., p. 88.

22.   Christina Stead, *For Love Alone,* Angus & Robertson, Sydney, 1966 (1945), p. 76.

23.   Christina Stead was denied the Encyclopaedia Britannica prize of £10,000 for outstanding contributions to Australian literature because she did not live in Australia. The fact that her books have been published abroad has always counted against their being favourably received in Australia, as it has also meant that Elizabeth Harrower has remained comparatively unknown even though she lives in Sydney. By contrast, the fact that *The Tree of Man* was first published in London did not prevent its being critically treated as an Australian work. Thus the fact of being female would seem to be more decisive than the status of expatriate. The case of Henry Handel Richardson does not constitute an exception because her reputation was secure before her sex was revealed.

24.   Kylie Tennant, *Ride on Stranger,* Angus & Robertson, Sydney, 1943, p. 9.

25. Margaret Dick, *The Novels of Kylie Tennant*, Rigby, Adelaide, 1966, p. 67.

26. In a lecture entitled 'Rooms of their Own' delivered at the University of Sydney in October 1972, Humphrey McQueen pointed out that a similar fate has befallen Eleanor Dark's 'feminist' novels, those early books, principally *Prelude to Christopher*, in which Dark delineated for women an alternative lifestyle where freedom to choose one's destiny was a paramount concern. These early books are forgotten and Dark is remembered mainly for her nation-building trilogy.

27. Anon., 'The novels of Elizabeth Harrower', *Australian Letters*, Vol. 4, no .2, January 1961, pp. 16 and 18.

28. The best of her works, in my view, are *The Long Prospect* and *The Watch Tower*, Macmillan, London, 1966.

29. For instance, Juliet Rolleston, *Pink is for Girls*, Angus & Robertson, Sydney, 1960, and the many female contributors to Anne O'Donovan, Jayne Sanderson and Shane Porteous, eds, *Under Twenty-five*, Jacaranda Press, Brisbane, n.d. (1967). Suzanne Holly Jones published *Harry's Child*, Jacaranda Press, Brisbane, in 1964. She has now published another, *Crying in the Garden*, Outback Press, Melbourne, 1974, but only after an interval of ten years.

30. Gwen Harwood, *Poems*, Volume Two, Angus & Robertson, Sydney, 1968, p. 29.

31. Hazel de Berg, taped interview with Charmian Clift, 8 June 1965.

32. ibid.

CHAPTER

TWO

MANZONE COUNTRY

We are in the terminal days of a sort of Menzies era of social criticism. But the new men of a new age are waiting on the sidelines. It won't be long.

MAX HARRIS, The *Australian*, 9 February 1974

The second 'level' of culture consists of theories and interpretations which intellectuals have devised to describe what they perceive as the quintessential elements of Australian life. For the most part these are – or used to be – expressed in semi-academic works or in journalistic essays, that enormous collection of commentaries which pile up annually.[1] More recently they are also contained in those newspapers and magazines which set themselves up as critical commentators of either the entire corpus, or of some particular facet of Australian society. Both modes of articulating interpretations of Australian life have to be looked at here for it is important to gauge the extent of the self-professed radicalism of the latter. Certainly many of these little magazines or newspapers set themselves up in opposition to the bland theories of their intellectual fathers but it is possible that the limits of their protest have been obscured by their flamboyant, seemingly iconoclastic style.

The first and the most influential post-Federation commentator on Australian life was W. K. Hancock whose book *Australia* was published in 1930. Hancock's analysis of Australian history pursued three main themes: the taming of the land, the emergence of sectional strife and the development of a nationalism which was democratic and egalitarian. R. W. Connell has pointed out that ' . . . the themes developed or crystallized by Hancock have been taken over by his successors with only minor modifications, though with many new illustrations. The result has been a homogeneous tradition of social comment and criticism.'[2] He argues that Donald Horne, J. D. Pringle, Peter Coleman, Max Harris, F. W. Eggleston, Sol Encel and Craig McGregor, the best known and hence presumably the most influential commentators on Australian life, have generally just elaborated on Hancock's themes. Yet, as he points out, Hancock's book was flawed

in many respects. It concentrated on rural history when in fact the
majority of Australians have always lived in the cities. He insisted
that Australian political life was devoid of ideas although, as Connell
shows, ideological clashes have been a constant feature of our politics,
beginning with religious conflicts in the nineteenth century and
persisting into the twentieth with the battles over conscription and
the Vietnam war. Hancock also plied the myth that Australia was an
independent nation, again a half-truth in the post-1918 era of distrust
of nationalism and the emergence of an international culture.[3] A
further, and more serious, flaw of Hancock's work, one which eluded
Connell and the Hancockians he selects, was that Hancock used the
terms 'Australian' and 'men' synonymously: the Australia he described
was a wholly male universe depicted from a man's point of view.
His basic framework partly precluded any other interpretation; had
he examined city life he might have had at least a cursory look at
'the family'; had he conceded ideology in politics he might have
been forced to glance at the emergence of the demand for equal
rights for women; had he placed Australia in an international context
it may have occurred to him that women in Australia were uniquely
tied to home and family when compared with their sisters in other
industrialized nations.

It has already been pointed out that most of the more recent
commentaries have paid some fleeting attention to 'the family' but
this has been the full extent of the revision of Hancock's ignoring
of women's role in the development of the Australian nation; in
every other instance they have been content to reproduce those
themes, particularly the assertion of egalitarianism, which Hancock
first articulated. The egalitarian thesis has been subjected to criticism
by recent writers who have pointed out that class and race divisions
have always characterized our culture, but what none of these writers
has done is to make the same comments about how we have been
divided on sex lines.

The standard example used by the commentators to illustrate our
supposed egalitarianism – 'Australians sit beside the taxi driver on
the front seat . . . '[4] – has become something of a joke among those
who reject the accompanying thesis, but what none of these critics
has noticed is that the example, and the way it is always written up,
applies only to men. Australian women do not as a rule sit in the
front of taxis. Certainly middle class women do not and any woman
who does open the front door and sit beside the driver is automatically
regarded as *déclassée*, or somehow disreputable and her action thrusts
a wedge through any posited female egalitarianism. An example

which supposedly proves something about men, proves exactly the opposite about women and therefore should cast doubts on the universal validity of the thesis. The criticisms of this thesis which point out its limitations on class or race lines, but which do not recognize its sexist implications, are not making a very radical challenge. They can be seen as merely demanding that the fraternity be opened up, and that more *men* be included in the definitions of national characteristics. They do not necessarily challenge the values, categories and deep-rooted assumptions based on sex which are part of our national self-portrait.

Most of the standard commentaries on Australian culture have taken up and reiterated the 'lucky country' theme, portraying a nation endowed with endless possibilities for national aggrandizement and the acquisition of personal fortune, a land free from bitter sectarian and racial conflict, a homogeneous paradise where sun-loving Australians, beguiled by their belief that they are 'Godzone' continually congratulate themselves on their good fortune at having been born in, or migrated to, this best of possible worlds. This vision of Australia has been arrived at by tabulating the vast physical expanses, the revealed mineral wealth and the absence of bloody wars or revolutions, and correlating these with a selective panoramic version of our history: the first country to receive the secret ballot, the eight-hour day and conciliation and arbitration. The resulting vision dovetailed nicely with the themes elaborated by colonial literature and gradually a consensus was arrived at. Even where this did not match the actual experiences of those who read about it, challenging the happy hegemony meant calling into question not merely the integrity of the dream-spinners but also of the generations for whom the vision was some kind of existential prop. The experiences of the first AIF as well as the industrial struggles of the early labour unions were both integrated into the egalitarian myth and eventually became seen as its basis. Therefore to challenge it involved at least questioning if not actually denying the seminal experiences of a substantial proportion of the male population of Australia.

It is notable that women have rarely participated in this kind of writing; they have written histories and historical biographies but no Australian woman this century has dared to participate in the intellectual exercise of trying to formulate theories about Australian life. A likely reason for this is that the dominant themes which, as we have seen, have been reproduced over three generations with little modification, are so patently at odds with the life's experiences of almost all Australian women. The one woman to even venture into this field, and her work is largely historical, has been Kylie Tennant with her book *Australia,* a volume which is ironically subtitled *Her Story.*[5] A more inappropriate title for a book which concentrates on pastoral, industrial, political and mining development, all processes which have not involved women or have engaged their energies only in a peripheral way, could hardly be imagined. This book devotes even less attention to those areas of social life inhabited by women than do those of Hancock, Horne *et al.* The book was commissioned by businessmen and this partly explains the focus, but Tennant's services, rather than those of an academic historian, were engaged because the sponsors of the book wanted a 'readable' account. Such a specification could have easily been interpreted to bring in the kind of material which the other works have neglected but Tennant obviously felt unable to do this.[6]

Her difficulties would have been manifold: she wrote the first draft in the late Second World War years, a period when even primary source material pertaining to social history was available only to the most intrepid archivist and secondary works were virtually non-existent. Secondly, it would have involved forging another furrow, elaborating a 'new' interpretation of our past and present at a time when Hancock's vision went completely unchallenged. The feminist movement, to the extent that it was able to exist at all in those years of self-protective solidarity, still confined its energies to campaigning for tangible, legally enforcible 'rights' and to recording the achievements of visibly successful women, women whose accomplishments were recognizable to a society which valued political, economic or altruistic achievements. The movement did not feel it necessary to question these successes, nor to relate them to the life chances of the majority of women. It did not attempt to identify as oppressive those sexist values which social theorists projected as national characteristics. The devastating effects of this sexist culture on the female psyche had not then been recognized. So there was little inducement for Tennant to write any other kind of book. In the post-war period the only commentaries on Australian mores written by women have come from visitors from other countries.[7]

As the previous chapter argued, women writers of fiction have had to work in a realm which was outside the mainstream of the development of Australian literature, but at least they have, even if at enormous personal cost, still continued to write. The complete absence of women commentators on Australian culture requires further explanation, one that is necessarily related to the exclusion of women from those areas of national life which preoccupy the male theorists. This exclusion has explicitly denied the contributions which women have made by declaring these unworthy of celebration or recording, or has assumed that the female role in national life has been an unchanging constant which need not be singled out for examination at any particular period.

Women have often been excluded, not merely from the books, but from celebratory events. A banquet held in 1914 to celebrate the simultaneous reaching of a railway, a water pumping scheme and a post office to Loxton, S.A. was apparently a riotous, Bacchanalian affair but one which, the *Murray Pioneer* of 20 February pointed out, was 'for men only': 'A storm in a teacup over the exclusion of women from public and semi-public jollifications raged for several weeks. Some were moved to institute reforms. But seven Institute Committee men voted, instead, to remove the *Pioneer* from the Reading Room of the Institute.'[8] When it was realized that the sesqui-centenary celebrations planned for New South Wales in 1938 did not include tribute to the efforts of the pioneer women, women's organizations made urgent representations to the organizers and, only after much astute politicking, succeeded in obtaining some official recognition for their planned celebrations. But even these were token recognitions and women in three states were moved to compensate for this official black-balling at their centenary or sesqui-centenary celebrations by publishing their own tributes.[9] When the Australian National Library was established feminist groups which had made representations on the subject were promised that a special women's collection, housed separately, would be established.[10] It has yet to materialize, and the researcher of women's history in Australia has to work through an inadequately indexed general catalogue in the hope of finding material germane to the subject. There is a general assumption that, before the recent upsurge of interest in women's issues, there had been 'nothing written about women in Australia' and yet in 1973 when I compiled a general bibliography on this subject I had no difficulty in amassing a collection, still very incomplete and dealing only with printed works from 1900 onwards, of 523 items.[11] Much material *is* there and the women whose lives it deals with have had existences as various and as difficult to categorize as men's. But to be able to utilize it, to thread it into coherent and illuminating patterns will require challenging the assumptions and frameworks so far employed by the definers of this level of our culture.

It will mean completely scrapping Hancock's thesis on rural, non-ideological and nationalistic themes and the assumptions of fraternal egalitarianism which they shored up, and developing a concern with family life and social and sexual mores. Already the egalitarian view of our past has received a heavy challenge from the work of people like Humphrey McQueen, and historians of the destruction of Aboriginal society such as C. D. Rowley, Peter Biskup and Lorna Lippmann.[12] But opening up the subject area with respect to Aborigines has not necessarily included a simultaneous recognition that a society dominated by narrowly circumscribed views on individual and group achievements has had other victims as well. It is no longer enough to note the absence of Aborigines or women or any other cultural minority (such as homosexuals) from our official history. We have also to ask what functions their exclusion served, both economically and ideologically, for the dominant hegemony, and whether or not these functions persist.

These questions are not asked by two recent works which give the superficial appearance of challenging the Hancock-Horne vision. Ronald Conway's work, an attempted psycho-history of Australian culture, does move right away from the old framework and does concentrate on those areas, such as 'the family' and sexual relationships, which necessitate taking cognizance of the activities of women. He writes with some sympathy of the wasted and ravaged lives of so many Australian women but his solutions lie in a reassertion of the traditional nurturing role and in trying to impose upon this a more egalitarian relationship between men and women. He fails to recognize that what he poses as a solution is in fact *the* problem for many women, and that his twin-headed panacea is, for many, a contradiction. The traditional mother/wife role has been structured around an unequal social and economic relationship between men and women, with the 'separate but equal' ideology cloaking a multitude of legally sanctioned and *de facto* inequalities. As will be outlined later, it is the very dissatisfaction and confusion engendered among women by the structural changes in their roles which is causing so many problems; they will not be solved by resort to a nineteenth century patriarchal fantasy.

Ian Moffitt's book, *The U-Jack Society*[13], is an experiential account of one man's Australia but it also has a savage lash at the old she'll-be-right-mate attitude and argues that our hapless drift has not brought about the benign Utopia painted by the myths. His book challenges the 'lucky country' thesis by insisting that we have to grasp the future and forge it for ourselves, for it will not magically unfold before our wondering eyes, but it does not go any way towards beginning the kind of reinterpretation which was posited above.

Conway and Moffitt are in a sense the new guard in the process of defining our culture, but they remain within the old tradition of articulating their themes in book form. They were preceded over a decade ago by a group which defined themselves as rebels for they attacked not only the ingredients of the vision but also the form in which it was propagated. *Oz* magazine burst onto the Australian publishing scene in 1963 with a satirical iconoclasm which speedily brought about a reaction in the form of an obscenity suit and condemnation by all kinds of social and political leaders. But the radicalism of *Oz* remained circumscribed; it was a men-only affair, edited by a triumvirate of talented men who have all become successful in publishing or artistic ventures since, and their satire and comment fitted fairly easily into the Australian tradition of 'knocking'. In 'An Australian Catechism' which appeared in a 1964 issue, the *Oz* credo was by implication outlined:

In Australia one may not read about, write about or think about sex. In fact, one may only practise it in so far as it is necessary to keep the population figures respectable. One should not mention urination, criticize Royalty or the R.S.L. or god, or do anything that might conceivably cause the least embarrassment to any single person. Soldiers have died for such freedom. May their souls rest in peace.[14]

It was a late-adolescent oedipal revolt, an assertion by a new generation of impatient young men that they were no longer content to subscribe to the view of the world defined by their fathers, that *they* had a few ideas on previously taboo topics which they were going to air and to hell with you oldies. *Oz* crystallized and for a while was the vehicle for a revised version of the national self-portrait. It cut through humbug and hypocrisy, voiced moderately radical postures on domestic and foreign policy and challenged, with its cartoons especially, the rampant puritanism of Australia in the mid-sixties. It devoted a lot of attention to the boorish and rapacious behaviour of drunken Australian men, particularly that of their generational contemporaries, but its attitude was only mildly critical; it contained a good lashing of indulgent tolerance:

. . . there were a few king birds there but they were holding hands with these fairies – So DENNIS *belted* them and we all got onto the birds and Frank got one of them so pissed that she passed out so we all dragged her out to the garage and went through her like *a packet of salts* – KING! Then the old lady of the bird who was having the turn said she'd ring the Johns so Sid chucked all over her and she got hysterical so *Dennis BELTED her* and then Phil did this king hambone on the kitchen table and ran round the house in *the raw* ripping the gear off all the birds – God he's KING!...[15]

The attack on sexual puritanism contained no explicit repudiation of the old Australian denial of female sexuality and the concomitant middle class view that women outside one's own acquaintance could be employed in whatever fashion was necessary to satiate male lust.

Women have rarely been engaged, except as girl-friends, wives or the operators of typewriters, mimeograph machines and tea-urns, in any of the radical/underground activities of the past decade. The little magazines and newspapers and the later anti-Vietnam and anti-conscription campaigns were organized and their ambit defined by men, and women had either to participate in accordance with terms already laid down, or to join other male-organized oppositional factions. It was not until women began to form their own groups, and the beginning of Women's Liberation in Sydney in late 1969 and in Melbourne, Adelaide and Canberra in 1970, that any real challenge to the old hegemony began to be articulated. A Women's Liberation newspaper, *Mejane*, was begun in 1971 and is still publishing, a remarkable feat for a publication which enjoys neither paid advertising nor government grant. Yet its accomplishments – both in staying alive and in the kind of world-view it is trying to expound – get little recognition outside the Movement. A recent survey of the underground press conducted by a national newspaper spent an inordinate amount of space on commercial newspapers devoted to surfing or rock music, both avenues that ensure advertising revenue, and barely mentioned *Mejane*.[16]

The limits of the challenge to the old definitions of Australian culture posited by *Oz* and its successors, or rather its irrelevance in terms of developing a *real* counter-hegemony to the Hancock-Horne vision, is demonstrated by the reactions of those women who were caught up in it. Many women, including myself, feel a peculiar intellectual schizophrenia in attacking the mid-sixties rebellion for we *did* identify with it, and it played a major role in our acculturation to a position of radical protest against many facets of old Australia. Yet it could never entirely accommodate us and our needs even though, for a long time, we were unable to identify precisely the source of our alienation and we felt caught in an excruciating double-bind. We passionately defended this rebellious posture against the criticisms of parents, teachers and other authorities for we certainly did not agree with *them* but there still remained an uneasiness that much of our protest was hollow for we defended something that gave us only honorary status. We felt like Catherine in *Seven Poor Men of Sydney*: ' . . . I've fought all my life for male objectives in men's terms. I am neither man nor woman, rich nor poor, elegant nor worker, philistine nor artist. That's why I fight so hard and suffer so much and get nowhere.'[17] It was only with the formation of Women's Liberation, when women began to discuss this discontent and to tentatively assign reasons for it, that we began to understand that our sensibilities had been split, our feelings fractured by trying to identify with a radical posture which had not thought it necessary to challenge, along with the other sacred cows it tore down, the view that it behoved Australian women to sublimate all their ideals and aspirations in dutiful wifehood and bountiful maternity. It was evident that *this* challenge would have to be made by women themselves and this was the reason that *Mejane* and, in late 1972, *Refractory Girl*[18], were begun by groups of women who needed media in which to begin to voice their dissatisfaction with current definitions of this level of our culture, and to begin to explore possible alternatives.

The need for such publications is continually reinforced by the intransigence of the now aging rebels. The 'vital importance' of Women's Liberation is conceded by all who have any pretensions to views left of centre in both the cultural and political spheres, but these token acknowledgements too often are accompanied by a continuance of the old chauvinist attitudes and practices. A case in point is that weekly newspaper which has in three years changed its name as many times and which is currently published as *Nation Review*.

Nation Review is *Oz* reached early middle-age, its brash iconoclasm now the nomenclature of a sizeable minority of the population and, having acquired a wealthy backer, at last able to indulge in all its adolescent fantasies. Its hallmark, a 'lean and nosy ferret' embodies an incipient phallic symbolism which can hardly be accidental. *Nation Review* prides itself in its 'liberated' attitude to women; it is the only large-circulation newspaper to have adopted Ms as a descriptive title for all women, regardless of their marital status, it occasionally exposes and denounces instances of discrimination against women and it supports 'women's issues' such as abortion. But if *Nation Review* thinks this is sufficient to undermine the sexist basis of our culture it has largely missed the point of the criticism. The complaint has been that women have had little to identify with in a critical tradition written entirely by men and concentrating on issues, activities and themes which these men have identified as important. *Nation Review* has done nothing to reverse this trend. Its distinctive features, particularly its regular columns, are all written by men. Moreover, most of them depend for their effects on a peculiar kind of humour which uses women as objects of scorn, derision or ambiguous sexual ambition. It is a strange food column which devotes paragraph after paragraph to descriptions of the state of the underwear, or the lack of sobriety, of the diner's female companion but this is the Sam Orr which *Nation Review* readers know and love. It is an even stranger film critic who appraises films in terms of whether or not they are likely to arouse a woman to maximum capitulation after minimal seductive effort on the part of the male escort. The reviewer of *Last Tango in Paris* wrote, 'Go and see it, and watch how scared your girlfriend waxes on the swift drive home,'[19] and implicitly exhorted his male readers to exorcise their violence and frustrations on the hapless body of whichever unfortunate woman happened to accompany them that evening. Whenever an item such as this appears letters of protest from female readers inevitably follow, as do the where's-your-sense-of-humour-ladies? justifications from the reviewer or columnist in question.

The 14–20 October issue of the *Nation Review* in 1972 was handed over to a group of women journalists to edit: the editor of the newspaper sat back and congratulated himself on his benevolence while these women slaved for months on a miniscule budget to produce this single issue. The cover misleadingly announced that 'This issue has been taken over by women', implying that, like the S.D.S. women who actually physically seized editorial control of the U.S. underground newspaper *Rat* a few years ago, these women had ousted the elders of *Nation Review* and had thereby gained access to all the resources of the publication. Actually what happened was that the $1,500 budget allocated to this issue had to cover not only contributors' payments but also the many air-fares for the Sydney-based temporary editor and sub-editors and lay-out people to fly to Melbourne where the paper is produced. The result was that contributors to this issue received well below AJA award rates for their articles while the regular male columnists all had a week's holiday on full pay. Such are the benevolent ways in which *Nation Review* supports Women's Liberation.

The *Living Daylights*, a counter-cultural companion to *Nation Review* and edited by another member of the *Oz* brigade, began publication in October 1973. Despite its proclamations to the contrary it too is heavily male-centred in its preoccupations. It has published articles which explore men's sexist attitudes and responses but their content has been consistently eroded by other features which have glorified a masculine, at times almost macho, cult.

When such blatant assertions of masculine self-importance and power appear in publications which ostensibly challenge the old cultural hegemony, even if the traditional 'ocker' image of the Australian males is embellished with new, 'alternative' guises, it is evident that this counter culture is no less repressive as far as women are concerned than that which it challenges.

It would be encouraging for women to conclude that this was why the *Living Daylights* enjoyed a life of only six months as a separate publication. But obviously financial considerations governed its demise and incorporation in *Nation Review* where its heady influence is still occasionally evident, and we cannot brashly imagine that women's disillusion had much to do with this. Rather, the answer would seem to lie in the fact that the counter culture is neither large nor wealthy enough to support an expensive weekly. The 'alternative' man is still a distinct minority—and he only pays lip-service to the ideas of Women's Liberation. The majority culture still rests serene, its misogynist ockerism unassailed. Which indicates that women's struggle to have the traditional images of Australian culture changed in order to reflect some of *their* experiences is going to be very difficult indeed.

NOTES

1. For example, Kylie Tennant, *Australia: Her Story*, Macmillan, London, 1953; Donald Horne, *The Lucky Country*, Penguin Books, 1965; Craig McGregor, *Profile of Australia*, Penguin Books, 1968; John Hallows, *The Dreamtime Society*, Collins, Sydney, 1970; Ronald Conway, *The Great Australian Stupor*, Sun Books, Melbourne, 1971; Robin Boyd, *The Great Australian Dream*, Pergamon Press, Sydney, 1972; Ian Moffitt, *The U-Jack Society*, Ure Smith, Sydney, 1972. These are in contrast to the more scholarly works such as A. A. Phillips, *The Australian Tradition*, Cheshire, Melbourne, 1958; Russel Ward, *Australia*, Ure Smith, Sydney, 1967; *Anatomy of Australia*, H.R.H. the Duke of Edinburgh's Third Commonwealth Study Conference, Sun Books, Melbourne, Revised edition, 1970.

2. R. W. Connell, 'Images of Australia', *Quadrant*, No. 52, March-April 1968, p. 15.

3. ibid., pp. 16–17.

4. McGregor, op. cit., p. 10. This example has also been used by Max Harris, Donald Horne and D. H. Lawrence.

5. Tennant, op. cit.

6. For an account of how this book came to be written and its rather chequered publishing history, see Kylie Tennant, 'A Moral Story', The *Australian Author*, Vol. 1, no. 4, October 1969, pp. 11–13.

7. For instance, Mary Gallati, *My Low-down on Down-under*, Hutchinson, London, 1953; and Jeanne McKenzie, *Australian Paradox*, Cheshire, Melbourne, 1961.

8. cit. Marjory R. Cassan and W. R. C. Hirst, *Loxton*, Hawthorn Press, Melbourne, 1972, p. 87.

9. Frances Fraser and Nettie Palmer, eds, *Centenary Gift Book*, Robertson and Mullens, Melbourne, 1934; Louise Brown et al. eds, *A Book of South Australia, Women in the first hundred years*, Rigby, Adelaide, 1936; F. S. P. Eldershaw ed., *The Peaceful Army, A Memorial to the Pioneer Women of Australia 1788–1938*, The Women's Executive Committee and Advisory Council of Australia's 150th Anniversary Celebrations, Sydney, 1938.

10. This information was provided by Ms Ruby Rich, one of those who made representations for the women's library.

11. This bibliography has been published in the Autumn and Winter 1973 issues of *Refractory Girl*.

12. Humphrey McQueen, *A New Britannia*, Penguin Books, 1970; C. D. Rowley, *The Destruction of Aboriginal Society*, Penguin Books, 1972; *Outcasts in White Australia*, 1972; *The Remote Aborigines*, 1972; Peter Biskup, *Not Slaves nor Citizens*, University of Queensland Press, Brisbane, 1973; Lorna Lippmann, *Words not Blows*, Penguin Books, 1973.

13. Ure Smith, Sydney, 1972.

14. *Oz*, March 1964, cover.

15. Cartoon by Martin Sharp, *Oz*, No. 6, February 1964.

16. Michael Byrne, 'The alternative press is alive . . . ', The *National Times*, 1–6 January 1973.

17. Christina Stead, *Seven Poor Men of Sydney*, Angus & Robertson, Sydney, 1971, (1934), p. 214.

18. *Mejane*, a Women's Liberation newspaper, available from Box 221, P.O. Glebe, 2037. Subscriptions: $3 a year for six issues. *Refractory Girl*, a women's studies journal, available from 25 Alberta Street, Sydney, 2000. Subscriptions: $3.50 a year for four issues. There have been, and are, other women's liberation publications pursuing similar ends. *Shrew*, a journal produced from Brisbane, lived for about a year. A Melbourne group began another paper, *Vashti's Voice* in 1972 and several issues have appeared so far, while Women's Liberation groups in each state produce newsletters which contain articles, letters etc. in which women discuss their alienation from our male-dominated culture. See Further Reading at the end of this book for details of more recent publications.

19. *Nation Review*, 25–31 May, 1973.

CHAPTER THREE

THE SPORTING WIFE

. . . it's easy to tell it's Saturday . . . The garish clubs are beginning to gird themselves up for the late afternoon rush, rapid-fire race broadcasts drift out of the pubs, surfboards are loaded on to the roofs of old jalopies, and in the parks the children's playgrounds and duck-ponds draw family groups, New Australians, toddlers, prams, dogs . . . This is the life Australians have created for themselves in their leisure hours, and in a way it shows them at their best. There is a sense of community . . .

CRAIG McGREGOR, *Profile of Australia,* 1966

The third 'level' of culture consists of those multifarious recreational activities with which Australian people, women and men, occupy their leisure time. Even more than with the other two 'levels' which are to some extent minority proclivities both in terms of the numbers of people either participating or influenced by them, activities at this level are circumscribed by class and generational preferences. Often the popular images we fondly believe to characterize our national profile are no more than images projected by cultural revivalists searching for symbols to serve as unifying rallying points for what they see as a diverse and directionless people. Many writers seem to imagine that such cultural jingoism is both possible and desirable. Yet individual reactions to a recreational activity such as football, uncritically upheld to be an engrossing national pastime, are diverse and complex; and it is facile to suppose that the Melbourne Cricket Ground on grand-final day holds a crowd whose presence can be appraised by a single slick standard. Similarly those who portray Australians as a nation of beer swillers discount the marijuana smokers, the wine and spirits drinkers, and the teetotallers. To cull from an increasingly heterogeneous society a small number of recreational activities inevitably does injustice both to those groups and individuals who do not indulge in these pursuits, and to those who deliberately oppose the erecting of these activities into the mythic proportions they have already attained.

Yet these stereotypes do persist, and they do reflect the actual behaviour of a large section of the population. Whether extolled or criticized, sport – particularly horse-racing, football and surfing – is recognized as being of particular significance to Australian men, and ranks along with (beer) drinking, gambling and an obsession with cars as national pastimes. All these activities thus earn a mandatory mention by the carvers of cultural myths and stereotypes.

Sport to many Australians is life and the rest a shadow. Sport has been the one national institution that has had no 'knockers'. To many it is considered a sign of degeneracy not to be interested in it. To play sport, or watch others play sport, and to read and talk about it is to uphold the nation and build its character.[1]

Australians drink with great relish, often with the sole idea of getting drunk; among young men the mark of a successful party is that everyone got drunk, several chundered (vomited) and half a dozen or so flaked (passed out) . . . In Australia drinking is an occasion for raucous bonhomie, yarn-spinning, laughter, swilling down schooners, middies and ponies of beer and, occasionally pumping drinks into the girl-friend or the wife – it is all part of that explosive good humour and companionship which Australians equate with 'the good life'.[2]

The Australian's loving preoccupation with his car has become a common-place: he fondles each nut and bolt in interminable conversations in the pub; strips it, lays it on the lawn, and greases its nipples while his wife wonders whether he will ever better his indoor average of one-a-month. But put him behind the wheel and he becomes the world's most heedless driver . . . So many Australians equate driving with masculinity: pass them and they suffer instant emasculation.[3]

The Australian mania for gambling can be documented by the vast amounts of money which are poured into bookmakers' bags, poker machines, lotteries and the TAB. In March 1973 the TAB turnover in New South Wales alone was more than $7 million a week[4], a total of $814,914,000 was invested in totalizators around Australia in 1970–71 while a further $813,318,000 was paid to licensed book-makers.[5] This was some $600,000 more than the amount expended on social service payments by the Australian Government in the same period.[6] A further $110,227,000 was spent in lottery tickets in 1970–71[7], while some $140 million was jabbed into poker machines in 1972 in New South Wales, the only state where this kind of gambling is permitted.[8] Altogether some $2,000 million was gambled legally in Australia in one year, almost one-tenth of the national wages bill.

In the quotations cited above, there is an unmistakable tendency in each of the writers to equate 'Australians' with 'Australian men'. To 'many Australians', Horne maintains, sport is life. What he really means is that to many Australian men, sport is life. Sport, drinking and gambling are upheld as the working man's prerogative, due recompense for his hard work in factory, office or wherever he may happen to earn his living. They are also espoused, more or less explicitly, by men of all classes even if their pursuit is couched in rituals designed to delineate the class differences. The members' stand or the public enclosure, the local pub or the executive bar, two-up or baccarat – the differences are finely shaded, elaborate measures designed to mesmerize those iconoclasts who might be tempted to lump them all together in the one inclusive fellowship. For while men may argue amongst themselves about whether they merit being classed with the fraternity, it is abundantly clear that women do not even have the choice. At every level in every recreational activity which is characterized as a crucial part of Australian life women are either physically barred or their participation is circumscribed by a *mélange* of rules, conventions and attitudes which ensure that these activities remain the preserve of men.

Male pre-eminence in horse-racing is specified at almost every level of participation: club membership, punting, riding and training.[9] Members' stands have special enclosures where only men may congregate to watch the finish; watchful attendants protect the fraternity from the trespasses of any unwitting female. In the past female jockeys have been able to ride only at picnic race meetings although city clubs are now beginning to allow women to ride the odd race. Unlike the situation in the United States, female jockeys – or 'jockettes' as they are derisively referred to – will not be able to ride against men.

There are women trainers in New South Wales, some of whom are fairly successful, but none has even looked like entering the galaxy of glamour trainers whose names are familiar to anyone who even glances at the sporting pages of any newspaper. Women are employed as track-riders, strappers and stable-hands, all jobs which receive equal pay but which are menial and low in status and which offer only vicarious opportunities to share in the mystique and glamour surrounding those, such as jockeys, who perform before the public and whose careers are kept before the populace by the Press.

There are no women on-course bookmakers at racing clubs -- although there have been a few at greyhound tracks – and when it is remembered that the 1906 Victorian Lotteries, Gaming and Betting Act, which first licensed bookmakers, did so on the condition that they did not accept bets from women[10], it appears that women have several rather intangible obstacles to surmount if they are ever to be able to follow racing with the same freedom as men.[11] The assumption that women were not interested in betting seems to have been the reason for setting lower admission prices to the tracks for women, and although approximately three times more men than women pass through the turnstiles at each meeting, the avidity with which women patronize the Tote would seem to belie any assumption that they have no proclivity for gambling. Given the extent of economic deprivation among women* it is not to be expected that very many women would have the money to become large-scale gamblers, but even if a woman did harbour an ambition to be a professional punter she would find several difficulties in her way. The rules of the Australian Jockey Club exclude women from the betting ring and although this is no longer enforced, the proscribing of women from membership of Tattersalls' Club prevents a woman from placing bets on credit unless she can find a bookmaker prepared to designate an alternative place for settling accounts: this would inevitably limit the number of bookmakers she could do business with, a serious obstacle to getting good odds.

In racing, as in most sports, there is active and overt discrimination against women, but this is probably less bothersome than the more elusive ways in which women are excluded. The entire sport is conducted on the assumption that only men wish to take it seriously. The very title of the leading form-guide, the *Sportsman*, assumes that only the male sex has any taste for the tensions and exhilarations of following the horses.

Women gamblers are notoriously considered to be governed by capricious inclinations rather than a careful studying of the form: they are said to choose horses by some intuitive response to its name, or by some confused and diffused sexual attraction for a particular jockey. Many bookmakers adopt a patronizing attitude to women, even when they are investing quite large amounts; some will pretend to adopt a protective stance towards women who frequent race-tracks, promising them tips or good odds. Occasionally they will sneer at a woman placing money on a long shot.

It is accepted that upper-middle-class women and attractive young women will play a decorative role at race-tracks, particularly at

* See Chapter Five

Carnivals when there is usually one meeting set aside for the fashion stakes. Then elegantly or outlandishly dressed women will attempt to attract the attention of a social notes writer, while the next day's Press will feature photographs of women wearing amazing hats or daring outfits, with jocular captions implying that this is the only level at which women can participate in racing. They may place bets, but they are not expected to care about the results; once the business of being noticed is over it is thought that women should retire to the bar to sip champagne, to wait until their escorts have completed their day's punting. (The positioning of the men-only enclosures opposite the winning post presupposes that women are not interested in watching the finish of a race, and in any case precludes them from doing so with the same facility as men.) Women from the lower-middle and working classes have no such carefully defined role. But the 1973 Autumn Carnival in Sydney was advertised in such a way as to suggest that it was a fine place to bring the family, implying that Mum and the kids could sit around on the lawns while their husbands got on with the serious business of losing a week's pay.

Yet women are indispensable in maintaining the comfort of racing crowds. They are the ones who serve food and drinks non-stop for up to seven hours to crowds whose main response is to complain about how long it takes to be served or how expensive everything is. Both charges are true but these women who bear the brunt of the hostility and irritability of tired punters are unable to control either factor, and certainly their rates of pay and working conditions are not enhanced by having to contend with churlish customers.

The other group of women who are indispensable to the gambling hordes are the clerks and cashiers employed in TABs. The TAB will rarely employ men below the level of supervisor as female labour is cheaper and more 'manageable'. The women themselves are grateful for a job which offers flexible hours and comparatively good money for casual work and TAB jobs are much in demand. But these inducements are mitigated by the responsibilities involved in the work. Foremost amongst these is that each cashier is responsible for the money she handles and if she is unable to balance it at the end of a day, must make up the deficit from her own pocket. The Clerks' Union has made the TAB a closed shop and has acquiesced in the penalizing of cashiers in this way. One union regulation states that if a woman works at a window for two hours she must take half an hour off. This means in practice, because of the penalty rule, that no one else may handle that cashier's money and take over from her for that half-hour, and so one window closes and the other cashiers have to cope with the extra volume of work, enhancing the likelihood that they will make an error in their calculations.[12] The cashiers are not allowed to set up a fund to cover possible losses, the argument against this being that because the cashiers are casual workers they could not be trusted: some of them might deliberately register a deficit and keep the money.[13] The irony of an enterprise whose *raison d'etre* is speculation and gambling adopting this kind of reasoning appears to have bothered neither the administrators of the TAB nor the officials of the Federated Clerks' Union. All of the things which comprise the mystique of racing are rather remote to these women, for whom each race meeting means simply another spell at an overworked, deadly monotonous job.

In other forms of gambling, where the odds are lower and where few skills are required – such as lotteries and poker machines – there are no prohibitions against women participating. Nor is there any longer any restriction against women patronizing TABs.[14] Where the simple and stated aim is to raise money, the sex of the sucker is unimportant. The various circumscriptions operating against women at race-tracks are related to the aura which surrounds this sport, to the traditions and rituals which have come to be associated with it. These were devised and developed by men and have come to be regarded as a male preserve, and many features of racing, and even of race-horses, seem at times to be posited by the devotees as pointers towards some kind of ideal existence. This was made explicit when the chairman of the Brisbane Amateur Turf Club at the farewell ceremony for the champion Gunsynd spoke of the horse's 'courage, determination and guts and what an example it is to mankind'.[15] The qualities he enumerated were those which at present in Australian society men rather than women are expected to strive for and so it cannot be concluded that he was posing a universal model. Rather he was simply stating the realities of horse-racing: it is a world inhabited overwhelmingly by men where the rewards and successes are invariably won by men.

A similar situation obtains with football, that other sport which occupies a special place in the tribal life of Australian men. There are two quite different elements in football – playing and watching – and while women are physically excluded only from the former, the total configuration of both elements of the game is once again very much a male preserve.[16] Only two kinds of football are accorded an integral place in Australian culture – Australian Rules and Rugby League. Other forms may engross thousands of people but have not been incorporated into our cultural mythology, probably because the other main games, soccer and Rugby Union, were not easily available to working-class Australian men and to elevate them to prominence would have meant denying a major premise of the egalitarian theory of Australian society.

The demarcation between the players and the spectators is an important feature of both forms of football; there is none of that unity between the teams and supporters of opposing sides which characterizes British soccer matches. This separation receives its ultimate expression in the hail of beer cans which angry crowds direct onto the playing field whenever some incident or referee's decision is found displeasing. Such aluminium ammunition indiscriminately injures players on both sides and reinforces the view that the battle is conducted as much across the picket fence as between the two teams of players: ' . . . there they are, the enemy, not the other mob but the watchers, the thirty thousand with violence in their hearts, tiny smoke-puffs everywhere.'[17] Violence is part of the currency of football and this crowd hostility is but one manifestation of it. Nor will it be vanquished simply by prohibiting fans from carting ice-boxes of cans into the grounds. They may be deprived of their weaponry, but to dissipate the passionate impetuosity of an aroused crowd would require the entire rewriting of both football codes.

Many sporting writers argue that it has been recent attempts to prevent violent encounters between players which has led to a decline in attendance at football, particularly Rugby League matches in Sydney. The language employed by sporting writers provides ample evidence of the explicitly violent expectations in players and spectators which these games foster. 'What does a Rugby League forward do,' wrote Sid Barnes, 'follow instructions from his coach or please the pacifists who are quickly killing the game? . . . the fans are unhappy for being robbed of a fair spectacle and League sinks even further into the pussy cat section of sports.'[18]

Despite the watchful eye of the referee the fans generally are rewarded with at least several spectacular and illegal tackles, and each week the football toll mounts: multiple injuries, often including permanent paralysis, and several deaths a year all occur, to the apparent concern of no one.[19] When it was proposed in Sydney in 1972 that junior league games should be abandoned, this was not because club officials were worried by the evidence of eight- and nine-year-old boys battering bodies and brains before these were even fully developed. Rather the officials were concerned that junior league was draining the energies of these children, burning them out too quickly and thus depleting the ranks of those eligible for the big league.

Women are, by reason of their relative physical frailty and their conditioning to avoid violent encounters, unable to participate in this ferocious fraternity. But if they suffer no regrets about missing out on the bruises and broken bones, they have several reasons to feel deprived because of the male bonding entailed in keeping a football team in peak physical and emotional condition. Although individual men may star for a day or even a whole season, the team is pre-eminent and the greatest hero is allowed no special treatment. What the coach aims for is a moving machine of eighteen (or whatever number) precisely integrated parts, a perfectly engineered, carefully co-ordinated and absolutely invincible team whose solidarity and group performance outshine any individual feat of brilliance. This precision and loyalty must be carefully nurtured and continually revitalized. The weekly clamorous communions on the playing field are the product of this rigorous conditioning:

'I want you to think win, eat win, talk win (smacking his fist each time). From now. From the word go. Right?' We nod agreement, mumble yair, yair, hypnotised in thirty seconds flat. 'Our first game? Like hell. We've been playing together for weeks, and now? We're run in, we're ticking over smooth. We know each other – where to look, where to kick. We got youth, right? We got experience, right? We got skill and we got muscle. We're going to bowl 'em over from the word go, knock 'em off balance. The Bears! (He shouts it, with his eyes shut, this is some mad revivalist meeting.) The Bears! The Bears!' Yair! Garn! Grrr! We're aroused, we make wild animal noises, snort and paw the ground, jump about, smack the fist.[20]

When this mad mass spills onto the ground it is the consummation of a long arduous process whereby individual uniqueness has been fused into an unprecedented alloy. To effect this, team members have had to follow exacting club rules governing their dress, their demeanour and their social and sexual behaviour. Recently, coaches have begun to concede that sexual activity on the night before the Big Game may be permissible: 'Sex on Fridays? "I'd say in moderation," says [Ron] Barassi. "I wouldn't be rapt in a single player having a new sexual adventure on a Friday night but a married man wouldn't lose any energy by it. With him it could be a regular thing and I don't think it could do him much harm." '[21] Only two years before one Rugby League official was quoted as saying, 'As far as going to bed with Mum is concerned, after about Tuesday the boys cut it down. Their wives co-operate, of course.'[22] It was perhaps never explicitly acknowledged or even recognized, but some deep psychological fear, a dread of emasculation – the subtle undermining of the team by drained energy expended on a woman – probably motivated this ban. Much of the high-pitched nervous energy which was translated into brilliantly co-ordinated play during Saturday's game was, and undoubtedly still is, the expression of a shared sexual repression. It was one more thing which united the team, which was fostered from early in the season, and which was compensated for after the grand finals by rewards ranging from ocean cruises to trips to Japan for the boys – without their wives and children of course.

Coaches try to ensure that the links between team members are deep, satisfying and sustaining. 'Beer . . . is the team-spirit builder. Coaches make sure that players get around a keg one day early in the season to get to know each other "as mates". "This mateship has been the secret of South Sydney's success", explains Sydney football writer Peter Frilingos. "They're dead-set mates who have stuck together socially, and that has kept the team going." '[23] A sartorial solidarity is also enforced by coaches such as Melbourne's Ian Ridley:

All my blokes are treated the same, regardless of ability. They all know they cannot wear beards or moustaches and that their hair must be no longer than collar length. I don't think it's healthy in our game to be otherwise. Too much hair makes players hot, sweaty and uncomfortable. And I don't think it becomes a top-line sportsman to look like that . . . I make them wear the club jersey in training to build up their pride and I wouldn't let anyone train with his socks down. Their boots must be clean They must look the part.[24]

It is clear that much of the success of the league footballer lies in his ability to subsume his entire existence for at least half a year under the accommodating umbrella of the team; this is done at the expense of physical and emotional relationships with other men and women. The role of footballers' wives is on the sidelines, cheering, probably with some bitterness since they cannot but realize that every success for the team is a set-back to their hopes for conjugal enjoyment. They must acquiesce in having a conglomerate husband, a man who lives and breathes in an induced environment of competitive unity, who brings the rest of the team home, even to bed, with him, and whose inadequacies socially and sexually are to be endured as a necessary sacrifice to sportsmanship. One could conclude that it is the wives who have to be the good sports. Of course to even suggest that a handsome, physically fit football player might be a less-than-perfect human being is tantamount to treason – a betrayal of one of the psychic props of so many Australian men – and few women would dare complain publicly. Their husbands are the objects of adoration and emulation for enormous masses of people who watch their weekly game and follow their careers with cannibalistic avidity. To question their manly credentials would undermine the self-assurance of the fans for whom vicarious identification with their on-the-field accomplishments is almost a mandatory part of Australian masculinity.

This identification is various and elusive and cannot be reduced to a single neat explanation but what is significant is the extent to which men from diverse groups in Australian society merge to form a tenuous fraternity of football followers. Football is the subject of an annual lecture delivered by Ian Turner at Monash University.[25] During a brief spell as football writer for the *Australian* Max Harris attempted to bring literary elegance and semantic precision to describe the game of the big men of Australian Rules. The disdain many intellectuals feel for the activities of the masses does not so often extend to football which secures often fanatical support from men one would not, from their pretensions in other areas, have suspected of harbouring a secret admiration for the game and the men who play it.

It is this kind of devotion, this mixture of intellectual appreciation of an intricate and skilful game and the sheer cathartic pleasure gained from watching others indulge in purposeful violence, which few women are able either to share or to understand. Women who watch football are seemingly motivated by less complex notions. They are there as sidelines supporters for husbands, sons or boyfriends, or as companions to devoted fans, or perhaps because they entertain secret sexual fantasies about one or more of the players. Rarely can women engage in the detailed technical discussions of rules, precedents and decisions which are an important part of following the game. And any woman who thinks that by acquiring such knowledge she will be admitted to the fraternity is likely to be disappointed, for men cherish and wish to retain as a retreat this avenue of self-expression. It is part of the pub-talk, the work-break chats and the other conversations men have in which they establish their clan credentials and strike up friendships with members of their sex. The woman who takes up this interlocution is likely to be resented for transgressing a sexual boundary, for intruding into the private and precious province of mateship, a precarious state of communality whose fragility is underlined by its antipathy to a female presence.

It is not just that men have their activities and women have theirs and that each sex can satisfy itself with the free and equal pursuit of its chosen recreations. Women have few areas of superiority of either skill or participation. Where both men and women engage in the same sport, it is invariably the men's which has higher status and attracts more attention. The only exception to this, and it may be a transient one, is women's tennis which is currently enjoying immense popularity. But this is at top tournament levels and this kudos has not filtered down to the Wednesday afternoon tennis games which occupy many suburban women. And in any case the popularity of women's tennis has not prevented discriminatory treatment for female players. During the 1973 Australian Open Tennis Championships the two women's quarter finalists were forced to play on a rain-saturated court. One of the players, Julie Heldman, had to stand in a puddle to serve. The men's singles match which followed immediately afterwards was transferred to a dry centre court. Ms Heldman protested about having to play in such conditions but the referee would not move the women's match. Both the women players told the Press that women had had to endure second-rate conditions in earlier rounds when they had been expected to play without ball-boys and with no drink facilities.[26]

Women's swimming is also very popular, although it is not usually considered 'more interesting' than men's in the way women's tennis is. Women swimming champions are the subjects of immense publicity and have huge followings, but much of this admiration may be diffused nationalistic gratitude; after all, Australia owes its modest tally of gold medals from the Munich Olympics largely to its female swimmers. But even where women playing a particular sport enjoy fame and success it is a very temporary phenomenon: once they have passed their peak they generally marry and, presumably, disappear into the suburbs never to be heard of again. By contrast, a large proportion of the male sports stars of former years manage to keep their names before the public by going into businesses, often those which deal with the equipment used in their former sport, or by acquiring jobs which ensure that their names, and the remnants of their former glory, are kept alive. With most other sports which both men and women play – cricket, athletics, basketball, hockey, baseball – the men's game is considered to be superior.

Women do have other recreational pastimes where their talents are acknowledged to be superior, but these are invariably activities which, having been relegated to 'women's sphere', are not things most men would care to show any interest in. Even when these skills are demonstrated competitively, they are not regarded as providing the kind of entertainment which draws crowds and evokes column inches of superlatives. Can we for a moment imagine 100,000 people packing into the Melbourne Cricket Ground to watch the Moonee Ponds vs St Kilda cake-decorating championships? One reason for this of course is that many of the singular skills which women possess are considered to be part of their housewifely 'duties' and such skills represent the attainment of a degree of perfection which is neither demanded of them by the role, nor rewarded when it is achieved. A good housewife should be able to bake, to arrange flowers, to run up clothes for her children and to possess a modicum of skill in a myriad of other areas. But if she should turn any of these into a craft to be pursued with loving skill and devotion she is likely to be cruelly disappointed if she expects accolades to be heaped upon her. Contests of housewifely skills are parodied by those whose job it is to provide day-time stimulation to suburban housewives. An ironing competition held in Melbourne in 1973 evoked guffaws and cynical gibes from the reporters the radio stations sent to cover it. They devoted their attention to the single male competitor and passed on uneasily when one woman participant remarked that seeing she had to spend so much of her day ironing she felt she might as well have some company, and the chance of a prize, while doing it.

Women's recreational activities are either disdained by men for their too close association with the mundane routines of domesticity, or for the amateur zeal with which they are pursued, or else men command the heights of skill and prestige in 'female' areas they consider worthy of their attention. Thousands of women play bridge, dabble in Cordon Bleu or Oriental cookery, design and make their own clothes, but the woman whose skills in any of these areas are such as to achieve public accord is a rare creature. Those men who choose to engage in these things usually elevate them to professional proficiency, underlining the distinction between *their* special prowess and the idlings of a mass of suburban women. There are of course many women who paint and pot, and sculpt and dye materials, with competence and professionalism even if they remain amateurs in the sense that they do not earn a living from their endeavours. Often their skills are recognized and praised – among their circle of family and friends and in the anticipatory eagerness of the adult education classroom. But for many, their little creative outpourings, all those landscapes and less-than-perfect pots, are the object of familial embarrassment, scorn or even mockery. Iris, the frustrated middle-aged woman in Thea Astley's *The Slow Natives* experienced this: 'She had been an Ikebana cultist for a while. "She can work at them half an hour before she achieves a climax," Bernard used to say unkindly.'[27]

Women who go to classes in arts and crafts are often desperately anxious to have their efforts noticed and, hopefully, commended and it is a pathetic recognition of the handmaiden status of most female art forms that such commendation is often only convincing to its recipient if it comes from a man. Male teachers of arts and crafts are in great demand and can gather large classes around them where they command the undivided devotion of their slavish students. During the couple of years that I worked in adult education I was at first astonished and then very much saddened at the obsequious attitudes many middle-aged women students showed towards young men just out of Art School. If the teacher was an artist of some repute this female flunkeyism reached depths of servility which was a tragic testimonial to the need these women had for the bestowal of dignity and worth upon their underrated selves. Where the classes were taken by women a more stimulating camaraderie existed. The distinction between teacher and student was less evident and it was possible for students to allow their individual predispositions to flourish, rather than fawning to the style or trend espoused by the male mentor.

Women's doings are relegated to the far corner of the national consciousness, their separatism confirmed by the special magazines and sections of newspapers which are devoted to them, and their objectification completed by their being treated as special categories of description and analysis. 'Women', 'migrants' and, lately, 'Aborigines' are singled out for attention, on the apparent assumption that these are united homogeneous groups. This is a legitimate enough technique if the concern is with the effects on individuals of being lumped together in a single, low-status group in this way, but this kind of consciousness is seldom the motivating force among writers such as Horne, who, unable to fit these groups into his major thesis adds them on as careless afterthoughts. Of the 'Lucky Country' he says, ' . . . it still *is* a man's country, but no more so than in comparable countries.'[28] He writes, 'Men and women go their own ways, but men get the best of the bargain because they have more ways to go'[29] but thinks this is the result of 'social awkwardness rather than male dominance'. Australian women, thinks Horne, inhabit a discrete and different world, and he feebly attempts to demonstrate this by devoting an entire page of his book to citations from the social pages and cookery notes of several newspapers and for some ineluctable reason seems to think that proves his case. Apparently it did not occur to him to conclude that the trivia which fills these pages is more at the behest of the men who own the newspapers than an accurate representation of the mores of Australian women.[30]

When the socially valued areas of our culture are either occupied by men or depend for survival on values which are associated with the male sex role, what and where is women's place? What alternatives do most women have but to subsume themselves within that permitted territory and strive for self-realization at the lower levels, in the shadowy areas of allowed art forms or in the homes and gardens where they are psychically imprisoned?

Before the recent resurgence of a feminism with strong emphasis on cultural forms of oppression, few people considered or questioned this ostracism, or the reasons for it. The basic 'maleness' of this 'level' of our culture was taken for granted. If anyone did query it, as did the occasional overseas visitor, perhaps taken aback at the sight of women sitting in cars outside pubs sipping the beers their husbands periodically lurched into their laps, then two kinds of responses were inevitable. One was the careless avowal that the women could join in if they wanted to, but they didn't so that settled that and whose shout is it boys. The second was a defensive justification of all-male activities and the ethos which surrounded them. Often the need for a man to 'get away from it all' – meaning away from his wife and children as much as from the memory of the tedium of his job – was offered as an explanation. No one considered where women might go to get away from it all.

The first response fails to recognize the legal and other barriers which do prevent women from participating in many of these pursuits. Many hotels will not serve women in the front bar, forcing them to patronize dingy 'ladies' lounges' where the discomfort is exacerbated by the higher prices charged for drinks. There is at least one city hotel in Sydney which will not allow women anywhere on its premises, a practice which its patrons, many of whom are journalists, delight in helping to enforce. Ritual attempts by groups of women to desegregate these hotels have rarely been successful: often they have involved the women being subjected to jeering and abuse while one recent attempt, at Manly in Sydney, ended with the arrest of four women.[31]

The tenacity with which so many men cling to segregated drinking requires explaining for it seems to be a habit unique to this country.

Complicated patterns of repression and guilt coupled with a hedonistic abandonment of social prescriptions have characterized the drinking patterns of many Australian men, a combination which is often attributed to the Irish-Catholic influence on Australian social mores. This ambivalence has been illustrated by attitudes male drinkers have exhibited towards women in hotels. The presence of female drinking companions was resented by the denizens of the old-style drinking dens and this was reflected in the way these places were sub-divided: the largest space was allowed to the utilitarian, tiled, men-only bar while women had to brave their way to dark, poky corners if they wanted to drink. In the 1950s the burgeoning of suburban hotels featuring large drinking halls, concrete beer 'gardens' and Saturday afternoon entertainments, enabled drinking, particularly at weekends, to become an integrated activity. But most old-style pubs have clung to their seeming misogynism. Some inner-city hotels have had their bars taken over by university or other non-conformist groups where women and men drink freely with each other, often in the face of disapproval or resentment from the original male patrons. There are also instances of all-women drinking scenes. For instance there are several pubs in Balmain, an inner-city Sydney suburb, where every Saturday sees groups of middle-aged working-class women congregate for an afternoon's drinking, following the form, listening to the races from transistors and placing bets with the pub's SP bookie. In the public bar, visible through the serving area, the men (many of whom are the husbands of the women) are doing exactly the same but it does not appear to occur to either group that they could get together. Even where individual men may enjoy the company of women the pub ethic has become so strong that all must profess to prefer getting drunk without the restraining presence of wives or girlfriends.

Yet opposition to the introduction of barmaids came not from the drinkers but from religious and temperance groups which anticipated the corruption of pretty young girls in these iniquitous, alcoholic havens. The drinkers appeared to welcome a female presence behind the bar and to accept from them the chidings and rebukes which coming from their wives would have been classed as unpardonable intrusions. It is not uncommon for a man to entrust his pay packet to the barmaid, instructing her how much he can afford to spend, and then accepting without argument her notification that his drinking for that night is over. In her book *Autobiography of a Sydney Barmaid*, the author recounts how the toughest characters in the bar where she worked in the 1930s afforded her a gently protective respect and admonished any stranger who attempted to 'get fresh' or swear in her presence.[32] On the other hand, any woman who ventured into the ladies' lounge was considered fair game to these drunken cavaliers.

It was perhaps a percipience of this which kept 'respectable' women out of hotels, but there has certainly never been any correlation between Australian women's frequenting of hotels and their willingness to drink, especially to engage in what is coyly referred to as 'social drinking'. A 1970 survey comparing drinking patterns of people in Sydney and San Francisco showed the women of Australia to be much more likely to drink, particularly to be light drinkers, than their American counterparts. Only 18 per cent of Sydney women abstained completely while 43 per cent drank lightly; in San Francisco 28 per cent did not drink at all and 35 per cent were light drinkers.[33] Australian women have been permitted, even encouraged, to drink but their imbibing has been circumscribed by rules and conventions which have prevented them from being able to freely and openly use drinking as the form of social release it so often is for men. There has always been, and remains, enormous social disapprobation for drunken women, and those women who do drink heavily must be secretive about it and their families will go to inordinate lengths to conceal their shame from others. But women are far less likely than men to become alcoholics. The survey already cited showed that while 48 per cent of male respondents were heavy drinkers only 15 per cent of women were.[34] The admission to psychiatric centres for treatment for alcoholism reflects this difference: in 1971–72, 1,053 men were admitted to centres in New South Wales for treatment related to excessive drinking, compared with 230 women.[35] Perhaps women alcoholics are less likely to seek treatment for this entails admitting to a form of socially unacceptable behaviour, but it is also likely that women, excluded from the culture of drinking and not accustomed to equating drinking with recreation, are less likely to develop a compulsive dependence on alcohol.*

The legal or traditional exclusion from physical participation in the various recreational activities outlined so far is perhaps less important, particularly in terms of women's social aspirations, than

* Since writing this, it has been drawn to my attention that there are in fact an enormous number of women alcoholics in Australia. Often their alcoholism is disguised by doctors who, either through compliance or ignorance, diagnose a psychiatric disorder. It also seems that alcoholism in women, especially in young women, is increasing rapidly. This can probably be attributed to the breaking down of the taboos against women drinking publicly, and many young women

their exclusion from that impenetrable freemasonry which male sport followers create for themselves. Participation means much more than being able to actually play whatever the game is – the number of spectators always far exceeds the players in any sport. It involves a vicarious identification, not simply with what is occurring on the track or field on that particular day, but with the evolution and refinement of the sport or activity to its present form, and, more importantly, with the mythologies and rituals which have arisen with it.

The rewards of the actual participants are of a different order. The sheer excitement of the successful demonstration of a prized skill can transport a footballer, a jockey or a surfer into a state almost mystical, of exultant heightened consciousness, a state of extra-terrestrial infinity where one moment of time contains a vision of boundless possibilities finite man usually remains ignorant of. Several Australian Rules footballers I have spoken to have, hesitatingly, self-consciously and awkwardly, tried to put into words those ineluctable ethereal perceptions which overcame them for a few seconds after capturing a ball from a high mark. And the champion surfer Midget Farrelly has described a similar reaction:

. . . it was a good day with the sun shining, and I was sliding off the peak into the deep water when suddenly I felt as though I could keep going and going, pushing on and on as though there was no end to it anywhere. You go into oblivion. Suddenly all your life is there in this long, long stretched-out wave; you're removed from the past, everything that has been on your mind becomes immaterial, everything goes to jelly, and you feel completely removed from the world around you. Nothing matters any longer but you and the board and the wave and this instant of time![36]

Few women experience this mystical exultation from the sports they play, just as watching a football match cannot play the same functions for women as for men. Women are less bound to the culture of violence and fraternizing amongst the female sex takes a different form; but these are the ingredients which fuse to form a mode of release of frustration and tension for men who watch the game.

---

are starting to develop the same compulsive dependence on alcohol which so many Australian men have. I have also heard of a number of cases of elderly women developing an addiction to alcohol. Often these are women who have been teetotal all their lives but who have started drinking to help them sleep or else simply to blot out the misery of being an old woman in a society which discriminates against both women and the old.

Unless a person can project themself onto the field, somehow place their body and mind into the context of the game, this kind of experience remains impossible. The spectator need not even be present at the game for this to operate. Often the most avid identifiers are those who watch the game on their television sets – and there is nothing to prevent women from doing this. But while for men physical remoteness is no bar to immersion in the mystique, it is difficult for women to identify with it and there is little question of their being admitted to the fraternity.

The myths and the enticements they hold out for a reassuring submergence in group solidarity, if not for individual glorification, begin to impinge on the boy-child's consciousness as soon as he is old enough to perceive the elevated status certain sports have in Australia. These facts of life will probably be acquired before any sexual information complicates his social life; if they are not imparted by a paternal zealot, they will certainly be rammed into his psyche by the daily newspapers, the television and the general drift of boys' games. Girls are subjected to the same barrage, but part of their indoctrination into the sporting way of life will include the knowledge that this is a male preserve, a fact initially made clear by the gender of the teams or the individual heroes, and reinforced by the sex-role proscriptions that condemn tom-boy activities. Even if she escapes the latter, the former is too evident a description of the state of play to enable her to carry any delusions about the opportunities for female participation. She may furtively follow a team, but it is unlikely that she will be able to emulate those boys who, before they are out of primary school, already have acquired impressive memories for scores, winning margins and other historical ephemera associated with their chosen sport. Girls will know that they can play their own sports, and often excel in them but that generally women's sports – as with all their recreational activities – are denied the status accorded to men's.

NOTES

1. Donald Horne, *The Lucky Country*, Penguin Books, 1965, p. 40.
2. Craig McGregor, *Profile of Australia*, Penguin Books, 1968, p. 135.
3. Ian Moffitt, *The U-Jack Society*, Ure Smith, Sydney, 1972, p. 112.
4. Article by Pat Farrell, *Daily Mirror*, Sydney, 30 March 1973.
5. *Official Year Book of the Commonwealth of Australia, 1972*, p. 532. The amounts

invested with starting price bookmakers, wagered in private card-games and expended in various illegal gambling clubs cannot begin to be estimated.

6. In 1970–71 the Commonwealth Government spent a total of $1,060,461,000 in welfare cash payments. This included money paid in the form of age and invalid pensions, child endowment, maternity allowances, widows' pensions, unemployment benefits, emergency assistance to wool-growers as well as other categories of assistance. *Official Year Book of the Commonwealth of Australia, 1972*, p. 392.

7. ibid., p. 531.

8. Information provided by Chief Secretary's Department, State Public Service, New South Wales.

9. All information in this section on horse-racing, unless otherwise acknowledged, was supplied by Reg Byrne, formerly a racing writer for *Nation Review*.

10. Keith Dunstan, *Wowsers*, Cassell, Melbourne, 1968, p. 277.

11. There are some women operating as illegal SP bookmakers, all of whom conduct phone rather than hotel businesses. Most of them are widows who seem to have simply carried on businesses begun by their husbands.

12. Lesley Gray, 'Casual Workers', *Mejane*, No. 6, February 1972, p. 5.

13. ibid. A further hazard of this job which is not compensated for in any way is the increasing risk that these women will be subjected to armed hold-ups and incur severe shock, if not physical injury.

14. When the Hogan Government introduced a Bill into the Victorian Parliament to legalize the Tote in 1928 it proscribed the use of the Tote by women: the belief was that mothers would teach their children to gamble. Dunstan, op. cit., p. 277.

15. Reported in the *Australian*, 8 May 1973.

16. There are sometimes games between opposing teams of men and women, usually organized by university colleges or similar groups, but the jocular way in which these are conducted simply serves to emphasize that this is pre-eminently a man's sport, and that a match involving men and women must necessarily be a comical occasion.

17. Barry Oakley, *A Salute to the Great McCarthy*, Penguin Books, 1971, p. 89.

18. The *Sun*, Sydney, 30 March 1973.

19. By contrast, in 1973 the Australian Government announced its intention to hold an inquiry into boxing on the grounds that it is a sport which causes injuries and deaths! In two hundred years of boxing in Australia there have been 98 deaths. (Figures supplied by boxing authority, Ray Mitchell.) Football authorities refuse to provide figures on deaths and serious injuries incurred by football players, but it is likely that football has taken many more lives than this. Yet no one has proposed an investigation into the violent nature of this game.

20. Oakley, op. cit., p. 88.

21. John Hurst and Ian Moffitt, 'Not tonight Josephine – it's the big game tomorrow', the *Australian*, 7 April 1973.

22. Ian Moffitt, 'To do or die', the *Australian*, 18 September 1971.

23. Hurst and Moffit, op. cit.

24. ibid.

25. This lecture, the Ron Barassi Memorial Lecture, is divided into four quarters; during the intervals Turner sips from a can of Carlton Draught, and the lecture generally closes to wild cheering from the crowd/lecture theatre.

26. Reported in the *Australian*, 31 December 1973.

27. Thea Astley, *The Slow Natives*, Sun Books, Melbourne, 1966, p. 32.

28. Horne, op. cit., p. 84.

29. ibid., p. 85.

30. In February 1972 the *Sydney Morning Herald*'s women's section underwent a dramatic change of face; adopting a new name, *Look*, its editor Suzanne Baker promised a livelier and more stimulating section, one that recognized that women were interested in things other than who wore what to some exclusive gathering of the bourgeoisie and how to prepare exotic foods. Its first few months were exciting ones in which well-researched and seriously written articles explored issues such as abortion, battered babies, the fate of children in children's courts as well as conducting in-depth interviews with local or visiting women of some repute. However *Look*'s demise was apparently inevitable. In spite of very favourable readership response to its new format and its new focus, gradually it began to revert to the old formula: the articles got shorter, certain topics became – apparently – taboo, by-lines disappeared (thus discouraging contributors from writing feature articles) and the cooking and social notes sections expanded. The same editor remains and she has not changed her ideas about what the section should be doing, so a reader can only conclude that the proprietors of the newspaper have insisted on this return to the practice of catering to the specialized interests of the idle rich. (She has since resigned. January 1973.)

31. See account in *Mejane*, No. 10, March 1973.

32. Caddie, *Autobiography of a Sydney Barmaid*, Sun Books, Melbourne, 1966, (1953).

33. S. Encel and K. Kotowicz, 'Heavy Drinking and Alcoholism, Preliminary Report', *Medical Journal of Australia*, I, 21 March 1970, p. 609.

34. ibid.

35. *Statistics of In-Patients in Psychiatric Centres*, Bureau of Census and Statistics, Sydney, 1973, p. 5.

36. cit. Craig McGregor, *People, Politics and Pop: Australians in the Sixties*, Ure Smith, Sydney, 1968, p. 118.

CHAPTER
FOUR
THE RAVAGED SELF

. . . the obsession of many Australian women with their homes goes beyond fashion or normal motherly concern; it represents an attempt to provide spiritual value in material things and modes of living.

DONALD HORNE, *The Lucky Country*, 1964

The fourth 'level' of Australian culture consists of everyday life – that constant set of activities involving work and familial and other personal relationships through which people define and sustain their lives. Most definitions of culture neglect this area. Some theorists, such as Raymond Williams[1], have tried to explore the relationships between society and culture but they generally confine their discussion of 'society' to wider communities. Thus the working lives of men often merit inclusion but men's family lives and women's working and family lives are passed over. Culture is too often circumscribed by definition to include only the public and easily accessible facets of people's lives and work. In Australia there are numerous writings about culture in this sense – the first three 'levels' of culture described in earlier chapters – but virtually the only writing about family relationships is to be found in fiction and, as I have already pointed out, this is only read and taken seriously if it comes from the pen of a man and deals with male perceptions of those relationships. The family lives of women remain largely unarticulated and unexplored.

I said earlier that most of the commentators on Australian society pay token homage to the institution 'the family' and note that the lives of women in this country are inordinately bound up with their families. None of them, however, dares lift the veil of illusion created by these platitudes to view the realities they conceal. Similarly, sociologists and moralists extol the institution while ignoring much that goes on within it. For instance, the introduction to one recently published book claims, '. . . it may still be affirmed that the family in Australia, although subjected to strains at the present time, remains the cornerstone of community stability and continues to exert a powerful influence in promoting the well-being of Australian society.'[2] Is 'the family' this? A cornerstone of community stability?

Those who make such assertions usually base them on generalities, or on idealized notions about the functions performed by families. Families, they consider, are places of retreat, private sanctuaries from the pressures of the world of work. Families are also places where children are physically cared for and where they learn to conform to the requirements of the adult world. In fact, sociologists and moralists do recognize that stability is not always synonymous with family and that there are conflicts and breakdowns and deviations; much of their prognosis is actually exhortation. This is what they think families *should* be like. But these assertions rest on a view of families and family functions which are derived from male expectations and which are based on men's needs. *Nowhere* in theories about families, in moralistic prescriptions about what families ought to be like, is there specific acknowledgement of women's expectations, needs or experiences. Nor is any attempt made to see whether the theories and prescriptions are compatible with women's needs, expectations and experiences. This fourth 'level' of culture is the only one where women have an acknowledged place and function and so it is important to explore their place in it in some detail. Such an exploration has to specifically recognize that women's participation may differ substantially from men's and that the generalizations made about men and families may be quite at odds with generalizations about women and families.

An exploration of women's family experiences is a major theme of this book and, as well as being begun here, is dealt with in detail in Chapters Six and Thirteen. The present chapter is concerned mainly with outlining what I see to be the differences. The later chapters will analyse these in more detail and suggest various reasons for these differences. The present discussion is also necessarily fairly abstract: in order to establish its main point it generalizes about 'men' and 'women' and minimizes differing experiences resulting from factors such as age, class, race, religion and so on. To subsume individuals into these over-riding categories is by definition sexist and, in the long run, not very elucidating. But as a starting point I need to establish that such sexist categorizations are imposed by society anyway and that they have discernible effects. Once that is recognized it is meaningful to pursue the varieties of human experience within each categorization.

Everyday life involves home and work, relationships with friends, neighbours and kin, contacts with institutions such as churches, schools and welfare bodies. This fourth 'level' of culture is the foundation on which the three other 'levels' rest but to view it as a 'cornerstone of community stability' is to emphasize idealized notions about what everyday life *should* be like and to overlook the many social processes actually at work within it. These processes include not only the maintenance of life, this entailing the constant maintenance of 'self' or personal identity, but also its acquisition. 'Self' is a social entity – it is socially constructed and socially maintained. If it is unable to be maintained, if a person experiences partial or total breakdown, then we need to examine the social processes which have contributed to this.

I want to examine three areas of everyday life, the three areas which I consider to be the most crucial components of existence, and to see how women's experience of these differs from men's. The three areas are the acquisition of 'self', or socialization; and two areas of adult 'self'-maintenance: home and work.

I am using 'self' to describe one's being-in-the-world, the way in which a person sees themself, the society in which they live and their relationship to that society. 'Self' is not a fixed and totally determined category. People can have several different 'selves' for different areas of their lives and although each of these 'selves' will be derived to a large extent from the imperatives of social existence in each area, people interact with and impose on that social existence. The resulting 'self' will be a product of this dialectic. But the social foundations of 'self' are acquired in infancy while the young person is physically vulnerable and totally dependent upon its carers and, as yet, unable to interact independently with the world. So much of the 'self' that is constructed in the very early years of life is indelibly imprinted on the psyche and, if it is able to be altered at all, only with considerable struggle. This struggle will itself be extremely threatening to the existing 'self': such an 'identity crisis' can seem to totally obliterate all existing conceptions and to leave a person devoid of workable 'self'-conceptions with which to even cope with the crisis. So while human beings always retain the power to change their social environment and, within it, their conception of 'self' – this, indeed, being a distinct and distinguishing attribute of humanity – this power is not easily exercised and, in fact, many people's socialization consists precisely in preventing them from realizing that they possess it.

Most children in Australia are raised by at least one of their biological parents. Because our society has strong notions of 'love' as a duty between parents and children, socialization of children by their biological parents is seen as being the most desirable form since it is the most efficient. Parental 'love' becomes an oppressive tool in the socialization process: the threat to withdraw it induces conformity to parental prescriptions. The child begins life as totally dependent on her or his parent(s) or whatever person has undertaken responsibility for the child's early development. While the child becomes aware very early of the social environment in which she or he exists, this awareness is preceded or obscured by its absolute dependence. She or he hardly has a separate existence and, therefore, only the most embryonic 'self'. The 'self' is acquired as that dependence is broken and as the infant learns to repress her or his instinctual drives to the demands of society as communicated by the parents.

The child learns she or he must conform to a whole range of things which are 'good', for example, obeying parents, eating food at prescribed times, using a toilet or pot; and must desist from other things which are 'bad'. As John Maze has pointed out, the aim of socialization is always the suppression of certain instinctual drives, usually sexuality and aggression but the process of suppression involves exhorting the child to act in certain ways not just because the parents have demanded it, but because these actions are meant to be good and desirable in themselves.[3]

This means that the child will find that very wounding epithets ('dirty', 'greedy', 'rude', 'cruel') are being applied to his behaviour or indeed to his own nature ('You dirty boy!') by persons whom he loves, and whose respect, affection and protection he urgently needs. This is an instance of psychological stress of the very first rank. The child feels himself in danger of being rejected as a *worthless* person. This is very different from just ordinary threats of punishment. One of the conditions of being worthwhile, as conventional parents set them up, is that the child is supposed to come to see that certain actions and wishes are *wrong in themselves*.[4]

These moral values will often (or usually) seem quite incomprehensible to the child who will submit to them in an effort to retain her or his parents' affections. And such submissions *will* be rewarded by affection: the child is rewarded for being worthwhile, as parents have defined this. Thus there will be confusion in the child's mind between the apparent arbitrariness of the acts in question and the contingent nature of the parents' affection. The child will calculate that, in order to survive in the social world of the family, she or he must become a good person who will be rewarded by love. This love or, rather, social approval will enhance the child's feelings of security, just as she or he will feel insecure if the social approval is withheld. The 'self' acquired in this process will be a more-or-less calculated combination of partly or fully repressed instinctual desires and actions and a morality acquired in order to gain social approval. The infant 'self' is a survival mechanism and is also a measure of the extent of its repression by externally imposed values. This pattern of submission and conformity is established as an integral component of a person's being-in-the-world.

This very brief description of how a child learns to behave in a social environment implies that the process is identical for each sex. Maze talks only of male children, and most other writers either do the same or merely make passing reference to the sexual differentiation that occurs when the infant must renounce total dependence on her or his mother. Yet this rupture is where sex differentiation begins to become a crucial part of the 'self' and therefore needs to be examined in some detail. The 'self' acquired in childhood is a sex-differentiated 'self' and the actual content of some of the morality imposed during the repression of instinctual drives differs for boys and girls. Within the general repression of aggression, for instance, current sex roles allow that boys may still display more aggression than girls.

The female child's experience of becoming an independent person (and no longer remaining a dependent infant whose 'self' is largely subsumed in that dependence) is different from a boy's experience. The boy's is often seen as being more traumatic because of the total renunciation and change of identification involved: the boy must learn to identify with his father as an agent of the male sex and in this way identify himself as a boy. But this change involves only one main process: the establishment of his own separateness. The girl can retain her identification with the female sex of her mother but her establishment of separateness involves another process as well. She learns at the same time that she is a female person and that she is also an inferior person. This is more than the temporary inferiority of children in a world governed by adults – something which children of both sexes must endure. The boy knows his inferiority is a function of age and will not obtain indefinitely. The girl knows she is inferior as a child but also as a woman and that, even when she is no longer a child, she will retain the low status her mother, in relation to men, has. She also learns that a further important part of being female is tending to the needs of others. The female child thus internalizes a maternal role as part of acquiring her separateness. By contrast, a boy's future is more open-ended: he learns that he will probably be a father but that fatherhood is not a full-time occupation. Nor does it require a structuring of the 'self' in the way that the acquisition of the nurturing qualities of motherhood does.

The female child has this sex role and an awareness of its low status imposed upon her in the same way as the general morality described above is imposed, and she is threatened with the same kind of insecurity and feelings of worthlessness unless she submits to it. But she is immediately caught within a contradiction. The low status of women induces feelings of worthlessness anyhow. Compared to the high status male sex, women are worthless. Yet, because she is born female, she must conform to female sex-role behaviour or she will be rejected as a worthless person and lose parental affection. The female child is made to feel worthless if she does not conform to her nurturant sex-role, but conformity to it means accepting a low status which engenders feelings of worthlessness. The female 'self' is, almost by definition, predicated on insecurity, anxiety and a proclivity to doubt one's worth. The female child copes with this contradiction by becoming excessively dependent upon her father and upon men generally: her dependence disguises her insecurity. And society helps disguise the contradiction, and at the same time endeavours to make it palatable to women by purporting to endow motherhood – posited as the fulfilment of the female sex-role – with a high and worthwhile status. By clinging to these two props, the female child can often escape having to confront the very precarious nature of the social foundations of her 'self'. Exactly how the female child attains her dependence upon her father and other men is unclear and existing psychological theories are not particularly helpful in explaining it. It is not possible here to speculate at length on the likely processes involved but this is clearly an area in need of research. Obviously, the female child is imitating her mother's sex role behaviour and part of that requires dependence on her husband, especially if she has no income of her own. The child is also drawn to her father *because* of his high status: the only way she can share this status is to become dependent upon him and allow him to be protective towards her.*

The female child becomes even more submissive than a boy needs to because such submission removes the need to examine her own

* The whole question of how women become dependent on men at the same time and by the same process, as they become separate individuals, needs further exploration. How can dependent women identify as separate individuals with a country whose physical and cultural dimensions are dominated and described by men ? Freudian explanations are now obviously inadequate but even those advanced

behaviour and question the contradictions involved. Such questioning would prove extremely threatening to her already fragile 'self' since, in a society in which women have low status, there is no absolute resolution to the contradiction. Her dependence on men, and the protective stance men assume towards her, removes the need for self-examination. Her dependence on men is reinforced by her mother's attitude towards her. Her mother withdraws total nurturance from her so that she can become a separate person and with this withdrawal a woman is permanently deprived of a close, loving relationship with members of her own sex. Nor is she compensated even with the kind of camaraderie which exists between men. Women learn not to really like each other, for this would threaten both their dependence on men (and the status men derive from this) and their ability and willingness to nurture men.

This basic model of submission, dependence and hostility between women – which leads to their social isolation from each other – is reflected in and reinforced by marriage and its supporting institutions. As Phyllis Chesler explains it:

Daughters don't turn to their mothers for 'sexual' initiation, or, as Freud would have it . . . they specifically turn away from them, for a number of reasons. 'Mothers' are conditioned not to like women and/or the female body. They are phobic about lesbianism; they are jealous of their daughters' youth – rendered so by their own increasing 'expendability'. Also, 'mothers' must be harsh in training their daughters to be 'feminine' in order that they learn how to serve in order to survive. The way in which female children grow up – or learn how not to grow up – is initiated by the early withdrawal or relative absence of the female and/or nurturant body from their lives. Nurturance-deprivation, and the sexual abuse of female children are possibly the two most important factors involved in making female children receptive to 'submission' conditioning – at a very early age. Female children move from a childhood dominated or peopled by members of their own sex to a foreign 'grown-up' world dominated, quite literally, by members of the opposite sex. Male children graduate from a childhood dominated or peopled by members of the opposite sex (women) to a 'grown-up' world dominated by members of their own sex. Unlike women, they

---

by feminist psychologists such as Phyllis Chesler leave many questions unanswered. Until these processes can be described and understood, the means by which female separateness can become independence from men cannot be arrived at. Juliet Mitchell's *Psychoanalysis and Feminism* (Allen Lane, London, 1974) has begun such a process of inquiry and understanding.

can safely go home again by marrying 'wives', who will perform the rites of maternal domestic and emotional nurturance, but who are usually younger, economically poorer, and physically weaker than themselves. In patriarchal society, the basic incest taboo (between mother and son and father and daughter) is *psychologically* obeyed by men and disobeyed by women. Psychologically, women do not have initiation rites to help them break their incestuous ties. While most women do not commit incest with their biological fathers, patriarchal marriage, prostitution, and mass 'romantic' love are psychologically predicated on sexual union between Daughter and Father figures.[5]

Whatever else a woman may do with her life, this basic model of female behaviour will be part of her 'self' and she will have to struggle to restructure this 'self' in adulthood. A total restructuring would be virtually impossible within the patriarchal institutions which reinforce it and since most women do marry, conceptions they acquired in childhood will continually be reinforced during their adult lives. As we have already seen, women's participation in other areas of cultural existence is either proscribed or has low status and would reinforce her 'worthless' status. Women are thus effectively imprisoned within family and marriage, dependent on men, and nurturing husbands and children, as their only means of psychic survival.

The world of work outside the home is an important part of men's lives. As protectors and providers they are obliged to earn money. Even though many married women now have jobs outside the home, this is a recent development and is still not institutionalized as part of the female role. For women, family life is a primary means of 'self'-definition and their family responsibilities persist even if a woman decides, or is forced, to take on an additional job. As is shown in detail in Chapter Thirteen, women are still not socialized to expect to have jobs after they marry, and this expectation is not part of their conception of 'self'. Thus, if they do have jobs, these are likely to be seen as temporary and contingent and as peripheral to their primary identification as wives and mothers. For men, however, their jobs are an integral part of their 'self'-identification and have a definite relation and status to their family lives.

In a capitalist society, workers of both sexes are exploited. They are both subjected to the alienating effects of the division of labour: they both are forced to sell labour power for which they are inadequately paid, thus creating a surplus which enhances the wealth and power of the ruling class. Beyond that, however, the situation of each sex differs. Because men are providers for families, they expect rewards for their labours from their families. They want families to be retreats, places to forget the drudgery of the boredom of work. They expect to be cosseted, their meals prepared for them, their clothes washed and ironed, their problems listened to. (This may not always happen, but this is the expectation which is acquired as part of the male sex role.) At the level of everyday life, men have two distinct bases for 'self'-maintenance, two separate areas in which they can earn the approval of others by conforming to the roles required in each area. At present few women have this. As pointed out above, women have not learned to see work outside the home as a means of 'self'-maintenance. This makes it easier for women to leave jobs, to be dilatory in their work-performance ('It doesn't really matter for me, because I can always go back to being a house-wife'), to be less upset by difficulties with the work itself or the people they work with. In fact, a husband who wants to remain secure in his provider role might encourage such feelings. The requisites of the Australian economy are probably slowly changing this situation and the next generation of women may begin to learn to see jobs outside the home as being essential to their 'self'-identification. But this has not happened yet, and I am concerned to look at what is happening with women in the present. And at present, their identities, their sense of 'self' rest insecurely on one area, their family lives.

Women are culturally impotent; they acquire a conception of 'self' which is based on a contradiction which they resolve by sub-mitting to male dominance; they are not yet able to value work outside the home as a valid activity for their sex.* This means that their family lives and relationships are critical. If their expectations in this area cannot be fulfilled they have not the safety valve of an alternative area of 'self'-validation and the fragility of staking their psychological well-being on one area will rapidly become apparent. They have not the diversions open to men, nor are they likely to receive much sympathy, for the ideology of 'the family' is so strong. The extent to which this ideology requires the compliance, or in other words, the oppression of women is explored in Chapter Six.

* I am mainly concerned here with the psychological question of 'self' and its relation to women's lives at present and have not, therefore, included in this section a critique of work within a capitalist system. I am aware of the deficiency this entails but I am not trying to suggest that women should learn to value work which is both exploitative and alienating.

For the present, I want to look at what is happening with women in families, to see whether or not their 'selves' are secure.

There are many indications that women are increasingly unhappy with their female, which are family, roles. Behaviour which suggests that they are unable to cope with the narrow range of existence available to them has reached pandemic proportions in recent years. There are at least three ways in which people signify that they have reached a nadir of despair and desolation: seeking psychiatric treatment, taking drugs which blot out awareness and engaging in self-destructive acts. In recent years there is inescapable evidence that women are resorting to these methods of signalling incipient breakdown in far greater numbers than men.

The *Statistics of In-Patients* for New South Wales psychiatric hospitals shows that by a small majority, there are more men than women in public hospitals.[6] But when the psychiatric diagnoses are broken down by sex some pertinent factors are revealed. The categories in which there is a clear majority of men are: alcoholic psychosis (477 men, 132 women), alcoholism (3,246 men, 585 women), 'other personality disorders' (666 men, 634 women), mental retardation (509 men, 378 women) and 'no psychiatric diagnosis' (151 men, 148 women). The only category in which the difference is significant and which does not involve a possible hereditary defect is alcoholism, which is clearly a men's disease in Australia at present. The diagnoses for women are rather different and while the contrast between men and women is not as dramatic as with alcoholism, the differences are significant in the following diagnoses: schizophrenia and other paranoid states (2,314 women, 2,171 men), depressive psychosis (893 women, 398 men), 'other functional psychoses' (369 women, 235 men), depressive neurosis (2,223 women, 1,090 men), 'other neuroses and psychosomatic disorders' (452 women, 350 men), and drug dependence (326 women, 280 men). A clear majority of children admitted for behaviour disorders is also female.[7] Statistics of in-patients in private psychiatric clinics are not available but if they could be added to the figures for public hospitals it is likely that the numbers of women would greatly increase. Women who require only short-term hospitalization and whose families can afford it, are more likely to enter private hospitals or clinics. There is still a stigma attached to having to resort to public psychiatric treatment where people are more likely to be labelled, by society and by friends and neighbours, as 'mad'. The person who enters a private hospital can use the more palatable label 'nervous breakdown'.

That the in-patient figures from public hospitals are imprecise indications of the numbers of women suffering from some degree of psychiatric disturbance was indicated by the findings of the Canberra Mental Health Survey. This survey, conducted on a sample of the population of Canberra by the ACT Health Services Branch in 1971 found that a total of 26 per cent of the population suffered moderate or severe psychiatric disturbances.[8] It is important that this survey was conducted from house to house rather than through doctors' waiting rooms or the admission centres or out-patients section of a hospital, for it can by no means be assumed that all persons suffering from some degree of psychiatric disturbance will seek this kind of assistance. The survey divided its results into three categories each of which revealed a higher rate of disturbance·amongst women: Not disturbed: 70 per cent men, 69.3 per cent women; mildly disturbed: 15.7 per cent men, 20.8 per cent women; moderately-severely disturbed: 5.3 per cent men, 9.9 per cent women.[9]

Most women who had been admitted to psychiatric hospitals were hospitalized for what was diagnosed as 'depressive neurosis' and most had comparatively short stays in hospital: a clear majority was admitted for a month or less.[10] We need more detailed figures on the psychiatric complaints of women in Australia, especially break-downs by age over a ten-year period, to see whether or not this 'illness' is increasing, and increasing at a faster rate for women than for men. But it is likely that this is the case. In the United States, where women's family lives are fairly similar to those of Australian women, 'national statistics and research studies all document a much higher female to male ratio of depression or manic-depression at all ages.'[11] Depression appears to be becoming *the* female disease of the 1970s.

Depression in women can be, Chesler points out, 'a way of keeping faith with their feminine role'.[12] Two very common instances of female depression are closely associated with women's mothering role: post-partum depression and menopausal depression. Even women who have accepted their female role willingly and uncritically often experience intense depression shortly after the birth of a child. This time of so-called female 'fulfilment' is very often accompanied by a realization of just what that fulfilment entails for a woman: whatever degree of freedom she had prior to the birth of the child has been subverted by the appearance of a totally dependent infant who will regularize her life and minimize her ability to be anything other than a full-time mother. Fulfilment means entrapment, and so while, for men, fulfilment generally means the satisfaction of having achieved something they sought after, and a release from the tension channelled into the project, for women maternal fulfilment is merely the beginning of a sixteen-year stint. The realization of this often engulfs a woman when she first returns home with her new child and she succumbs to her fate by experiencing depression. Were she to renounce full-time care of the child, put it in a nursery or engage a nurse-maid (if she could afford to), she would be in a much better position to feel fulfilled. Having accomplished the pregnancy and birth she would not have to totally subordinate her existence to the demands of the baby.

Large numbers of women experience depression on reaching menopause. It is difficult to know the extent to which this is a learned response to the idea that already 'worthless' women have even less value once they are no longer able to fulfil the main role of women in a patriarchal society, and how much of it is hormonally induced. But the former idea is difficult to suppress, especially for a woman who has devoted her whole life to her family. Children are usually grown-up and often have already left home when their mothers begin menopause. It is often also the time at which the husband's job is most demanding and requires him to be away from home for long periods each day. Or the husband may well have decided to seek the company of a younger woman. All too frequently the menopausal woman cannot but see her life as over: she knows of little else to do with her life except care for husband and children yet now they barely need this care. It is too late for her to have another child to fill the gap and, in any case, the middle-aged woman having a baby is a subject of mirth or ridicule.

A third form of depression which is endemically female is what is inaccurately referred to as pre-menstrual tension. As there is virtually no medical and only sparse psychological and psychiatric research into this it is impossible to ascertain how great a proportion of women endure this monthly misery. But informed research amongst women of my acquaintance and conversations with sympathetic doctors suggest that the numbers are very high. 'Tension' is an inaccurate term since it is only one of many symptoms which afflict women for several days before their menses. Women who suffer from this affliction are overwhelmed by feelings of depression, moroseness, and irritability and are often so severely incapacitated that they are unable to go about their daily lives and work. There has been some speculation as to its causes and some doctors consider that it is related to increased hormonal activity which leads in some women to a retention of body fluids. But a not uncommon medical attitude is that it is psychosomatic and either deserves no treatment or can be alleviated by tranquillizers or anti-depressants. This view is an arrogantly ill-informed attitude to what is a real and constant debility for large numbers of women and one that is not relieved by drug therapy. (Some women report getting some relief from taking diuretics which activate excretion of fluids but this is the only form of drug treatment which appears to have much effect.)

The extent and the seriousness of this form of depression is underrated because only women have to endure it. This is evident when we compare this – as well as the paucity of research into other problems such as vaginal infections which only women suffer – with the high status and well-endowed research programmes devoted to heart disease, alcoholism and other afflictions to which men are more prone and which, therefore, have a more marked and discernible effect on the functioning of the economy. Women's debilitations, on the other hand, are used to criticize them for being unreliable, irrational, and frequently absent employees, or for being neurotic housewives. Whatever the physical and psychological causes of pre-menstrual and other forms of female depression they are obviously related to the stresses and contradictions involved in being a woman in a sexist industrialized society. Such afflictions are, to the best of my knowledge, unknown amongst women in non-industrialized societies, societies which while still being organized around a sex division of labour and which often discriminate very harshly against women, nevertheless do not seem to involve them in the kinds of anxieties and uncertainties about their 'selves' which are so common in countries like Australia.

Women are caught in an enveloping double bind when they devote their entire lives to their families: their 'selves' are constructed on this premise, yet their 'selves' are threatened when they do it. The hostility, bewilderment or despair experienced by women who realize this is often turned inwards against themselves – depression – rather than outwards against the cause of their 'self' dislocation – aggression. The quiet and passive endurance of anguish is typically female behaviour. And it is also because of women's social conditioning that they are more likely than men to end up in psychiatric hospitals for conforming to their imposed sex roles. As Phyllis Chesler says:

The mental asylum closely approximates the female rather than the male experience within the family. This is probably one of the reasons why Erving Goffman, in *Asylums*, considered psychiatric hospitalization more destructive of self than criminal incarceration. Like most people, he is primarily thinking of the debilitating effect – on *men* – of being treated like a woman (as helpless, dependent, sexless, unreasonable – as 'crazy'). But what about the effect of being treated like a woman when you *are* a woman ? And perhaps a woman who is already ambivalent or angry about just such treatment ? Perhaps one of the reasons women embark and re-embark on 'psychiatric careers' more than men do is because they feel, quite horribly, at 'home' within them. Also, to the extent to which *all* women have been poorly nurtured as female children, and are refused 'mothering' by men as female adults, they might be eager for, or at least willing to settle for, periodic bouts of ersatz 'mothering', which they receive as 'patients'.[13]

There are large numbers of women who periodically capitulate to their extreme discontent and, no longer able or willing to control their frustration, disappointment or misery, manifest their feelings in such a way that they have to be temporarily incarcerated in an asylum. This is because they themselves request respite and demand to be taken from whatever situation it is which has precipitated the breakdown, or because their relatives cannot endure this constant demonstration of dolour, which is perhaps a reminder of the precarious state of their own psychic health. Sometimes people end up in psychiatric hospitals and are diagnosed without their being able to participate at all in the process. In a study of psychoses among female migrants it was reported that one depressed woman had been tentatively diagnosed as psychotic. Her certificate read 'The patient is lying in a bed, weeping bitterly. She does not respond when addressed in English, nor in Italian.' She was later found to be Ukrainian.[14] For many of the women studied in this survey, even though most suffered from a degree of psychosis – many due to war-time experiences in labour camps – their depression and frustration was exacerbated by their being unable to communicate their feelings to the medical staff. The hospital had, prior to this study, apparently acted on the assumption that all migrants were either Greek or Italian and had only employed interpreters in these languages: it was found that these migrant women were among the noisiest and most difficult to handle in the entire hospital *until* they began being treated by nurses of their own nationality.[15]

This example may provide a clue to the psychiatric problems of many women. Even when actual illness exists it is exacerbated, and thus in the eyes of the medical staff is diagnosed as being more serious, by the inability of the woman to communicate to those around her what is wrong. Possibly she does not know herself, in which case even the most sympathetic husband or friend is likely to lose patience. It is rather unrewarding to have constantly to deal with a person who weeps continually and can only respond with an 'I don't know what's wrong with me these days . . .' Vast numbers of women, often with advice or pressure from impatient families, cope with this by imbibing massive doses of what they see as soothing panaceas: sedatives and tranquillizers.

This resort to drugs can take two courses. A woman can simply supply herself with large quantities of non-prescription drugs, thereby circumventing the need for doctors' visits which involve high costs and the chance of censure for her dependence on these substances. The Senate Select Committee on Drug Trafficking and Abuse found evidence that synthetic bromides – 'bromureides' – which it was submitted were major drugs of dependence in Australia, were not only freely available, but were consumed in enormous quantities. In the Melbourne area alone, 720,000 bromureide tablets were sold without a prescription *each week* in 1969.[16] Drug companies were reluctant to co-operate with this investigation and supply exact figures of their own production of various drugs, but the written submission of one manufacturer stated that ' "An analysis of known industry sales figures shows that the usage of mild analgesics in Australia is 0.63 tablets per person per day". By simple calculation this reaches the staggering figure of 2,904.3 million tablets used by the Australian community in a single year.'[17] The same committee heard evidence that suggested that there were 180,000 drug dependent females – 4 per cent of the population – in Australia, compared with 90,000 drug dependent males, and that the people treated for abuse of depressants including bromureides were predominantly female, mostly in the 40–50 age group.[18] It was also reported that Australia is the third highest consumer *per capita* of codeine in the world.[19] A survey conducted at Sydney's Prince Alfred Hospital and the Department of Social and Preventive Medicine at Sydney University in 1972 found that 7.9 per cent of men and 14.7 per cent of women take aspirin daily; men were found to take a slightly higher daily dosage than women but the numbers of women who were regular takers was substantially higher. The 1,057 housewives interviewed gave the following reasons for taking aspirin daily: headaches, nerves, tension, habit, arthritis and joint pains.[20] The survey also found that regular ingestion of preparations containing aspirin had been associated with both gastric ulcer and kidney damage. So the fact that women are taking non-prescription drugs, that is, drugs which are presumed not to be dangerous if taken in small quantities, is no guarantee that they are not doing substantial physical damage to themselves, nor can they be assured that the pain for which they sought the drug in the first place will be alleviated.

The New South Wales Health Education Council executive officer claimed in 1972 that an estimated 30 per cent of Sydney housewives were daily users of barbiturates or other drugs of dependence and that many of the social workers from his department had been shocked to discover that 'Mum gets stoned at 6 a.m. and stays that way all day.'[21] The Canberra Mental Health Survey found that 6.7 per cent of women compared with 2.9 per cent of men took headache pills or powders daily, and that 5.1 per cent of women compared with 2.4 per cent of men took sleeping pills or tablets each day.[22]

Any person who is tempted to use non-prescription drugs, especially pain-killers, to deaden psychic pain will find this resort encouraged by those who profit financially from such drug consumption. In May 1973 the Pharmacy Guild of Australia made Panadeine its Product-of-the-Month. That month's issue of the *Australian Journal of Pharmacy* carried a full-page advertisement headed: 'Panadeine Promotions give a Real Lift to *Your* Analgesic Sales'. The advertisement then went on to inform chemists of the most effective ways to sell more Panadeine.[23] Since women assume most responsibility for shopping in Australia, they are more likely to be aware of, and to respond to, such a high-pitched sales campaign and their already existing susceptibility to abuse these drugs is encouraged.

The second form of drug consumption amongst women is the taking of prescribed drugs. Here the acquiescence of a medical practitioner is required but this seldom seems to be difficult to obtain. Most doctors are unable to do more with the constant stream of women complaining of elusive aches and pains or of general depression than write out a prescription for a substance which will at least lessen the woman's awareness of her pain. Recently, since the dangers of kidney failure associated with overdoses of barbiturates began to be recognized, and with tranquillizers being made available on the NHS list, there has been a switch to prescribing tranquillizers, anti-depressants and non-barbiturate hypnotics. These are being seen by both doctors and patients alike as the latest panacea in the battle against tension and unhappiness.

In the year April 1970 to March 1971 over eight million prescriptions were written by general practitioners for psychotropic drugs, sedatives and hypnotics; they amounted to 13.8 per cent of all prescriptions written by general practitioners for that year.[24] The actual amounts prescribed would have been considerably higher than this since these

Percentage of Prescriptions given for Sedatives, Tranquillizers, and Anti-depressants to Males and Females of Different Ages in the Period January to March 1972[25]

	Barbiturates (e.g. Nembutal, Amytal)		Non-Barbiturates (e.g. Mogadon, Doriden etc.)		Psychotropics Neuroleptics (e.g. Largactil, Melleril)		Psychotropics Other (Valium 91%, Librium 9%)		Psychotropics Anti-depressants (Tofranil, Tryptanol)	
Total No. of Prescriptions	587,620		360,967		153,157		396,197		338,914	
Sex:	Male %	Female %	Male %	Female %	Male %	Female %	Male %	Female %	Male %	Female %
Under 1	0.2	0.1	0.3	0.5	0.5	0.2	—	—	—	—
1–4	0.4	0.2	1.0	0.7	0.9	0.4	0.6	0.2	0.4	0.8
5–14	0.3	0.3	0.2	0.3	3.5	1.3	0.3	0.2	4.3	2.4
15–24	0.6	3.2	1.1	2.9	1.2	5.2	1.6	3.8	0.8	3.2
25–34	1.6	4.5	1.2	3.8	3.3	4.9	3.0	7.7	2.9	9.3
35–44	2.2	6.1	3.0	8.0	4.2	4.0	5.0	9.8	2.7	11.6
45–54	4.8	8.8	6.8	12.3	6.0	10.3	7.7	11.5	6.4	13.0
55–64	6.5	11.8	7.3	13.1	7.2	10.8	6.7	13.0	5.9	11.3
65–74	7.0	17.6	6.5	12.4	3.9	14.1	4.7	10.7	1.9	10.7
75 and over	5.3	14.7	4.4	11.3	3.5	12.0	2.0	7.9	1.8	7.6
Total	28.9	67.3	31.8	65.3	34.2	63.2	31.6	64.8	27.1	69.9

Source: Macquarie University, School of Behavioural Sciences

drugs are frequently prescribed by specialists and by doctors in public and private hospitals. Each of these drugs is more frequently prescribed to women. A study of prescriptions written in Australia between January and March 1972 made by Anne Winkler at the School of Behavioural Sciences, Macquarie University found that two-thirds of the prescriptions for the drugs in each category were for women.[25] (See Table on p. 151)

Of these drugs prescribed by general practitioners in the year 1970–71 55 per cent were given to patients diagnosed as having mental disorders.[26] Within this category of 'mental disorders' women constituted almost 70 per cent of patients.[27] The sex differences in patients with mental disorders is set out in the table below:

Mental Disorders*[28]

Age Group	Male		Female	
Under 5	55,562	(1.0%)	52,153	(0.9%)
5 to 14	103,872	(1.8%)	75,753	(1.3%)
15 to 24	97,861	(1.7%)	283,073	(5.0%)
25 to 34	154,124	(2.7%)	434,261	(7.7%)
35 to 44	203,033	(3.6%)	493,561	(8.8%)
45 to 54	338,277	(6.0%)	620,837	(11.0%)
55 to 64	298,891	(5.3%)	650,475	(11.6%)
65 and over	413,853	(7.3%)	1,210,371	(21.5%)
Not stated	13,999	(0.2%)	29,460	(0.5%)
Total	1,679,472	(29.8%)	3,849,943	(68.4%)

* Sex was not stated in 101,537 cases (1.8%).

The patients receiving prescriptions for what were diagnosed as mental disorders were, with the exception of alcoholics, predominantly women. Women greatly outnumbered men in attendance for psychosis; they constituted more than double male attendance for anxiety neurosis; they comprised 70 per cent of attendances for hysterical neurosis, and over 60 per cent of attendances for depressive neurosis.[29]

These figures, as with those for in-patients in psychiatric hospitals, can indicate that women actually suffer from mental disorders in far greater numbers than do men *or* that, in the opinion of the diagnosing and prescribing doctors, such labels are appropriate to describe the behaviour of large numbers of women. It has already been pointed out that there are weighty social reasons for women to be susceptible to depression, that even the faithful fulfilling of the prescribed female role can result in feelings of depression.

The female 'self' is based on a narrow range of activities which are confined to the one physical location. Its maintenance is very much contingent on continual male protection and approval yet the activities which comprise the area of female 'self'-validation are carried out in the isolation of the home with the husband absent for long periods of time. Women are socially isolated from each other as the withdrawal of the mother's nurturance from the female child produces distrust and incipient hostility towards other women. Thus women have only the continued presence of their children – and not even this once they have grown up – to reinforce their feelings of self-esteem and worth. This is too flimsy a support for many women, especially if her children are excessively demanding and energy-draining and her husband remote or even critical of her efforts. This is the 'fulfilled' life of many women who have accepted their female role – small wonder the already insecure 'self' disintegrates into depression.

But what of the woman who partially or totally rejects her female role? Her 'self' has been socially constructed to require validation through motherhood: the process of reconstructing that 'self' to thrive by other means is slow, painful and subject to frequent retrogression if not shored up by an actively supportive and understanding circle of people. But even such support can be threatened or invalidated by the existence of institutions which reinforce the sexist *status quo* and which try and impose patriarchal notions of normality upon recalcitrant women.

Medicine in general (and psychiatry in particular) is just such an institution. Apart from the fact that the vast majority of its members are men who receive considerable personal benefit from the existing sexual division of labour (which is reflected in hospitals, clinics and surgeries as well as in their families), the psychological theories employed in medical training impute scientific validation to the socially derived system of sex differences. Both as men and as medical practitioners, most doctors have strict and traditional notions of what is appropriate behaviour for women. If a female patient displays behaviour which the doctor considers to be 'unfeminine' he is likely to label her 'neurotic'. The dangerous double-bind women find themselves in is that they are labelled thus if they reject their female role *or* if they adhere too stringently to it. If a woman does the latter she is likely to be periodically or even chronically depressed and this thereby challenges the idea that the dutiful wife and mother is a happy and contented being. If she is aggressive, argumentative and rational; if she eschews childbearing and demands an abortion; if she spurns sexual or emotional dependence upon men; if she refuses to be a full-time child-minder, takes a job and puts her children in day-care; if she has extra- or pre-marital affairs – if a woman does all or any of these things she is seen as rejecting all or part of her female role and is subject to 'self'-threatening social censure. If she confesses all or any of these things to the doctor from whom she is seeking medical assistance she is, at the very least, likely to be subjected to moralizing and risks being labelled 'neurotic' and treated as such. Rather than allow women to choose what they will do with their lives, and recognize that any degree of restructuring of the childhood-acquired female 'self' will produce some psychological stress, the medical profession dictates that contented compliance to the female role is a measure of mental health.

Men are subjected to strain and stress and seek medical assistance yet are far less likely than women to be categorized as 'neurotic'. Maybe this is partly because, as men, doctors can identify with the complaints of their male patients. Men are more reticent in consulting doctors than women; one survey of the use of health services in Sydney's western suburbs found that of the total population who had consulted a doctor in the two months preceding the survey, women comprised 46.4 per cent and men 35.4 per cent.[30] The Canberra Mental Health Survey found that 32.0 per cent of women and only 16.9 per cent of men were having regular treatment from a doctor.[31] Yet neither of these factors adequately accounts for the massive majority of women who are categorized as mentally ill by general practitioners and psychiatrists. The explanation would seem to lie in the fragile nature of the activities assigned to validate the female 'self', and in the refusal of the medical profession to accede to women any independence from patriarchal definitions of how women should behave.

These definitions are imposed by drug therapy even upon women who have not been classified as neurotic. It was noted above that only 55 per cent of the prescriptions for sedatives, hypnotics and psychotropic drugs were for people who were diagnosed as having mental disorders.

This means that nearly four million prescriptions for these drugs were written for people who, even in the opinion of doctors, were not mentally unsound. Many of these drugs, particularly the anti-depressants, are potentially dangerous. Drug-abuse is generally blamed on the patient who is said to have treated as a chemical panacea what the prescribing doctor intended as a palliative. Yet doctors continue to write millions of prescriptions without apparently considering the possible consequences this enormous dependence on drug therapy is producing.

Between 5 and 15 per cent of patients in Australian hospitals suffer from some drug-induced disease.[32] A study of suicide attempts admitted to the Alfred Hospital, Melbourne in 1973 found that three out of five people had taken overdoses of drugs prescribed by doctors for insomnia or depression and that 86 per cent had consulted a doctor in the two months prior to the attempt.[33] Dependence upon drugs to alleviate social problems is actively encouraged by the manufacturers of these drugs. Although they cannot be promoted direct to the public, these drugs are portrayed as miraculous cures in expensive advertisements in journals read by medical practitioners. These advertisements continually reinforce notions about what is 'normal' behaviour in women: they almost always show women – usually in family situations – in states of depression, anxiety or total breakdown. For instance, the anti-depressant Tryptanol, for which 884,473 prescriptions were written out in 1971[34], has recently been advertised in four-page glossy supplements in the *Medical Journal of Australia*. The first page shows a desolate-looking woman with small children around her saying 'I just can't cope with things anymore'. The 'medical' advice contained in the centre pages warns doctors against prescribing tranquillizers 'when the diagnosis is mixed anxiety-depression' for this 'may sidetrack the patient even deeper into depression'. Instead 'When mixed anxiety-depression is the diagnosis. Tryptanol. An effective anti-depressant with an inherent tranquillizing effect can be more useful in relieving target symptoms such as *Anxiety *Agitation *Insomnia *Functional gastrointestinal disorders *Loss of interest *Functional somatic complaints *Loss of confidence and sense of importance.' Page four shows the same woman, smiling gaily (even if doped to the hilt) responding to her children – obviously able to cope.[35] Many other tranquillizers and anti-depressants are promoted in the same fashion.[36] With this kind of promotion it is not surprising that the general practitioner, confronted by a woman mouthing almost identical complaints, will respond by prescribing one of these drugs.

By far the most popular drug in Australia is the tranquillizer diazepam, which is sold under the trade-name Valium. Usage of this drug has increased rapidly since it first appeared on the market. In the year April 1970 to March 1971, 941,090 prescriptions for Valium were written by general practitioners.[37] Sixty-three per cent of these prescriptions were written for women.[38] On 1 December 1972 Valium was placed on the NHS benefits list and since then its usage has increased spectacularly: by the end of December it had been prescribed more times than most other drugs were for the entire six-month period ending that month.[39] In 1973–74, 4.6 million prescriptions were written for Valium, making it the most prescribed drug in Australia.[40]

One of the reasons these drugs are so heavily prescribed, and one that has accounted particularly for the enormous rise in the consumption of Valium, is that they are non-toxic. 'The lack of fatal outcomes from overdoses of benzodiazepines is a great factor in explaining their popularity'[41] as one journal succinctly phrased it. No risk of overkill. But there are a great many other risks, especially with Valium, and these appear to be overlooked by the prescribing doctors and to be unknown to the supplicant patients. Nothing on the bottle itself, the advertisements for Valium appearing in most medical journals, or the general practitioners' pharmacological compendium mentions them.[42] MIMS, the Monthly Index of Medical Specialties, which is sent free of charge 'to all doctors in active practice' lists the following special precautions to be taken with Valium: 'Moderation with alcohol; as with other drugs, precaution during the first three months of pregnancy.'[43] How many women are aware of the latter warning? In effect it means that any woman who is likely to become pregnant – a substantial proportion of the female population – ought not to take Valium or any related drug. MIMS reports in relation to this group of tranquillizers that 'Safety in pregnancy is not yet established although some have been used with apparent safety.'[44] It could be argued that in order to avoid the slightest possibility of a tragedy similar to that caused by Thalidomide, Valium should not be prescribed to women who wish to have children. Other side-effects of Valium include 'Drowsiness, mental confusion especially in aged, appetite stimulation, Agranulocytosis' and doctors are advised that patients should be warned of a possible impairment of their ability to drive a motor car, the possible potentiation of alcohol, plus the possibility of physical dependence in patients using Valium.[45] Yet not one of the dozens of the Valium-using people, men and women, I have spoken to has ever been warned of any of these dangers.

Valium is prescribed for a wide variety of problems experienced particularly or solely by women and this usage is encouraged by Roche Products, its manufacturer. One booklet produced by this company gives a list of 'psychological problems of marriage'.[46] These include: frigidity, dyspareunia (painful intercourse), fear of pregnancy, childlessness, the tensions of mothering and fathering, and divorce. The cover of the book depicts the Chinese symbol for 'trouble' which is made by combining the symbols for 'women' and 'roof'. The 'problems' listed are all experienced mainly by women. The last page of the booklet provides pharmacological details of Valium. The unspoken implication of this booklet is that when women suffer anxiety about any of these 'problems' then Valium is the answer. A new pharmacological panacea has emerged which has the most insidious implications. It would seem more sensible to prescribe contraceptives to a woman who is frightened of pregnancy, and the Roche booklet does not dispute this, but it argues that 'modern contraceptive measures are often fraught with emotional conflict'. The message seems to be: forget the problem, just assuage the anxiety.[47]

Women account for nearly two-thirds of the consumers of Valium – it is now widely prescribed by gynaecologists as well as by general practitioners and other specialists – and they are clearly being forced to resort to it as a means of blotting out awareness. Because Valium and these other much-consumed drugs *do* work. They anaesthetize, they dull responses, they create a sense of well-being. Problems no longer seem so threatening or overwhelming. No matter that they mute one's psychic awareness, that they insidiously undermine a person's capacity for acting upon the world and working to change their 'self' and social environment – that potential which defines our humanity. They keep people functioning – humanoid robots perhaps – but at least alive and 'able to cope'. The distraught 'self' already ravaged by the contradictory demands of the female role, is lulled into quiescence and quietism. The possibility of restructuring is removed, and the doctors who glibly prescribe these mind-stoppers are guilty of something like mass psychic murder of the women of this country.

The third resort of people in distress is to engage in self-destructive acts, behaviour which is risky to life or which is likely to incur strong social reproof, or punishment. These acts can be seen as instances of 'mayday' behaviour: they are engaged in to draw attention to a person's plight. The most dramatic of these – for there is always the risk that it will misfire and become a grotesque confirmation of a person's urgent need for aid – is what researchers on the subject are increasingly referring to as 'suicidal behaviour'.[48] The rate of successful suicides has increased dramatically in Australia since 1955 while it has remained constant in comparable countries like the United

Kingdom.[49] This increase has been in part because of the very large jump in the percentage of female suicides. These have increased from 5.4 per 100,000 in 1955 to 10.8 in 1965; by contrast the male rate increased by 3.7 per 100,000.[50] But this statistic only obscures what has been an extraordinarily large rise in the number of women engaging in suicidal behaviour, particularly by means of self-poisoning. More than three-quarters of these attempts involve overdoses of drugs, especially barbiturates, which have been prescribed by a doctor.[51] During an eight-year survey of patients attending a Melbourne western suburbs hospital after suicidal behaviour, it was found that there was a mean ratio of one man to every 2.4 women, that women made up 71 per cent of those who had used this means of drawing attention to their plight.[52] The overwhelming majority of the women, many more than amongst the men, said afterwards that they had not wanted to die[53] – their swallowing of massive doses of pills was a desperate attempt to get someone (anyone?) to recognize that their complaint was *serious*, that they *had* to have help, and that, everything else having failed, this seemed to be the most efficacious means of signalling this.

There are many other forms of 'mayday' behaviour, many of which may not be recognized as such for not every instance of such behaviour will necessarily be a cry for help. But when a person, particularly a woman who has no other means of venting her frustrations, engages in a form of behaviour which for her is atypical, then it must be asked whether or not she is – even if subconsciously – calling attention to her malaise.

It has been found that women are more likely to shoplift than men, and that the greatest number of 'offenders' occurs in the 15 to 39 age group.[54] If many of the younger girls can be classed as acting on dares – common among school children – the same cannot be said of women aged 20 to 39 and this was substantiated by the extreme readiness with which women admitted their guilt and gave no reason for the theft: 232 women compared with 179 men gave no reason, while a further 23 women (and only 4 men) gave 'health' as a reason.[55] Over a quarter of the shoplifters came from suburbs of high social standing, and of these, 77 per cent were women, a further indication that this was not typical behaviour (assuming that people living in such suburbs are likely to have money and not be forced to steal for this reason).

A woman who neglects, or who physically attacks, her children may also be crying 'mayday' – saying 'Look I'm a bad mother, what's wrong with me, why doesn't someone help me.' The incidence of 'baby-battering' has risen greatly in recent years although it is often not detected unless the child has sustained serious and often permanent injury. In a society which professes to hold motherhood in high esteem, the woman who is a 'bad' mother receives swift condemnation. Where maltreatment is persistent and publicly observable the children are usually taken away and placed in State custody: they *are* cared for, but what happens to the mother? Is she left, bereft and alone, to find yet another means of calling attention to her plight? It may be the case that it is the children who *are* the problem and that she will be happier without them, but this cannot merely be assumed. When women learn the qualities of nurturance as part of the process of acquisition of 'self', they do not bash their children without suffering enormous guilt. Such action, even if induced by extreme anguish, can precipitate total breakdown of 'self' for it will appear to the woman that she has negated one of the fundamentals of her personality, her 'nature' even. When women engage in behaviour that is so totally at odds with their expressed 'self'-conceptions they do not need punishment or censure. Rather they require sympathy and someone to whom they can try to articulate the immediate cause of their actions. Not someone who will push away their problems with a prescription but a person (or group) who has some insight into the enormous ravages wrought upon the female psyche in a culture which is sexist and patriarchal.

It is only at this fourth 'level' of culture – everyday life – that women have an explicit and acknowledged place. Even here their status is low and their activities, because they are so taken for granted, are not incorporated into definitions of Australian culture. Yet here we find women engaged in an enormous variety of activities. Women are wives and mothers and grandmothers. They are child-minders and housekeepers, cooks and cleaners, gardeners and laundresses, decorators and dressmakers. These activities have been allocated to women and they are their lives and their work. They form, in a sense, a female culture which possesses its own history and traditions. It has accumulated skills and wisdoms which are transmitted from one generation of women to the next. But it has not been given the status of a culture, or even a sub-culture, by any intellectual tradition in this country. This lack of status makes the already flimsy foundations of women's 'selves' even more precarious.

It has been shown in this chapter that large numbers of Australian women are unhappy and that they are trying to assuage this misery with a variety of remedies, many of which are potentially dangerous and none of which will, of themselves, resolve the basic existential problem. While men in a male-defined culture are to a large extent cut off from the sources of life and the material processes that sustain it, women are so deeply embroiled in them that they are unable to move beyond them and enter those areas of cultural expression whereby individuals and groups define their present situations and articulate their futures. Women are denied this experience. They are forced to be silent. Australian culture provides women with a very narrow range of validating areas of existence. Women are invisible in Australian culture and they are supposed to accept that their existence is denied. Those who extol the revered place which 'the family' has in this country rarely consider the toll taken by the physical and psychic imprisonment of women within families.

NOTES

1. Raymond Williams, *Culture and Society*, Penguin Books, 1963; *The Long Revolution*, Penguin Books, 1965.

2. Jerzy Krupinski and Alan Stoller, *The Family in Australia: Social, Demographic and Psychological Aspects*, Pergamon Press, Sydney, 1974, pp. 1-2.

3. John Maze, 'The Family and the State', *Search*, July 1974, pp. 339-42.

4. ibid., p. 340, original emphasis.

5. Phyllis Chesler, *Women and Madness*, Avon, New York, 1972, pp. 19-20. Also published in Allen Lane, London, 1974.

6. In 1971-72 there was a total of 10,911 men and 10,076 women admitted to psychiatric hospitals in New South Wales. *Statistics of In-Patients in Psychiatric Centres*, Bureau of Census and Statistics, Sydney, 1973.

7. All figures from *Statistics of In-Patients in Psychiatric Centres*.

8. B. L. Hennessy, W. J. Bruen and J. Cullen, 'The Canberra Mental Health Survey. Preliminary Results', n.p., n.d., Table Three.

9. ibid.

10. *Statistics of In-Patients*, op. cit.

11. Chesler, op. cit., p. 41.

12. ibid., p. 45.

13. ibid., p. 35.

14. Frieda Schaechter, 'A Study of Psychoses in Female Migrants', *Medical Journal of Australia*, II, 22 September 1962, p. 459.

15. ibid., p. 461.

16. *Drug Trafficking and Drug Abuse*, Report from the Senate Select Committee. Australian Government Publishing Service, Canberra, 1971, p. 35. As a result of this report bromureides are no longer available without a prescription.

17. ibid., p. 37.

18. ibid., p. 19.

19. ibid., p. 17.

20. Reported *Sydney Morning Herald*, 6 May 1972.

21. Reported *Sydney Morning Herald*, 13 June 1972.

22. Hennessy, Bruen and Cullen, op. cit., Table Twelve.

23. Reported in the *Australian*, 14 May 1973.

24. Ian L. Rowe, 'Prescription of Psychotropic Drugs by General Practitioners', *Medical Journal of Australia*, I, 24 March 1973, p. 589. Psychotropic drugs are those capable of altering a person's emotional state. They include anti-depressants, tranquillizers and neuroleptics.

25. Anne Winkler, 'Incidence of Analgesic Usage in Australia', unpublished paper, Macquarie University, May 1973.

26. Rowe, op. cit., p. 590.

27. ibid.

28. Reproduced from Rowe.

29. Rowe, op. cit., p. 591.

30. Anthony Adams, Alan Chancellor and Charles Kerr, 'Medical Care in Western Sydney: A Report on the Utilization of Health Services by a Defined Population', *Medical Journal of Australia*, I, 6 March 1971, p. 509.

31. Hennessy, Bruen and Cullen, op. cit., p. 6.

32. David S. Watson, 'Some Factors Influencing General Practitioner Prescribing', *Australian Journal of Pharmacy*, November 1973, p. 789.

33. Reported *Sydney Morning Herald*, 21 March 1973.

34. Trevor Hawkins, 'The Most Prescribed Drug in Australia is a Tranquilliser', *National Times*, 19–24 March 1973.

35. *Medical Journal of Australia*, I, 21 March 1970.

36. For instance, an advertisement for Tofranil (use 'In an emotional crisis') shows a woman similarly overwrought, neglected children crying in the background, while she is saying, 'I was so wretched I burst into tears. And I couldn't stop crying. I felt so irritable. It wasn't as if he'd shouted at me. He only asked me to iron his blue shirt. But at that moment anything was too much for me. Lately I keep getting these headaches. And I wake up so early. I'd give anything for a good night's sleep. It makes me so tired and short-tempered during the day. The children get on my nerves. Yet really they're good kids. Financially things are a bit rough at the moment. But we've had problems before and I've always been able to cope. I just wish I could pull myself together.' *Medical Journal of Australia*, I, 21 March 1970.

37. Rowe, op. cit., p. 591.

38. ibid., p. 592.

39. Hawkins, op. cit.

40. Trevor Hawkins, 'Australia, the nervous nation of pill poppers – and paying for it', the *National Times*, 11–16 November 1974.

41. L. E. Hollister, 'The Clinical Use of Psychotherapeutic Drugs, Anti-anxiety Drugs and Special Problems in the Use of Psychotherapeutic Drugs', *Current Therapeutics*, November 1972, p. 76.

42. *Australian Drug Compendium 1972–73*, A.D.C. Publications, Seaforth, N.S.W., 1973. A copy of this is issued free to every doctor. It contains the various dosages of Valium but says nothing about its possible side-effects.

43. *MIMS*, April 1973, p. 61.

44. ibid., p. 58.

45. G. B. Chesher, 'The Pharmacology of Psychotropic Drugs', *New Ethicals*, April 1967, p. 252.

46. *The Roots of Marital Tension*, Roche Products Pty Ltd, Dee Why, N.S.W., n.d.

47. This practice of mass sedation of an anxiety-prone populace has proved extremely profitable to the manufacturers of Valium. In April 1973 the British Government ordered Roche Products to reduce the prices of Librium and Valium by about 40 per cent because the company had made what the Government considered to be the excessive profit of some £24 million on these two drugs alone since 1966. Reported *Sydney Morning Herald*, 14 April 1973. The price of Valium in Australia is from 100 to 120 per cent higher than the British price – *before* the cuts were ordered.

48. This term is favoured in preference to 'attempted suicide' because it is evident that a large percentage of people who take overdoses or slash their bodies do not want to die. An attempted suicide should properly refer only to a real effort to end one's life which, for some reason, was unsuccessful.

49. Basil S. Hetzel, 'The Epidemiology of Suicidal Behaviour in Australia', *Australian and New Zealand Journal of Psychiatry*, Vol. 5, No. 3, 1971, p. 157.

50. ibid.

51. R. G. Oliver et al., 'The Epidemiology of Attempted Suicide as seen in the Casualty Department, Alfred Hospital, Melbourne', *Medical Journal of Australia*, I, 17 April 1971, p. 835.

52. ibid., p. 834.

53. ibid., p. 836.

54. Tony Maiden, 'Profile of a Shoplifter', *Australian Financial Review*, 20 October 1971. This article is a comprehensive report of a survey of shoplifters conducted by two Melbourne criminologists.

55. ibid

CHAPTER
FIVE

THE POVERTY
OF DEPENDENCE

Australia is not the wealthy country that many of the glowing commentaries of our national characteristics would have us believe. Our apparent affluence harbours an enormous amount of desperate material poverty, and in the midst of the two-cars-and-swimming-pool suburban prosperity there exist well over two million people who find it difficult to ensure adequate housing let alone the complacency of a full belly.

That such poverty exists, and that its true dimensions ought to be publicly known, was acknowledged by the Federal Government in 1972 when it established a Commission to inquire into poverty in Australia. The Commission, headed by Professor Ronald Henderson has, at the time of writing, released its Interim Report and several research reports but its final report has not yet been published. This has been the first inquiry on such a comprehensive scale ever conducted in this country and it is to be hoped that its full report will acknowledge something which all previous poverty surveys have apparently not recognized and that is that *the vast majority of the 'poor' are women.*

The euphemistic categories we use to describe material depriva tion – 'pensioner', 'deserted wife', 'single mother', 'low-income family' etc. – obscure the fact that these terms refer either exclusively or overwhelmingly to women and the children for whom they are responsible, and that virtually the entire social security system of Australia exists as a monumental testament to our systematic refusal to grant women economic independence. No previous survey has seen that poverty is a likely consequence for almost every woman who has been unable, or unwilling, to procure for herself a male provider/protector. The irony of the promise of 'social security' is apparent only to those who realize that no such security is assured for women. It is not until the age of sixty that women are guaranteed a fixed income in their own right – in the form of the old age pension. Before that age, the economic well-being of *all* women, of any social class, is determined by sheer chance. A series of 'ifs' will decide her fate. *If* she is able to obtain an appropriate education and *if* she can secure a job which pays well and *if* it is not threatened by redundancy or male competition or an unforeseen pregnancy, or *if* she is prepared to get married and rely on her husband to ensure her economic survival and *if* her husband's income remains adequate and *if* they stay together he gives her a reasonable share of it and *if* they part she is provided for by him, then a woman can be reasonably secure economically. But a lot of things can go wrong – if any of the 'ifs' do not prevail, a woman can find herself in sudden and unprepared-for poverty.

Many women grow up with this realization; for others it can come, at any stage in their lives, as an unanticipated and shattering recognition that their lives are out of control, they are economically impotent, unable to gather together the resources, or denied the tangible opportunities, for sheer economic survival.

It is true that many men are similarly unable to direct their lives, fall victims to accidents or are in other ways prevented from pursuing economic self-determination, and a great many women live their entire lives without knowing material deprivation. But individual instances from either category do not contradict the basic proposition that, as a sex, women are systematically denied an independent place in our economic structure: the money that women of pre-pension age receive is money for them to mother their children with – not geared to their personal needs or aspirations – and those women who are able to support themselves do so in spite of the system, not because of it.

A comparison between male and female wages demonstrates the slender chances the majority of women have of enjoying economic security.* (See the Table on the opposite page)

The proportion of women workers earning above $4,000 in 1969 was miniscule. While 65.4 per cent of males earned less than this amount a huge 94.2 per cent of women were concentrated in the two lowest income brackets with nearly half of all women full-time workers earning less than $2,000 a year.

* The figures used in this Chapter are the latest available to June 1975. Where statistical material relating to earlier years is used this is because these figures have not been updated by the Australian Bureau of Statistics. It can be expected that most of the actual figures relating to incomes and pensions will be out of date by the time this work is published but unless major structural changes are made to the Australian economy – and this does not seem likely – then the argument made in this Chapter remains valid.

Male and Female Full-time Workers; Total Income, 1968–1969[1]†

	Males		Females	
	Proportion with stated income			
	Cumulative %	Class Interval %	Cumulative %	Class Interval %
Total Income				
Up to $2,000	10.3	10.3	48.6	48.6
$2,000 to $4,000	65.4	55.1	94.2	45.6
$4,000 to $6,000	89.5	24.1	98.3	4.1
$6,000 to $8,000	95.5	6.0	99.5	1.2
$8,000 to $10,000	97.3	1.8	99.7	0.2
$10,000 to $12,000	98.5	1.2	99.8	0.1
$12,000 to $20,000	99.7	1.2	100.0	0.2
$20,000 and over		0.3		0.0
Total	100.0	100.0	100.0	100.0
Numbers	3,161,800		1,009,000	

† Although this table appears rather ancient in 1975 it has proved impossible to obtain a more current rendering of it from the Australian Bureau of Statistics even though it has been asked for repeatedly. I decided to leave this table in because it illustrates so graphically the concentration of female workers in low-income jobs. Even though the actual incomes have increased markedly it is unlikely that this pattern has altered.

Women are considered *a priori* to be dependants, just as men are assumed almost from birth to be wage-earners/breadwinners and the wage-structure of our economy has been arranged around this basic assumption. People's lives will not obediently follow this charter, of course, and it is when it breaks down, particularly when a man fails to provide for those for whom he is legally responsible – because he dies or deserts – that women's dependent status, and the perpetual poverty that threatens, are made most clear. For when a dependent woman is deprived of her male provider, the State – in the form of a welfare agency – steps in and assumes the protector role, thereby perpetuating women's dependent status, and since welfare payments are notoriously meagre, ensuring that poverty will continue to be a likely accompaniment to this dependency. This reinforces without questioning the stereotypes of dependency and protection. Not every instance of State monetary relief transforms its recipient into a handmaiden: relief to wool-growers obviously does not assume this status. What is being suggested is that the State will only pay to women money which, in its view, their husbands (or some other supportive male) should be paying them *and for the same purposes*: it is money which is earmarked for a specific task – the raising of children. The State assumes the husband's financial role only as long as a woman remains a full-time mother.

Unless there were a full-scale inquiry directed specifically to this question, it would be impossible to delineate with any great accuracy the extent of poverty amongst women in Australia. Certainly it would be hazardous to try to estimate the numbers of women involved, but it is possible to designate those areas in which poverty is most likely to occur and then to gain some idea of how many women are possibly suffering within those areas. However, the actual numbers involved are less important than the general point that so far even those most concerned with discovering the extent of poverty in Australia, and with trying to eradicate it, seem unaware of the fact that they are dealing mainly with women. This oversight has important implications for proposed 'solutions' to poverty. If, as I am suggesting, endemic poverty is concomitant with being female unless male financial support can be obtained, then structural solutions which move beyond the 'more money' approach are essential. Although higher pensions would alleviate much poverty, governments are unlikely to spend the vast amounts which would be required to bring pensioners past the poverty line. In any case, it will be suggested that the structure of the Australian social security system does little to alter the posture of dependency which women must assume in order to gain financial support.

The fact that the majority of poor people are women has been partly disguised because researchers in the past have always been preoccupied with 'the family'. Economists who try to set a poverty line income have always pitched this to family needs, yet it is women who live outside ordinary family situations who are most likely to be poor.

Although those who study poverty now have adjusted income scales which apply to people outside 'the family', most of their discussions are still addressed to poverty amongst family groups thereby implying the presence of a husband/father or a *de facto* male provider, and there is rarely explicit recognition of the special problems encountered by people who do not live in this fashion. For instance, the 1966 Henderson survey began by stating, 'We

have deliberately confined ourselves to a study of poverty as determined by the relationship between the income of a family and its
normal needs.'[2] It was stated that a basic-wage concept of poverty
would be used, albeit one where 'the incomes of different-sized
family units have been standardized to make them comparable with
a unit of the basic size.'[3] This theoretical framework assumes that
most of the population can be accommodated by a 'family-unit'
analysis. Such a preoccupation prevents the study from acknowledging, or maybe from even observing, the existence and, more
important, *the causes*, of several important areas of poverty.

For instance, although the Henderson survey devoted a great deal
of attention to the poverty of aged people, there was no specific
mention made of the fact that more than two-thirds of the recipients
of aged pensions are women, and that in talking of the poverty of
the aged, the survey was in fact dealing primarily with the poverty
of old women. The family-oriented framework thereby disguised
the existence and extent of poverty amongst one group of women.

More recent thinking has begun to recognize this although so far
no full-scale survey of poverty amongst women has been attempted.
In its evidence to the Commission of Inquiry into Poverty, the
Australian Council of Social Service submitted that ' . . . to ignore
the extent to which sex discrimination operates to cause and to
reinforce poverty, is to ignore issues which are a vital part of anti-
poverty politics.'[4] It recommended 'That the Poverty Inquiry give
detailed attention to the needs of those specially disadvantaged
groups . . . older single women, lone parents (including lone fathers),
homeless women, women outside families and Aborigine women.'[5]

Some of this advice has been heeded and the Interim Report shows
that the family-unit analysis has been abandoned in favour of a
potentially more flexible concept 'income unit':

The 'income unit' was chosen to correspond to the family group normally
supported by a pension or benefit. It was decided that the household was
too heterogeneous a unit, particularly if it contained boarders or consisted
of an 'extended' family. Moreover, it was felt that persons such as aged
relatives should be treated as individuals with a right to income regardless
to whether they live with friends or relatives.[6]

Such a recognition of the right to an income is not extended to
women. The only special group singled out as suffering considerable
poverty because of their dependent status is children.[7] So the previous
surveys' short-sightedness in respect of women has not been completely overcome theoretically although in practice the Report does

recognize the existence of single women with or without children as having special needs. Moreover the new concept 'income unit' could be extended to women fairly easily were the researchers into poverty to realize the need.

Much of the poverty of women is contingent. It is the direct result of their dependent status within Australia's economy and society generally and the fact that they are not paid an independent income or allowance. If a woman's continued material well-being is the result of her dependent status – and the consequences of abdicating this dependency would be dire poverty – then a discussion of poverty must broaden its perspectives to include some recognition of the economic bondage many women find themselves in. Therefore the following will be as concerned with those women who have no income and who are dependent on others for support, and the various factors which perpetuate this situation, as it will be with the more traditional concerns of the investigators of poverty in Australia.

Many women are forced to remain in domestic situations that they would prefer to leave simply because they have no ready cash and no financial resources to draw upon to enable them to find new accommodation. This is especially the case with women who have dependent children and who therefore must ensure that, before they leave, they have another house or flat to go to. Although emergency relief is paid to women who are totally destitute, the amounts are paltry and they will not be paid *until after the woman has left home*. She cannot obtain money in advance to enable her to leave. The State will spend money to stop women and children sleeping in the streets but it will not be party to encouraging the break-up of families, even *de facto* families. So unless a woman can find free emergency accommodation for herself and her children until she can obtain some money, it will be almost totally impossible for her to leave and she is, in fact, enslaved to a man with the State condoning her enslavement.

Stark confirmation of this judgement has been provided by the stories of many of the women who have sought temporary accommodation at the Elsie Women's Refuge in Sydney.[8] In the first nine months of this refuge's operation more than six hundred women and children spent at least one night there and a substantial number of these had been in exactly the position described above. Until the refuge opened – offering them free accommodation, food and clothing – these women had been imprisoned in homes with husbands whom they wanted to leave. But unless the woman had been able to save a little money or unless the man was so violent that she just waited for him to go to work, picked up her children and ran, escape was very difficult.

What she would have to go through would be something like this: once he had gone to work she would collect her children and as many of their belongings as she could carry and leave home; if she were lucky enough to have somewhere to leave the children and the suitcases she would go into the social welfare offices alone. Otherwise she would have to manage to get herself, children and belongings – often on public transport – into the nearest centre; there she would be interviewed by several people and after a wait of up to eight hours would be given a sum of money; the amount she would receive varies from $10 to more than $60 and, from my experience, appears to be awarded very arbitrarily; she would then have to find accommodation for the night and even if she had received quite a large sum of money much of this would be used immediately in eating in a restaurant or cafeteria and in paying for a hotel room. Many of the women who stayed at Elsie Women's Refuge have described going through this process: the next day they would probably return home, exhausted and embittered at the obstacles put in the way of a woman seeking to make her own life. Thus, when talking about poverty and about poverty amongst women in particular, it is important to take account of this kind of economic bondage.

In 1973–74 the Australian Government spent over $1,944 million under the Social Services Act, an increase of 24 per cent on the previous year. This expenditure was distributed as follows:

Expenditure under Social Services Act, 1973–74[9]

Age Pensions	$1,146,387,000
Invalid Pensions	$226,022,000
Widows' Pensions	$180,957,000
Supporting Mothers' Benefit	$40,586,000
Maternity Allowances	$7,782,000
Child Endowment	$225,392,000
Orphans' Pensions	$458,000
Unemployment and Sickness Benefits	$106,637,000
Rehabilitation Service	$7,078,000
Sheltered Employment Allowances	$1,418,000
Funeral Benefits	$1,578,000
Total	$1,944,295,000

Some of these benefits, such as Child Endowment and Maternity Allowances, are paid to all those eligible regardless of income and these need not be considered here except where they apply as supplementary income for women on low incomes.

Age and invalid pensioners make up the largest group of claimants from the welfare pool and here the majority of the recipients of pensions are women. Although 59 per cent of invalid pensioners are male, 68 per cent of age pensioners are female[10], and since the number of age pensioners is considerably greater, we can see that the total percentage of female pensioners is greater: women constitute 65 per cent of all age and invalid pensioners. (They are of course 100 per cent of all widows' pensioners and those in receipt of the Supporting Mothers' Benefit.)

Number of Age and Invalid Pensioners, 30 June 1974[11]

	Female	Male
Age	706,200	321,400
Invalid	64,700	92,100
Total	770,900	413,500

The Interim Report of the Poverty Commission found that in August 1973 the pension for every pension-receiving group was *below* its austere poverty line.[12] At that time the single Age and Invalid Pension was $5.50 below the poverty line, while a widow with three children received $11.90 less than was required to subsist. Also it was found that half of all single age pensioners and just over a third of all married ones were poor.[13] The Commission reported that of aged single men 36.6 per cent were 'very poor', that is, below the poverty line, while 13.3 per cent were 'rather poor', that is, less than 20 per cent above the poverty line. Thus a total of 49.9 per cent of the men could be described as poor.[14] With the women 31.0 per cent were 'very poor' and 19.8 per cent were 'rather poor', a total of 50.8 per cent.[15]

Pension rates increased three times between October 1973 and May 1975 and at the last increase the rate for single people was $36 per week while married couples received $60. These rates would need to be compared with a new poverty line to see if there has been any absolute improvement in pensioners' financial condition. However it is unlikely that this has occurred and we could not expect it until the final Henderson report is tabled and its recommendations acted upon.

Although poverty appears to be a highly likely consequence of being a pensioner of either sex, the percentage of women totally dependent on their pensions is far greater than of men. At 30 June 1974, 15.85 per cent of female age pensioners had no means at all apart from their pensions whereas this was true of only 5.15 per cent of male age pensioners.[16] And when we recall that there are two and a half times as many female age pensioners, the actual number of aged poor women is substantially greater. The majority of the aged poor is female.

The only survey of the plight of single women age pensioners ever, to my knowledge, carried out, revealed that in 1971 elderly single women were living in conditions of appalling poverty and loneliness, neglected or exploited by relatives.[17] They were even worse off than childless widows of similar age, sometimes suffering malnutrition and physical neglect. The survey found that high rents were the biggest factor in elderly single women's poverty but it also pointed to the relentless loneliness which befalls these women and which many compensated for, often at enormous material cost, by maintaining pets. Some of the case histories cited show the devastating deprivation of these friendless old women:

Age, 78 years; income $19.25 per week (pension and supplementary allowance); expenses, rent $18 a week. No assets. Cared for a blind father for 15 years until his death . . . rent recently raised from $10 to $18 a week. Will not leave small house with garden because of seven-year-old dog . . . he is her best friend.

Age, 76 years; income $19.25, rent $12 a week for room, use of kitchen; food and clothing $6.50. She suffered appendicitis and was admitted to public hospital 18 months ago, transferred to private hospital to recuperate. Is so lonely in her room, and was so happy in the private hospital that she threatened to break her leg to force them to keep her. She fell out of bed every night for a week, so her bed was made up on the floor; she threw herself out of a window on to a concrete path and succeeded in breaking her leg, which secured her a further twelve weeks in the hospital.

Age, 67 years; income $19.25; expenses, $12 a week for rent for one-bedroom house. No bath in house, only a coldwater tap in bathroom, floorboards rotten. Refused to move because of her four cats.[18]

Women in situations such as these probably constitute the worst instances of poverty amongst women. Physical frailty accompanying old age becomes yet another scourge they must endure: it prevents them from having access to those supplementary welfare agencies which do exist, unless the agencies are somehow led to *them*, and where they have neither friends nor family to help them, they are likely to be totally dependent upon their pensions. The few dollars left over after the rent has been paid allow no indulgence in luxuries and, on current prices, would preclude many basic foodstuffs. Thus when a coat becomes so threadbare that it no longer serves its purpose, or a pair of shoes wears paper-thin, the woman in poverty must choose between replacing them and eating that week. If she is fortunate enough to live within walking distance of a second-hand clothing place and if she can find there a garment which fits her and which she can afford, her plight may be less drastic. But for many women, old age is likely to exacerbate their poverty. No longer fit enough to be able to chase up bargains in food or clothing, they must patronize the nearest shop. I have often watched elderly ladies in neon-lit supermarkets, clutching a tin or two under their arms, their myopic eyes unable to focus properly on the prices, searching pitifully amongst well-stocked shelves for a product which is recognizable to them, their eyes resting for a wistful moment on those laden trolleys wheeled past by women for whom each purchase is not a matter of vital calculation.

Many of the non-rent-paying women, that is, those who are living in houses they have either purchased themselves or which they have acquired through marriage, are also likely to be living in some degree of poverty. A woman who owns her house would be expected to be better off since she pays no rent, some rates and taxes can be deferred and paid from her estate and she is in possession of a realizable asset. But unless she rents rooms to boarders a house provides no current income. Her assets may preclude her from receiving a full pension and she could be as poor as a rent-paying woman who receives the full pension. Many old women cling tenaciously to dilapidated and deteriorating homes, often living in only one room, the garden an overgrown jungle, because this constitutes an ever-present reassuring reminder of days past when things were better, a psychological prop against capitulating to the despair of their current deprivation. They *could* sell and use part of the money to buy their way into a retirement village or similar form of housing for the aged – assuming they have had the foresight to put their names on a waiting list, for these are often five or more years long – but many old women resent being forced to do this. Just as many single women pay high rents so they can keep their pets, often the widow will live in poverty in a house she has known for many years rather than risk a major rupture at this stage of her life.

A further group of women who are likely to have to subsist in material poverty are those who head what are referred to as 'fatherless families', the negative description aptly summarizing the situation of the mother who has no husband.* She is removed from dependency on her husband's bread-winning but must now supplicate for State largesse, her entitlement resting solely on the fact of her never having, or having been deprived in some way of a male provider. Thus widows, deserted wives, wives of prisoners and *de facto* wives in each of these categories have been able to receive from the Commonwealth Government a Widows' Pension.

A total of 115,200 women were receiving Widows' Pensions and 26,268 were getting Supporting Mothers' Benefits at 30 June 1974.[19] Women eligible to receive these pensions include widows, divorcees, women whose husbands are in prison or a mental hospital and deserted wives. The maximum amount payable to a woman with one dependent child in May 1975 was $52.50, made up as follows:

Standard rate	$36
Mothers' allowance	$6 (if the mother has custody of at least one child under six or a child who is an invalid; otherwise the allowance is $4)
Children's allowance	$5.50 for each child
Supplementary assistance	$5 (available if the mother pays rent and meets a stringent means test)
	$52.50

Obviously many supporting mothers receive less than this: $2 less if her youngest child is over six, a further $5 less if she is living in her marital home – even if it has not been paid off. A woman trying to rear a growing child on about $45 a week will experience almost insurmountable difficulties: children's clothes become too small with alarming rapidity, our 'free' education system makes continual demands on parents' purses, children demand entertainments which invariably cost money. And a majority of widows are solely dependent on their pensions for income. In June 1974, 52 per cent of Class A widows[20] had no means apart from their pensions, and 63 per cent did not own homes.[21] But until recently the widow with dependent children was the only one who had even a chance of survival. It is only since December 1972 that Class B and C widows have received

* The term 'single-parent family' is now being used more frequently partly in recognition of the fact that many men are 'single parents'.

the standard rate pension ($36 in May 1975); prior to that they received a pittance of about 75 per cent of the standard pension, an amount which must have made eking out an existence a precarious undertaking for even the most frugal woman. But the rationale behind it was clear.

Women's main function in Australia has been defined as child-raising and they are seen as being entitled to support while they carry out this task; if the husband or father fails to provide it, the State will step in. But support from the public purse is neither automatic nor immediate. The Social Services Act, 1947–72 which sets out Widows' Pensions defines a deserted wife as one 'who has been deserted by her husband *without just cause for a period of six months*'.[22] One effect of this definition is to exclude the deserted wife from assistance from the Commonwealth for the first six months of her husband's desertion. During this period she can apply to State welfare agencies for assistance and the amount she will receive will vary, depending on the state where she lives, but will always be less than the Widows' Pension.[23]

As one researcher into State welfare relief found:

The (means) tests ensure that no recipient of State assistance (typically a deserted wife or unmarried mother) is able to rise significantly above the poverty line, even if she is willing to enter the work force. The tests reinforce the feelings of humiliation, utter dependence and hopelessness that often characterize persons driven to seek relief in circumstances of extreme personal distress, by imposing near (or complete) destitution as a condition of assistance. The unstated assumption behind the tests appears to be the notion that the recipient has only herself to blame for her predicament and consequently she must accept as her lot a perpetual state of poverty, with little or no incentive or opportunity to improve her economic position.[24]

All the states require women to have dependent children and to be virtually destitute before they will render assistance. For those who qualify for the Widows' Pension this period of state-sponsored mortification will last six months and then they can transfer to the better-paying and more liberally administered Federal scheme.

Until 14 June 1973 single mothers were completely excluded from the Federal benefits and for them perpetual poverty was their only prospect. Under legislation introduced into the Australian Parliament in 1973 single mothers became eligible from 3 July 1973 for the Supporting Mothers' Benefit which is paid at the same rate as the Widows' Pension, but they still have to endure the first six months after their child's birth under the parsimonious patronage of the states.*

While the Commonwealth benefits are, in comparison to those proferred by the states, rather more generous financially, they are by no means a step towards relieving women from the paternalism which their dependency status entails. To obtain these benefits and pensions, women have to sign maintenance orders against their husbands or the child's father and they will not receive payment if they refuse to do this. They are thereby forced to retain a relationship with that man and to remain financially dependent upon him, the only difference being that the Government becomes an intermediary and supplements the amount if the husband cannot afford the full pension payment.

A censorious and oppressive moralism pervades the administration of the Commonwealth scheme, the effect of which is to turn the Government into the most rigidly authoritarian of husband/providers. Under the Social Services Act an applicant is not to receive the pension '(a) unless she is of good character; (b) if she is not deserving of a pension; or, (c) if she directly or indirectly deprived herself of property or income in order to qualify for a pension.'[25] The first two conditions in particular are obviously open to abuse, for they require that the administering officer adopt a judgemental attitude on factors other than the applicant's basic situation of having lost her husband. If a recipient of a Widows' Pension gives birth to a child after the death of the man with whom she was living, and the child's father was not that man, that child is ineligible for benefits.[26]

Further, the Government has an evident horror of being cuckolded; it requires the undying sexual fidelity of the women it is supporting. One of the strongest complaints of single mother claimants of welfare has been the practice of welfare officers searching their houses for evidence of a man's presence; if such evidence is discovered welfare payments are stopped.[27] The Commonwealth Minister for Social Security gave no assurances that this practice would stop when single mothers began to receive the Widows' Pension, and recent protests by single mothers indicate that such snooping is still practised. Indeed it can be surmised that this practice will be retained as a political defence against those critics who abhor what they see as the Government condoning immorality.[28]

* In his policy speech before the 1974 elections, the Minister for Social Security announced that he intended to amend this to provide for single mothers to start receiving the pension from the date of birth of the child.

The morality of forcing women into what is a situation of virtual prostitution by demanding that a man with whom they may have formed only a temporary alliance support them does not seem to perturb the Government, yet this is the effect of the practice of stopping welfare payments if it is decided (often on very meagre evidence) that a single mother or a deserted wife is living with a man. The Government demands that that man pay for the woman's sexual favours by undertaking to support her and her child(ren). It is an expensive proposition for any man and one which few would willingly accept. Thus a single mother receiving a pension is forced to engage in clandestine affairs, ever fearful of that early-morning knock on the door, to embark upon a forced-choice marriage, or else to live in nun-like chastity. The social security agencies of this country exact a merciless penance from women who have, willingly or otherwise, borne a child out of wedlock or have been deserted by their children's father.

Three other groups of women who are likely to be poor but the extent of whose poverty we know very little of are Aboriginal women, derelict or inebriate women and women with physical disabilities of some sort. All of these women are victims of race or circumstance in such a way as to be automatically precluded from obtaining the financial support of men and therefore, on the argument advanced here, can be said to be almost by definition in poverty.

According to the ACOSS submission to the Poverty Commission:

. . . perhaps nowhere can be found more horrifying examples of deep poverty than among Aborigine women. They are discarded by the community for not being the right colour, the right sex – lacking in language, in education, in training, in available or accessible job opportunities, ill-prepared to function in a white society, unable to get into the white service systems, unreached by birth control methods, producing children many of whom are destined for early death and the rest to live a life of poverty. If she does have the support of a husband it is 90 per cent sure that he will be a minimum wage earner.[29]

White men in this country have almost always treated black women as whores, as women to have sex with (and maybe leave with half-caste babies) but not as women to marry. So black women have, almost by definition, less chance of finding a white male protector than white women. While they may marry black men of course, as the ACOSS submission points out, black men are rarely likely to be earning more than the minimum wage themselves, and are subject to all the vagaries of the unskilled job market, and if they have more than one or two children are likely to be below the poverty line themselves.

The only way a black woman can find temporary escape from poverty is to follow the vocation which white society has said is all she's good for and to prostitute herself. But this will only be possible while she is young and still able to attract white men. Within a comparatively short time the ravages of alcohol and disease are likely to restrict her ability to earn in this way. So for black women the chances of avoiding poverty are even more difficult than for white women. The sexist stereotypes which are applied to all women in Australia clamp the lives of black women more firmly in one direction than is the case with white women. The stereotypes work as polar opposites, either a woman is a madonna figure or she is a whore and, as we have seen, women are seen as being entitled to income only for mothering. If a woman is precluded from this, as black women have been since white colonization of this country, she is automatically cast as a whore and will probably have to become one in order to survive. As a whore she receives money from men but she is not guaranteed an income and is even more dependent upon men than the mother-woman is.

It is impossible to determine just how many homeless women there are in Australia although their numbers are probably surprisingly high. Women can be found sleeping in parks and railway stations in Sydney, and a social worker from the NSW Department of Health informed me that there are dozens of women who are either temporarily or permanently homeless. As with examining women's poverty in general, it is necessary to consider the nexus of sex discrimination and the assumptions which underlie it when considering homeless women. Permanently homeless women are almost by definition in poverty. They are likely to be inebriates or women who through some misfortune have been separated from their families and have been unable to gather together the necessary resources for a new start. (There is a small and enterprising group of homeless women in Sydney who do not fall into these categories, who would be best described as gypsies and who have either through fate or choice found themselves homeless but who have made this state a positive lifestyle. They are unlikely to have much money but they are rarely destitute because they know the city and its resources well and are always able to find food, clothing and shelter without having to prostitute themselves. Bea Miles, usually described as Sydney's famous 'eccentric', was such a woman but she is by no means a sole example.)

Many women would like to become temporarily homeless while they look for alternatives to unsatisfactory present living situations but are deterred, even prevented, from leaving the 'homes' they are forced to share with brutal and violent husbands because of the virtual absence of emergency shelters for women in Australian cities. In New South Wales a survey of such temporary accommodation found that in October 1973 ' . . . there appear to be only *four* hostels for destitute women, and together these can accommodate approximately *73 women and 75 children*, whereas for destitute males there are *seven* hostels providing accommodation for approximately 1,379 men.'[30] Since then Elsie Women's Refuge has opened in Sydney and it rarely has fewer than thirty women and children there each night and is forced to turn away many others for lack of space. But the experience of the refuge has demonstrated very clearly that the absence of such shelters has prevented many women from leaving home, and that once such a temporary shelter is available to them it is possible for them to contemplate a clear alternative to their current situation. The number of temporarily homeless women will rise sharply as more refuges open in capital cities round Australia. Over 90 per cent of the women who have sought refuge at Elsie have been totally destitute when they arrived, most bringing only a few clothes with them. Their stories have borne out the contentions of this chapter about the poverty of women. The enormous difficulty these women have in trying to transfer from financial dependence on their husbands to State support reinforces the argument that the State would prefer the poverty of women to remain within 'the family', and thereby hidden, rather than have it exposed publicly by adding to the numbers already receiving social security pensions.

The ACOSS evidence found that 'there is little or no help' for inebriate women.[31] The few night shelters will not take them, arguing that they are dirty, uncontrollable and a nuisance to the other women. Institutional confinement is possible only on condition that the women agree to undergo treatment. Their only other option is a night in the cells and a short gaol sentence. Social prejudice against drunken women is so great that it impedes recognizing it as a problem when it does occur and thereby prevents special provision being made for short-term shelter for inebriate women.

A further social assumption which has prevented more shelters being made available for women is the sexist view, held by many police and some social workers, that 'any woman can get herself a bed for the night'. The hypocrisy of this attitude is manifold. Lack of alternatives often ensures that women have to prostitute themselves in return for a bed, but it is the women, not the men, who are then charged with soliciting. Many social workers are quick to condemn the morality (or what they see as the lack of it) of deserted wives or single mothers who move from one *de facto* relationship straight into another. What these critics do not seem to consider is that given women's economic dependency and the lack of emergency accommodation and the difficulties of getting social security relief quickly, many women have no alternative. If they can get housing and support from a man who promises to treat them better than the previous one this is a more attractive proposition than to face destitution and the probable loss of their children to State welfare custody.

In a culture which regards women as objects of sexual gratification – and much of our advertising attests to this being a pervasive feature of Australian society – then it is fairly easy for any woman to sell her body in return for money or material support. Many marriages are contracted on this basis: it is mainly when the woman has absolutely no resources beyond her sex that the crude realities of the sexual barter are most apparent. They are also thrown into sharp relief with those women who are unable to obtain male protectorship.

Black women and inebriate women have already been mentioned; a further group who are totally ignored by society are women with some kind of physical disability. A surprisingly large number of women seeking refuge at Elsie have been women, often as young as sixteen, who have been abandoned by their parents and who are totally unable to attract men because of a disability which lessens their attractiveness. These women are serving life-sentences of poverty and neglect. Their only hope is to find sympathetic women companions or supporters. They have to exist on invalid pensions; often they are physically incapable of caring for themselves and rarely have an alternative to an institutional life.

The refusal of the State to pay women pensions if they are living in *de facto* relationships forces women into prostitution, even if this is glossed over with the label 'common-law marriage'. The total neglect of women who are unable – even if they wanted – to prostitute themselves is evidence of the view the State has of women and poverty.

The State reflects and reinforces the ubiquitous notion that woman's dependence on a male bread-winner is the 'natural' order of things and that he who pays ought to be able to determine the lifestyle, and hence define the limits of freedom, of the recipient of this protection.

The majority of adult women in Australia spend at least ten years of their lives as dependent housewives – and for many women this is their entire life's destiny – and this means that their economic well-being is totally contingent on whatever amount their husbands choose to pay them as 'housekeeping money'. There is no minimum amount, nor even a fixed proportion of the husband's income, which a woman can legally expect to receive in return for her services of keeping house, cooking meals, rearing children, shopping, washing and doing the innumerable other tasks which are the usual lot of the housewife. The determination of the female wage at 54 per cent of the male rate at the beginning of this century – which contained the assumption that since women did not have to support families they needed smaller incomes – could perhaps be said to have implied that married men were expected to spend 46 per cent of their wages on the extra rent, food, clothing etc. involved in maintaining a family. A certain proportion of this perhaps was designed to be given to the wife for her personal disposal. But Justice Higgins did not specify this when awarding the Harvester judgement, which outlined the basic wage concept, and it has never been publicly demanded of men.

The wife whose husband considers it a mark of his own social standing that his wife be expensively dressed, turn on exotic parties and embellish his house with costly *objets d'art* but who fails to provide her with cash which she may spend in whatever way she pleases is not rich. Even if her husband is generous and provides her with unlimited cash and credit facilities, she is not economically independent. She may live in a gilded cage but it is a cage nevertheless, and she may be less free economically than the female factory worker who, from her meagre wages, can retain a proportion to dispose of at her whim. Very few women amass money they have earned themselves. Most rich women are rich because they have inherited money which their husbands or fathers earned, or they have been made nominal owners of property and other assets in order to reduce the husband's tax liabilities. Even though many women do of course reap the benefits of their ruling class husbands' or fathers' exploitation of the labour force, very few are actually engaged in that process. While women who hold paid jobs outside the home can be classified in terms of a classical Marxist class analysis, this framework does not fit so easily the situation of women who have no paid employment.

The economic dependency of all wives who do not have their own incomes – and women who have these without engaging in paid work outside the home are rare – reduces them to a common economic status. There is no relationship between the actual work done by a housewife and her husband's occupation; even when a woman has every labour-saving device at her disposal, and is therefore presumably married to a wealthy man, the actual nature of the work is unaltered. It remains a service job which is unpaid. If a machine or a paid domestic does much of the work for her she may gain extra time, but unless she uses this time to earn an income of her own, her dependent status is unaltered. Thus the wife of the managing director of a multi-national corporation is in the same position of economic dependency as the wife of a factory worker.

The *social* status of the two women is of course very different but their objective economic position is the same and this is what the traditional Marxist analysis, in its failure to recognize household work as productive labour, has neglected to take into account. Thus while it might be true in a propagandist sense to maintain that the wives of ruling class men are collaborators with that class, and that they have access to the wealth accumulated by their husbands' exploitation of other workers, such a statement is not an accurate representation of the economic power and independence of these women. It is necessary to analyse the productive labour of housewives separately and *then* to assess the class position of women who are at present assigned putative class on the basis of their husbands' positions.

Women in Australia who are full-time housewives are engaged in two kinds of productive labour. They perform the socially necessary work of cooking, cleaning, washing etc. which are essential to maintaining the physical and emotional comfort of a household. The second form of productive labour which the majority of housewives perform is that of reproduction. The woman who bears children is engaged, as the Italian Marxist-feminist Mariarosa Dalla Costa points out, in the socially vital task of reproducing the labour force:

Woman . . . has been isolated in the home, forced to carry out work that is considered unskilled, the work of giving birth to, raising, disciplining, and servicing the worker for production. Her role in the cycle of social production remained invisible because only the product of her labour, *the labourer*, was visible there. She herself was trapped within pre-capitalist working conditions and never paid a wage.[32]

In fact, in Australia, this is the only part of the housewife's work which is acknowledged and rewarded, albeit parsimoniously, in monetary terms. All mothers receive a maternity allowance at the birth of each child, and child endowment is paid for each child until at least the age of sixteen, or twenty-one if the child remains a dependent student. But these payments are minute in size and have declined enormously in value since they were first introduced. And so while token acknowledgement of women's mothering role exists, it can hardly be said to constitute a just payment for the labour involved.

Inasmuch as the State does not recognize a woman's right to an independent income it assists in the perpetuation of this dependency. The allowances mentioned above are payments for *mothering* or are intended, as with child endowment, to be spent on the child's welfare. There is no provision at all for women under sixty to be paid allowances of any kind which are intended purely and simply for their *own* life's maintenance. For instance, a housewife who seeks work in the paid labour force but who is unable to find a job can register for work but if her husband is working and earning more than a pittance she is not entitled to unemployment benefits. An unemployed husband whose wife works is also in theory denied this benefit. In fact the incomes of most women are so low that the unemployed husband would usually collect at least a few dollars so that he would rarely be totally dependent on his wife. In any case it is likely that the entire salary of the wife (because it is generally lower) would be needed to house and feed the family and it is therefore unlikely that she would have any money left for herself. The main point however is that employment services discriminate against women in their definition of unemployment and in the manner in which they fail to recognize the differing needs of male and female workers.

There is evidence to show that even more married women than presently work would take jobs if these were available and if suitable child-care facilities existed. A government publication on female unemployment concedes that during most of the post-war period the incidence of unemployment in Australia has been considerably higher among women than among men: 'In 1969, for example, female unemployment averaged 1.5 per cent of the total female labour force while male unemployed averaged 1.0 per cent of the male labour force.'[33] A survey conducted in 1969 by the (then) Department of Labour and National Service found that the incidence of female unemployment in four country industrial cities was very high due to a shortage of jobs appropriate to the skills possessed by women in those areas and because fewer jobs for women existed in these towns.[34]

But, as Steinke points out[35], unemployment amongst married women is likely to be much greater than the official surveys show since they take as their criteria 'persons who when registering with the Commonwealth Employment Service claimed that they were not employed and were seeking regular full-time work'.[36] Many married women who are searching for jobs do not bother registering with the Commonwealth Bureau since, if their husbands are working, they are not entitled to unemployment benefits and their chances of finding a job via this avenue are no greater than pursuing the usual routes of answering newspaper advertisements and applying to local firms.

In any case, several surveys have shown that married women, especially those with young children, seek part-time work[37] and such women are not defined as being unemployed. If 'unemployed' was defined to mean 'absence of any income' then the percentage of Australian women falling into this category would increase dramatically. In February 1973, 80.6 per cent of women working outside the home had part-time employment; and four-fifths of all part-time workers are women.[38] The lack of enough part-time jobs prevents many more women from engaging in paid employment. A further deterrent to married women working is the absence of suitable, cheap child-care facilities and there is evidence that this prevents many women who would like to from taking jobs.[39] A small survey conducted in a Sydney suburb by the Women's Electoral Lobby in late 1973 found that 33.9 per cent of married women interviewed would take jobs if they could find suitable child-care facilities.[40] A Morgan Gallup Poll conducted in late 1973 found that 32 per cent of women interviewed said they would go out to work if there was a convenient day care centre available.[41] Thus it is probably impossible to begin to estimate the numbers of women who would like to work, or feel they need (for whatever reason) to work, but who are unable to find either suitable jobs and/or child-minding facilities and who do not register with the Commonwealth Employment Service. The pressures and conflicts facing married women who take jobs, or who are seeking them, are complex, but it is clear that the need for money is one of the major motivating factors. Often a woman will rationalize her working to what she perceives as a critical society by saying that her family needs the money. This is usually quite true but an important part of earning money for her family is also that it provides the woman herself with at least a few dollars which she can spend on herself, which she does not have to account for to her husband or to anyone.

Almost every survey has shown 'financial reasons' to account for the majority of women returning to work. For instance, a 1971 survey on the responsibilities of working women conducted by the Department of Labour and National Service for its Report for the United Nations Commission on the Status of Women found the following reasons:[42]   (See Table overleaf)

Reasons for Married Women Returning to Work

	Main choice %	Multiple choice %
Money to support self/family	46	59
Children's education expenses	5	13
Money for extras	16	38
Enjoyment of working	8	35
To avoid boredom	7	31
To meet and be with people	1	38
To use skills and abilities	13	53
Other	4	18

It cannot be assumed, however, that a paid job will necessarily elevate a woman from poverty nor alleviate her dependent status. Many single, childless women who live outside families have difficulty in supporting themselves due to a combination of low wages and high rents. For married women to be economically independent, the money they earn from their job must be sufficient to support themselves – and their children if they have any – independently of their husband's income. This does not mean that in practice the husband's and wife's incomes will not be pooled in most families, but unless a woman is able to support herself on her own earnings the possibility of her leaving an unsatisfactory marriage or *de facto* relationship and being able to survive materially does not exist; and although she may have some money of her own to spend as she likes, her economic bondage has not been completely undermined.

In the past the refusal of the Arbitration Court to award women an equal minimum wage with men has meant that hordes of women working in unskilled jobs earn meagre incomes which would be insufficient to support themselves. The 1974 National Wage decision awarded women an equal minimum wage to be phased in over two years and this will mean an uplifting of women's wages. The possibility of women receiving a living wage now exists but we will have to wait to see whether this will be the consequence of the award. It is quite likely that more women than men will never rise above the stated minimum because men are more likely to have loadings and margins added to their pay and they are also more likely to supplement their incomes with overtime. Often they do this to raise their family income and were women receiving living wages it would not be necessary.

At present, and in the past, the wages the majority of working women receive have not been adequate for self support let alone to support children as well. In February 1975 the prescribed average minimum weekly wage, excluding overtime, paid to adult females in industry was $92.31 whereas the comparable wage for men was $104.23.[43] These are *average* earnings for the whole of Australia and provide only a rough indication of the actual earnings of many women in particular jobs under varying state awards. Many women would earn more than $92.31 but more would earn less. For instance at 30 June 1974 in New South Wales, the state where the cost of living is highest, an adult female working in a biscuit-making factory received $72 per week, while a furniture machinist got only $62 and most jobs in the textile industry paid wages of between $63 and $67.[44]

Although most adult female jobs pay minimum wages of over $70 a week there are dozens of different jobs which pay less. The woman who earns this amount would, after tax has been deducted, receive about the same amount as a widow or single mother with two children and, as has already been argued, this is barely sufficient to support three people, particularly in Melbourne and Sydney. (When assessing the real value of women's wages we have to take into account whether they are sufficient to maintain herself and her children, since in practice women retain responsibility for their children if a marriage breaks up. In theory the woman's wages should be supplemented with maintenance payments from her husband but a woman cannot guarantee that these payments will be forthcoming. If we are discussing the economic possibilities of women becoming independent our calculations must be based on her guaranteed income for this is the minimum amount with which she will have to try to manage.)

Thus being in paid employment does not of itself guarantee escape from poverty nor can it ensure economic independence. For the woman deprived of educational and occupational skills and forced to take a low-paying factory or service job the 'reward' is forty hours of virtual slavery, for her labour will not allow her a sufficient income to survive independently of the economic support of some other agency.

The full extent of poverty amongst women has never been investigated. Those studies which have examined poverty in Australia have, directly or indirectly, indicated that it does exist on a massive scale amongst certain groups of women. But what has to be acknowledged is that the institutionalized arrangements which exist ostensibly to alleviate it do in fact perpetuate it by ensuring that women will remain as supplicants to the State welfare system and will be forced to live on or close to the poverty line. The present economic and cultural system decrees that a woman must obtain a male protector/provider to avoid the probability of destitution. In practice this means that women are classified by whether or not they are worthy of such protection and support and the usual criteria applied are those of sexual attractiveness and maternal status.

Mothers are automatically seen as deserving protection while non-mothers are seen as suspect. Mothers who do not have husbands – for whatever reason – are in a half-way category. Their maternal status is praised, their inability to attract or to keep a man is regarded as cause for suspicion and they are awarded sufficient money to ward off starvation but not enough for them to enjoy economic security. Unless all women, whether they are mothers or not, married or single, are accorded both in theory and practice the right to economic independence – and not depressed wages, allowances for child-raising or trifling rewards for having survived to the age of sixty – then poverty will continue to be a normal condition, or a constantly threatening possibility, in the lives of vast numbers of Australian women.[45]

NOTES

1. Adapted from Table 43 in *Facts and Figures*, Women and Work, no. 11, Women's Bureau, Department of Labour, Melbourne, September 1973, p. 28.
2. Ronald Henderson, Alison Harcourt and R. J. A. Harper, *People in Poverty: A Melbourne Survey*, Cheshire, Melbourne, 1970, p. 1.
3. ibid.
4. *Poverty: The ACOSS Evidence*, Australian Council of Social Service, Sydney, 1973, p. 317.
5. ibid.
6. *Poverty in Australia*, Interim Report of the Australian Government's Commission into Poverty, Australian Government Publishing Service, Canberra, March 1974, p. 21.
'The income unit comprises:
* An adult income unit head, spouse (if head married) and dependent children for whom the head or spouse is responsible. A dependent child is defined as a person not married and either less than 15, or 15–20 and still engaged in full-time secondary schooling. An adult is a person 21 and over, or a person 15–20 who is at present married and/or is responsible for a dependent child (e.g. an 18-year-old single mother and child is an adult income unit).

OR

* An independent juvenile, who is a person 15–20, not engaged in full-time schooling, not at present married and not responsible for a dependent child. However, a full-time *tertiary* student is always defined as an independent juvenile even though the person may be partly or wholly financially dependent on his or her parents.

Thus, a household consisting of a man and wife (both working), two school children, an unemployed 28-year-old son, an 18-year-old daughter attending university full-time and an aged mother, comprises four income units:

* husband, wife and two school children
* unemployed son
* university daughter
* aged mother'

7. ibid., p. 11.

8. Elsie Women's Refuge was opened as a women's shelter in Glebe, Sydney on 16 March, 1974 by a group of women from the Women's Movement. It is two small houses which are open to any woman in need and which will offer free temporary accommodation to women and their children. It is the first of several proposed women's refuges, places which are non-institutionalized and which will take women in without requiring forms to be filled out or any other bureaucratic rigmarole. Women can leave their children there during the day while they go to arrange their social security allowances, look for somewhere to live or seek legal advice.

9. Department of Social Security, *Second Annual Report of the Director-General, 1973–74*, Australian Government Publishing Service, Canberra, 1974, p. 128.

10. ibid., pp. 8, 10.

11. ibid., pp. 149–50.

12. *Poverty in Australia*, op. cit., p. 15.

13. ibid., p. 9.

14. ibid.

15. ibid.

16. Department of Social Security, *Second Annual Report . . .* , p. 149.

17. *A Personal Enquiry into the Poverty of the Older Single Woman*, The Executive Officer, Council of Social Service of WA (Inc.), December, 1971. The study examined the living conditions of single women aged 50 and over whose incomes were less than $50 per week.

18. ibid., pp. 7–8.

19. Department of Social Security, *Second Annual Report . . .* , pp. 151, 154.

20. The three types of Widows' Pensions are as follows:

CLASS A: A widow who has the custody, care and control of one or more eligible children under the age of 16, or eligible student child.

CLASS B: A widow who has no eligible children under 16 years of age or eligible student children and who is not less than 50 years of age, or who, after having attained the age of 45 years, ceases to receive the Class 'A' pension because she is no longer caring for a child.

CLASS C: A widow who is under 50 years of age, has no children in her care but is in necessitous circumstances within the twenty-six weeks after the death of her husband. She receives a pension for not more than twenty-six weeks. If the widow is pregnant this time may be extended until after the child's birth. She may then become eligible for the Class 'A' pension.

21. Department of Social Security, *Second Annual Report* . . . , p. 151.

22. Ronald Sackville, 'Social Welfare For Fatherless Families in Australia: Some Legal Issues', Part I, *Australian Law Journal*, December 1972, p. 611.

23. The allowances paid to a woman with one child in April 1972 were as follows: NSW – $25.50; Victoria – $26.00; Qld – $27.75; SA – $27.75; WA – $27.75; Tasmania – $27.75, ibid., Part II, *Australian Law Journal*, January 1973, p. 10.

24. ibid., Part II, p. 14.

25. Section 62(1).

26. Section 59(1).

27. This practice is referred to by Departmental Officers as 'bed-sniffing'.

28. When the single mothers' pension was introduced it was denounced by many people. One clergyman claimed that it made 'promiscuity a paying proposition' while Dr Clair Isbister told the 26th Biennial Conference of the Australian Council of Catholic Women that girls were having babies as a source of income: 'You and I are paying for this, yet married women accepting their responsibilities and making homes for their families cannot receive this allowance.' Reported in the *Australian*, 19 September 1973.

29. *Poverty: The ACOSS Evidence*, op. cit., p. 316.

30. Dorothy Smith and Betty Harding, 'Report of a Survey carried out to prove the needs of women for Hostels and Rehabilitation Centres', roneoed, Sydney, October 1973.

31. *Poverty: The ACOSS Evidence*, op. cit., p. 317.

32. Mariarosa Dalla Costa, *Women and the Subversion of the Community*, Falling Wall Press, London, 1972, p. 26.

33. *Female Unemployment in Four Urban Centres*, Labour Market Studies no. 3, Department of Labour and National Service, Melbourne, 1970, p. 1.

34. ibid.

35. John C. Steinke, 'Some Problems in the Measurement of Unemployment', *Journal of Industrial Relations*, March 1969.

36. *Female Unemployment in Four Urban Centres*, op. cit., p. 2.

37. e.g. Business and Professional Women's Club of Sydney, *Pilot Study of Married Women in the Work Force with Children Under Eighteen*, Sydney, July 1968.

38. *Facts and Figures*, Women and Work Series no. 11, Women's Bureau, Department of Labour, Melbourne, September 1973, p. 22.

39. L. A. Cox, 'Review of Current Research on Children of Working Parents', Address to 43rd ANZAAS Congress, Psychology Section, Brisbane, 25 May 1971, p. 22.

40. Reported in NSW Women's Electoral Lobby Newsletter no. 18, January 1974, pp. 17–18.

41. Morgan Gallup Poll, *Findings No. 26 and 27*, November 1973.

42. *Report for United Nations Commission on the Status of Women on Family Responsibilities of Working Women*, Department of Labour and National Service, Melbourne, 1971, p. 4. The Business and Professional Women's Club *Pilot Study* found: '70% returned to work mainly for financial reasons. Of the remaining 30%, nearly half expressed boredom and wanted an outside interest. Others thought it a waste not to use their training . . . ' ibid., p. 5.

43. *Wage Rates and Earnings, February 1975*, Australian Bureau of Statistics, Canberra, 1975, pp. 12, 14.

44. *Award Rates of Pay and Prescribed Hours of Work, Adult Males and Adult Females, State Capital Cities, 30 June 1974*, Australian Bureau of Statistics, Canberra, 1975, pp. 11–12.

45. The statistical information and references in this chapter have not been updated since 1975. However, in spite of the alterations in the social welfare system since then, the argument presented here remains all too true.

CHAPTER

SIX

THE FAMILY OF WOMAN

A young woman becoming a wife should think of her new state not as one that is to make her happy but as one in which she is to make her husband happy. Her own happiness will be a by-product of that determination, and will be assured in no other way . . . The good wife realizes that in becoming a wife she contracts to forget self and put her husband's happiness above her own wishes and desires . . . In the marriage contract she handed over the right to her body for the actions of marriage; she does not try to take that back again. She contracted to make a home for her husband in whatever place his work might call him; she does not proclaim any spurious independence in that regard . . . In dress she tries to please, even in the privacy of the home; in speech she encourages, comforts and shares her husband's interests; in her household tasks she tries to be perfect that he may think of no place as more pleasant than his home.

Catholic Weekly, 26 February 1953

The extreme differentiation of the sexes in Australia frequently puts the female child, like her mother before her, in the position of moral censor. This even reflects itself in child play where it is invariably the little sister who runs and 'tells' about the misdemeanours of her brothers, whose main feeling is not of guilt but the pragmatic hope that they can 'get away with it'.

RONALD CONWAY, *The Great Australian Stupor*, 1971

Australian culture ignores women except in its taken-for-granted assumption that they are all safely enshrined within families as wives and mothers. And unless women have male protectors and providers in the form of a husband or some other man who is legally obliged to support them and their children, they will be very lucky to escape at least periodic, if not perpetual poverty. These two factors alone provide compelling reason for women to want to marry and to secure for themselves both the status and the economic security which is necessary to survive physically and psychologically in a country like Australia. Women's cultural impotence and their economic dependence are a twin-pronged manacle which forces them into families and ensures that while they remain within them they conform to quite rigidly defined roles. Conformity to these roles is the main insurance most women have against exclusion, poverty and neglect.

It could similarly be said that men, too, are forced into marriage – if only to accommodate women's urgent need for a partner. It is probably indisputable that most men *want* to marry – although the persistence of the cultural stereotype of the gay bachelor not only suggests that there is a high-status alternative to marriage for men, but also that many men feel that they have been coerced into marriage and that in marrying they have surrendered some of their freedom. And it is true that many women resort to desperate and distasteful measures in order to ensure that they will marry: many do attempt to literally ensnare a mate. There are a variety of measures that a skilled seductress can employ although the simplest and probably most commonly used method is to become pregnant. The man faced with the inevitability of supporting a child for the next sixteen years might just as well marry the woman – and thereby be able to claim the child as his legitimate progeny – and accumulate the benefits of marriage. For most people it does not really matter whom one marries, especially in the case of men for whom the idea of romantic love is less important than the assurances of the domestic services automatically guaranteed by the marriage contract.

Just over 20 per cent of all brides are pregnant at the time of marriage although this figure increases markedly the younger the bride: two out of three brides aged under seventeen, and one quarter of brides aged nineteen are pregnant when they marry.[1] Not all such marriages entail the coercion suggested by the phrase 'shot-gun' marriage but a pregnancy can be one means of dragging an otherwise reluctant man to a marriage ceremony. *Any* measure used by a woman to secure a marriage vow from a less than willing man inevitably degrades the woman who has forsaken her pride and her independence in her quest to find a provider. But Australian women have never been encouraged to have high self-esteem or permitted to be truly independent. Their sheer need to have a husband, legal or *de facto*, is merely one indication of this, and explains why some women feel compelled to get one – at whatever cost to their pride.

For men, the need is not so great. Whereas the status of marriage is valuable for a man, it is *vital* for women, and the cultural importance attached to it in Australia (and some other European countries) is reflected in the titular forms applied to men and women. All men are addressed as Mr regardless of their marital status whereas there is a clear and rigidly enforced distinction between Miss and Mrs.

In some European countries all mature women are accorded the same title. For example, in France all adult women are addressed as Madame, but in Australia the adult single woman is still burdened with the girlish appellation, Miss. Married women themselves often proudly perpetuate this status distinction: the young bride's loud insistence on being called Mrs – to ensure that everyone acknowledges her newly acquired status – is an illustration of the importance attached to this title, one that is as important as being able to flash a gold-ringed left hand. There has been mighty resistance – much of it from women themselves – to feminists' efforts to have the status-neutral term Ms replace Miss and Mrs. (Not all the resistance has been from married women: those early feminists who fought for the right to remain single and still have status in Australian society determinedly cling to Miss, and although we can admire their pride and valour, their efforts have done little to erode the still existent status distinction that accompanies these two forms of address for women.)

It is generally assumed that men are married but rarely is this status relevant to their occupation or recreational activities. A few occupations, usually senior executive positions in national or multi-national corporations where the job includes social as well as business activities, insist that men are married – and often interview the wives of prospective employees. But this is comparatively rare. Men have automatic status – as men. They retain their names and their class in marriage (which is why middle-class parents oppose their daughters marrying working-class men while working-class parents will often welcome their daughter marrying a middle-class man) whereas it is customary – although not legally obligatory – for women to assume their husband's family name upon marriage.

Nor do men need marriage for financial security; indeed they will generally be better off if they remain single. Men's salaries are the same regardless of their marital status and although married men can be taxed at a slightly lower rate and can claim deductions for dependent spouse and children, these compensations are not significant enough to offset the financial responsibility entailed in supporting a family. The desire to retain all of his income for his own disposal may in fact deter a man from marrying at least until his middle twenties, so that he can enjoy the lifestyle that his higher income confers before grudgingly 'settling down'. By contrast, even women who have paid jobs can be in poverty, as Chapter Five pointed out. The Australian economy perpetuates a wage structure which is geared to family needs and is based on sexist assumptions about these needs: it assumes that men are breadwinners and has always paid men more, even when they have done exactly the same work as women. The 1974 National Wage Case determined that an equal minimum wage for women be introduced by mid-1975. The effects of this judgement have yet to be felt but one possible outcome is that, now that female labour is no longer cheaper, employers may prefer to hire men. Equal pay might well result in unemployment for women thus indicating that basic sexist assumptions and prejudices are a long way from having been undermined.

Men need marriage in other respects: the domestic and sexual services provided by their wives give a degree of security and continuity to their lives which they lack as single men. They also gain the emotional security of a close relationship with another person, as well as the feelings of pride and even aggrandizement associated with fathering and supporting children. Families provide an entire little world in which the man is the legally acknowledged boss; and this can be a powerful compensation for the man who has a menial or boring job, especially one where he is continually forced to obey other people's orders. At home he is king and his dependent wife and children accord him love, honour and obedience. Or, at least, that is how it is supposed to be. In the ideal family. Within this ideal, men's and women's needs are supposed to dovetail: the 'natural' differences are supposed to complement each other in a perfectly conceived symmetry of needs and fulfilment. This grand design is sanctified by religion, endorsed by the State, taught as obligatory in the schools and clumsily emulated by the majority of people.

But like any ideal, it has been so mythologized and romanticized that its actual purposes have been obscured. According to the romantic myths, marriage and family enable the fusion of male and female, a fusion whose accomplishment and aim are the reproduction of the human race. What the myths do not elucidate are other aspects of that fusion. Women gain in status and acquire economic security while the man's reward for conferring these is an increase in his personal power: he is able to perpetuate himself and his name by producing children, and his financial support of his wife enables him to exact whatever he wishes from her. The rather cruder realities of this barter are disguised by the myths of marriage which are only able to extol marriage and family in this romantic way because they ignore the elements of power involved in male/female relationships. They assume, or pretend, that this fusion is based on equality of needs and they gloss over the power of the husband and the dependency of the wife and the far from romantic consequences attendant upon such an unequal union.

Marriage for most women is not a matter of choice but a desperate necessity – their only means of survival. This absence of choice is also disguised by the romantic myths of marriage, myths which are so persuasively propagated that each generation of gullible girls grows up believing that the best thing they can do with their lives is devote them to marriage and motherhood, and that following this vocation will bestow its own rewards of satisfaction and happiness.

The power of these myths is so great that they can obliterate from the consciousness of a young girl's mind the cautionary warnings which could be served by her own observations of marriage which run contrary to the myths. She may be aware of, and even have witnessed, husbands beating or raping their wives, husbands depriving their families of sufficient money for food and other necessities, husbands deserting their families. She will almost certainly know of marital relationships where bitterness, resentment and mutual hostility have replaced affection. She will know of families which are more like battle-grounds than the tender unions of love and respect described by the myths. Yet seldom does such knowledge impinge sufficiently upon a girl's consciousness to make her resolve to avoid marriage: the myths successfully convince her that such instances are rare, that they are the fault of the individuals concerned – rather than of the structure of the unequal union – and, most importantly to an impressionable and anxious mind: *that it can never happen to her*. And so girls go on to repeat the experiences of their mothers or of other women whose disastrous or miserable marriages they have witnessed.

Even where a girl manages to avoid succumbing to the romantic myths, her alternatives are few for, as already pointed out, women in Australia have never been encouraged to acquire the necessary pre-requisites for an independent existence. Without the transitory consolation of such romantic expectations a girl can only confront the starkness of her situation: there is an absence of real choice for women and it is this which makes women's need for marriage and family so different from men's.

Once in a marriage both partners can suffer – and sometimes the man may suffer more. To express her resentment and frustration at her overall situation of impotence, an unhappy woman may dredge up whatever subversive weapons she can find to take what is inevitably a petty retaliation. A woman who resorts to constant nagging, to refusing to have sexual intercourse, to neglecting the housework or the care of her children will not, by these means, remedy or escape from her cultural prison. Her revenge is ignoble because it can only create guilt and self-hatred in herself – and can in no way alter the structural iniquities of her situation. Such measures can usually only be taken against a meek and acquiescent husband – for a brutal or domineering man can simply terrorize his wife into conformity to his will – and are thus directed against an individual rather than the institution. Their main result will be an increase in mutual misery. A woman who is constantly beaten or raped by her husband can do little except endure it – or run. But the momentary relief of her escape will soon be tempered by the realization that she has merely fled to a different form of oppression: the perpetual poverty of being a recipient of State-provided social 'security'. Once again, women's lack of real alternatives to marriage and family is underlined.

Yet this is continually disguised by various cultural factors which reinforce the idea that women must marry. Chapter Thirteen discusses in detail the multitude of social pressures which conspire to cajole women into seeing marriage and maternity as their sole vocation. Here, it is important to examine a still more fundamental level at which this pressure is exercised. Built into Australian culture are several images of women. These exist at the level of barely conscious and thus rarely articulated certitudes about what are appropriate vocations for women. (There are also cultural images of men but since, as Chapter Two points out, most commentaries about Australia devote considerable attention to them it is not necessary to dwell on them here.) It is the curious combination of certitude and subconscious which has enabled these images to exist unexplored and unchallenged for so long, and which now makes a detailed examination of them necessary. When we consider the range of possible lifestyles available to women in Australia it does not take long to conclude that the images of women which exist in our culture, and which are of course derived from what women have been able to do in the past, are very restricted in ambit and few in number. This becomes clear if we attempt to draw them from their cultural recesses in order to describe and elucidate them. We find that they consign women to only two possible destinies and that these are defined by whether or not their lives are family-oriented. These images are in fact stereotypes and, as such, they exaggerate. They slur over variations in aptitude and ambition and they distort the actual activities of women. They also ignore the absence of choice in most women's lives. Chapter One showed that women themselves are either ignored or viewed as stereotypes in many areas of our culture: especially in the Arts the image and the reality are merged and the stereotypes are thus perpetuated. It would seem that women can only exist as stereotyped creatures. And since the stereotypes of women are so restrictive, this sexist form of categorizing and circumscribing people is more discriminatory in the case of women than it is with men.

The strength of the stereotypes is made clearer if they are named and their effects on women's lives examined. We can identify two stereotypes and see that one is positive and prescriptive, outlining the familial roles women *ought* to perform, while the other is negative, defining women purely in terms of not fulfilling these roles, and hence is pejorative and punishing. The pro-family stereotype is called 'God's Police' while its antithesis is 'Damned Whore'. (The specific Australian origins of these terms and their connotations are described in Part Two.)

This means of assigning women into dual categories of good or evil is not unique to Australia. It has been a basic tenet of the Judaeo-Christian tradition and hence of most Western intellectual thought and social practice. The actual content of each stereotype differs from country to country and sometimes changes with time and social or economic conditions. For instance, in Australia until the 1960s a married woman who took a paid job was considered to be con- travening the God's Police stereotype (except during World War Two when a relaxation of the prescription was enforced by wartime exigencies). Various economic and sociological factors contributed to an alteration of this content of the God's Police stereotype during the 1960s and it became permissible for mothers whose children were at school to enter the paid workforce. But variations such as these in no way alter the rigidity of the dichotomy between the two stereotypes. Working mothers with pre-school age children were condemned as 'bad' mothers while women who in no way conformed to the approved female role were still regarded as 'evil'. Eva Figes suggests a reason for this:

. . . since the standard of womanhood is set by men for men and not by women, no relaxation of standards is allowable, she is either an absolute woman or nothing at all, totally rejected. This is one of the reasons why the male image of woman has a tendency to split into two, into black and white, Virgin Mary and Scarlet Woman, angel of mercy and prostitute, gentle companion and intolerable bluestocking. A rigid image must of necessity split, since the most compliant reality can hardly fit in absolutely.[2]

In many societies the stereotypes derive from woman's relationship to man, from whether or not she is a sex-object, but in Australia the stereotypes are tied to family and it is this which has given them their distinctive cast. Although they include women's relations with men, they are more widely defined than that and involve a broader social function than is often permitted to women in other countries.

GOD'S POLICE

The God's Police stereotype describes and *prescribes* a set of functions which all Australian women are supposed to fulfil: the maintenance and reproduction of the basic authority relations of society. The prototype of these is found within 'the family' and it is here that women ideally perform their task, but the task of shoring up these authority relations requires extensive support systems, among them the education and social welfare network. The God's Police stereotype permits women to work within these areas, so long as they perform the prescribed functions and do not contradict any other fundamental tenets of the stereotype.

Women do not therefore necessarily have to be married in order to earn this label; the kind of work they do and their social/sexual lives will determine this. For instance, a single woman teacher or social worker would be seen as God's Police. So would nuns who teach or do other forms of charitable work. Single women who live with men without being married to them constitute an increasingly large group, and as their numbers increase so does the acceptability of their lifestyle. But at present we cannot say that their mode of living is totally accepted by society at large and so their status is uncertain. If it is counter-balanced by their working at one of the above-mentioned jobs then some sections of society are prepared to regard it benignly; for other groups this in itself is sufficient reason to condemn them and they argue about the undesirable moral influence such women could exert.

But the God's Police stereotype applies primarily to women within families and has as its *raison d'être* the perpetuation of the bourgeois family.

This stereotype describes a socially and politically conservative function: the policing and preservation of existing relations. That they need to be policed suggests that they are not very firmly implanted in Australian social practice, but while it is the case that they need to be transmitted to each generation, this policing notion is historically derived and arises from the peculiar conditions existing at the time of the formation of 'the family' in Australia. This is outlined in detail in Chapter Nine. The main task of God's Police is to instil in husbands, sons, daughters or pupils the necessity of submission to existing class, sex and race authority structures. So long as such submission is maintained these oppressive and exploitative relations persist. Women are thus called upon not merely to perform an authoritarian function within a society – and within institutions such as family, school etc. – where they have virtually no power, but also to police the perpetuation of the very authority structures which oppress them. Women are specially prepared for this task when, as young girls, they are taught to be submissive and passive, to conform and obey, to imbibe the morality of their generation and class and to impart its contents to the more recalcitrant of their peers.

Women are caught in a contradictory situation whereby they pass on and police a morality which they did not devise and which includes as one of its precepts the notion that women are inferior. They can only perform this schizophrenic role if they are unaware of the authority they possess and, having internalized their roles obediently and unquestioningly, they equate their tasks with what is 'natural' to their sex. Women are further duped by the superficial status which is accorded to conformers to the God's Police stereotype: they are rewarded with a degree of respect from the men whose consciences they are.

The other singular attribute of the God's Police stereotype is that it is asexual. This is why it can simultaneously accommodate married, single and widowed women so long as they perform the policing function. It is conveniently forgotten that married women must have sexual intercourse in order to reproduce: a general Australian puritanism has managed to convince itself that Mothers are not sexual creatures and female sexuality is either denied or else relegated entirely to the Damned Whore stereotype. (This curious attitude can be partly explained by the historical circumstances which led to the Damned Whore stereotype dominating white society in Australia for the first fifty years of its existence; the eventual revulsion against it as the bourgeois family and its concomitant God's Police notion of women gradually became dominant, led to a denial of women's sexuality even within marriage. See Chapters Eight and Nine.)

The authority which women possess within families, schools and as social or welfare workers is not absolute. It is contingent authority which is why it does not carry any power. It can only be exercised while it is recognized and upon those who are prepared to recognize it. Women are incapable of enforcing it upon anyone, even their children, if their authority is disputed. And of course it often *is* disputed and then women are, once again, left hapless and helpless, stripped of the one means by which society allows them to gather status and respectability. A woman in this position will be described as being unable to control her children, as having committed some wrong so as to have lost her husband's respect (or why else would he spend each night in the pub?) and she will thus negate some of the meagre benefits which accrued to her upon marriage.

The God's Police stereotype by itself could barely win any woman's allegiance, even with its enticements of status and respectability. But the point of the polarized stereotypes is, as Figes pointed out, their rigidity: if you don't conform to one you are automatically cast into the other. The alternative stereotype often affords women substantially more personal freedom but it does not possess the comforting mantle of status and respectability. It is, rather, a punitive stereotype which entails relegating women classified by it to the *demi-mondaine*. The God's Police stereotype, on the other hand, is posited as the apotheosis of womanhood, as that to which all women strive. This idealization of women's vocation is peddled to unsuspecting women while the contradictory aspects of the role itself, as well as the unequal nature of the meeting of needs in the marriage union, are disguised by the accolades poured upon the stereotype and the superficial status afforded to women who try to conform to it.

DAMNED WHORES: PROSTITUTES, LESBIANS, WOMEN IN PRISON

The Damned Whore stereotype is a negative one; it is used to describe women who do not appear to be engaged in maintaining existing authority relations and is most often applied to women who are seen as actively contravening these relations – especially those governing women themselves. In practice it is often punitive as the very labelling of a woman as 'unrespectable' deprives her of any status and, as is shown below, often involves her losing many of the rights she is supposedly guaranteed as a citizen. The very fear of being castigated as Damned Whores keeps women in line; most women have no option but to conform to the God's Police stereotype in order to guarantee societal approbation and thus try to avoid these punitive measures. This stereotype is mainly applied to three groups of women: prostitutes, lesbians and women in prisons or detention homes. It is *assumed* that there is a necessary contradiction between being a prostitute or a lesbian and fulfilling the God's Police function; women in custody are actively *prevented* from doing so.

In contrast to God's Police, the Damned Whore stereotype is avowedly, although not exclusively, a sexual category. The prototype is the prostitute and, with her, any other women who trade on their bodies, such as strippers, as well as call girls, hostesses, massage parlour workers and the host of occupations which are euphemisms for selling some form of sexual service. But also included in this stereotype are any women who are sexually 'liberated', women who have extra-marital sexual relationships and especially those who bear children out of wedlock. There are obviously many, many women included in this stereotype but their numbers are partly disguised by further labels or descriptions which are used to categorize them, for example, gangsters' molls, bikies' girl-friends, groupies.

Many male groups like surfers or the men who congregate around a particular pub or a social or even political activity have names for the women who attach themselves to the group, proffering sex in return for some recognition and status as a group member. These names, like the ones mentioned above, are always denigratory and serve to differentiate *those* women from respectable women. The latter are the women these men would marry, and the labels they assign to the women who trail after them are designed to be constant reminders of the low esteem in which they are held. Other labels are used to identify women who are seen as 'fair game' to rapacious men. The purpose of such labels is always to single out sexually active or acquiescent women and to contrast them with the sisters, mothers or girl-friends of these men. In this way they both perpetuate the dual stereotypes and also tend to relegate the women so labelled to inconsequence. The latter tactic only works if the women accept the labels – but they often have little choice, especially if they are very young, very poor, come from certain suburbs or if they are black.

Women, too, have internalized the stereotypes and have accepted men's right to decide which one they belong to and it is only very strong women who can assert their right to be sexually active and not be treated purely as sex objects. The fear of being labelled a 'moll' or a prostitute deters many young women from using contraceptives: they argue that if they take 'the Pill' they are admitting (to themselves) that they are promiscuous and that their boy-friends will think this of them. Their reasoning often leads to a pregnancy which, if they cannot marry to 'legitimize' the child, confers on them the very label they were trying to avoid.

PROSTITUTES

Prostitution is as old as patriarchy. It occurs inevitably in a society where women are seen as sex objects and are also denied economic independence. When women are paid even less for their labour power than men are, they cannot usually survive in the labour market except by selling the one commodity they possess for which men are willing to pay a good price: their bodies. Women are thus forced to sell their bodies in return for economic support. If they are fortunate, the market nature of this transaction is disguised by the myths and rituals of love, courtship and marriage. Many women who do not have this opportunity, or whose marriages fail, are forced to sell their bodies to a series of men.

All pretence of affection and romance is stripped away with the prostitute and the purely sexual nature of the transaction is laid bare. This means that she is in a better position than the married woman for she runs no risk of disenchantment. Unless she works totally in isolation – and very few do – she is better protected from rape and other forms of sexual violence than the woman alone in the marital bedroom with her husband. She also has far more independence for she can reject a customer, and can determine the extent of the sexual activities with one whose custom she has accepted. The prostitute is of course exploited by those who prey on her. A large industry hovers behind her and most prostitutes are forced to pay for 'protection' as well as continually lining the coffers of the State with regular fines for soliciting, and the pockets of individual policemen who demand monetary consideration for regulating the number of times they are arrested.

Prostitution can only exist where men are prepared to pay for sexual gratification, and so men both create and perpetuate prostitution. Yet it is women who are punished for working as prostitutes. Patrons are immune from prosecution while prostitutes are hauled before the courts and treated by male police, magistrates and court officials with disdain and contempt. Preying on the bodies of women is a privilege patriarchy bestows on men: there is no comparable industry where women may buy men's sexual favours. Patriarchy sees the prostitute as being necessary to protect the virtue of 'good' women and it is this argument which is generally advanced by those who advocate legalizing prostitution.

Those who favour legalizing prostitution often argue that their proposals would ensure better treatment for the women by removing their need for protection, by abolishing the need for police payments and by introducing trade union arrangements for hours, working conditions, wages etc. But in fact these arguments are designed to make conditions better for the patrons of prostitutes: legalization is always accompanied by the introduction of compulsory venereal disease checks for the women – thus removing the risk of infection, and of the client having to tell his wife that he has been with prostitutes – and the unionization of prostitutes is designed to keep the price down, again benefiting the customers. The only honourable alternative to the present prostitution scene is its total abolition and that can only come about when women are well paid for jobs which do not involve commercializing their sex. To enable this to happen men must cease seeing women as sex objects. It is unlikely that a patriarchal society would ever realize these pre-conditions but that is no argument in favour of institutionalizing the sexual exploitation of women by legalizing prostitution.

Yet these arguments involve several admissions about the oppression of women. Firstly, they expressly exploit the sexuality of all women: the 'good' women are denied sexual expression, while prostitutes are regarded and treated merely as sexual vessels. Secondly, they are an admission of the alienation of the sexes from each other. Those people who cannot sanction the thought that mothers can also be sexual creatures are denying the possibility for mutually satisfactory sexual relations between wives and husbands. This attitude condemns the wives to sexual misery and frustration. Their husbands are similarly condemned but at least have the choice of patronizing prostitutes.

This attempt to repress women's sexuality is such a blatant thwarting of basic human needs that it is inevitably a very precarious undertaking and one that can only succeed during periods when women's lives are totally regulated by men. Every woman who breaks the taboo threatens its existence – which is why sexually 'liberated' women are castigated as sluts, tramps, harlots and any other label which men hope will deter other women from following their example. But it is obvious that this taboo is rapidly being broken by women themselves. Once they obtain the use of fairly effective contraception, and thus remove the fear of unwanted pregnancies, women can fight this tenet of patriarchy.

Women were repressed in order to protect men's property and their egos. The idea of the chaste woman was seen as necessary to maintain the bourgeois patriarchal family since that institution has as its cornerstone the rule of the husband and the submission of the wife. This power relationship necessarily extended to sexual behaviour as the husband felt he had to ensure that he had actually sired the children who bore his name and whom he was bound to provide for.

Once women can control their fertility – and it must be stressed that this means women determining whether or when they will reproduce, not men imposing this decision upon them – then they can demand sexual satisfaction and the argument about unwanted pregnancies cannot be used against them. Women themselves can say, and are doing so increasingly, that they too have sexual needs which must be gratified and that the distinction between 'good' and 'bad' women is yet another means of oppressing women.

In the past this distinction between women on the basis of their sexual activities has been maintained in order to preserve 'the family'. In Australia there has always been a profound fear of so-called sexual anarchy undermining established social mores, and this has created the polarized stereotypes of women as either maternal figures who are not seen as sexual or as whores who are seen as exclusively sexual. The effect of this has been to ignore or actively repress married women's sexual needs -- particularly by denying them access to contraception and abortion facilities and by encouraging them to internalize an image of themselves as asexual and puritanical maternal creatures (see Chapters Ten and Eleven) – and to view sexually active women as nothing but prostitutes.

Again, women's lack of choice has been glossed over and the polarized stereotypes have been posed as descriptive of reality as well as being prescriptive (in the case of God's Police) and proscriptive (in the case of Damned Whore). Yet they are patently inaccurate descriptions of reality and it is in the censoring of any information which would contradict the stark polarization that the social purpose of the stereotypes is revealed. Both mother and whore are posed as mutually exclusive categories. Yet many mothers have active and satisfying sex lives and many prostitutes are also mothers, some of whom try to bring up their children to conform to the God's Police prescriptions. But so rigid are the stereotypes that they refuse to accommodate such realities and the images projected on to women – images which they internalize while they are very young and still denied access to knowledge or information which would undermine the polarization – perpetuate the myths of exclusivity. The effect is that the mother will keep silent to her children and friends about her sex life, and the prostitute will not tell her children how she earns her money or she will be so consumed with shame and guilt about her occupation – blaming herself rather than a society which forces women into prostitution – that she will give up her children or have them cared for by another, more overtly respectable woman.

LESBIANS

Lesbians are also seen as belonging to an exclusively sexual category and the label 'lesbian' is supposed to be a sufficient description of a woman. Yet a woman who is a lesbian may also be a wife, a mother and have a job as, for instance, a secretary. Of course many lesbians are not, and have never, married. They may set up house and live with another woman but they have to have jobs to support themselves so the purely sexual label is still inaccurate.

It is the rigid sex roles, based on marriage and family, of a patriarchal society which lead to the condemnation of lesbians (and of male homosexuals). They are seen as rejecting 'the family' because they engage in non-reproductive sexuality. Lesbians are regarded as being even more subversive than male homosexuals because they are not sexually or emotionally dependent on men and their sexual preference is a living defiance of the patriarchal precept that men are superior to women and indispensable to women's survival. And for this reason lesbians are held in far more disrepute than prostitutes who are patently dependent on men for survival.

Lesbians are subjected to two forms of discrimination: the first is to deny that they exist and the second is to brand and persecute them. The law does not recognize the existence of female homosexuality and thus lesbians are safe from legal prosecution for their sexual activities but this does not imply that these activities are condoned. Rather, the absence of legal proscription has been part of a tactic of annihilation by non-recognition. The same tactic is used by parents who hope that refusing to recognize that their daughter is a lesbian will make 'the problem' disappear: they will change the subject if ever she raises it and will repress any information they might stumble across which would confirm beyond doubt that their daughter is a lesbian. This non-recognition annihilates the identity of the daughter and this, combined with the second tactic of branding and persecution, in the past has been sufficient to keep most lesbians from being visible to the world.

Lesbians are branded as 'sick', 'perverted', 'unnatural' and many other labels which contrast them to the 'natural' female who bears children and is subservient to men. It is almost impossible for a lesbian not to internalize some of these attitudes and, especially when her parents and society generally refuse to grant her even a hostile recognition – which would be better than totally ignoring her identity – as a lesbian, she inevitably suffers contortions of guilt, shame and self-hatred. Many lesbians are unable to endure this combined rejection and condemnation and resolve the situation in a way which conforms to society's death-wish for them. It is unlikely that a prostitute would suicide *because* she is a prostitute: she has social recognition, even though she has no status, and that recognition is sufficient to bestow some identity on her.

Lesbians are relegated to the *demi-mondaine* because they do not usually live in bourgeois families and, it is therefore assumed, they are not fulfilling the female role of maintaining existing authority relations. A woman who lives in a sexual relationship with another woman is contravening the prescription that women should accommodate men's needs. In this sense, the stereotype can be an accurate description of reality but only because it is applied selectively. If it were extended to encompass a lesbian's entire life it would not match reality so conveniently (just as the God's Police stereotype breaks down if mothers' actions and attitudes within families are examined a little more closely).

Many lesbians feel totally incapable of marrying and having sexual relations with men but a great many 'compensate' for this inability to conform to the prescribed female role by working in jobs which enable them to act out variations of that role: nursing, social or welfare work, teaching. They have to hide their lesbianism to hold these jobs as society's attitude is such that it is assumed that because they are non-conformers in one respect they are total revolutionaries who are intent on subverting 'the family'. Those people who fear that lesbians in schools or hospitals will influence women in their charge away from the prescribed female role do not realize that, in order to be a revolutionary, a person must have a strong self-image and a positive conviction that what she or he is doing or advocating is right. And, as we have seen, that same society which fears lesbians also actively prevents them from having these certitudes. At present a woman's homosexuality is seen as sufficient reason to grant her husband a divorce and to take her children away from her. She is regarded as a pariah – as a total negation of everything that is desired (by men) in a woman.

WOMEN IN PRISONS

Both lesbians and prostitutes are seen as failing to fulfil the God's Police functions and are condemned for this reason. But women in prisons are actually prevented from doing so and this is then used as a rationalization for depriving them of any future opportunity to do so. This is especially the case in girls' detention homes where, it would be assumed if we expected social attitudes to be consistent, girls would be rigorously drilled into conformity to the female role. But this is not the case.[3] Girls are sent to girls' homes (shelters, training schools or whatever euphemism is currently in use to disguise the fact that they are prisons) either because they have been charged, or found guilty, of some offence, because their families cannot care for them, or, for some other reason, they have been put into State custody.

A large percentage of the girls who come under the first category, that is, they have committed an offence, are there on the charge of 'being exposed to moral danger'. This can mean they have been guilty of being sexually active while still under the legal age of consent (which ranges between sixteen and eighteen according to each state law) or that, in the eyes of the police or the court or a disapproving relative, they look as if they might be. A Sydney journalist who worked at an inner-city girls' shelter in order to investigate conditions there reported

The most common charges were 'Exposure to moral danger', vagrancy and 'uncontrollable'. In none of the cases I heard about had any of the girls involved done any harm to anyone else. They were guilty of arguing with their parents, feeling unwanted at home, going off with their boyfriends for a weekend, hitching to Sydney from Purfleet, Melbourne or Newcastle – hardly crimes against society.[4]

Until recently, all girls entering these prisons in New South Wales were subjected to compulsory examinations to determine whether or not they were virgins. After protracted protests by the Women's Movement, including demonstrations outside several girls' homes in Sydney, the authorities announced that this practice would be stopped.

Although the stated aim of these prisons is 'rehabilitation', in practice they are punishment centres. The girls have to spend their days performing senseless repetitive tasks such as scrubbing already spotless floors. There are no educational facilities – even for girls under the school-leaving age – and a girl's formal education ceases the moment she enters one of these institutions. But another form of education commences immediately: the girls very quickly learn that they are already considered beyond reform, that in society's eyes they are criminal. Their initiation into crime begins, encouraged by the regulations and practices of the institutions.

Rather than being homes, or even rehabilitative institutions, these girls' prisons are in fact training schools for adult criminality. The official attitude to the girls assumes that they are already criminal, they are treated as criminals and most of the girls, not surprisingly, go on to fulfil this expected role. Girls' prisons can be seen as prostitution fodder factories since, as the girls are denied an education, this is practically the only way they can earn a living. One third of adult women in New South Wales prisons have a history of juvenile crime, with 70 per cent of these having spent time in a girls' prison. None of this 70 per cent has had any secondary education.[5] Men are employed at some girls' prisons and at one place in Sydney, girls have become pregnant as a result of sexual assaults by these employees.[6] These girls are prepared, at an early age and in a very brutal fashion, for their adult lives of sexual abuse and exploitation.

Several criminologists have predicted recently that as women become 'more liberated' the female crime rate is likely to rise.[7] What they mean is that women are becoming more assertive and are hence more likely to adopt violent methods of crime. So far there has been little indication of this happening in Australia and it seems a remote possibility: these experts in crime have misunderstood the nature of women's 'crimes'. Angela Weir, who spent several months in a British prison, wrote after her release in 1973 that most women in prison, far from being deviant, were often incarcerated because the effort to play out their roles as mothers and wives had led them to commit 'crimes'. Women who did not have the material means to make a decent home for their children stole to provide for their families, and women who were overcome by the stresses and tensions of their domestic responsibilities took too many pills or too much alcohol, which led to some form of anti-social behaviour.[8]

About half of female prisoners in Australian prisons are convicted of crimes of the kind described by Weir above; a substantial proportion of the remainder are serving sentences for vagrancy or prostitution – both, as has already been shown, almost inevitabilities for women outside marriage in a patriarchal society. It is a crime to have no money and it is also a crime to sell one's body in return for money. Prison statistics show that the women at the Detention and Training Centre for Women at Silverwater in Sydney (the one women's gaol in that state) are far less likely to be married and if married, far more likely to be separated than the general female population. They are women who, lacking a male provider/protector, find it very difficult to survive economically. And if a women has spent

some of her youth in a girls' prison she will have absolutely no
training – intelligence tests on a sample of women at Silverwater
showed them to have a higher level of illiteracy than the general
population – to enable her to earn a living at any kind of job which
would keep her above the poverty line.

But it is also evident that the majority of women do strive to avoid
criminal solutions to their poverty. Even though women are far more
likely than men to be poor, the proportion of men in gaols (for all
crimes) is far greater: in 1972 a total of 12,056 men were received
into gaols in New South Wales, compared with only 1,279 women.[9]
Of those female prisoners who had children, few had shown signs
of neglecting them. Only one of the sample of forty-six women at
Silverwater had a child in the custody of the Child Welfare Department; four had grown-up children while a great majority of the rest
had left their children in the care of their mother, mother-in-law,
husband or other relatives while they were imprisoned.[10]

Women who give birth while in prison or who have very young
infants when they commence their sentences are permitted to place
the child in the prison hospital and care for it themselves. But once
the child is about nine months old it is taken from the mother and
placed in State custody. If the aim of imprisonment is rehabilitation,
and in the authorities' eyes rehabilitation for women obviously means
'settling down' to domesticity, then it would be expected that women
in prison would be encouraged to care for their own children, and
would perhaps receive encouragement to learn to cook and to care
for a house. But the women have to work at washing and sewing for
the entire prison population of the state and at cooking for the local
hospital – hardly jobs which will encourage them to want to be
full-time housewives. When the sample of women studied at Silverwater were asked to state their preference for employment or home
duties when they finished their sentences, only 17.5 per cent opted
for staying at home. Almost 70 per cent preferred to go out to work
while the rest wanted to work at home, to continue with prostitution,
or wanted to go out to work but would be unable to.[11]

Prisons exist to punish women for not conforming to their female
roles and this punishment purpose far outweighs any effort to change
the women. The effect of prison is to convince women that the road
to respectability is closed to them forever. Women in prisons, like
lesbians and prostitutes, are seen as damned, as totally beyond
redemption. No attempt is made to 'rehabilitate' prostitutes; rather
they are encouraged to return to their profession, for society still
prefers to overtly exploit some women while pretending to protect

others. Lesbians and women imprisoned for 'crimes' other than prostitution are hidden away, ignored and rejected as blights on the seemingly benign face of womanhood.

WHY THE STEREOTYPES ARE NECESSARY TO 'THE FAMILY'

The continued existence of these two stereotypes and the romantic myths of marriage which reinforce them have prevented people, and especially women, from taking full cognizance of women's position and all of its implications. So we need to ask, why are they perpetuated? Something large must be at stake if successive generations of women have been unable to recognize and to challenge this stranglehold which society keeps them in. The stereotypes in operation amount to massive coercion: that such coercion should be necessary undermines the argument that what women do in families is 'natural' to them.

Nature has never been so universally cruel and selective in its application as what we witness if we lift the veils of illusion from the marriage relationship and the family responsibilities of women. Yet an even worse fate awaits the woman who rejects this vocation. So we are led to conclude that the functions women perform in families must be of critical value to our society. Therefore we need to examine the structure of that society and try to determine just how necessary the oppression of women is to its continuation.

This I will attempt to do by looking at the main functions performed by families in Australia, and at the nature of women's involvement in the performance of these functions. At the same time I will analyse whether these family functions need to be performed at all and, if so, whether they must necessarily occur within families as they are presently structured, that is, families in which a sexual division of labour is the essential organizing principle. In other words, must they occur within families and must they be the responsibility of women?

There are six major functions which are currently performed within families: (1) Production (2) Reproduction (3) Consumerism (4) Privatization (5) Sexual repression and (6) Socialization.[12] These functions are examined in detail later in this chapter.

Some of these functions must be performed within any human society while others are a product of specific historical and cultural conditions. These latter ones are closely tied to the evolution of a specific form of family structure common to Western industrialized nations – the 'nuclear family'. It is this group of reproductive couple and their progeny which is what is usually meant when social scientists and others refer to 'the family'. As already stated, this term has a strong prescriptive flavour to it: the 'nuclear family' is seen as the *ideal* family and it is this view of family which is used as a model in schools and other educational institutions and is employed by the media, advertising, the churches and other cultural institutions which influence people's ideas. While I have already pointed out that this ideal does not match the reality of many people's lives in Australia, it is also important to remember that because this ideal is propagated as the most desirable way to live, it is often striven for or emulated even by groups whose structure or composition makes such efforts futile or even ludicrous; for instance, a homosexual couple who try to reproduce male/female role stereotypes. The adoption by a non-procreative couple of roles which assume a reproductive situation and the presence of children is obviously unnecessary, but it is some indication of the social strength of these role prescriptions which leads 'deviant' families to try to win social recognition and approval by imitating them. The ideal family is recognizable and is recognized even by people who have no wish to conform to it, so the functions performed by it are also recognizable and often even form the basis of many of the non-conformers' objections. It is, therefore, possible to discuss 'ideal' functions as 'ideally' performed by 'the family' even while recognizing that not all people live in this fashion.

HISTORY OF THE 'NUCLEAR FAMILY'

This entire discussion is only sensible if we realize that the 'nuclear family' both as an ideal and as a partially-accomplished reality for large numbers of people is of comparatively recent origin. It might seem unnecessary to suggest that family structure and functions can, and should, alter if we were dealing with an institution which had existed for many centuries. But this is not the case. 'The family' developed into an idealized institution less than two hundred years ago – since the white colonization of this country – and it was evolved in order to fulfil fairly discernible social and economic functions. If these functions were no longer seen as being necessary, or as having to be performed within families, then we could expect the institution to alter and, perhaps, disappear. At present, however, a major impediment to the recognition of the social and historical nature of 'the family', and thus its susceptibility to change, is the idea that 'the family' is a private area of existence. Most people for whom 'the family' serves as a primary arena of self-expression believe it to be inalienable, to a large extent removed from societal interference, an arrangement freely chosen by themselves (inasmuch as they chose their marriage partners), in short, as a private realm. It is this contradiction between the existence of 'the family' as a *social* institution – serving definite, prescribed social functions – and people's perception of it as a *private* world, which needs to be resolved before change is possible. This notion of privacy, and the accompanying idea of the sanctity of 'the family', have enabled the oppression of women within families to escape comment or condemnation and, until very recently, its consequences for women to be largely ignored.

The 'nuclear family' as an ideal and as an actual institution developed in Europe around the beginning of the eighteenth century. It was evolved by the mercantile middle class as an institution appropriate to its social and economic needs and aspirations. The 'nuclear family' is the creation of the bourgeoisie and its extension to other classes in society is a measure of the control of that class over the means of production and social relations; we can say that acceptance of the ideal of the 'nuclear family' by other groups is an indication of their perception of inclusion within the capitalist system.

Phillipe Aries, whose book *Centuries of Childhood* chronicles the spread and acceptance of this ideal way to live, concludes: 'Between the eighteenth century and the present day [the family] remained as [it had developed] in the town and country middle classes of the eighteenth century [but] it extended more and more to other social strata.'[13] Aries argues that two ideas were crucial in the evolution of this middle-class family: the development of privacy and the concept of childhood. Previously, sociability was literally enforced on people: home and work were not always physically separated, married couples and their children coexisted within larger households and there was little physical separation of houses into rooms with particular functions. Privacy for individuals or for families was thus impossible.

Prevailing social mores were reflected in the design of housing: rooms opened into one another, bedrooms were not seen as private sanctuaries, servants frequently slept in their masters' bedrooms. There was no clear separation between childhood and adulthood and therefore no concept of childhood as a preparatory period for adult life in which young people are seen as inferior and denied many of the civil rights which adults possess. Children were regarded merely as small people. They worked along with everybody else, and they were granted adult rights, such as the right to marry, at what today would be regarded as the very early age of twelve years. There was no notion of children being intrinsically good (or bad) and therefore needing to be isolated from society in order to spend years being inculcated with social norms.

With the middle-class family came the desire to separate family groups from the wider society and to enshrine the nuclear group in its own private world. Thus it was seen as necessary that each family have its own house and land, that rooms be allocated for specific purposes, that they be separated from each other by corridors, that special quarters be built to accommodate servants. This retreat to privacy was motivated by economic considerations: a market in land and housing was quickly developed and became the source of great wealth to those who specialized in property. With the development of middle-class family private property – as distinct from feudal estates owned by a few noble families and common land held by whole villages or communities – came the desire to accumulate property, as a source of speculation and added wealth, to signify the owner's affluence to the world at large.

Nineteenth-century wives of the middle class were seen as property. Women of this class were not permitted to work, even within the home, but had to spend their time entertaining or visiting, wearing as many different outfits as it was possible to display in a single day, in order to demonstrate not only their husbands' wealth but also their generosity in spending it so freely on these idle creatures known as wives.

The notion of childhood as a period of existence separated from the adult world entailed the development of new institutions to accommodate young people during their period of transition from infancy to adulthood. Principal among these were the school and 'the family'. The child was now seen by the middle class as a helpless and malleable creature who spent its infancy in the nursery at home, its care undertaken by servants acting under the remote supervision of her or his mother. The child was then sent to school where, under a strict disciplinary system, he (for girls were educated at home by emulating the inactivity of their mothers and acquiring, in a roundabout and haphazard fashion, the 'feminine' accomplishments of pianoforte and embroidery, as well as moral instruction) was inculcated with information and ideas designed to aid his moral development and equip him to take his place in the mercantile world. A necessary accompaniment to the concept of childhood was the idea that each child was unique and irreplaceable and that there should be equality between children. Infant deaths were now mourned rather than accepted as part of the scheme of things and the old custom of primogeniture, or favouring the first-born, gradually was replaced by treating all sons equally – and all daughters a little less equally. With these developments, 'the family ceased to be simply an institution for the transmission of a name and an estate – it assumed a moral and spiritual function, it moulded bodies and souls.'[14]

It can readily be seen how this new institution 'the family' meant that women were to be confined in a way that they had not experienced before. Domestic work was now seen as a separate productive enterprise, rather than one integrated with other work, and religious and social sanctions gave it a relatively high status:

The rise of the bourgeoisie entailed a simultaneous advance and retrogression in the position of women. In the economic life of medieval England women were closer to equality with men than they later were under capitalism. For example, women participated as equals in many guilds in the fourteenth century. With the rise of capitalism they were excluded and, in general, economic opportunities for women not in families – such as spinsters and widows – declined. On the other hand women were given a much higher status within the family. For the Puritans, women's domestic labour was a 'calling', a special vocation comparable to the crafts and trades of their husbands. Like their husbands, women did God's work. As the lesser partner in a common enterprise, a woman was to be treated with respect . . . Wife-beating was now forbidden.[15]

The two key ideas of the modern family – privacy associated with separate household, and childhood as a period requiring special care and training – entailed women assuming new functions, both of which removed them from wider society and confined them within the household. The new 'nuclear family' strongly enjoined that married women should not work outside the home, but while this family form was still a middle-class phenomenon it had no objection to using the labours of married women from other classes. The wife in the bourgeois family until the late nineteenth century was not called upon to care for her own children, nor even to supervise her household, as she had swathes of servants who assumed the tasks that were later to be taken over entirely by the wife.

The period of the formation of the middle-class family was also the era during which the industrial working class was formed. It was a period of massive human misery as the transformation from an agricultural to an industrial economy entailed the movement of people into towns; as old family-based crafts were transformed to large-scale production in factories; as the family-determined rhythm of work and sharing of tasks was changed by the division of labour and the brutalizing speeding up of production in large, dehumanized factories. Initially whole families had to work in factories as a man's wages were insufficient to support a family. Women and children of all ages, as well as men, spent long hours in factories and mills, but even the combined labour of a family did not earn sufficient to rent decent accommodation or to buy sustaining food.

At the same time as the bourgeoisie was extolling the family of its creation as a moral imperative for all classes, its other creation – the capitalist system – made the idealized family institution an impossible attainment for the labouring class. Engels noted in his study of the English working class in the 1840s that:

. . . the social order makes family life almost impossible for the worker. In a comfortless, filthy house, hardly rain-tight nor warm, a foul atmosphere filling rooms overcrowded with human beings, no domestic comfort is possible. The husband works the whole day through, perhaps the wife also and the elder children, all in different places; they meet at night and morning only, all under perpetual temptation to drink; what family life is possible under such conditions? Yet the working-man cannot escape from the family, must live in the family, and the consequence is perpetual succession of family troubles, domestic quarrels, most demoralizing for parents and children alike. Neglect of all domestic duties, neglect of the children, especially, is only too common among the English working-people, and only too vigorously fostered by the existing institutions of society. And children growing up in this savage way, amidst these demoralizing influences, are expected to turn out goody-goody and moral in the end! Verily the requirements are naive, which the self-satisfied bourgeoisie makes upon the working man.[16]

E. P. Thompson says that there was a drastic increase in the intensity of exploitation of child labour between 1780 and 1840 and remained so until the child 'was rescued by the school'.[17] The conditions of life for the working class were reflected in their average age of death. In 1842 the average age of death for labourers in Manchester was seventeen (compared with twenty for tradesmen and thirty-eight for gentry) while in Liverpool it was fifteen for labourers (twenty-two for tradesmen and thirty-five for gentry).[18]

Thus while the bourgeoisie was urging the family institution upon the population it was simultaneously preventing the working class from adopting it. In fact the exploitation of the working class was essential to the bourgeois style of family life in the first half of the nineteenth century. While industry remained labour intensive, it required hordes of workers to create the profits it could then use to increase its industrial wealth and to expend in conspicuous consumption, and it also demanded the labour of servants to maintain its lavish lifestyle. Only as industry became more mechanized, and the labour of women and children was no longer essential, could the ideal of 'the family' begin to be adopted by the working class.

The confinement of working-class women in households thus occurred much later and even then there have always been regional and other differences: single working-class women have almost always had to work before marriage – in contrast, until recently, to middle-class women. There have always remained class differences in family and marriage patterns, and variations in the married and single women's working habits in different regions and different periods.*

But the main ideas of the 'nuclear family' – those about privacy and household, childhood and women – have been accepted, and some attempt has been made to conform to them since the late nineteenth century, by a substantial proportion of the populations of Western industrialized countries.

The almost simultaneous development of the 'nuclear family' and of capitalism was not merely fortuitous: this new family form obviously had advantages for the newly evolving economic system and the two have developed an interdependent relationship. Zaretsky points out:

The organization of production in capitalist society is predicated upon the existence of a certain form of family life. The wage labour (socialized production under capitalism) is sustained by the socially necessary but private labour of housewives and mothers. Childrearing, cleaning, laundry, the maintenance of property, the preparation of food, daily health care, reproduction, etc. constitute a perpetual cycle of labour necessary to maintain life in this society. In this sense the family is an integral part of the economy under capitalism.[19]

This interdependence had to be fostered – it was not a spontaneous occurrence. Many women resisted being forced into full-time dom-

* This is necessarily an extremely abbreviated account of the development of the 'nuclear family' and is forced to schematize developments and patterns which took over a century to develop and which displayed regional, national and class

esticity, just as many men resented being forced to support a number of dependent and unproductive family members. But gradually 'the family' assumed its own imperatives and rationales which encouraged people to view it as a 'natural' institution. The very existence of a closed, private and, as knowledge of birth control spread, smallish family group generated notions of affection and responsibility amongst its members. The male worker gradually incurred the notion that he was responsible for supporting his family (and this was legally enforced late in the nineteenth century) and he was thus provided with a powerful motive to be a diligent and reliable labourer. Schooling gradually was made compulsory and education became a vehicle for inculcating masses of young children with the values required by the capitalist system. These values included the ideology of 'the family' as well as submission to authority and were established by the very structure of the education system as well as by the content of the syllabus.

At the same time, 'the family' became an authoritarian body: a system of reciprocal rights and duties evolved but these were determined by a sexual division of labour. Wives and children were dependent on the husband's economic support and this enabled him to exert greater authority over them, an authority which was enhanced by his ability to draw on his experience in the world outside the family to justify his opinions and behaviour. Wives and children, confined to home or school, had become unfamiliar with this world and were forced to interpret it through the eyes of their husband and father. Women's subordination was effected by their being denied equal education, so that they were even less familiar with the world outside than their male children were. Denied paid employment outside the home, and unpaid for their domestic labours, women were economically totally dependent upon their husbands who could regard wives as property – which they had bought – and demand domestic and sexual services in return for economic support. The status afforded to child care and domestic work was meagre compensation for the lack of freedom which was now women's estate. The more 'the family' came to dominate personal life the less were women's opportunities for self-assertion and independence; they had no choice but to stay within, and make the best of, their domestic prisons.

---

variations. Part Two deals with the development of 'the family' in Australia in more detail.

Through 'the family,' the capitalist system now had at its disposal a vast army of labourers who had a strong motive to earn a wage, and whose families would provide them with the necessary refurbishment and retreat from the ardours of work to enable them to turn out again each working day. Yet the physical and emotional work done by women which enabled the workforce to keep working was obtained at no extra cost to the capitalist. Ties of duty and affection obscured the fact that both sexes had been duped: the system was in effect getting two people's full-time work for the price of the male wage.

The next major development in 'the family' was again an innovation of the middle class but this time was precipitated by its women. In the second half of the nineteenth century in England there was a vast surplus of women and it was simply demographically impossible that all could marry. Yet the 'nuclear family' creed denied them the opportunity to work. Women had not been educated for any accomplishment beyond the home and nor were there sufficient jobs for which they were equipped – such as needlework or governessing – to accommodate them. Many middle-class women, unable to work and unable to marry, could not obtain life-long support from their fathers who, especially if they had large families or if they were impecunious, were quite unable to meet what had formerly been their responsibility. So middle-class women demanded the right to work and the right to an education which would give them the qualifications to obtain jobs.

The initial refusal of these demands prompted women to begin consciously and critically to examine the roles patriarchal society expected them to fulfil, and to conclude that they were unjust. Soon the demands swelled to the right to vote in order to be able to influence society to take women's needs into account. After a protracted struggle these three demands – to vote, to learn and to work – were granted but even then women were not afforded full equality with men: their maternal and family responsibilities had always to come first. It was only if they were unmarried, or in times of national emergency, that they were permitted to engage in paid work and then they were usually confined to jobs which were either especially menial or which were seen to be compatible with women's maternal destiny.

A second mass questioning of their roles by women is under way at present and, again, it has been precipitated by middle-class women. It has been partly a reopening of some of the debates and demands of the earlier agitation and this has occurred because, once again, large numbers of women are under-employed. A greatly lowered birth rate has meant that women's family responsibilities are largely fulfilled before they reach middle age and they are left with little to do. Economic motives have also been important as the male wage is today seldom sufficient to provide the commodities and services which an increasingly affluent society is beginning to decree are essential to family well-being. This new wave of women's agitation is only a few years old and what it will accomplish remains to be seen. But unless it is directed at the sexist structure of family and society, rather than merely at some of its manifestations – as the first wave was – then it will not achieve fundamental changes. At the moment family practices and ideals are being questioned but the institution itself is still functioning. It is against this brief background that we can consider the functions performed by the 'nuclear family' in Australia.

PRESENT FUNCTIONS OF THE 'NUCLEAR FAMILY'

These are, as we have seen, Production, Reproduction, Consumerism, Privatization, Sexual repression and Socialization.

1. PRODUCTION: HOUSEWORK, CHILD-CARE, EMOTIONAL SUSTENANCE

The huge amount of domestic work performed within each family is not usually thought of as production. It is not included in the calculations of the Gross National Product nor, if it is performed by a housewife, is it paid for – unless we can call the $364 taxation concession allowable to her husband a payment. This work is almost invariably done by women since it is viewed as part of the contractual obligation undertaken by a woman in return for the economic support of her husband. The actual amount of labour performed by women within the home, and the time they devote to it, are totally out of keeping with modern workforce practices. A survey on housework conducted by the National Council of Women in Britain found that a total of 85 hours per week was required to run a home and that even if a woman had family or paid help she was likely to spend about 65 hours a week doing housework.[20] A more detailed American analysis of housework took account of the number and ages of children and whether or not the wife also had a paid job outside the home.[21] It found that a non-employed wife devoted the following time to housework:

one child – under one year old	56 hours
one child – over two years old	49 hours
four children – any age	58 hours
four children – one under five	64 hours
six or more children	63 hours
eight or more children	84 hours

If a wife had employment as well she generally spent about two hours less per week on housework, but she also had more help from her husband. This study calculated that if women were paid for each task on the basis of the cost of employing casual labour they would be entitled to an annual salary of between $A3,940 and $6,620. The British study estimated that women would earn $8,000 a year. The longer hours attributed to British housewives are perhaps due to the relative lack of modern labour-saving appliances in many British homes. The Australian times would be somewhere in between, but probably closer to the American ones.

If we categorize as domestic production all those tasks which are necessary to maintain the individuals within families then there are clearly several different types of work involved. The most important of these are: housework, child-care and emotional sustenance. All of these are usually performed by women but not all of them are seen as 'work'. Many of the activities involved in child-care, for instance, would not be regarded by women themselves as 'work', nor would the multitude of functions which come under the label of emotional sustenance. These tasks are performed, according to family ideology, from love, devotion and sense of duty. This might be true with many women but does not alter the fact that the ideology masks the essential nature of these tasks. They are 'work' in the sense that effort and energy must be expended on them – they will not take care of them-selves – and furthermore, their performance is essential to the maintenance of the 'nuclear family' in its present form. Given the current division of labour where men are required to work outside the home, this work could not be carried on within families unless women did it. (This is clear from the experiences of single, widowed or deserted fathers who attempt to do housework, raise children and provide emotional sustenance at the same time as holding a full-time job. They invariably must employ housekeepers or else give up their jobs. If they do the latter they are not entitled to receive either unemployment benefits or the equivalent to the supporting mothers' pension.*)

Need this work be performed within families – and must it be done by women? Of course the staunch defenders of traditional family ideology (a tradition, it might be pointed out, less than a century old) are adamantly positive about both of these questions. They generally argue that women are intrinsically and even 'naturally' inclined towards this work and advance theories about maternal 'instincts' (as opposed to learned behaviour) to emphasize that this work, but especially child-care, must be done by women.

But if these emotive and largely unscientific arguments are rejected[22], are there further reasons? Obviously much housework exists because families exist and because of the division of labour within them. If all family members took responsibility for their own cleaning and washing, or if these jobs were rostered amongst members, the woman's workload would be considerably lightened. She would do some of this work as her turn came around, but she would no longer be solely responsible for it, nor would it occupy all her time. She could no longer claim the occupation 'housewife'. Alternatively, outside labour could be employed: cleaning could be done by contractors, washing and ironing by laundries, meals could be eaten at cheap local restaurants such as exist in some European countries. Either of these, or a combination of them, would see the work done and women released from full-time devotion to it. There is nothing intrinsic about the work which dictates that women must do it, and it could be a matter of choice whether it was shared by family members or contracted to outside agencies.

Child-care could also be undertaken outside the family and need not necessarily be done by women. Many children are already cared for from infancy in private or government centres (although many more are deprived of this care because of the Government's tardiness in instituting a national child-care scheme). The concept of extra-familial child-care is already largely accepted although there is still much argument about the advisability of caring for very young children in this fashion, and there is also resistance to the notion of employing men in this job. There is no inherent reason why men cannot undertake child-care. Several alternative child-care centres in Sydney include men on their rosters and these men are not necessarily

* In August 1974 the then Minister for Social Security, Mr Hayden, announced that an allowance, similar to that paid to supporting mothers, would be paid to supporting fathers.

the fathers of any of the children. Resistance to allowing men to care for young children is often based on fears of molestation; but while such fears may be realistic at the present time in a society whose repressive sexuality encourages the development of fetishes, it would be possible to take precautions against this. That a few men are child-molesters is not a sufficient reason to prevent men from undertaking this work. We could just as easily argue that because some women batter their children, no woman should be allowed to care for children.

More frequently, however, the insistence that women care for children, and the prejudice against very young children being placed in child-care centres, is based on notions of maternal instinct and maternal deprivation. Yet the idea that children who are cared for (as distinct from socialized which is a different concept and will be discussed later) by people other than their mothers will grow up to be unstable adults, is a cultural notion rather than a universal fact. 'Child care arrangements which differ from the traditional intense mother-child relationships assumed as an ideal by many in our society do not produce "unhealthy" personalities – merely different ones, depending on the range and nature of the relationships the child encounters.'[23]

The third area of work involved in production is the emotional sustenance of the members of families. Bound up in both housework and mothering is that nexus of action and reaction which is incorporated within the God's Police stereotype. Within families women engage in this function at its most particularized and most concrete level. They are rightly referred to as 'the emotional hub of the family', expected to act as a buffer zone between husband and his fractured ego when *he* has problems, moving to prevent squabbling children from engaging in open warfare, conciliating between rebellious children and outraged father. Women are expected to perform this kind of diplomacy outside as well as within the home: a top secretary is as much defined by her ability to shield her boss from the routine pestering of the rest of the world, by her skill at lying and manoeuvring for him – even against his wife – as she is by her prowess at the typewriter. But it is seen in its most essential form within families where it often emerges as the most important work which a woman does. It is in the performance of this work that she enables 'the family' to perpetuate itself as an institution. She consoles the child who is bullied at school, the husband who has problems at work, the daughter who is in the throes of a teenage passion, the son who didn't make the football team. The woman alleviates stress between family members and thus enables *them* to keep going at whatever work they are engaged in outside the home, and to the extent that she is successful in keeping them going they value 'the family'. The institution itself is credited with the individual work of one of its members.

We tend to confuse the emotional sustenance derived from 'the family' with that which is necessary to maintain 'self'. This confusion arises, as was pointed out in Chapter Four, because most of us have acquired 'self' within a family and retain a strong association between that institution and individual emotional stability. We are thus socialized to expect to receive a great proportion of our emotional sustenance from our current family and from that family which we expect, as adults, to establish. We learn to expect our 'self' to be maintained from a close relationship with one other person, coupled with relationships with the progeny produced by that union. We learn that friendships, acquaintances and other social interactions are less important than those with a chosen mate. We therefore expect that our emotional lives would disintegrate if we were to be deprived of coupling, marriage and family.

But these are *learned* expectations; had we grown up on kibbutzim or communes we might have acquired rather different perceptions of how to meet our need of social sustenance. If we recognize the degree of social conditioning involved in what are assumed by many people to be basic needs then it is possible to realize that marriage and family are not the only means of obtaining emotional sustenance. We could derive similar sustenance from several close relationships and a number of friendships. Thus what has often been viewed as a function which can only be fulfilled within families is capable of being met by other people.

Much of this work of emotional sustenance performed by women within families is generated by the intensities and inequalities of families themselves. In other words, if families did not exist there would be less need for such extensive sustaining. The very confining of four or five people of differing ages and aspirations within an institution which is circumscribed by notions of parental responsibility and filial respect is likely to cause conflicts. These will be more or less severe depending on the extent to which family members conform to the roles of their age and sex.

The powerlessness of women can be expressed by self-destructive behaviour, as pointed out in Chapter Four, or it can be directed against other family members. Continual nagging, emotional blackmail and other retaliatory tactics are employed by many women who are bitter or resentful about their lives. In such cases, a woman may totally refuse, or be incapable of, providing emotional sustenance to her family and so what is seen as a necessary function, and one that ought to be fulfilled by women, is either undertaken by another family member or is not performed at all. In such families conflicts are likely to be more naked and to be articulated; without the inter-vention and preventive tactics of a mediatrix the tensions and clashes which attend every family group will be unleashed and are likely to lead either to resolution or to family breakdown. Either result illustrates the overburdening of women with this responsibility. If conflicts can be coped with without the woman's mediations then her role is shown to be unnecessary; if her efforts are directed towards holding together a precarious and hostile group of people she is defeating her purpose since none will gain sustenance in the presence of these latent tensions.

While women continue to shoulder this job, other family members can avoid the responsibility of managing their own emotional lives, of acquiring emotional maturity. This is why we have the phenomenon of so many men who are totally unable to relate to women, except to place them in a maternal role, or to other men. They have been mollycoddled and cosseted by women all their lives and have never learnt to direct their own emotional lives. And for the women who spend a lifetime attending to other people's emotional needs there can also be devastating effects. As long as this function is seen as being exclusively women's preserve (and this idea is reinforced by such jobs as nursing and social work being mainly women's jobs) and, as Chapter Four argued, women are taught early in life to be wary of other women and hence often find it difficult to form close friendships with each other, how are women to receive emotional sustenance? Who comforts the comforters? Many women have little recompense except the vicarious satisfaction of being able to sustain the lives of their husbands and children.

2. REPRODUCTION

This is a function essential to species-survival and hence cannot be dispensed with. It is also essential to 'the family'. We have to distinguish between marriage and 'the family': a married couple does not constitute a family. A major purpose of 'the family' is to reproduce itself both physically and psychologically and there is considerable pressure applied to young married couples to start their families early. Similarly, young couples who live together without being married almost always decide to legalize their union once the birth of a child is imminent. Married women who delay having a baby for too long are criticized for being 'selfish'. For instance, a doctor wrote in an Australian sociology book about 'the family':

It is wise for a young couple to start a family as soon after marriage as possible. Perhaps three to six months can be used in which to 'get to know' one another under ideal conditions . . . A marriage is incomplete without children and yet the longer a pregnancy is postponed the greater the danger of selfishness developing.[24]

Women are not yet in full control of their fertility while methods of contraception remain unreliable or a risk to health, and the uneasy legal status of abortion makes termination of pregnancy available only to women in capital cities who know where to go. Until women gain full control of their fertility they will still be subjected to un-wanted pregnancies and, often, unanticipated and unwanted marriages. But whatever degree of fertility control is obtained, present methods of reproduction still require women to bear children. Some radical feminists have argued that only the development of artificial means of reproduction will totally free women[25] but this view is neither widely accepted by women nor is yet technologically feasible. (Such a view also ties the liberation of women and the abolition of sexism rather determinedly to technological innovation which would confine it to small sections of the world population. This view therefore is open to many objections on political as well as other grounds.)

In our currently over-populated world there is no danger of species-extinction so there is no justification for enforcing compulsory motherhood. Denying women access to facilities for contraception and abortion amounts to this. If women could control their fertility they would then have a real choice about whether or not they wished to bear children. But if vast numbers opted not to have any then 'the family' would be threatened. This is one reason why non-procreative forms of sexuality, such as homosexuality, are so abhorred by advocates of 'the family'. 'The family' is dependent on women being prepared, if not forced, to bear children.

Extra-marital reproduction could also undermine 'the family'. Whether or not this is a real possibility could only be gauged by considering several variables over a lengthy period of time. The statistics on extra-marital births do not, in themselves, indicate whether or not 'the family' is being threatened by recalcitrant women even though their number has increased quite markedly in recent years. Until the late 1950s extra-marital births in Australia amounted to about 4 per cent of annual births; between 1966 and 1970, 7.88 per cent of births were 'illegitimate' and they have increased slowly every year since, from 8.30 per cent in 1970 to 9.77 per cent in 1973.[26] But the figures alone provide no guide to whether this trend threatens 'the family'. We would need to know what percentage of women kept their children – or had them adopted by families – as well as those who subsequently legitimized them by forming legally recognized families. At present some 90 per cent of child-bearing women are preferring to have legitimate babies, and a substantial proportion of those babies born outside marriage are adopted. Women themselves, therefore, are perpetuating the convention that reproduction should occur within marriage and as children are the starting point of 'the family', we can say that women are choosing to perpetuate the institution.

3. CONSUMERISM

Consumerism is the regular and almost compulsive purchasing of goods or services which are not essential to human survival. This is a function which is quite specific to societies which produce a surplus of commodities apart from foodstuffs and the basic require-ments of clothing and shelter. It assumes that basic scarcity has been overcome, for at least a large proportion of the population, and that people can be induced to buy non-essential goods. In a society where families constitute the dominant form of social organization and where an expanding capitalism seeks to increase its profits by increasing markets for its products, it is obvious that families are going to be encouraged to consume as *families*. The association of private space (the family home) with family life has meant that each family buys a large number of essential goods which could easily be shared among larger groups of people. Such things as cars, washing machines, lawnmowers, books etc. which are purchased by each family unit could be shared between several households.

But in a competitive society, where people compete against each other for status as well as money, the family home becomes more than a retreat from the outside world. It assumes a demonstrative function whereby people can display their wealth by adorning their houses and gardens with every conceivable appliance, gadget, piece of furniture and arrangement of artistry that the market allows and their incomes can afford. In a society where the over-production of non-essential goods occupies a vital part of the economy and where time payment enables instant possession if not ownership, great effort is expended by producers to encourage families to consume. The advertising industry encourages and reinforces excessive buying, especially status consumption, as well as trying to induce people to accept advertisers' definitions of what goods and services are essential to family well-being.

Consumerism is a function which involves mainly women. Men probably decide when a new car is necessary and choose the make, but women are reputed to have a decisive say in spending up to 90 per cent of the family budget. A bored housewife is a very susceptible target in a consumer society which tries to equate happiness with purchasing. (See Chapter Thirteen.)

Consumerism is not a function which is essential to family survival, even if this is how advertisements often portray the products they brandish. Poor families obviously consume much less than rich ones and this does not necessarily impede their performance of other family functions. It can be expected as inflation reduces the spending power of low and fixed income earners that there will be a growth in co-operative buying amongst some family groups. This already occurs with foodstuffs and could easily be extended to cover some consumer durables. Although our present economy is very dependent on multiple family consumption, this is not essential to the survival of the capitalist system. Were new forms of families to develop, we would expect a rapid adjustment by manufacturers to cater for new needs. Obviously the trend of many young people leaving the family home and sharing flats or houses with others of their age has led to an *increase* in consumption of many essential household items by people who are not setting up new nuclear families.

The only real challenge to the consumerism ethic comes from groups which deliberately set out to exist on as few material possessions as possible: some communes, especially rural ones, operate in this fashion and they obviously contribute little to the creation of surplus value and the profits accrued by manufacturers of household and other goods. Were such non-consumption to become widespread, the capitalist system would be under some threat, but such an occurrence appears highly unlikely at present since most people cherish the comforts of their abundantly stocked houses and see no reason beyond the limits of their incomes to curtail their consumerism.

This is a highly specific function of families, one which is totally contingent on historical and economic circumstances. It is, in a sense, an excrescence on 'the family' since it serves no essential function for the institution. The values which have become attached to family consumerism – and which are manifested in such things as family shopping outings and the deliberate commercialization of Mother's Day and Father's Day – are cultivated ones. Their existence reminds us of the strength of family ideology, but families would not collapse if they ceased to consume. However, if this function ceased to exist, women within families would discover how great a proportion of their time was devoted either to consuming, or to planning to consume, and many women could find that the paid employment they now take for 'economic reasons' is perhaps not essential to maintaining (i.e. feeding, clothing, educating etc.) their families.

4. PRIVATIZATION

Privatization refers to the actual retreat of the marital couple from society and to the emotional processes which attend it. It has already been stated that the physical separation of 'the family' from society is one of the definitive characteristics of the bourgeois family. This retreat takes the form of the couple establishing a separate household which they view as an inviolable domain. Such retreat is seen as increasingly necessary in a world that is violent, exploitative, and racked with the tensions of overcrowded cities and the nebulous fears induced by international conflicts or political or industrial unrest. Individuals seek refuge from what they fear or dislike in society within the closed world of 'the family', and especially in close relationships with other family members.

From early this century 'the family' has been increasingly seen as a sphere of self-realization, as an autonomous realm where individuals might express themselves in ways which are usually denied to them at their place of work. As Zaretsky remarks,

. . . the contemporary family threatens to become a well of subjectivity divorced from any social meaning. Within it a world of vast psychological complexity has developed as the counterpart to the extraordinary degree of rationalization and impersonality achieved by capital in the sphere of commodity production. The individualist values generated by centuries of bourgeois development – self-consciousness, perfectionism, independence – have taken new shape through the insatiability of personal development in developed capitalist society. The internal life of the family is dominated by a search for personal fulfilment for which there seem to be no rules. Much of this search has been at the expense of women.[27]

I have already pointed out that the role of emotional sustenance is undertaken almost entirely by the wife/mother, and that the women's self-maintenance is also self-abnegation since women maintain self by conforming to roles which render them subservient and secondary. The stress on self-realization which forms much of the current ideological rationale for 'the family' allows women this bounty only in their function as child-bearers. At the same time, the weight of the emotional sustenance role has increased the more the role of family in individual self-realization is stressed, and so women have had to shoulder additional burdens for ever diminishing rewards – since women now bear fewer children and, in terms of the ideology, are thus afforded fewer opportunities for *their* form of self-expression.

Women with paid jobs have to juggle their time and their energy between working at those jobs and continuing to be mothers, housekeepers and wives. They are in an excruciating position: since they are exposed to the outside world and the frustrations of the workplace they need to retreat to 'the family' in the same way as their husbands do, but they are the ones who bear the main responsibility for ensuring that 'the family' is a haven. Men do not learn to fulfil this role and most find it extremely difficult to adopt, particularly if they have never been called upon to perform it until comparatively late in life – which is when their wives are most likely to resume paid employment. Many men thus resent their wives taking jobs since it means that, even though the material benefits for the family group might be enhanced, their wives' ability to give them emotional sustenance is likely to be diminished.

Marital and family relationships are now afforded a value which they have never before had to possess. Until this century it was not considered necessary to love one's marriage partner, or to have to relate to her/him at more than a functional level. It is now considered paramount that 'a good relationship' form the hub of every family.

Yet the sex division of labour within 'the family' means that women's quest for fulfilment within the conjugal relationship inevitably fails to reach her expectations. Although both sexes now desire and expect a rewarding and sustaining relationship, the structural inequalities of the marriage-family institution make this expectation difficult, if not impossible, for women to attain. Women are still taught to expect their major area of fulfilment to be through bearing and raising children, and the demands of this role are often totally at odds with having the time, energy and disposition to devote to developing and maintaining the conjugal relationship. By the time the children are old enough not to need constant care and attention it is often too late: the husband has found another partner.

Secondly, while women are expected to play the role of soothers, comforters and mediators within 'the family' and the primary responsibility for managing personal relationships rests with them, men do not learn, or see the need to, develop any of these traits or skills themselves. They can rest secure in their legal and economic dominance of 'the family' and expect that their role as provider entitles them to constant cosseting and devotion.

Women have learnt to expect their familial roles to constitute their major, if not their sole, mode of self-expression and satisfaction. But women are overburdened with responsibilities within 'the family' (and these do not diminish, but are increased, if they have a paid job as well) and some of these responsibilities are often, in practice, mutually exclusive or contradictory. This means that women must almost always agree to settle for less: they must apportion their energies and their emotions between children and husband. Rather than this leading to a rich relationship enhanced by its involving several people, it often results in the woman feeling her loyalties to be divided and she can begin to resent the many and varied demands made upon her emotions. The husband is not similarly divided since he is not expected to have such a close relationship with his children.

The basic inequality between husband and wife is critical when it comes to the enhanced expectations each now has of the conjugal relationship because these expectations have been grafted on to a structure which cannot really accommodate them. Yet this inequality is integral to maintaining 'the family': if women refused to submit to their diverse familial roles it is unlikely that the institution could survive. To date there is no widely accepted alternative to the inequalities of family relationships, and so when people leave one relationship because they find it unsatisfactory and seek to establish another one, what they actually seek to reproduce is this inequality – which they equate with fulfilment. The closed private world of 'the family' with its ever-increasing stress that it can provide avenues for individual fulfilment and mutual happiness can in fact only provide this to the extent that women consent in relinquishing some of their expectations and then collaborate in disguising this fact. The inequalities and their consequences persist *because* 'the family' is a closed and private area of existence. If when a relationship fails to meet people's expectations they began to question the structure of the institution rather than just blaming the other person, then perhaps the ideology of 'the family' could be challenged. But one of the primary purposes of maintaining privatization is to avert such a challenge and, in this way, perpetuate 'the family'.

5. THE REPRESSION OF SEXUALITY

The repression of sexuality is one of the most important functions of 'the family' since it is one of the means by which 'the family' is reproduced. Sexuality in our society is controlled and managed. Until very recently only one form of sexuality was permitted: procreative sexuality within marriage. Although not all sex within marriage was expressly aimed at conceiving another child, it occurred within a procreative framework. Marriage was seen as the only legitimate state in which to have a child, and 'the family' required marriage as a precondition for its existence. In the last decade with the development of fairly effective forms of contraception, and with an exploding world population providing a reason to restrict fertility, it has no longer been possible to confine sex to marriage or to view it as primarily procreative. So-called 'recreational sex' has become increasingly acceptable and this state of affairs has been labelled 'the permissive society'. But this very phrase illustrates that limits still exist: it describes a society which *permits* more forms of sexual expression than was previously the case. The very words reveal the authoritarian nature of the situation: if a society can permit, it can also prohibit.

Individuals are still subject to social controls. Male homosexuality, for instance, is still outlawed as are various other forms of sexuality which are labelled as 'perversions': incest, sodomy, bestiality and sex between adults and children. There is an 'age of consent' for girls, demarcating the age at which they are legally permitted to have sexual intercourse. If a girl below this age is discovered to be having sexual relations she is usually confined to a State institution and her male partner is charged with having carnal knowledge and often imprisoned.

All societies restrict sexuality to some degree, although there is considerable variation between different societies in what is permitted and prohibited. But some amount of control has always been seen as necessary and usually justified in terms of perpetuating that society. Freud, for instance, maintained that the very existence of civilization depended on sexual instincts being repressed:

. . . society must undertake as one of its most important educative tasks to tame and restrict the sexual instinct when it breaks out as an urge to reproduction, and to subject it to an individual will which is identical with the bidding of society. It is also concerned to postpone the full development of the instinct till the child shall have reached a certain degree of intellectual maturity, for, with the complete irruption of the sexual instinct, educability is for practical purposes at an end. Otherwise, the instinct would break down every dam and wash away the laboriously erected work of civilization. Nor is the task of taming it ever an easy one; its success is sometimes too small, sometimes too great. The motive of human society is in the last resort an economic one; since it does not possess enough provisions to keep its members alive unless they work, it must restrict the number of its members and divert their energies from sexual activity to work.[28]

This view assumes a scarcity of resources and an inability to control population except through sexual abstinence, but it also uses an argument which is widely subscribed to in capitalist countries: that people must curb their sexuality so that they will work. Sex must be routinized and pushed into the far corners of people's lives. It must be an activity which is totally separated from work – which is seen as people's main activity – and must submit to the routines imposed by that.

The sex instincts are not totally repressed, they are organized. They are channelled into genitality (in contradiction to the human potential to respond sensuously over her or his entire body) and they are subjugated under the function of procreation. All other forms of sexual expression are outlawed as 'perversions'. In most civilizations this genital procreative sexuality is only permitted to be expressed within one institution, that of monogamous marriage. Moreover, the expression of even this limited form of sexuality is controlled and organized by the demands of the labour market.

Sexuality is relegated to one corner of life, while the 'realistic' needs of the labour market are elevated to prime importance in the individual's life. Adults spend most of their day at work, or preparing for or recovering from work, and have only a few hours each day in which to relax. Sexuality must be confined to this small temporal space. It must take place at times when people are tired from their day's work, or it cannot take place because they are tired or because they must be up early for work the next morning. People are excused from work if they are sick – but not if they merely feel like pursuing their sexual inclinations.

Probably the only occasion when sexual activity is regarded as totally legitimate and is ritualistically enforced on people is on a couple's wedding night, but even here the apparent unease with which most people view sexuality is made evident by the coarse and ribald jokes and suggestions which are likely to be directed at the newly married couple. Far from being viewed as natural and enjoyable, sex is seen as a furtive, even dirty activity which, if it must take place at all, should be confined to darkened bedrooms and accomplished with a minimum of delay. The various terms Australians use for sexual intercourse – having a 'naughty' or a 'poke' – amply illustrate this.

For people to view a basic instinctual drive in this fashion – the same attitudes are not applied to eating for instance – it is evident that a process of repressing that instinct must have taken place. This process begins in early childhood and occurs within 'the family'. Children are discouraged from touching their genitals, or from being interested in those of other children or adults. Their provocative and often perverse sexual questions and conversations invoke admonition and punishment from shocked parents whose own sexuality has been so successfully repressed that they cannot remember that they acted in exactly the same fashion. Most parents will not permit their children to see their naked bodies and they are careful lest they witness any sexual activity. Once children have reached the age of sexual curiosity they are not usually allowed to bathe with siblings of the opposite sex, nor to share bedrooms with them.

'The family' is obviously an ideal place to effect the repression of sexuality. It possesses natural limits of size and variability which make strict supervision and control of children easy. Children are subjected to the control of their parents in every other respect so the repression of their sexuality can occur as just one further process of their 'bringing up'; it fits easily and unobtrusively into the overall parent-child relationship. The small size of the Australian family reinforces parental authority as there are seldom more than two or three children, a number which can be supervised fairly rigorously. Similarly the small size generally means that there is not a great variation in the children's ages which again makes curbing their sexuality easier. A mixture of very young and adult children tends to blur the child/parent distinction and perhaps subvert parental authority to some extent. It can also contradict the dictate which parents try to enforce that children should be asexual, since the adult 'children' will undoubtedly be dating and engaging in some forms of sexual activity.

A further reason for 'the family' being seen as a suitable place for repressing sexuality is that it is not supposed to provide opportunities for sexual contact between its members – except, of course, between husband and wife. It is not known how widely the taboo on incest is observed since this is not a subject which has attracted the interest of researchers in Australia. It is likely that it is broken far more frequently than we would expect (given the horror which this form of sexuality generally evokes) but it is also probable that most incest is in fact rape, with fathers forcing themselves on their daughters. Other forms of incest, between mothers and sons and sisters and brothers are probably far less common.

As the person who bears the major responsibility for 'bringing up' children, the mother is the primary agent in their sexual repression. It is she who will explicitly instruct and restrict, who will urge her children away from sexual games and punish them for 'playing with themselves'. As part of what she sees as her maternal duties of ensuring that 'the family' reproduces itself, she will generally take particular care in the instruction of her daughters, leading them to believe that sexuality merely justifies its end which is motherhood and has little else to commend it. She will teach her daughters that it is their duty to curb the 'uncontrollable passions' of the boys she goes out with, that the woman must set the pace in any encounter since women are less troubled by such passions. In instructing her daughter thus, a mother is bequeathing to the next generation of women her own sexual miseries and fears and frustrations.

As the next chapter points out, women are the ones who have suffered most from the particular form sexual repression takes in Australia. Sex engaged in purely for procreation or for male satis-faction and seen as an illicit activity to be got over with as quickly as possible is rarely satisfactory for a woman. Small wonder, then, that many mothers are not eager for their daughters to be sexually active. Others pragmatically put their daughters on the contraceptive pill. Both responses are designed to ensure that their daughters will not bear children outside the legitimate bounds of 'the family', the first by trying to discourage daughters from any but marital pro-creational sexuality, the second by ensuring that the daughter does not get pregnant as she flails through 'the permissive society'.

Mothers pay less attention to curbing their sons' sexuality once the initial childhood repression is completed; they confidently rely on women continuing to fulfil the God's Police role which, as we have seen, denies female sexuality and places women in the position of regulating the sexuality of the men with whom they live or go out. Sons who 'sow their wild oats' are regarded indulgently, whereas a pregnant unmarried daughter is still regarded as being immoral and casting shame on her entire family. So even though the processes of sexual repression encompass all members of Australian society, men and women are assigned different roles within that repressed state. Men are undeniably afforded more sexual freedom while women inherit the unhappy task of monitoring both their own and their men's sexuality, and of trying to ensure that the next generation of women will perpetuate 'the family' by avoiding procreational sex outside marriage.

Their effectiveness can be relied upon whereas that of more traditional agencies such as the churches cannot, because women have little option but to perpetuate and strengthen the one social arena which gives their lives some legitimacy and function – 'the family'. If women were to refuse to be moral guardians and to be sexually circumspect, so long as the view that sexual repression is necessary to maintain civilization were maintained some other agent of repression would be found. But it is difficult to envisage any other agency where this repression could be effected so easily and so unobtrusively as within 'the family'.

6. SOCIALIZATION

Socialization is the process whereby individuals learn the norms, values and behaviour codes of society and of the particular group into which they are born or into which they come to spend their lives. As children we learn broad social conventions as well as more specific ones related to sex, class, and race and also those deriving from the region where we live, the religion to which our parents belong and the ethnic group into which we are born.*

Socialization, as the term implies, is the *imposition* of society's values and demands on to the individual. This occurs for two reasons. Even in a society such as Australia which professes to value the freedom of the individual, social needs are seen as over-riding those of the individual if there is conflict between the two, and one of the purposes of socialization is to minimize this conflict by having the individual voluntarily conform to social dictates. Secondly, this imposition is almost inevitable when the process of teaching these values begins when the child is physically dependent and psychologically malleable and is therefore incapable of disputing what it is

* Socialization can be seen as a continuous and life-long process, for as long as we encounter new situations or are called upon to perform new roles we must learn how to act within these situations or roles, but I am here only concerned with childhood socialization. This is because the focus here is on 'the family', the site of a great part of childhood socialization, and also because of my argument that what occurs during childhood socialization is not merely the absorption of knowledge and attitudes but the formation of a psychic structure and the channelling of instincts into conformity to the demands of the *status quo*.

taught. This does not mean that individuals are incapable of later rejecting or at least questioning some or all of the content of what they are taught as children. We would have no rebels, and no possibility of widespread individual social change, if this were the case. Similarly, the content of each child's socialization is not identical. It is informed by the various group differences mentioned above and also by the extent to which the socializing agents concur with the broad social values. Thus some children are taught to be devoutly religious while others are taught to reject all religion; some learn that the existing class system is natural or inevitable and others learn that it is exploitative and unjust.

But despite a plethora of individual and group variations among families some common patterns emerge. Although what we can call primary socialization occurs within families whose cultural affiliations are more or less diverse, a secondary socialization of a far more uniform kind takes place within schools. Here the State exercises a considerable degree of control over what is taught (and over who is permitted to teach – many teachers are dismissed for stepping beyond these prescriptions) and the pressures of succeeding at school examinations and conforming to peer group norms often combine to subvert parental inclinations.

From the time of birth it is difficult to distinguish just what constitutes merely caring for a child and what is guiding her or him into what the carer considers appropriate behaviour. As the infant grows this guidance becomes more evident, but what is important to recognize is that very little, if any, of the behaviour the child learns is culturally neutral. The child learns restraint (from aggression), control (over its bowels), moderation (in eating, playing) and, above all, obedience (to adults, mainly its parents and older relatives but also to authority figures such as policemen, teachers, clergy and any others which are selected as appropriate by its parents or placed before the child by society through one of its agencies such as the mass media).

These are all characteristics required by a society which needs to exact loyalty and conformity from its members so that they will perform the tasks which perpetuate that society *in its present form*. That form includes the current economic system and those institutions such as 'the family' and the education system which support and reinforce it. Thus socialization is a conservative function which is directed to ensuring the perpetuation of the existing form of the society and the institutions which comprise it. Since the greater part of socialization occurs within 'the family', we can say that 'the family' has as one of its most important jobs the maintenance of the *status quo*. This task is virtually identical to that described as the God's Police role of women: the maintenance of existing authority relations. It is therefore in the processes of socialization and sexual repression that we see most clearly the congruence of 'the family' and the approved female role; and the importance to the capitalist system of women performing the God's Police role within 'the family'.

In Australia, as in most Western nations, 'the family' is seen as the best place to 'bring up' children, and people who have children, or intend to have them, usually establish families for this reason. Couples who live together almost always marry if a child is expected. The State attempts to find foster homes for children placed under its care, and there are adoption facilities for 'approved' families to take over the care of children unwanted or unable to be cared for by their natural mothers. 'The family' is regarded as a hallowed haven, as the *only* suitable site for child-development, and those unfortunate children who find themselves being 'brought up' in an institution or some other family substitute are usually made to feel aware of their deprived situation.

But this *family* idolatry is rather curious when we remember that the actual child carers, and those who are given the main charge of socializing children, are *women*. The father's main role is seen as being provider and protector for the woman and her brood, and he is expected to be a model of masculinity which his sons can emulate. It is the mother who spends most time with her children, who nurtures them and guides their physical, spiritual and cultural development. And I have already shown that this guidance cannot be culturally neutral: the mother's directives are always towards socially valued ends, ends which coincide with the characteristics demanded of people by the system.

Thus it would seem that it is women as mothers, rather than 'the family' who are the instruments of socialization. The mother is charged with child-care and it is she who is constantly present and struggling with the child. The father remains an authority figure but he is only present for a few hours a day; indeed if he works a long distance from home the children might only see him at weekends and although he might be called upon to administer severe discipline it is usually on the mother's behalf and for some action which has occurred while he was not present ('just wait till your father gets home!'). Because the father is not continually present he is less aware of the daily battles and tends to see his children at the end of the day, after they have been bathed and fed, when they are tired and less boisterous. He can relate to them as a kind and indulgent figure, someone to play with, a contrast to their nervy and irritable mother.

It is mothers rather than 'the family' who are held to be responsible for how their children develop and even for what they do as adults. If a child becomes a delinquent, a homosexual, a sex offender or demonstrates any form of criminal or anti-social behaviour, the mother is seen to be somehow to blame. In the case of delinquency and homosexuality there are all kinds of specious psychological theories which try to 'prove' her complicity. If she 'neglected' her child – by going out to work, for instance, – then she has created a delinquent; if she smothered her (male) child – by paying him too much attention – then she has made him a homosexual. The mother too often responds to these charges with guilt-stricken agreement since she accepts her socially-assigned role as child-minder but is not always fully aware of the strategic role she, as socializer and repressor of sexuality, plays for the maintenance of the existing system.

Thus women do all the work and if the results are as the system wants them then the institution in which they work, 'the family', receives the credit. If they are not successful, however, it is they rather than the institution which tends to receive the blame.

'THE FAMILY' AND DIVORCE

Rather than seeing the institution of 'the family' as breaking down, as many contemporary moralists bemoan, we can see that its reputation has never been higher. A distinction is now posited between the institution and the individuals within it, and this separation enables that institution to endure in the face of individual defections or disenchantment. One of the primary objects of 'the family' is to reproduce itself. This means more than merely producing children; it also means ensuring that they will form families themselves, and parents are starting to be as self-conscious about this responsibility as they are about their relationship with each other. A good relationship between the conjugal couple is seen as necessary to socialize the children of the marriage successfully. The idea of a couple remaining together at all costs is starting to be replaced by the search to find 'what's best for the children'. If the intention is to persuade the child that one's physical and emotional well-being is best provided for within the closed private world of 'the family' then it is obviously undesirable for a child to have to witness and endure constant conflict and hostility between its parents.

The parents themselves have acquired strong expectations for a fulfilling conjugal relationship and their view of 'the family' is likely to be prejudiced if they do not experience this. Greater life-expectancy now means that people spend a considerably longer period of time in families than they did a century ago, and fewer and fewer people are now prepared to spend what could be as long as fifty years imprisoned in an unhappy marriage. This combination of wanting self-fulfilment and feeling a responsibility to instil a favourable disposition towards marriage and family in their children may lead a couple to decide to separate and obtain a divorce.

Such a decision, in these circumstances, is likely to be encouraged by marriage guidance counsellors who are now beginning to recognize that a good conjugal relationship is 'what's best for the children'. Whereas divorce used to be abhorred by upholders of 'the family', it is increasingly being seen as integral to preserving it. This change in attitude is reflected in divorce statistics. It should be pointed out that a majority of families remain together if not forever, at least until children reach adulthood, and the number of children involved in divorce cases remains very small. In 1973, 16,095 marriages were dissolved in Australia and nearly one-third of these, 5,210, involved no children.[29] The 15,584 marriages dissolved in 1972 involved 22,061 children[30] while in 1973 this number had only risen slightly, to 22,952 children. At the 1971 Australian Census, the total number of children aged twenty and under was 1,075,817[31] so the proportion of children involved in divorce cases is very small.*

But it is also clear that the presence of children in a marriage has, in the past, deterred couples from divorce. Until 1971 most divorces were granted to couples who had been married less than five years or more than fifteen years; in 1971, 9.3 per cent of divorces were to couples who had been married less than five years while 40.7 per cent were to those married fifteen years or more.[32] This suggests that half of all divorced couples either had no children, or had only one, or that they waited until their parental responsibilities were discharged before dissolving an unsatisfactory relationship. This is borne out by

* This number could be substantially larger if those children involved in desertions and separations could be accounted for. This would entail obtaining statistical information on the number of children whose mothers are in receipt of the supporting mothers' allowance – and this information is not readily available. Even this would not complete the picture, however, as we would also need to add those children who are cared for by their father as well as those whose mothers are not in receipt of a social security allowance.

the 1972 divorce figures: there were only 143 children involved in the 401 divorces granted to couples married five years or less.[33] Since 1971 the number of divorces granted has risen by about 30 per cent and most of that rise has occurred amongst couples married five to nine years[34], and who are thus likely to have young children. It is clear that the relationship between the conjugal couple is being seen as extremely important and that fewer people are prepared to endure an unfulfilling marriage simply for the sake of the children. Couples now separate with less guilt as they begin to realize that their children are likely to be happier, and to have a better chance of acquiring a pro-family disposition.

Most people do not divorce because they are disenchanted with marriage and 'the family'. Rather, they divorce because they have learned to value these relationships so highly that they are discontented if they do not match their hopes and expectations. The very closeness and intensity of the privatized world of 'the family' exacerbates relational tensions which perhaps would be less evident if there were continuous interaction with a wider group. Yet people have learned to expect emotional fulfilment from just such a closed and intense relationship so if one relationship is unsuccessful they will usually attempt to form another. Because they have learned to expect to find emotional sustenance in marriage and family, most people attribute an unsuccessful relationship to the individuals involved and not to the institution itself and so they are not deterred from attempting to establish another relationship. Divorced people generally seek, and a great many manage, to marry again, or to at least form a stable *de facto* relationship.[35]

CONCLUSION

The foregoing has argued that virtually every function of 'the family' is dependent on women's work for its performance. Yet while women are accorded a certain amount of status for doing so, the institution remains a patriarchal one. Legally and economically it is dominated by the husband/father. It bears his name and requires his financial support, if not his presence. If either of these is withheld then women must founder in a world which gives them scant recognition because they are unmarried or because they have been abandoned by their provider/protector. In return for giving his name and his financial support, the husband/father assumes dominance within an institution which plays a key role in perpetuating the present system, a system which is both capitalist and patriarchal.

The pious and sentimental attitudes and conventions which surround 'the family' disguise the connection between it and the system by representing it as a privatized sphere, and as an arena of individual assertion. They also obscure the work that women do within families as well as the fact that women have little choice but to engage in this work. 'The family' survives on the conscripted labour of women.

The functions fulfilled by 'the family' as outlined in this chapter are all interlocking and mutually dependent. Not all of them are socially necessary, and they need not all be performed within an institution such as 'the family'. The common link between them is provided by women who, as mothers and wives, devote the greater part of their lives to ensuring the perpetuation of existing authority relations and, hence, 'the family'.

NOTES

1. Ladislas Ruzicka and Lincoln Day, 'Australian Patterns of Family Formation', *Search*, July 1974, p. 303.
2. Eva Figes, *Patriarchal Attitudes*, Faber & Faber, London, 1970, pp. 17–18.
3. The information in this section has been gathered from a variety of sources, including talking with women who have been in homes and prisons. The written sources include the following: accounts of girls in homes and prisons in *Mejane*, no. 8, August 1972, and no. 10, March 1973; Shirley Lewis, 'Sheltered Lives', *Nation Review*, July 27–August 2, 1973; Elisabeth Wynhausen, 'Suffer the Little Children', *Bulletin*, 8 April, 1972; Virginia Duigan, 'Liberation turns more women to crime – now for equal penalties', *National Times*, August 27–September 1, 1973; Department of Corrective Services, New South Wales, *Women in Prison*, Sydney, 1971.
4. Lewis, *Nation Review*, op. cit.
5. *Women in Prison*, op. cit., p. 45.
6. *Mejane*, no. 10, March 1973.
7. Duigan, *National Times*. See also 'Women's Lib. link with crime rise', *Sydney Morning Herald*, 18 July, 1973.
8. Angela Weir, 'When the key turns', *Spare Rib*, May 1973, p. 26.
9. *Prison Statistics 1971–72 New South Wales*, Bureau of Census and Statistics, Sydney, 1973, p. 7.
10. *Women in Prison*, op. cit., p. 20.
11. ibid., p. 34.

12. The use of these six functions has been adapted from Anna Yeatman, 'The Marriage-Family Institution', *Australian Left Review*, no. 28, December–January 1971, pp. 21–37.

13. Phillipe Aries, *Centuries of Childhood*, Penguin Books, 1973, p. 390. The following account of the development of the nuclear family is based on Aries; and on Eli Zaretsky, 'Capitalism, the Family and Personal Life' Part I, *Socialist Revolution*, January–April, 1973, pp. 69–125.

14. Aries, op. cit., p. 396.

15. Zaretsky, op. cit., pp. 95–6.

16. Frederick Engels, *The Condition of the Working Class in England*, Panther, London, 1969, p. 159.

17. E. P. Thompson, *The Making of the English Working Class*, Penguin Books, 1968, pp. 366–7.

18. ibid.

19. Zaretsky, op. cit., p. 79.

20. Reported in the *Australian*, 18 April, 1973.

21. Reported in the *Sydney Morning Herald*, 19 June, 1973.

22. I do not propose to undertake the lengthy discussion which would be necessary to demonstrate that these attitudes are socially determined rather than inherent to the female of the species. These arguments are adequately covered in Michael Rutter, *Maternal Deprivation Reassessed*, Penguin Books, 1974; Lee Comer, *The Myth of Motherhood*, Nottingham, 1972 (Spokeswoman pamphlet available from Women's Liberation, Sydney).

23. Julie Rigg et al., *Child Care: A Community Responsibility*, Media Women's Action Group, Sydney, 1972, p. 7.

24. Dr Lorna Lloyd-Green, 'Family Planning' in Allan Stoller, ed., *The Family Today*, Cheshire, for the Victorian Family Council, Melbourne, 1962, p. 160.

25. e.g. Shulamith Firestone, *The Dialectic of Sex*, Jonathan Cape, London, 1971, p. 263.

26. Australian Bureau of Statistics, *Births 1973*, Canberra, 1975, p. 5.

27. Zaretsky, op. cit., pp. 122–3.

28. Sigmund Freud, *Introductory Lectures on Psychoanalysis*, Penguin Books, 1974, pp. 353–4.

29. Australian Bureau of Statistics, *Divorce 1973*, Canberra, October 1974, p. 12.

30. Australian Bureau of Census and Statistics, *Divorce 1972*, Canberra, July 1973, p. 12.

31. W. G. Coppell, *Australia in Figures*, Penguin Books, 1974, p. 15.

32. ibid., p. 28.

33. *Divorce 1972*, op. cit., p. 12.

34. *Divorce 1973*, op. cit., p. 13.

35. Elizabeth Kelly, 'Sociological Aspects of Family Life', in Jerzy Krupinski and Allan Stoller, *The Family in Australia*, Pergamon, Sydney, 1974, p. 21.

CHAPTER SEVEN

A COLONIZED SEX

The subjection of women to men being a universal custom, any departure from it quite naturally appears unnatural.

JOHN STUART MILL, *The Subjection of Women*, 1869

Rape is an act of aggression (by a man or group of men against a woman) in which the victim is denied her self-determination. It is an act of violence which, if not actually followed by beatings or murder, nevertheless always carries with it the threat of death . . . rape is a form of mass terrorism, for the victims of rape are chosen indiscriminately but the propagandists for male supremacy broadcast that it is women who cause rape by being unchaste or in the wrong place at the wrong time – in essence, by behaving as though they were free.

SUSAN GRIFFIN, 'Rape: The All-American Crime',
Ramparts, September 1971

At the Women's Commission [in Sydney] last March, much time was spent listening to the expression of hostility towards the doctors in women's lives. The cost of treatment was rarely mentioned. The complaints were about male chauvinism and its pervasive effects on women's treatment and their well-being.

CAROLINE GRAHAM, 'Women and Doctors',
Nation Review, 8–14 June, 1973

During life it is inevitable that a woman will have her share of anxiety, of illness, of strain, as well as her share of satisfaction and happiness. But because she is biologically different from man, she may develop conditions unique to woman. Many of these are minor, but require attention. In most instances a woman should consult her doctor, but as doctors are busy men and all too often do not explain adequately to the patient the nature of the condition from which she is suffering, she often remains anxious.

DEREK LLEWELLYN-JONES, M.D., *Everywoman*, 1971

When the British invaded the continent of Australia in 1788 they did more than colonize a continent and its Aboriginal inhabitants.

They also colonized an entire sex – the female sex. This means of exploiting women was not a unique form developed especially for the Antipodes although, as Part Two outlines, it has taken on various unique features in this country. The argument that women are a colonized sex can be generalized to include all industrialized Western countries, and is probably applicable to women in all known societies. However no such universal claim is being advanced here: my intention is to try and show how women in Australia are colonized and some of the effects of this.

The classic colonial situation has four major components which can be described in abbreviated fashion as (1) the invasion and conquering of a territory, (2) the cultural domination of its inhabitants, (3) the securing of effective control of the inhabitants by creating divisions amongst them, thus preventing their uniting to oppose the invasion, a political tactic traditionally known as divide and rule, and (4) the extraction of profits from the colonized territory. Colonization is accomplished by the brute force of invasion and by the partial or complete destruction of the native people's culture. It is the latter which is often decisive both in accomplishing control and in preventing revolt against the invading power. The native people is persuaded, or forced, to concede that its own culture is inferior and that it should strive to emulate and adopt that of the colonizing power.

The process of cultural colonization is seldom accomplished without resistance since there is usually a religious or spiritual value attached to the indigenous culture by the native people. In such cases the colonizers will try to provide a substitute religion – such as Christianity – which both compensates for the loss of the old one and also, because it is associated with the power of the invaders, can be posed as superior to the myths and superstitions previously adhered to. But the old culture is ultimately destroyed by the 'benefits' which the invaders proffer, 'benefits' which could not possibly be acquired in any other way. The people are offered individual rewards, such as wages for labour (in comparison to the vagaries of commodity exchange which characterize a peasant economy), which enable them to purchase consumer items which the colonial masters persuade them are necessary to a satisfying existence. The invaded people is also supplied with collective benefits in the form of schools, hospitals and other services which, they arc informed, will be of immeasurable advantage to them. (What they do not often recognize immediately is that all of these 'benefits' are in fact slowly inducting them into the ways of life of the colonial power and, at the same time, destroying forever their own heritage and wisdoms.)

No matter with what seeming ease the colonial invasion is accomplished there is invariably some resistance. This usually comes from the older people who either have memories of previous invasions, or instinctively resist this wanton destruction of their own way of life. The tactic adopted by the colonizing power to thwart and neutralize such resistance is the classic one of divide and rule. Some sections of the native people, usually the younger people who want to be 'progressive', are almost always responsive to the rewards dangled before them by the invaders, and it is these groups which are selected for special treatment. They are given privileges, allowed to share some of the status of the colonizers and are persuaded that their capitulation to the mores of the powerful group is to their own personal, as well as their country's, advantage.

The colonizers always make use of ideological weapons. No matter whether this ideology is religion, philanthropy, a 'civilizing mission' or whatever, it is intended to mask the true intent of the invasion. That intention is always to pacify the invaded people and to convince them that the colonization is for their own good. Yet, if there were not substantial benefits to be accrued by the invaders, colonization would not have occurred in the first place. The primary purpose of colonization is always and without exception to enhance the wealth and power of the ruling class of the colonizing country.

At first sight it appears that there are some similarities between the position of women in a patriarchal society such as Australia and that of a colonized people. Both are denied self-determination, and both spend their lives working to enhance the power and wealth of a group to which they can never belong. But this similarity extends much further than has been previously recognized.[1] To say that women are a colonized group is no metaphor. It is a salient political description of women in industrialized countries like Australia, if not of all women everywhere.

The limits to women's freedom and self-determination described in the previous chapters amount to a massive physical and psychological circumscription of their ability to decide what to do with their lives and would, in themselves, present a strong case for describing women as a colonized group. But, it could be objected, women possess no separate territory. They have not been invaded, and various other crucial criteria for colonization have not been met. Can we say that women have had an alien culture imposed upon them? Have they been divided in order to secure a more effective domination? Who profits from their subjugation?

Yet women do possess a territory: their bodies. Women's bodies are territories in two senses. In a society which denies them economic independence and hence precludes them from ownership of land – isolated examples to the contrary do not disprove this since most women with wealth have inherited it from men – their bodies are all that women indisputably possess. Secondly, their bodies are hosts to new life and, to date, no amount of technological innovation has been able to make them redundant in this respect. When human lives are seen as resources – and most societies view population this way, however much they might disguise it with ideological or religious sentiments – it becomes imperative for the survival of the human race that women's bodies continue to serve this function. Women's bodies are seen as territory to be cultivated, the product reaped being a new generation of human beings.

Once women's bodies are recognized as a form of territory the description of their position as being one of colonization stops being metaphorical and assumes the status of political analysis. *Women are colonized by being denied control over their bodies.* The main purpose of colonization is to ensure that women will continue to reproduce. But most societies also require that reproduction does not occur indiscriminately: they want population to be produced in accordance with what are viewed as desirable kinship patterns and methods of socializing new members of that society. In a country such as Australia 'the family' is considered to be the only appropriate institution into which children can be born and reared. Thus the specific aim in colonizing Australian women is to ensure that they will marry and bear children, thus perpetuating 'the family'.

The colonization of women contains the four elements which are present in the colonization of a continent or a tribal people. These are (1) invasion and conquering, (2) cultural domination, (3) divide and rule, and (4) the extraction of profits.

THE COLONIZATION OF WOMEN

Women are denied control and self-determination of their bodies in three separate ways. Their bodies are violently invaded by the act of rape which is a political means of terrorizing and conquering them and controlling their movements. They are denied full expression of their sexuality and the freedom to explore their unique sexual responses by the demands of reproduction. And they are denied free access to those technological means which are available for controling their biology by the stranglehold the medical profession has over these means and their distribution. The cultural domination of women comes about by the imposition of the code of femininity and the male dominated, professionalized practice of modern medicine. Women are divided by the Damned Whore and God's Police stereotypes and, their potential solidarity undermined, patriarchy's control over women is facilitated. Both the patriarchal and capitalist systems and individual men reap substantial profits from women's colonized state.

INVASION AND CONQUERING

THE POLITICAL CRIME OF RAPE

Rape is viewed by most people and by the organs of the mass media as a terrible crime. According to a public opinion survey it is considered by a great majority of people to be second only to murder as the most serious crime that can be committed.[2] But there is a contradiction between this professed public horror and the various means by which rape in Australian society is either overlooked, excused or considered a subject of mirth. These means also disguise the enormous incidence of rape and the fact that it is increasing rapidly.

Rape is defined at law as the forcible penetration of a woman without her consent. This definition is a narrow one which does not encompass or even recognize several kinds of undesired sexual violation which women commonly encounter. The legal definition assumes a degree of violence, or threatened violence, beyond the penetration and overlooks the violence involved in the act of penetration itself.

The heterosexual act of intercourse is, by its very nature, the invasion by a man of a woman's body.* It is not necessarily a coercive

---

* This statement is not intended to imply that all heterosexual intercourse is rape, or that women do not gain pleasure from intercourse. As will become clear as the argument develops, the point being made is to stress the potential for violence which the biological facts of intercourse embody. Much of what is said could also apply to homosexual intercourse, although in a society where heterosexuality is the norm and homosexuality is either proscribed or considered to be immoral or a deviation, then it is to be expected that homosexuality will incorporate many features of heterosexuality, including male/female power relations and the incipient violence that these possess. Thus homosexual rape also exists.

act, nor one which women do not seek or enjoy, but in a political system where differences of sex also describe differences of power and status it becomes not merely one aspect of that power difference, but a tangible expression of it. The heterosexual act of intercourse is the unique activity which encapsulates the polarity between the sexes: the male must actively desire it before it can be accomplished, while the female's acquiescence is not physically necessary. This activity is also the means by which the female is impregnated and thus enabled to perform her unique function for civilization. Yet again it is at the male's behest that this occurs: a woman cannot demand of an unwilling male that he perform this task for her. In other words, biology ordains that a woman's body must be invaded for her to be able to reproduce, yet while she is able to prevent conception she is unable to effect it without the consent of a male. Patriarchal society demands of women that they reproduce, and it is men who have the social and the biological power to decide when *and whether* they will do so. The desire of the male is an essential pre-requisite while female passivity, indifference or resistance is not an impediment. Rape is a biological possibility for the male, while no such conquistadorial power is possessed by the female. This biological fact, when situated in a culture in which men monopolize political, economic, legal, military, religious and other forms of power, has the potential to create a disposition amongst men to view sexual intercourse as one additional piece of weaponry in their armoury of power, one that they can use whenever and upon whomsoever it pleases them.

Rape, however, is not seen as having any connection with 'normal' sexual intercourse. It is seen as a crime, and a very serious one which in Australia carries a maximum penalty of life imprisonment. It is a violent act which occurs very infrequently, people believe, and then is committed only by a minority of deviant men. Rapists are not regarded as ordinary criminals, but as a specially abhorrent group apart. Or at least that is the popular mythology, and it is reinforced by the fact that rape is a subject studied by criminologists who devise all kinds of theories to account for its incidence and to suggest ways of reducing the rape toll.

This is how rape is popularly viewed. This is our means of distancing rape from our everyday lives, of defining it out of the province of normality into the region of deviance and, therefore, of spasmodic and infrequent occurrence. This is patriarchal society's way of de-emphasizing rape. At the one time it is demarcated as the most serious crime short of taking a person's life, and yet also proclaimed to be an offence which is rarely perpetrated and then only by a minority who are seen as deviant.

This view excludes from recognition the common everyday occurrence of rape, denies that it is a constant fear and a far from uncommon reality in the lives of almost all women, and totally overlooks the fact that some instances of rape are actually sanctioned by law while others are deliberately placed outside the ambit of the law.

There is no legal recognition of rape within marriage. Marriage gives a man 'reasonable' access to his wife's body and she is not free to refuse him intercourse if he insists – although she can refuse to participate in some sexual acts, such as sodomy, which are legally proscribed in all circumstances. Marital rape need not only be the brutal forcing of sexual submission from an unwilling wife, although this occurs with a frequency which, if it could be incorporated into the official rape statistics, would increase them to horrendous proportions. Any sexual encounter involving an unwilling woman is a violation of her body and a denial of her self-determination. Marriage provides many occasions for such violation because of the constant physical proximity of husband and wife.

The husband who insists on obtaining his 'rights' when his wife is too tired or for some other reason uninterested, is guilty of rape. These other reasons can include a husband's brutish and selfish lack of consideration for his wife's sexual satisfaction which can leave her totally unmoved or even disgusted by sexual activity. The following letter from a reader to a woman's magazine described such a case:

I am now one of the supine hurry-up girls. Why? Simple. I am tired of 33 years (I am now 50) of trying to get my husband to apply a little gentleness, coupled with loving, prior to sex, but it's always the same old caper. I can be asked anytime. While I am peeling the spuds, playing the piano, reading a book, or as soon as I hit the sheets at night, especially on my busiest day – I am a working wife . . .[3]

A wife is legally obliged to accede to any reasonable demand her husband may make for intercourse. But what is reasonable can be interpreted in different ways. If their interpretations vary her only recourse when she is tired or unwilling is to appeal to his better nature. If he does not heed her request and insists that she submit, he is guilty of rape. The marriage contract says nothing about a wife's entitlement to enjoyable sex; if she has the misfortune to be saddled with an uncaring husband all she can do is submit and get it over with – or else pack up and leave him. If, after years of unrewarding sex, a woman has developed a complete disdain or repugnance for intercourse but is still forced to endure it, she is a constant victim of marital rape.

There are two other kinds of rape which are not recognized as such by the law. These are what Germaine Greer has labelled 'petty rape' and 'rape by fraud'.[4] With both these forms of rape, the woman's consent is extracted – and so they do not meet the legal definition of rape – but this consent is not given freely or from a position of equality or independence. Both these kinds of rape escape being labelled as such because men exploit their superior social and economic power to obtain the woman's submission. To realize the extensive incidence of rape in our society, it is necessary to distinguish between the willingly-agreed-to invasion of a woman's body which is inherent in intercourse, and an invasion which is a violation, a denial of her self-determination, an abrogation of her freedom and independence, an imposition of masculine power upon her female body. In order to make this distinction meaningfully, we have to situate a consideration of rape within the entire landscape of social, and especially sexual, mores which prevail in the society in question at the time.

Because men possess the pre-emptive strike capability, so to speak, and because they also possess the financial, political and other kinds of power which accrue to men in a patriarchal society, the social and sexual relations between the sexes are not equal. The constant manifestations of this unequal relationship as it occurs in marriage were outlined in the last chapter, and the legal immunity which a husband has from being charged with the rape of his wife gives to this a dimension of coercion and terror which cannot be overstressed. The situation between single people is very similar: a basic inequality pervades our sexual universe and is constantly demonstrated, under-scoring the colonized status of women under patriarchy.

Men, the colonizers, not only regard women as sex objects but they continually remind women that this is how they see them. The existence of beauty quests, contests for women with the best bodies, legs, breasts and so on, are but ceremonial testaments to this objecti-fication. Far more insidious are its everyday manifestations. Any newspaper story which happens to mention a woman will describe her by her sexual attributes: by her age, the colour of her hair, the cut of her dress. Women cannot walk even crowded city streets without being whistled at, being cat-called or having their bodies subjected to evaluative scrutiny by the men they pass. The whole repertoire of 'jokes' used by radio and television 'entertainers' depend for their appeal on the audience agreeing that woman equals body, and this view is constantly reinforced in advertising as well as in men's conversations. So confident are men in their status as colonizers that even when they are alone they feel free to make insulting comments to women they pass, to brush their bodies against those of women they do not know, to hiss 'I'd like to *fuck* you' to women they encounter in the street. In groups, especially outside pubs, men acquire the bravado of numbers and increase the number and loudness of their comments. Such instances are not expressions of sexual attraction or desire: they are declarations of menacing intent. And far from being isolated occurrences they are, as any woman who has to use public transport or who has occasion to walk in the streets knows, more of an ever-present hazard than being knocked down by a motor car or being robbed. It is impossible for women to move around, even in the daytime, without being accosted in this manner. They are petty outrages but they are an indication of the power men possess to threaten and insult women, and of the freedom they feel to exercise it and to continually remind women that they possess it.

This power lurks around every male/female encounter but is most likely to emerge in its naked form in situations where the encounters could involve a sexual liaison. It is against a background of this reality that we can discuss petty rape and rape by fraud. Rape by fraud is the exacting of a sexual encounter from a woman by a phony tenderness or by phony promises, such as assurances of marriage or a long-term relationship, or even the likelihood of seeing the man again. In this way a woman may be persuaded to have intercourse, or even to surrender her virginity, because she has been led to believe that the man loves her, or at least that he likes her, and that she is not losing her self-respect or his esteem by agreeing. Under law, this is not rape, since the woman has consented, but her consent has been contingent, has rested on assumptions which are unfounded, which have been assiduously cultivated by a man who merely wants access to her body. This kind of rape is part and parcel of the sexual mores of Australian culture. Those who would object that the consent, however it was obtained, removes the charge of rape from such situations, ignore the inequalities inherent in the encounter. They might charge the woman with excessive credulity or stupidity but they ignore the excruciating position women find themselves in.

The desperate need women have to find husbands places the single woman – especially one who does not measure up to current images of beauty – in a very vulnerable position. She has to devise ways to attract, and then keep, a man's interest and convince him that she is suitable wife material. But no matter how attractive, or how adept, a woman is, she is ultimately placed in a dependent position by the social customs of dating. Men are supposed to be the initiators: they ask the woman for the date, they usually own the car which provides the transport, they pay the cost of the outing, and they are afforded the role of instigating any sexual intimacy which may occur. Women are captive to the need to secure male approval and they have to calculate just what degree of response will earn them a further date and the hope of the man developing some affection for them.

In the past, a woman's role was clearer: if she wished to retain respectability and eligibility for marriage, she had to remain a virgin.[5] Today, with apparent changes having taken place in our sexual code, women are less certain about how (and how far) to respond. While some changes have definitely occurred, it is still men who are the arbiters, who define the limits of permissiveness and decide when a woman has transgressed them. So the woman who is eager to gain the affection of a man whom she likes has to decide if his professed ardour is genuine or merely a ploy. Few young women have the sophistication or the assurance to detect the difference and their own romantic yearnings will probably determine their decision to agree to what, for the male, may be his sole objective: to get her into bed. When she subsequently discovers that his avowals were fraudulent, that he has got all that he wanted from her, and being anxious not to entangle himself with a woman he does not care for, either does not want to see her again or makes it clear that all future involvement will be solely sexual, the woman realizes that she has been conned.

What she may not be conscious of is that she has also been raped, that the man exploited her dependent situation in order to invade her body. She has also possibly been permanently tainted. The man will boast of his conquest, drop the girl's name to his friends, informing them that she is 'an easy lay', that 'all you have to do is spin her a line'. The girl will possibly be pleasurably surprised at her new-found popularity – until she discovers its cause.

Conduct of this kind on the part of men is so integrated into the *modus operandi* of most young men that it is accepted by both sexes as perfectly normal. Men pride themselves in developing a convincing and irresistible seduction patter – their 'line' – and persuade themselves that it is the 'line' which has won them what they want. They exploit the patent inequalities of the situation but seldom make any conscious acknowledgement that this is what they are doing; instead they personalize it and take pride at the ease with which they can get women into bed. Women, on the other hand, realize these inequalities only too well, but they also know that they have little alternative but to take a gamble on reaching through the 'line' to the human being they assume, or hope, exists behind it.

Petty rape is very similar to rape by fraud except that it is stripped of the pretence of affection. The petty rapist capitalizes on the inequality between the sexes by insisting that he deserves sexual repayment for having taken a woman out or even for having driven her home. The petty rapist is a calculating man who does not wish to waste his time or attention unless he can be pretty certain of gaining what he wants. Unlike the rape by fraud man, he considers a seduction patter to be extraneous and will put his proposition to the woman in direct and crude terms. Sue Rhodes, a Sydney journalist who wrote a book about Australian sexual mores, described this phenomenon:

I know men, and talked to them at some length about it, who freely admit that six dates is the limit with them. If she hasn't come across by then or strongly indicated that she will next time, they're not about to waste any more time or money on her. 'But why?' I asked one of them. 'Surely if she came across early you'd only think she was too easy anyway?' 'Oh yeah,' he admitted. 'But then I'm not gonna marry her anyway, am I? I'm only taking her out.'[6]

That was seven years ago: nowadays the petty rapist expects the woman to 'come across' on the first, or at most, second date. Many petty rapists prefer not to have to expend any time or money at all; the most they are prepared to pay is a gallon or so of petrol. Women need to be up to date with the conventions and argot of Australian men if they are not to misinterpret a situation. For instance, when most Australian men say to a girl they have just met at a party 'Do you want a ride home?' or if they ring her and say 'Do you want to go to a drive-in?' what they generally mean is 'Do you want a fuck?', and any girl who takes the invitation at face value is likely to find herself landed on a lonely road and forced to walk home or else spend the evening fighting off a genuinely amazed male who refuses to believe that she did not realize the contract she had entered into. Both the petty and the fraudulent rapists are aware of the legal definition of rape and are clever enough to ensure that they are never culpable in that respect. Their strategies are designed to extract consent, however grudgingly or reluctantly. The petty rapist, in particular, will take a woman's 'No' as a challenge rather than as signifying the end of his attempt to conquer her. He will cajole, persuade, threaten (but not with violence – he is not so naive; rather he will merely threaten to withdraw his esteem of her) and, often present himself as immobilized by sexual frustration, appealing to the woman's kindness and generosity to put him out of his misery. Eventually he is likely to succeed. Worn out by the verbal struggle and the constant battle with predatory hands, most women who have had previous sexual experience (and for whom, therefore, the intercourse holds no additional fears of an unknown quantity) are likely to mutely submit with a hurry-up-and-get-it-over-with attitude. At least that way they will get driven home.

Variations of this tactic are the sexual conventions which operate in many groups. Especially in those which are professedly opposed to the mores of bourgeois society, such as bikie gangs, surfies, and various hippie and other counter-cultural groups, sexual permissiveness is posited as being among the ways in which opposition to 'straight' society can be demonstrated. These groups are always dominated by, if not entirely composed of men, and their credos are devised for their own benefit. Women who wish to be associated with these groups (for, although they may not immediately realize it, they can never *belong* to them) must accept this sexual ethic. Many willingly do so for they, too, wish to escape the stultifying effects of family and suburban attitudes and the ways in which these confine women. But it is illusory to think that they can flee from the colonization of their sex. The conventions might differ in form but their result is the same: to deny women self-determination.

Most of these groups have a definite hierarchy amongst their members and a woman's status is derived from the man she is sexually involved with. In order to increase her status, a woman must form a liaison, or at least have a casual encounter, with a man who occupies a higher rank than her current lover. The men at the top thus derive considerable benefits as they can choose from any of the women attached to the group. To maintain their connection with the group, women must comply with whatever is demanded of them, and such dependence is by definition demeaning. Members of these groups seldom want to marry so the main criteria they seek in their women is sexual attractiveness. The women's involvement with the group can only ever be transitory, can only last while they remain young and attractive or until the entire group has, literally, been through them.

None of these three kinds of rape – marital rape, petty rape or rape by fraud – is legally acknowledged as such, but each is as much a violation of a woman's body, and of her integrity, as the violent rapes which occupy the statistics. Each is part of the colonization of women for each is an everyday happening or possibility, and each a constant reminder to women that their bodies are not their own to control or to give. And each contributes to the creation of total passivity and even masochism amongst women who realize that so long as they have any social encounters with men, they risk being raped. As Germaine Greer put it:

Sexual rip-offs are part of every woman's daily experience; they do not have the gratifying strangeness of disaster, with the special reconstructive energies that disasters call forth. They simply wear down the contours of emotional contacts and gradually brutalize all those who are party to them. Petty rape corrodes a woman's self-esteem so that she grows by degrees not to care too much what happens or how. In her low moments she calls all men bastards; she enters into new relationships with suspicion and a forlorn hope that maybe this time she will get a fair deal. The situation is self-perpetuating. The treatment she most fears she most elicits. The results of this hardening of the heart are eventually much worse than the consequences of fortuitous sexual assault by a stranger, the more so because they are internalized, insidious and imperceptible.[7]

What we can call illegal rape, that is the rapes recognized as such by police and courts, differs in several important ways from the three kinds of rape mentioned above – although all four kinds combined are part of the colonization of women. Illegal rape is committed by one or more men and invariably involves threatened or actual violence as well as brutal penetration. The illegal rapist is also very likely to increase the shame and repulsion his victim inevitably feels by forcing several kinds of perverse sexual acts upon her. Anal rape and forcing the victim to perform fellatio on the rapist often accompany, or occur instead of, vaginal penetration. The victim of illegal rape is far less likely to know her attacker – although she may possibly have noticed him lurking in her neighbourhood. American studies have shown that most rapes are pre-meditated and rapists go to considerable trouble to watch their victims' movements and routines before they attack.

If the other forms of rape can be seen as relatively peaceful colonization, illegal rape is mass terrorism which has a dual purpose: to caution women against stepping outside their permitted sex-role boundaries, and to punish them for purportedly doing so. Illegal rape brings home to women most forcefully that they are a colonized group. It can occur any time, anywhere, and there is virtually nothing women can do to prevent it. They are not safe even within their own homes as about 50 per cent of such rapes occur within the victim's home[8], and rapists can go to extraordinary lengths to gain access to their victim. I know of one example where six men kicked in the front door of a house to reach a woman (a stranger to them) whom they all raped; and of another where the man cut off the woman's electricity and telephone before stealing into her bedroom late at night and holding a knife to her throat while he raped her. Some victims are abducted from bus-stops; others are attacked as they walk home down well-lit streets. In other instances, the victim has accepted a lift or gone to a party with a man or group of men who have subsequently raped her.

It is rapes of this kind which are held in abhorrence by the public, which are characterized as 'a fate worse than death' and which evoke vengeful cries for the rapist to be castrated. Yet even in cases such as these, the violation and the outrage are tempered by a farrago of myths and prejudices which attempt to extenuate the attacker and to implicate the victim. At the same time as rape is considered to be an horrific crime, there exists the myth that it is impossible for a woman to be raped. Related to this belief are the corresponding ones that if the woman submitted to the rapist, rather than risk incurring additional physical injuries, then she did not really resist and that she must have enjoyed the experience. The basis of this collection of myths is that all women secretly want to be raped, that women harbour a deep-seated longing to be violently conquered. This myth affirms and reinforces the fundamental sexist dichotomy between women and men which colonization seeks to create and sustain: that women are passive receptacles and that men are active *conquistadores*. Yet these myths are patently untenable as the existence of several other, contradictory myths demonstrates. Women are said to provoke rape: by being alone in the streets, by wearing certain kinds of clothes, by acting in a fashion which is contrary to the code of feminine behaviour, for example by being drunk, or by accepting lifts from strangers. This myth, that women are responsible for rape, directly contradicts the notion that rape is impossible. Rather, the placing of blame on the victim attempts to absolve the rapist from full culpability for his actions.

A further myth which lessens the man's responsibility for his crime is the prevalent notion that men cannot help themselves, that they are subject to sudden, uncontrollable sexual urges which are generally provoked by the sight of a woman acting in one of the ways mentioned above. Here the rapist is excused by a combination of biological determinism and allotting the victim a share of responsibility for the attack. It is salient that there are no corresponding myths about other violent crimes in which men can be victims. There is no myth, for example, that it is impossible to be robbed, that all men secretly want to be murdered, or that men enjoy being bashed. Nor are child victims of sexual assaults ever accused of provoking their attacks, of perhaps enjoying the violation of their bodies or of having desired the assault. It is only women who are held to be at least partly responsible for the one crime in which they are always the victim.

A further way in which the supposed horror in which rape is held is shown to be false is the preponderance of jokes about rape. These jokes utilize the myths, underscoring the wide social recognition they enjoy, but more importantly, lessening and even negating the horror and the terror and the violence and the violation that rape is. Rape jokes are not those ironic devices people develop to ease pain or to make an horrific situation or memory bearable. Rape jokes all suggest that rape is a joke, and are yet another way of absolving rapists from culpability. The way the law collaborates in hiding the huge incidence of rape, the myths which exonerate the rapist and the humour which hides its criminality all highlight the contradictory attitudes to rape which exist in Australian society. Despite the public profession of horror, rape is condoned and even encouraged and for many men it is seen as perfectly normal male behaviour. Criminologists Greg Woods and Paul Ward found in their study of pack rapists that few considered that they had committed a crime: 'The "pack" make no attempt to hide their indentities and on apprehension seem surprised by the fuss made about a "normal" activity.'[9]

Everyone is against rape. Even rapists. They exonerate themselves by calling it something else, by employing those myths which can ease whatever conscience they may have, or they can hide behind the law which says that forcing your wife to have sex is not rape. Or they exploit the sexist stereotypes to denigrate their victims and implicate them in the crime. Unless a raped woman is very young, very old, a virgin, demonstrably respectable (a nun, for instance) or has incurred severe physical injuries she is not automatically seen as a victim and is even blamed for the attack she suffered. This view has been given the authority of judicial sanction in many rape trials and has resulted in rapists either being discharged or receiving very lenient sentences.

One case which was heard in Sydney in October 1973 before Mr Justice Lee involved two trainee nurses who had been trying to get back to their hospital for duty at midnight. The hospital in question is in a remote part of Sydney which is ill-serviced by public transport and after being unable to catch a bus the two women had accepted a ride in a car containing three men. Instead of taking them to the hospital, the men drove the girls to isolated bushland where, after threatening them, they raped them. When passing sentence Mr Justice Lee said that the law went to great lengths to protect women. He then pronounced:

It is a serious question to ask, however, when two intelligent young women who get into a car in the early hours of the morning with three totally strange men, really deserve much sympathy when the inevitable happens and they get raped . . . These young women, who are prepared to get into a car late at night, or in the early hours of the morning, are so often seen by young men as an invitation to take liberties. It is like placing a saucer of milk before a hungry cat and expecting it not to drink it.[10]

The one man who was being tried received a two year sentence with a non-parole period of six months.

In another case heard in Perth before Mr Justice Virtue in July 1974 a woman who had 'streaked' through a nightclub, gone moonlight swimming with two men and was then raped by them, was said by the judge to have 'asked for trouble'. The woman had run through the nightclub wearing only her panties and had then accompanied the two men to a hills reservoir where all three had stripped for a swim; the two men then each raped the woman twice. The judge said:

The woman's loose and abandoned behaviour both at the nightclub and after she had accepted without demur the suggestion of an early morning frolic in the hills was clearly calculated to encourage you both to conclude that she would not be averse to accepting advances from either of you. On the contrary, they were calculated to arouse your passions to an extent that not surprisingly though reprehensibly, you would not take 'no' for an answer.[11]

The men were placed on a three-month good behaviour bond.

In both these cases the judges disapproved of the women's actions. In the latter case, the judge apparently found it inconceivable that people could swim naked together without this being regarded as lascivious conduct. What judgement would he have reached, I wonder, if the woman had become so sexually aroused at the sight of the men's naked bodies that she attacked one of them? In the first case, the judge showed no consideration for the inequalities of women's social and economic situation which so often leaves them vulnerable to attack by a rapist. Most women do not own cars and if taxis or public transport are not available, how are women to get to work or to wherever they might need to go?

The situation of women being stranded without transport is exceedingly common. For instance, there is *no* public transport to Sydney's Macquarie University, and students without cars or unable to make transport arrangements with other students are literally forced to hitch-hike to and from university each day. I know several women students in this position and two of them have been raped while trying to get to university. In fact there is evidence that a number of men who are aware of the students' predicament deliberately prey upon it and cruise past the university each day looking for young women hitch-hikers.

It is clear from these judicial statements – and they merely reflect widely held social opinions – that the supposedly hallowed prerogative of a woman to refuse a sexual invitation has all sorts of qualifications attached to it. It is not, as women are led to believe, an absolute prerogative but is a privilege afforded to women who unprotestingly acquiesce in their colonization. Even then a woman is not protected from rape: she is merely afforded the right to be considered a victim rather than a provocateur if she is raped by a stranger. This is a petty reward for having submitted to a colonized state and it in no way lessens the enormous incidence of rape. What it does contribute to, however, is disguising the political nature of rape. If we examine the effects that rape itself, and the fear of rape, have on women we can see that, rather than being merely an outrageous criminal offence, rape is a political weapon of the colonizers. It is used to reinforce patriarchy, to confine and curb women and, finally, to punish those who have refused to conform to the God's Police role.

Patriarchy denies women a separate and independent existence: they are the property of and appendages to men. First their fathers, and then their husbands, are the formal custodians of women. The father's duty is to protect his daughter's virginity so that she can be given away intact at the marriage ceremony. The husband receives the wife in a ceremony which legitimizes his having total access to her body and to her labour. Only in a society where women are regarded as property and as chattels, could men exchange women amongst themselves in this way. The myths of love and the cultural value attached to marriage simply disguise the basic nature of the transaction. Because men view women as their property, they take it as a personal outrage and affront if a woman who belongs to them is raped. They feel it is incumbent upon them to avenge the act and if they can find the offender are likely to take some kind of vigilante action against him. This reaction takes little account of the woman's suffering, humiliation or shame; it is the reaction of a property-owner who finds his property has been tampered with and his proprietorship challenged. When the police decide to take up a rape case and press charges against a rapist, they are often acting from similar motives; they can be seen as agents of the father or husband of the raped woman. They sometimes take violent revenge upon the rapist themselves, by beating him up while he is in the police cells, or they will invite the male relatives of the victim to do so if they wish. Yet if their motives were purely and simply outrage and anger at what the woman had had to endure, they would not prolong her ordeal by subjecting her to brutal and prurient questioning as they do.

Where rape is viewed as an outrage against the male relatives of the women who are violated, rape becomes a weapon men can use against each other. Men rape women in order to assert their power over the other men. This occurs most commonly in war-time when invading armies engage in mass rape of the women of the city or territory they are invading in order to underscore their defeat of the defending army. Often the women victims of these rapes are ostracized by their families and fellow citizens and are relegated to ignominious isolation, forced to endure their shame – and, very often, to care for the resultant children – alone. The mass rape of the women in Bangladesh was given very wide publicity because those women were treated as pariahs, but this was simply a very wide-scale instance of a very common war-time occurrence. The fact that invading armies seek out to violate women who, in other circumstances, would be relatively immune from rape (such as nuns, very young girls, wives of prominent men etc.) shows that their actions are not motivated merely from the lust which undoubtedly results from long periods of sexual deprivation, but by a desire to assert their military power in a way which every individual soldier and citizen can understand and suffer from.

The fear of rape, and the knowledge that a rape victim who does not have a male custodian is so often seen as having provoked or deserved the rape, impels women to seek male protectors. Marriage does not protect a woman from being raped by her husband, but it lessens her exposure to petty and fraudulent rape, and while it cannot guarantee her immunity to illegal rape, it reduces her risk and ensures that if it does happen, she will have some legal redress. She is also far less likely to be accused of having deserved to be raped. In this way, the existence of rape reinforces patriarchy by making it necessary for women to have protectors.

It is necessary to ask why it is that only one form of rape, what I have called illegal rape, is widely accepted as such. Why are the three other kinds of rape described in this chapter condoned or overlooked and one form, the least frequently perpetrated form, singled out, labelled as rape and pronounced as being the most terrible deprivation of a woman's integrity, when women's bodies are being violently invaded daily by other kinds of rape which are accepted as normal patterns in our sexual mores? The immediate and obvious answer is that colonizers never label their actions as such, but always disguise their intentions with a variety of subterfuges which are intended to increase the potency and success of colonization by making it acceptable to a majority of the colonized people.

The existence and increasing incidence of illegal rape are used by the colonizers to keep women confined so that they will perform the work required of them, and will do it without too much resistance or complaint. If they want to avoid illegal rape, women must be constantly wary. They can try to avoid it by not walking in the streets at night, by not hitch-hiking, by not wearing tight or revealing clothes. In effect, women must observe an unproclaimed curfew and obey unofficial ordinances. Like any colonized group their movements are restricted and their activities regulated. Women do not have the freedom of the streets, or the freedom to wear what they like, or the freedom to meet new people in unfamiliar surroundings. Women cannot travel cheaply (and few can afford, therefore, to travel at all), they cannot go into a pub alone for a drink. Men can hitch-hike round the country, walk into any pub, talk to anyone they choose, wear whatever they want to, say and do whatever they feel like. If women do any of these things, they are said to be inviting rape.

The fear of rape is instilled in women so that they will remain indoors. If a known illegal rapist is active in a particular area, police issue warnings to women to remain indoors and to lock their doors and windows. This is obviously a wise safety precaution, but it nevertheless means that women are locked up, virtually imprisoned, because of the actions of one man. Yet even if women remain inside they are not fully protected from rape. Marital rape occurs, by definition, within a woman's home, and so can any of the other three forms of rape. The professed intention of the curfew is evidently a camouflage for some other object. Why, we might ask, should women have to remain locked away when it is men who rape? If the objective were to protect women from rape, surely this would be more likely to be accomplished if a curfew were imposed upon men and they were prohibited from engaging in such predatory behaviour as prowling the streets in cars. Instead the proffered rationale links, and thereby suggests a connection between two distinct things: preventing rape and confining women. It seems obvious that it is the latter which is intended.

If men ceased to rape, if they elected not to exercise their pre-emptive strike capacity upon reluctant or unwilling women, there would be no need for women to be confined. If women had no reason to fear rape they could enjoy the freedom of movement now possessed by men. This would mean that women could have more choice about what they did with their lives. It might mean that many women would decide that they did not wish to devote their lives to bearing children and maintaining families. If rape were not a threat, women would have less motive to marry. The patriarchal system derives considerable benefit, then, from the existence of rape and it is able to use this to confine women. It instils in women a fear of rape, a fear which is realistic in terms of the risk women are at; but one which is extremely hypocritical since it does not acknowledge the most frequently perpetrated kinds of rape. But the fear is there and it does keep women in line, it does restrict their movements and their actions.

Conversely, rape can be used as a weapon to punish women who do not conform and, as the judicial statements quoted earlier made clear, such refractory women obtain little sympathy if they are raped. One judge said that rape was 'inevitable' if women acted in certain ways. It seems that men feel free to abuse and punish women who, in their eyes, are acting in a way which is contrary to the God's Police role. The steep increase in reported rapes in the past few years could be accounted for in this way. In the last seven or eight years more and more women have elected to ignore the confining feminine role and have tried to live their own lives without the protectorship of a man. Such women are seen as a challenge and a threat to the patriarchal system: if these women can get by without men and can try to control their lives and their bodies, they could become an inflammatory example to other women. Rebellion could spread. The institutions of patriarchy could be endangered. To prevent this, women who try to be independent of men are punished in various ways. Chapter Five showed how they invariably have to endure poverty. It can also be suggested here that another thing they have to endure is the threat of rape.

It is generally admitted by police, criminologists and others who concern themselves with illegal rape that only a tiny fraction of the illegal rapes which take place are reported to the police. As will be pointed out later in this chapter, there are several good reasons why women are reluctant to press charges if they are raped. There has been no reason for women to become more willing to do so in recent years for police procedures have not changed appreciably and nor have social attitudes towards rape victims. Yet there has been a discernible increase in the number of rapes reported in Australia – with a corresponding decrease in the number of convictions obtained – so it can be inferred that the incidence of illegal rape has considerably increased.

Rapes Reported and Cleared, Australia, 1966–1972[12]

	1966	1967	1968	1969	1970	1971	1972
Rapes Reported	251	311	363	364	416	578	544
Rapes Cleared	205	228	281	286	315	375	380

The singling out of illegal rape as a crime, and the pious pronouncements of horror which accompany it, also serve to de-emphasize other forms of rape. These other forms of violation are not rape, women are persuaded, and a whole range of individual and social reasons are advanced to justify why one form of sexual violation is rape while an identical form is, because of a slightly different circumstance, normal sexual intercourse. After all, he's not a rapist – he's your husband, and he is entitled to demand sex from you. Or, you should not have gone out with that man, you *must* have heard of his reputation for taking 'no' to mean 'yes'. So we have the situation where the form of rape which women are least likely to experience is treated seriously while the others, which they encounter or risk every day, are seen either as trivial or as ordinary, and certainly not illegal, sexual activity.

The occasional much-publicized rape trial, with its ritualized pronouncement of (a usually light) sentence on one rapist while thousands of other known rapists walk the streets is rampant hypocrisy. Such trials are probably thought to be good public relations for patriarchy, meant to persuade women that most men mean them no harm and that the odd 'deviant' one who attacks women will be punished. It is like the trial of Lieutenant Calley for the My Lai massacre in Vietnam; neither he, nor probably the violated Vietnamese, could quite understand why one man was being tried for something which was regarded as normal war-time behaviour on the part of the invading troops. While that trial proceeded, the Americans continued to saturate the country with bombs, to kill and to capture Vietnamese. The trial was a hollow, hypocritical sham which did nothing to stop the war. Similarly, rape trials single out the odd rapist – in many cases men who cannot afford to buy their way out of the charges – as a scapegoat for the system, but they do nothing to stop rape.

SUPPRESSION OF WOMEN'S SEXUALITY

Women are denied control over their bodies in other ways besides the violent invasion of rape. Women are kept ignorant about, and unable to fully express, their sexuality, and the technological means which do exist and with which women could more adequately control their biology are not made freely available to them.

The sex education most children receive is usually sparse and is phrased in such remote clinical language that it is puzzlingly irreconcilable with the sexual urges experienced by the recipient of the information. Moreover 'sex education' is an erroneous label: few children ever receive more than reproductive education and this is not, in the case of women, the same thing. Children learn how babies are made, which means they learn about copulation and, specifically, the vagina and the penis which are posited as the only sexual organs. Seldom is either sex told about the female clitoris which is the principle organ for women's sexual arousal and satisfaction. This omission invariably leaves girls confused and wondering, for few can reach adolescence without becoming aware of the pleasurable sensations which an accidental brushing against the clitoris produces, and once these sensations have been triggered, most women will engage in some form of clitoral self-stimulation even if reticence, shame or fear prevents them from prolonging their masturbation to orgasm.

At the same time, however, most women are abysmally ignorant about what their sexual organs actually look like. Few women have thought, or been encouraged, to take a mirror and examine themselves and so they have little idea how closely the line-drawings in sex education books resemble the organs they are meant to represent. Even women who masturbate regularly often have little occasion to explore their entire genital area; most women insert tampons by 'feel', often without fully understanding exactly where the tampon rests. Modern methods of contraception absolve women from having to touch their genitals: users of the douche or the diaphragm were obliged to be familiar with their internal genitalia, but most women today either use the contraceptive pill or rely on a doctor to insert an intra-uterine device. With adult women being confused or ignorant about their genitalia, it is not surprising that young girls are imparted inadequate information and are left to try and resolve for themselves the puzzling contradiction between the 'facts' of sex education and their own cursory experience.

Women who, seeking to try and resolve this puzzle, consult a sex manual might, depending on the author and date of publication of the book, gain some rudimentary information about the clitoris. Books published in the last decade are likely to inform them of what they already know: that the clitoris is highly sensitive and that it must be stimulated if the woman is to achieve orgasm. Prior to that sex manuals treated the clitoris as if it were a vestigial organ, or else relegated any discussion of it to the Freudian notion that clitoral sexuality is 'infantile', and that to achieve sexual maturity a woman must transfer her sexuality to the vagina.

It now seems highly probable that Freud's formulation was based on an inadequate understanding of female biology and especially of the mechanisms of the female's sexual arousal[13], yet this notion has been overlaid by countless psychiatrists who have diagnosed women unable to experience vaginal orgasms as frigid or neurotic. Generations of women have grown up with the information that there are two sorts of orgasms and that one is infinitely superior to the other. In the absence of any scientific or other contradiction to this proposition, thousands of women have thought themselves frigid, have felt guilty about their persisting clitoral fixation or have been denied sexual satisfaction because of their partner's adherence to the idea of the superiority of the vaginal orgasm. It was not until the early 1960s with the publication of Masters and Johnson's clinical studies on the physiology of sexual response that it was irrefutably demonstrated that the clitoral-vaginal dichotomy is a false one, and that anatomically all orgasms are centred in the clitoris no matter whether they are produced by manual stimulation or through vaginal intercourse.[14] This finding was followed by a spate of writing by women in which they endorsed the discovery and denounced the ill-informed view it replaced.[15]

Neither scientific discovery nor psychiatric orthodoxy is always available to wide numbers of people, however, and the majority of women has almost always had only their own experience to inform them. Human sexuality has never been a high priority amongst researchers in Australia and so our knowledge of people's sexual experience is not very great. But what we do know suggests that a very large percentage of Australian women have only rarely, or never, experienced orgasm and this in turn implies that the clitoris has been neglected in perhaps a majority of heterosexual relations in this country, at least until recently.

The only survey of Australian women's sexuality so far published found that of its sample 47 per cent of women said they experienced orgasm all or most of the time during sexual intercourse, 41 per cent said they did sometimes or occasionally, and 12 per cent had never had an orgasm.[16] The survey found also that the older a woman was, the more likely she was to have never experienced orgasm.[17] It is doubtful if the findings of this survey can be generalized to the whole female population since the sample was selected rather unsystematically, and it included a higher proportion of highly educated women than is found in the general population – and most sex surveys have found orgasmic capacity to increase with level of education. Thus it seems likely that the percentage of women who never, or only occasionally, experience orgasm is considerably higher than is suggested by the figures cited above. This seems to be borne out by the statement of Sydney gynaecologist Derek Llewellyn-Jones that: 'A few women reach orgasm at every episode of sexual intercourse, and some of these have multiple orgasms during the episodes; but most women only have orgasms occasionally, a few rarely or never.'[18] If this statement is not based on clinical information then it amounts to a gross example of male chauvinist medical endorsement and perpetuation of female frustration.

The only other evidence available is impressionistic – based on conversations with women and with doctors – but the overall picture suggests that women's sexual satisfaction has been sacrificed to the imperatives of reproductive sexuality, that is, sexual intercourse involving only the vagina and the penis. This has occurred partly through ignorance in both sexes about how to engage in forms of sexual activity which sufficiently stimulate the woman – and such ignorance is a by-product of the initial rejection of the clitoris as a sexually important organ – and partly through male reluctance or refusal to try and ensure that his sexual partner is satisfied. This last reason is undoubtedly a major one for it is decidedly in the interests of the colonizers to keep women ignorant about their sexuality and thus prevent that sexuality from erupting as a demanding and consuming force.

The object of colonization is to ensure that women reproduce, and that they do so within an approved kinship structure. The target of the colonizing process is therefore, women's bodies, their wombs in particular, and the womb can only be reached, and the woman impregnated, through the vagina. As already pointed out, it is not biologically necessary for women to be even sexually aroused, let alone satisfied, for them to conceive. Male arousal, on the other hand, is an essential pre-requisite. Male ejaculation does not always coincide with, or produce, a totally satisfying orgasm but an ejaculation will generally give the male some pleasure and satisfaction.[19] The failure of the male to experience full orgasm may be related to male denial of female sexuality:

Ann [sic] Koedt in her pamphlet *The Myth of the Vaginal Orgasm* argues that men created this myth to deny the sexuality of women and therefore their personality, and to perpetuate male dominance, symbolized by the centrality of the penis in the sexual act. The myth has a rebound. The negation of female sexuality and the female as a person, psychologically rebounds on the male and deprives him of full male potency – of orgasmic potency. The male ideology of virility is anti-female but also denies the relationship the dynamic necessary for male orgasm and the male thereby loses orgasmic potential. This, I think, explains the emphasis on quantitative measurement in male ideology. Part of the rebound is the creation, unconsciously and also consciously, of fear of women. There is the fear of her rebellion against her submissive role, fear of her use of her frustration against him by destructive subtlety and deeply, the fear that she could expose him as sexually negative. This becomes an impediment to full male sexuality.[20]

If this is the case, then it should provide a powerful motive for men to begin to recognize women as human beings with a unique and responsive arousal mechanism. But the above writer has suggested a further reason why men are reluctant to do so: fear of women and, although he does not say so, especially fear of their sexuality and the effects that allowing it to flower could have.

While male sexual capacity is physiologically limited inasmuch as a man is only capable of a finite number of arousals and orgasms in any sexual encounter, women's sexual capacity, once aroused, is unlimited. Mary Jane Sherfey who has conducted research on female sexuality, particularly on their orgasmic capacity, writes:

I urge the re-examination of the vague and controversial concepts of nymphomania and promiscuity without frigidity. Until now, it has not been realized that regular multiple orgasms, with either clitoral or vaginal stimulation, to the point of physical exhaustion could be the biological norm for women's sexual performance . . . It could well be that the 'over-sexed' woman is actually exhibiting a normal sexuality . . .[21]

She hypothesizes about:

. . . the existence of the universally and physically normal condition of women's inability ever to reach complete sexual satisfaction in the presence of the most intense, repetitive orgasmic experiences, no matter how produced. Theoretically, a woman could go on having orgasms indefinitely if physical exhaustion did not intervene.[22]

No wonder men are reluctant to assist in the arousal of female sexuality! Their inability to either match the woman's sexual appetite, or to provide her with total satisfaction, would make rather drastic inroads in men's self-conceptions of their superiority.

It may also be the case that the sexually aroused woman would refuse to acquiesce in her subjugation to the passive and domestic roles assigned to her in all patriarchal societies. It is likely that the repression of female sexuality is a pre-condition for the existence of 'the family' and for women accepting responsibility for the care of children. Says Sherfey:

Many factors have been advanced to explain the rise of the patriarchal, usually polygynous [sic], system and its concomitant ruthless subjugation of female sexuality (which necessarily subjugated her entire emotional and intellectual life). However, if the conclusions reached here are true, it is conceivable that the *forceful* suppression of women's inordinate sexual demands was a pre-requisite to the dawn of every modern civilization and almost every living culture. Primitive woman's sexual drive was too strong, too susceptible to the fluctuating extremes of an impelling, aggressive eroticism to withstand the disciplined requirements of a settled family life – where many living children were necessary to a family's well-being and where paternity had become as important as maternity in maintaining family and property cohesion. For about half the time, women's erotic needs would be insatiably pursued; paternity could never be certain; and with lactation eroticism, constant infant care would be out of the question.[23]

The colonization of women is usually disguised or justified by the arguments that maternity and domesticity are natural to the female. Yet there is evidence to show that modern women have not bio-logically adapted to child-bearing, and that the 'natural' method of childbirth does considerable physical damage to women which seriously impedes their capacity for sexual enjoyment. Sherfey reports on

. . . the fact that the female sexual and procreative apparatus was evolved for mothers giving birth to small-headed babies. Man is much too recent an evolutionary innovation for the female pelvic adaptations necessary to deliver big-headed babies without trauma to the birth canal. (Of the 75,000,000 years the primates have been working themselves up to us, men with heads big enough to produce consistent maternal damage have been around for only the past 500,000 years at most – and probably much less – perhaps .6 to .3 per cent of the total.) Obstetrical damage to the sexual structures is far more frequent than most psychiatrists [who diagnose frigidity in women] realise, I believe. Without the best of modern obstetrical care, it occurs to a greater or lesser extent in close to 100 per cent of all women bearing their first full-term babies; and even with that care, it occurs to some degree in a very large number of them.[24]

The two most common forms of perineal tears either reduce or totally remove women's orgasmic capacity.[25] It is difficult to label as 'natural' a process which causes such damage to women's sexual and reproductive organs. In this context, 'post-partum' depression assumes yet another dimension: the very understandable misery of a woman who has fulfilled what society ordains is her natural role, only to find that it entails her body being lacerated and perhaps permanently mutilated. Yet what measures are taken to try and prevent or reduce the appalling toll taken by maternity? Why is there no advocacy by the medical profession that women have their babies delivered by Caesarean section so as to preserve their sexual organs intact? How many so-called frigid women realize that their inability to enjoy orgasm may in fact be due to their dutiful complicity to the motherhood imperative? Were more women in possession of this knowledge it is likely that they would refuse to give birth in the 'natural' fashion and would demand that their babies be delivered by Caesarean. Why is it that doctors do not point out to pregnant women the danger they face in giving birth?

The only plausible answer to this question in the face of the evidence available is that the medical profession is no more interested in women obtaining knowledge about, and power over, their sexual capacity than any other group of men. (It will be shown later in this chapter that despite the increasing number of women doctors, medicine can still be regarded as a male-dominated profession.) Rather, the medical profession can be seen as a principle agent in the colonization of women, as a body which not only is uncaring about women's ability to express and enjoy their sexuality but does not wish women to control their bodies in any way.

THE PILL: THE NEW OPPRESSOR

The Pill is posed as a panacea to all women's worries about unwanted pregnancies: the daily swallowing of a tiny tablet will ensure that fertility can be controlled with none of the risk of failure which accompanies every other method of contraception. The Pill is the most commonly employed form of contraception in this country and it has such popularity here that in the late 1960s Australian women were reported to have the highest *per capita* consumption of the Pill in the world.[26] A survey conducted in late 1971 of a sample of 1 per cent of the population of Melbourne to yield information about married women's contraceptive practices found that in 1970–71 the Pill was used by 38 per cent of the sample, and was at least twice as popular as any other method of contraception.[27] If the number of single women also taking the Pill were added to this, the percentage would be much higher. In late 1973, more than 750,000 Australian women were using the Pill.[28] But these figures showing an apparent high acceptance of the Pill by Australian women do not reveal the dark side of Pill-taking, the plethora of problems experienced by women who have to use this method of contraception.

One of the questions asked of women in the Melbourne survey was designed to elicit women's opinion of the Pill: the statement 'The Pill has brought more benefit to women than any other modern invention' was affirmed by 52 per cent of respondents.[29] This was a clear majority – and to a very strongly worded statement. But when we ponder on the benefits that the Pill has supposedly brought to women, is this a very high response? When we consider that, for the first time in history, women are at last freed from the monthly horror of waiting to see if they were pregnant yet again, the affirmation seems less than enthusiastic. Perhaps it is the case that many women who feel their lives to be indelibly imprinted with their domestic duties could only respond unambiguously to items such as washing machines or vacuum cleaners which have reduced the workload of those duties. But most women who are burdened with such work have also to face the worry of unwanted pregnancy – and each pregnancy brought to term means an incalculable increase in the daily workload of any housewife. So perhaps the failure of a higher number of women to give the Pill the Invention of the Century award is due to other factors. To dissatisfaction with this supposed liberator of women, perhaps?

The Pill indisputably does what it claims to do: it prevents pregnancy. It does this so reliably that if a woman does get pregnant while taking the Pill, the fault invariably lies with the user (she must have missed several days of taking it) rather than with the product. But in addition to fulfilling its professed function, the Pill does a lot of other things, and very unpleasant things, to women's bodies. One of these 'side-effects' is so serious that it can cause death. Professor H. M. Carey, who researches the Pill at the University of New South Wales, writes:

Thrombosis is the most serious, although a relatively rare, complication of oral contraceptives. The risk of thrombosis is related mainly to the dose and type of oestrogen used in the formulation, but the type of progestogen employed probably also influences the magnitude of the risk.[30]

He cites the following table:

Deaths per 100,000 women per year[3]

	Age in Years	
	20–34	35–44
Non-users of oral contraceptives	0.2	0.5
Users of combined contraceptives	1.5	3.9

The risk admittedly is slight, and it can be reduced by using lower doses of the two main components of the Pill, but it is still there and women have died from taking the Pill. But in addition to this comparatively rare side-effect, Professor Carey lists twenty-six other known side-effects.

Many of these are experienced so commonly by women that it is worth listing most of them:

glucose tolerance and chemical diabetes (one in eight women develops chemical diabetes within a short time of taking combined oral contraceptives; this is reversible if use of combined preparations is discontinued);

hypertension (in about 1 per cent of women a rise in blood pressure has been observed with higher dose pills);

migraine (induces migraine headaches in women who have not suffered them previously and increases the attacks with those women who have);

some types can exacerbate *cardiac disease*;

plasma concentration of zinc levels lowered and copper levels increased (similar to that experienced in the last trimester of pregnancy);

iron metabolism (increase in serum iron, total iron binding capacity and transferrin in women taking combined preparations);

thyroid function changes (similar to those that occur in pregnancy);

liver function is affected (oral contraceptives should not be used by women who have a history of cholestatis jaundice of pregnancy);

water and salt retention (leads to weight increase);

leg cramps (muscle spasms similar to those which can occur in pregnancy);

nausea (likely on commencing course of some preparations, especially with young women who have not been pregnant and women who experience nausea in pregnancy);

leucorrhoea (increased vaginal secretions and discharges);

reduction of lactation (experienced when using an oestrogen-based pill);

fibroids (can be enlarged with high dose of oestrogen);

cancer ('Oestrogens are not carcinogenic. However the probability of malignant change is related to the number of cell divisions. Oestrogens by increasing cell division may increase the opportunity for abnormal cell division. If this occurs in the endometrium usually no harm is done provided the endometrium is shed at regular intervals.'[32]);

hyperpigmentation of the face (blotches on face, especially during summer);

depression, chronic fatigue, loss of libido, irritability (Professor Carey lists these as one; in my opinion they should constitute four separate side-effects. Various studies show that 5 to 30 per cent of women experience one or all of these side-effects when taking the Pill; women taking high dose progestogen preparations are the most susceptible, but the nausea induced by high oestrogen pills can also lead to depression, irritability, fatigue and loss of libido);

pre-menstrual symptoms (breast discomfort, headaches, migraines, a 'bloated feeling' and tension result from the action of progestogens);

weight gains (fat deposit is facilitated by all types of progestogens);

breakthrough bleeding (likely while taking any hormone preparations, and especially progestogen);

acne and skin texture (women with tendency to acne should avoid high-dose progestogen preparations);

menstrual flow (reduced flow occurs in most women on progestogens when these are given over a sufficient length of time to produce a reduction of thickness in the endometrium);

failure of withdrawal bleeding (occurs most commonly with high progestogen formulations);

post-pill infertility (a small number of women can fail to re-establish ovulation and menstruation after even a very short time on oral contraceptives; some undergo spontaneous cure after a variable length of time extending up to two years, while most require treatment).

Many of these side-effects are rare, but none of them can be taken lightly. Even the most 'minor' of the symptoms can cause considerable discomfort or anguish to women, while the most commonly experienced ones are sufficient for women to decide that the disadvantages of the Pill far outweigh its advantages. One study cited by Professor Carey reports that one in three women using oral contraceptives stops using them for reasons other than desiring a pregnancy.[33]

The main reasons for discontinuing to take the Pill were listed by the following percentages of women: weight increase – 35 per cent; headache – 31 per cent; decreased libido – 27 per cent; depression – 21 per cent. We have already seen (in Chapter Four) that depression is practically *the* female disease of the twentieth century. Women already have numerous sociological and personal reasons to succumb to depression without having it foisted on them as a penalty for being able to control their fertility. Similarly, some of the pills which women already swallow to reduce tension, anxiety or depression, such as the much-taken Valium, have as reported side-effects 'headaches, nausea, skin rashes, decreased libido . . .'[34] identical to those of the Pill.

Together, these two most-taken pills place an intolerable burden on already harassed women and spin their lives off into a relentless spiral of trying to avoid compounding their misery. Women can choose all right: between pregnancy and depression, between depression and nausea, between nausea and lost libido, between lost libido and pregnancy, between pregnancy and so it goes on. Yet these side-effects are scoffed at by most doctors who continue to write prescriptions for the Pill as if they were jelly-beans, often without taking the woman's blood-pressure, enquiring about her medical history or giving her a pelvic examination. They smoothly assure women that the Pill is the best thing that has ever happened to them, and brutally inform them that they have to endure the side-effects or else risk pregnancy. Other doctors threaten. I have been told by a doctor not to come asking for an abortion just because I am too 'pig-headed' to take the Pill. That I might have valid objections to taking it was not considered worthy for discussion.

Most doctors are so pro-Pill that they will not countenance a word against it, yet if they are closely questioned few possess much knowledge of its side-effects and the dangers associated with taking it. Few have seen, let alone read, Professor Carey's pamphlet listing the side-effects and the ways to counter some of them.* And if these statements sound rather sweeping and seem not to be backed with hard statistical evidence – this is hardly surprising. Who could – or would – conduct a survey designed to show doctors' ignorance or lack of feeling? What doctors would co-operate with such a survey? My opinions on this subject have been formed not just from personal experience but from that of a large number of women I have talked to and whose opinions about the Pill and about doctors who prescribe it I have sought.

My generation, aged thirty in 1975, has had the Pill since we were eighteen. We have had twelve years of trying it. Most of us grew up thinking 'the Pill' was synonymous with 'contraceptive'; we had no experience of any other method but abstinence. Yet I know scarcely any women who still take the Pill. All of my friends and acquaintances have rejected it because they are unable to bear the depression, the weight-gains, the constant feelings of irritability, the loss of sexual feelings.

* Professor Carey's prescribed remedy to counter these side-effects is to 'tailor-make' a pill for each individual woman who wishes to use this form of contraception. By charting a woman's daily temperature levels and correlating these with her known medical history and other details such as her weight, it is possible for a doctor to calculate the exact compound necessary to prevent ovulation. By contrast, commercially mass-manufactured pills contain often vast overdoses of either or both of the main ingredients of oral contraceptives and it is this dosage *beyond* the amount required to prevent ovulation which is responsible for many of the side-effects. Both doctors and the manufacturers of mass-produced contraceptive pills are reluctant to inform women that individually-tailored pills are a possibility. To prescribe them requires a doctor to spend more time and care with a woman than most are prepared to do, while the manufacturers undoubtedly see reduced profits as a result of women eschewing a product which while manufactured in mass numbers can be produced cheaply.

The last reason figures highly in their rejection of oral contraceptives. One of the promises the Pill supposedly holds out to women is that, at last, free from worrying about whether each sexual encounter could produce a pregnancy, they will be able to relax and enjoy sex. What is offered with one hand, however, is cruelly taken away with the other. The Pill while it protects women from the consequences of sexual relations, all too often stops them wanting any. They are afforded protection from something they no longer desire. No wonder so many women feel cheated, feel that this so-called liberator of women is just one more agent of their oppression.

Yet the Pill is still promoted to women by doctors who assure their patients that it is the safest and most reliable form of contraception. While the latter claim is true, in the view of a great many women this benefit is negated by the twenty-seven known side-effects, especially the two most sinister ones – depression and loss of sexual feelings – which conspire with so many other facets of patriarchal society to rob them of the power to control what happens to their bodies. Yet many women feel horribly trapped; by not taking the Pill they risk losing that control in the traditional way – becoming pregnant.

The main alternative method of contraception advocated by doctors at present is the intra-uterine device (IUD) which is not so reliable in preventing pregnancy and which causes unbearable cramps in many women. Although more and more desperate women are using IUDs as an alternative to the Pill they often find themselves equally dissatisfied with this method, and in particular, experience deep revulsion at the barbarity of having to tolerate metal or plastic foreign matter inside their wombs.

While doctors can rightly claim that they can only prescribe what is available and that they have no choice but to advise women who need contraceptives to use either the Pill or an IUD, some other factors need to be considered. Medicine is a solidly male profession which has shown little concern for the dilemmas women face in trying to protect themselves from unwanted pregnancies. It should not be thought extraordinary to expect that doctors, avowed healers of the sick, would at least experience some qualms about prescribing remedies which are known to have such side-effects. The reason why a pill for men has still not been marketed is that so far all trial versions have had marked side-effects. These included shrinking testes, enlarged breasts, change in liver function, weight increase and alcohol intolerance. With the exception of the last one, these side-effects are almost identical to those experienced by women. They were considered sufficiently deleterious to prevent the male pill from being marketed, but did not stop the female pill from being introduced to millions of women. This decision was a medical one, which also means that it was a male one. It was reached by male researchers and policy-makers (the health department authorities in each country who approve the release of new drugs). It was evidently considered that these side-effects would be intolerable to men but that women, having no choice, would have to endure them.

The main medical criticisms of female contraceptives are those which are voiced when further research reveals that these contraceptives might jeopardize the colonial function women are meant to serve. When the often fatal side-effect of thrombosis was detected in the late 1960s, many doctors stopped prescribing the Pill until a combination which reduced this risk was developed. Since then the only reported medical disquiet concerning the Pill has centred around recent reports that some forms of oral contraceptives could cause infertility.[35] It seems that the only time the side-effects of the Pill are taken seriously by the medical profession is when these could permanently impede a woman's reproductive ability – either by rendering her sterile, or by killing her. All other side-effects are considered to be trivial, or at least endurable – unless, of course, they are expected to be endured by men.

Nor can women easily solve this dilemma by divesting themselves of their reproductive function. It is a salutary index of women's lack of freedom to determine the uses to which their bodies are put that they are not permitted to become sterile until they have provided the State with a requisite number of progeny. It is virtually impossible for a single woman to obtain a sterilization until she is at least thirty years of age, and, even then, she will have to shop around for a compliant doctor. Married women of any age, medical condition and with any number of children must have the written consent of their husbands before a doctor will perform a sterilization. It is not uncommon for a churlish husband to withhold his permission, even when the operation is medically imperative – for instance, on the grounds that the woman would not survive another pregnancy. In such cases, a doctor must be prepared to risk being prosecuted if she or he proceeds with the operation with only the wife's permission.

The consent of the wife is also required when a husband undergoes a vasectomy. Until about three years ago, vasectomy was virtually unheard of in Australia. Its legal standing was uncertain and it was generally considered by most men, and undoubtedly by many doctors, to be emasculating. It is probably because of the unpleasant side-effects of the Pill that increasing numbers of men are resorting to vasectomies, and at present about 14,000 men are having the operation each year.[36] The husband who is sympathetic to his wife's suffering from the Pill can alleviate her burden by having himself sterilized. But it is also probable that a selfish motive propels many of them to the operating table: once their wives can stop taking the Pill their interest in sex is likely to be revived.

Male sterilization cannot be seen as a solution to the problem of how women are to regain control of their bodies. It does not give women sexual freedom. It does not give them the freedom to have more than one sexual partner (unless male sterilization becomes very widespread indeed), nor does it offer any promises for women's sexual enjoyment. The sterilized man can guarantee not to impregnate a woman but this does not necessarily signify that he is interested in ensuring that she gains pleasure and satisfaction from their sexual activities. Male sterilization could become a further means of curbing women: a sterilized man whose wife or girlfriend becomes pregnant or who still uses a contraceptive will have definite proof that she has more than one sexual partner.

The availability of contraception, abortion and sterilization to Australian women is not necessarily an indication of the freedoms they possess. These matters have always been viewed as part of the overall question of population control rather than as part of women's right to control their bodies. The early family planners in Australia were frankly eugenist and wanted population reduced, especially among the working class, because of their belief that healthy national development was only economically and physically possible in small family groups. This view still informs many advocates of the ready availability of contraception and abortion. The Family Planning Association of New South Wales retains a eugenist plank in its articles of association, and many of the speakers in favour of the Medical Practices Clarification Bill, which was introduced in the Australian Parliament in 1973 in an attempt to legalize abortion in the Australian Capital Territory, couched their arguments in terms of the need for small families if every child is to receive proper mothering. The movement for zero population growth propagates similar notions. In none of these movements or bodies has there been a constantly voiced concern for women's right to control their bodies. Even these so-called progressive reformers view women as tools to be utilized for wider, national goals.

The key role of the medical profession in this manipulation of women's bodies (and of their lives) derives from the power it has to determine and regulate the degree of access women have to the means of controlling those biological processes which might impede their ability to be full and free members of society.

Doctors might merely be agents of the patriarchal order but they have a very wide determining power to either ease women's problems or to exacerbate them. With their concerted backing it might be possible to stir research scientists into a fast search for an alternative to the Pill and the IUD. Women's voices alone evoke no response. With their backing, abortions could be made widely available – and the laws outlawing abortion swiftly changed. With their backing, sterilization could become a matter of individual request. But the medical profession has shown no signs of wishing to mount a campaign for the right of women to control what happens to their bodies.

THE MEDICAL PROFESSION AS A COLONIZING AGENT

A common rationalization for the inferior status of women is that they are slaves to their biology: 'Anatomy is destiny', as Freud once remarked. This rationalization has acquired the legitimacy of scientific canon, thereby making it difficult for non-scientists to challenge or change.

It is impossible to determine the extent to which women are controlled by their biology, the degree to which hormonal activity or other biological factors determine their behaviour, while a uniform code of behaviour is foisted upon women, and while women only receive status and respectability so long as they conform to that code. At the same time, it is very convenient for a society to maintain that women are governed by their biology when one of their biological functions is of essential value to that society, and when it is realized that the pursuit of other activities might impede or even prevent the performance of that function.

This argument has been used against every advance women have sought to make into the general activities of society. Education for women, votes for women, employment for women, have all been opposed on the grounds that they might physically weaken women and make them incapable of performing their major social function of reproducing the race *or* (and this was the main fear) that if they engaged in other stimulating activities they might be less inclined to want to devote all, or even any, of their time to bearing and raising children.

These arguments were so patently unjust that they were not able to be maintained once a determined onslaught was made against them, but they have not disappeared. What has happened is that these bald arguments which stated honestly and openly the intention for which women were subjugated have been replaced by more subtle and devious means of ensuring that women will comply with what society requires of them. Women are permitted now to do a wide range of things: to receive an education, to participate in politics, to take paid employment. Women's participation in any of these areas is never quite the same as men's – there are definite discriminatory differences of status, level of participation and remuneration. This inequality is exacerbated by the fact that women are required to *prove* that these activities do not prevent them from performing their child-bearing role. The argument has been turned around and posed as a challenge to women: show us that your biology is not all-determining, prove to us that you can share the man's world and still be feminine, still bear and raise babies, still be a woman.

Everything is so easy for you now, women are told. You have the Pill, and so no longer need worry about unwanted pregnancies. You have fewer children than your mother or grandmother did, so your housework and child-care responsibilities are easier. With everything on your side ('You've come a long way, babe') you have only yourself to blame if you fail. Only yourself – or your body. If you cannot succeed with all the advantages you now possess, it can only mean that you are biologically incapable of full and free participation in the world and our original opposition to your leaving the home is vindicated.

What is so cunning about this situation of challenge is that not only does it put the onus on women to succeed at two jobs, and thereby gets a double amount of labour performed by one person, but it also manages to define the terms of that situation so that it is difficult for women to disagree with any of its tenets and not appear to be unable to meet the challenge.

In a society such as Australia, technological innovation has made it possible for some biological processes to be regulated or controlled. It is now possible to regulate fertility, to perform safe and painless abortions, to make childbirth relatively pain-free and to reduce or remove the pain and discomfort associated with a large number of illnesses and disorders suffered only by women. But women do not have direct access to the means of controlling these processes; they are forced to plead for access to them, and that access is regulated by the medical profession. Freud's aphorism could more accurately be reformulated as 'doctors are destiny' because it is totally up to individual doctors, and to the medical profession as a body, to decide whether or not women are given the means to regulate their fertility (and what means they are given), to ease or remove irritating diseases and infections, have comfortable and pain-free childbirths, and be permitted to rid themselves forever of their reproductive ability.

All of these matters are seen in our society as being within the province of medical competence and women are given very little opportunity to determine them for themselves. The fact that healthy women have to go to doctors – curers of the sick – for their contraceptive needs* is not considered to be bizarre in this country, nor is the fact that doctors have the power to arbitrate whether or not these needs should be met. The two most effective methods of contraception, the oral contraceptive pill and the various intra-uterine devices (IUDs), can only be obtained through doctors. Women are, therefore, totally dependent on the doctor concurring with what they see as their contraceptive needs. It is still not uncommon for young girls seeking prescriptions for the Pill to be refused by doctors who make moral judgements about whether or not girls of that age should be having sexual relations. Rarely, though, does the doctor's judgement affect the girl's behaviour: all that she or he has the power to determine is whether or not a pregnancy might result from that behaviour. And here the doctor's power is very great indeed.

A woman who does not wish to continue with a pregnancy must obtain the permission of at least one doctor – most states stipulate two (see Chapter Thirteen for details of various state abortion laws) to be able to secure a legal abortion. Even when the law permits abortion for 'social' reasons, that is, on the grounds that continuation of the pregnancy could cause damage to the woman's emotional stability, it still endows doctors with the power to pronounce whether or not the woman deserves an abortion. In some cases a psychiatric opinion is required, but the most common procedure requires the agreement of two general practitioners that an abortion is warranted. Seldom is the woman's own opinion that she does not want a child considered sufficient reason for terminating her pregnancy.†

There are strict penalties awarded to women who attempt to take control of their bodies and, for example, abort themselves or their

---

* I am indebted to Judy McLean from the Leichhardt Women's Community Health Centre for this observation.

† In the last year (1974) several abortion clinics have opened in Sydney and Melbourne and while they usually insist that a woman be counselled about her reasons for wanting an abortion, they are far more inclined to co-operate with a woman who has already formed her opinion on the matter than are most general

friends. The necessary equipment is not available for sale to the general public, which is an understandable precaution against unqualified people obtaining it. But this legal proscription means in practice that desperate women who are refused abortions will often resort to dire methods, using instruments such as knitting needles or coathangers. Thus the proscribing of the proper instruments does not secure the desired end of preventing unqualified people from operating on themselves or upon others. The extreme professionalism of medicine in Australia has meant that lay people, especially women such as midwives who are recognized in similar cultures like the United Kingdom, are regarded here as scurrilous old wives or worse, and are not permitted to work. The power to determine women's access to the means of regulating or controlling various biological processes is thus vested solely in the hands of a profession, the majority of whose members are men and whose professional socialization strongly reinforces a traditional view of women's role.

Doctors' dealings with women as patients are almost invariably conducted with their own convenience in mind and with little consideration given to women's comfort or dignity. Many doctors still use the lithotomy position (where the woman's spread-eagled legs are raised over stirrups on either side of the table) for pelvic examination – a position which is not necessary for access but which exposes the woman to feelings of shame and ridicule. A series of articles in the *National Times* in late 1974 raised the issue of doctors inducing births so that they would occur at times convenient to them – so that they would not be called out at night or weekends – and evoked a stream of letters from regretful women who had agreed to have their babies' births induced and who now complained that their babies had been born too soon and often suffered adverse effects because of this.[37]

Other women have complained of doctors' brutality towards their suffering or distress. Caroline Graham, in a newspaper article about women's experience with doctors, investigated the conditions in labour wards and quoted one obstetric anaesthetist as saying that labour wards were an 'untapped reservoir of pain in the community . . . if the RSPCA saw what went on, they'd shut them down.'[38] She reported the reluctance of doctors to administer an epidural anaesthesic,

practitioners. They do not of course throw the woman off their premises for asking for an abortion – as some doctors still do – and they do not subject the woman to severe cross-examination about her motives as many supposedly 'sympathetic' doctors do.

a painless injection in the spine which dissipates the pain of labour but allows the woman to be conscious and aware of the birth. At the time of her article only 40 per cent of women in Sydney hospitals were being given epidurals although the doctor quoted above felt that 80 per cent of women could benefit from them. Women who are not given pain-killers during labour and who demonstrate their pain are often abused by hospital staff: they are expected to bear the pain silently and stoically.

The other area of complaint by women concerns the callous and uncaring attitude of doctors to commonly experienced vaginal infections and to menstrual pain. Many doctors are disinclined to believe that the latter even exists and although there are two drugs available which relieve it, few of the women who could benefit from them have ever even heard of them. Both Buscopan and Merbentyl are drugs which can relax the uterine muscles, thereby relieving menstrual cramps without adversely affecting the woman's activities.

Women consulting doctors about vaginal infections such as monilia (also called thrush) are often treated with distaste and are led to believe that they have contracted a venereal disease[39], an insinuation which many – young girls especially – have no knowledge with which to counter. Yet monilia is a fungal affliction which is related to the state of the bacteria in the vagina and *not* to a woman's sexual activities. It can occur while taking the Pill, during pregnancy or after taking a course of antibiotics. While remedies exist which can get rid of simple cases, many women suffer monilia chronically and get little relief from these pessaries and creams. These are most likely to be Pill-taking women, on whom the remedies are virtually wasted as the Pill continues to produce the symptoms. Monilia, and the slightly rarer trichomonas, are both intensely irritating and often extremely painful complaints which, if suffered for a long period of time, can often send women quite deranged with the discomfort. They also make sexual activity either very painful or totally impossible. One Sydney gynaecologist informed me that monilia is so common at present that she estimates that up to 90 per cent of women suffer it at some stage of their lives. Yet it is a non-talked about, virtually taboo subject. Women themselves are often extremely reluctant or embarrassed to admit that they suffer from it, an attitude they have adopted following the way doctors regard them when they describe their symptoms. Women's magazines, which could play a very useful role in explaining the causes and the extent of these complaints to their readers, almost never mention them. The more traditional magazines devote pages and pages of discussion to pregnancy yet manage to omit any reference to this common accompaniment to pregnancy. And the distressed woman who takes her symptoms to a doctor is likely to be treated as dirty or immoral, the doctor exhibiting an obvious distaste at being forced to examine her, and refusing to believe that the prescribed remedies have not been effective in curing it.

All of these complaints about doctors affect women *as women*. In addition women have to suffer the range of afflictions to which all human beings are susceptible, and which doctors are often unable to treat, or whose treatment involves side-effects which are almost as debilitating as the complaint. Women are no more vulnerable in these cases than are men. But as well as this general impotence most people experience in the face of illnesses and the men who treat them, women must suffer the indignity and the frustration of being expected to function as well as men in the world outside the home yet not being able to receive the benefits which our technological capacity could provide. This is because the men who control that capacity or who provide women's access to it collaborate in the colonizing of women, in denying them control over their bodies. They ensure by demarcating the areas of health in general, and gynaecology in particular, as being within the province of their expertise that women do not gain the power of knowledge of or control over their bodies and what happens to them. Women's hazy understanding of the processes of menstruation, contraception and childbirth makes them dependent on the assessments and pre-scriptions of doctors. In general the doctors are very reluctant to surrender their professional monopoly of information and provide women with anything more than a cursory explanation of how their bodies work and, therefore, how some of these processes can be regulated or, where they cause discomfort, made less painful. Lacking this very basic power, women are rendered even more susceptible to the other kinds of invasion and denial of control already described.

CULTURAL DOMINATION

So far I have concentrated on describing how the colonization of the female sex is accomplished. We have to look also at how it is per-petuated and who profits from it. The colonization of women, like that of a native people, is perpetuated by the two classic weapons of cultural domination and divide and rule. We will look first at the cultural domination of women.

THE IMPOSITION OF FEMININITY

Women have been stripped of their own culture and have had an alien one imposed upon them. That colonial culture is referred to as 'femininity' and is so thoroughly and pervasively propagated to women that they have been persuaded to accept many of its precepts as being inherent and 'natural' to their sex. Femininity is a cultural imposition upon the female sex, an artificial contrivance designed to replace natural conduct and appearance with conventions which make their governing easier.

This has been done so successfully that women no longer know what their own culture is, what natural female behaviour and appearance might be; in accepting femininity they have collaborated so completely in their colonization that they have risked losing forever the possibility of perceiving the violation of their integrity and self-determination that it entails. Femininity has both social and physical components and is a total culture in the sense that it is intended to provide rules of conduct for every facet of a woman's life. (If the same can be said of masculinity, which is also a cultural overlay guiding men's conduct, the difference is that men have created it themselves and can therefore alter it. As we shall see, the notion that femininity and masculinity are complementary codes and that both are equally oppressive is a fiction which serves to disguise the benefits to men, and the disadvantages suffered by women, resulting from the imposition of femininity. There are few reciprocal benefits to women from the masculinity code – it is devised by men for themselves.)

Socially, femininity decrees how women should walk, what they should wear, the conversations they can have, the places they may go, the people they might associate with – in short, their total demeanour, movements and social conduct. The actual content of the culture of femininity varies slightly from place to place and over time. For instance, it used to be an abrogation of femininity for women to smoke or to wear trousers. Most social groups within Australia now permit their women to smoke cigarettes (but not pipes or cigars), and to wear trousers (but only to certain places) but changes such as these do not subvert the overall authoritarian intent of this imposed culture, and it is illusory for women to think that minor extensions to the list of permitted activities amount to an erosion of that culture.

It is like the South African Government's propaganda which documents the things which coloured people in that country are now permitted to do and which is meant to try and persuade the critics of apartheid that it is being eroded. Even to take this propaganda seriously entails adopting a subservient attitude, accepting that that Government has the right to demarcate areas of permitted activity, to give and to take away the freedom of a group of people to do as it likes. If there were no apartheid there would be no need for the propaganda. So long as the propaganda is produced we will know that apartheid exists.

A significant difference between apartheid and the cultural domination of women is that many women are not conscious of that domination, that they accept their separate and inferior status as natural. They will tend to see changes in the code of femininity as evidence that they are not oppressed. They do not recognize that in allowing such changes, the colonizers are merely making political calculations about the steps necessary to keep women deluded about the existence and the extent of their colonization. Femininity has not varied or altered in its essential form: women are expected to be socially dependent and physically passive because this state is claimed to be necessary for their maternal role. In fact it is because it enhances the power of men.

The code of femininity is spelt out fairly clearly through a variety of agencies: individual men's requests or demands to the women they associate with (as husbands, boyfriends, fathers, employers etc.), collective male requirements as these are embodied in laws, religions and mythology, and that specific vehicle for coercing women into conformity to the current content of the code: women's magazines.

The popular magazines have as their principal *raison d'être* the codification and constant updating of femininity. By consulting these magazines women can gain a pretty good idea of how to behave and dress and whatever else is deemed to be consonant with or compulsory to being a woman.

Essentially, femininity entails women stripping themselves of their sexuality and their individuality and trying to conform to a uniform image. That image is remarkably constant through class and other differences although it varies according to age. The ultra-feminine woman is a bland creature who has acquired the ultimate in passivity: she does not act, she merely reflects. She slavishly adopts whatever appearance or demeanour she believes will earn her the approval of men and, also important, other women. Even though she is aware that it is her sex which makes her desirable to men, she knows that this must not be brandished brazenly but has to be secreted behind an alluring and seductive facade. She therefore carefully removes most of her body hair, disguises all body odours with perfumes and sprays, and wears 'foundation garments' or diets diligently in order to acquire an approved shape. She will disguise the fact that she menstruates or suffers from monilia, cystitis or any of the other debilitating complaints which women endure, and although she might allude to her sexual encounters she will never admit to being a creature who could be engulfed by sexual passion.

Women who want to be feminine must devote an enormous amount of time to self-maintenance – to tending their hair, their fingernails, their skin. These are all activities which are conducted privately, at home. The acquisition of femininity demands that women confine themselves even further. It also means that women are continually prone to anxiety about their appearance, and they often endanger their health in the effort to be feminine. Such dangers are seldom pointed out by the merchants who profit from the cultural domination of women. Instead they reinforce female anxiety in the attempt to peddle their wares. Virtually every women's magazine is guilty, through both their editorial and advertising content, of making women feel fearful that they might not be sufficiently feminine. In almost every issue of every magazine readers are urged to diet: the amazing array of different diets being surely intended to persuade each woman that there is one that must suit her. Yet there is little recognition given to the hazards that can accompany compulsive dieting: an over-scrupulous dieter can develop a total aversion to food, a sometimes fatal medical condition known as anorexia. Readers are told through endless advertisements that all body odours are repulsive, and a certain deterrent to male approval, and that they must be destroyed with deodorants. It is never pointed out that many underarm deodorants cause skin irritation and that vaginal deodorants can destroy the natural balance of chemicals in the vagina and lead to infections or irritations. There is a multi-million dollar industry in telling women how they can, and must, be feminine. Obviously it is not going to jeopardize the enormous profits it reaps off women's bodies by informing them that their products are not necessary and that some of them are indeed harmful.

Femininity is not an option for women. They must adopt this alien culture if they want to attract men – and, as we have already seen, few women can survive without the protectorship of a man.

The woman who eschews femininity, who is content with her natural shape and size and smell, who is impatient with the lengthy rituals of femininity, is condemned by both sexes. To women, she is an uncomfortable reminder of the extent to which they have abandoned themselves to the demands of men. To men, she is a threatening warning that their domination is not total and that women still have the power to regain themselves. But few women can afford to forego the demands of femininity for it means disapproval and ostracism.

As will be seen below, often the most ardent enforcers of the alien culture are other women. The ultimate sign that women accept their colonization, that they accept the domination of men, is when they agree to police other women and try to ensure conformity amongst their daughters, sisters, friends and acquaintances. Rather than their oppressed state engendering a solidarity and mutual sympathy amongst women, the all-too-urgent need to attract male protectorship makes women competitive. They see each other as rivals and often become hostile to one another. The opportunities for solidarity with other women are not very great because although women as a group are colonized, each woman lives out her colonized state in isolation. She must spend most of her time at home alone – making herself feminine, looking after husband and children, doing housework – and her isolated state leaves her feeling vulnerable and insecure. She does not acquire the confidence that comes with daily social intercourse and is often frightened as well as resentful of other women, especially if they seem to be happier, or more successful with their lives than she is. She envies these women for they appear to have attained femininity whereas she feels that she is inadequate or that she has failed.

For there is a catch to femininity. It is not something women are born with, but is posed as something they must strive for. The closer they come to attaining it, they are told, the more pleasing they will be to men. And even though much of the content of femininity is spelt out and is accessible to women to try to attain, there is one element which cannot be codified, and that is the ineluctable aura of fascination and mystery which is supposed to surround the truly feminine woman. This is what is referred to as 'the eternal feminine', 'woman's mystery', 'the essence of womanhood' and various other indefinable names. It is this which must be striven for if a woman wants to be 'truly feminine'. But because it cannot be precisely defined, because it is a mysterious and arbitrary *something* which men judge whether or not women have achieved, a woman does not know exactly what she is reaching for. This creates further anxiety and leads women to perpetual self-scrutiny and comparison with other women. It is this anxiety and this incipient rivalry between women which is exploited by the women's magazines and by the manufacturers of clothing, cosmetics, perfumery etc. who advertise in their pages.

Women can only assuage this anxiety by increasing their subservience to the code of femininity and hoping that, in this way, they will achieve the accolade of male approval. What they often do not realize is that femininity equals vulnerability, and the more subservient they are, the more easily their colonization is effected and strengthened. Women wear clothes which are deemed to be feminine and which please men – and which are usually cumbersome or uncomfortable, which inhibit circulation or which ruin foot or leg muscles. Most importantly, the clothes that are deemed the most feminine are those which are the most confining and which make it impossible for women to run and escape from an attacking man.

Women participate in the dating game which is tailored to enhance men's self-esteem and their power over women. In a typical date the man assumes total control of everything that happens. As we have already seen, this is the scenario for many a petty rape when the man feels that the woman 'owes' him a sexual favour for the time and money he has spent. The inequalities built into dating rituals need to be analysed one by one before their oppressive nature becomes apparent for, so successfully has the code of femininity been propagated to women, they feel insulted if the man does not take all of these initiatives. That is, women feel insulted if they are not patronized, treated as creatures without arms or wits, and steered through a social occasion as if they were ventriloquists' dolls.

Every social facet of femininity means aggrandizement for the male and isolation, dependence and anxiety for the woman. No matter how much it is masked by romance or ritual, no matter how cloaked by notions of duty or respect, no matter how much genuine affection infiltrates, the social code of femininity robs women of their self-determination and abets in their colonization. They give inequality and dependence an aura of legitimacy and naturalness thereby obscuring the real intent of this imposed culture.

When applied to female sexuality, femininity is clearly an alien culture which denies women their independence and the right to sexual satisfaction. The feminine woman is supposed to be sexually ignorant and, therefore, passive until initiated by her husband. (Nowadays, with extra-marital sex becoming the norm, a woman can no longer pretend total ignorance, but if she wants to be regarded as really feminine she must proclaim that all previous sexual encounters pale before the pleasures afforded by her current lover.) The forms of sexual expression permitted to the feminine woman are limited and are designed to enhance the pleasure of the male and to guarantee the purpose for which women are colonized – reproduction – rather than to give the woman satisfaction. To achieve this dual aim, women are kept ignorant about their sexuality and about their bodies generally, and the code of femininity is invoked to persuade them that this is a desirable state of affairs. 'Nice' women, they are told, do not reside at the level of carnality and ought not to be preoccupied with their bodies or their sexuality. *That* is the preserve of men, and they display an incessant concern with women's bodies, viewing and discussing them as sexual objects.

At the same time though, women are aware of a pervasive distaste, and repulsion even, which men direct towards their bodies and which directly contradicts the value in which they are supposedly held. There is something ambiguous, to say the least, in the men who profess a desire for frequent sexual contact with women and who also use the word 'cunt' as a term of vile abuse. Why has the word which denotes the female sexual organ become the most vituperative word in Australian argot? The contempt conveyed by the word does not simply carry over to women, it derives its pungency from the contempt in which women are held. The worst thing in the world any man would wish to be is a woman – since they are weak, and have no independent status and barely an existence without men – and as women are viewed foremost as sexual objects, men curse each other with the word which describes women's sex. Thus no amount of effort women make to disguise their sexuality will succeed in raising their esteem in the eyes of men because, to them, woman is a sexual category whose only value derives from the need men have of her. The woman who aspires to femininity, to this dependence on men, is cheated. The weaker she becomes, the more she is despised.

THE DESTRUCTION OF FEMALE CULTURE

There are further instances in which a female culture has been destroyed and replaced by an alien one designed to impede the colonizing process. Part of the suppression of female culture has been the rewriting, or total censoring, of the history of pre-patriarchal eras and so it is difficult to write with any confidence or authority about the origins of patriarchy and the colonization of women, or to know just how much of women's culture was destroyed in the process. Those anthropological studies of historic matriarchies, such as the work of Morgan which Engels used in his study, *The Origins of the Family, Private Property and the State*, have been regarded as spurious by the apologists for patriarchy. But Mary Jane Sherfey's suggestion, cited earlier, that female sexuality was forcibly suppressed as part of the beginnings of the rule of men is supported by several works which have tried to recover the lost history of women.[40] Elizabeth Gould Davis, for instance, documents the widespread existence of castration (removal of the clitoris) performed on women by men who wanted to suppress their ability to have orgasms.[41] The legendary tale of the mass rape of the Sabine women by Roman men illustrates the measures apparently adopted by the first overtly patriarchal state to subjugate women of the matrilineal Sabine clans.[42] Men later founded families within these clans and they called themselves patricians: *qui patres scire possunt* – those who know their fathers[43] – signifying that men now headed these families and gave their names to their children, and that men had, therefore, now established firm control over women's 'promiscuous' sexuality.

These are probable instances of forcible suppression of practices or other cultural norms belonging to women. A further example which can be supported by research conducted by women attempting to uncover their past is the beginning of medicine as a profession. This provides a clear instance of a female culture being destroyed and an alien, male-derived one imposed in its place. Medicine as a profession requiring university training developed in the thirteenth century. The fact that it was a university degree made it easy to bar women legally from practice: 'With few exceptions, the universities were closed to women (even to upper class women who could afford them), and licensing laws were established to prohibit all but university-trained doctors from practice.'[44] The new masculine medical profession sought, along with its allies the Church and the State, to discredit the lay healers and midwives who had, until then, been the only dispensers of cures to the sick. A great many, if not the majority, of these healers were women. They had acquired considerable facility in curing a variety of illnesses and were especially sought after as midwives. They were stamped out by a three-pronged strategy: (1) the licensing laws which forbade them to practise, (2) denouncing them as witches and drowning or burning them, and (3) a relentless campaign to brand them as sorcerers and dispensers of evil.[45] This strategy gradually succeeded in destroying women's healing culture: those women who escaped death as witches were discredited, their remedies sneered at as 'old wives' tales', or they were labelled as immoral – because they performed abortions and gave advice on contraception.

For four centuries medicine remained a stolidly male profession which staunchly resisted the instruction of women into its ranks. The first woman to obtain a medical degree in modern times, Elizabeth Blackwell, was refused admittance by twenty-nine medical schools in three countries before a small college in Geneva, New York, finally agreed to accept her as a student and from which she graduated in 1849.[46] Her graduation still did not enable her to practise in her native England where she was refused admittance to the medical roll, but it heralded the beginning of a protracted campaign by women wanting to practise medicine to be admitted to medical colleges and to practice. (The battle fought by Australian women wanting to be doctors is described in Chapter Ten.) Parallel with this fight was that by women to enter a different level of medicine: nursing.

The second campaign was far more successful than the first; once the initial battle for respectability and professional status had been won by Florence Nightingale and her co-fighters, women slid easily into the secondary and subservient position nurses occupy in relation to doctors. If anything, this success undermined the efforts of would-be women doctors, because women with medical ambitions could be persuaded that nursing was more ladylike, more compatible with femininity, and entailed sufficient devotion to the sick to satisfy their helping aspirations.

Although women have in the past few decades joined the medical profession in increasing numbers, their entry has not been without resistance and attempted obstruction. Women now comprise between one-third and one-half of medical students in Australian universities but almost every year some quarters of the medical profession instigate the cry for sex quotas to limit the intake of female students. Their cry, which is always taken up by the newspapers and so receives considerable publicity, is invariably justified by the spurious and sexist claim that medical training, like almost any other form of higher education, is 'wasted' on women because they tend to marry, have children and thus either drop out of practice or else devote fewer hours to this work than their male counterparts. This claim is demonstrably false and, in any case, is a graphic illustration of the colonizers' attitudes to the responsibilities and capabilities of the colonized.

A survey of women who had graduated from Australian medical schools between 1910 and 1969 carried out by Ione Fett at Monash

University found that 56 per cent of these doctors practised full-time and only 14.7 per cent were not practising at all at the time of the survey.[47] Several of them had reached retiring age, and of those who were not practising, a significant number had young children and planned to return to practice or to post-graduate studies in the future. The number of women doctors who had dropped out of practice permanently was thus shown to be very small, probably no higher than the male drop-out rate. But then that is never surveyed. If it was, it would probably be discovered that the percentage of men who give up practice because of disillusionment with the profession or because they want to become farmers, wine-growers, politicians or hippies is as high as the percentage of women who give it up to become wives and mothers.

This attitude towards women doctors illustrates the hypocrisy of much of the profession. As a body it is conservative to the point of atavism, and tends to subscribe to and advocate a very traditional role for women. A very great number of men doctors prescribe maternity and full-time housewifery for their female patients. Yet when a small number of their own profession chooses, or is forced, to adopt that role, all female participation in the profession is castigated. Little or no effort is made to create facilities for women doctors to be easily able to combine a professional career with motherhood and so the woman doctor who wants children is virtually forced into at least temporary retirement unless she has a husband who is prepared to do more than a token part of the child care. Opposition to women within the medical profession is evidently not so much that some women drop out to become mothers, but that most of the profession think that all women *ought* to forget all ideas of obtaining professional training and devote their lives to domesticity. Female participation in the profession is still resented, and a great many men doctors would like to see their profession revert to being an exclusive all-male fraternity.

Despite the increased numbers of women doctors, the concerns and practices of the medical profession as a whole remain, if not misogynist, certainly designed to prevent women from having any meaningful control over their bodies. Medicine as it is currently practised is, therefore, both the imposition of an alien culture upon women and an attempt to deny them self-determination. The care and efforts of individual female or male doctors does not invalidate this generalization, for these individuals are forced to work within a profession which cares little about women beyond ensuring that they are kept alive so that they can fulfil their colonized role as childbearers. Doctors I have spoken to have told me that there was very little attention paid in their training to contraception or to other areas of women's special needs such as gynaecological complaints. A great deal of attention was devoted to obstetrics however. General practitioners learn a lot about bringing babies into the world, but very little about preventing conception.

In addition, all doctors undergo at least six years socialization into their profession. This induction process occurs almost imperceptibly but it underpins the content and the method of teaching – and, by implication, what is learned. Students learn that medicine is oriented towards curing existing illnesses rather than anticipating or preventing them. It is a profession which accepts the *status quo*, not only in medicine, but in society generally. Most doctors graduate having internalized the goals of wealth and success, as well as a traditional notion of what women's place in society is. The students who commence a medical course inspired by humanitarian ideals will be very lucky if they complete the degree without having had these ideals replaced, or at least severely tempered, by cynicism and impatience or even contempt for patients. Once in practice, these attitudes are likely to be reinforced when the doctor has to cope with a never-ending stream of people many of whom bear to the consulting room trivial complaints or problems more suited to the training of a social worker or community welfare worker than to that of a medical general practitioner. A majority of these patients are women, and so they are likely to become the main recipients of doctors' impatient and uncaring attitudes. Instead of the empathetic treatment they once received at the hands of women healers and midwives, women must accept treatment from a male-dominated profession which not merely believes, but actively abets and perpetuates the colonization of the female sex.

DIVIDE AND RULE

Divide and rule is the technique employed by the colonizing powers to ensure the allegiance of a strategic majority of the colonized, to convince them that colonization is beneficial to them, and to persuade them to collaborate in the task of pacifying or punishing the more recalcitrant of their sex who refuse to accede to the demands of the invaders. By imposing divisions amongst the colonized sex, and allowing privileges to the favoured group, the colonizing power is able to prevent the colonized from forming a united opposition and from refusing to perform the labour required of them by the invaders.

THE ORIGIN OF THE STEREOTYPES

It is in this colonizing technique that we discover the origins of the Damned Whore and God's Police stereotypes. Women are divided according to whether or not they are prepared to uphold the colonial order. The women who are called God's Police are those who do not (or cannot see how they can) resist their female socialization, which can now be called – more accurately – induction into colonial mores, and who adopt the code of femininity, seek a male protector and remain faithful to his will while raising children within the prescribed family institution. The women who are called Damned Whores include those who were discussed in the last chapter – prostitutes, lesbians and women in prison – and any other women who demonstrably have, or who are thought to have, contravened the code of femininity or in some other way not conducted themselves in accordance with the role required of women by the colonizers. Single mothers, for instance, fulfil the colonial imperative of producing offspring but because they have done so outside the prescribed institution their babies are labelled 'illegitimate' and they and their children are usually subjected to some form of social disapproval. Women who subscribe to counter-cultural values and customs and who, therefore, dress in ways which are considered to be 'unfeminine', who live with men but do not marry them, and whose language and general demeanour are not consonant with feminine propriety are condemned – often merely on the meagre evidence of their appearance.

As we have already seen, adherence to the God's Police role affords women status and some degree of protection from poverty and from illegal rape. It also gives them the psychological security which comes with conforming to majority values. Certainly the majority of men continue to affirm these dual categories of women because they are of considerable advantage to them, and it is difficult for women to mount the kind of resistance which would be necessary to transcend them. With women divided as they are, men can have it both ways. They are able to have both a wife and a mistress. Even if the mistress subsequently becomes his wife, the man is still able to acquire yet another mistress, and there is always a clear distinction in his mind about the different functions of each woman. Even if a man does not have a mistress or visit prostitutes, he is still aware of and able to utilize the social distinction made between 'good' and 'bad' women. What most Australian men seek from their wives after the first couple of years of marriage, is the provision of domestic comforts. The Australian wife is expected to be primarily a good mother, to both her children and her husband. Australian men acknowledge this in the way they so often refer to their wives as 'Mum'. It is very common for them to address their wives in this fashion – they are so identified with their role that their names and their identities are totally hidden behind it – and even more frequently men refer to their wives in this way when discussing them with their friends or work-mates. Most men maintain a firm distinction between their wives/sisters/daughters/mothers and other women who are all seen as potential if not actual sex-objects.

Men have different standards for and expectations of wives and of women they consider to be whores, and they treat the two very differently. This is most apparent in their sexual behaviour. They will often accord their wives a 'respect' which amounts to gross neglect of the women's sexual desires, while visiting a prostitute to satisfy the yearnings they have for what they regard as perversions. The same men who are protective and respectful towards their wives often see all other women as fair game for their predatory behaviour, be it an attempted seduction, an aggressive cat-call or merely a heavily insinuating leer. Yet should any man, even his friends, attempt such behaviour towards the women the man regards as *his*, he will quickly leap to defend them or their reputations, often demonstrating his proprietorship with his fists.

The effect of this division on women themselves is to create anxiety and uncertainty about how to behave – just as the code of femininity does – and to engender a competitive and unfriendly rivalry towards other women. Since the benefits and protection afforded by the God's Police designation are so essential to women's security, they strive to earn it and are careful that their transgressions are discreet. They also learn as a self-protective measure to subtly denigrate other women in the company of men they want to impress. In this way they hope to enhance their own impeccability and hence their suitability to be a wife/mother. Women engage in bitchiness towards each other in an effort to unsettle the other's assurance, hoping she will thereby discredit herself in front of the men by losing her composure or by engaging in unfeminine retaliation. This kind of behaviour is most pronounced in single women who are still husband-hunting, but even married women cannot afford to let down their guard and they are prone to making sure that any woman in whom their husbands show an interest has her virtue undermined so that their matrimonial security is not threatened.

Women who act in this way totally accept the validity and justice of the way in which their sex is divided and set against itself and they are thus collaborators with the colonizers. They not only agree with the two stereotypes but they are quick to condemn one of their sex to the ignominy of the Damned Whore category, knowing only too well what the consequences of this are likely to be. Their actions are prompted by a raw survival instinct, and for this reason are understandable, but they do not realize that they help perpetuate the stereotypes by making use of them and that they are both continuing their own oppression and undermining any attempts by rebels to end the colonization of women.

HOW THE STEREOTYPES SUBVERT FEMINISM

The success or failure of feminist movements has always rested to a very large degree on whether or not they were able to make significant inroads into these divisions between women. Chapter Eleven discusses the turn-of-the-century Australian feminist movement and its response to the sexist stereotypes. Like all feminist movements to date, the Australian women were unable to transcend these divisions: they accepted that there were 'good' and 'bad' women and tried to rehabilitate the latter, thereby reinforcing the patriarchal condemnation of them and their behaviour. It is impossible for unity amongst women to be forged while credence is still given to these two opposing categories. To have any chance of success, a feminist movement – which is, by definition, a movement for the liberation of women from their colonized state – must reject the stranglehold of these spurious stereotypes and affirm the common bond of the oppression which all women experience.

Such a task is supremely difficult however because the colonization of women is so complete that few women themselves recognize it; they accept the colonizers' ideology that women's separate and unequal position is 'natural' and that feminists are trying to tamper with something which has divine sanction. Feminism itself is dismissed by men as a trite and unnecessary ideology and feminists are disposed of by the very labels they are trying to subvert. They are accused of being lesbians, or man-haters, or bearing resentment against men because they have been unable to find one for themselves. The ideology itself is not considered seriously – for to do so would be an admission that it contains some validity – and the often successful tactic of personal persecution of its adherents is pursued. To identify with feminism thus takes considerable courage, for in doing so women almost inevitably incur the displeasure of the men they live and work with and risk being relegated to the Damned Whore stereotype themselves. While feminism remains a minority idea, few women are willing to take such a risk and indeed will join in, or even lead, its denunciation. In doing so, these women help perpetuate the patriarchal fallacy that women are not oppressed. Men can then say to the desisting women: your complaints are not valid, otherwise all women would agree with you; the fact that other women denounce you undermines your arguments.

Women who have become famous or successful within the patriarchal system are sometimes quick to heap scorn on feminism. Such women are called Aunty Toms by feminists and fulfil exactly the same function for sexism as black Uncle Toms fulfil for racism: they deny the existence of the oppression which makes their success so very conspicuous. If our society were not sexist then there would be nothing remarkable about their achievement. To be successful in a system which denies women virtually any opportunities outside the domestic sphere, a woman must have remarkable talent, persistent determination and/or be prepared continually to seek male approval for what she is doing and to alter her course of action if she incurs insurmountable disapproval. Such women must ensure that they are also successful in the domestic sphere. They are the women who, when they give newspaper interviews about their achievements always stress their wifely devotion and their maternal achievements and imply that their success is secondary and perhaps not even terribly important. They will often deny that any obstacles exist to prevent other women from following in their footsteps yet they usually pose beside the kitchen sink and demur that feminism is unnecessary since they succeeded without it. What they do not acknowledge is that feminism exists because so few women are able to achieve fulfilment outside the God's Police role. The anxiety these women show lest they be thought bad wives and mothers is a testament to the enveloping hold this stereotype has on women. And, as I have already attempted to show, its demands prevent most women from participating in the world as freely as men do.

Until very recently most women were prevented from doing anything else at all by the demands of motherhood and domesticity. This has changed in the post-war years as women have smaller families but even though this gives many of them the time to take a job or further their education or engage in some other activity outside the home, they are still required to discharge their domestic duties first and anything they do must be compatible with this primary responsibility. As I have attempted to show elsewhere, this in itself creates a schizoid-like anxiety as women try and juggle their ambitions or desires with the imperatives of the God's Police role. They cannot risk failing at the latter because of the known consequences of being relegated to the Damned Whore category. It is this constant anxiety which contributes to women's confinement, which inhibits their ambitions, deters them from aiming too high or reaching too far – in case they overstep the boundaries of the God's Police role. Because if they do, or even if it appears that they might have, the condemnation is quick and cruel and the woman has literally to fight to have herself reinstated in the favoured category.

A variety of things can provoke such condemnation. If a child has an accident, the mother can be blamed for not watching its movements more closely. If an adolescent 'gets into trouble' with the police, the mother's devotion and home attendance are scrutinized by critics to see if some action or omission on her part can be held responsible. If a husband drinks a lot or is seen in the company of other women, it is assumed that his domestic situation must be unbearable and his wife's behaviour somehow responsible for his failing to be a devoted husband and father. If a woman bears a child outside marriage, she is almost automatically assumed to be a slut. And if a woman is raped, she is invariably considered to have done something to invite the attack and to be, therefore, besmirched by it.

HOW RAPE DIVIDES WOMEN

The treatment of rape victims is a very striking example of how women's reputations can be sullied and their status altered by an action for which they were not responsible. Women who have been raped are set apart from other women: they are condemned and ostracized by both sexes.

It is a situation in which only women find themselves since men are seldom raped, and when this does on rare occasions happen their attackers are always other men – not women. So rape itself is a microcosmic instance of the unequal power relations between the sexes but, as was pointed out earlier, it is the expression of a very particular aspect of men's superior power. Women are powerless both to prevent the phenomenon of rape – and thus ensure that it can never happen to them – and to stop the physical and psychological aftermath which the victims suffer.

Rape is the only crime in which the victim has to prove her innocence. Earlier in this chapter I described the various ploys which patriarchal society has for absolving the rapist and implicating the victim. In practice the woman is assumed to have 'asked for it' which, in patriarchal parlance, means deserved it. She is assumed to have acted in such a way as to have made the attack possible and as the feminine code proscribes any behaviour which could be construed as being provocative, it is concluded that the woman must have been acting in an unfeminine manner. In other words, that she has abrogated her God's Police status (if she possessed it before the attack) and can now be considered to be a Damned Whore. And as such she is no longer entitled to the respect and cordiality which a God's Police woman can demand. She is therefore subjected to a brutal and humiliating cross-examination by both the police and the courts in which she is required to retell every detail of her ordeal.[48] In court she must relive the experience in front of her attacker(s) whose sober and spruced-up appearance will give no indication of how he (or they) appeared and acted during the actual rape. And she is subject to cross-examination on her testimony by the defence lawyer(s) who will overlook no opportunity to try and force her to contradict details of what she has testified, or to discredit her personally.

According to law, rape is a very serious charge. It carries a maximum penalty of life imprisonment although in practice sentences of over ten years are very rare and most convicted rapists at present seldom get more than five or six. Yet although the practice is nowhere near as severe as the letter of the law, an alleged rapist is afforded every opportunity to acquit himself of the charge. These opportunities extend far beyond those which are the civil rights of persons charged with any other kind of crime.

The rape victim's story is not automatically believed: the fact that she has complained is not deemed sufficient proof that the attack occurred and first the police and then the courts will subject her to extensive questioning about what happened. If the police are satisfied that the woman's complaint is justified and that there is sufficient evidence to convict the rapist – providing he can be identified and arrested – then the police will prosecute him. Since rape is a criminal offence it is heard in a criminal court before a judge and jury, but first the evidence must be presented before a magistrate who decides if there is a case against the alleged rapist. The rape victim appears as a police witness and must appear at both hearings. In order for her assailant to be punished, therefore, the victim must endure two court cases each of which will necessarily involve a brutal and insulting inquisition into her personal life.

There are only two possible defences against rape: (1) that penetration did not occur or (2) that it was not in fact rape, that the woman consented. Since the court is required to pass judgement on the word of one woman – for there are seldom witnesses to rape – against one or more men, the defence will usually try to argue or to imply that it was not rape. And it is in this process that the unique position of the rape victim is highlighted. Unlike the victim of any other crime, the woman is cross-examined not merely about the actual rape but about her entire lifestyle. The defence lawyers will cleverly play on what they can safely enough rely upon to be the sexist prejudices of the jury to try and suggest that the woman is promiscuous or has at least engaged in extra-marital sexual relations previously. He will then insinuate that since she has consented in the past to men to whom she was not married that there is no reason to believe that she did not consent this time. Victims of assault are not cross-examined about whether or not they have been in fights before, nor is it implied that they invited robbery by walking the streets with wallets in their possession. Yet a rape victim is often practically accused of having incited the attack, and the cross-examination can be so gruelling, and irrelevant to the charge, that it often seems that it is the victim who is on trial. Even if the rapist is convicted the victim is left with the experience of the rape and the court cases engraved indelibly in her mind.

Some reformers who recognize and abhor the humiliating and tortuous experience a rape victim must endure if she wants to press charges have argued that it would be preferable for the woman to merely charge the rapist with assault and thus save herself from cross-examination about the details of the rape and her previous sexual experience. While the sincerity of such reformers is usually beyond question, the effect of such a practice would be to increase the ways in which patriarchal society can deny the extent of, or excuse, rape. I have already described the three forms of rape which the law does not recognize; this measure would pave the way for denying the existence of the one form which the law does take into account. Such a move would not stop rape. If anything, the incidence of illegal rape would increase as men, who already can rape with virtual impunity since so few rapists are caught and even fewer convicted, would have only the lesser charge of assault with its lighter penalty as a deterrent. Moreover, this 'reform' would in no way lessen the shame and humiliation and degradation and stigma

which all rape victims feel because although these are heightened
and made unforgettable by a court experience, they occur with all
rape victims whether they press charges or not.

One woman who went through this process described in the
following poem just how she was left feeling after a court case:

<blockquote>
stinking sperm
ran down my legs
mingling with gutter sewage
and pavement spittle
as the animalman
limped off into his inflamed infested world
i picked
my torn and battered
vagina
up from the red earth
and took it to the local gestapo
who tortured it
and threw it into the courts
where
it lay on display
for animalmen to starejeer
and spit venomous taunts at
– Shouldn't have taken your vagina
into the streets that night –
– Leave your vagina behind next time –
my vagina
was discharged from
the animalmen's bench
charged first
with inciting penises
and causing erection
– sentenced to lifetime
servitude to seedysperm
and penispersecution.[49]
</blockquote>

The court experience merely highlights and crystallizes the prevailing social attitude to rape and its victims, and a woman does not
have to go to the police or endure a court hearing to be marked by
these attitudes. All women have been taught to fear rape and to
curb their activities and behaviour because of it. If a woman is raped,
therefore, one of her first reactions will be guilt. She has internalized

the myths of rape described earlier and it is impossible for her not to apply their import to herself. Even if her rational mind can reassure her that she did absolutely nothing to provoke the attack, her subconscious is likely to quibble and question, to turn over every word or action which could perhaps have sparked off the rape.

Few women have learnt to view rape as a political act – in the way that it has been portrayed in this chapter – and they can only interpret it in terms of the patriarchal myths which lessen or remove the culpability of the rapist and implicate his victim. But a political consciousness is not necessary to feel degradation and humiliation and this is what every rape victim feels. Her body has been violently invaded; she has usually been subjected to, or forced to perform, sexual acts which she might enjoy with her lover but which with a violent stranger are repugnant and perverse. Most rape victims report that they feel soiled and dirty after the attack. Many wash themselves compulsively, shower up to a dozen times a day for weeks or months afterwards, trying to wash away the memory and the taint. For many women their sexual behaviour is irreparably altered. Some become absolutely frigid and cannot endure a sexual advance; for them rape and sex are inseparably associated and sex takes on all the horrors of rape. Other women become self-destructively promiscuous, consciously or otherwise reckoning that the guilt imputed to them by the myths must be justified and they therefore embark on proving it a prophecy.

Women who have been raped are also made to feel tainted, to feel that they bear a stigma. Again a court experience will heighten this because the woman's shame and guilt will become public knowledge, reported upon in the newspapers and listened to by prying crowds in the public gallery. But the stigma is still there even if the woman does not press charges. Her family and friends have internalized the myths too and however much sympathy they feel for her, they will find it almost impossible not to secretly believe that she did not somehow invite the attack. She will thenceforward be known as a 'rape victim', a status which invites prurient and speculative curiosity. The association of sex and violence – a bestselling combination as every Sunday newspaper proprietor knows – incites a curiosity of mingled horror and excitement. People want to know all the details and will often feign extreme sympathy for the woman to prise them from her and then use this knowledge to condemn her. When a rape is reported in the newspapers, most people react almost instinctively with a combination of pity and a 'but she must have asked for it' response. They regret what she was forced to endure but they nevertheless still suspect that somehow she invited the attack. Any woman who is known as a rape victim bears this stigma. If the woman becomes pregnant or contracts venereal disease as a result of the rape, the stigma is even worse because a testament to what happened remains. Even after the disease is cured, and pregnancy aborted or the child given up for adoption, the woman's memory and her reputation are seared with shame.

Rape Crisis Centres which have been established in the United States and more recently in Australia, report that a large percentage of their calls are from women who were raped as long as ten years previously and who still live with the horror of the memory. In April 1974 the American feminist Elizabeth Gould Davis wrote a letter of testimony to a seminar on rape in which she described in the third person her ever-present memories and reactions to a violent rape she had endured, while aged in her late fifties, three years earlier:

It was two or three days before the shock wore off and the full impact of the experience hit her. She became very ill, and now, nearly three years later, she has not yet recovered. The police told her she was lucky not to have been murdered. But that remains an unanswered question in her mind. Simple murder would not have involved the horror, the insulting degradation, the devastating affront to the dignity, and the sensation of bodily filth that time has not washed off. Nor would it have led to years of startled awakenings from sound sleep, the cold sweats at noises in the dark, the palpitations of the heart at the sound of a deep male voice, the horribly repeated image of two large muscular hands approaching her throat, the rumbling voice that promised to kill her if she struggled or tried to scream, the unbearable vision of being found on the floor of her own home, lying half naked and dead with her legs ridiculously spread. What was lucky about it was that it happened nearer the end of her life than the beginning. What torture it must be to *young* women who have to live with such memories for fifty years! This older woman's heart goes out to them . . .

The stigma does not exist merely in the raped woman's mind; it also has a tangible social existence. But it is one which is rarely articulated. It is like a prejudice which is alluded to, and which everyone recognizes, but which is rarely upheld for rational examination. Women are very aware of its existence and if they, or a member of their family, are raped they will try and hush up what happened, will try to preserve their reputation behind a mask of silence. While this is their only resort if they want to avoid being labelled Damned Whores, such reticence means they internalize the horror of the experience. Much of it could be exorcized from their memories if they could externalize and discuss it, express their anger and their outrage. But to do so invites condemnation. Secondly, their silence disguises the extent of rape in our society. It is acknowledged by police and by criminologists that probably 90 per cent of illegal rapes are not reported. The comparatively small number reported which are on public record can lead apologists for patriarchy to dismiss women's outcries about rape. They are likely to retort that rape is a rare occurrence and that women are more likely to be run over by motor cars than to be raped – so why all the fuss?

While women themselves are afraid to shout loud and clear about their rape experiences – and there are few women who have not endured at least one of the four forms of rape – then its ubiquity and its political nature can remain hidden. And while they are hidden, the extent of women's oppression by rape – and the other ways in which they are denied control over what happens to their bodies – is also disguised.

Women are afraid to disclose that they have been raped, are timid about questioning the benefits they supposedly reap from modern medicine, are too reticent to complain about their feelings of sexual frustration or the irritating gynaecological problems they are constantly beset with. They are afraid to discuss these things with each other because of the physical barriers and the psychological space which exists between women. They are afraid to trust one another in case their confidences are betrayed and the information they have revealed is used to castigate them. While women remain divided like this, and feel they must compete with each other, they are unable to unite and realize the common oppression they share. Such a recognition is a necessary pre-condition to starting to fight against it, to launching a campaign for women's liberation.

THE EXTRACTION OF PROFITS

The patriarchal system has every reason to fear such unity amongst women, and is consequently most reluctant to listen to the demands of feminists or to heed the complaints of less politically motivated women. It has every reason to try to keep women divided and wary of each other because the profit to the system, and to individual men, from the continuation of the colonization of the female sex is very great indeed. The way that colonization is maintained makes it palatable to a majority of women: they can take comfort in the security and status that marriage affords them, and the code of femininity has its own inner logic and appeal to women who do not cherish independence and self-determination – or who have never been given the opportunity to taste them and thus decide their value. Were any of the fundamental demands of women's liberation to be heeded, and women given the taste of freedom, large numbers of them might join the fight for liberation. They would refuse to perform the major task for which their sex has been colonized – the repro-duction of 'the family' – and thus place patriarchy in jeopardy. It is unlikely that women would refuse to bear children altogether but the possibility of large numbers of them having babies outside marriage and of refusing to name the father is not so remote. This would be a small but significant inroad into the patrilineal system and would be a symbolic assault against patriarchy. As has been stated previously, women are colonized not just so that they will continue to bear children, but to ensure that they will do so within the approved kinship pattern which in Australia is the bourgeois, patriarchal family. That institution confers power on men, a power which both mirrors the relative power of men over women in society at large and compensates those men who are dominated by other men in that society. All men, therefore, derive considerable benefit from 'the family'. In addition, they enjoy the domestic comforts and sexual benefits their wives are obliged to provide.

The colonization of women creates other forms of profits as well. All men can take advantage of the way women are divided by the stereotypes. They can enact all of the contradictory and contrary attitudes and impulses without having to face the likely psychological stress entailed in expecting one woman to be all things. They can enjoy the services which both wives and whores are expected to give. Having two kinds of women (as they see it) available, they can simultaneously love and respect women and at the same time hate, abuse and exploit them.

The close links between patriarchy and capitalism were discussed in the last chapter, and the colonization of women has obvious advantages to the capitalist system. In producing children, women are reproducing the labour force; in reproducing them within 'the family' they are ensuring that those children receive the kind of socialization which will tend to make them compliant workers whose own family commitments and involvements will enforce their loyalty to the system. While the benefits of capitalism to individual men are clearly unequal because of class differences, all men profit from capitalism more than women do. The majority of them are exploited as workers, but at least they receive a wage. All women are exploited as women and they do not even receive the minor compensation of an income of their own. Those women who are also exploited as workers by the capitalist system are more grossly exploited than their male co-workers since they receive lower wages (or, if they receive equal pay, are more likely to be sacked in an economic recession) and they have to manage their domestic responsibilities as well as their paid job.

There are also enormous monetary profits involved in women's colonization. The industries which prey on the feminization of women – the manufacturers of cosmetics, perfumery, women's clothing (especially foundation garments, hosiery and luxury clothing such as furs) and the many other forms of frippery which are deemed to be part of femininity – all reap huge fortunes. The medical profession's coffers owe much of their plenitude to women's misery and to their need to consult medical advice on matters such as contraception. The drug companies which manufacture the pills which keep women able to cope or which prevent pregnancy amass great profits from women's colonized state. The exploitation of women is a multi-million dollar industry. It probably provides sufficient employment to be a major sector of the economy and this, together with the multifarious benefits which each and every man derives from women's colonization, combine to make a compelling reason to ignore the dissatisfaction and the misery of the colonized sex.

NOTES

1. Some feminist writers have made the point that women are a colonized group, but most of these writers have confined their analysis to pointing out that women as a group are denied self-determination and this, by itself, is merely a metaphor and not an adequate political analysis. See for instance, Barbara Burris, 'The Fourth World Manifesto', in *Notes from the Third Year: Women's Liberation*, N.Y. Radical Feminists, New York, 1971.

2. A. A. Congalton and J. M. Najman, *Who are the Victims?*, Statistical Report 13, Department of the Attorney General and of Justice, NSW Bureau of Crime Statistics and Research, Sydney, 1974, p. 15.

3. *New Idea*, 10 March 1973.

4. Germaine Greer, 'Seduction is a four letter word', *Playboy*, January, 1973.

5. At least this is what we are led to believe, especially by parents who reinterpret their own pasts in order to impose what they profess to be the correct sexual code upon their children. In fact, the stress on female virginity at marriage while being

continually prescribed until the present generation – where we can say it has definitely broken down – was probably advocated far more than it was observed. It is probably more accurate to say that a woman was obliged to remain a virgin until she became engaged; once she had a publicly announced assurance of marriage then it was fairly safe for her to surrender her virginity.

6. Sue Rhodes, *Now You'll Think I'm Awful*, Gareth Powell Associates, Sydney, 1967, p. 98.

7. Greer, op. cit., p. 178.

8. Katherine Whitehorn, 'Rape: fact and fantasy', *Bulletin*, 31 August 1974.

9. Paul Ward and Greg Woods, *Law and Order in Australia*, Angus & Robertson, Sydney, 1972, p. 93.

10. *Sydney Morning Herald*, 5 October 1973.

11. *Sunday Mirror*, Sydney, 28 July 1974.

12. Table compiled from the *Official Year Book of the Commonwealth of Australia*, various years. 'Cleared' means that the police investigation has been completed, either because a suspect has been brought to trial or for some other reason.

13. Mary Jane Sherfey, *The Nature and Evolution of Female Sexuality*, Random House, New York, 1972, p. 116.

14. William H. Masters and Virginia E. Johnson, *Human Sexual Response*, Churchill Livingstone, Edinburgh, 1966.

15. See Sherfey; Susan Lydon, 'The Politics of Orgasm' in Robin Morgan (ed.), *Sisterhood is Powerful*, Vintage, New York, 1970; Anne Koedt, 'The Myth of the Vaginal Orgasm' in Leslie B. Tanner (ed.), *Voices from Women's Liberation*, Signet, New York, 1971; Mette Ejlersen, *I Accuse!*, Tandem, London, 1969.

16. Robert R. Bell, *The Sex Survey of Australian Women*, Macmillan, Melbourne, 1974, p. 121.

17. ibid., p. 122.

18. Derek Llewellyn-Jones, *Everywoman*, Faber & Faber, London, 1971, p. 72.

19. 'The Myth of the Male Orgasm', article by Frank in *Sex Tharunka*, University of New South Wales, 1971, p. 9.

20. ibid.

21. Sherfey, op. cit., p. 134.

22. ibid., pp. 134–5.

23. ibid., p. 138.

24. ibid., pp. 127–8.

25. ibid., p. 128.

26. John C. Caldwell et al., 'Australia: Knowledge, Attitudes and Practice of Family Planning in Melbourne, 1971', *Studies in Family Planning*, March 1973, p. 50.

27. ibid., p. 54.

28. Gerri Sutton, 'The Pill – ten years on', *Daily Mirror*, Sydney, 12 November 1973.

29. Caldwell, op. cit., p. 52.

30. H. M. Carey, *Inhibition of Ovulation*, School of Obstetrics and Gynaecology, University of New South Wales, n.d. (c. 1971), p. 8.

31. ibid.

32. Carey, op. cit., p. 23. The endometrium is the lining of the womb which is shed each month during menstruation. The warning contained in this statement is against women continuing to take the Pill month after month without having a week's gap every three weeks to allow for menstruation to occur.

33. ibid., p. 29.

34. *MIMS*, April 1973, p. 58, listing side-effects of benzodiazepines.

35. A symposium on oral contraception at the 1975 ANZAAS Congress evoked several criticisms from medical researchers about side-effects of the Pill. The criticism given the most extensive press publicity was the claim by gynaecologist Dr G. D. Parkinson that the combined oestrogen-progestogen pill – the formula used by most women today – had a permanent or long-term infertility rate three times higher than the older type single hormone (oestrogen-based or progestogen-based) pill. Reported *Daily Telegraph*, 23 January 1975.

36. Reported by Janet Hawley, in 'A Pill for Everyman', *Australian*, 1 February 1975.

37. See the *National Times*, 16–21 December, 1974.

38. Caroline Graham, 'Women and Doctors', *Nation Review*, 8–14 June 1973.

39. This has been reported to me by innumerable women, and was a frequent complaint of women who testified at the Women's Commission in Sydney, March 1973. See Caroline Graham's article for further confirmation.

40. See Helen Diner, *Mothers and Amazons: The First Feminine History of Culture*, Anchor, New York, 1973; and Elizabeth Gould Davis, *The First Sex*, Penguin Books, 1975.

41. Davis, op. cit., p. 158ff.

42. Paul Tabori, *The Social History of Rape*, New English Library, London, 1971, p. 51.

43. Diner, op. cit., p. 195.

44. Barbara Ehrenreich and Deirdre English, *Witches, Midwives and Nurses: A History of Women Healers*, The Feminist Press, Old Westbury, U.S.A., 1973, p. 15.

45. ibid., p. 4ff.

46. See Dorothy Clarke Wilson, *Lone Woman: The Story of Elizabeth Blackwell, the first woman doctor*, Hodder & Stoughton, London, 1970.

47. M. Ione Fett, 'The Monash University Survey of Australian Women Medical Graduates', *Medical Journal of Australia*, 24 April 1971, p. 920.

48. As with criticisms made of doctors' attitudes to women, the complaints of rape victims about how they are treated by the police are based mainly on the accounts of women who have endured the ordeal of making a complaint. Periodically

the treatment of rape victims by police and courts becomes a subject of interest to newspapers. For instance in late 1974 Mr Don Chipp MHR publicly announced that he had advised the parents of a young rape victim not to report the crime to the police. His complaint, and the complaints made by women involved in the Sydney Rape Crisis Centre, are always criticized by the police who while admitting that they have to establish the veracity of the complaint, claim that their treatment of rape victims is not as harsh as the complainants make out.

Further accounts of police, court and social attitudes to rape victims can be found in the following: Susan Griffin, 'Rape: The All-American Crime', *Ramparts*, September 1971; June Bundy Csida and Joseph Csida, *Rape: How to avoid it and what to do about it if you can't*, Books for Better Living, Chatsworth, California, 1974; Ann Wolbert Burgess and Lynda Lytle Holmstrom, *Rape: Victims of Crisis*, Robert J. Brady Company, Bowie, Maryland, 1974.

49. Untitled poem by Miranda, *Broadsheet*, (N.Z.), no. 23, October 1974, p. 35.

SEXIST STEREOTYPES
PAST AND PRESENT

The origins, development and consolidation of the 'Damned Whore' and 'God's Police' stereotypes of women.

CHAPTER
EIGHT
'DAMNED WHORES'

... the damned whores the moment that the[y] got below fel a fighting amonst one a nother and Capt Meridith order the Sergt. not to part them but to let them fight it out ...

> – LT RALPH CLARK of the First Fleet,
> *The Journals and Letters of Lt Ralph Clark 1787–1792*

Though how many [of the female convicts] were prostitutes will never be known, almost all contemporaries regarded them as particularly 'abandoned'; and even if these contemporaries exaggerated, the picture they presented is a singularly unattractive one!

> A. G. L. SHAW, *Convicts and the Colonies*, 1966

The social and economic conditions of the first fifty years of white colonization of Australia fostered whores rather than wives. The traditional Judaeo-Christian notion that all women could be categorized as being exclusively either good or evil – with the Virgin Mary and Mary Magdalene being the prototypes of each kind – was brought to Australia with the First Fleet. But its application to the women in this country was totally lop-sided. From 1788 until the 1840s almost *all* women were categorized as whores – or 'damned whores' – as Lt Ralph Clark called them. This categorization was initially based on the fact that virtually all of the white women to come here in the first two decades of colonization were transported convicts, but it was continually reinforced by the social structure which evolved in the penal colony. Thus even female convicts who had served their sentences had little chance of having their status redefined and the stereotype came to be applied to many other women in the colony who had not been transported.

The First Fleet consisted of 1,480 people more than half of whom were convicts. There were 586 male and 192 female convicts as well as a large number of seamen, marines, servants and officials.[1] Only a tiny fraction of these were accompanied by their wives and children. Governor Arthur Phillip hoped he was to be the first superintendent of a new outpost of British civilization. He wanted free settlers to be encouraged to migrate and he wrote, 'As I would not wish convicts to lay the foundations of an empire, I think they should ever remain separated from the garrison and other settlers that may come from Europe.'[2] The British Home Office had other ideas, however, and intended New South Wales to be little more than a dumping ground for the excess of convicts which British gaols could not accommodate. Within this penal colony, women were assigned only one main function – they were there primarily as objects of sexual gratification. The main difficulty, as far as the British authorities were concerned, was to find a sufficient number of women convicts, and to do this they had to impose preponderantly harsher sentences on women: 'Whereas only the more hardened male offenders under sentence of transportation were actually transported to the Colonies, all women under sentence, provided they were healthy and under forty-five were transported.'[3] Even this measure could not secure enough women and Governor Phillip's instructions included the following order:

And whereas, as from the great disproportion of female convicts to those of the males who are put under your superintendance, it appears advisable that a further number of the latter should be introduced into the new intended settlement, you are, whenever the *Sirius* or the tender shall touch at any of the islands in those seas, to instruct their commanders to take aboard any of the women who may be disposed to accompany them to the said settlement.[4]

Phillip declined to obey this instruction but he did not disagree with its underlying assumption about women's role in the penal settlement. Four months after landing at Port Jackson he wrote to Lord Sydney in England: 'The very small proportion of females makes the sending of an additional number absolutely necessary, for I am certain your Lordship will think that to send women from the Islands, in our present situation, would answer no purpose than that of bringing them to pine away in misery.'[5]

The sexual abuse of female convicts began on the ships. Although after 1811 the women travelled on separate ships from the male convicts, they had the crews to contend with. W. H. R. Brown told the Select Committee on the State of Gaols in 1819 that:

These women informed me, as well as others of their shipmates, that they were subject to every insult from the master of the ship and sailors; that the master stript several of them and publickly whipped them; that one young woman, from ill treatment, threw herself into the sea and perished, that the master beat one of the women that lived with me with a rope with his own hands till she was much bruised in her arms, breasts, and other parts of her body. I am certain, from her general good conduct, she could not have merited any cruelty from him.[6]

He also reported that 'the youngest and handsomest of the women were selected from the other convicts and sent on board, by order of the master, the king's ships . . . for the vilest purposes . . .'[7] One convict woman, Elisabeth Barber, accused Thomas Arndell, the assistant surgeon of the ship on which she was transported of being 'a poxy blood-letter who seduced innocent girls while treating them for the fever, using his surgery as a floating whore-house.'[8] Some convict women did not even reach their expected destination. In 1797 the military guard and several of the sailors aboard the female transport *Lady Shore* seized control of the ship and sailed it to Montevideo. There the mutineers were made prisoners of war and the 65 convict women were distributed as servants to Spanish ladies of the port.[9] After this incident guards were no longer placed on ships carrying female convicts[10], but the transportees could do little to escape the advances of the surgeons or sailors.

When the First Fleet arrived at Port Jackson, the female convicts were kept aboard for five days while the other ships were unloaded and elementary shelters were constructed. Governor Phillip turned a blind eye to the riotous two-day debauch which ensued when the women landed.[11] This Bacchanalia, and Phillip's response, signalled the kind of treatment which was to be the lot of the female convicts. One settler wrote to England:

It will perhaps scarcely be believed that, on the arrival of a female convict ship, the custom has been to suffer the inhabitants of the colony each to select one at his pleasure, not only as servants but as avowed objects of intercourse, which is without even the plea of the slightest previous attachment as an excuse, rendering the whole colony little better than an extensive brothel . . .[12]

The 1812 Select Committee on Transportation reported that female convicts 'were indiscriminately given to such of the inhabitants as demanded them, and were in general received rather as prostitutes than as servants.'[13] The women were distributed to the men almost as part of the daily rations. In 1803 forty women were listed, baldly, as 'women allowed to the New South Wales Corps'.[14] In a penal settlement where there were at first no gaols – since the entire island continent was regarded as a prison – and which was both physically and morally remote from England, the usual sexual division of labour assumed a particularly brutal and oppressive form. The men were set to work at constructing the basic requirements of a new settlement – buildings, roads, fences – or to farming or manufacturing. They were forced to work hard, on near-starvation rations in the first few years, and were brutally punished for even minor transgressions. There was little employment for the women. Since there were so few free settlers the demand for servants was minimal and light manufacturing or other industries which could have absorbed them developed rather slowly.

The women's punishment comprised transportation plus enforced whoredom. For at least the first twenty years they had no means of escaping this fate. The best a woman could do was to form an attachment with one man and live with him as his wife and in this way protect herself from the unwelcome attentions of any other man who fancied her. But whether she was concubine to one man or available to all she was still considered a whore. Since there was virtually no escape from the colony which required women to be whores, there was no escaping whoredom. Even those convict women who formed attachments with Governors or other prominent men, and bore them children, were unable to shake off the common status and assume anything matching the social standing of either these men or the wives and daughters of men of similar rank. The list of time-expired male convicts who were able to cast aside their past and acquire wealth and respectability is long and impressive. Very few women could match their success. Mary Reiby, who inherited her husband's merchant business and expanded it successfully, is conspicuous because she was unique.

Marriage did not automatically ensure that women could flee from the whore stereotype. The taint borne by the female convicts seems to have been more permanent than it was for men. In any case, not many female convicts had the opportunity to marry, especially in the first three decades. Although the British authorities had made a perfunctory recommendation to Governor Phillip that he encourage 'the promotion of matrimonial connexion between the unmarried people – a measure which must tend to the improvement of their morals'[15] in practice women were transported solely to serve as sexual commodities and the British Government acted as imperial whoremaster. Its attitude was one of sheer hypocrisy. Although Phillip, who wanted to govern a new society not just a penal settlement, did encourage marriage, there was little incentive, and several obstacles, to these first settlers marrying. Soon after landing in 1788 Phillip had approved the marriage of thirty couples but many of these marriages were contracted in the expectation that married people would receive comforts and privileges denied to single people. When these hopes proved false many asked to be released from their contract and after 24 February 1788 the percentage of marriages per population was greatly reduced.[16] Time-expired convicts and other free settlers received grants of land in Phillip's time, and married men received larger grants if they had a wife, as well as getting an additional ten acres for each child. But this was a limited inducement. The majority of convicts had come from cities and had little interest in land cultivation. Many admitted signing over their land holdings – at no charge – because they had no use for them.[17] Neither was marriage encouraged by the legal position prior to 1834 whereby a marriage was invalid unless an Anglican clergyman officiated and where a licence from the Governor was necessary.[18] Roman Catholics, Presbyterians and other non-Anglicans were thus prevented from being married within their religion because of the first provision while the high cost of the licence deterred others.[19]

During his governorship from 1809 to 1820, Lachlan Macquarie made some attempt to alter the situation of female convicts. Viscount Castlereagh wrote to Macquarie:

It has been represented to me that upon the arrival of female convicts in New South Wales, the unfortunate females have been given into the possession of such of the inhabitants, free settlers and convicts, indiscriminately, as made a demand for them from the Governor. If a practice so extraordinary and disgraceful has not been abolished, you will by no means suffer it to continue, and I am to desire you will take the proper means for having the female convicts, upon their arrival, kept separate until they can be properly distributed in such a manner as may best encourage attention to industry and character.[20]

But neither pompous-sounding instructions from across the ocean, nor Macquarie's efforts, could substantially alter what was by then a deeply entrenched attitude. The men of the colony were accustomed to having convict women at their disposal, even if there were at least three men to every woman, and it was impossible to prevent servants being regarded as prostitutes both by their employers and any other men on the place. Single men were supposedly not able to have female convicts assigned to them, but in 1837 James Mudie, a colonist, reported to the Select Committee on Transportation that 'they generally manage to get them'.[21]

The major obstacle to reform was the strength of the Damned Whore stereotype. The ideology had become so powerful that it was confused with reality. Even if large numbers of women did not conform to the attributes of the stereotype, their behaviour was overlooked and the ideology that all convict women were whores remained unchallenged. Female convicts were universally condemned. Thomas McQueen, a magistrate and a former convict himself, described the women he sentenced as 'the most disgusting objects that ever disgraced the female form'.[22] Governor Darling wrote in 1830 – a decade after Macquarie's term of reform had ended – that 'the women sent out to this country are of the very worst description, not in general being transported until there is no longer any hope of their reformation at home.'[23] James Mudie thought that they were 'the lowest possible . . . they all smoke, drink and in fact, to speak in plain language, I consider them all prostitutes.'[24] Even Macquarie was condemnatory and he wrote to Earl Bathurst in 1813 that the female convicts were 'so very depraved that they are frequently concerned in the most dreadful acts of atrocity.'[25] Although he wanted more male convicts to be sent out since the prosperity of the Colony depended on labour being available for public works and agriculture, he considered that 'female convicts are as great a drawback as others are beneficial'.[26]

None of these men tempered their vilifications with any recognition of the lack of choice open to the women. They had been transported to service the sexual needs of the males of the Colony and were then condemned for their behaviour. This has always been the fate of prostitutes in a patriarchal and sexist society: the women are chastized while their male patrons, without whom prostitution would not exist, escape criticism or punishment. Governor Macquarie indicated that he was unwilling to perpetuate the enforced whoredom when he requested that no more women be transported. This plea was ignored and women continued to be sent out. But neither did Macquarie show much sympathy for women. It could have been expected that, in his zealous attempts to transform the penal colony into a civilized society, he would have applauded female convicts marrying and leaving the colony. But he reported to Castlereagh in 1810 that he had been 'induced to grant more free pardons than I could have wished; in order to enable a number of women, who had lived for many years with and had children by soldiers of the 102nd regiment, to marry those men, and accompany them home.'[27] Although he regretted having to take this course of action, he was comforted by the thought that it had at least saved the Government the expense of victualling the women and their progeny, and since economy was being demanded of him by England he could be assured that his actions would be approved.

Like the contemporary observers, historians of the convict period have condemned the female convicts. A. G. L. Shaw was quoted at the beginning of this chapter: he evidently found the picture too horrifying even to allow further investigation. L. L. Robson, the other main authority on transportation, is less reserved and reinforces the contemporary judgements by reinvoking them in modern terms of moral abuse. He finds evidence of 'indiscriminate love-making'[28] by some of the women, and notes that 'some female prisoners, particularly those from the cities of Britain, were accustomed to loose living.'[29] A tone of disapproval pervades his descriptions of the convict women: he clearly agrees with the Damned Whore stereotype. That many of the women *were* whores is beyond dispute. What historians have failed to appreciate is the extent to which the women had any choice about this. Nor have they distinguished the extent of the reputation from the extent of the 'crime'.

Even the contemporary evidence makes it clear that the women had no option but to prostitute themselves. Commissioner Bigge, who was sent to report on the colony at the end of Macquarie's governorship, drew a vivid picture of the fate of women sent to the old Female Factory* at Parramatta. All women who were not selected as servant/bed-mates when their ships arrived were sent to the Factory:

On their arrival there, they are allowed to remain in a wooden building that is near the factory; and if they have succeeded in bringing their bedding from the ships, they are permitted to deposit it in there, or in the room in which the female prisoners are confined for punishment. The first of these apartments is in the upper floor of a house that was built for the reception of pregnant females. It contains another apartment, on the ground floor, that is occupied by the men employed in the factory. It is not surrounded by any wall or paling; and the upper room or garret has only one window, and an easy communication with the room below. No accommodation is afforded for cooking provisions in this building; nor does there exist either inducement to the female convicts to remain in it, or the means of preventing their escape. The greater portion, therefore, betake themselves to the lodgings in the town of Parramatta, where they cohabit with the male convicts in the employ of Government, or with any person who will receive them . . .[30]

* The Female Factory will be described in more detail later in this chapter.

Such was the accommodation offered by the authorities! The women who had just arrived had no opportunity to earn any money as they came straight from imprisonment in England. They were thus unable to pay for lodgings in Parramatta. The Government did not provide beds for them so what was their option but to sell their bodies in return for a bed?

The Molesworth Report on transportation in 1837 amassed evidence of the iniquities of the system of assigning convicts as servants or labourers to colonial settlers. Lord Molesworth said of the female convicts:

At times they are excessively ferocious, and the tendency of assignment is to render them still more profligate; they are all of them, with scarcely an exception, drunken and abandoned prostitutes; *and even were any of them inclined to be well-conducted, the disproportion of the sexes in the penal colonies is so great, that they are exposed to irresistible temptations:* for instance, in a private family, in the interior of either colony, a convict woman, frequently the only one in the service, perhaps in the neighbourhood, is surrounded by a number of depraved characters, to whom she becomes an object of constant pursuit and solicitation; she is generally obliged to select one as a paramour, to defend her from the importunities of the rest; she seldom remains long in the same place; she either commits some offence, for which she is returned to the Government; or she becomes pregnant, in which case she is sent to the factory, to be confined at the expense of the Government; at the expiration of the period of confinement or punishment, she is reassigned, and again goes through the same course; such is too generally the career of convict women, even in respectable families.[31]

These two Reports are tantamount to an official admission of the enforced whoredom which was the punishment endured by the convict women. Molesworth also drew attention to a further discriminatory feature of the women's punishment. No matter what length of sentence had originally been imposed, in practice women were often transported for life. Time-expired male convicts could work their passages home aboard a ship. Women could not do this – except, again, by prostituting themselves to earn the fare. This was likely to earn them another pregnancy and another year at the Female Factory, thus effectively extending their sentences.

Not even these official acknowledgements of the situation of female convicts could make much impression on the Damned Whore stereotype. It was continually reinforced both by the now entrenched ethos of the colony and by the numerical disparity between the sexes.

The two continually reacted on each other. The following table sets out the numbers of convicts transported to New South Wales during the convict period.

Convict Population of New South Wales[32]

Year	Males	Females	Total
1788	529	188	717
1790	297	70	367
1800	1,230	328	1,558
1805	1,561	516	2,077
1819	8,920	1,066	9,986
1828	16,442	1,544	17,986
1836	25,254	2,577	27,831
1841	23,844	3,133	26,977
Total	78,077	9,422	87,499

Before 1840 the convicts always numbered at least one-third of the total population. Before 1800 they amounted to over 60 per cent but even in 1828, 46 per cent of the total population were convicts.[33] Transportation to New South Wales stopped in 1840, and by the time of the 1841 census, convicts comprised only 20 per cent of the population but the free population included many ex-convicts and it was difficult for women to escape from the reputation they had acquired as convicts. Given the numerical disproportion of the sexes, it would ordinarily be expected that every woman who wanted to would have the opportunity to marry. Yet Commissioner Bigge had reported that:

The marriage of the native born youths with female convicts is very rare, a circumstance that is attributed to the general disinclination to early marriage that is observable amongst them, and partly to the abandoned and dissolute habits of the female convicts, but chiefly to a sense of pride in the native born youths, approaching to contempt for the vices and depravity of the convicts even when manifested in the persons of their own parents.[34]

By 1828 only 42 per cent of those women transported prior to 1826 had married.[35] Nearly one-quarter of these already had husbands in England and were not eligible to marry. But many apparently wished to, and by this time the authorities were trying to promote marriage and discourage concubinage. Some married women convicts used to write letters informing themselves of the death of their husbands, post them to friends in England who would send them back to the Australian authorities so that their names could be entered in the widows' register.[36]

On 24 February 1810 Macquarie had issued a Proclamation designed 'to reprobate and check . . . the scandalous and pernicious custom so generally and shamelessly adopted throughout the territory of persons of different sexes cohabiting and living together un-sanctioned by the legal ties of matrimony.'[37] The main point of the Proclamation was to inform the populace that in the case of a man dying intestate, the 'mere circumstances of illegal cohabitation, for whatever length of time, with any man, confers no valid title upon the woman to the goods and effects of that person.' Thus it was definitely in the material interests of women to marry rather than cohabit. Marriage also afforded women some protection against the advances of other men. So if women who were convicts or ex-convicts failed to marry it is unlikely to be because they chose not to; rather, as Bigge suggested, it was because they were not seen as worthy women. They were whores, not wives.

At the end of the transportation period in New South Wales the rate of marriage began to increase. Between 1841 and 1846 the ratio of married to unmarried increased by 3.3 per cent.[38] By this time, an alternative stereotype, that of God's Police, was replacing the Damned Whore as the dominant one. This will be discussed in the next chapter. Before the 1840s however few women escaped the taint of the Damned Whore stereotype.

The stigma of the stereotype shackled the female convicts as firmly as any leg-irons. It could be seen as a female equivalent to the chain gang except that there was less hope of being released from it. So strong was the idea that all women in penal colony Australia were whores that women who were not convicts became its victims too. Aboriginal women carried a double burden. As women, they were seen as sexual objects and fair game for white men; as members of a subject people they were also victims of the whole range of indignities bestowed by a brutal invading colonialism which considered itself to be the master race.[39]

A further group of women who were seen as whores were the female immigrants. In 1831 the Government began to use revenue from the sale of land in Australia to assist the emigration of single women between the ages of eighteen and thirty. They were wanted as domestic servants and as wives. But this attempt could not immediately alter either the social mores of colonial society nor the dominant view of women. Even if the scheme had been supervised more rigorously, its success under the social conditions prevailing in Australia would have been purely fortuitous. For forty years the dominant ethos of the colony had been one of individual self-assertion within a framework, first of the military discipline which regulated the penal system, and later of the exactitudes enforced by the opportunistic battle for prosperity. Transportation had created a social system characterized, as Humphrey McQueen points out[40], by a self-interest which often manifested itself in brutality and treachery towards one's fellows. The arbitrary introduction of a few hundred more women was not immediately going to alter this.

Female immigrants* were subjected to the same kind of treatment as the women convicts. Whenever news spread that a ship-load of female immigrants was due to arrive hordes of men would assemble at the docks, waiting to claim their share of the imported goods. Employers seeking domestic servants had to battle with lustful men who had no intention of paying for the services they required. Some of the women received proposals of marriage before they disembarked, but mostly they had to face proposals of a different nature.

When in August 1834 the *Strathfieldsay* berthed at Hobart Town, several thousand men were waiting to greet the female immigrants on board.

As soon as the first boat reached the shore, there was a regular rush towards the spot, and the half dozen constables present, could scarcely open a passage, sufficient to allow the females to pass from the boats; and now the most unheard of, disgusting scenes ensued – the avenue opened through the crowd was of considerable length, and as each female passed, she was jeered by the blackguards who stationed themselves, as it were, purposely, to insult. The most vile and brutal language was addressed to every woman as she passed along – some brutes, more brutal than others, even took still further insulting liberties, and stopped the women by force, and addressed them, pointedly, in the most obscene manner . . . scarcely a female was there, but who wept, and that most bitterly; but this, again, was made the subject of mirth, by the brutes that were present.[41]

This behaviour was considered reprehensible by the reporter and so it is evident that there was opposition to women being treated in this

---

* Although contemporary accounts described all migrants to Australia as *emigrants*, this work will employ the modern distinction of describing arriving or settled migrants as *immigrants* and will use the term *emigrant* only to designate a prospective migrant from England (or whatever country).

fashion. But the point is that no one, not even the police, was able to prevent it. The men in this case pursued the women to the house in which they were billeted and remained there for three days, making continual attempts to break in. Although the constabulary was able to maintain a guard on the house it could not disperse the crowd. Authority was in a defensive and therefore unstable position.

The same incident illustrates the dilatory nature of the arrangements which the authorities made for the arrival of free women. These women had to wait six-and-a-half hours before being given any food and their sleeping arrangements consisted of 'a few dozen blankets (for nearly 100 women) and as many bed ticks, in which the girls were set to put straw, so that they might have something better than the bare boards to lie down upon.' By contrast the 320 convicts who had landed that same morning had been immediately provided with clothing and rations. The Governor had welcomed them and they were given sleeping berths.[42]

Ultimately the arrival of free immigrants was going to totally change the social structure of the colonies but this was to be a slow process and one that met with considerable resistance. The fate of women was, meanwhile, one of exploitation and abuse. While women remained a numerical minority, and the authorities took no special measures for their protection, they had little hope of being treated any differently from female convicts. The population of New South Wales and Van Diemen's Land (Tasmania) in 1833 was as follows:[43]

New South Wales

Free Males	Free Females	Convict Males	Convict Females
22,798	13,452	21,846	2,698

Van Diemen's Land

Free Males	Free Females	Convict Males	Convict Females
12,524	8,561	13,664	1,874

D. D. Heath, giving evidence on these figures to the Select Committee on Transportation in 1837, claimed that 'if transportation were abolished, and the free emigration of families encouraged, the effects would soon be sensible.'[44] He estimated that if 4,000 to 5,000 convicts, 85 per cent of them men, were still transported annually, while the free immigrants were overwhelmingly male, 'it cannot be expected that for a century to come any approximation to equality can be made.' Without such an approximation, the chances for a change in the treatment of women appeared remote.

The attempts at change instituted by Governor Macquarie during his eleven years in the colony were short-lived. He had hoped to see a society based on the efforts of peasant farmers, independent traders and artisans.[45] His policy of promoting the emancipated convicts – by giving them land grants and appointing them to positions of authority – was bitterly resented by the exclusivist and anti-emancipist 'Pure Merinos' who wanted a pastoral industry resting on convict labour to form the foundations of the new colony. He received more support for his policy of promoting education and, by the time of his departure in 1820, one-fifth of all local official spending was on education.[46] But the comprehensive system of charity schools which Macquarie instituted did not long survive the end of his administration. The blueprint for the new society which Macquarie had espoused was implicitly rejected by the recommendations of the Bigge Report which established the guidelines for the administration of the colonies for the next two or three decades.

Macquarie's priorities had been thwarted by those who rejected his idealism in favour of a colony based firmly on the principles of punishment and profit.[47] For a time at least, Bigge's general estimations had seemed vindicated. Only 730 free immigrants had come to Australia during the twelve years between 1810 and 1821 and of these 310 were the wives and children of transported convicts.[48] Before 1831 only two types of settlers arrived: those who had no choice in the matter, and those men of property who had the means to extract a quick fortune from the new land. The original land policy was reversed: henceforth only 'respectable capitalists' received grants and these were large, in proportion to their available capital.

Such immigrants saw little advantage in altering the role of women. They wanted to employ men 'with no encumbrances'[49] so they would not have to provide rations for unproductive women and children. They were happy with the existing situation whereby there was a supply of whores who could keep their men from becoming too restless and whose offspring could be supported by the Government.

Bigge, it will be remembered, had criticized the treatment of convict women but he also supported the exclusivist view of the immediate future of the colony. He did not, therefore, advocate either the abolition of transportation for women nor that they no longer be used as sexual fodder. Rather he implicitly endorsed the views of the Select Committee on Transportation which had reported a decade earlier. It had said that the convict women were 'of the most abandoned description and that in many instances they were likely to whet and to encourage the vices of the men, whilst but a small proportion will make any step towards reformation.'[50] The Committee took a 'realistic' view of this behaviour; 'But yet, with all their vices, such women as these were the mothers of a great part of the inhabitants now existing in the Colony, and from this stock only can a reasonable hope be held out of rapid increase to the population; upon which increase, here as in all infant colonies, its growing prosperity in great measure depends.' In keeping with Castlereagh's instructions to Macquarie all that was done was to build a new Female Factory so that the women would be accommodated and not forced to prostitute themselves simply to get a bed for the night.

In 1821 the new Female Factory at Parramatta was opened; it was a three-storey stone building designed by Francis Greenway to accommodate 300 women. It was both a prison and a place of employment; until 1835 women were employed spinning and weaving. (There were two similar factories in Tasmania: one at Launceston and the Cascades Factory in Hobart.) Women in the Factories were divided into three classes. The First Class consisted of women who had recently arrived from England, women who had been returned from service with good character reports, and women who had undergone a probationary period in the Second Class. Women in the First Class were eligible for assignment and to marry. In the Second Class were women who had been sentenced for minor offences and who could, after a period of probation, be transferred to the First Class. The Third, or Crime, Class consisted of women who had been transported a second time or who had been found guilty of misconduct during the voyage out or since their arrival. Convict women who became pregnant, and female immigrants convicted of vagrancy or other offences were also confined in the Factories.

But while the Female Factories would appear to resemble conventional imprisonment, they did not abate the enforced whoredom of the convict women. Rather they removed the women from the sight of the free population – so that they could ignore the ill-treatment and degradation of the convicts – and enabled their systematic abuse to be conducted more efficiently. Even within the new Factory conditions were appalling and, as the number of women transported grew, very overcrowded. The infant mortality rate at the Factories, especially at the Cascades Factory, was high, in contrast to the low rate for the colony generally. Life at the Cascades Factory has been described as follows:

Situated in a morass, surrounded by lofty hills, the sun's rays bringing with them health and cheerfulness do not penetrate into the yards of that miserable prison for a great portion of the entire year. The capacity of the building is so unequal to the number of the wretched inmates, that their working rooms resemble the hold of a slave-ship . . . So foetid, so wholly unfitting for the human being is the atmosphere after the night's halations, that if we are correctly informed, the turnkeys when they open the doors in the mornings, make their escape from the passages with the utmost expedition to escape semi-suffocation.[51]

Within the Factories women were subjected to punishment as well as incarceration. Most despised by the women was the shaving of their heads as punishment for refractoriness. Women were supposedly not allowed to be flogged, but the Rev. Samuel Marsden, a member of the Managing Committee of the Parramatta Factory had one woman, Susanah Denford, flogged and then dragged through the streets of Parramatta behind a dray.[52] In 1836, one hundred small dark cells were built at the Factory 'in order to try the effect of solitary confinement on recalcitrant females'.[53] A frequent form of punishment in Van Diemen's Land prior to Governor Arthur's administration was to force around the women's necks an iron collar which had a long prong on each side of it. This, says Robson, 'gave them the appearance of horned cattle.'[54] Evidently this was considered an eminently suitable mode of apparel for what was, in the 1812 Select Committee's opinion, a herd of prime breeders. In 1837 a treadmill was erected at the Cascades Factory; such punishment had been meted out to women in Sydney since 1823. This horrendous form of torture had especially deleterious effects on those women sentenced to periods on it. An English surgeon, Dr John Goode, who reported on its effects found that its main consequence was 'a very horrible pain in the loins' which precipitated a greatly intensified menstruation.[55]

The Factory at Parramatta functioned as a brothel and as a marriage mart. James Mudie told the 1837 Select Committee that many more women were retained in the First Class than was necessary for the size of the establishment. He recounted that Ms Gordon, the matron, had several times refused to allow him to take as servants women he had selected. It appears that Ms Gordon unofficially employed the women herself and that she had made 'thousands of pounds' from her enterprise. Mudie intimated that she had acquired influence with the authorities by the late 1820s and thus ensured that all reports made of her management of the Factory would be favourable. She was, he evinced, 'notorious'.[56]

Any man, emancipist or free settler, could visit the Factory and choose a wife:

(the eligible women) are turned out, and they all stand up as you would place so many soldiers, or so many cattle, in fact, in a fair; they are all ranked up . . . The convict goes up and looks at the women, and if he sees a lady that takes his fancy, he makes a motion to her, and she steps to one side; some will not, but stand still, and have no wish to be married, but that is very rare. Then they have, of course, some conversation together, and if the lady is not agreeable, or if the convict does not fancy her from her conversation, she steps back and the same ceremony goes on with two or three more.[57]

It is not known how many women secured husbands in this manner although in 1830 Governor Darling attributed the marriage of 163 women prisoners during the first half of that year to 'the system of management which has been pursued'.[58] But even if some women could leave the Factory by this respectable route, they left behind them many more in miserable conditions. Little was done to help them, and some of the attempts that were made were subjected to ridicule or criticism. The female convicts were so universally despised that any effort to alleviate the conditions that led to their wild and licentious behaviour was held to be suspect. It should also be remembered that the male colonists had a definite interest in seeing that the female convicts were not allowed to change their ways.

In 1841 Lady Jane Franklin, wife of the Governor of Tasmania, tried to form a ladies committee to visit the women in the Cascades Factory. Lady Jane had been commissioned by Elizabeth Fry, the reformer of women's prisons in England, to try and do something for the female convicts. When the proposed committee was announced in the Press it was mercilessly ridiculed and was attacked because there were some unmarried women amongst its members.[59] The Press attacks were so fierce that the committee disbanded much to Lady Jane's chagrin. She wrote:

it has been *the one* object I have thought most about, and cared for most, since I have been in this Colony – yet what have I done – what have I been allowed to do? . . . These women, these outcasts, for whom no man careth, how willingly would I spend my life in their service, how ardently would I devote the remnant of health and strength I yet possess to their amelioration. It would be worth living.for to have such a work before me. I could wish to be the Governor of Van Diemen's Land for that *alone*, but with anything short of *his* power . . . there will be nothing done.[60]

Lady Jane made frequent visits to the Factory to speak to the women and she was publicly criticized for this. Her efforts appear to have been grounded on a realistic appraisal of the female convicts' situation. She did not attempt to moralize to the women nor, like Governor Darling's wife in Sydney, try to bribe them to reform. Her concern was that they receive some education and better food and clothing and that conditions within the Factory be improved. She criticized the benevolent reformers:

There are many good but weak people who think if you only read to and pray with [the female convicts], they must be amended by it – will it do any good to pray amidst the howlings and blasphemy of a brothel or what is worse hushed for the moment you are there, but recommencing before you are out of hearing? – The weakness of some of these excellent people is astonishing.[61]

Even though the Factories were crowded and oppressive places, they afforded the women some measure of protection from the vagaries of being a lone woman in the rough colonial society outside. There is evidence that many of the women looked upon the Factories as their home and did their best to remain in them. There at least they had the companionship of other women in similar circumstances and, together, they were in a better position to protect themselves or to initiate things, than if they were isolated within a household as servant and sexual fodder. James Macarthur gave evidence to the 1837 Select Committee that the medical officer who attended the Factory had told him that the women would rather be there than out on assignment.[62] James Mudie claimed that when women were assigned to someone they did not like they would commit any offence so they would be sent back to the Factory. In his capacity as magistrate he had one such woman come before him. She thanked him profusely for sentencing her to Parramatta and begged him to increase her term of incarceration. When he realized her intention, he said, 'I must make an example of that woman, and I must return her to her master.'[63] Such attempts to determine one's own fate were intolerable as far as Mudie and his ilk was concerned: a constant supply of whores was necessary to maintain a quiescent male workforce.

Within the Cascades Factory was a group of women known as the 'Flash Mob'. They apparently stood up to the authorities within the

Factory and would leave the Factory whenever they chose to visit nearby inns and taverns. Instances of revolt amongst the united women within the Factories were quite common. A group of visitors to the Cascades Factory one day comprised Sir John and Lady Franklin, the Aide-de-Camp and several ladies, as well as the Rev. Bedford, the man who had been recommended by Commissioner Bigge as a suitable person to try and infuse some morality into Van Diemen's Land. The women convicts listened patiently to addresses from Lord and Lady Franklin but not to Rev. Bedford:

These women had had quite enough of Mr Bedford; they were compelled to listen to his long stupid sermons, and knew his character, and that he loved roast turkey and ham with a bottle or two of port wine much better than he loved his Bible, and when he commenced to preach they with one accord endeavoured to cough him down, and upon the warders proclaiming silence they all with one impulse turned round, raised their clothes and smacked their posteriors with a loud report. The Governor was shocked, and the parson was horror struck, the Aide de Camp laughed aloud, and even the ladies could not control their laughter.[64]

The most dramatic revolt occurred at the Parramatta Factory in October 1827 when a riot and mass escapade took place. The riot was precipitated by the women in the Third Class who complained that they were being starved and that their ration of tea and sugar had been taken away. At the time there were over 200 women in the Third Class and a larger number than usual in the First Class as more women were being transported than could be absorbed into employment. One newspaper described what happened:

Several of the more refractory spirits were . . . taken from among the gentler ones, and clapped in cooling cells under lock and key. The factory continued in a state of agitation until Saturday morning when the storm raged fiercer than before. The ladies, by some means, got possession of tools, with which they belaboured most unmercifully the hinges and panels of one of the gates, till it left an opening, through which, in a joint and corporate body, all rushed, and dispersing through the town, proceeded to beat up the bakers' and the butchers' quarters.[65]

Only three or four women actually escaped. Most submitted to capture once they had obtained food. Their actions seemed to have been designed to protest about conditions at the Factory and they had no desire to escape – where could they go? Another account of the riot is significant for it shows how the women stood up to the soldiers who were sent in to quell them and how on their recapture they demonstrated a solidarity with each other to protect the ringleaders from being singled out for punishment:

A Captain, a Lieutenant, two serjeants, and about forty rank and file, were in immediate requisition by the Magistrates, and were seen flying in all directions with fixed bayonets, for the purpose of securing the fugitives, and staying the mutiny; but so violent were the Amazonian banditti, that nothing less was expected than that the soldiers would be obliged to commence firing on them. After a little time, however, numbers of those who had broke loose were secured, and conducted back to the old quarters under a military escort, shouting as they went along, and carrying with them their aprons loaded with bread and meat, for which, after the manner of a conquering army, they had laid the inhabitants of Parramatta and its vicinity under contribution. On their arrival at the Factory, Major Lockyer, the Superintendent of Police, at Parramatta, directed the ring-leaders be selected and confined in the cells, but so determined were the rioters, that, though opposed by a military force, they succeeded in rescuing their companions, declaring, that if one suffered, all should suffer.[66]

In 1847 the need for the Parramatta Factory ceased to exist. No convicts had been sent to New South Wales for seven years and the women still remaining at the Factory were described by the Governor as 'the dregs of the convict system'.[67] The following year the Factory became the Convict, Lunatic and Invalid Establishment at Parramatta. Most of the women had been discharged or given tickets-of-leave and the place was 'thus cleared except for those women who were invalids and lunatics'.[68] Two years later its name was changed to the Parramatta Lunatic Asylum and in 1852 it began to receive male patients as well. In 1855 the records showed it had 187 male and 92 female patients.[69]

With the beginnings of mass immigration to the colonies and the development of an alternative ideology about the function of women, the enforced whoredom of women could no longer be so blatantly maintained. It was replaced by the more subtle controls of the institutions of marriage and motherhood.

Transportation to Australia ceased in 1852 and by that time the Damned Whore stereotype was no longer dominant even though it persisted as a label for the *demi-mondaine* who became outcasts, forgotten or ignored by respectable society. The 'invalids and lunatics' who remained at Parramatta probably died there since the administration of lunacy in New South Wales was such that although measures to commit people were devised, no provision was made for discharge procedures.[70] Many of these convicts were probably refractory women who had had to endure solitary confinement as this was known to send many women – more so than men – permanently insane.[71] In 1855 the female population was still outnumbered by males by over two to one, so there was a disproportionately high number of women confined to the Parramatta Lunatic Asylum. These women were indeed the dregs of what by now was a prosperous respectable society which had no wish to be reminded of its recent history during which female prostitutes had helped lay the foundations of that prosperity.

The female convicts were not as evil and as depraved as they were painted. In Tasmania, where the 'worst' women were sent, only 4 per cent were convicted for crimes committed after their arrival whereas 10 per cent of the men were.[72] A statistical study of a sample of women sent to Tasmania found that 28.5 per cent were not normally criminal before transportation, that is, they had committed only one offence which had led to their being sentenced, that 37.5 per cent were occasionally criminal, that is, had a small number of convictions, while only the remaining third could be classed as habitual criminals.[73] It needs to be pointed out that what was called criminal then would be classified as a misdemeanour today. By far the most common crimes were larceny and theft of wearing apparel.[74]

It is difficult to ascertain how many had been prostitutes before coming to Australia: Robson calculates that about one-fifth had engaged in full- or part-time prostitution.[75] So the wholesale adoption of whoredom on coming to Australia has to be explained in terms of the social climate of this country and the expectations held of women. It was deemed necessary by both the local and the British authorities to have a supply of whores to keep the men, both convict and free, quiescent. The Whore stereotype was devised as a calculated sexist means of social control and then, to absolve those who benefited from it from having to admit to their actions, characterized as being the fault of the women who were damned by it.

NOTES

1. Margaret Weidenhofer, *The Convict Years*, Lansdowne Press, Melbourne, 1973, p. 27.
2. ibid. cit., Weidenhofer, p. 24.
3. ibid., p. 74.

4. Instructions to Phillip, 25 April 1787, *Historical Records of Australia*, Vol. 1, p. 14.

5. In C. M. H. Clark, *Select Documents in Australian History 1788–1850*, Angus & Robertson, Sydney, 1965, p. 48.

6. ibid., p. 114.

7. ibid., p. 114.

8. Frederick C. Folkard, *The Rare Sex*, Murray, Sydney, 1965, p. 69.

9. Charles Bateson, *The Convict Ships 1787–1868*, Brow, Son & Ferguson, Glasgow, 1959, p. 156.

10. ibid., p. 26.

11. C. M. H. Clark, *A History of Australia*, Vol. 1, Melbourne University Press, Melbourne, 1962, p. 88.

12. T. W. Plummer to Colonel Macquarie, Park Street, Westminster, 4 May 1809, *Historical Records of New South Wales*, Vol. 7, p. 120.

13. Clark, *Select Documents . . . 1850*, p. 114.

14. Brian Fitzpatrick, *The Australian People 1788–1945*, Melbourne University Press, Melbourne, 1946, p. 108.

15. Rt Hon. W. W. Grenville to Gov. Phillip, 19 June 1789, *Historical Records of Australia*, Vol. 1, p. 120.

16. ibid., p. 739.

17. Weidenhofer, op. cit., p. 38.

18. C. H. Currey, 'The Law of Marriage and Divorce in New South Wales (1788–1858), *Royal Australian Historical Society, Journal and Proceedings*, Vol. 41, Part 3, 1955, pp. 96–102.

19. ibid.

20. Viscount Castlereagh to Gov. Macquarie, 14 May 1809, *Historical Records of New South Wales*, Vol. 7, p. 146.

21. *Report of the Select Committee on Transportation, 1837, British Parliamentary Papers, Vol. II*, 1837, Evidence of James Mudie, p. 38.

22. cit. Michael Cannon, *Who's Master? Who's Man?* Nelson, Melbourne, 1971, p. 55.

23. Gov. Darling to Rt Hon. Sir George Murray, 14 July 1830, in Appendix 6 of *Report . . . on Transportation 1837*.

24. *Report . . . on Transportation 1837*, Evidence of James Mudie, p. 38.

25. cit. M. H. Ellis, *Lachlan Macquarie*, Angus & Robertson, Sydney, 2nd rev. ed. 1952, p. 130.

26. ibid., p. 237.

27. Governor Macquarie to Viscount Castlereagh, 30 April 1810, *Historical Records of New South Wales*, Vol. 7, p. 351.

28. L. L. Robson, *The Convict Settlers of Australia*, Melbourne University Press, Melbourne, 1970, p. 135.

29. ibid., p. 135.

30. cit. R. C. Hutchinson, 'Mrs Hutchinson and the Female Factories of Early Australia', *Tasmanian Historical Research Association, Papers and Proceedings*, Vol. 11, No. 2, December 1963, p. 52.

31. cit. Kathleen Fitzpatrick, *Sir John Franklin in Tasmania, 1837–1843*, Melbourne University Press, Melbourne, 1949, p. 83. My emphasis.

32. Taken from Weidenhofer, op. cit., p. 93.

33. ibid.

34. cit. *Report . . . on Transportation 1837*, p. 262.

35. Robson, op. cit., p. 142.

36. ibid., p. 75.

37. Proclamation . . . 24 February 1810, *Historical Records of New South Wales*, Vol. 7, pp. 292–4.

38. Ralph Mansfield, *Analytical View of the Census of New South Wales for the year 1846*, Kemp . . . and Fairfax, Sydney, 1847, p. 61.

39. See C. D. Rowley, *The Destruction of Aboriginal Society*, Vol. 1, Penguin Books, 1972, p. 30f.

40. Humphrey McQueen, *A New Britannia*, Penguin Books, 1970, p. 126.

41. *Colonial Times*, 19 August 1834.

42. ibid.

43. *Report . . . on Transportation 1837*, p. 261.

44. ibid.

45. Marjorie Barnard, *A History of Australia*, Angus & Robertson, Sydney, 1942, p. 106.

46. Ellis, op. cit., p. 442.

47. This phrase is taken from John Ritchie, *Punishment and Profit*, Heinemann, Melbourne, 1970.

48. R. B. Madgwick, *Immigration into Eastern Australia 1788–1851*, Sydney University Press, Sydney, 1969, p. 33.

49. Russel Ward, *The Australian Legend*, Oxford University Press, Melbourne, 1970, p. 95.

50. *Report of the Select Committee on Transportation, British Parliamentary Papers*, 1812, p. 12.

51. cit. Fitzpatrick, op. cit., p. 81.

52. Denton Prout and Fred Feely, *Petticoat Parade*, Rigby, Adelaide, 1965, p. 226.

53. cit. Cannon, op. cit., p. 56.

54. Robson, op. cit., p. 133.

55. cit. Cannon, op. cit., p. 65.

56. *Report . . . on Transportation 1837*, pp. 50–52. (A similar situation may have existed at the Cascades Factory as the *Hobart Town Gazette* reported in May 1833 that of the one hundred inmates only four were eligible for assignment.)

57. ibid., pp. 39–40.

58. Darling to Murray, 14 July 1830 in Appendix 6 of *Report . . . on Transportation 1837*.

59. Frances J. Woodward, *Portrait of Jane: A Life of Lady Franklin*, Hodder & Stoughton, London, 1951, p. 216.

60. cit. ibid., p. 217. Original emphasis.

61. cit. ibid., p. 218.

62. *Report . . . on Transportation 1837*, Evidence of James Macarthur, p. 196.

63. ibid., p. 48.

64. cit. Fitzpatrick, op. cit., p. 81.

65. The *Australian*, 31 October 1827.

66. *Sydney Gazette*, 31 October 1827.

67. cit. C. J. Cummins, *The Administration of Lunacy and Idiocy in New South Wales, 1788–1855*, Department of Public Health, Sydney, 1967, p. 21.

68. ibid.

69. ibid., p. 22.

70. ibid., p. 10.

71. Cannon, op. cit., p. 56.

72. Robson, op. cit., pp. 96, 130.

73. H. S. Payne, 'A statistical study of female convicts in Tasmania, 1843–53', *Tasmanian Historical Research Association, Papers and Proceedings*, Vol. 9, 1961, p. 59.

74. Robson, op. cit., p. 213.

75. ibid., p. 78.

CHAPTER NINE

'GOD'S POLICE'

If Her Majesty's Government be really desirous of seeing a well-conducted community spring up in these Colonies, the social wants of the people must be considered. If the paternal Government wish to entitle itself to that honoured appellation, it must look to the materials it may send as a nucleus for the formation of a good and great people. For all the clergy you can despatch, all the schoolmasters you can appoint, all the churches you can build, and all the books you can export, will never do much good without what a gentleman in that Colony very appropriately called 'God's police' – wives and little children – good and virtuous women.

CAROLINE CHISHOLM, *Emigration and Transportation Relatively Considered*,
1847

. . . Caroline Chisholm was to set a pattern for women who followed her into public life in Australia. Her work was philanthropic, but practical; it opened up a new field which official policy had neglected; it led to changes in both legislation and administrative policy; it was directed to ensuring public and private morality and ensuring a more stable foundation for family life; and it did a great deal to offset the rough masculinity of colonial society. All this, moreover, was achieved without a head-on clash with Victorian conventions, and without raising any issue of principle about women's rights.

NORMAN MACKENZIE, *Women in Australia*, 1962

Our business being to colonize the country, there was only one way to do it – by spreading over it all the associations and connections of family life.

HENRY PARKES, NSW Legislative Assembly, 14 August 1866

As Australia evolved from penal colony to respectable society, those influencing and determining the change wanted women to be wives, not whores. They wanted to alter the social conditions which had forced women to be whores, and to eradicate the evidence of the colony's far from illustrious recent past. This was not possible while the colony was regarded by the British Government as a continental gaol and by the wealthy pastoralists as a giant grazing pasture. But once it became clear that Australia was going to be able to attract and absorb free settlers and to cast off its penal function, new ideas about what kind of society could develop became important. The 1840s saw the first wave of Australian nationalism. Transportation to the mainland ceased, a distinctive land policy which had important enduring effects on the country's future social and economic patterns was implemented, and the first stage of self-government was intro-duced. A new nation was beginning to emerge and its citizens were anxious to determine its social, economic and political perimeters as well as their place within it.

It was as part of this process that the first moves to redefine the position of women in the nascent nation were made. This was confirmation of the trend established in penal colony days: women's status and their allotted functions were always to be tied to national needs. Women in Australia have never been treated as individuals able to move more or less freely within those boundaries which all societies erect to ensure that their citizens ultimately conform to what are defined as social necessities. Men in Australia, while being repressed in the way that all societies repress their citizens, have almost always had a degree of choice about which repressive route they would follow: their individuality has been recognized. Women have been treated as a group – a group defined purely on grounds of gender – and rarely have had more than a single vocation imposed upon them.

It was inevitable that the social engineers of Australian society would look to England rather than to another colony, or former colony like the United States, for the values they wished to implant. The great majority of the immigrants who peopled Australia in this nation-building era came from the British Isles, most of them from England, and the greater proportion of settlers in Australia were of British descent. However much they aspired to a new way of life or wanted to declare their political and economic independence from Britain, they retained links with the parent nation which were founded as much in cultural obsequiousness as in simple nostalgia or the desire to maintain contact with relatives. The English immi-grants came to Australia convinced that the British political and economic system deserved emulation; what they also brought with them was the hope that this system would work more successfully for them in the new land than it had, for the majority of them, in the old.

Virtually all previous writers on immigration to Australia have devoted their attention to economic development, especially land use, or to the political ideas which the immigrants reputedly brought with them. In arguing against the theory usually culled from this approach – that radical labour politics originated from these immigrants, Humphrey McQueen cites one radical newspaper's views of the aspirations of the immigrant of the late 1840s: 'The mechanic who emigrates to this colony has the same object as the capitalist. Ask anyone what he came to the colony for, and his answer will be: to better his condition.'[1] Rather than bringing in his baggage the predisposition to establish a socialist Utopia, the immigrant came hoping to imitate the bourgeois class whose monopoly of the wealth in England had forced him to leave his native land. What enticed him, argues McQueen, was 'the prospect of establishing, not a class*less* society, but a one-class society, and that one class would be petty-bourgeois in orientation. Even those who failed were subject to the attitudes of those who succeeded.'[2] But like those he is attacking, McQueen's sights are still pinned to the labouring activities of men, and he defines the immigrants' ambitions narrowly, restricting them to their political and economic aspirations and attainments. The only departures from this tradition have been those historians who have traced the influence of religious ideas on Australia's social and political development.

C. M. H. Clark, for example, has drawn attention to the way in which Anglican ministers were regarded as moral policemen during the penal period and how their religion had 'an obvious social usefulness in a convict society, for it preached in favour of subordination and against drunkenness, whoring and gambling.'[3] Similarly, it has been pointed out that when, in 1820, the first Roman Catholic chaplains officially tolerated by the authorities were allowed to pursue their pastoral duties, it was in the belief that Catholics would thus be more easily controlled. Governor Macquarie hoped that the Blessed Sacrament would expel forever the spectre of the 1804 Castle Hill rebellion. Fear of Irish Catholic sedition and subversion prompted the erosion of the Anglican hegemony. These motives were made clear by the fact that whereas Protestant chaplains were paid direct from the Treasury, the salaries of the priests came from the Police Fund.[4] But to attribute the changes which occurred in the socio-economic and authority structures solely, or even mainly, to the labouring or political activities of men and the moral exhortations of ministers of religion ignores huge tracts of human intention and experience. It entails totally excluding from consideration one group who by now comprised nearly 25 per cent of the population. In these accounts, women assume an ethereal existence and are apparently subsumed within the activities of men. But even the accounts of the men are inadequate. What were these men working for? How did they actually see their changed environment and status? How did a few ministers succeed in taming what most commentators concurred was an ubiquitously amoral and rebellious populace? The historians of labour and religion have myopically concentrated overmuch on the public lives of men and have not made the obvious connections between these and family developments in colonial Australia. Such a recognition would have enabled them to perceive some of the motives influencing these men and to recognize the new functions and status women were starting to assume.

Many of the proponents of the 'Whig interpretation' of Australian history have relied very heavily on the fragment thesis of Louis Hartz. In his attempt to explain the genesis and development of the governing ideologies of new societies, Hartz proposes that the new society be viewed as a fragment of the parent nation, the fragment encapsulating the dominant political and social ideologies prevalent at the time of the founding of the new society.[5] Thus he sees the United States as a fragment of pre-capitalist mercantile England, whereas Latin America and French Canada, founded earlier, are fragments of the feudal period. What is important about the fragment is that although it imports the dominant ideology, this is not accompanied by either the forces which gave rise to it or those which subsequently arose to counter it; the history of the parent nation and the new society thus will differ even if at one point in chronological time they were virtually identical. The new society will exhibit in a pure, crystallized form some of the ideas plucked from the mass of conflicting ideologies fighting for hegemony in the parent nation.

Hartz and his followers see Australia as a fragment of the radical democracy of Cobbett and the Chartists, as a society which incorporated within its origins ' . . . the proletarian spirit which came out of the early convict establishment and the subsequent waves of radical migration, both British and Continental, which characterized Australian development.'[6] They postulate the fragment in almost pure political form, forgetting that this may not match the perceptions of the ordinary people they champion. Yet if the fragment thesis is applied to social ideas it appears more fruitful, and is a more plausible representation of the actual motives impelling mass migration to Australia. In particular it can be used to view the introduction, unfolding and subsequent entrenchment in Australian society of the idea that the bourgeois family should be the basic unit of social organization, that it was the most satisfactory institution yet devised for organizing reproduction, rearing children, controlling sexuality and affording maximum opportunities both for individual self-realization and conjugal happiness. Hartz notes that the social ideas of the Old World invariably influence each other and merge together in some kind of compromise conflation

. . . because [the Old World] locks them together in a seething whole, it gives none of [these social ideas] the freedom to evolve. The fragments provide that freedom. By extricating the European ideologies from the European battle, by cutting short the process of renewal which keeps that battle going, they permit precisely that unfolding of potentialities which the Old World denies.[7]

Australia, it can be argued, became the fragment within which the bourgeois ideal of 'the family' was able to flourish, and to be adopted by all classes long before it would have been possible for them had they remained in Britain. Australia became the place where, from the late 1840s onwards, thousands of immigrants were able to turn their aspirations of emulating middle-class lifestyles into some kind of reality. The fragment which broke away from the Old World was something simpler, more concrete and infinitely more portable than the complex notions of radical democracy and unionism. Such views could be carried only by a politically aware minority, they would have to be imposed on a largely disinterested population, and a protracted struggle with an entrenched ruling class would be necessary before a propaganda process could even begin. By contrast, the idea that the bourgeois family was the ideal way for men and women to live and reproduce was shared by ruling class and immigrants alike. It was one of the bases on which immigration agents in England sought to select prospective settlers: married couples and young people of marriageable age were given priority for assisted passages. And it was an idea that did not require a lengthy process of induction or preparation. The Australian economy was already particularly receptive: it had few labour intensive manufacturing industries to require the labour of women, and boom conditions ensured that men were paid wages high enough to support a whole family in a degree of comfort only dreamed of in England.

But although conditions in Australia were potentially receptive to establishing the bourgeois family, during the early period of mass migration there were several obstacles lying between the immigrants' aspirations and their fulfilment. They were hampered by the chaotic arrangements of the early emigration schemes, and the depression of the early 1840s proved to be a temporary set-back, but foremost amongst the retarding forces was the entrenched attitude to women lingering on from transportation days.

As was shown in the last chapter, the early female immigrants were subjected to the same treatment as the female convicts and this resulted in the Damned Whore stereotype remaining even after transportation had ceased. This, as we have seen, excluded the women tainted by it from marriage or at least from the respectable status that marriage and family were now intended to bestow. The position of women was the key to family development. The bourgeois family required wives who were sexually faithful and who, ideally, were virgins at marriage. Wives were seen by the bourgeois class as a form of property and as instruments of reproduction; husbands wanted their property to be untainted and they wanted a guarantee that they had fathered the children they were obliged to provide for. In addition, as the wife's functions increased and she undertook the moral guidance and elementary education of the children, it was seen as essential that she conform to bourgeois moral standards. So, although a woman characterized as a Damned Whore could marry and raise children, the stigma of the stereotype would brand her forever, in the eyes of society if not her husband, and her fitness for performing these functions would always be called into question. The kind of women who were seen as being ideal wives in the bourgeois family were those who had led thoroughly respectable lives, who knew little of the world and especially of its seamier, that is, sexual, side, and who were prepared to submit to the authority and opinions of the husband who was regarded as the undisputed master of the bourgeois family.

This at least was the way things were seen in England. In Australia there were differences, and these differences led to an altering of emphasis placed on the wife's position and on the husband's authority. The Damned Whore stereotype and the social conditions which produced it were so intertwined that its critics considered that more than the processes of time and gradual social evolution were needed to eradicate it. Colonial society needed to be totally restructured and those who urged the facilitation of the establishment of the bourgeois family all saw the securing of a safe and respectable position for women as integral to this process. But where they differed from their English counterparts was in their opinion that women themselves could play a major role in restructuring society. All of them saw reform of the immigration system as an essential pre-requisite.

The three main articulators of this idea were the founders of

South Australia, particularly the social architect of that colony, Edward Gibbon Wakefield; and Caroline Chisholm and John Dunmore Lang in New South Wales. All three argued for, and devised schemes to implement family colonization as opposed to the government schemes of selective immigration which tended to increase the already large imbalance between the sexes, and to lead in their view to moral degeneracy and chaotic employment arrangements.

Wakefield had pointed out in his plan for the new colony that the great need felt in all infant colonies where there was neither convict nor coloured slavery 'and that which leads most of the other wants which then suffer in its train, is the *want of labour*.'[8] His solution to this shortage was also designed to alleviate the other wants, and it was on the basis of his attempt to grapple with the labour problem that he devised a theory of colonization which formed the basis of the new settlement in South Australia in 1836. His primary considerations were economic:

It is obvious . . . that great as has been the augmentation of the value of land in the Australian Colonies, it would have been much greater if, every thing else remaining the same, the expense which has been incurred in sending *convicts* to them in the proportion of at least ten males to one female, had been employed in furnishing them with young couples well selected from the classes of agricultural labourers and workmen.[9]

Lang and Chisholm began by criticizing the female immigration system. In the opinion of Lang, Minister of Scots Church, Sydney: 'The female emigration system has added greatly to the immorality of the colony . . . the total amount of licentiousness has greatly increased, and the outrageous form it has assumed is certainly much more prominent . . .'[10] Caroline Chisholm had similar misgivings about the scheme:

Shiploads of females from parishes thrown on the shores of Australia! It is far from being complimentary to the feelings or character of the Australians, and knowing the settlers and the manner of living in that colony as well as I do, I cannot but feel apprehensive that a greater evil may arise from such a system than even from the present partial disparity of the sexes in the colony.[11]

Wakefield was able to engage in the luxury of planning an entire social system from scratch. He was able to see the virtues, and the errors, of other colonies, and once he was able to gain the backing of a substantial group of influential Englishmen who were prepared to finance the founding of the new colony, he was able to expound his principles of colonization as a practical activity, not merely a theoretical endeavour.

What Wakefield did – and his plan was largely adopted by the founders of South Australia – was to provide a framework for a colony designed to suit the moral, economic, political and religious needs of the rising class of mercantile capitalists.[12] He proposed that, in contrast to the colonies of the eastern states of Australia, land would be sold, thus providing revenue for some internal development and to finance immigration. He advocated that the population be concentrated in towns, rather than dispersed all over the countryside, for such concentration would enable manufacturing and service industries to develop and would constitute a secure base for social development. But most importantly, he stressed the need for an equal number of the sexes in order to provide a source of labour and to secure a future population. He calculated that if this policy had been followed in New South Wales from 1788, its population in 1834 would have been ten times more numerous than it was.[13] Along with a population increased in this natural manner, Wakefield expounded, would develop the social cohesion necessary for the smooth evolution of the colony, and with it, the bourgeois form of 'the family'. The Plan for South Australia stressed that 'no woman there would be without a protector, and no man would have an excuse for dissolute habits.'[14]

That 'the family' was now seen as an integral economic feature of mercantile capitalism was made clear by Wakefield's rationalization for sending whole families, or young people of marriageable age, to the new colony: 'If males only are sent, the expense of conveying each person purchases for the Colony but one labourer. If young couples are sent, their cost of passage is paid for them, and all their progeny, their five or six children, fifteen or eighteen grandchildren, and for the succeeding generations which descend from them.'[15] And Colonel Torrens who, along with Wakefield, was responsible for much of the philosophy of colonization which was implemented in South Australia, saw this scheme as invalidating Malthus's 'demoralizing doctrine that the working classes ought to delay their marriages'. Now, he said, 'that doctrine would be blown to the winds. In South Australia a large family would be a large source of wealth, and happy is the man who has his quiver full of them.'[16]

The reformers in eastern Australia, by contrast, had to contend with a society where males greatly exceeded females and where government attempts to alter the situation had simply compounded the problem. In New South Wales in 1833 there were 44,688 men and 16,173 women[17] while in Van Diemen's Land the following year there were 22,240 men and 10,496 women.[18] The first census taken at Port Phillip, the embryonic Victorian settlement, in September 1838 showed a total of 1,580 men, 431 women and 267 bonded servants, the sexes of whom were not distinguished.[19] The government did not have an official view of the likely consequences of continuing this situation but the fact that attempts were made to try to reverse the trend indicated that it wished to equalize the population. In 1831 the government began to finance the immigration of single girls but, as already pointed out, these women were treated similarly to the female convicts. In 1835 a new immigration scheme was introduced which granted settlers bounties to bring out the number of immigrants they required. The colonists had complained about the women sent out under the old scheme and had also said that the labourers and artisans who had been sent out to fill urgent labour shortages were unsatisfactory. Under the new scheme the onus was now on the future employers to ensure the suitability of prospective immigrants. No single criterion of eligibility existed, for different employers had different needs, and these were often at variance with what the reformers saw as conducive to the long term needs of the colonies. The squatters wanted single men 'with no encumbrances', whereas the religious and other reformers wanted to import young married couples and suitably chaperoned single women. The latter's views were shared by the Government to the extent that these two classes of immigrants were given assistance with their passages. But in 1840 the Government ceased to subsidize fares, and the bounty scheme, with substantially increased bounties, became the only means of enticing immigrants to Australia.

Since it was impossible for the colonists to select the immigrants themselves, they began to rely on a newly arisen vulture class of immigration agents, and the bounty permits were eventually transferred to the English ship-owners. A booming new enterprise was soon underway. Emigrants were supposed to furnish certificates of good character but the ship-owners, anxious to cram full their specially reconstructed ships, were willing to provide forged references. Thus while the volume of immigrants increased considerably, they were a potpourri of people whose motives for immigrating were undoubtedly to improve their current fortunes, but who could not always be assimilated into the schemes of the main employers of labour in the colonies.

The immigrants themselves had good cause for dissatisfaction during this period. On reaching Sydney they found scant welcome.

They were permitted to remain on board ship for ten days on full rations; whether they had found employment or not they were turned loose to fend for themselves after that. There were no hostels or barracks to accommodate them, and no employment registration office nor any means whereby prospective workers could be directed to existing jobs in the country.[20]

The immigrants who fared worst in these circumstances were the two groups which the authorities claimed were needed most – families with young children, and single women. The former were often unable to find work because employers were usually unwilling to provide rations for unproductive labour, that is, pregnant or nursing women and children aged under seven, while the single women were subject to the vagaries of an erratic employment system in a city crushed by a depression. Even if jobs were available, the women were often unable to find them as there was no body which concerned itself particularly with the employment arrangements of domestic servants. Groups of penniless women, often very young, were to be found sleeping on the Sydney Domain during the early 1840s, completely at the mercy of whoever might decide to prey upon them.

The initial government immigration schemes failed to substantially alter the social structure of the colony because they were piecemeal and made little attempt to secure employment and accommodation for the people they had enticed out to the colony. It became evident that, if things were to change, direct intervention was required. This came – in the person of Caroline Chisholm. She arrived in Sydney from India with her husband in the late 1830s and was horrified to discover the plight of the single women immigrants. She went round the streets and parks of Sydney, gathering up distressed women and took them into her home, but she soon recognized that large scale measures were necessary to alleviate the plight of what she estimated to be six hundred women.[21] She had children of her own and recognized her responsibilities to care for them but she also became convinced that she had received a divine-appointed mission to do something about the needs of immigrants. She began by pressuring Governor Gipps who grudgingly gave her the use of a building where, on 26 October 1841, she opened a Female Immigrants Home.[22]

Chisholm's aim was to find employment, not merely provide shelter for the women, and she established the first free labour registry in Sydney. Other registries which were in operation by then charged employers five shillings (or a guinea if they lived in the country) and employees two and sixpence. These were large amounts to pay during a depression, particularly when there was no guarantee that the contracts arranged would be mutually suitable. It also quickly became evident that although there was insufficient employment available in Sydney, plenty existed in the country, and so Chisholm began what became regular trips to the bush, escorting cart-loads of prospective employees.

Although she had begun her work with single women, she extended it almost immediately to include any unemployed person. She persuaded country people to allow her to use their empty drays returning from the city to carry men, women and children to their jobs in the country. She devised a form of employment survey and, bypassing the squatters completely, sent questionnaires designed to reveal existing employment opportunities to ministers and to farmers and other small employers. The *Sydney Herald* encouraged her work by urging the public to support her with subscriptions, and asked for the co-operation of settlers in the interior in lending their drays.

Within a year Chisholm had established employment centres at Parramatta, Moreton Bay, Liverpool, Maitland, Campbell Town, Wollongong, Scone, Bong Bong and Yass. Persons requiring servants or other labour could apply to these centres and each week a suitable supply of people would be directed to the available jobs. As well as simply placing people, Chisholm acted as a broker in securing them fair wages and she insisted that contracts for service be drawn in triplicate, copies going to employer, employee and herself. At the end of her first year of work Caroline Chisholm claimed that she had been 'the instrument either directly or indirectly of serving upwards of 2,000 persons'; 1,400 of these were women, including 76 whom she said were 'reclaimed' prostitutes.[23]

Chisholm wanted the employment she found for the women to be temporary. What she wanted was for them to become wives and mothers, and she went to great lengths to encourage marriage between single women and respectable settlers. She described her trips to the country placing employees as 'my matrimonial excursions in the Australian bush'.[24] Whenever she found a comfortable farm owned by a reputable bachelor or widower, she placed a suitable woman with the nearest married neighbour and 'in the natural course of events many suitable and happy marriages were the result'.[25]

Chisholm had strong views on the contribution respectable married women could make to a restructuring of Australian society. As the quotation at the beginning of this chapter shows, she considered women to be 'God's Police', a civilizing and moderating influence in an intemperate social environment. She saw women as actively complementing, if not taking over, the policing role played by chaplains during the penal era. Wives, she considered, could have a much greater and more direct influence on their husbands than any once-a-week contact with religion could ensure. She thought that even wild colonial Australia would be elevated if men could be rescued from their 'enforced bachelorism': 'Give them helpmates and you make murmuring, discontented servants, loyal and happy subjects of the State.'[26] She was confident that 'the influence of . . . one hundred wives in the Bush would soon be visible in the improved sympathy and feelings of their husbands . . .'[27]

This view of women as moral police was not new – it was a basic tenet of Christianity, and Caroline Chisholm was a devout Roman Catholic; but it was not a facet of feminine ability which was stressed much in England at the time. It undermined the absolute authority of the patriarchal husband, for instance, and was seen as superfluous in England where respectable society had a solid enough base to be unconcerned with the vast lower strata of people who were forced, by grim economic conditions, to eke out wretched lives of squalid poverty where crime was the only means of acquiring food and clothing. In Australia, the embryo of a respectable society existed but it was necessary to protect it, and allow it to expand and perpetuate.

Caroline Chisholm was not so naive as to imagine that the mere presence of women would alter things; she knew only too well the fate of the unchaperoned female immigrants and this is what prompted her to endeavour to secure respectable posts for the women she hoped would become the mothers of future generations of middle-class Australians. But her early efforts entailed settling immigrants who either arrived privately or else on the government scheme, and she could do no more than tinker with what was still an ill-conceived means of acquiring a balanced population.

Both Chisholm and Lang soon recognized that if their dreams of an Australia based on the bourgeois family were to be realized they would have to select suitable immigrants themselves. In 1843 Chisholm left Australia for England. She had three principal aims: to locate and arrange passages for the wives of emancipated convicts; to do likewise for the children immigrant couples had been forced to leave behind, and to found a 'national colonization' scheme. To aid the latter aim she had collected nearly seven hundred statements from settlers.[28] These were to provide evidence of the bountiful life one could lead in Australia, and to assuage the fears of prospective emigrants. She had some success in her attempts to reunite families but the third aim took much longer to effect and it was not until 1849 that her Family Colonization Loan Society was born. The immediate aim of the Society was to 'relieve the distressed and to help the poorer classes of people to emigrate'; wherever possible the reunion of families was to be encouraged and the ultimate aim was to raise the moral standard of the people.[29] Chisholm ascertained the respectability of the prospective emigrants and obliged them, as proof of their sincerity to want to start a new life, to contribute part of their passage money in advance. The balance was repayable after they had established themselves in Australia.

John Dunmore Lang was suspicious of Chisholm's motives: he accused her of trying to people the colony with Papists, but the two were agreed on basic principles. Lang wrote

. . . nothing less than a speedy or rather an immediate, and extensive emigration of virtuous and industrious families and individuals from the mother country to the Australian colonies can possibly relieve these colonies from the baneful effects of past mismanagement . . . or ensure to them a reputable moral character and a healthy tone of society for the future.[30]

During the 1830s Lang had arranged for the passage to Australia of over four hundred carefully selected Scottish immigrants. They were mainly mechanics and agricultural labourers, but also included several ministers and school teachers.[31] Lang recognized the need to import both respectable hard-working labouring immigrants and also to provide the means for their moral and practical education. Later he, like Chisholm, saw that it was necessary to select immigrants personally, and from September 1848 to November 1849 he toured England and Scotland lecturing on the desirability of emigrating to Australia. Like Chisholm, he published a series of pamphlets and newspaper articles extolling settlement in Australia and eventually was responsible for the departure of six ships containing 1,424 immigrants, the quality of whom was 'unimpeachable'.[32]

In his survey of British immigration to Australia, Crowley concludes with an attack on the 'Whig interpretation' of Australian history:

It would be a mistake to regard the history of this migration as an expression of revolt against exploitation and social restriction, and to create a legend of high ideals and unselfish industry among these new Australians would be to extol and dramatize a movement which was seldom more than a search for higher wages, conditions and more of the comforts of life.[33]

The immigrants who came to Australia were only a tiny proportion of the more than eighteen million people who left the British Isles in the second half of the nineteenth century. Our knowledge of them is sparse but we do know that the majority came from the labouring classes, virtually none of them were paupers and that most were under forty-five years of age.[34]

It is difficult to agree with the proponents of the Whig interpretation that these immigrants viewed their flight to Australia Felix as an ideological exodus. Government attempts to entice immigrants had succeeded mainly in attracting people from the lumpenproletariat, a group so oppressed by conditions in England that no matter what hopes individuals within it may have had for their new life, existing conditions in Australia were scarcely conducive to radical changes in their previous mode of living. For most of them, it was only the location of their lives that changed.

The systematic enticement of respectable immigrants to eastern Australia was mainly the work of private individuals like Caroline Chisholm and J. D. Lang, and although they were responsible for the immigration and settlement of many thousands of families and single people, their efforts suffered many setbacks. Chisholm reacted with dismay to the news in 1850 that gold had been discovered. She knew that the lure of a quick fortune would attract bands of single men intent only on extracting what they could from the country, that it would break up families and would erode the precarious beginnings of the respectable, family-based society which had started to develop during the 1840s. Very few of these three groups of immigrants – government-sponsored paupers, family groups and fortune hunters – could be seen as coming to Australia with the aim of establishing a radical egalitarian democracy. It is possible to impute more plausible motives to those immigrants who intended to stay, and who had planned their immigration with a view to realizing in Australia what was denied to them in England.

The British Isles in the 1840s and 1850s were not, for the working class, a propitious place in which to marry and raise children. As one immigration handbook put it 'Marriage is either a luxury, or an imprudence. Married men are congratulated by their friends when their wives prove childless.' It added, enticingly ' . . . in Australia the working man, with a few acres of corn-growing bushland, sees in every child the source of an income. They prove useful at seven and eight years old.'[35] Most of the immigration propaganda, and much of that literature which is more effective than any official propaganda – letters from people already settled in Australia to their relatives in Britain – stressed the warm, sunny, healthy environment, the economic opportunities for acquiring a small plot of land or a cottage, the availability of fresh food of a quantity and quality unknown in

England – 'meat three times a day' – which the colony offered. These proved to be powerful inducements to people for whom marriage was either impossible or for whom it meant poverty, high child mortality, constant hunger and sharing crowded living quarters with other families.

For many, women especially, marriage was simply impossible. In England there was a huge surplus of women; between 1851 and 1871 there was a 16.8 per cent increase in the number of single women of marriageable age and there was a surplus of over 125,000 single women.[36] Thus a large proportion of the female immigrants were obviously in search of husbands. The problem was greater for middle-class women. Few of them were trained to earn an income to support themselves and if they were unable to find husbands, many were threatened with destitution. Those few occupations which middle-class women were able, and willing, to undertake could not accommodate the numbers seeking work. It was not uncommon for an advertisement for a governess to receive up to seven hundred applications, while the demand for delicate embroidery from the needles of gentlewomen was not high enough to provide a living for very many.

While female immigrants were subject to such abuses as met most of the women who came to Australia in the 1830s, few middle-class women would risk venturing abroad. But the problem of how these women were to survive became so severe that they banded together to try to tackle it. In May 1862 the Female Middle-Class Emigration Society was formed in England by Ms Rye.[37] Prior to this Ms Rye had arranged for large parties of working-class women – mainly servants and dressmakers – to emigrate to Queensland, New Zealand and British Columbia. When she took up the cause of middle-class women, she found what was most needed was money for passages, and also protection for the women when they arrived at their destinations; and the initial efforts of the Society were directed to organizing these essentials. After a year of operation the Society had obtained employment and accommodation for more than one hundred women.[38] But even after the women could be assured of protection when they arrived in Australia, there was no guarantee that even with the huge surplus of men, they would be able to find husbands.

Many of the single men who immigrated both before and during the gold rushes planned merely to amass a quick fortune and return to England. The adventurous types one meets in the pages of the many accounts of colonial life during this period, working their way through various jobs, accumulating exotic experiences to recount back home, seldom seem to have marriage on their minds. Lt Col Mundy, a chronicler of mid-century colonial life noted:

Strange to say, too, the well brought up and pretty maidens of the middle and servant classes of Sydney do not appear to be much sought in marriage. Yet it is undoubtedly in these classes that the well-known preponderance of males exists. The single men do not want wives, and the responsibilities and encumbrances of family life. They prefer working hard – working like slaves – four or five days, and 'larking' the rest of the week.[39]

As the century progressed, however, family life became more widespread as colonial society began to be organized around this institution and it became more difficult for these free spirits to avoid matrimony. Of those men aged between 25 and 29 in 1871, 24 per cent had never married; by 1901 this had dropped to 20 per cent and ten years later was 15 per cent.[40]

Indeed, the taming and domestication of the self-professed independent man became a standard theme in late nineteenth century fiction, especially that written by women. It seems that the initial reluctance of the wild colonial boys to marry was eroded fairly quickly: most of the women who immigrated to Australia in the 1840s and 1850s eventually did find husbands, and the overall marriage rate for women in Australia was much higher than in Britain. In 1881, 96 per cent of women aged between 45 and 49 had married; a great many of these women would have come to Australia as single immigrants. Had they stayed in Britain their chances of marriage would have been significantly less. The percentages of women aged 45 to 49 who were married by 1881 are as follows: England and Wales – 87.7; Scotland – 80.6; Ireland – 82.4.[41]

For working-class families in England the contrast between their current lives and what Australia offered must have seemed irresistible. These families had by now internalized the ideal of the bourgeois family but economic conditions made its realization in England virtually impossible for them. Few could afford to buy, or even rent, their own home and most were forced to live in the warren-like slums depicted by both Engels and Dickens in their accounts of poverty in Victorian England. The average number of inhabitants per house in the major cities of Britain was as follows: London (1831) 7.48; Edinburgh (1841) 5.94; Dublin (1831) 12.74.[42] By contrast, in Sydney in 1841 there was an average of 6.67 people per house and this had dropped to 5.96 by 1846; in the suburbs of Sydney it was only 4.79.[43] The building of houses progressed rapidly during

this period: in the five years between 1841 and 1846 there was a
92.0 per cent increase in the number of new houses completed and
an 82.2 per cent increase in the habitation of these houses.[44] Mansfield
claims that, in the same period, infant mortality in Australia was less
than half of that in England.[45]

Wages for workmen were high in Australia. Professor N. G. Butlin
has shown that in the second half of the nineteenth century, Australian
incomes per head were substantially higher than in Britain or even
the United States.[46] In 1852 a wage-earner wrote that he 'had no
prospects in England but here thank God I have, and I have never
yet regretted leaving my native country and I hope I never shall do.'[47]
And McQueen notes that sections of the workforce were prepared to
accept a 10 to 20 per cent wage cut in 1856 in order to maintain their
recently won eight-hour day – how many workers could afford such
reductions today?[48]

Thus conditions in colonial Australia enabled working-class individuals and families to adopt the bourgeois family as their lifestyle.
They could inhabit, and often purchase, their own cottage, thereby
fulfilling the requisite of family privacy. Wages were high enough
for a man to be able to support his wife who need no longer slave in
factory or mill but could remain at home, engaging in the never-
before-experienced task of having an entire house to care for, and
babies – who thrived instead of dying in their first year – to look after.

The idea that women ought to be homemakers and full-time
mothers was beginning to gain credence in England at this time.
In the 1830s and 1840s a host of books appeared, written by both
men and women, which sought to establish the precise place of
women in society and to set out the exact duties of the wife and
mother of a family. The most common line of argument was that
'the sphere of Domestic Life is the sphere in which female excellence
is best displayed' and advocates of this thought that it was a woman's
fundamental task to create a home that would provide an environment
of emotional stability for her husband and children.[49] In Australia
after the 1840s, working-class people could realize these goals and it
was these concrete aspirations involving their everyday lives, rather
than abstract political notions, which brought thousands of immigrants
flocking to these shores and which enabled 'the family' to be
established as a basic unit of social organization with a widespread
rapidity that was probably unequalled anywhere else in the Western
world.

Both Lang and Chisholm were infinitely aware of what these
immigrants sought and both believed that the budding colony could

meet their needs if sufficient efforts were made to accommodate them. Both had religious convictions which impelled them to want the penal colony's rough and wild ways replaced by what they considered to be a more moral civilization. Ultimately the Government was to agree with them. Although 'the family' would have been established, albeit more slowly, as the basis of colonial life, their endeavours served as a catalyst. And it is important to recognize Caroline Chisholm's specific contribution, not only in promoting family colonization, but in articulating a role for women.

Caroline Chisholm was no feminist and she was well aware of the contradiction between her own political and public activities and the function she wanted other women to fulfil. But she felt compelled to act, and to neglect her own family, in order to see other families established and within them, women policing the morals of their husbands and, indirectly, the entire colony. Thus her public life in no way set a precedent for women to follow. She herself was opposed to any measures which would discourage women from marrying. While arranging employment for single women, she wrote:

. . . the rate payable for female labour should be proportional on a lower scale than that paid to the men . . . high wages tempt many girls to keep single while it encourages indolent and lazy men to depend more and more upon their wives' industry than upon their own exertions thus partly reversing the design of nature.[50]

Her philosophy of women's role was rapidly and widely accepted for she was voicing a view which was evidently compatible with the rapid and stable growth of colonial society.

Once the British Government conceded that a new nation was emerging where once had stood a conventional gaol, and British and local capitalists began to realize the rewards which could be reaped from this outpost of the Empire, it became essential to ensure that the population would increase with some degree of predictability, and that it could be harnessed to the needs of an evolving capitalist economy. As was shown in Chapter Six, the bourgeois family had become almost synonymous with ensuring these requirements were met. Obviously this form of organizing people had to be introduced to Australia if its rulers were to prosper. That Chisholm's efforts were not radical ones, that she was in fact serving the needs of the bourgeoisie, was evidenced in the kind of support she received. Although the colonial authorities were slow to recognize her work, local capitalists were not: they could see the advantages of securing a family-based population. An extravagant editorial in the *Empire* in 1859 was evidence of the esteem in which she was held at the time:

If Captain James Cook discovered Australia; if John Macarthur planted the first seeds of its extraordinary prosperity; if Ludwig Leichhardt penetrated and explored its before unknown interior; Caroline Chisholm has done more: she has peopled, she alone has colonized it in the true sense of the term. To her influence, her untiring efforts, her self-sacrificing devotion is owing, in great measure, the spreading over the land of a prosperous – a happy – a teeming population . . . hundreds of homes have been founded . . . families throughout the length and breadth of Australia by her untiring efforts.[51]

Henry Parkes is quoted at the beginning of this chapter as saying that the only way to colonize Australia had been to spread over it 'all the associations and connections of family life'. This occurred in the form of laws and social or industrial practices which complemented or reinforced the bourgeois family and which were often implemented long before they were adopted in Britain. The need for a plentiful supply of wives in a colony where men were still a distinct majority obviously influenced the passing of legislation to enable marriage to a deceased wife's sister – long before it was enacted in Britain. An integration and balance between work and family life was secured for men with the introduction of the eight-hour day. The sexual division of labour and responsibility was confirmed by the granting of universal manhood suffrage in all colonies – women, who were by now increasingly confined to the home, were presumably supposed to be represented by their husbands' or fathers' votes. Early industrial unionism was designed to secure better wages and conditions for men and was conducted on the apparent assumption that only men were in need of this protection. Women workers had to toil without such benefits.

By 1890 there were large numbers of women, especially single working-class women, in the workforce. In 1891 over 40 per cent of all women in New South Wales between the ages of 15 and 24 were in employment; most of them worked as domestic servants but increasing numbers were going into factories.[52] The majority, in both occupations, had to labour long hours for pittance wages. In 1888 William Lane, the radical socialist who was later to found a Utopian colony in Paraguay, wrote:

The position of working women in the cities of the colony is becoming worse and worse every year . . . They are becoming herded in stifling workshops and ill-ventilated attics . . . They are forced to stand all day behind the counters of large emporiums . . . They are 'sweated' by clothing factories, and boot factories . . . the children too are being dragged into the slave-house of toil; little ones are working in factories and shops, and the Law, instead of rescuing them . . . stands by to ply the whips on their backs if they revolt.[53]

In 1891, 3 per cent of females aged 5 to 14 in New South Wales were in the workforce.[54] Commissions into conditions in Shops and Factories which were conducted in various states around 1890 confirmed Lane's description of the conditions of women in industry, but the infant trade union movement, while it made ritualistic condemnations, did little to alter these conditions and evinced little desire to include women workers in its ranks. At a series of Inter-colonial Trade Union Congresses held between 1879 and 1891 the position of women as unionists, or as members of the labour move-ment, was barely considered.[55]

Women workers had either to endure this gross exploitation or else attempt to organize themselves to fight their employers. Most of their attempts to do the latter met with interference, if not opposition, from the male trade union movement. In the 1880s and 1890s several women's unions were formed within specific trades, and in 1891 an embracing Female Employees Union began. It was intended to accommodate waitresses, barmaids and laundresses. Four months after its inception, the FEU organized a strike of laundresses in Pyrmont, Sydney, after the dismissal of a girl they believed had been victimized because she was a unionist.[56] The strike generated considerable public support and the Union gathered more members but in July 1892 the Trades and Labour Council announced that it intended bringing charges against the FEU and shortly afterwards the Union collapsed.

In 1882 tailoresses in Victoria went on strike against sweating in their trade. This strike lasted a long time and was sympathetically reported in considerable detail in the *Age* and this elicited nearly £2,000 in donations to help the striking women. As soon as the strike began, officials from Trades Hall organized the women into a union whose membership soon reached 2,000.[57] However, it has been suggested that the formation of the union was instigated by male tailors who wanted to protect themselves against being undersold by cheaper, female labour and was not motivated by a unionist concern for the conditions under which the women worked.[58] Two women represented the union at the Second Intercolonial Trade Union

Congress in 1884, but they did not appear again – men represented the Union at subsequent congresses.[59]

The much vaunted militancy of early trade unionism in Australia rarely was extended to protect women and this can largely be explained by the ascendancy of the idea that women ought not to work outside the home. The ideology of the bourgeois family was strongly entrenched by 1880, nearly fifty years after the initial efforts of the immigration reformers in the eastern colonies and the establishment of the family-based colony of South Australia; and men now staunchly defended their role as bread-winners. In doing so they ignored the position of the single woman and of those married, widowed or deserted women who were forced into employment.

The God's Police stereotype had by now become so widely accepted that it was taken to be descriptive of what all women were actually doing as well as being prescriptive about what they *should* be doing. There had been a radical change in the position of women since the convict days; most women could expect to marry and to acquire a respectable status as they worked as mothers and housewives within their own homes. Once married, the great majority need not work outside the home because they could rely on the economic support of their husbands. The condemnations and abuses associated with the Damned Whore stereotype had been replaced by the respectful tributes seen as being the due of women fulfilling a moral policing and civilizing role within family and society. But this change was mainly one of status and in ideas about how women should be regarded; the ideals did not always match the reality.

This is made clear in the idealization of Australia's women pioneers. This standard theme in Australian literature and history occurs as a token subsidiary to the romantic idealization of outback life which is the basis of the Australian Legend. There are countless tales of the hardships endured by bush wives, Henry Lawson's 'The Drover's Wife' being but one of the more well-known examples. C. M. H. Clark, in the latest volume of his *History of Australia*, continues the tradition of idealizing the women who lived and bore children in remote parts of the colonial wilderness:

. . . contemporaries coined the phrase that the bush was 'no place for a woman'. Yet, paradoxically, those who possessed the pluck and the will to endure acquired a prestige and a power in a society whose composition seemed designed to confer a power on the men even in excess of that on which Moses and the apostle Paul had conferred a divine sanction. Out of such squalor and hardship, which drove the menfolk into erratic, unsteady ways in the primitive huts of the gentry, a matriarch quietly took over the central position in the family, and in the huts of the servants a 'Mum' came into her own.[60]

A curious evasiveness pervades the myths surrounding the outback women: their ability to cope with a hostile environment and to survive months, even years, of unremitting loneliness is acknowledged. What has been glossed over were other hazards these women had to endure: the men of the outback, including, often, their husbands. A savage corrective to the romantic myths of bush life comes from the pen of Barbara Baynton who, in story after story, depicts the hardships, miseries and even murderous attacks experienced by bush women from unsympathetic husbands, lecherous employers and rapacious swagmen. Unlike most male writers of the fiction of the outback, Baynton does not resort to symbolic representations of these threats: she does not write about snakes or fires or Aborigines. Her depictions are real. In 'The Chosen Vessel' she writes of a young wife isolated in terror in a primitive hut throughout the week while her husband was off shearing, terrified of a swaggie who importunes customary bush hospitality from her and who returns that night and murders her:

More than once she thought of taking her baby and going to her husband. But in the past, when she had dared to speak of the dangers to which her loneliness exposed her, he had taunted and sneered at her. She need not flatter herself, he had coarsely told her, that anybody would want to run away with her.[61]

The myths of the bush women evade such realities and they also ignore the lives of the majority of women in Australia at the time. In 1871 the six capital cities of Australia contained one-quarter of the population; by 1901 this had risen to one-third.[62] A further proportion lived in rural towns. A majority of women lived solely in urban areas and their experiences are totally neglected by this concentration on women in the bush. The life of the nineteenth century suburban housewife remains hidden and unexplored; there is not, to my knowledge, a single piece of writing outside one or two novels which even begins to investigate what women's new roles entailed.

We have already seen that the working life of the single woman was one of exploitation and trade union neglect; the lives of bush women were fraught with hazards that extollers of the Legend dare not even contemplate (for they would destroy the myths they have constructed about the men of the bush). It would be naive and unrealistic to conclude that the lives of urban married women were as contented and rosy as Caroline Chisholm predicted they would be. Middle-class values now dominated the cities, and these included the God's Police stereotype of women. Caroline Chisholm had thought that the mere presence of large numbers of women would be sufficient to alter the mores of convict Australia; she was confident that what she considered to be women's innate desires for marriage, children and homes would, if encouraged by the authorities, secure a reversal of the Damned Whore stereotype. What she did not see was that the God's Police stereotype was just as much an imposition on women as the one it replaced.

There was an important difference, of course, in that the new stereotype was seen, especially by women themselves, as a vast improvement. But the situation was a very rigid one which allowed only two possible choices to women about what to do with their lives. They could be wives and mothers, or workers in surrogate-mother jobs, and win respectable status – and lose all independence to the authority and economic support of their husbands. A subtler form of exploitation but exploitation nevertheless: because women were doing what was supposed to be 'natural' to them, they were not expected to want any monetary reward or even any independent identity. They had status and the kind of power, formerly held by priests, that is acknowledged but resented by men, but their lives were now firmly circumscribed by the limits of home and family. They had lost all powers of self-determination. There remained another alternative, although class and other factors mediated to determine the extent of choice involved in its adoption. The Damned Whore stereotype did not disappear but was now applied to women who were outside the confines of family and maternity; it applied to the *demi-mondaine* who were, by definition, unrespectable. These were the women who worked in pubs, or as prostitutes, who were sexually free, who had 'illegitimate' babies. They were still victims of exploitation although, ironically, many of them were more independent than their more respectable counterparts.

In the 1880s, women who worked as nurse-maids or in similarly esteemed jobs earned from £18 to £25 per annum; by contrast, women in such disreputable occupations as barmaid earned between £40 and £70 per annum.[63] Thus, while the women who fulfilled the God's Police role were idealized and given a token status, they had no economic independence, and there has been a steadfast refusal to investigate just what their lives entailed. It is these women who are the predecessors of the majority of women in Australia today: economically dependent and culturally impotent, their activities and their influences were hidden within the home and hence could be overlooked. The price of being rescued from the ignominious fate of the female convicts and immigrants was to disappear from society, and from history.

NOTES

1. cit. Humphrey McQueen, *A New Britannia*, Penguin Books, 1970, p. 122.

2. ibid., p. 125.

3. C. M. H. Clark, *A Short History of Australia*, Heinemann, London, 1969, p. 22.

4. Patrick O'Farrell, *The Catholic Church in Australia*, Nelson, Melbourne, 1968, p. 16.

5. Louis Hartz, *The Founding of New Societies*, Harcourt, Brace & World, New York, 1964.

6. ibid., pp. 41–2.

7. ibid., p. 9.

8. E. G. Wakefield, *Plan of a Company to be Established for the Purpose of Founding a Colony in South Australia*, Ridgway, London, 1831, p. 43. Original emphasis.

9. ibid., pp. 17–18.

10. *Report of the Select Committee on Transportation, 1837*, British Parliamentary Papers, Vol. II, 1837, Evidence of J. D. Lang, p. 255.

11. Caroline Chisholm, *The ABC of Colonization in a series of Letters*, J. Ollivier, London, 1850, p. 22.

12. The first publication of Wakefield's views, *A Letter from Sydney* (1829) had been addressed, not to 'a poor Lieutenant; nor a broken farmer; nor a labourer; nor a mechanic'; but to 'young men of rank and connection', men of the professions and 'those in the intermediate ranks of life'. Cit. Douglas Pike, *Paradise of Dissent*, Melbourne University Press, Melbourne, 1957, p. 77. Wakefield was, in other words, offering a scheme which would extend the scope for profitable investment for those men whose moderate capital would perhaps be insufficient to accrue wealth in a fiercely competitive *laissez-faire* England.

13. *South Australia: Outline of the Plan of a Proposed Colony*, South Australian Association, London, 1834, p. 16.

14. ibid.

15. Wakefield, op. cit., p. 55.

16. cit. Pike, op. cit., p. 164.

17. Ralph Mansfield, *Analytical View of the Census of New South Wales for the year 1846 . . .*, Kemp and Fairfax, Sydney, 1847, p. 20.

18. Report . . . on Transportation, *1837*, Appendix 10, p. 261.

19. Michael Cannon, *Who's Master, Who's Man?*, Nelson, Melbourne, 1971, p. 95.

20. Margaret Kiddle, 'Caroline Chisholm in New South Wales', *Historical Studies*, April 1942 – November 1943, p. 188.

21. Margaret Kiddle, *Caroline Chisholm*, Melbourne University Press, Melbourne, 1950, p. 39.

22. ibid.

23. ibid., p. 61.

24. Chisholm, op. cit., p. 22.

25. Margaret Swann, *Caroline Chisholm*, Government Printer, Sydney, 1925, p. 16.

26. Chisholm, op. cit., p. 31.

27. ibid.

28. Kiddle, *Caroline Chisholm*, op. cit., p. 82.

29. ibid., p. 134.

30. John Dunmore Lang, *Transportation and Colonisation*, A. J. Valpy, London, 1837, p. iv.

31. Kiddle, *Caroline Chisholm*, op. cit., p. 53.

32. ibid., p. 91.

33. F. K. Crowley, 'The British Contribution to the Australian Population: 1860–1919', *University Studies in History and Economics*, July 1964, p. 78.

34. ibid., passim.

35. S. & J. Sidney, *Sidney's Australian Handbook*, Pelham Richardson, London, 1848, p. 30.

36. J. A. and Olive Banks, *Feminism and Family Planning in Victorian England*, Schocken Books, New York, 1964, p. 26.

37. Jane E. Lewin, 'Female Middle-class Emigration', *Transactions of the National Association for the Promotion of Social Science*, London, 1863, p. 612.

38. ibid., p. 616.

39. Lt Col Godfrey Charles Mundy, *Our Antipodes*, Vol. 1, Richard Bentley, London, 1852, p. 374.

40. Ladislas Ruzicka and Lincoln Day, 'Australian Patterns of Family Formation', *Search*, July 1974, p. 300.

41. This information was provided by Peter McDonald of the Department of Demography, Australian National University. I would like to thank Dr McDonald for making this material from his Ph.D. thesis available to me.

42. Mansfield, op. cit., p. 125.

43. ibid.

44. ibid., p. 122.

45. ibid., p. 131.

46. cit. J. W. McCarty, 'Australian Cities in the Nineteenth Century', *Australian Economic History Review*, September 1970, p. 117.

47. cit. McQueen, op. cit., p. 122.

48. ibid., p. 123.

49. Banks, op. cit., p. 58.

50. Caroline Chisholm, *Prospectus of a Work to be entitled Voluntary Information*, W. A. Duncan, Sydney, 1845, p. vii.

51. The *Empire*, 15 August 1859, reproduced in *What has Mrs Caroline Chisholm done for the Colony of New South Wales?*, James Cole, Sydney, 1862, p. 17.

52. J. E. Cobb, *The Women's Movement in New South Wales 1880–1914*, M.A. thesis, University of New England, 1967, p. 120.

53. cit. D. P. Crook, 'Occupations of the People of Brisbane: An Aspect of Urban Society in the 1880s', *Historical Studies*, November 1961, p. 59.

54. Cobb, op. cit.

55. Cobb, op. cit., p. 153.

56. ibid., p. 160.

57. J. Hagen, 'Employers, Trade Unions and the first Victorian Factory Acts', *Labour History*, November 1964, p. 9. There is some dispute about exactly when this Union was formed and some researchers claim it was established *before* the strike; T. A. Coghlan puts its formation as early as 1874.

58. Peter Biskup, *The Female Suffrage Movement in Australia*, B.A. Honours thesis, University of Western Australia, 1959, p. 21. I would like to thank Dr Biskup for kindly allowing me to quote from his thesis.

59. Cobb, op. cit., p. 154.

60. C. M. H. Clark, *A History of Australia*, Volume III, Melbourne University Press, Melbourne, 1973, p. 272.

61. Barbara Baynton, *Bush Studies*, Angus & Robertson, Sydney, 1965, (1902), p. 134.

62. McCarty, op. cit., p. 107.

63. Crook, op. cit., p. 52.

CHAPTER TEN

EDUCATION FOR MOTHERHOOD

. . . though we do want a higher standard of female education it is not in order to fit us for professions, but that we may better perform those home duties that are undoubtedly a woman's work.

Ladies column in the *Australasian*, 27 April 1872

As bearing upon the subject of child-birth, it may be mentioned that the conditions of life in Australia necessitate much separation of husbands and wives. On the night of the Census of 1901, 30,379 husbands out of 206,186 in New South Wales were not under the same roof with their wives and this is the habitual condition throughout Australia. The advent of a more settled life will prevent this breaking up of families and conduce to a higher birth-rate. But . . . these remedies, if operating to their full extent, would not go far to restore the former birth-rate nor would anything be effective unless a radical change takes place in the mental and moral attitude of women towards child-bearing.

T. A. COGHLAN, *The Decline of the Birth-Rate in New South Wales*, 1903

Among the most neglected areas in the study of Australian nationalism has been the radical reappraisal of the role of women and the place 'the family' was to occupy in the new nation in the period which began in the 1880s and continued to the beginning of World War One. This period of the gestation and birth of the nation was characterized by a self-consciousness which prompted the critical examination of the institutions and ideas which had evolved during the past century. The devastating depression of the 1890s had called into question the effectiveness of existing economic arrangements while the political and social ferment of the 1890s had given lie to the consensus which complacent colonials assumed to govern their social existence. An urgent soul-searching ensued by those who were determined to launch a nation which would leave behind it forever the uncertainties of the previous decade.

Although this process was by no means confined to determining the future of 'the family', and women's role in relation to it, 'the family' was viewed as a fundamental unit of social organization and changes which occurred in its role had implications for many areas of life. These changes are important in illustrating that sexism in Australian society has not been static. The dominant ideas about women's role in society and ideas and practices affecting relationships between the sexes have been reappraised several times in the past two hundred years. These reappraisals have produced some important changes but they have not led to the erosion of the fundamental sexist assumptions which have always circumscribed the freedom of women. The changes which occurred during this period are especially relevant to today because although many of these changes paralleled those of other countries, the context of conscious nation-building in which they were forged were to endow the resulting ideas and practices with a distinct and enduring character. Almost all of the social and ideological factors which are seen as constraining women today were fashioned during this period and thus their development is of more than historical interest.

The bourgeois form of family, as described in Chapters Six and Nine, was advocated by State, Church and other bodies and individuals with power to influence social relations, as the most desirable way for people to live and reproduce, and this form of family was being adopted by more and more of the population. But although the outlines of this family form were generally agreed upon, many of its details were still in dispute. If the populace was going to be marshalled into predictable patterns of behaviour and response – as a newly-formed nation obviously sought as desirable – these details had to be resolved and this required State intervention. This family form, with its strict sex-based division of labour and responsibilities, was still not structurally integrated into the Australian economy. The God's Police ideology, which prescribed the roles of women which underpinned this family form, still required precise definition. Although it was by now the dominant stereotype, it was being interpreted in a variety of ways by women themselves and in ways which the authorities considered could undermine its basic rationale.

It was the area of birth-control and family size that saw the most decisive clash between women and the State. Between 1886 and 1901 the birth-rate in New South Wales declined by nearly one-third.[1] Similar falls were recorded in all states and as there had been no significant decline in the marriage rate to account for this, it was evident that women were controlling their fertility themselves. Neville Hicks, the writer of an excellent doctoral thesis on the subject, remarks that between 1888 and 1903 the fall in the Australian crude birth-rate was as great as any Western nation except France had known in modern times and it was even more rapid than the French decline had been.[2] There is evidence that women used contraception, abortion and infanticide to limit their families.

Contraceptive devices and abortifacients were freely available in Australia from the 1880s. They were sold over the counter at chemist shops and were explicitly advertised in newspapers and magazines. The most commonly advertised artificial contraceptives and aborti-facients were condoms ('French goods'), pills (to 'prevent irregulari-ties'), pessaries and vaginal douches. Also available were primitive intra-uterine loops and spermicidal solutions designed to be soaked up by a sponge which was inserted in the vagina prior to intercourse. Newspapers carried large advertisements such as the following:

LADIES! MARRIED OR SINGLE can Obtain Immediate Relief for irregularities etc., by Sending for Dr C's Famous Treatment. No Failures. PRICE: 10s; and Extra Strong £1. It is Perfectly New, and is as much Superior to the Remedies usually advertised as the Express Train is to the Mail Coach. They act within a few hours with Perfect Safety and Comfort, and a Positive CURE is effected in EVERY CASE undertaken. This Treatment is prepared with the advice and under the immediate supervision of a Legally Qualified Medical Man. All Consultations by Letter or Personally are FREE. Call or write, as a Friendly chat costs nothing. Send stamped addressed envelope for Testimonials and particulars. DR CARTWRIGHT, 7 Wynyard Square.[3]

Contraceptives and abortifacients of all kinds were sold in copious quantities. In October 1903 more than 21,000 sheaths and pessaries were imported to New South Wales, and three wholesalers in that state reported sales of over 200,000 items each year.[4] Since they were sold openly, these contraceptives and abortifacients were available to all classes, and women had no hesitation about going to chemists and asking for them 'as openly and indifferently as they would ask for a toothbrush'.[5] There is also evidence that women were adept at making their own contraceptives from the basic ingredients used in those available commercially.

A special Commonwealth Royal Commission on Secret Drugs, Cures and Foods, established in 1907 to investigate the plethora of patent medicines and other goods freely available in Australia at the turn of the century, reported that many of these devices were injurious to women's health and could impair their reproductive capacity.[6] This was undoubtedly true[7] but the zealous moralism and insistence that a high birth-rate was essential to national greatness, which pervaded the Report, must have left women feeling sceptical. The depression of the 1890s had made it economically impossible for large families to survive. Infant mortality in all states but South Australia was very high, and the numbers of women dying in child-birth had increased significantly between 1880 and 1900.[8] Women must have recognized the futility of enduring endless pregnancies which risked their own lives, which often produced a still-born child and where, even if mother and child survived, the opportunities for feeding and clothing them adequately did not exist. Thus women were forced to use contraceptives and abortifacients or, if these failed, to resort to surgical abortion and infanticide.

In 1898 the Australian Medical Gazette editorialized alleging that surgical abortion was widely available and sought after in Sydney.[9] Advertisements from 'accouchement' and 'lying-in' homes, claiming to have qualified nurses and midwives in attendance, appeared in newspapers beside the contraceptive advertisements. A letter to the *Bulletin* in 1895 claimed that

. . . in a recent Saturday issue of a Southern daily there were 20 advts. from well-known abortionists. In the majority of cases, a stranger may call, and, on payment of 10s down, the balance by instalments, time-payment in fact, without any inquiry, the operation will be performed there and then. The majority of these practitioners live along the train-lines, and, the other week, one woman operated upon experienced the result before she was able to get to her home![10]

Although many doctors performed abortions, the methods used were primitive and undoubtedly were not conducted in sterile conditions and it is probable that large numbers of women were inadvertently sterilized as a result.

Infanticide was widespread in Australia at the turn of the century.[11] It was still not legally proscribed to kill a child in the process of birth; and death certificates were not required for still-born babies, nor did they have to be buried in a cemetery. It is highly probable that 'a high proportion of the "still-born" were killed in the process of birth or shortly afterwards, while in some cases, children of one, two or even three years old were classified in this way.'[12] Another form of infanticide was to give children overdoses of various patent medicines. 'Mother's Friend' and other 'soothing syrups' contained chloroform and opium and as the Royal Commission on Secret Drugs, Cures and Foods reported that 15,000 babies died each year in New South Wales from these formulas, 'it is reasonable to assume that many of the deaths were deliberate.'[13]

The use of these remedies to limit progeny was not confined to married women, and there is evidence that single women were not inhibited about engaging in sexual activities. Between 1891 and 1900 one quarter of all first births were 'illegitimate' while a further quarter were born within nine months of marriage.[14] The percentage of ex-nuptial births in relation to population between 1900 and 1910 was higher than it was in 1967 – in the so-called 'permissive' society.[15] Yet there was little overt condemnation of this. All the public controversy raged over the propriety of limiting births *per se* and it was even intimated that single girls could contribute to the falling birthrate by having babies. Although illegitimacy and forced marriages were not condoned, some quarters considered that the resulting births compensated more than adequately. The *Bulletin* waxed eloquently with this opinion when it editorialized over the death of a young girl from an abortion:

The knife of the abortionist may have slain Jessie Nicholls, but Society placed the knife in the abortionist's hands. So long as social traditions make motherhood out of wedlock a social shame, so long will the trade in abortion flourish, and so long will ignorant girls risk death rather than 'disgrace'. 'Disgrace!' The 'disgrace' of being a mother, of performing the sacredest and most necessary function of humanity. The 'disgrace' of the supreme self-sacrifice which lights the Madonna's face with its ineffable glow – that mystery of beauty which a thousand men of genius have vainly sought to place on canvas, while Nature mocks them from the eyes of the humblest peasant girl who bends over her babe! The 'disgrace' of being a woman, of flowering into perfect womanhood, of going down into the Valley of the Shadow of Death to bring up the jewel of a new life, of making the race one's debtor, and placing in the hands of Existence another torch to light the path through the voids of Eternity. Motherhood a 'disgrace' under any circumstances whatever! What a grotesque perversion of ideas.[16]

There was loud spoken and authoritative opposition to the use of contraceptives, especially by married women. In his Presidential Address to the Medical Society of Victoria in 1907, Michael O'Sullivan declaimed:

. . . when a wife defiles the marriage bed with the devices and equipment of the brothel, and interferes with nature's mandate by cold-blooded preventives and safeguards; when she consults her almanac, and refuses to admit the approaches of her husband except at stated times; when a wife behaves in so unwifelike and unnatural a manner, can it be otherwise than that estrangements and painful suspicions of faithfulness should from time to time occur? Can a home with such an environment be a happy one? Many husbands so situated are, I fear, tempted to seek elsewhere the pleasures denied them at home. Such are nature's reprisals; such, indeed, her unfailing retributions.[17]

Condemnations such as this one were more concerned that men were to be denied the opportunities to satisfy their sexual appetites than they were with a falling birth-rate or the medical dangers of many contraceptive measures, but all three reasons generally informed most opposition. What was in dispute was not only the size most appropriate for the family form which the authorities wanted established in Australia, but also the extent to which women were to be arbiters of this. In the Victorian middle-class family where the wife was debilitated from annual childbirth and where, in any case, female sexuality was denied, the existence of armies of prostitutes had served to satiate the sexual desires of husbands. The distinction between mothers (madonnas) and sexual creatures (whores) was clear and, as has been argued so far, was embodied in sex stereotypes which categorized and described women's functions. Once women could control their fertility this distinction could no longer be so rigidly upheld: the possibility of wives engaging in sexual activities without pregnancy being a probable consequence meant they could start to value sex for its own sake. It also meant that single women could be sexually active without having either to bear an unplanned child or else be forced into marriage.

The idea of wives as sexually active, and moreover, sexually interested creatures, was abhorrent to the God's Police stereotype as articulated by Caroline Chisholm. Even more so was the notion of single women 'losing their virtue' since virtuous wives were seen to be the foundation of 'the family' and of the nation. And if women were to curtail their fertility to the extent that they were having only three or four children, instead of the huge families of the mid-nineteenth century, then, prophesied many, the race itself was in danger of extinction. There was a lot of lamenting about race suicide and the dangers of Australia being over-run by the more fertile Asian races to the north but behind most of this moralizing was the fear that 'the family' was in jeopardy. If the rigid distinction between madonna and whore could not be enforced, and if women refused to bear more than a few children, how could the mother remain the central figure in 'the family' and how, without her dominating maternal presence, could 'the family' survive? These were the kinds of reasonings employed by the authorities of Church and State and it was these questions which were to be resolved during the first decade of the new nation.

It is clear in retrospect that what was occurring was a modification in both women's roles and in the form of family which had been adopted fifty years earlier. Some women wanted changes, especially in their educational opportunities and political rights, but many of the more vocal ones, including many feminists, wanted to uphold the madonna/whore distinction even if in a redefined form. They considered sex to be an impure, animal drive which it did not become women to indulge in. The Sydney Mother's Union, for instance, quoted the Bishop of Carpentaria's opinion that ' . . . impurity . . . is eating out the heart and destroying the vitality of the Australian race. It is *the* national sin. The birth-rate is declining at an alarming rate, and the proportion of illegitimate births increasing as steadily . . . '[18] It was agreed by most authorities that women had to alter their attitude to their maternal vocation while at the same time useful employment or other activities had to be provided for women who could not or would not marry.

During the 1880s large numbers of single women had moved into the workforce as the State Public Services opened a range of commercial employment to women. Four high schools for girls were established in NSW after the passing of the 1882 Public School Act[19] and they provided their pupils with an identical education to that given in boys' schools and thus were a real alternative to the various academies and young ladies' seminaries which during the seventies and eighties groomed their students in accomplishments but did little to stimulate the intellect. These newly opened avenues accommodated only a small number of women but they pointed to the need to reformulate the kinds of vocations women should be free to pursue and to alter women's opportunities accordingly.

The issue was first raised with the struggle to have matriculation examinations and then the universities open to women. It was not a feminist consciousness which informed the campaign to admit women to universities. This is not to say that women did not want this avenue opened to them, or that there was no opposition to the proposal, but the move was not seen as improving the status of women generally. It was probably because it arose before discussion of women being given political rights was widespread and before secondary education was made compulsory (and thus only a very small number of middle-class women were involved) that it was achieved relatively easily. All but the most reactionary legislatures could respond to the appeal that higher education would provide them with more stimulating female companionship. One champion of the cause in Victoria, C. H. Pearson, made this point to the parents at the opening of the first school in Australia to provide girls with an education equal to that of boys, the Presbyterian Ladies College, of which he was the first headmaster: 'Dismiss all theories about the admission of women to political rights. Assume that the married will remain as in England, barely able to own property . . . still women exercise . . . a most tremendous direct influence over children, husbands, lovers . . . ought we not . . . to "educate" our rulers ?'[20]

The University of Adelaide had permitted women to attend lectures from its opening in 1874 but it decided to withhold issuing them with degrees until 'the event of the existence of a clear and general demand on the part of Female Students for admission to Degrees', provided that the Legislature and the colony deem it advisable.[21] Both conditions were apparently met by 1880 when the Act of Incorporation was amended to enable the University to confer degrees of Bachelor and Doctor of Science, and to confer degrees on women.[22] The year before, the liberal schoolmasters on the Council of the University of Melbourne had taken advantage of the absence of half of their reactionary colleagues to sneak through 'two of the most significant motions in the university's history: one admitting women . . . and the other recommending the creation of three chairs in the pure and applied sciences.'[23] It was a further two years before Pearson, now a parliamentarian, was able to get his University Constitution Amendment Bill passed in the Legislative Assembly and thus remove any legal doubts about whether women could attend university, but by this time the first female students had already begun their courses. The question of admitting women had first been raised in 1872 by Dr John Madden and the nine year Victorian campaign made it the longest in Australia: 'No campaign in the university was fought so doggedly, or faced such indifference and so many untenable prejudices.'[24]

Sydney was the last university to admit women when, three years after the matter had been first raised in 1878, the Chancellor, Sir William Manning decided to declare the principle of women's rights to equality within the University: ' . . . it would be better to open the portals at once, so that the sex might plainly see their way to enter whenever they should be disposed to climb up to it by the necessary paths of preparation – rather than that the Senate should wait till they came to our gates knocking for admission.'[25] Once the established universities had conceded the principle, all future universities automatically followed suit and women were accepted as equal students from their inception.

The paternalism in Manning's declaration was also evident in the other states where almost all the men who shepherded in the reforms had daughters, sisters or students who were qualified for university. These men were generally acting in accord with J. S. Mill's conception of equality between the sexes as well as from a narrower concern for the women of their immediate acquaintance to be able to acquire an education. The linking together of the admission of women and the granting of degrees in science in Adelaide and Melbourne suggests that it was viewed as an enlightened and progressive measure, an opinion that is strengthened by the fact that the University of London had admitted women to degrees in 1878 and liberals in both these colonies were anxious to follow England's lead in legislation in respect of women as rapidly as possible.[26] But economic motives were also important in the decision, as more and more women were being forced to earn their own income or at least to prepare against this possibility, while women themselves had publicly deprecated the 'accomplishment-oriented' education they were expected to endure. As early as 1841 a Sydney woman had complained that 'the pursuits of poetry and romance . . . instead of filling [women's] minds with useful knowledge – instead of fitting them to become agreeable companions to men of sense and education, have merely been training them for a romantic existence in the land of Utopia.'[27] In 1878 the South Australian feminist Catherine Spence claimed that changes in population growth and movement were forcing unprecedented numbers of women into the labour force and that they, as well as the housewives being left increasingly idle as mechanization reduced housework, should have access to a more useful education than 'the pretentious programme of the young ladies seminary'.[28]

These advocates of vocational education for girls were not thinking only of tertiary education. In 1875 Pearson delivered a lecture entitled 'The Higher Culture of Women' in which he attacked the conservative view that women should not be trained for those professions, such as teaching and nursing, which many of them were destined to pursue. But his progressivism was tempered by his conviction that 'four-fifths of women would marry and spend the greater part of their energies in rearing their family, and that, even when the university did come to admit women to degrees, no more than a tenth of their number would wish to avail themselves of the opportunity.'[29] Like many of his contemporaries Pearson was prepared to argue for the right of women dispossessed by demographic accident of their opportunity to marry to receive an education which would equip them to support themselves. He also followed through his conviction by providing afternoon lectures at PLC for older women who wished to continue their education, especially those who wished to gain sufficient proficiency to undertake work as teachers or governesses.[30] But, being a true 19th century gentleman, Pearson could not conceive of any woman actually choosing this independent path in preference to marriage; nor was he prepared to allow that it might be desirable for a woman to do both.

Enabling a few women to receive an education that was substantially the same as men's raised questions about the kind of education the majority of women should have. Theoretically the 'free, compulsory and secular' Education Acts which were introduced in most states in the early 1870s had conceded the principle of equal education. But because they provided only for an elementary education designed to provide basic literacy and because it proved impossible to enforce the compulsory clause anyway[31], the question was discussed and resolved at the tertiary level. The attitude to female education which emerged influenced the entire direction of girls' secondary schooling when it came to be discussed in the early years of the 20th century, and it is for this, if for no other reason, that the entry of women into higher education is more properly discussed in the context of the evolution of the Australian education system than in connection with the campaign for women's rights. Although the two are ultimately part of the whole question of the roles women were expected to play in the new nation, the two issues were worked out separately.

The critics of women's entry into universities were concerned mainly with whether or not such intellectual exertion would decrease a woman's capacity to fulfil her maternal responsibilities, and the defenders of the women went to great lengths to argue that this would not happen. Carruthers, the NSW Minister for Public Education in 1889, concluded his introducing of the Bill to provide an endowment for the proposed Women's College at the university – the first women's college in the Commonwealth to be of equal status with male colleges[32] – by saying:

We must recognize the fact that the women are the mothers of the nation . . . it behoves us to see that we strengthen their judgement; that we so improve their mental faculties and so raise their intelligence that they will be better able to perform their duties in training the rising generation. If we wish to have better men we can only hope to have them by giving our children better proclivities, and giving their mothers increased powers to promote their intelligence.[33]

This kind of argument was sometimes used by those who believed in women's right to an equal education *per se* in order to win over opposition, but it soon became the major argument for girls' education and, as an article in the *Bulletin* demonstrated, began to replace the earlier ideal:

Women cannot be too learned, provided the learning she has helps her to fulfil her varied functions of mother, nurse, educator and trainer of her children . . . Woman, as woman, cannot be too much or too well educated; but her education must have the future well in view. On her the nation's future depends. Any education which unfits her for the fulfilment of her maternal responsibilities is not only useless – it is most emphatically a curse.[34]

The advocates of equal education had to be careful to demonstrate that what were seen as women's essential qualities of gentleness and refinement would in no way be subverted. The Board of Studies at Sydney University which had approved the admission of women to the same lectures as males in all subjects undertook to censor classics texts when there were objections to women being expected to read what were considered ribald passages in mixed company.[35]

In such actions they received the complete support of the women students themselves. Bella Guerin, the first woman to graduate from an Australian university – she received her B.A. from Melbourne in 1883 – wrote in her old school magazine in 1886, 'This Arts course is one against which the most jealous conserver of purely feminine graces can find no just objections. The subjects are elevated and ennobling in themselves, and their study in the chaste atmosphere of a convent, must be productive of solid benefit on the character of girls thus trained.'[36]

Most controversy had occurred on the question of admitting women medical students to mixed classes. In Melbourne a clause in Pearson's 1881 Bill leaving it to the discretion of the University Council to exclude women from any lectures it chose was used to prevent women from doing medicine until 1887.[37] When the first women demanded admittance, Professor Allen, Dean of the Medical Faculty, expressed the fear that teaching before mixed classes might embarrass the lecturers who would be inclined to avoid delicate subjects, such as venereal disease, and thereby narrow the range of teaching[38]; but he supported the application of women students for admission to the medical school. Allen claimed that to duplicate the lectures in question would be too expensive; enquiries to Sydney had revealed that mixed classes were held there and this apparently made Allen adamant that women should do likewise in Melbourne.[39] He had already admitted the first female students before the question was finally resolved and it was the intervention of the women them-selves which eventually decided the issue. They wrote to the University Council on 27 September 1887 explaining that they had chosen to study medicine 'believing that there is an urgent need of educated women to attend women, and that very great suffering, and, in some cases, death even occurs through such attendance not being avail-able . . . As women, we claim therefore the right to qualify ourselves to attend upon the sick and suffering of our own sex.' This fine ambition did not imply however that they had sacrificed any of their feminine qualities, and they claimed that 'to insist upon our attending dissection, hospital practice and certain courses, or certain portions of certain courses with men would have the effect of rendering the permission you have granted us to study practically worthless, and would be repugnant not only to our feelings, but to those of the majority of this community.'[40] This letter was made public and the *Argus* supported their stance; the Council resolved to grant the women a separate dissecting room and separate hospital instruction. The Alfred Hospital refused to comply with the latter arrangements but the women were apparently satisfied with the compromise and the separate dissecting room was retained until the mid-1890s.[41]

Although these pioneer women university students could not fail to see themselves as trail-blazers, they were not feminists. As one of the early students put it: 'Everything was so new and exciting: the lectures and the gay social life, and we as frivolous young girls did not worry too much about the significance of women's rights.'[42] Although they were undoubtedly anxious to see their footsteps followed by other women, they did not perceive their venture as necessarily widening women's sphere in any way. Almost without exception, they reaffirmed that woman's basic calling was to mother-hood and that their education was important for the way it would equip them to perform this task more adequately.

In her speech at the opening of Sydney University's Women's College in 1894, the first principal, Louisa MacDonald, herself a remarkable woman with a distinguished scholastic record, looked forward to a future Australia 'when the mother may guide her household, and train her children the better in that she has studied more deeply the history and expression of human thought, and has learned the principles of nature's laws, and the duty of obedience to them.'[43] She favoured girls receiving practical training in household arts and in 1896 put a resolution to the first meeting of the National Council of Women 'that a knowledge of the domestic arts be included in the curriculum for girls in public schools.'[44] In Melbourne the husband of the main benefactoress of the Women's College, Lady Janet Clarke, claimed at the opening ceremony that her £6,000 donation had been motivated by her 'strong desire to advance the higher education of women, believing that a well-educated woman made the best wife and the best mother.'[45]

The early students were generally very successful scholars, most of them taking a post-graduate degree[46] and a large percentage of them going on to careers of some kind. The educational achievements involved were considerable but they tended to be treasured only by the women themselves and by those feminist groups who enthusiastically recorded women's attainments in public life.[47] By arguing, whether from conviction or from circumstances, that equal education for women could best be justified by the way it equipped them more adequately for their mother roles, these pioneers and their supporters established the attitude that women's intellectual ambitions and accomplishments were not to be valued for their own sake, but for the use they could be in educating a future generation. What was initially proposed as an enlightened liberal measure designed to enable at least a few women to develop intellectually – and, conceivably, to extend the number of activities women were able to pursue – started to assume the proportions of a new form of oppression as two related attitudes were fostered.

First, was the notion that a woman's academic qualifications were to be measured in terms of her maternal, which then amounted to her marital, status. The educated woman who, perhaps after a short period of pursuing a career, renounced all to become a wife and mother was deemed to have successfully carried out her 'highest' vocation, but the woman who chose to follow her profession and did not marry was regarded as not being a 'real' woman. While the educational pioneers did establish that it was possible and even desirable for women to obtain university degrees, and to practise careers such as law and medicine which had previously been closed to them, they made no progress in establishing the right of such educated women to continue at their chosen occupations after marriage. They were in effect denying that women, like men, have multi-faceted natures, each part of which desires satisfaction. While it was never questioned that a man had the right to enjoy love, fatherhood, home and the job by which he made his living, the patriarchal assumptions of the 19th century attributed to women one over-riding vocational desire and elevated it to the status of an instinct. Motherhood defined women and represented their ultimate fulfilment; any other activity on the part of women was activated by economic necessity or because of frustration of this 'natural' destiny. Thus these educated women were faced with what one English feminist labelled 'the intolerable choice'; the desire for an intimate human relationship with the satisfaction of bringing up children, and the wish to fulfil those ambitions which her vocation-oriented education had instilled in her. Those who chose the latter might be praised for their professional capabilities, as many of our early doctors were, and their altruistic endeavours received high social sanction, but the insulting epithets 'bluestocking' and 'spinster' were continual reminders that in society's eyes they were only half-women, part of whose essential natures remained frustrated.

The pervasiveness of this attitude was revealed in a circular appealing for funds for extensions to Sydney's Women's College, which was sent out in 1920. It listed the fortunes of the nearly two hundred women who had already graduated from the College and contained impressive documentation of their successful careers; it concluded however with effusive praise for those fifty-seven past students who had married 'to engage upon the most important public service a woman can perform, that of bringing up children to serve their day and generation as useful members of the State.'[48] Those who were lecturers, researchers, medical practitioners, welfare officers, teachers, librarians, and headmistresses were being told by their old College that their public services paled in comparison to rearing another generation of girls to face exactly the same intolerable choice.

The early female university students did establish the right of women to obtain an equal education with men, but it was a pyrrhic victory. Those who succeeded in the male academic world and who wished to reap the benefits of this success in a profession were banished to an existential limbo. They paid dearly for that right to education. For those women who decided to use their education in professional employment it involved abdicating the right to marry and inevitable social disapprobation. These women tried to alter the social image of the single woman, to establish by their example an alternative image of an independent and fulfilled existence. But their efforts were not assimilated into the repertoire of roles available for future generations of Australian women; the pervasiveness of the God's Police stereotype condemned these women to defensive eccentricity. The social world they constructed around themselves was either ignored or ridiculed; they were pitied because they did not have children, they were assumed to have no opportunities for sexual expression and were categorized as frustrated. They were pointed out as warnings to young girls who read too many books or entertained ideas of professional achievement.

The two ideals, the right of women to remain single and not become social pariahs, and the right of married women to work, involve a similar set of assumptions. Both require the erosion of the sexist characterization of women in terms of their relationship to a man, and in terms of their success in the motherhood stakes. Women must have the same freedom to combine various sets of activities that men do and not have their social worth assessed by one suffocating standard. The battle for the educational rights of women did very little to change this. That the struggle was not carried through is hardly surprising for it was not difficult to perceive the social revolution involved in that proposition. Those who argued for women's equal education on the grounds that it would better equip them for motherhood helped ensure that the battlegrounds would not be drawn. It was conceded that women might have to support themselves if they were unable to find husbands, or if they were widowed, but this contention simply reinforced the idea that women, particularly middle-class women, worked not from choice but through personal misfortune. The rights of the single woman to a secure social status were rarely discussed except in terms of the 'problem' they posed to embarrassed families. By the early 1890s it was starting to be recognized that married women might engage in a wide range of activities outside the home, but these must always be altruistic activities performed in a spirit of bourgeois benevolence and never for monetary reward.

The second attitude engendered by the campaign for equal education was that it was not only desirable that women be educated for motherhood, but that it was *necessary*. This perception was shaped gradually but its first manifestations were in criticisms of girls receiving equal schooling. The Church of England *Messenger* on 12 October 1885 decried the amount of school work demanded of girls as it encroached 'perilously on the home life'.[49] This line of attack was developed by those who thought that excessive schooling was detrimental to girls' health. In this view conservatives were able to cite the authority of Herbert Spencer who had claimed that health was more important than intellectual training for women. Social Darwinism which relied heavily on Spencer's sociology was part of the armoury of Australian conservatives at the beginning of the 1890s.[50] Pearson had had to reassure parents of students at P.L.C. that he was well aware of the tendency of the girls to overwork and that provision would be made for physical culture to ensure a well-balanced development.[51] A Sydney doctor, Walter Balls-Headley claimed in his *Evolution of the Diseases of Women*, published in 1894, that modern education placed physiological restraints on a young woman and 'should she have capacity for higher mental attainments, her nervous system is apt to develop at the expense of her body', and had concluded that 'high mental culture is antagonistic to healthy sexual development and childbearing.'[52] The solution to this alarming prediction entailed the repudiation of the earlier principle that girls receive equal schooling, and the introduction of special syllabuses which explicitly prepared girls for their future mother roles and which did not involve heavy intellectual exertion.

Part of the post-1890s self-examination by the architects of Australia's future involved a thorough scrutiny of the education system, and, by every possible criteria, it was found to be a dismal failure. The Fink Commission into the general administration of public education in Victoria in 1899 had concluded that 'there could be no doubt that as far as public education was concerned this colony has been living in a fool's paradise.'[53] A similar condemnation of the New South Wales system was made in 1901 by the Professor of Philosophy at Sydney University, Francis Anderson, who claimed that 'a radical alteration' in the whole system was needed.[54] The entire public system of education was completely reformed in every state and the comprehensive system which we have inherited today was instituted in the early years of the 20th century. Teacher training was introduced, the syllabus was revised and diversified to cater for a wider range of subjects and levels, the compulsory nature of education was strictly enforced and a series of State-controlled examinations ensured standardized progress of all children up to school-leaving age.

The fate of the girls within this new system was influenced by several factors. In October 1898 the National Council of Women had sent a deputation to the NSW Minister for Public Instruction requesting that domestic arts be included in girls' curriculum in State schools.[55] Their frequent representations to this effect received support from some teachers; a Ms Chandler told a meeting of the North Sydney District Teachers' Association in 1910, 'The real direction of a girl's education must be towards the house. We are developing the home workers of the future in whose hands will be the well being of our nation.'[56] This view that girls should be educated for motherhood received wide support. The heavily vocational nature of the entire education system since its inception in Australia[57] gave impetus to the notion that girls' education could perhaps be tailored to meet their natural vocation, and this view received final confirmation by the experiences of the depression.

During the 1890s teachers' salaries had been cut, and female teachers had been dismissed, teacher-training had been restricted and school building had been limited.[58] Even more importantly, the view of education being directed towards purely pragmatic ends was vindicated by the fight for economic survival; there could be no question of enabling women who were not economically distressed to compete for male jobs. The traditional male/female division of labour was asserted to be the only possible way to arrange the economy and if education for girls was to be compulsory then it would have to be a form of education which would equip them to perform their traditional female functions. Thus schools providing technical and domestic arts training for girls were introduced in all states while the syllabuses in high schools were altered for those girls who did not plan to go to university.

The old principle of equal secondary education was reversed and the majority of girls, their future vocations assumed, received what was considered appropriate training for fulfilling their female destinies:

The old system with its divisions into full high schools, intermediate high schools, domestic science schools, involved far more differences than mere changes of names. The actual content of education differed, subject matter varying both in nature and degree of treatment. Mathematics, science and languages were three important areas that were treated superficially or ignored in the intermediate highs and domestic science schools catering only for girls. Even in such an apparently common subject area, English, vast differences in types of text books were clearly evident. The whole stress in girls' education in such schools was on a commercial/domestic level, but with a commercial course designed to produce lower level office personnel, certainly not executive staff, and a domestic course basically designed as a general background course for girls who would eventually marry, having filled in their time up to then in that vast army of unskilled female labour on which many areas of our economy still rely.[59]

This course of events was influenced by more than the depression. By the turn of the century Social Darwinism in Australia had moved from being a conservative rationalization for *laissez faire* economics to justifying radical State interventionist policies.[60] Those people who advocated education for motherhood were radicals who based their demands on what they saw as the firm scientific ground provided by Darwin and Spencer tempered by Rousseau's notions of education. The unit of analysis in the survival of the fittest moved from the individual to the State and the theorists concerned themselves with ways in which the new nation could produce a fine race of civic-minded Australians.

In its more radical version, the idea of education for motherhood was pinned to firm feminist principles and it was a variety of this notion, propounded by the Swedish writer Ellen Key and supported by Havelock Ellis[61] which was argued for in Australia. Key's main principles were that children were to receive fuller attention from their mothers than had hitherto been the practice and, to attain this, she advocated 'a renaissance of motherhood'. The latter could only come about, she claimed

. . . through a new marriage, where the perfect equality and liberty of both husband and wife are established; through a strict responsibility towards society in regard to parentage outside as well as within marriage; through education for motherhood; and, lastly, through rendering motherhood economically secure, recognizing it as a public work to be rewarded and controlled by society.[62]

A major exponent of such theories in Australia was Maybanke Anderson, wife of Francis Anderson. She recognized that the claims that had been held out for the old public education system – that it would substantially reduce crime – had not been successful, and proposed that a new approach be tried, 'the building of character in the home, by the person who alone can lay its foundation – the mother'.[63] She was active in a wide range of social and political activities, from the Kindergarten Union to the Womanhood Suffrage League and edited the suffrage newspaper *Woman's Voice* from 1894-5 and so it can be assumed that her views were widely known and supported. It was she who stated the Australian version of the Key/Ellis recipe for successful social evolution: 'In an ideal State every prospective mother should be so educated that she may not only bear a healthy child, but may also know how to train her family in virtue and the duties of citizenship. Without such an education a woman is only partially qualified for the duties and pleasures of life.'[64] She was sufficiently feminist to avoid arguing that all women should bear children; she argued however that 'preparation for the woman's natural duty' would do no harm to a woman who chose to remain single but would 'tend to make her more sympathetic, a more useful member of society'. Such views were widely endorsed and the teaching of Domestic Economy was considered to be as important as any other subject.

One of the earliest courses had been introduced in 1887 at Loreto Convent in Victoria – it was set up after the school principal returned from Europe where she had seen similar courses in operation. It was seriously thought out and was considered to be parallel to a university course.[65] During the first years of this century it was advocated that a chair of Domestic Economy be established at Sydney University. The proposal was backed by the Women's Progressive Association – a post-suffrage feminist group – by the Women's Central Organizing Committee of the Labor Party and by the Women's Liberal League.[66] By 1914 the idea had even been endorsed by the state Liberal Party of New South Wales.[67]

The support given to the idea of education for motherhood indicated that society was acknowledging certain changes in the structure and functions of the family. Since the early Industrial Revolution the family had been defined by the gradual differentiation from the wider society of the conjugal couple and their children, and by their assumption of specialized functions which had been performed in a haphazard way previously, by a variety of agents or not at all. One of these functions was the children's material and spiritual welfare. In practical terms this was coped with by a division of labour between husband and wife whereby in the ideal-typical family (that is, one that had emulated middle-class practice) the husband worked to provide the economic support for the children and for the wife who in return performed domestic work for him and attended to the spiritual and perhaps elementary educational development of the child. This arrangement characterized the ideal family in the mid-19th century where economic and other circumstances permitted and it was given implicit social sanction, but it was not until the last two decades of the century that the precise boundaries of these obligations were spelt out and their concomitant responsibilities defined.

It was not, for instance, until the Child's Protection Act was passed in 1899 in England that fathers became legally obliged to maintain their children[68] even though until the passing of the Guardianship of Infants Acts, initially in England in 1886 and subsequently in all Australian states, a father had absolute guardianship and custody rights over his children. The latter Act gave the mother some rights in this respect and gave the Courts power to over-ride the common-law rights of the father and award the mother custody of the children if it was considered, and it usually was, that it was in the children's interests to do so.[69] This was the first legal acknowledgement of motherhood and its rights and marked the acceptance of the elevation of a woman's maternal role to the almost reverential status that it came to have in Australia. The idea that some education was necessary for motherhood was an acknowledgement that 'the family' was expected to perform the specialized task of socializing its children and that it was the mother who was to undertake major responsibility for this. The older notion that the mother was responsible for a child's spiritual development was now given a more explicit cast and nurture became child-rearing, a new and exacting science.

The institution of compulsory education was the major means of ensuring that girls were sufficiently educated to be able to fulfil what was now a vocation: their roles as mothers of the nation. But a range of supporting activities, influenced by the environmental determinists who advocated education for motherhood, reinforced the new conception of the tasks of the family. The Kindergarten Union established in New South Wales in 1895 and Victoria in 1908[70] founded free kindergartens in inner urban slum areas which were designed to compensate for what were assumed to be the inadequacies of the family lives of working-class children. Even before standardized education tried to ensure uniformity of values across class lines, the instigators of kindergartens were trying to instil middle-class attitudes to child-care and family living in working-class children and their mothers. Mothers' Clubs were attached to most kindergartens and the teachers – who were invariably the daughters of wealthy parents and were working for pocket-money wages[71] – visited the homes of their pupils to instruct the mothers in the emotional and physical care of their children.[72] In Victoria, the Women's Christian Temperance Union established its own free kindergarten in the suburb of Richmond; associated with it was the first School for Mothers in Victoria and at the opening ceremony there was much stress on the power of motherhood and the influence for good that both institutions would have in that neighbourhood.[73] In 1903 the Sydney City Council established a baby health service designed to guide mothers 'in the care and feeding of young children'.[74]

Just as Ellen Key had advocated, this renaissance in motherhood was produced by a new attitude to children: they were increasingly seen as weak and malleable creatures who, if exposed to the right influences, could join the ranks of civic-minded citizens. Maybanke Anderson had seen the kindergartens as being 'for children who might otherwise become larrikins, and eventually criminals'.[75] The theories of environmental determinism encouraged reformers to regard working-class children, not as condemned by their birth to physical and social debilitation but, if correctly nurtured, as capable of salvation. By the turn of the century educationalists were seriously seeking to prevent children from engaging in paid employment before the legal school-leaving age. In country areas particularly they met with considerable resistance from farmers who wanted to use their children as cheap labour and even after the principle had been established, a petition was sent to Parliament from five school committees in northern Victoria requesting that the Christmas holidays be moved to March and April so that child labour could be obtained during the fruit packing season.[76] A new protective attitude to children was evidenced in Bills such as those passed in all states to prevent juveniles from buying tobacco, cigarettes or cigars[77] and which prevented them from purchasing alcoholic liquor. A special children's court was introduced in South Australia in 1895[78] and reinforced the idea that children required special treatment even when they had committed 'adult' crimes and that they should be punished less severely. They were considered redeemable while their parents, especially their fathers, often were not.

The reassessment of the role of motherhood had important implications for 'the family' which was now viewed as a key social institution wherein the citizens of future generations acquired their training in civic virtues. Women were seen as playing a vital part in this. Motherhood became a special vocation which required special, scientific training; it had attached to it a high status since mothers were seen as the people who instilled these civic virtues in their children. Within the new family parents' responsibilities were more sharply defined and sexist differences given the validation of legal statute. Men were the providers of financial security while women were responsible for emotional security.

This sexual division of labour and the new small size family were explicitly integrated into the Australian economy with the determination of the first basic wage in 1907. Justice Higgins, in handing down judgement in the Harvester Case, said that a basic wage should be sufficient to maintain an unskilled labourer, his wife and three children in frugal comfort. Higgins had used as his evidence of the actual wage necessary the budgets of several labouring families, and in laying down the basic wage had, in fact, formulated a family wage. This concept was clearly accepted by the terms of reference of the 1919 Royal Commission on the Basic Wage which deputed Commissioner A. B. Piddington to establish the minimum amount on which an average Australian family could maintain what might be called the Australian standard of living.[79] Justice Higgins also stated that women were not entitled to the same wage as men except where they were employed on exactly the same work as men – and were therefore competitors for men's jobs. In the Rural Workers' Case of 1912 – usually referred to as the Mildura Fruit Pickers' Case – Higgins restated the principles of the Harvester Judgement and then said that whereas the normal needs of a man included domestic life and that he was legally obliged to support a family if he had one, the same was not usually true of women. He concluded that women were not therefore entitled to equal pay, but merely to a wage that would enable a single woman without dependants to 'find her own food, shelter and clothing'. It was only in industries where women competed for male jobs that women should be paid the male rate in order to prevent men from being ousted from those jobs. Higgins did not approve of women being employed and said, ' . . . fortunately for society, however, the greater number of breadwinners are still men. The women are not all dragged from their homes to work while the men loaf at home.'[80]

This judgement had, as Norman MacKenzie points out:

. . . far-reaching implications, for it made the sharp distinction between the rates of pay suitable to 'men's work' and those for 'women's work'; it explicitly stated that job protection for males was desirable, and if necessary should be ensured by equal pay; and it expressed the view, still widely held, that if women are offered wages comparable to those earned by men they would be 'dragged from their homes' by this inducement and the traditional roles of the sexes and the stability of family life would be imperilled.[81]

At the same time the Report of the Royal Commission into the Hours and General Conditions of Employment of Female and Juvenile Labour in New South Wales in 1911 stated six main objections to married women working:
1. It encouraged the practice of prevention (contraception)
2. Women risked miscarriage
3. Women had to stop breast-feeding and this led to infant mortality
4. Their day's energy was given up to making money to the neglect of the home

5. It encouraged idle and extravagant men
6. Often married women had a bad influence on single girls[82]

Married women were thus discouraged by social attitudes and by inferior wages from taking jobs and were compelled by the new notion of motherhood as a vocation to devote their entire lives to their families.

Motherhood was seen to be an all-consuming vocation, one that could not properly be combined with any other career. The mother was also urged to be responsible for her own housework, a neat ideological solution to a chronic shortage of women willing to work as servants. The 'new' mother of the early 20th century family was supposed to be a capable, responsible woman who wanted nothing more than to keep her family satisfied: she was cook and cleaner and educator of children as well as wife. Her vocation was clearly defined and socially valued. What was not considered was that, despite the opening of tertiary education and membership of the professions to women, the lives of the majority of women were more governed and determined by sexist notions than ever before. Whilst a handful of women could receive an education and follow a career, most women had absolutely no choice but to adopt the career of motherhood which, society said, was their 'natural' vocation.

In the early years of this century a rampant puritanism descended upon Australian society. It was the product of a family-oriented petty bourgeois mentality and its object was to promote and protect family life and, particularly, to enforce its morality on single women. The pervasion of this puritanism marked a victory for Church and State and signalled its success in having imposed upon a substantial segment of the population the view that 'the family' was an institution to be elevated to the highest national respect. As the next chapter argues, much of the pro-family crusading was undertaken by middle-class women in the feminist movement. They particularly concerned themselves with advocating the God's Police role for women and with attempting to redeem those women who were characterized as Damned Whores. But the pro-family puritanism was not confined to women; by themselves women lacked the power to enforce change. Its prevalence was a class phenomenon, an indication that the middle-class had achieved political and economic power and had ousted the last remnants of the pre-capitalist squattocracy. This class, as was shown in Chapter Six, required a small privatized family whose internal organization was based on a sex division of labour. This conception of 'the family' had been promulgated in Australia since the 1840s: sixty years later it was firmly entrenched and its advocates and practitioners felt able to enforce this family form and its supporting mores on those remaining recalcitrant areas of society.

The early years of the 20th century saw a mass of puritanical legislation introduced. Bills to raise the age of consent (for girls) were introduced in all states. The advertising of contraceptives, abortifacients and birth-control information was suppressed. Brothels were outlawed. When in 1907 the South Australian Parliament passed a Suppression of Brothels Bill, the Premier, Tom Price, moving the second reading, said there was no necessity to discuss the Bill since it was not wise to advertise the evil, and that although he was tabling a report on the subject he hoped that no unmarried members would think of reading it.[83] Such reticence at times proved dangerous. Immediately after the war it was realized that an enormous proportion of the population of Melbourne was infected with venereal disease. The Committee Concerning Causes of Death and Invalidity in the Commonwealth reported in 1916–17 that 'fully 25 per cent of the sick children in Melbourne are tainted with Syphilis and that about 10 per cent of the total number of children are syphilized.'[84] Between 1 July 1917 and 30 November 1918 there were nearly 10,000 registered cases of venereal disease in Melbourne but since only a fraction of infected cases were registered, it has been suggested that there may have been as many as 80,000 people (of a population of 743,000 in 1919) afflicted.[85] However when the suggestion was made in the Victorian Parliament that medical examination of both parties be compulsorily effected before marriage, the response was that it was more important to protect the modesty of decent women than to protect society from the contamination of promiscuous ones.[86]

These measures to suppress what was seen as illicit sex were accompanied by attempts to limit the availability of alcohol. A large number of temperance groups were in existence and they pressed among other things for provision for local option polls to enable residents to determine how many hotels should operate in their area. The temperance groups and their supporters succeeded in winning several victories against the powerful liquor trades. For instance, in New South Wales the 1905 Liquor Amendment Act increased ratepayers' local option powers; this Act reflected a growing public concern about the free flow of alcohol and its effects on families. Between 1907 and 1913 three local options were held and resulted in the closing of 12 per cent of hotels in New South Wales.[87] The birth-rate did not rise significantly but the numbers of 'illegitimate' births and births occurring within nine months of marriage declined markedly. Although contraceptives were no longer advertised in the daily Press, women now had the knowledge that control of fertility was possible and they could still buy contraceptives or devise their own. None of these methods was totally reliable, and some were medically dangerous, but gradually contraceptive technology became more sophisticated and developed products, such as the diaphragm, which if used properly afforded a greater degree of protection from unwanted pregnancies. Abortion was always available although it was removed from shop front to backyard and women required know-how and money to find a safe operation. But it also seems likely that, in accordance with the descent of puritanism, women who wanted to avoid pregnancy abstained from sexual intercourse. 'Illegitimate' births and 'shot-gun' marriages now carried even more social stigma than previously and signalled a victory for those who wanted sexuality restricted to a procreative act. A good mother could not also be a sexually active person: God's Police and Damned Whores women were seen as polar opposites.

Women who wanted to share the status now attached to maternity had to take care not to preclude themselves with an illicit pregnancy. Those who feared race suicide had to bow before the evidence of a new family size, a size which was pioneered by Australian women, and which was evidently more suitable for local economic and social conditions than the large Victorian family which still straggled on in Britain. They were forced to recognize that the new small family heralded an expanded maternal role for women and not, as some traditionalists had feared, a decrease in women's responsibilities. Women were now expected to be far more conscientious mothers and to attend to the child's social as well as physical formation. This increase in maternal responsibilities enabled the State to exert a greater degree of control over the entire population. Women's economic dependence on men was now enshrined in the wage structure and women were thus firmly tied to their husbands and families. They now had a strong vested interest in ensuring the fidelity of husbands (and hence their opposition to alcohol and prostitution) and the perpetuation of 'the family'.

NOTES

1. T. A. Coghlan, *The Decline of the Birth-Rate in New South Wales*, Government Printer, Sydney, 1903, p. 3.

2. Neville Hicks, *Evidence and Contemporary Opinion About the Peopling of Australia, 1890–1911*, Ph.D. thesis, Australian National University, 1971, p. 268. I would like to thank Dr Hicks for his kind permission to quote from his thesis.

3. Appearing in Sydney's *Evening News* in 1898; reproduced in Rosemary Pringle, 'Octavius Beale and the Ideology of the Birth-Rate', *Refractory Girl*, No. 3, Winter 1973, p. 21.

4. Hicks, op. cit., p. 259.

5. cit. Pringle, op. cit., p. 21.

6. Report of Royal Commission on Secret Drugs, Cures and Foods, 1907, *Commonwealth Parliamentary Papers*, Session 1907–8, Vol. 4, p. 61.

7. See discussion of the various devices by Pringle, op. cit.

8. Coghlan, op. cit., p. 67.

9. Hicks, op. cit., p. 157.

10. The *Bulletin*, 26 October 1895, p. 10.

11. Pringle, op. cit., p. 24.

12. ibid.

13. ibid.

14. Coghlan, op. cit., p. 9.

15. Geraldine Spencer, 'Pre-marital Pregnancies and Ex-Nuptial Births in Australia, 1911–66 – A Comment', *Australian and New Zealand Journal of Sociology*, October 1969, p. 126.

16. The *Bulletin*, 21 September 1895.

17. M. U. O'Sullivan, 'Presidential Address', *Intercolonial Medical Journal of Australia*, 20 February 1907, p. 67.

18. cit. Hicks, op. cit., p. 172.

19. Peter Biskup, *The Female Suffrage Movement in Australia*, B. A. Honours thesis, University of Western Australia, 1959, p. 13.

20. cit. J. A. Hone, 'The Movement for the Higher Education of Women in Victoria in the Later Nineteenth Century', M.A. thesis, Monash University, 1966, p. 37.

21. University of Adelaide, *Calendar*, 1880, p. lxix.

22. ibid.

23. Geoffrey Blainey, *A Centenary History of the University of Melbourne*, Melbourne University Press, Melbourne, 1957, p. 59.

24. ibid., p. 87.

25. cit. W. Vere Hole and Anne H. Treweeke, *The History of the Women's College within the University of Sydney*, Halstead, Sydney, 1953, p. 32.

26.   A similar trend was observable in the school system where in the late 1870s science subjects were included in the syllabus for the first time and became examinable for matriculation; at about the same time several corporate schools were established for girls in which they could study subjects previously limited to boys' grammar schools. A. Barcan, 'The Australian Tradition in Education', in R. W. T. Cowan (ed.), *Education for Australians*, Cheshire, Melbourne, 1966, p. 13.

27.   Letter signed 'Currency Lass', *Sydney Morning Herald*, 7 January 1841.

28.   Catherine Spence, *Some Social Aspects of South Australian Life*, The Register, Adelaide, 1878, p. 10.

29.   John Tregenza, *Professor of Democracy*, Melbourne University Press, Melbourne, 1968, p. 79.

30.   ibid., p. 83.

31.   A. G. Austin, *Australian Education 1788–1900*, Pitman, Melbourne, 1961, p. 179.

32.   Hole and Treweeke, op. cit., p. 41.

33.   ibid., p. 57.

34.   The *Bulletin*, 10 May 1890.

35.   Hole and Treweeke, op. cit., p. 33.

36.   In *Loreto Eucalyptus Blossoms*, December 1886; cit. Hone, op. cit., p. 177.

37.   Ernest Scott, *A History of the University of Melbourne*, Melbourne University Press in association with Oxford University Press, Melbourne, 1936, pp. 99, 103.

38.   Hone, op. cit., p. 142.

39.   ibid. What was probably not revealed was that the Sydney Medical School did not then provide a very warm welcome for its female students. One professor consistently failed all women in their final year and it was not until he went on sabbatical leave in 1893 that the first woman doctor graduated from Sydney, two years after Adelaide and Melbourne had produced their first graduates, even though they had opened their schools to women much later. Hole and Treweeke, op. cit., p. 35.

40.   Hone, op. cit., p. 144. Scott, op. cit., p. 104.

41.   Hone, op. cit., p. 144.

42.   cit. Hole and Treweeke, op. cit., p. 94.

43.   ibid., p. 87.

44.   J. E. Cobb, *The Women's Movement in New South Wales, 1880–1914*, M.A. thesis, University of New England, 1967, p. 116.

45.   cit. Hone, op. cit., p. 108.

46.   See Scott, op. cit., p. 102; and Appendix in Hole and Treweeke, op. cit.

47.   e.g. papers like *The Australian Woman's Sphere* (1903 to 1909) edited by Vida Goldstein and its successor, also edited by her, *The Woman Voter* (1909 to 1919) both in Victoria, and to a lesser extent *The Dawn* (1888 to 1905) edited in New South Wales by Louisa Lawson, had regular notes on women who pioneered or were otherwise successful in any field of endeavour outside the home.

48. Hole and Treweeke, op. cit., p. 118.

49. cit. Hone, op. cit., p. 172.

50. Craufurd D. Goodwin, *Economic Enquiry in Australia*, Australia and New Zealand Book Company, Sydney, 1969, pp. 330–9.

51. Tregenza, op. cit., p. 79.

52. cit. Hicks, op. cit., p. 141.

53. cit. Austin, op. cit., p. 255.

54. ibid., p. 256.

55. Cobb, op. cit., p. 252.

56. Reported in the *Australian Journal of Education*, June 1910.

57. When King's School was established in Sydney in 1832, the principal was forced 'to compromise with colonial practicality' and instead of the purely liberal education he had hoped to give his students had to introduce scientific and commercial subjects alongside the classical studies. Barcan, op. cit., p. 7. Similarly when Sydney University was founded in 1850 the foundation professors fought against a hostile Press and public which favoured an instrumental kind of education designed to keep society supplied with a constant stream of professionally qualified graduates in the shortest possible time. The Arts degree which was all the University initially offered was considered to be time and money wasted. J. J. Auchmuty, 'The Idea of a University in its Australian Setting. A Historical Survey', *The Australian University*, July 1963, p. 148.

58. Barcan, op. cit., p. 15.

59. Nance Cooper, 'The Education of Women' in Donald McLean (ed.), *It's People that Matter: Education for Social Change*, Angus & Robertson, Sydney, 1969, p. 73.

60. Goodwin, op. cit., pp. 339–45.

61. Ethel Puffer Howes, 'The Meaning of Progress in the Woman Movement', in William L. O'Neill, *The Woman Movement*, Allen and Unwin, London 1969, p. 210. Havelock Ellis gave enthusiastic support to Key's theories of motherhood in several of his works while she returned the favour by dedicating one of her books to him.

62. Ellen Key, *The Renaissance of Motherhood*, G. P. Putnam, New York, 1914, p. 132.

63. Maybanke Anderson, *Mother Lore*, Angus and Robertson, Sydney, 1919, p. 5

64. ibid., p. 12.

65. Hone, op. cit., p. 171.

66. Cobb, op. cit., p. 252.

67. ibid., p. 254.

68. M. J. Wood, 'Reforms in Law Affecting Women and Children' in Louise Brown et al., eds, *A Book of South Australia: Women in the First Hundred Years*, Rigby, Adelaide, 1936, p. 131.

69. ibid., p. 130.

70. Peter Spearritt, 'The Kindergarten Movement, c. 1890–1972', unpublished paper, Department of Government, University of Sydney, 1972, pp. 2–3. The first kindergarten in New South Wales had been established in the grounds of the Methodist Ladies College, Burwood in 1891. Methodist Ladies College, *Jubilee Souvenir 1886–1936*, Sydney, n.d., p. 17.

71. Spearritt, pp. 4, 12.

72. ibid., p. 5.

73. Isabel McCorkindale (ed.), *Pioneer Pathways*, W.C.T.U., Melbourne, 1948, p. 121.

74. Spearritt, op. cit., p. 5a.

75. Maybanke Anderson, 'Women in Australia' in Meredith Atkinson (ed.), *Australia: Economic and Political Studies*, Macmillan, Melbourne 1920, p. 296.

76. Jessie Ackermann, *Australia from a Woman's Point of View*, Cassell, London, 1913, p. 91.

77. 1903 in New South Wales and South Australia, 1905 in Victoria; Keith Dunstan, *Wowsers*, Cassell, Melbourne, 1968, p. 132.

78. S. M. Eade, 'A Study of Catherine Helen Spence 1825–1910', M.A. thesis, Australian National University, 1971, p. 221.

79. Peter Macarthy, *The Harvester Judgement: An Historical Assessment*, Ph.D. thesis, Australian National University, 1967, p. 550.

80. cit. Norman MacKenzie, *Women in Australia*, Cheshire, Melbourne, 1962, p. 172.

81. ibid.

82. cit. Cobb, op. cit., p. 263.

83. Dunstan, op. cit., p. 164.

84. cit. Dennis Shoesmith, ' "Nature's Law": The Venereal Disease Debate, Melbourne, 1918–19', *A.N.U. Historical Journal*, December 1972, p. 20.

85. ibid., p. 21.

86. ibid.

87. G. T. Caldwell, 'From Pub to Club: the History of Drinking Attitudes in New South Wales (1900–1945) and the Growth of Registered Clubs', *A.N.U. Historical Journal*, December 1972, p. 25.

CHAPTER ELEVEN

FEMINISM AND
THE SUFFRAGISTS

We women must bring a new element into political life, an element which no sectional party can represent . . . Remember that a woman's mission is to inspire man and to help him build up our young nation upon all that is righteous. Brute force and intellectual force have in the past dominated the world. Let us control both these forces with moral force. The safeguards of the nation will then rest on the individual conscience of its women.

ROSE SCOTT, writing in *The Australian Woman's Sphere*, December 1903

What we want is not less parental responsibility, but more, and the great aim of the Woman Movement is to secure equal justice between man and woman, and to uplift the sacred responsibility of parenthood, which has too long been sacrificed to the insatiable Moloch of Lust.

Letter signed 'A New Woman', the *Bulletin*, 12 October 1895

The story of the entry of Australian women into political life has been distorted by three persistent myths. The first, still perpetrated by politicians of all persuasions who seem to think it absolves them from initiating any further progressive legislation, is that Australian women were the first in the world to obtain the vote. Apart from the imputations of masculine benevolence contained in this claim there is the further implication that all Australian women received the vote simultaneously. This is true of the Federal sphere where all women were enfranchised in 1901 and were able to vote in the first Federal elections of 1903, but what was considered more important at the time, the right to vote in state elections[1], was obtained slowly state by state, often after protracted campaigns which were hampered by considerable resistance. The women of South Australia had the vote for fourteen years before their sisters in Victoria were finally enfranchised in 1908. Australia was the second country to give women the right to vote at national elections eight years after New Zealand, but several American states and Finland had enfranchised their women before the state right to vote was obtained throughout Australia.[2]

The claim that we were the first to enfranchise women is partly true if we consider the badly drafted Victorian Electoral Act of 1863 which enabled all those on municipal rolls to vote at parliamentary elections. The honourable gentlemen had overlooked the fact that they had given some women the right to vote in municipal elections earlier that year and that the names of women possessing property were on the rolls. When it was realized that a large number of women had thus been inadvertently enfranchised, the provision was repealed on the grounds that 'women had not obtained it through deliberate intention'.[3] Those who boast of our pioneering effort in this field generally omit to add that this legislation was an accident and that it was repealed two years later – in time to prevent those women from exercising the franchise.

The second myth is that the awarding of the vote to Australian women was a gratuitous gesture on the part of enlightened legislators and that women themselves had neither requested nor fought for it. Ian Turner, for instance, compounds ignorance of when the vote was actually obtained with this view: ' "Votes for women" was not the burning question, as it was in the United Kingdom. Unlike their British sisters, Australian women were, in the 1880s, handed the vote on a plate.'[4]

Related to this is the third myth which proclaims that Australian women have made little use of the vote:

Australian women have had access to the ballot box for almost three-quarters of a century. But today they have little to show for it. There are currently no women in the House of Representatives. Female involvement in state and Federal parliaments has been pitifully inadequate over the last 70 years. Women continue to encounter discrimination in the workforce. They continue to suffer from laws which unrealistically deny them the right to control their biological destiny.[5]

While contemporary feminists mourn this state of affairs and resolve to correct it, the detractors of women's claims declare it is the result of their not having had to fight for the vote; because it was handed to them on a silver platter they have neither appreciated nor used it, the argument goes. The second myth attempts to deny the existence of an Australia-wide feminist movement which agitated for the vote. The third is a product of this: in suppressing the existence of the movement the myth-makers have buried its ideas, including its views on the uses to which the vote was to be put. While it is true that we have elected fewer women to Parliament than have English or American voters, this has not been for the reason suggested above. Rather it can be traced to the role women elected to play in our political life, a role which was defined by the early 20th century feminists and which received substantial support from other women.

Feminism on anything more than an individual scale first appeared in Australia with the demand for the vote and while not all those who advocated female suffrage were feminists, all feminists wanted votes for women. The campaign for the vote involved thousands of women and many men; suffrage societies existed in all cities and in many country towns and while the agitation never matched the militancy of the English suffragettes*, a relentless and tenacious struggle was carried on for well over a decade in most states. Yet this movement has been neglected by historians of the 1890s: the granting of the vote often rates a passing reference but the campaign itself and the activities of its most dogged fighters are seldom mentioned.[6] Feminism has apparently been viewed as a foreign affliction which may have been periodically imported to our shores, but it has never been seriously considered by labour historians to have flourished as an indigenous ideology in much the same way, *and for very similar reasons*, as the movements whose activities they so prodigiously record.

The details of the suffrage campaigns in each state are not widely known, as the pervasiveness of the three myths demonstrates; certainly they are not taught in schools or universities. There are however several accounts available and so it is not planned to reproduce them here.[7] It is more important in the present context to outline the ideas of Australian feminists, particularly their view on the roles women should play in Australian social and political life, and to examine some of the political issues which engaged their energies. This abbreviated account cannot, and does not pretend to, be more than a fleeting glimpse which attempts to put Australian

* The term 'suffragette' was not used in Australia until the vote had been obtained here; Australian suffrage fighters were known as 'suffragists'. The term 'suffragette' is reputed to have been coined by a London newspaper in 1907 as a pejorative attempt to trivialize the militant agitational tactics of Ms Pankhurst and the radical members of the Women's Social and Political Union. The WSPU however decided to take up the term themselves and used it proudly and defiantly to distinguish themselves from the more conservative, constitutional reformers, the suffragists. 'Suffragette' was used in Australia after 1907 to describe the Pankhursts and their followers, but was not in currency when the main Australian battles were under way.

feminism into its context in the crucible of Australian nationalism. A detailed history of feminism and of the campaign for the vote in this country has still to be published.[8]

In 1869, in a letter to the Melbourne *Argus*, Harriet Dugdale became the first Australian woman on record to advocate full citizenship rights for women but she appears to have received little support until 1884 when she was joined by Annette Bear who had recently returned from involvement in suffrage activities in England. Together they formed the first Australian group, the Woman's Suffrage Society. This was followed in Sydney in 1889 by the Dawn Club, formed by Louisa Lawson as a social reform club for women. It aimed, in the words of its manifesto, to 'gain the definite sympathy and strength which comes from combination, to afford an understood channel for the expression of opinion and translation into practical effort, in connection with Woman's life and work', and it intended to discuss such subjects as 'health, temperance, woman suffrage, social purity, education, dress reform and physiological matters'.[9]

In May the previous year Lawson had founded a newspaper, the *Dawn*, which described itself as 'a journal for the household, edited, printed and published by women' and which was to survive until 1905 despite vehement opposition and physical obstruction by members of the Typographical Union which objected to her employment of female, non-union labour.[10] Lawson had little choice in this since the Union refused to admit women to its ranks even though she employed women who had qualified as printers overseas. From its inception the *Dawn* was abrasively feminist, pointing out the injustices women suffered at the hands of male legislators, demanding that women be given the vote, and proudly listing the achievements of women in any extra-domestic activities.

In 1891 the organization which became the chief body for suffrage agitation in New South Wales – the Womanhood Suffrage League – was established. The League's secretary for its entire life was Rose Scott. She and Vida Goldstein, who was initially in Dugdale's society in Melbourne but later formed her own Woman's Federal Political Association, are probably the best known Australian feminists. By the early 1890s there were suffrage societies in all states. They were composed of women who substantially supported the ideas of Scott and Goldstein on the place of women in society and what they hoped to achieve for women with the ballot. Feminism in Australia created and sustained these suffrage societies. They existed for one purpose – to obtain the vote – and, unlike other organizations which also campaigned for the vote, they were not committed to other goals which might clash with their desire to alter the position of women in Australian society.

The Women's Christian Temperance Union, formed initially in 1882 in New South Wales and in all other states within five years, was an important element in the suffrage campaign, but its influence is often overstated. It has been the only women's organization of that period to leave extensive records of its activities – there are official histories of each state branch – and some writers have tended to equate the amount of written material inherited with its influence on the feminist movement. There was usually co-operation between the temperance women and the suffrage societies, and many of the former would have considered themselves feminists, but to designate the suffrage societies as front movements for temperance reform is inaccurate. The two bodies had very similar views on the role they hoped women would play in political life however. Only those organizations formed by, or existing under the aegis of, existing political parties had different opinions.

The Women's Equal Franchise League, created by the Labor Party in Queensland and the Australian Women's National League, which was closely connected with the Liberal Party in Victoria, were more concerned with organizing women and channelling them into useful political activities – useful politics being defined by the parent party – than with pursuing feminist policies. One exception to this was the NSW Women's Liberal League which, under the presidency of the indomitable Ms Molyneaux Parkes, firmly resisted any party directives to its all female membership.

Feminism in Australia developed within a few years of the first women graduating from university although few of the early graduates associated themselves with the movement.[11] Although the feminists supported the opening of the universities to women, they saw as their special task the reappraisal of the whole range of activities then available to women. This involved challenging the male hegemony which was reflected in the legal and social system and demanding that women's interests be heard and heeded. Women's total dependence on men in every sphere of life was illustrated somewhat sardonically by Louisa Lawson when she was asked to write for the Red Page of the *Bulletin*, not because she had struggled against every possible form of opposition in her attempt to lead an independent and fulfilled existence in her own right, but because she happened to be the mother of a well-known Australian writer.[12] Anticipating the introductory editorial paragraph which patronizingly noted that 'many gifted men have had remarkable mothers', she wrote:

Women are what men make them. Why, a woman can't bear a child without it being received into the hands of a male doctor; it is baptised by a fat old male person; a girl goes through life obeying laws made by men; and if she breaks them, a male magistrate sends her to a gaol where a male warder handles her and looks in her cell at night to see she's all right. If she gets so far as to be hanged, a male hangman puts the rope round her neck; she is buried by a male gravedigger; and she goes to a Heaven ruled over by a male God or a hell managed by a male devil. Isn't it a wonder men didn't make the devil a woman?[13]

Feminism has always been sneered at as Messianic man-hating. The most common charge against the suffragists was that they were soured spinsters. The *Bulletin* labelled them 'disappointed childless creatures who have missed their natural vocation, the ill favoured ones, the bitter hearted'[14] who assuaged their frustrations in acrimony. These charges provided a convenient justification for both ignoring the criticisms of the social system advanced by feminists and for refusing to consider feminism as a valid ideological position in the way, say, socialism is.

The critics have consistently avoided recognizing the distinction between hatred for a male-dominated system which denies women recognition as complete human beings, and hatred directed against the male sex *per se*. Both responses can be, and often are, considered justifiable in other circumstances; the socialist has never questioned the reasonableness of the industrial worker's hatred of an exploitative factory owner, but somehow a woman's hatred of a particularly oppressive husband, or of a legal system which systematically refused to recognize the individuality of women is considered irrational. The former is considered a valid response to an intolerable situation and it is even encouraged by those socialists who consider hatred a decisive spark in fanning the flames of class struggle. Women are expected to respond to similarly intolerable situations with resignation, if not with magnanimous love for the oppressor. Too often those demagogues who maintain that a happy slave is a contradiction in terms and that no Negro could have had anything but hatred for the plantation owners, adroitly shift their ground when the slave analogy is applied to women. It is usually denied that the analogy is even justified, for the sufferings of women are not *real* sufferings; if the occasional injustice is revealed we, your benevolent protectors, can be relied upon to remedy it. One speaker in the Victorian Parliament in 1901 epitomized this argument when he proclaimed, 'If we look at our legislation, we see that a lot has been done by men for women:

married women's property act, local government act, divorce law . . .
They only had to ask for anything *reasonable*, and men were only
too glad, on all occasions, to pass what was necessary for their well-
being.'[15] Such a statement in defence of black slavery even in 1901
would not have been tolerated; it was an indication of how petty
and unimportant the demands of women were seen to be that such
a speech could have been made.

The labour movement in Australia refused to recognize female
suffrage as a legitimate demand until it had first obtained its prime
objective: the abolition of plural voting. Immediately after its
inception, the WSL wrote to the Parliamentary Committee of the
Trades and Labour Council asking that womanhood suffrage be
included in the labour platform; this was refused point blank[16] and
it was not until 1894 when one man one vote was established that
Labor would alter its platform. It would be difficult to find a clearer
example of male affirmation of the inconsequential nature of feminist
demands. The meticulously literal way in which one man one vote
was interpreted by the labour movement exemplified the contempt
in which the women's demand was held. The principles of equality
and justice were not apparently seen to apply to women, the matter
of *their* political representation could be attended to after the important
demands had been won. In a characteristic display of forbearance,
the WSL expressed its disappointment at this response but its
conviction that women would have to do their own fighting was
doubly reinforced.

Labor's antagonism to feminism was, it claimed, based on class
objections. The suffrage organizations were composed of middle-class
women and Labor was unable to reconcile itself to an alliance with
the wives, mothers or daughters of its class enemies. Both the
WCTU and the major suffrage organizations were almost exclusively middle-class in membership but this did not signify an
automatic anti-labour bias. The feminists represented their policies
as being in the interests of women of all classes and certainly as long
as they were the sole champions of female suffrage and a host of
other issues affecting women it was not possible to assign a class
label to any of these policies. It was as much Labor's intransigence
on the question of female suffrage, and its continued suspicion of
feminists' efforts to organize working women, as any ideological
position which led the feminists to view men, and organizations
composed mainly of men, as their enemy.

Certainly, many of the more prominent feminists came from
families of high social standing. Lady Windeyer was the first president

of the WSL and both she and Rose Scott were on personal terms with a large number of parliamentarians. Rose Scott's celebrated Friday night salons were frequented by politicians of all persuasions and it is reputed that the Early Closing Act was actually drafted in her home.[17] Scott worked hard to convince these men that shorter hours for shop assistants were necessary. She arranged for shop girls to come to her home on Sundays – their only free day – and recount the details of their industrial conditions to the law-makers. This tactic proved so successful that the Bill was drafted on the spot – in her sitting room. Similarly, Henry Parkes who was friendly with the Windeyer family is supposed to have asked Lady Windeyer to draw up the Boarding Out Bill.[18]

Yet even this degree of intimacy with the framers of legislation was insufficient to ensure the passage of the Woman's Suffrage Bill. By 1895 there appeared to be sufficient support from liberals in NSW to carry it but no Premier was willing to make it a Government measure and although the Labor Party by this stage supported the principle, it was not prepared to assist the Bill through the House.[19] In this way, the measure was delayed until 1902 when the Labor Party finally agreed to actively support it. In NSW the WCTU was one of the few supposedly middle-class organizations which sought, and was refused, vice-regal patronage.[20]

The inability of the feminists to influence their male class compatriots – and this influence would on paper appear formidable as the wives of the editors of both the *Sydney Morning Herald* and the *Daily Telegraph* were involved in the suffrage campaign – to grant them one of their most sought-after objectives should have convinced the Labor Party that other factors besides class were operating here. Instead it continually condemned such organizations as the Factory Girls Club, and the Women's Industrial Guild because they were organized by middle-class women.[21] Such bodies undoubtedly were limited because of this, and probably reached only a small number of working-class women, but the point remains that at the time such middle-class women were the only ones who were aware enough of the difficulties experienced by their sex to even attempt to alleviate them, and they alone possessed the resources of time, money and organizing abilities to be able to try.

The Labor Party came eventually to support female suffrage as a matter of principle but it was scarcely able to comprehend the general case for independence from male domination which the feminists presented. In the early 1890s unionists had expressed their opposition to the numbers of single women who were taking jobs in shops and offices and, they argued, depriving men of work. Their response to this situation was either to deny that women should have equal employment opportunities, or to urge that women receive equal pay. This they knew would almost guarantee an all-male workforce since employers were more attracted to the greater value they obtained from their female staff than to the notion of the right of women to economic independence.

The other main source of opposition to suffrage came from the powerful liquor interests and others who, like the *Bulletin* and John Norton, editor of *Truth*, managed to tar all the feminists with the temperance brush and declare them to be a bunch of man-hating kill-joys. Although they were to lose the battle to have unlimited alcohol flowing freely at all times, they were so successful in their propaganda campaign against the feminists that the image of them they created still lingers on today. In 1895 the Sydney Licensed Victuallers' Association declared themselves against women's suffrage while later in the year a much stronger protest was recorded by the Newcastle branch of the Association which declared that suffrage would ruin their trade as, they believed, it had already done in New Zealand.[22] Their identification of the suffragists and the WCTU was incorrect for they were never organizationally linked and dual membership appears to have been rare, but it is true that many feminists tended to attribute to alcohol most of the abuses women suffered from their husbands.

But if the temperance women were misguided in their attributing of practically all social evils to the demon drink, nor is it easy for us today to appreciate the extent of the alcohol problem. The term 'wowser' which Norton is reputed to have coined to denigrate those who would deny a man his few beers has now attained such powerful imagery that we can only conceive of anyone described by that term as being solely intent on preventing people from enjoying themselves. But Australia had long been renowned as an inebriated island. When in 1854 the Victorian Parliament had appointed a select committee of the Legislative Council to inquire into intemperance, the president of the Victorian Liquor Law League claimed that one in 10 of the population had been committed for drunkenness; this compared with one in 220 in London and one in 25 in Glasgow and we had even managed to outdrink the Irish who recorded only one in 14 arrests.[23] Thirty years later an English visitor, R. E. N. Twopeny, noted that although statistically drunkenness in Australia was not very much worse than in England 'the difference lies in the class who gets drunk. Here it is not merely the lower classes, but everybody that drinks.'[24]

Even the *Bulletin* was forced to agree that this judgement was correct. In 1880 it calculated that Victoria had managed to outdrink the other states and that judging from the total amount of liquor consumed annually in that state, 'The average drinker filled himself 96 times with beer, 12 times with whisky and water and 6 times with wine, 114 times in all or about once every third day.'[25] A practice which required the investigation of several Royal Commissions – there was another one in South Australia in 1906, commissioned to collect evidence as to the cause and cure of inebriety in Victoria, NSW and S.A.[26] – could hardly be dismissed simply as people having a good time. Alcohol was used in voluminous quantities for medical purposes; in 1882 the Melbourne Hospital prescribed 350 gallons of wine and spirits and about 3,000 gallons of porter – small wonder that the out-patients department was regarded as a free grog shop.[27]

As well as objecting to the free availability of alcohol – it was on sale to anyone, including children, virtually twenty-four hours a day – the temperance women decried the use in hotels of barmaids who were, they claimed, employed solely as sexual objects to attract drinking customers. They also thought that hotels were no place for women because they were forced to witness swearing, gambling and other forms of 'moral danger'. Even Labor should have been alerted to the employment conditions of barmaids. Since women did not use hotels there were no lavatories provided, not even for employees; the Victorian Royal Commission on Employees in Shops in 1883 heard evidence that one barmaid had died from constipation because of long hours at the bar.[28] The WCTU women were not alone in their attack on intemperance, and local option polls and Sunday closing had been established before women were enfranchised. A referendum on six o'clock closing held in 1915 in South Australia surprised even the WCTU which had agitated for it when 100,418 votes, a clear majority over all other options, were recorded in favour of early closing.[29]

In drawing attention to and campaigning against the evils and injustices they identified, these women transgressed the boundaries of womanhood as it was then defined. The Australian feminists regarded the vote as a potent symbol of the freedom to determine issues which they thought were women's special preserve but few of them equated suffrage itself with emancipation; it was only a precondition, a necessary tool with which to force legislatures to recognize their demands. These were raised continually during the suffrage campaign but tended to be overshadowed by the polarization of opinion which surrounded the issue of giving women the vote.

One member of the Victorian Parliament in 1896, by which time women in two states were already enfranchised, objected to handing over the destinies of this country to 'the most unthinking portion of humanity'.[30] When the feminists had to contend with opinions such as these it was only to be expected that they would spend most of their time simply arguing for the justice of the vote. They did so defiantly, scorning the reprobation they knew would follow for it had become evident that if women were to have any kind of freedom, if they were to break through the paralysing effects of the polarized stereotypes of womanhood, they would have to define and seize a new life for themselves. Maybanke Anderson, a prominent and vocal member of the WSL, pointed this out in a pamphlet she published anonymously in answer to anti-suffrage attacks:

Women ask to be enfranchised because they see that just as class rule in the past was fatal to freedom and to progress, so sex-rule is still fatal to the woman, hindering her development, marring her usefulness, and injuring her children; while it is equally fatal to the moral and spiritual development of the man.[31]

The English common law principle as enunciated by Blackstone that 'husband and wife are one, and that one is the husband' denied women any personal, social or political rights. Once women realized the injustices of this situation and saw that it was not an inevitable human condition, they were inspired to do something about it. This perception was precipitated by the extension of personal liberty to American slaves and of political liberty to working-class men. The agitation for women's rights began in the United States with the fight for the abolition of slavery and the first women's rights convention, held in Seneca Falls, New York in 1848 was organized by veterans of that campaign. It was to take nearly forty years before the same consciousness of their slave-like status in relation to men emerged in Australia and by this time there was already a history of agitation for female independence in both England and the United States with which the Australian feminists could identify. The slow process of altering the legal status of women had already begun in England and those Acts which had been passed, for example, the Married Women's Property Act and the Guardianship of Infants Act, had been quickly copied by the colonial legislatures.

These legal changes undoubtedly aided the awareness of Australian women of their own position. Once a few concessions were made women were quick to perceive that extensive changes were possible, especially when the new legislation was, as in the case of the 1873 NSW Marriage Act, still discriminatory. This Act, a close copy of the English one, did establish the position of the wife as *femme sole* in respect to her property, enabling her to dispose of it herself, a right which was fully conceded with the Married Women's Property Act; but the grounds for the dissolution of marriage still favoured the husband and perpetuated the notion that the wife was his property. He could divorce her on the grounds of adultery alone – that is, property tampered with – while she was obliged to prove adultery *plus* incest, rape (of another woman – wife-raping was, and still is, permissible), bigamy, sodomy, cruelty or desertion for two years without reasonable cause.

Feminism in Australia was an indigenous response to indigenous conditions. Where there were similarities with England this was because the legal position of women was identical. When Australian feminists explained what inspired their involvement it was almost always because of a sudden realization of their inferior legal position. Dora Montefiore, who convened the first meeting of the WSL, discovered when her husband died in 1889 that because his will made no provision for guardianship of their children they were allowed to remain under her care – he could if he had chosen entrusted them to some other person and she would have had no legal redress. She told the lawyer who informed her of this: 'You don't know how your horrible law is insulting all motherhood.' 'And from that moment I was a suffragist (though I did not realize it at the time) and determined to alter the law.'[32] It was not until 1916 and the introduction of the Testator's Family Maintenance and Guardianship of Infants Act that widows in NSW automatically became their children's legal guardians.[33]

Rose Scott's induction into public life came when she joined a committee which was agitating for the age of consent – and consequently the age at which girls could legally be employed in brothels – to be raised from fourteen to eighteen. When the Bill was introduced into the NSW Legislative Assembly in 1890 it was greeted with gales of laughter: 'Then came the thought that if women had the vote children would be protected, and such insulting conduct could be put a stop to for ever! I read all I could, for and against the Woman's Vote and finally John Stuart Mill's "Subjection of Women" made me a convert and an enthusiast!'[34]

Australian feminists were extremely prolific in their production of journal articles, speeches, propaganda leaflets and contributions for their own publications. Several of them left personal accounts of their involvement in the movement[35] but none of the major figures apart from the South Australian Catherine Spence (and her pioneering efforts were largely before a wide-scale movement arose) left autobiographical accounts of their intellectual development as feminists. It appears that some contact with overseas activities was maintained and the Australian women read John Stuart Mill, Mary Wollstonecraft (whose *A Vindication of the Rights of Women* published in 1792 was one of the first feminist tracts), Henrik Ibsen[36] and Olive Schreiner.

The formation of the Women's Literary Society in NSW in 1891, a prestigious and intellectually lively association which had the distinction of being the first women's organization to meet at night[37] had encouraged women to read critically and to write papers on a variety of topics. The programme for 1894–95 shows that the society discussed such subjects as the life and work of George Sand, contemporary women writers, Elizabethan dramatists and Emerson.[38] Many of the women in this society joined the WSL. Each issue of Vida Goldstein's paper the *Australian Woman's Sphere* carried an advertisement for the *Woman's Journal*, a United States feminist magazine founded in 1870 by Lucy Stone, a pioneer American woman's rights worker, and reprints from this and similar journals as well as tributes to American activists were frequent. When Adela Pankhurst, daughter of the British suffragette, migrated to Australia she was enthusiastically welcomed into the movement by Victorian feminists.

But the Australian feminist movement was above all an activist body. The women were reacting to injustices they readily perceived and fighting for ideals they wished to implement: reading theoretical tracts could only reinforce what they already knew from observation to be true.[39] Their campaigns were mostly pragmatic exercises designed to introduce, or to repeal, specific pieces of legislation. They wanted the vote because they saw this as a weapon in that struggle: until they had political representation and thus at least theoretical power to influence election results they recognized that they were destined to remain in bondage to the paternalistic whims of all-male legislatures.

Thus the campaign for the vote became symbolic of the self-determination which women sought in all areas of life. Enfranchisement would mean the recognition of their political independence and, it was hoped, this would provide the leverage for demanding independence in other spheres. There was also the fundamental principle of justice, of women being denied the vote when every man in the country could vote. While the franchise applied only to propertied men, women could be persuaded that the theory of representation had some merit, but once working-class men obtained suffrage both class and race prejudices were revealed. Ms Euphemia Bowes, a leading member of the WCTU protested during a delegation to the Premier that every larrikin in Woolloomooloo could vote but that she, a lady, could not. And both NSW and Victorian feminists objected to Chinese and 'Blackfellers' being able to vote when they could not. The issue of the *Australian Woman's Sphere* for 8 April 1903 carried a front page poster showing a huge procession of men of all colours and classes marching under a banner emblazoned with a brimming beer mug and opium pipes. The heroine of the poster, an upright young woman was chained to a convict and a demented old woman under the banner, 'Thou shalt not vote Womanhood, Madness, Criminality.'

Prior to suffrage women had no equity in the political system and in the case of women with property this involved a blatant contradiction of the principle that had been violently established by the American War of Independence although it was partly resolved by giving propertied women the vote in municipal elections.[40] But women with property were still subject to the iniquitous 'taxation without representation' in relation to Parliament and this motivated some women to join the suffrage agitation. A printed letter addressed to the Commissioners of Taxation and stating that the Land Tax was being paid under protest was made available by the WSL to women who wished to make a point about this injustice. But for the majority of women, who had no property, this was no argument of course and it was never advanced as the major reason for wanting the vote by any group.

The leaflets produced by the various suffrage organizations covered every possible reason, polemical or otherwise, for enfranchising women. There was basic agreement between them; and the following, selected from WSL, WCTU and the Australian Women's Franchise Society leaflets provides a fair selection:

Because women are equally entitled with men to 'life, liberty, and the pursuit of happiness'. Because the denial of this right is a denial of justice to half the human race. Because no social system which represses one-half of the community by unequal laws can be just, wise or safe. Because no truly free race of men can be reared from slave mothers.

Man claims the Vote for his PROPERTY and upon his MANHOOD: it is conceded to Women in Municipal Matters Only, on the first, and denied her, either as a property holder or her Womanhood in all Matters Political.

Because it is the foundation of all political liberty that those who obey the law, should be able to have a voice in choosing those who make the law. Because a Government of the people by the people, and for the people, should mean all the people and not one half. Because some [laws] set up different standards for men and women. Because the vote of women would add power and weight to the more settled communities. Because the possession of votes would increase the sense of responsibility amongst women towards questions of public importance. Because, to sum up all reasons in one – it is just.[41]

In 1891 the *Woman's Suffrage Journal of NSW* ran a competition inviting women to write in giving their reasons for wanting suffrage. The printed replies covered the arguments most commonly used by the feminists. They ranged from asserting enfranchisement as a fundamental principle of justice: 'because I believe in equal liberty and opportunity for every human creature, male and female, and because I have never seen the document by which God authorized men to decide what women may or may not rightly do', to pointing out the injustices women suffered under laws they could not influence, to the hope that 'the spirit of purity and unselfishness, with which women have inspired domestic life, will in its expansion, now inspire public life; changing the guiding principle of nations, classes, and individuals, from self interest to love . . . '[42]

Each of these three reasons was considered important by all advocates of suffrage but the last is especially significant as it gives expression to the conception of women, and to the relationship between domestic and political life, which the feminists sought to universalize. They saw women as a moral force for good within 'the family' and they wanted this influence to filter through into political life. They considered that 'the family' was the most important of society's institutions and that the superior qualities they believed women to possess emanated from their constant involvement in family life. Margaret Windeyer had pointed out, in a paper delivered to the Dawn Club, that the life of girls from childhood onwards showed 'a common tendency to be helpful, sympathetic and self sacrificing in the service of Mother, Brother and Husband'.[43] There were no similar observations made about boys' socialization but they did assume that men were victims of a social process that few of them had power to alter, and whenever any individual or group of men sought to alter the status of women this met with their approval. Loud applause followed the announcement at the first annual general meeting of the WSL that 'the adventurous pioneers who are shortly going from Australia to form a communistic settlement in Paraguay all sign articles of association which will give the women equal rights with the men in the "New Australia".'[44]

Their prime objective however was to enable the civilizing and humane influences which they considered to be women's special virtues to have as wide an influence as possible. In advocating this, the feminists were restating Caroline Chisholm's theory of women's mission which had formed one of the fundamental bases of the Australian family. This notion of women's contribution to society had been absorbed into the value-system of the country and so was widely accepted in principle, if not always interpreted in the same way. When the *Bulletin* finally reversed its editorial opinion on female suffrage, which it had previously opposed, on the grounds that 'the evil is evidently becoming unavoidable and must be endured in the best way possible', it bemoaned the fact that the woman's vote would be a 'danger to the cause of Democracy. The tendency of the feminine mind is almost invariably towards Conservatism . . . '[45] But the feminists, many of whom were radical politically, saw conservatism as a positive virtue. Maybanke Anderson wrote:

Every woman knows that she is fulfilling one of the highest, if not the very highest, of her possible duties to her country and herself when she maintains in purity the home whence good and healthy children pass into the world. The women's vote must evidently be so far as the home is concerned, conservative in the highest sense.[46]

The God's Police conception of women was still valid as far as the feminists were concerned but changes in the social system were required if it was not to be neutralized. One of the constant complaints of the feminists was that the good work they performed in socializing their children, especially their sons, was undermined by the free availability of alcohol and by the sexual double standard. Not only were mothers denied legal guardianship of their children but their moral influence over them was constantly subverted. The feminists were demanding nothing less than a radical reappraisal of the relationship between domestic and social existence and they realized that, as their protectors-in-law were not going to act without a good deal of prompting, it was necessary for women themselves to take public, political action.

Lady Beaumont, the President of the Sydney Women's Club in 1901, said to a meeting of the club:

. . . it is most important that at this period of the country's history that its women should stand clearly for the highest standards in everything. The responsibility of keeping up such standards lies always very largely with the women of any land . . . woe the land whose women are less high minded than the men . . . [47]

The insistence that the domestic and social spheres be more closely intertwined did not entail women abrogating their maternal functions. Although the feminists attacked the idea that women should be defined solely in terms of these functions as this cruelly left the single woman without a social function, the import of their demands was to enhance the maternal role for those who chose to adopt it. The plea for the economic independence of the housewife – by means of a maternal endowment – together with their philosophy of the importance for the nation of the socializing of the next generation being undertaken by women who were physically and legally un- fettered by the domination of their husbands was a plea for recognition of what they considered to be women's unique contribution to humanity. As one feminist put it:

We need not go back to the old fallacy that marriage is the aim and end of a woman's existence, and absolutely necessary for further happiness. Some women are doubtless called to be mothers of the race, and to do the social work which is so necessary to our complex civilizations. Some women may feel themselves called to some literary or artistic pursuit, for which they require the freedom of unmarried life. But most women will agree that for the ordinary woman marriage is the happiest state, and that she rarely realizes the deepest and highest in her nature except in wifehood and motherhood.[48]

The desire of *fin de siècle* feminists for women to retain a separate sense of identity had to be expressed by arguing for social recognition of a claim to expertise that only women possessed. Hence the stress on motherhood, even by those women who were not, and did not want to be, mothers themselves. 'Separate but equal' is the phrase used today to express what they aimed for. That the fight for political and social independence was not a fight to be able to do the same things as men was borne out by their attitudes to two important areas. The battles to have the age of consent raised to seventeen or eighteen[49] from twelve (in Victoria) and fourteen (in New South Wales) and to repeal the Contagious Diseases Act were seen as direct attacks on the double standards of sexual morality which burdened and prematurely aged women with numerous pregnancies and which prostituted poorer women.

The Contagious Diseases Acts were ostensibly to suppress prostitution and to control the spread of V.D. New South Wales, Queensland and Tasmania had each introduced Acts in the 1870s and while they did not receive the amount of opposition that similar Acts in Britain generated, there was protest from individuals who recognized that these Acts merely victimized women and enabled the male patrons of prostitutes to evade prosecution. These Acts could not suppress prostitution: all they could do was enforce licensing of prostitutes and regular medical examination – for women only. Critics of the Acts rightly pointed out that this was a humiliating, authoritarian and futile means of obtaining either of their stated objectives and that they victimized women while enabling their customers to spread V.D. with immunity.

The feminists saw prostitutes as victims of male lust and scandalously low wages[50] and they wanted both to delay as long as possible 'the age at which a girl can consent to her own ruin', as one petition put it, and to prevent the institutionalization of the double standard which the Contagious Diseases Acts effected. They advocated rehabilation farms in the country for prostitutes; and their demands that girls receive adequate training for gainful employment, together with their support for institutions like the YWCA and Louisa Lawson's Darlinghurst Hostel for working girls were evidence of the comprehensive manner in which they tackled the problem.

The feminists accepted implicitly the social stereotypes of God's Police and Damned Whore which characterized women in Australia. It did not occur to them to argue for an amalgamation of the two 'types' into an independent, sexually active 'new woman' whose maternal status was irrelevant. They had internalized this derogatory dualistic notion of womanhood so completely that they could only envisage trying to totally eliminate the Whore conception and turn all women into God's Police. They were not prepared to echo societal condemnation of women labelled as 'whores' but adopted a redemptive attitude towards them; hence the various rehabilitative measures they proposed or established.

Although in both England and the United States minority groups of feminists argued for, and practised, free love, the Australian feminists' universally shared conception of the higher mission of women completely precluded the development of a similar challenge to established sexual mores. Vida Goldstein issued a formal repudiation against a rumour perpetrated during the first Federal elections that she was in favour of free love.[51] Although this was rarely stated outright, many feminists opposed artificial methods of contraception in favour of self-restraint. A rare and courageous exception to this was the Melbourne WCTU activist Ms Bessie Lee who shocked many of her contemporaries in the early 1890s by advocating that married women restrict their child-bearing by using contraception.[52] Birth control was widely practised in Australia by this time and hence the technological means existed for women to start demanding recognition of their sexuality as well as being able to control their fertility. But the cultural means did not yet exist: sexual freedom, or licence as most of the feminists would have it, was too closely associated with the Whore conception for it to be even contemplated. Rather than argue that women enjoy the same sexual freedom as men, the feminists wanted men to acquire the same degree of chastity which they believed women to be blessed with: ' . . . we believe that the stability of marriage and the home depend on our having an equal standard for men and women' said an article in the first issue of Goldstein's post-suffrage paper the *Woman Voter*.[53]

In the birth-rate controversy which raged in the early 1900s – the decline in the birth-rate had raised fears of race suicide among some – the feminists agreed that families should be limited in size, mainly because this reduced the physical burden for women. Smaller families meant that women could devote more time to each child and this would ultimately be better for the nation. But when it came to discussing how family size was to be limited, those feminists who tended to view sex as abhorrent, recommended abstinence. Rose Scott thought that 'licensed or unlicensed vice can only mean evil, and . . . a really great nation can only be built by inculcating the virtues of self-control and purity.'[54] These virtues they hoped to propagate widely as new social norms, not merely for the pragmatic end of family limitation. One feminist wrote:

the sowing of 'wild oats' by the young man is regarded as a necessity by some and as a trivial offence by others. And yet there will be no hope of a higher marriage relationship until this miserable falsehood be swept away. When a young man has been trained to rigid self-control before marriage, and has enshrined within his heart a high ideal of womanhood, he will approach the marriage relationship in a very different way to what he does now. He will realize that restraint is as necessary now as before, and his former training will stand him in good stead.[55]

The second way in which the feminists sought to distinguish themselves from men was by refusing to participate in party politics. Many of them regarded the party system as manifesting the cynical bargaining for party strength at the expense of principle which had denied women effective representation in the past. Goldstein and Scott were the most trenchant opponents and fought vainly to prevent female enfranchisement from contributing to the perpetuation of the system. 'Our place as women', said Scott

is not as camp followers to a corrupt system of Party politics, but as women to be men's inspiration to higher and nobler methods of governing a country. The blind worship of man and his methods never did any man any good, although it may soothe his vanity, but to help man realize his ideals is the work of every true woman.

She urged women to 'think for yourselves, belong to no party, accept no dictation as to your vote'.[56]

The non-party ideal was strong in all states and enfranchisement was generally followed by the setting up of organizations designed to educate women in political matters so that they could use their vote discriminatingly. The feminists believed that by being non-party they could also be more effective politically. They could lobby all parties without their demands being dismissed as partisan for they could argue that women of all political colours filled their ranks. But non-party affiliation was primarily an ideal which, as Goldstein explained, could restore principles to politics:

By adopting (a non-party) policy it is not to be supposed that we are a body of gelatinous creatures, who have no definite views. We have all got very decided views as to the merits of the various political parties – some of us are protectionists, some are free-traders, some are single taxers, some are labourites, some are socialists, but we differ from those organized on party lines in one important particular. We believe that questions affecting honour, private and public integrity and principle, the stability of the home, the welfare of children, the present salvation of the criminal and the depraved, the moral, social and economic injustice imposed on women – we believe that all these questions are greater than party, and that in nine cases out of ten they are sacrificed to party interests.[57]

The S.A. Women's Non-Party Association had been founded in 1909 on the principle that 'women of all parties or none are on common ground in the realization that the things that unite women are greater than those that divide them, and that matters affecting all homes and all citizens should be approached without party bias', and this principle guided all post-suffrage women's organizations.

Although they were fighting an already lost battle in attempting to abolish the party system, the belief that women of different political views could fight together for feminist aims was quite consistent with their conception of the role of women. One common feature in the demand for the vote by all feminist bodies was the absence of any claim for personal or group power; they wanted representation and influence and for most this simply meant using their votes judiciously. None of the feminists initially sought the right for women to sit in Parliament and only in South Australia was this provision included in the suffrage Bill – an amendment which was in the words of one observer, an 'invention of the enemy, put in to wreck the measure'[58], but which misjudged the political temper of the Government and hence misfired.[59] Most feminists saw the advantage of possessing the vote to be, as Jessie Ackerman put it: 'If the social problems demanding legislation do not receive the attention of members, women are in a position to unseat them, and fill their places with *men* who will carry out their wishes.'[60]

But there were some, like Vida Goldstein, who not only thought that women should take seats in Parliament but who actually stood for election. She argued that having women in Parliament would prevent injustices in legislation concerning women and children which men, however well-intentioned, were unable to completely understand, and that such representation would save women's organizations the enormous amount of time they currently spent 'on the often Herculean task of educating members up to the point of seeing the injustices in certain measures affecting women'. Her main point however rested on an argument, used frequently, though without the conclusions she drew, by other feminists:

It is suicidal to divorce the home and the State, and that is what we have done in the past, in insisting on man-governed institutions. The State is only an aggregate of families, and as the best-governed family is where husband and wife work together in the highest interests of their children, so the best-governed State will be that where men and women work together in the highest interests of the people, the country, the race . . . [61]

Goldstein stood as an independent candidate in Victoria five times between 1903 and 1917 and although she was never elected she polled very well the first time, in the first Senate elections. Her position was shared by Ms Martel and Ms Moore in New South Wales who both stood as candidates; but the majority of feminists felt they should restrict their political activity to voting, pressure group tactics and attempting where possible to act upon some of the reforms they advocated.

In terms of ideas about 'the family's' place in Australian society, the feminist movement signalled the end of a decisive phase. The demands of the feminists coincided with, and when they were implemented, marked the social recognition of, the necessity of certain reforms to the Victorian-era patriarchal family. The feminists had identified as the two most important tasks of the modern family the socialization of children and the control and confinement of sexuality. They argued that 'the family' was in danger of becoming ineffective because these two functions were being jeopardized by the disjunction in the relationship between domestic and political life. Both functions were in need of reform, reinterpretation or reconfirmation and they saw women in their God's Police role as providing the linchpin to this social renovation. They saw that women needed avenues of political expression to be able to effect domestic reforms.

The harmonizing of the relationship between domestic and political life which occurred in Australia prior to 1914 was not principally due to pressures from the feminists – they never attained that degree of influence. But they were important in enforcing some legal reforms in women's status and family responsibilities. The modern family is the creation of the middle-class and any changes which have occurred in its organization or prescribed functions have been initiated by that class. Middle-class feminism can thus be viewed as one stage in the reform of 'the family' to a more egalitarian unit where spouses were legally equal and where children were considered to be in need of special treatment for a protracted period of time. As pointed out in the last chapter, theories of child-care began to be expounded at a popular level about this time.

The Australian feminists quite consciously wished to retain and strengthen 'the family'. The kind of criticisms of the institution launched in Australia by Tom Mann[62] and other radicals received no support from any feminist. They were influenced by the same ideas which motivated the advocacy of specialized education for girls to enhance and perfect their performance of the mother role. Motherhood as a vocation was a late nineteenth century invention; the feminists argued for legal changes which would enable women to fulfil this vocation more effectively and at the same time elicit from society just recognition of their contribution to the world. It was the link between family and society which the feminists perceived which enabled them to declare that women were performing their duties as citizens by producing and educating children who could contribute actively to the development of the nation

But the feminists carried this further than the educational reformers. They insisted that marriage should not be necessary for women to gain social recognition of their individual worth and they argued very strongly for the right of women to support themselves. They also demanded the opportunity to express opinions and take actions in government matters which they saw as germane to their ideal of raising the status of women, children and the family. The Women's Political Association, formed in August 1909 in Victoria to educate women in the use of the vote, had the following platform:

1. Equal Federal Marriage and Divorce Law
2. Equal Parental Rights over Children
3. Equal Rights in the Disposition of Property after death
4. Equal Pay for Equal Work
5. Pure Food and Pure Milk Supply
6. Education Reform
7. Protection of Boys and Girls to the age of twenty-one against the vicious and depraved
8. Reforms of Methods in dealing with neglected and delinquent children
9. Establishment of a State Children's Council, a Central Children's Court, and the appointment of a Special Children's Magistrate
10. Stringent Legislation to protect the child wage-earner
11. Appointment of women as: (a) Police Matrons, (b) Sanitary Inspectors, (c) Inspectors of neglected and boarded-out children, (d) Inspectors of State Schools and Truant Officers, (e) Inspectors of all State Institutions where women and children are immured, (f) Members of Council of Education, (g) Members of Municipal and Shire Councils
12. Reform in the Liquor Traffic
13. Cessation of Borrowing, except for reproductive works
14. International Woman Suffrage
15. International Peace and Arbitration.[63]

What the feminists failed to perceive was that their two ideals were contradictory. They could not strengthen 'the family' and *also* win for women the right to a new independent identity. In practice this was solved by elevating motherhood – a reformed idea of motherhood as a vocation deserving high status – to a universal ideal; but what this did in effect was to ensure the perpetuation of a considerably strengthened sexism which differed little in substance from the older variety. Women were still seen as being able to be encompassed by one of two stark categories, something which the feminists themselves contributed to by their missionary-like attitudes to women classed as Damned Whores.

It is telling that most feminists seemed to be more concerned by *this* division between women than by any other and this would constitute one explanation for their tardiness in trying to attract working-class women to the movement. They had perhaps unconsciously retained the middle-class assumption that all lower-class women were Whores unless they proved otherwise and while they were ready to bestow benevolent advice on working-class women they do not seem to have actively solicited them to join the movement. There were no Annie Kenneys in the Australian movement.*

And so the feminist movement did not succeed in carving out an alternative option for women. This would be partly explicable by demographic factors. In Britain where there was a large excess of single women over men, it was necessary to create a lifestyle for such women, and their numbers were sufficiently large and included enough forceful individuals to endow it with legitimacy and respect, even if its status never matched that of the married brigade. In Australia, however, there was still a shortage of women at the turn of the century and so most women had at least the theoretical opportunity to marry. There was little demographic stimulus to argue that a single life could be a rewarding state for a woman and feminism created little cultural impetus for such an argument. The feminists insisted that a woman need not marry and most of the leading feminists remained single, but their continued emphasis on the God's Police conception as the sole desirable one for women, married or single, neutralized the possibility of women being able to choose from a wider variety of socio-cultural options. Instead of enlarging the sphere of sexism, as it could be argued British feminism did, Australian feminism had the perhaps unintended effect of strengthening the old dualistic mode. Women were classified as being different from men with numerous social and personal consequences for behaviour attending this difference, and women themselves were still viewed as being able to be categorized by two stereotypes.

One important consequence of this has been that large numbers of

* Annie Kenney was a militant English suffragette. She was a cotton mill worker in Oldham until she met Christabel Pankhurst in 1905 and became a full-time worker for votes for women. She was the only working-class woman to hold a prominent full-time position in the Women's Social and Political Union.

women who undoubtedly were living lives which did not conform to the God's Police stereotype have been hidden within our history and we can guess that they suffered the miseries, self-denigration and uncertainties which attend being excluded from socially valued groups. Single women could hover on the fringes of families and be granted the honorary membership status of maiden aunt. Those who chose more independent lives were regarded as eccentric spinsters to be pitied or, if their lives touched the daring or the unrespectable, relegated to black-sheepdom.

If they were lesbians they would have had either to disguise this, their lovers referred to always as secretaries, companions or such-like, or to face ostracism. Most seem to have chosen the former and there are innumerable instances in our history and literature of celebrated women who lived with other women under a variety of pretences. Jill Johnston makes the point that until very recently there was lesbian activity but no lesbian identity[64] and such women would probably not have called themselves lesbians even if they were involved in a close emotional and/or sexual relationship with another woman. It simply would not have been possible to forge a positive, strong and assertive lesbian identity in a culture which was so insistent that women ought to be wives and mothers. The consequence of this for a self-styled lesbian was to face a life of risk and no doubt a fair amount of mental anguish. Some tried to live as men. It is not possible to guess how many women would have done this since it is only the few who were charged with some criminal activity or whose transvestitism was publicly exposed who are known to us, but one can speculate that the two who became notorious about the turn of the century were not isolated cases.[65]

Generally though, women were not aware of any alternatives to the God's Police role and the majority seem to have adopted it or at least aspired to it. After the initial movement of large numbers of mainly single girls into the workforce in the 1880s, the number of women working outside the home remained fairly constant and small until the War. At the 1891 census 82.6 per cent of all women were classified as dependants. The 1901 and 1911 censuses both showed 82.4 per cent of all women in this category. The major changes in the female workforce had occurred within the categories of those employed, with the percentage employed as domestic servants declining slightly while the percentage engaged in industrial work rose.[66]

Once the vote was granted, organized labour continued to criticize the feminists for being bourgeois but it could find few among their policies to disagree with apart from the non-party stance. Since the 1870s Labor had seen the bourgeois family as a desirable lifestyle for Australian workers. Labor men had opposed the importation of cheap coloured labour on the grounds that it would undermine the structure of the workforce: this now reflected the division of labour between home and work which reinforced the bourgeois family. Men worked, some single women worked – but only until they married. Married women were full-time mothers and housewives. An influx of single men to a country where there was already a shortage of women could undermine the stability of family life, the Labor men argued. Their racist sentiments meant they could not sanction the possibility of Asian labourers marrying Australian women so they drummed up the Yellow Peril scare and propagandized against these men entering Australia. They would turn young girls into opium-smoking prostitutes, thereby reducing the number of women available for marriage and motherhood, and threatening the newly-established stable relationship between family and workforce.

Although Labor might describe things differently, in their support for 'the family' they and the feminists were fighting for the same thing. In the historical context in which it occurred, feminism was a reformist ideology, one that insisted on women's equality as citizens while maintaining their different (and superior) qualities. It was also a remarkably successful movement in that it managed to obtain most of the legislative changes it sought. 'By 1914', writes Joan Cobb, 'the women's movement in New South Wales had achieved most of its immediate aims in regard to legislation affecting the social and legal status of women. It had done so without particularly altering the ideals of those concerned with it or enlarging their vision of themselves.'[67] The Annual Report of the Women's Political Association for 1916 claimed success in the following areas:

☐ the retention of British nationality by women marrying foreigners
☐ equal pay for equal work (had been awarded to commercial clerks in Victoria)
☐ equal property rights (under the intestacy laws) for children under twenty-one years
☐ equality of measures for the prevention of vice (the introduction of compulsory cures for venereal disease for both sexes)
☐ protection of children (four female WPA probation officers had been appointed)
☐ the appointment of women police (this had been promised by the state Government)[68]

Many of the ideas and institutions which today's radical feminists decry are the inheritances of the first feminist movement. They fought hard for women's prisons, and women police, and to discourage women from enjoying their sexuality. They wanted special regulations for women workers and separate syllabuses for girls at school. They fought for the dignity of womanhood but their ideal of womanhood was one which still depended heavily on the Victorian characterization of women as pure and noble, as superior to men and as needing special protection. There was a contradiction between this characterization and the ideal of independence and self-determination they sought, but their failure to delve more deeply into the causes of women's oppression, and to examine the differing aspirations of women themselves, obscured this. They should have realized that the readiness with which the male legislatures acceded to their post-suffrage demands signalled their failure to provide a radical alternative vision for women.

The women who received the most opposition were those, like Vida Goldstein, who transgressed some or all of the sexist conventions about what was appropriate behaviour for women. In standing for Parliament she cut through the prescriptions of both stereotypes and was, theoretically, in a good position to decry sexist categorization. She and several others did succeed in winning approval for their individual stances but they were unable to establish these as the bases of a new tradition of what was permitted to women. Reasons for this were suggested earlier.

The early Australian feminists succeeded in defining, and acquiring social approbation for an enlarged sphere of special women's activities, rights and privileges, but they did not recognize that it was the very fact of erecting such special realms which constituted a large part of female oppression.

They had no consciousness of what is now called sexism and it is because they did not recognize that while society divides power and responsibility on the basis of sex some of their sought-after aims were impossible to achieve. While they advocated a God's Police role for women, arguing that they were morally superior to men, they could not then expect to make public life more moral since men were, by definition, morally inferior. Nor could they remove the double standard or attain real independence for married women while they extolled 'the family'. They had equated these aims with changes in legislation not recognizing that factors other than simple male dominance were involved.

NOTES

1. The first demands for female suffrage were made before Federation and it was to changes in legislation for which the states were responsible that the feminists first addressed themselves. Even after Federation the state right to vote remained an urgent priority, for most of the issues which concerned women remained state responsibilities.

2. The vote for women was obtained in the following sequence: Wyoming, U.S. – 1869; Colorado, U.S. – 1893; New Zealand – 1893; South Australia – 1894; Utah, Idaho, U.S. – 1896; Western Australia – 1899; Australia – 1901; New South Wales– 1902; Tasmania – 1903; Queensland – 1905; Finland– 1906; Victoria– 1908; England – 1918 for women aged thirty and over, 1928 for full adult suffrage; United States – 1920.

3. Peter Biskup, *The Female Suffrage Movement in Australia*, B.A. Honours thesis, University of Western Australia, 1959, p. 68.

4. Ian Turner, 'Prisoners in Petticoats: A Shocking History of Female Emancipation in Australia' in Julie Rigg, ed., *In Her Own Right*, Nelson, Melbourne, 1969, p. 20.

5. Sally White, 'Women's Electoral Lobby', *Dissent*, no. 28, Winter 1972, p. 40.

6. R. Gollan's *Radical and Working-Class Politics* (Melbourne University Press, 1967) is one labour history which devotes some attention to the feminist movement, but he is a singular example of an historian caring to comment upon this phase in our political history. By contrast, there is hardly an aspect of union and parliamentary politics involving men which has not been eagerly taken up, rigorously examined, carefully analysed and passionately dissertated upon by the hordes of historians of the 1890s who inhabit Australian universities.

7. The most accessible secondary accounts of the Australian suffrage campaign are Norman MacKenzie, *Women in Australia*, Cheshire, Melbourne, 1962, Chapters 1–3; Dianne Scott, 'Womanhood Suffrage: the movement in Australia', *Journal of the Royal Australian Historical Society*, Vol. 53, part 4, December 1967, pp. 299–322; Peter Biskup, 'The Westralian Feminist Movement', *University Studies in History*, Vol. 3, no. 3, October 1959, pp. 71–84. MacKenzie's account is inadequate because of its virulent anti-feminism; Scott's is more reliable but because of the enormous field she has to cover concentrates only on the progress of the egislation in the various states; Biskup discusses only one state.

8. The activities of the feminist movements in New South Wales, Victoria and South Australia have been the subject of several higher degree theses but unfortunately these unpublished works are not accessible to general readers. The feminist movements of Britain and the United States have been meticulously examined and voluminous accounts have been published. The New Zealand suffrage campaign was the subject of a recent book, Patricia Grimshaw, *Women's Suffrage in New Zealand*, Oxford University Press, Wellington, 1972. Australian

students still do not have the basic tools – scholarly histories, popular accounts and biographical works – with which to begin researching and assessing the first wave of feminist politics in this country.

9. Gertrude O'Connor, *Genesis of Women's Suffrage*, Typescript, Mitchell Library, QA920.7/L, June 1923, pp. 5, 6. Ms O'Connor is Louisa Lawson's daughter.

10. For accounts of the harassment Louisa Lawson suffered because of her championship of women workers in the printing trade, see J. Hagan, 'An incident at the *Dawn*', *Labour History*, no. 8, May 1965, pp. 19–21.

11. These graduates chose either to form small self-protective groups within the women's movement, as they did within the Sydney Women's Club, or they completely rejected any form of union in favour of individually striving to achieve their particular ends. Their fear of being labelled feminist, and perhaps jeopardizing their marriage chances, or reinforcing the frustrated spinster image, probably motivated this attitude. The difference between the feminists, few of whom had a tertiary education, and the university women, was illustrated by their contrary attitudes to Tennyson's 'The Princess', a poem about a college for women whose founders had vowed never to marry and who banned men from the premises. Quotations from this poem appeared frequently in the newspapers and in the speeches of Australian feminists, especially the following couplets:

'The woman's cause is man's; they rise and sink
Together, dwarfed or god-like, bond or free . . . '
(which was one of the mottoes of the Womanhood Suffrage League)
'For woman is not undeveloped man,
But diverse . . . '
The first women's club at the University of Melbourne was called the Princess Ida Club, the title taken from Gilbert and Sullivan's satire of the Tennyson poem. The Sydney women were more ambivalent, using one enigmatic line from the poem – the single word 'Together' – for their college bookplate.

12. Brief accounts of her life can be found in Sylvia Lawson, 'Edited, Printed and Published by Women', *Nation*, no. 3, 25 October 1958 and Sue Bellamy, 'The Dawn', *Mejane*, no. 1, March 1971. The *Bulletin*'s comment that, 'Despite all, Louisa Lawson is essentially a womanly woman, of a characteristically feminine type. Her nature is the groundwork of her son Henry's; but there is in him the additional element of restless male intensity . . . ' completely discounted the restless intensity which had enabled her to physically survive, bring up a family, engage in political activities and continue to write poetry in addition to bringing out a newspaper for seventeen years.

13. Louisa Lawson, 'A Poet's Mother', *Bulletin*, 24 October 1896.

14. In fact the majority of Australian suffragists were married or, like Rose Scott and Vida Goldstein, had refused several offers: 'Life is too short to waste on the admiration of one man . . . ' wrote Scott – and expressions of contempt for the male sex were rare.

15. cit. Biskup, *The Female Suffrage Movement in Australia*, op. cit., p. 92. My emphasis.

16. Womanhood Suffrage League of New South Wales, *Annual Report 1892*, p. 5.

17. Article on Rose Scott, Sydney *Daily Mirror*, 6 September 1972. The Factories and Shops Act of 1912 was introduced into the Legislative Assembly by Attorney-General W. A. Holman. Holman was a frequent visitor to Scott's salon.

18. J. E. Cobb, *The Women's Movement in New South Wales 1880–1914*, M.A. thesis, University of New England, 1967, pp. 70–71.

19. ibid., p. 228.

20. ibid., p. 112.

21. ibid., p. 193.

22. ibid., p. 205.

23. Keith Dunstan, *Wowsers*, Cassell, Melbourne, 1968, p. 37.

24. R.E.N. Twopeny, *Town Life in Australia*, Elliott Stock, London, 1883, p. 70.

25. Dunstan, op. cit., p. 43.

26. Isabel McCorkindale, ed., *Torchbearers*, WCTU, Adelaide, 1949, p. 20.

27. Dunstan, op. cit., p. 43.

28. ibid., p. 75.

29. McCorkindale, op. cit., p. 113.

30. cit. Biskup, *The Female Suffrage Movement in Australia*, p. 98.

31. 'A Citizen' who has no Vote, *Woman Suffrage: A Refutation and an Appeal*, Australian Christian World Publishing House, Sydney, n.d., (c. 1897), p. 5.

32. Dora Montefiore, *From a Victorian to a Modern*, E. Archer, London, 1927, pp. 30–31.

33. Similar rights were granted in other states as follows: Victoria – Marriage Act, 1912; Queensland – Guardianship and Custody of Infants Act, 1916; South Australia – Guardianship of Infants Act, 1887; Western Australia – Guardianship of Infants Act, 1920; Tasmania – Guardianship and Custody of Infants Act, 1934. Enid Campbell, 'The Legal Status of Women in Australia' in Norman MacKenzie, *Women in Australia*, op. cit., p. 418.

34. Rose Scott, *Address to the Feminist League*, Sydney, 12 April 1921, Typescript, Mitchell Library, AS75/2.

35. For example, Maybanke Anderson, *Woman's Suffrage in Australia*, August 1924, Typescript, Australian National Library, Ms. 3447.

36. Ibsen's play *A Doll's House*, whose passionate defence of the right of women to determine their own lives even at the expense of husband and children caused a furore when it was first produced in Europe, was staged in Sydney in 1890, six years after the first English production.

37. Cobb, op. cit., p. 92.

38. Women's Literary Society, *Programmes*, Mitchell Library, 374.23/W.

39. One of the weaknesses of the first feminist movement was its failure to develop a body of theory. John Stuart Mill's and Mary Wollstonecraft's books, and some

of the writings of Charlotte Perkins Gilman in the United States, constituted almost the total volume of theoretical writing. This was partly because feminists in most countries were too busy fighting identifiable wrongs to have much interest in what they regarded as mere exegesis. It was probably because few of the early feminists had had a university education that there was no group of intellectuals providing theory as there was in the socialist movement, but this lack of theory was undoubtedly one reason why feminism was not taken seriously by the labour movement. The principles and ideals which guided their fight can be discerned in articles they contributed to journals, and were expounded in pamphlets and manifestos but the purely theoretical accounts of women's oppression – attempts to articulate this oppression and relate it to a wider theory of revolutionary change – have all been written by socialists, viz: August Bebel, Charles Fourier, Alexandra Kollontai and, more recently, Simone de Beauvoir and Juliet Mitchell. It has only been with the development of Women's Liberation that some attempt to expound feminism as a serious theoretical position has been made, in for example, Shulamith Firestone, *The Dialectic of Sex*, Jonathan Cape, London, 1971.

40.   This franchise had been given in the following years: New South Wales – 1867; Queensland – 1878; South Australia – 1861; Tasmania – 1884; Victoria – 1863; Western Australia – 1876.

41.   Pamphlets from the Mitchell Library pamphlet file Q324.3/1.

42.   *Woman's Suffrage Journal*, Vol. 1, no. 6, 17 November 1891, p. 4.

43.   cit. O'Connor, op. cit., p. 6.

44.   Womanhood Suffrage League of New South Wales, *Annual Report 1892*, p. 5.

45.   The *Bulletin*, 9 March 1899.

46.   'A Citizen' who has no Vote, op. cit., p. 7.

47.   cit. Cobb, op. cit., p. 101.

48.   Alice C. Wilson, writing in the *Australian Woman's Sphere*, 10 June 1903.

49.   Between 1890 and 1910, when the Bill which raised the age of consent to sixteen and excluded girls under eighteen from working in brothels was finally passed, this single issue elicited more petitions to the New South Wales Parliament than any other issue apart from the Land Tax Bill.

50.   Florence Gordon had shown that the wages paid to dressmakers, the largest occupational group of women apart from domestic servants, were so low that 'the average payment of the trained hand is barely self-supporting . . . so low is the average wage paid to grown women that it is astonishing that parents consent to their daughters working at such payment, when it does not relieve their fathers of the burden of their support.' Florence Gordon, 'The Conditions of Female Labour and the Rates of Women's Wages in Sydney', the *Australian Economist*, 23 August 1894, pp. 425–6.

51.   Norman MacKenzie, 'Vida Goldstein: the Australian Suffragette', *Australian Journal of Politics and History*, November 1960, p. 203.

52   See Ms Harrison Lee, *One of Australia's Daughters*, H. J. Osborn, London, 1906.

53.   The *Woman Voter*, no. 1, August 1909.

54.   Rose Scott, *President's Address to the Women's Political Education League*, 1904, Mitchell Library, Q324.3W.

55.   Alice C. Wilson, op. cit.

56.   Rose Scott, *President's Address . . .* , op. cit.

57.   The *Woman Voter*, no. 1, August 1909.

58.   McCorkindale, op. cit., p. 31.

59.   Women received the right to take seats in Parliament in the following years: New South Wales – 1918 (Legislative Assembly) 1926 (Legislative Council); Queensland – 1915; Tasmania – 1921; Victoria – 1923; Western Australia – 1920. New Zealand's first franchise Bill did not allow for women to sit in Parliament.

60.   Jessie Ackerman, *Australia from a woman's point of view*, Cassell, London, 1913, p. 221. My emphasis.

61.   Vida Goldstein, 'Should women enter Parliament?', *Review of Reviews*, 20 August 1903, p. 136.

62.   See, for example, Tom Mann, *Socialism*, 'Tocsin' office, Melbourne, July 1905, pp. 35–6.

63.   The *Woman Voter*, no. 1, August 1909.

64.   Jill Johnston, *Lesbian Nation*, Simon & Schuster, New York, 1973, p. 80.

65   See Anne Summers, 'Marion/Bill Edwards', *Refractory Girl*, no. 5, Summer 1974, for an account of the woman of that name; and Hugh Buggy, 'The Woman who had Two Lives' in a magazine entitled *Daughters of Death*, Melbourne, n.d., which is sold in newsagents, for a rather sensationalist account of the life of female transvestite (and murderer) Eugene Falleni.

66.   Cobb, op. cit., p. 120.

67.   Cobb, op. cit., p. 381.

68.   cit. Rachel Cookson, *The Role of Certain Women and Women's Organizations in NSW and Victoria between 1900 and 1920*, M.A. thesis, University of Sydney, 1959, p. 64.

CHAPTER TWELVE

THE MOBILIZATION OF MUM

They sit and spin together, this fair united band,
Not to dispute on politics and laws,
But to sit and work each day, for dear lads far away,
Just spinning, spinning for the Cause.

National Leader, No. 9, 1916

The percentage of women out of work has never been as great as that of men in Victoria, nevertheless there are many women, particularly those between the ages of 18 and 25, and those over 40 years who require assistance . . . health problems amongst unemployed girls and women constitute one of the greatest difficulties. When serious ill-health or even minor illnesses are associated with bad housing and inadequate food, medical treatment becomes practically ineffective . . . Nervous and mental disorders are becoming more noticeable amongst the women . . .

Muriel Heagney, *Are Women Taking Men's Jobs?* 1935

Men have always endeavoured to restrict the field of women's employment and now that the war is over there is an effort being made to push women back into what is called 'her sphere of influence' – the home, its cares and its manifold duties – and thus ignoring the fact the majority of women who do work, work because it is an economic necessity. Women have been forced into a kind of 'blackleg' position in industry in that man has determined that they are inferior workers and therefore should be paid less. It is this exploitation of cheap labour, female labour, which, I believe, affects the position of the male. This is particularly evident in periods of depression when women are usually retained in jobs because their labour is cheaper. Hitler's cure for unemployment was to confine women's interests to the home. We have fought the bloodiest war in history to demonstrate the wrongs of Nazism, among them surely, the doctrine of women as

I would like to acknowledge the assistance of Mary Murnane in researching and writing this chapter and to thank her for contributing many valuable suggestions.

breeders of warriors. Women of the United Nations in this war have been
subject to conscription, service and death and have endured these things
as fellow citizens with the men. They have earned rights as citizens and
therefore their economic position should be no less secure.

Grace J. Cuthbert, 'Filling Australia's Empty Cradles' in W. D. Borrie,
A White Australia, 1947

The First World War did not provide an opportunity for Australian
women to step beyond their traditional roles. Unlike the situation in
Great Britain, there was no wide-scale mobilization of the civilian
population which would have enabled large numbers of women to
undertake occupations or engage in activities previously barred to their
sex. Instead, the Great War – as it came ironically to be called – had
the effect of cementing and consolidating the notion that women's
main social function was to bear children and to influence those
around them into dutiful civic submission. The war elevated the
God's Police role of women to semi-heroic status ensuring that it
became incorporated into that body of war-generated cultural canon
and mythology which was seen to be almost sacred, certainly unchal-
lengeable, for at least three decades.

For the first two years of the war, enlistment in the Armed Forces
was voluntary and pro- and anti-war forces both mounted determined
campaigns to try to influence able men's decisions about whether or
not they were going to fight. Women entered these campaigns with a
vigour and an assertiveness which probably had some source in their
still new status as fully enfranchised citizens. In each case, they invoked
their maternal status and responsibilities in their efforts to persuade
men to enlist, or to desist from participating, in the imperialist war.
Carmel Shute says of the effects of the war in Australia:

The mythology engendered by the Great War affirmed the dichotomy of
the sexes and re-established and enshrined the inviolability of the traditional
sexual stereotypes of man, 'the warrior and creator of history', and woman,
the mother, the passive flesh at the mercy of fate (or rather, man). The
nature of womanhood was stripped of any remaining pretence of emancipation and reduced to its quintessential biological function, that of maternity.
The battlefield, the new symbol of sexual definition in imperialist mores,
was proclaimed the sole preserve of man and thus while men went off to
war, to decide the fate of nations and to achieve 'fame, glory and manhood'
(and incidentally, death, injury and disease), it was the lot of modern
women, as it had been through history, to deliver up unconditionally to
the 'Moloch of War' the fruit of their wombs.[1]

The pro-war, and thus generally pro-enlistment, women maintained that the supreme sacrifice for women was to persuade the men they loved to go and fight for King and Country. As one woman, who signed herself 'Sister of Soldiers' when she wrote to a Brisbane newspaper in 1916, expressed it: ' Any right-minded woman would rather be the mother or sister of a dead hero than a living shirker . . . If we fail in our duty by wanting to keep our men at home then we do not deserve the name of British women.'[2] Women were encouraged in this attitude by the authorities and other pro-war forces. A 1917 issue of the *National Leader*, the organ of the Returned Soldiers' and Patriots' League of Queensland, carried an article which enthused:

The mother who gives her son in war is noble, sublime . . . the noblest thing on earth today . . . sometimes I go to the Coo-ee cafe and I chat to women who are suffering a noble martyrdom and my heart thrills with pride at a heroism that seems to me to be stupendously great. They tell me of their boys, of the letter they have had from them and I feel that I am breathing in an atmosphere cleansed by the spirit of a nobility that is sacred.[3]

FEMINISM AND PACIFISM

Anti-war women held similar assumptions about the centrality of motherhood in women's lives and of mothers' prerogative to try to influence their sons' actions. Adela Pankhurst and Cecilia John, two English suffragettes who came to Australia and became activists in the feminist and anti-war movements, used to sing the following song at anti-war rallies:

'I didn't raise my son to be a soldier
I brought him up to be my pride and joy,
Who dares to put a musket on his shoulder,
To kill some other mother's darling boy ?'[4]

The Government evidently found this particular form of exploiting maternal sentiments unpatriotic, and was doubtless perturbed by the great popularity of the song. It was banned under the powers of the 1915 War Precautions Act, but this authoritarian proscription was seen as a challenge by the singers of the song who defiantly sang it, and persuaded huge audiences to join in, whenever they had the opportunity.[5]

As argued in the preceding chapter, the Australian feminists' ideas and campaigns gave impetus and validation to the emerging orthodoxy that women's special social function was to nurture and influence the young through what were supposed to be their unique civilizing and moral proclivities. When war broke out, the feminist movement divided into pro- and anti-war factions but, because of their common assumptions about women's powers and responsibilities, were able to use similar arguments to support their differing conclusions. The fatuity of ascribing to women certain innate qualities and then using such ascriptions as the sole basis for political judgements was under-scored by this situation. The Victorian National Council of Women, a post-suffrage association of various women's groups, resolved in 1917 to discourage women and girls from playing tennis or any other kind of sport with eligible men who refused to serve[6], while the Women's Political Association, which Vida Goldstein had formed after the vote was given in Victoria and which had always been strongly pacifist, split on the issue of support for the war.[7] Goldstein then formed the Women's Peace Army which was militantly anti-war and which, despite continued police harassment and censorship of its newspaper the *Woman Voter*, formed branches in Sydney and Brisbane and did not cease its campaign for peace and against war.

Vida Goldstein, Adela Pankhurst, Cecilia John and the other members of the Women's Peace Army were brave and determined fighters who all endured abuse and insult and some of whom, once the anti-conscription campaign unfurled in all its vitriolic civil-war-like fury, were imprisoned for their fight against the war. Yet they did not appear to recognize the irony and the ultimate anti-feminism of their basic assumptions. Goldstein declaimed rhetorically, 'What can a boy think of the mother who teaches him one thing, and then countenances this legalized murder? The time has come when the women, the mothers of the world shall refuse to give their sons as material for shot and shell.'[8] Although she was a political radical on the issue of the war (and on many other issues), Goldstein and the other members of the Women's Peace Army were endorsing a con-servative, if not outright reactionary, view of women and their social functions. What feminism overtly sought was independence for women. I have already pointed out how most feminists' upholding of the structural inequalities of 'the family' (however much they sought to obtain legal equality and special protection where it was necessary for wives) contradicted this aim. The anti-war campaign made graphic a further contradiction between this aim and the upholding of the God's Police view of women's role.

What the God's Police view essentially maintains is that women actively uphold the *status quo*, that they instil its values in children and that they police adherence to it amongst the people with whom they are in contact. The *status quo* is not always easily identified or defined and since women are seldom given the social or political opportunities to participate in determining its social and ideological perimeters they must invariably accept what they consider to be an authoritative interpretation. Some women choose a particular religion, others a political party, yet others draw on their family's inherited values or upon a mixture of sources such as newspapers or other media. The latter is always a voice for already vested interests and so most newspapers never express anything but opposition to any political attitudes or actions which threaten the existing social and economic order. Whatever avenue they seek, women are in the position of accepting – often simply on faith – a set of values which they did not themselves help formulate and yet which they are expected to disseminate and ensure conformity to. They are always deputies and never commanders. The battle for their allegiance is thus a propaganda war in which existing authorities, and those aspiring to replace them, engage in contest to try and persuade the women who will be their faithful deputies that they deserve to wear the crown and that women owe them fidelity.

Given this fundamental disparity in the power of the sexes, what does it mean to apply the word 'radical' to women? Is a 'radical' woman one who is radical as a feminist, radical in relation to the position of her sex? Or can we call a woman 'radical' who merely accepts the values and gives her allegiance to a group or party which is against the existing *status quo*? Often an aspiring power will try to win women's allegiance by promising to give them a share in that power once they attain it. Labour and socialist parties particularly have often done this, have promised to give women greater equality or at least to institute certain specific reforms. Such promises are often made for strategic reasons rather than from a sincere desire to change the position of women and rarely are they fully honoured. Because of their powerlessness, women are never able to enforce the keeping of such promises and the crafty politician or party generally awards just those minor reforms which, it calculates, will prevent women from shifting their allegiance and will ensure thereby that its view of the world is disseminated by them and its political power consequently made more secure.

To maintain, as the Women's Peace Army was inclined to, that pacificism was a particularly female proclivity, was absurd in the face of the reality of large numbers of male pacifists and even larger numbers of female militarists. Australian feminists found themselves in the awkward and damaging situation of using the same arguments for different causes because they had not considered sufficiently how it is that women can be radicals for their sex. Vida Goldstein and several others were aware of the problem and had thought that by being non-party, by making their primary affiliation to feminism, that they could attain independence. This kind of opportunistic stance enabled the Australian feminists to attain many of the reforms they sought but, as I have already argued, it could not enable them to win any fundamental alterations to the sexist division of labour and power. It could not allow them to realize fully the ways in which sex oppression is linked to other kinds of oppression and exploitation. They had no concept of liberation. What they strove for was independence and equality for women but they failed to resolve the contradiction between independence for individuals – or for a sex – and the interdependence required to maintain a social existence.

Nor did they fully comprehend the implications of demanding equality for women within a society which has many other inequalities besides those of sex. Few political groups have ever been able to devise even preliminary solutions to these contradictions so it is not surprising that the Australian feminist movement was unable to grapple with them. The overwhelming middle-class composition of the movement, and its upholding of the dual sexist stereotypes, were probably mainly responsible for them not having to confront these contradictions before 1914. There was virtually no class conflict within the movement and where it did erupt it was a clash of ideas rather than a personal confrontation between people of different classes. So long as the feminists subscribed to the God's Police idea that certain kinds of women were superior – both to some other women, and to all men – and the accompanying moral precept that all women *ought* to be this way, then they did not have to cope with the reality of the heterogeneity of their sex.

The war shattered their political confidence and underscored the naivety of seeing women's oppression in isolation. But it also demonstrated women's powerlessness and the way in which the God's Police prescriptions perpetuate it. It was possible to see the war 'from a woman's point of view' and support or oppose it on sex-role related grounds, but such arguments were largely irrelevant to what was going on. Woman had little alternative except to attach their allegiance to a pro- or an anti-war group and act as deputies for that group. The only other alternative would have been to disavow the war altogether, to denounce it as a war between men which had nothing to do with women. But such a stance would have totally removed feminists from the political arena and would in any case have been virtually impossible to maintain since most women had male relatives or friends who were fighting and risking death or who were opposing the war and conscription and risking imprisonment. It is difficult to be detached when people close to you are in danger. Bodies like the Women's Peace Army or, on the other side, the One Woman One Recruit League, might maintain an independent identity and organization but this could not obscure the fact that feminist aims had been pushed aside, that the feminists had been unable to make a connection between their struggle and this international occurrence. All they could resort to was the God's Police role: to singing 'I didn't raise my son to be a soldier'. They were forced to retreat – and found themselves affirming the same attitudes about women's sphere of influence as their opponents. The chance of formulating a truly radical feminism, which could have entailed as a first step refusing to accept the God's Police role, had been lost.

SEXISM IN THE WAR EFFORT

A strong sexual demarcation of permitted war efforts was maintained and when various groups of enthusiastic women militarists sought to translate their pro-war attitudes into concrete preparations for fighting, they were either scorned or firmly dissuaded. Even though women formed an enormous number of voluntary agencies to service soldiers – both those returned and still fighting – with the exception of the Red Cross and the nursing corps they were not permitted to adopt a uniform.[9] Carmel Shute describes the attempts of some women to be active beyond the sock-knitting front: The Australian Lady Volunteers which formed in Sydney early in the war 'aimed to enrol one thousand "efficient" girls who were to train to become "real rifle women and real soldiers under expert tuition" '[10] but they were not permitted to do more than welfare work. The Australian Women's Service Corps began in November 1916 and

its members repeatedly offered their services to the military as 'woman orderlies, woman clerks, woman cooks, laundry workers, as woman ANYTHING' and were on every occasion refused with the admonishment that they should devote their energies to some more 'appropriate' cause and let the men get on with the real business of the war.[11]

Shute writes of how the principal medical officer of the Commonwealth forces in Victoria, Colonel Charles Ryan, considered that women were a nuisance on the battlefield – even when fulfilling a truly female role such as nursing – and said that 'the average woman could do far greater service for her country by making bandages, pyjamas, warm clothing for the men, and by keeping within their own sphere to the best of her knowledge and ability.'[12]

While men fought the war, women were expected to maintain the home front and this phrase was interpreted very literally. The frustration at not being able to do more must have caused some of the zealous female patriots to feel at least a little impatience at the limitations imposed by their sex but all that they could do was to redirect their zealousness. The most obvious avenue, and the one that received positive social sanction, was the home. Women had already learnt to see motherhood as a vocation; now, in an effort to accumulate a little glory to reward themselves for four years of waiting, anguish and deprivation, they seized upon homemaking – a rather wider vocation than motherhood – and bestowed upon its mundane labour a spiritual quality.

Homemaking was more than housekeeping: it was the creation of a microcosmic world from which could radiate the love, devotion and labour which the woman poured into it. Complementing perfectly the God's Police prescription to instil civic values in those around her, the homemaker could create a physical and spiritual retreat from the outside world. This world was symbolized by the hearth, the warmth around which a family clustered in order to escape the cold outside and to forget the horrors of the war. Ethel Turner, author of *Seven Little Australians* and many other books which made her a popular and much-read writer, endorsed this notion in the introduction to a war-time book which was designed to raise money to aid returning soldiers:

The Voluntary Workers are men and women who have discovered a very great and very simple truth, viz., that the best stone in the entire structure of civilization is the hearthstone. Seized of this truth they have joined forces to see that the most deserving men of the community, the soldiers who are fighting for our existence, do not go short of one of their very own.[13]

The view of woman as homemaker was a readily acceptable one, to women themselves (who had little else they could do and had thus to make a virtue of necessity), but also to ordinary men (who had something to come home to) and to the men in power who could, at absolutely no cost to that power, bestow their blessing upon these women who so eagerly collaborated in their powerless situation. They could easily endow it with a semblance of power by disseminating such homilies as 'the hand that rocks the cradle rules the world' – a patent untruth as my analysis of the intrinsic powerlessness of the God's Police role has attempted to show. If women could be persuaded to place credence in such aphorisms, and the fact that they cleaved so neatly with the feminist view of women's special qualities ensured that *those* potential dissidents would be pacified, then any rumblings of female rebellion were unlikely to erupt into a potent challenge to the sexual division of labour and power. It was a cruel and a cheap way to buy women's compliance.

They were given none of the rewards which the men who went to war received. Those rewards were seldom as munificent as the promises made to enlisting soldiers during frenetic recruiting campaigns, and many returned to poverty, permanent disability and social uselessness. But all were given access to a heroic status which was permanently enshrined, not just in war memorials all around the country, but in a national day of remembrance and, as the memories of the realities of battle receded further and further, of braggadocio. Women were given nothing. They were prevented from fighting, or from doing more than extending their domestic skills from the home to the war effort, and so there was supposedly nothing for them to remember or to celebrate. *Their* contribution to the war, and *their* sufferings – especially the agony of going through casualty lists – were not considered comparable to the efforts of enlisted men.

The work that women did, the money raised, the voluntary soldier service organizations they operated mostly went unrewarded. Some women did an enormous amount of physical work as their contribution to the war effort: one Sydney woman, for instance, knitted 600 pairs of socks and sent a personal message with each pair as she despatched them.[14] But such efforts were rarely acknowledged. It was what was expected of women. And even when they did receive official acknowledgement, it was generally a lower order than that which men were awarded. The Order of the British Empire system of honours had been established in 1917; the following year it was divided into military and civil divisions. The latter had six rankings for civilian war effort but when the first list of honours was published most of those women whose work for Red Cross and similar bodies was acknowledged were concentrated in the lower rankings.[15]

Although Anzac Day is purportedly for service women as well as men, the First World War did not allow Australian women to serve in the only way which was recognized as important, and so for two decades it was solely a male affair. In that time it accumulated a mystique which was so identified with what men did that even when, during World War Two, thousands of women were mobilized into active service and hence theoretically received the right to regard Anzac Day as theirs too, they could never be seen as anything more than intruders – or else as irrelevant. The women who patriotically battled on at home during World War One were given nothing. Not even thanks. After 1918 what else could women do but fervently affirm the role and the work that they had no option but to accept?

THE 1920s: GENERATION OF HOMEMAKERS

During the 1920s women were visible mostly in connection with their efforts to perfect the role of homemaker. Early in the decade Housewives' Associations were formed in all states. Their function was explained by Ms Polkinghorne, President of the South Australian Association:

There is . . . one striking difference between the Housewives' Association and other amalgamations. The housewives do not (as well they might) agitate for higher wages or shorter hours. The old saying that 'women's work is never done' is as true now as ever it was, and, as for wages, well, they are still non-existent. No, we have to admit that this organization, now quite a power throughout the Commonwealth, is out purely for the good of the community at large, to protect first the sanctity of the home, and after that to fight the consumer's battle against wrong conditions. And we are all consumers.[16]

The Country Women's Association was formed after a meeting in Sydney in April 1922.[17] The meeting, which was organized by Robert McMillan of the *Stock and Station Journal* and Florence Gordon, editor of its women's page, decided to form an organization which 'pledged to break through the wall of isolation that hemmed in so many women'. Later that year a similar body was formed in Queensland, in Western Australia in 1924, South Australia in 1926 and Victoria in 1928. (The Tasmanian branch was established in 1936 while the Northern Territory's Country Women of the Air was not set up until 1953. The CWA of Australia organized itself as a federation in 1945.)

More women were now housewives than at any time earlier this century. Although the percentage of women workers in relation to the total workforce had remained static since 1901, in 1921 a smaller percentage of women were in employment as the following table sets out.

Women in the Workforce[18]

Year	1901	1911	1921
Percentage of women at work	30.7	28.5	26.7
Female workforce as % of total workforce	20.5	20.1	20.3
Married female workforce as % of total female workforce	n.a.	11.1	9.2
Percentage of married women at work	n.a.	6.1	4.4

In 1925 Ms Flora Mackay formed the Business and Professional Women's Club in Melbourne with the object of providing a link for girls who were beginning careers with women who were already established in different businesses and professions.[19] But while this infant association implicitly asserted women's right to work – or at least recognized that many women had to do so from necessity – from other quarters came cries for women to stay at home. These pleas emerged in the debate about whether or not women should receive equal pay, and followers of this controversy were subjected to the strange spectacle of one-time feminists arguing a case which implied that women ought not to be employed. Florence Gordon who was quoted in the last chapter decrying the scandalously low wages of working girls, in 1923 was bemoaning the situation of single girls earning a wage high enough to bedeck themselves with finery while married men were unemployed. She supported the principle of equal pay in order to eradicate the practice of using women as cheap labour, which she saw as depriving men of jobs, but her reasoning was not based on the desire for wage justice for women. Rather, she saw female employment as

a serious menace to the race. While marriage itself offers less attraction, [since these young women would no longer be able to afford to adorn themselves with the latest fashions], the actual chance of marriage is lessened. There is less material prosperity for married people in the lower ranks of the industrial class, while there is greater hardship in bearing and rearing children, owing to the difficulty in obtaining domestic assistance.[20]

Gordon's fears that young women would not want to marry were unwarranted. The rate of marriage increased sharply in 1921 and continued to rise until 1928. Women began marrying at a younger age than in previous decades and the proportion of women remaining unmarried declined.[21] True, the hopes of traditionalists that after the war women would revert to having nineteenth century sized families were not to be fulfilled. The small Australian family of only two or three children had definitely become established as a norm. Quality, not quantity, had come to be seen as the most desirable state to strive for as women's maternal and domestic responsibilities could not be discharged adequately if they had to bear and raise large numbers of children. This view of 'the family' was, as we have already seen, one which the middle class had tried to promulgate to all sections of society during the early 1900s. The efforts of these reformers, who included many feminists, continued during the 1920s. But whereas before the war the feminists especially had concentrated on trying to improve the relationship between mother and child, their post-war efforts were more concerned with fighting for social changes which they believed would enable 'the family' as an institution to flourish, especially amongst economically or physically disadvantaged groups. The three major campaigns were concerned with preventing race degeneration, with fighting to have the sale of liquor prohibited, and with trying to have a child endowment scheme implemented. Each of these reforms, it was felt, would undermine or eradicate evils which were seen as threatening the stability, or even the very existence, of family life.

SPREADING 'THE FAMILY'

In 1926 the Racial Hygiene Centre of New South Wales was formed and had as its objects 'the Teaching of Sex Hygiene and the Prevention and Eradication of Venereal Disease'.[22] The Centre was at first comprised entirely of women but at its second meeting, on 25 May 1926, it was resolved to try to interest men in joining and assisting with its proposed work. That work included honest and informative sex education lectures and films. One of the Centre's co-presidents, Ruby Rich, urged mothers to give their children correct sex information and 'no more sham and humbug, no fairy tales of cabbages and stories, no more cant and hypocrisy of life's development but simple Truth, which is not a menace but a safeguard . . . Remember Ignorance is not Innocence.'[23] The women printed leaflets about sex education and placed them in library books, thereby gaining a wide dissemination of their ideas. They wrote to all broadcasting stations and department stores asking to be allowed to advertise their aims and, in 1927, obtained the permission of the Teachers' Federation to speak to meetings of headmasters and headmistresses. But their beliefs also included eugenist notions about race improvement. The group had originally called itself the Race Improvement Society of New South Wales but at a public meeting held in June 1926 had adopted the less eugenist-sounding 'Racial Hygiene' name. At its first committee meeting, one woman had queried the use of the word 'eugenist' in the group's draft constitution but after some debate it was retained. Ruby Rich spoke at a Mother's Day service at Bourke Street Congregational Church of the need for racial hygiene: 'If sex education was spread and understood I think there would be considerably fewer of these cases [of "compulsory marriages"], and many mistakes would be eliminated. The trouble is partly due to alcoholism and partly to mental deficiency.'[24]

The Centre aimed to prevent both immorality and race degeneration by a combined policy of sex education and moral exhortation (to prevent young girls from being seduced or from wanting to experiment with sex), by trying to curb prostitution and the spread of venereal disease, and by urging that 'before the release of any prisoner, man or woman, guilty of sex aberrations, steps should be taken to prevent the said prisoners being a further menace to the public.'[25] They collected evidence of the relationship between venereal disease and mental disorder and estimated the cost to the community, in terms of maintaining mental asylums, of such disease. In order to try and curb its spread they urged that all immigrants should obtain medical certificates furnished by Australian doctors in England, and that similar certificates be obtained prior to marriage.

Their obsession with venereal disease was not merely a hangover from the war. As Chapter Ten pointed out, syphilis had reached near epidemic proportions in the immediate post-war years. Despite the efforts of health authorities and voluntary bodies such as Racial Hygiene it was not easily or quickly contained. In 1935 it was found that 10 per cent of all women who were confined in three public hospitals in Melbourne and Sydney had syphilis.[26] In May 1927 Sir Charles Rosenthal addressed the Sydney Legacy Club on the subject of V.D. and said that medical authorities estimated it to be directly or indirectly responsible for 80 to 90 per cent of lunacy and that the sum of half a million pounds annually that was needed to maintain New South Wales asylums was largely a consequence of the disease.[27] Within a short time, the Racial Hygiene Centre (later Association) had attracted a good deal of prestigious support. In June 1927 the Governor and his wife agreed to become Patron and Patroness of the organization and the Governor's wife, Lady de Chair, volunteered to approach the Minister of Education about showing the group's sex education films in schools.

A similar concern for the social and moral well-being of families inspired the various temperance groups to pursue their activities into the 1920s. A proposal to introduce early closing of hotels during the war had been widely supported by the general public and by the War Committee, the Minister for Defence, Federal Parliament and various other authorities. Legislation for six o'clock closing was enacted in Western Australia, South Australia, Victoria and Tasmania. This inspired some women's groups to urge total prohibition of the sale of liquor – at least for the duration of the war. They were not successful, but the introduction of Prohibition in the United States in 1920 gave impetus to the struggle for peace-time prohibition here and provided many women with an opportunity to pass an opinion on the effect of alcohol on the home. Ms Maybanke Anderson declared her voting intentions for a Prohibition plebiscite in terms of support for 'the family':

Emphatically, I must vote for Prohibition for the sake of the children of to-day, and for the future of the race; for the children – the ill-born and often deficient offspring of vice. One may see them everywhere – in mean streets, in fine homes, as well as in hospitals, where doctors and nurses will tell you that though statistics are impossible, they know that the greater part of their patients suffer because of the vice of their parents, and because of poor food and foolish clothing. The drunkard, father or mother, is seldom wise and careful.[28]

The demand that the State pay a child endowment was also motivated by a desire to uplift the conditions of family life by ensuring that children were adequately fed and clothed. The first system of child endowment in Australia was begun within the Commonwealth Public Service in November 1920 when, following the recommendations of the Royal Commission on the Basic Wage, an endowment of five shillings a week for each dependent child was paid to all officers who received a salary of £400 per annum or less.[29] In 1923 these allowances were confirmed as a permanent part of the salary scheme and the fund to meet them was created by deducting the average value of the payment from the basic wage of all officers. But this measure was of little use to the majority of the population who were not, or who were not married to, Commonwealth public servants. In June 1927 a Premier's Conference in Melbourne considered the question and then referred it to a Royal Commission appointed by the Commonwealth Government. The Commission filed two separate reports, a majority report (submitted by three Commissioners) claiming that such a scheme was 'both unnecessary and unjustifiable', and a minority report (submitted by two Commissioners, including the only woman) which argued that a child endowment scheme was 'the logical corollary of the living wage doctrine' and 'a measure of justice'. The Prime Minister told a Conference of Commonwealth and State Ministers in Canberra in May 1929 that the Government was not prepared to adopt a scheme financed entirely from the proceeds of taxation as recommended in the minority report; the Government agreed with the majority report that child endowment could not be separated from the control of the basic wage which was a power the Commonwealth did not possess and which the states were not prepared to relinquish. The Government did not, therefore, propose to establish an endowment scheme and the matter was left to the states.[30]

New South Wales was the only state to adopt a scheme; it had in fact already done so. The Family Endowment Act of 1927 allowed the amount of five shillings per child to be payable to all families with dependent children under fourteen years, subject to a means test.[31] The scheme was financed by a payroll tax and 'where practicable, the endowment is paid to the mother'.[32] Excluded from eligibility were most illegitimate children (in certain cases an exception would be made), also children whose fathers were aliens, Asiatics, or aboriginal natives of Africa, the Pacific Islands or New Zealand unless born in Australia, and children who received endowment from the Commonwealth scheme for its public servants or from the NSW Widows' Pension scheme. By 31 March 1928, 23,310 claims had been granted, 5,245 refused and 371 withdrawn.[33] Two years earlier the Widows' Pensions Act had provided for an endowment of one pound per week plus ten shillings for every dependent child under fourteen to widows in New South Wales. This was also subject to a means test and every claim had to be investigated by a police or stipendary magistrate. The scheme began from 10 March 1926, and by 30 June 1927 pensions were being paid to 5,449 widows and 11,654 children.[34]

All these reforms, whether they were achieved or still being sought, were designed to consolidate, improve and strengthen 'the family', especially among groups of people who were poor or who were considered to be disadvantaged in other ways. But, as the NSW Family Endowment scheme made brutally clear, they were *only* to be made to what were considered to be acceptable family groups. The single mother and her child were both excluded from assistance.

These campaigns recognized that not even the most ardent homemaker could keep her family together and be able to instil in them civic virtues if she had to contend with such uncontrollable forces as drunkenness, disabling disease or poverty. The so-called sinners – the anti-family forces – were not to be helped except, as in the case of venereal disease, where they were a potential social danger. They were to be either prevented from access to their crime, in the case of drink, or were to be punished with poverty as happened to single mothers. None of the campaigns had more than a token success in attaining the changes or reforms they sought but they were successful in drawing public attention to the ills they identified and were at least partly responsible for creating the heightened consciousness about the *quality* of family life which existed in the 1920s.

The 1920s in Australia did not produce a sexual revolution comparable to that which occurred in the United States or even in Great Britain. Certainly women shortened their skirts and bobbed their hair. Many took up cigarette smoking and danced the Charleston. They went unchaperoned to dances and had 'dates' with men they had no interest in marrying. But the 'jazz age' and all that that phrase implied for sexual emancipation in America never reached our shores. The wave of repression and Puritanism described in Chapter Ten was still very much in evidence.

The rate of 'shot-gun' marriages declined sharply in 1921 and although it began to rise again, by 1932 it had still not reached the pre-war level.[35] There was also a sharp decline in the birth-rate, as the following table shows, and although the general birth-rate dropped less sharply than the nuptial rate – suggesting that ex-nuptial births had far from disappeared – the figures are not high enough to imply that the renowned sexual emancipation of the American flapper was much in evidence in Australia.

Birth-rate in Australia 1880–1922[36]

Period	Births per 1000 women aged 15–44	Nuptial Births per 1000 married women aged 15–44
1880–82	170	321
1890–92	159	332
1900–02	117	235
1910–12	117	236
1920–22	107	197

It *could* be the case, perhaps, that single women in Australia were well equipped with contraceptive information and equipment, but this seems unlikely. The dissemination of published sex information was not explicitly prohibited but the moral orientation of the publication seems to have determined whether or not it was allowed distribution. Farmers' Department store in Sydney had refused to display material from the Racial Hygiene Centre[37], but generally this body had little trouble in distributing its pamphlets. This was undoubtedly because it advocated chastity for both sexes and countenanced the use of contraceptives for married couples only. Other publications which dared suggest that sexuality was something to enjoy, and that *this* criterion was important when choosing a contraception method, were far less likely to reach a wide audience. A pamphlet called *Parenthood Controlled* written and published by a Ms S. J. Marsden in Melbourne in 1923 had to be privately circulated. Ms Marsden was an enthusiastic promoter of the female orgasm as well as of birth control methods and products. Her pamphlet contained a catalogue of contraceptives for both women and men which could be purchased by mail order and she gave an address to which readers could write to her for further information about sexual and contraceptive techniques. She explained in detail how a husband could delay his orgasm so that his wife could enjoy satisfaction as well, and she roundly denounced the 'coitus interruptus' method of birth control because 'unless the woman has reached the culminating point before the withdrawal she is left in a disappointed, nervous state, which leads to irritation and lack of sexual desire.'[38]

Such views were articulated rarely however for they could be construed as undermining the dualistic view of women as either mothers or whores. Australia in the 1920s was not willing to accept a blurring of the distinction, and to acknowledge the sexuality of women implicitly challenged the view that motherhood was a totally fulfilling vocation. The war had re-emphasized the traditional division of labour between the sexes as it is enshrined in the bourgeois family and, with the inability of feminism to convert the gains it had made in the early 1900s into a challenge to the sexist *status quo*, had provided further justification for that division. Daring views such as Marsden's were disturbing for they undermined a fundamental tenet of that division and their dissemination was not encouraged.

Although there were variations to some of the patterns of family and marriage considered usual in the nineteenth century, by the end of the 1920s the basic structure of 'the family' was unchanged and had evidently become stronger and more widespread. Divorce began to increase after 1921 as the following table shows, but although the *number* of divorces rose substantially in 1921, there had been an even larger increase in the number of marriages, so the actual divorce rate had risen only slightly.

Divorce Rate in Australia 1891–1936[39]

1891	8.0	Divorces per 1000 existing marriages
1901	14.4	Divorces per 1000 existing marriages
1911	13.1	Divorces per 1000 existing marriages
1921	32.0	Divorces per 1000 existing marriages
1931	50.3	Divorces per 1000 existing marriages
1936	42.9	Divorces per 1000 existing marriages

In 1911 there were 0.1 divorces per thousand of population and by 1921 this had only risen to 0.3 so that fewer than one in a thousand people were divorced.[40] According to the 1921 Census, there were 4,298 women and 4,230 men described as divorcees[41] – fewer than 10,000 people in a population of almost five and a half million. It was impossible to see this divorce rate as threatening marriage and 'the family' while the marriage rate continued to rise and while many divorcees tended to re-marry.

THE DEPRESSION: MYTHS ABOUT MEN AND REALITIES FOR WOMEN

The 1930s were the years of the Depression. My generation, born during the next decade, has been presented with a collection of cultural lore about this time of great economic catastrophe. We have received images of thousands out of work, often for years, forced to beg and steal while trying to eke out an existence on the dole, their psyches seared forever with a 'Depression mentality' which led them to value the certainties and securities of a steady job and close family bonds. However, the images which have been handed down convey almost exclusively the male experience of the Depression; we have been told little about what it was like for women during the 1930s. None of the folklore tells us whether women's experience of the Depression differed from men's and, if so, how. Nor do we know if women have inherited a different 'Depression mentality'.

Most historians of the Depression do not mention women. One account, for instance, states:

In the 1930s, even more than today, Australia was culturally and ethnically homogeneous; there were not – at least by international standards – profound divisions of religion, wealth or opportunity. The effects of the Depression were widespread, and to some extent indiscriminate: many businessmen, professionals and farmers lost their incomes; not all the unemployed were unionists. To the extent that the Depression was seen as an external calamity, a visitation from outside – and it *was* thus commonly portrayed – then it may have acted as a unifying rather than as a divisive influence. Instead of setting class against class, it may have made Australians aware of their common nationality, or desperateness. In any case, it seems likely that the fact that the calamity was shared tended to mute rather than exacerbate class antagonisms.[42]

The authors do not think to consider whether sex antagonisms were created, or exacerbated, by the Depression. In looking at some of the consequences of the Depression, Gollan writes:

For governments of all persuasions the Depression became a nightmare which must not be permitted to recur. Public policy must be directed towards this end and, in the thirty years following the Depression, one of the main criteria on which the performance of governments has been judged is the extent to which they have maintained a high level of employment.[43]

He does not inquire whether governments have found it politically necessary to maintain a high level of employment for women, nor does he consider what effects the Depression had on women's participation in the workforce. Russel Ward describes one aspect of the Depression: 'For a time nearly 30 per cent of breadwinners were unemployed. Thousands tramped the bush roads again with swag and billycan, often ready to work for their keep if only work of any kind could be found.'[44] He does not say if any, or how many, of those breadwinners were women and he does not specify that those who took to the roads were all men, although his footnote describing a swag as 'a bushman's rolled-up bundle of belongings' certainly implies this.

These recent historical accounts of the Depression have served to perpetuate myths and to obscure realities. Women's experience of the Depression differed from men's in several fundamental ways. They had to endure several particular forms of suffering or deprivation which were a consequence of being female. They did not have access to the same range of compensations or escapes which enabled men to forget temporarily the devastation around them; and those who were married were expected to summon up resources to try to alleviate the physical and psychological distress of their husbands and families in ways which were rarely expected of men.

The main image we have of the Depression is of thousands of (male) breadwinners out of work. Our knowledge of women's activities during this period is confined to the information provided by census reports and one or two books, and so it is not possible to postulate theories with great certainty. But it does seem to have been the case that, in the two most populous states at least, the employment of women actually *increased* during the Depression. The 1933 census revealed that since the previous census in 1921 the total number of male breadwinners in Australia had increased by 15.4 per cent whereas the total number of *female* breadwinners had risen by a massive 27.9 per cent.[45] The figures for Victoria showed that the percentage of female breadwinners had increased by 2 per cent since 1921 and that there had been a similar decline in the percentage of female dependents; there was an exact reversal of this position in the figures for male breadwinners and dependents.[46] The figures for all occupations in Australia showed that the proportion of women to the total number of persons employed in various occupational groups had increased in almost all groups, with the largest increases being in transport and communication (an increase of 63 per cent), commerce and finance (56 per cent) and in public administration and professional occupations (28 per cent).[47]

While these figures for the twelve-year intercensal period do not reflect rises and falls in employment, and could therefore be seen as applying mainly to the increased entry of single women into the work-force during the 1920s and not reflecting a rise in women's employment during the critical Depression years 1931 to 1933, this possibility seems unlikely for several reasons.

Throughout the Depression the percentage of female breadwinners who were unemployed was far smaller than the corresponding percentage of men. In 1933 for instance, 24 9 per cent of male workers were recorded as being unemployed compared to only 14.7 per cent of female workers.[48] Moreover, the duration of women's unemployment tended to be shorter which suggests that it was easier for them to obtain work. The reason for women being able to find jobs while large numbers of men were out of work lies in the by then well-entrenched sex-demarcated division of work and remuneration obtaining in the Australian workforce. Unemployment during the Depression was greatest in the areas of manufacturing, heavy construction and building. Women were totally excluded from the last two occupations and so were not subjected to the vagaries of those sectors of the economy. They were employed in manufacturing but mainly in the production of textiles and light consumer goods. These areas suffered a great decline in the first year of the Depression but an increase in tariff protection and the 1931 devaluation produced increased demand and re-opened employment opportunities in what were female-intensive manufacturing occupations. At the same time, other occupations which engaged large numbers of women workers, such as domestic service and public administration, did not produce wide-scale unemployment although in many cases wages were drastically reduced.

A further and equally cogent factor in explaining the lower rate of unemployment, and the possibility of increased employment opportunities for women, lay in the almost ubiquitous practice of paying women only a little over half the wages which could be demanded by men. These factors were all overlooked and instead unemployed men bitterly accused women of taking jobs which rightfully belonged to them. Muriel Heagney, a socialist and feminist who spent her life fighting for equal pay for women attempted to refute this accusation in her book *Are Women Taking Men's Jobs*? which was published in 1935. Her main argument was that it was the tardiness of unions in supporting equal pay which had produced the situation of women being kept on while men lost their jobs. She pointed out that the Clothing Trade Union's claim for an equal basic wage in 1926 was refused by Judge Drake-Brockman who set the female basic wage at a little less than 55 per cent of the male wage.[49] Other applications for equal pay during the 1920s generally had a similar result. The only exception was one section of the metal trades industry. In 1925 a Victorian firm, H. V. McKay, had introduced girls to work on small cores and on nut and bolt machines; the men working at the firm threatened to strike against this encroachment of cheap labour. Both employer and employees agreed to have the matter subjected to a Government investigation and in 1927 the Minister for Labour appointed a special committee of women, which included Heagney, to look at the question of the employment of women in the iron, steel and other industries at the works of H. V. McKay. The committee recommended certain safety features and a male rate of pay for all operations. This was accepted by the firm and by the male employees.[50] Despite this finding, however, equal pay was not granted to women in other areas of the metal trades industries.

The position Heagney chose to argue in her book was a difficult one – especially during an economic crisis. Many men were happy to support equal pay on trade union grounds, as they had at H. V. McKay, because it prevented the use of cheap labour and thus secured men's jobs. But Heagney believed in 'The right of every woman to economic independence . . . Every worker should enjoy the highest possible standard of living in her own right, and not merely share in the pleasures and comforts of life through the beneficence of her menfolk.'[51] Such an argument propelled her into outright confrontation with the sexist division of labour and all that it implied for the cultural and social traditions of Australian life. As had happened during the war, many feminists found it difficult to maintain their militancy in the face of great suffering being endured by men. Heagney was obviously reluctant to push her point too far, but the material she presented spoke for itself. It was not women's *fault* that because they had to work for 54 per cent of the male wage, many women still had jobs while men had to subsist on the dole. But nor would she concede that, even if equal pay existed in all occupations, women should necessarily step down from their jobs in periods of wide-spread male unemployment.

The issue of equal pay obscured then, as it still does today, the more fundamental question of women's right to work and right to economic self-sufficiency. This was the thorny path through which Heagney tried to steer her argument. Where equal pay was sought or opposed in the Arbitration Court, these considerations were never voiced. Most unions supported the principle – because they saw it as protecting men's jobs. It is less certain however whether most unionists saw it this way. For the male worker on low wages any decision for equal pay would be likely to have direct consequences in his own home; his wife and daughters might find jobs they would otherwise have rejected attractive for economic reasons, his own status as breadwinner would be eroded and the one area of his life where he had any power would be cut from under him.

The employers opposed equal pay, citing the judgement of Mr Justice Cullen in March 1913 who had stressed the lower physical strength of women which supposedly made them less productive and efficient and of inferior endurance; he had also pointed out that if equal pay were granted men would be employed in preference to women.[52] The employers of course did not mention such trivial considerations as the fact that they could often extract almost twice the productivity, as the experience of H. V. McKay had proved, for only half the cost. Their arguments were couched in terms which evoked a mute sympathy from many a basic-wage-earning male unionist, and even if equal pay were a union aim, no union ever took the kind of industrial action to fight for it that they would take to secure or improve men's jobs or wages and working conditions. What was really at issue in the discussion about equal pay, although it was rarely articulated in these terms, was whether relationships between the sexes should be premised on the traditional breadwinner/dependent arrangement where there was a clear division of labour, status and power based on sex, or whether a new form of relationship, based on the economic independence and freely chosen interdependence of each sex, should be permitted to evolve. But the early 1930s was not a good time to be proposing such radical changes even though it was largely the traditional division of labour, and the expectations it had created for and from each sex, which caused a great deal of misery. Both sexes were accustomed to seeing the male as breadwinner and one judge of manliness was whether or not a man could provide for his family. If a man were out of work and his family suffering because of it, he and those around him felt he had failed – as a husband, as a father, and as a man. Such a judgement was harsh and unrealistic since the unemployed men were mostly victims of economic processes they could in no way control. Nevertheless it was a prevalent one. Men felt shame and frustration if they could not find work and the family had to be supported by the earnings of a wife or daughter.

The Depression could have provided an occasion for rejecting the traditional means of dividing and judging people on their sex-role prescriptions. Instead, it tended to reinforce them.

The way unemployment relief and rations were distributed to men mirrored the basic wage concept of the man as breadwinner and, relegating his wife to half-person status, assumed her needs to be less. A single man received 5/10d worth of food rations a week in New South Wales in 1932; a married couple got only 9/5d, while a man with a wife and one child got 14/8d.[53] It was apparently calculated that while a man needed 5/10d worth of food, and a child 5/3d worth, a wife could get by on 3/7d worth. The allowable incomes per fortnight before the food rations were reduced assumed that double a single man's earnings would support three people: husband, wife and child. Rather than economic necessity forcing role-sharing or even swapping – which could have been a prelude to a questioning of their justice and utility – the men tended to wallow in their supposed personal failure. This was partly because women allowed them to. One woman, herself a breadwinner, and unemployed during the Depression, said:

I felt more sorry for the men, somehow. I found that men on the whole felt worse about things than women. For a man there was always the feeling of personal failure in losing his job even though it wasn't his fault. And all most of them wanted was a job and a chance to earn a living – not this humiliating charity.[54]

It was the by now deeply internalized God's Police view of women's role and responsibilities which led most women to disguise their own hardship and suffering, to pity the men's plight and to act as props for *their* fractured egos despite the additional burdens it endowed them with and the injustices it exposed.

UNEMPLOYMENT OF WOMEN

Historians' preoccupation with men's sufferings has meant that many economic injustices endured by women during the period have been totally ignored. Even though women were not threatened with unemployment to the same degree as men, there was still considerable female unemployment. Much of it was simply not recorded. Then, as now, unemployed women could drop from sight back into the home. Yet in certain occupations women were the first to be dismissed – again reflecting the widespread conviction that men must be bread-winners. The passing of the Married Women (Lecturers and Teachers) Act in New South Wales in 1932 led to the dismissal of about two hundred and twenty women from the permanent staff of the Depart-ment of Public Instruction[55], and from this time until the Act was repealed in 1947, women had to resign from the permanent teaching staff upon marriage. This Act, however, specifically allowed for the continuation of the practice of certain teachers' wives giving instruc-tion in needlework or domestic arts in fifth or sixth form schools. Their wages for this work were paid to their husbands. A Trade Union Women's Committee Report on Sustenance for Unemployed Women estimated that in 1930 there were between 5,000 and 6,000 unemployed women in Melbourne alone.[56] Yet unemployed women found that their eligibility for sustenance (unemployment relief) was more tenuous than men's. Rosalie Stephenson claims that single women were simply not eligible for the dole.[57] In Victoria, the one state for which detailed information exists, women discovered that their assumption that they would be eligible for sustenance was unfounded. The Trade Union Committee quoted above stated that in most muni-cipalities 'the bodies distributing sustenance are under the impression that provision for unemployed women is not their function.'[58] Women were shunted from municipal body to head office to charity organiza-tion to trade union before they received any assistance. In an attempt to alleviate the dire economic position of these unemployed women and to draw public attention to this injustice, Muriel Heagney and Ms G. C. Henderson organized a 'Girls' Week' fund in August 1930 which resulted in direct contributions of £5,000 in less than a month.[59] This facilitated the inauguration of the Unemployed Girls' Relief Movement (UGRM); it was to work in conjunction with the Minister

THE MOBILIZATION OF MUM | 449

of Sustenance and was organized by a committee consisting of six women and one man. Heagney acted as organizing secretary and handled all claims.

The UGRM set up twenty-one centres in Melbourne and in several large country towns, to which unemployed women could come and work in return for a small amount of money. Women living with their families or relatives could work one day a week at a sewing centre and received 7/6d; women living in lodgings were entitled to attend twice a week and were paid 12/6d. Women from families whose combined weekly income exceeded 20/- were ineligible. The women worked at sewing garments for unemployed families and produced an average of 4,000 items of clothing each week. Between 10,000 and 12,000 women attended the UGRM centres between their inception in August 1930 and July 1932. The movement received Government funding to pay the women's sustenance and to provide materials for the sewing centres but had to raise all other income itself; in May 1932 however, the Government began to meet the administrative costs of the centres as well. As well as maintaining these centres, the UGRM started a jam-making centre which during the first twenty-three months produced 163,120 lb of home-made jam. The UGRM also arranged employment for girls, ran post-primary courses to retrain women for employment as domestic servants and organized a great many fund-raising functions.[60] Heagney felt that their effort 'in building up a women's co-operative movement . . . is without parallel in Australia.'[61]

Despite its demonstrable success, the UGRM's life was short. The May 1932 state elections saw the Government ousted by the Nationalist Party and the new Minister for Sustenance (Wilfred Kent Hughes) was of the opinion that 'whilst domestic work was available at any wage, under any conditions anywhere in Victoria, the Government was not obliged to provide assistance for unemployed women.'[62] The types of houses where domestic service was still available generally imposed such a draconic order that few women were prepared to submit to it: they had no days off, were expected to give extra service and devotion during entertainments or sickness (for no extra wages) and usually had to endure intolerable loneliness and monotony. The new Government had little sympathy for such problems. Kent Hughes changed the name of the UGRM to 'Girls' Employment and Welfare Movement', sabotaged the old committee by creating an advisory board consisting of six men and five women, and displaced Heagney with a conservative member of a benevolent society whose only previous experience was honorary charity work. The sewing centres were closed and what was left of the UGRM was transferred to the Sustenance Department to the 'charge of a male clerk whose experience in pre-depression days comprised that of an obscure railway clerk.'[63] All the social services for women which had been fought for in 1930 were withdrawn by 1935, although the Government continued to accept a nominal responsibility for the employment of out-of-work girls – as domestic slaves. Whereas in 1931 one woman was claiming sustenance for every fourteen men, by 1935 the ratio was one woman to every one hundred and forty men.[64] The days of the dole for women were over.

In her book, which was written at this time, Heagney was defiant and determined. She argued that the day for philanthropic and unofficial handling of this problem was past, and that the Victorian Government must be forced to take responsibility for establishing a central organization to work for the welfare of unemployed women, and that such a body must be staffed by young women with business training and experience.[65] But there was little she could do, for she had virtually no support. She railed against the women's organizations of Victoria which, she felt, had betrayed the unemployed of their sex by their apathy and indifference to the changes in the Government's administration of relief.[66] Heagney was exceptionally astute in her analyses of the situation and the means needed to remedy it; few other feminists at the time, and certainly not the majority of women, would have agreed with her. Her ideas implicitly challenged the existing sex division of labour, and although some other women might have agreed in principle with her about women's right to economic independence, few were able or prepared to do much about it at a time like that. Most of them were too busy – helping their families survive or else engaged in voluntary relief work.

The Depression, like the Great War, provided an opportunity for women to 'help' others in distress and most of these women were either so busy or so self-congratulatory about their benevolence that they seldom had time to consider the political implications of what they were doing. Governments were prepared to endorse the efforts of women who gave unpaid labour to relieve the distress of others – especially if it involved helping their own sex – so long as their work did not involve a perceived threat to the existing social order.

In 1930 a group of Sydney Labor women who were alarmed at the number of unemployed girls sleeping in parks and doorways approached Premier Lang for help. He sent them to the Repossessed Buildings Commission and the women were given the use of part of the MLC Building on the corner of Martin Place and Elizabeth Street. They ran it for eight years as a hostel able to accommodate forty homeless women, without any further Government assistance.[67] (Just as, ninety-two years earlier, Governor Gipps had given Caroline Chisholm the use of a Government barracks to start her Female Immigrants' Home – see Chapter Nine.)

In most cases, the voluntary relief work done by women acting out of concern for their sex helped obscure glaring disparities and injustices in the entitlements of women in distress. They unwittingly collaborated in the perpetuation of these injustices by devoting their energies to trying to alleviate the symptoms of that distress, rather than fighting for social changes which might remove them. They responded to appeals in situations of crisis, agreeing to forget their long-term aims for the duration, not recognizing that it is the very disruption generated by such crises which often enables radical proposals to become palatable to people who in periods of stability would reject them.

Women's voluntary work invariably involves tasks which are identical to, or an extension of, the work they do as housewives and mothers: making clothes or food, arranging shelter and other basic needs, comforting people – or else fund-raising. None of these activities in any way challenges women's sex role prescriptions. The UGRM attempted to do so by insisting that all work should receive a wage but, at the same time, the nature of the work they provided and the post-primary courses they taught reinforced the sex *status quo*. They were in a dilemma: how could they provide enough work except by utilizing skills which all women would have, and what was the point of training girls for jobs for which they would never be accepted?

Had it survived longer, the UGRM might have been able to grapple with this dilemma but in its short life it probably had little effect on women's self-conceptions about their role in Australian society. The acquiescence or self-abnegation of most women meant that no challenge to the sex division of labour occurred during the Depression. This must often have involved a considerable amount of self-delusion since many women were in effect challenging it by holding a job while the traditional breadwinner was unemployed. Yet the implications of this situation were not pursued and the traditional conceptions of appropriate sex roles remained as forceful as ever, so that even when women experienced the same problems as men – unemployment and trying to obtain sustenance – their suffering was not seen as warranting equal treatment.

SPECIAL PROBLEMS FOR WOMEN

This also meant that many of the special problems women had to deal with – those arising from being women – barely surfaced to be acknowledged as part of the suffering of the Depression even though they must have affected nearly all family groups. Foremost among these problems was the urgent need to avoid unwanted pregnancies. In a time of threatened or actual unemployment and of large cuts in wages and salaries, all but the wealthy had to engage in penny-pinching. For large numbers of people, the struggle simply to survive was a relentless daily battle to find enough food, to be able to pay rents and replace worn-out clothing. There was no money for extras or luxuries. And in a period like the 1930s, even those who had sufficient food and money to enjoy a comfortable life were affected by the uncertainties of the future. It was not a propitious time for marrying, and to have babies seemed sheer foolhardiness.

There is evidence that some people delayed marrying. McCarthy notes that:

From 1928 . . . the probabilities of marriage began to decline; they rapidly reached their lowest point in 1931 after which they again rose, almost as rapidly, and regained their pre-Depression level by 1935 . . . The long-term effect of the Depression upon proportions [of men and women] never married . . . seems to have been virtually negligible.[68]

This delaying is readily explicable by the large numbers of young, single men unemployed; for them marriage was simply an impossibility unless they married a working woman and were prepared to begin married life as a dependant. To most Australian men this was unthinkable.

But married or not, the most urgent problem was to prevent pregnancy. This meant either abstaining from sexual relations, using contraception or, if this failed, trying to secure an abortion. The two most common methods of contraception used required the co-operation of the man, so it was his problem too. But if an abortion was needed, or even if the pregnancy was brought to term, it was the woman who ran all the risks. The father, married or not, was legally obliged to support the child; but it was the mother who would ensure it did not starve.

The Melbourne survey of the contraceptive habits of married women found that during the 1935–39 period (the earliest time span covered by the survey) only 46 per cent of all fecund married women were using any form of contraception; of these, over half used condoms or coitus interruptus while a further 12 per cent employed the unreliable rhythm method.[69] Only a few years before, in 1933–34, the birth-rate had plummeted to the lowest ever recorded level of 16.7 births per thousand population (compared with 25.0 births per thousand in 1920–22).[70] This low birth-rate is difficult to reconcile with the low use of contraceptives generally and the fact that over 40 per cent of users employed methods (withdrawal and rhythm) which are notorious for their unreliability. Admittedly, by 1935 the birth-rate had begun to rise again as the worst years of the Depression were over, but it was not until the post World War Two 'baby boom' that the rate ever approached anything like the 1920–22 level. Other explanations have to be sought to account for the low birth rate and the generally low use of contraceptives. It seems likely that large numbers of people were forced to abstain from sexual relations in order to avoid pregnancy.

Safe methods of contraception were not widely available. The Racial Hygiene Association ran a birth control clinic in Sydney and there was at least one in Melbourne, but these tended to play God in deciding who was eligible to receive the methods (diaphragms mainly) they dispensed. Ms Goodisson, a member of Racial Hygiene, in discussing the Sydney clinic, wrote:

We do not advertise indiscriminate Birth Control. We only help people to use the best methods. We consider that – (1) Hereditary Diseases, (2) Mental Deficiency on the part of one or other of the parents or their near relation; and (3) Want of finance to support any further children are justifiable reasons why Birth Control should be used.[71]

Needless to say, single women were not eligible to receive help from the clinic. Unfortunately, the Melbourne survey did not investigate the contraceptive habits of single women. Yet single women also contribute to the birth-rate, and the level of extra-nuptial births declined at about the same rate as nuptial births during the Depression. So it seems that single women, and those married women who did not fit the birth control clinics' criteria for eligibility, had to seek other means to prevent pregnancy.

Writing about the use, or failure to use, contraceptives among Australians, Dr Norman Haire pointed out that all kinds of home-made contraceptives were in use and also that there was no check on the sale and advertising of mechanical and chemical contraceptives even though many of these were either worthless or harmful.[72] He also pointed out that the safer devices available from more reputable clinics:

. . . are sold to the women [at a price] so high as to put it beyond the reach of a great many. Why a contraceptive pessary which can be sold at a clinic in England for 1s 6d should cost as much as 15s at one in Australia, I cannot understand. Chemists here charge as much as £1 1s for the same article . . . Actually it is manufactured in this country, and, even allowing for higher costs of labour and material, the prices charged here are extortionate.[73]

He was writing in 1943 but it is unlikely that the situation was very different a decade earlier; where safe and reputable birth control means are restricted, quackery and extortion generally flourish. The same is true of abortion, and it seems probable that a great many women were forced to go to backyard butchers, or else to induce abortions themselves, when they were unable to procure cheap and reliable contraceptives and when safe abortions were prohibited by the Crimes Act.

The high rates of maternal deaths and of still-births both suggest that abortion was widespread. Even Ms Goodisson was forced to admit that since the Racial Hygiene Clinic had opened they had begun to realize just how many women had undergone illegal operations.[74] In 1931–32 in New South Wales one in every 200 women confined died in childbirth while if the number of women who died after illegal abortions is included, the figure is one in every 180.[75] The following table shows just how greatly abortions contributed to maternal deaths in New South Wales during the 1930s:

Maternal Deaths[76]

Number of deaths

Period	Including Criminal Abortion		Excluding Criminal Abortion		Deaths from Criminal Abortion	
	Married Women	Single Women	Married Women	Single Women	Married Women	Single Women
1931–35	1,197	158	1,040	85	157	73
1936–40	1,040	125	892	60	148	65

Rate per 100 Live Births

Period	Including Criminal Abortion			Excluding Criminal Abortion		
	Married Women	Single Women	Total	Married Women	Single Women	Total
1931–35	5.60	14.08	6.03	4.87	7.57	5.00
1936–40	4.55	12.44	4.89	3.91	5.97	3.99

Between 1922 and 1936 the rate of maternal deaths increased but began to decrease in 1937.[77] It can be seen from the above table that single women – who would have experienced the most difficulty in obtaining contraceptives – died in far larger proportion to their rate of pregnancy as a result of abortions than did married women. The highest rate of deaths coincided with the Depression years and was most probably connected with the desperate need both married and single women felt to prevent at any cost – even their own lives – the bringing of another baby into a hungry and uncaring world.

The high number of still-births in this period could provide another indication of the extent of abortions, especially self-induced ones. Muriel Heagney had commented on how many unemployed women were suffering from malnutrition and other poverty-related forms of ill-health (see quote at beginning of this chapter) and undoubtedly the wives of many unemployed men were in a similar condition, and this could be one factor explaining the high rate of still-births. But it seems likely that abortion was also a factor. Women who attempt to abort themselves often manage to kill themselves, but they are equally likely to kill the foetus. It was not compulsory to register still-births in New South Wales until 1 April 1935 (much later in other states; for instance not until 1967 in Tasmania) and so reliable figures are only available from 1936 onwards. Between 1936 and 1940 28.71 in every 1000 births were still-born and of these, 5.10 per cent were to single mothers.[78] The ex-nuptial rate was in fact higher, with 34.45 in every 1000 births being still-born. It is also probable, especially before compulsory registration was introduced, that a proportion of ostensible still-births were actually instances of infanticide.

Whatever means they sought to prevent either conception or giving birth, women during the Depression had to shoulder a burden of anguish and often to risk, or lose, their lives in a form of suffering that men did not have to endure. The constant worry about becoming pregnant, and then of what to do if they did, and the effects it must have had on the psyches of these already overburdened women is probably impossible for us to imagine today. For men who were out of work and who thus felt they were failures as men, sex was one of the few areas left in which they could still assert their masculinity and, because they were not working, they had more free time to engage in sexual activities. For women anxious to try and prevent the total collapse of their husbands' masculine egos, yet at the same time in constant dread of another pregnancy, the anxiety must have been virtually intolerable. No wonder Heagney noticed that: 'Nervous and mental disorders are becoming more noticeable amongst the women at the Centres, and [that] several serious cases have occurred.'[79]

For as well as worrying about unwanted pregnancies, married women's workload during the Depression increased in commensurate proportions to the rise of male unemployment and its attendant shortages of food and other necessities. Whereas the arena of the traditional male role contracted once a man lost his job, his wife found the arena of hers expanding. This is one reason why women did not exploit the breakdown of the sex division of labour to press for permanent changes: they were just too busy trying to keep their families fed and clothed and their husbands from lapsing into total gloom and despair. Whereas the Depression precipitated one-third of Australian adult males into inactivity it called upon women to work harder and to exercise a resourcefulness as homemakers that had never before been required of them. One woman questioned about her experience of the Depression said, 'I believe the Depression was much harder on men than the women. We had to exert our ingenuity and all our powers to survive. The men just rotted, in soul-destroying idleness and frustration.'[80] The men might have to go out daily and scrounge food or firewood, but 'making ends meet' and keeping up family morale rested mainly with the women. In D'Arcy Niland's *Gold in the Streets* there is a description of the imaginative efforts of one housewife:

For months they lived on nothing in the way of meat but mince, and Costello praised his wife for the things she could do with it. He referred to it as the miracle of mince, and he said he would write to the Pope and put in an application to have her canonized on the strength of her ingenuity: What'll be for Tuesday, Liz? Relief-worker's turkey. And what for Thursday, just for a change? Dole man's chicken. And all the time it was mince: mince disguised and travelling to the mouth incognito, hashed, stewed, grilled, curried; back to front mince, upside down mince, mince croquettes, mince à la buggalugs, mince murphy, which owed its great success to its potato content; and much as they got fed up with mince in general, they would have been fed up a lot quicker if it hadn't been for Mrs Costello's way with it.[81]

Women went without so that their husbands could have a bit of tobacco, or enough for a few beers and perhaps a couple of sixpenny bets with the local SP. Premier Lang says of those years:

One community activity that didn't seem to have suffered much was horse-racing. Meetings lasted from early morning until dark and attracted big crowds and Randwick, Canterbury and Rosehill racecourses carried on as usual with the bookmakers appearing to have escaped the hardships common to most of their clients. So I decided to introduce a Winning Bets Tax based on bookmakers' turnover . . . [82]

These compensations were not much, but they provided a small escape route for unemployed men; they were able to get together at the pub and maintain some sort of cameraderie as an armour against capitulating to their individual despair.

The legends of the Depression accord the greatest quotient of suffering to men; they take no account of either the similar or the additional suffering which faced women, nor of the efforts women made to prevent men from feeling that they were failures. The God's Police role took on a more intensive and urgent cast during the Depression. Its essence had always been to maintain the *status quo*, primarily 'the family'. Now it had to do this while the traditional division of labour which was the basis of that institution had, at least temporarily, broken down. Women immured themselves from this reality and enhanced their efforts to maintain a semblance of 'the family's' traditional forms by insisting that their unemployed husbands still receive the benefits they were used to as breadwinners. Hence the sacrifices so the husband could still have his few beers. They suffered their own anxieties and deprivations in silence – which is one reason why they have never been recognized, applauded and incorporated into the lore of the Depression.

What took place during those years was a massive but mute mobilization of Australia's housewives to fight for the survival of the institution which gave them their special role in society. Its effect was to prevent the temporary collapse of the male breadwinner role from developing into a permanent erosion of the traditional sex division of labour. In this way women helped ensure that even during a period of economic turmoil some basic form of social cohesion was maintained and that any threat of widespread revolt against the political and economic order which had caused the Depression was contained.

Those married women who had paid jobs during the Depression probably did not see them as permanent, but merely as one further means of providing for their family's well-being. They were encouraged in this attitude by the *Australian Women's Weekly*, a revolutionary new publication in the area of women's magazines because of its use of colour and its topical news content, whose first issue appeared in 1933. It had declared:

There are plenty of papers that deal purely with social events. We deal with these also. But no other paper surveys the important field covered by women's organizations. There are powerful organizations in every State in the Commonwealth working to improve women's status. The work and problems of these organizations will be effectively dealt with in our columns.[83]

But this promising, almost pro-feminist, beginning did not last once the Depression receded and men resumed their traditional roles. In 1934 the Editor wrote: 'The partnership of man and woman is the real meaning of sex equality. It implies equality in two separate but inseparable spheres. To ask for anything more is to ask for sex abolition; a race of neuters, like working bees.'[84]

Those women's organizations which engaged in political activities directly connected with protecting their families' interests were encouraged. For instance in 1935 the Housewives' Progressive Association of New South Wales decided to fight the Federal Government's decision to ratify a new sugar agreement with sugar combines which involved a tax which made sugar a very expensive commodity. Urging women to boycott sugar until the price dropped, and pointing out that sugar consumption was much higher in Australia than any other country, the HPA recommended: 'Do not be a slave to the sugar habit. Cut your sugar bill in half or less. Eat honey, dried and fresh fruit. This is your fight – you pay the tax. Join us now, do not delay. 100,000 members speak louder than words to politicians.'[85] The same issue of the journal carried articles on bee-keeping and extolling the virtues of honey; the cooking page compiled a collection of recipes using honey as a sugar substitute. The Association's efforts against the Colonial Sugar Refinery received high praise from the *Womens' Weekly*.

Once the Depression was over, however, the magazine began to reinforce the old stereotype of woman as full-time and busy housewife. Andree Wright in her study of the *Women's Weekly*'s history described the change:

As the *Women's Weekly* had always been divided into sections – each under the control of a sub-editor – which had to be planned around advertising quotas, increased sales meant that more firms wished to advertise their products in the magazine, especially those wishing to make a direct appeal to homemakers with their household goods. Therefore the Homemaker's Section introduced in October 1934, expanded rapidly. It centred around homemaking advertisements, and articles on personal appearance, child care, cooking, knitting, sewing, interior furnishing, decorating, and other aspects of housekeeping. It catered for the woman who felt that she belonged at home. Children were regarded as a full time occupation, otherwise they grew into 'nervous, restless, irritable little beings simply because they are deprived of their mother's care and attention'. Such a mother would one day be punished for her negligence: 'The time comes when the mother craves for the love she has pushed aside, and who can say that which is the sadder – the almost motherless child, or the almost childless mother.' (*A.W.W.* 2 November 1935, p. 35, Homemaker's Section) Advertisements encouraged women to emphasize their femininity and wifely capabilities. They made feminine subservience and masculine dominance appear legitimate.[86]

THE MOBILIZATION OF WOMEN INTO ACTIVE SERVICE

After only a few years of this post-Depression drive to reassert the more restricted female role of homemaker, the outbreak of World War Two demanded a renewed mobilization of women. In 1941 the three armed forces all formed women's services and began to recruit women for active service. The RAAF was the first of the forces to employ women full-time on work formerly done by men, and the Women's Auxiliary Australian Air Force decided to recruit 20,000 women.[87] The Women's Royal Australian Naval Service and the Australian Women's Army Service were established and began recruiting shortly afterwards. The WRAAF provided women with the greatest scope of skilled employment, enabling them to work as aircraft mechanics, X-ray technicians, meteorological assistants, instrument repairers and at similar trades but all the services gave woman telegraphic operator and signalling and driving jobs as well as the more traditional female jobs involving cooking, cleaning and sewing.

The ranks and rates of pay for women in all services were fairly similar.[88] There was, however, a great disparity between the rates of pay and entitlements given to men and those awarded to women. Servicewomen received approximately 66 per cent of the male rate or, if under twenty-one years of age, only 57 per cent; under-age men enlisting in any of the forces were entitled to adult pay from the start. Both men and women received similar entitlements in the form of coupons, clothing and free medical and dental treatment. But single men were entitled to claim a dependant's allowance if they had someone dependent on them, whereas women – married or single – who had dependants, were unable to claim such an allowance.[89] A further instance of discrimination was the double standard applied to the sexual behaviour of male and female service personnel. Unless a servicewoman who got pregnant was able to procure a quick and safe abortion, and thus prevent the authorities from discovering her condition, she was dishonourably discharged. Commenting on this, one woman character in the war-time novel, *Come in Spinner*, expostulated, 'I can never see why, when they regard V.D. as an occupational disease for men in the army, they shouldn't regard pregnancy for servicewomen in the same light.'[90]

Between 1939 and 1941 the war was something most Australian women could ignore: the more patriotically inclined could enlist in one of the services but a war in Europe did little to impinge on the daily lives of those who had no sons, fathers or brothers in the AIF. In December 1941 the Japanese assault on Pearl Harbour and, one month later, its invasion of the Malay peninsula dramatically altered this. The possibility of an invasion of Australia existed and drastic measures were taken to put the country in a state of readiness. The National Security Act of January 1942 provided for the mobilization of all available labour, male and female, into the workforce and instituted a system of 'essential' and 'reserved' industries; all inessential industries and occupations were to be phased out and the Government was to control industry and production. These Manpower regulations decreed:

that the resources of man power and woman power in Australia shall be organized and applied in the best possible way to meet the requirements of the defence forces and the needs of industry in the production of munitions and maintenance of supplies and services essential to the life of the community.[91]

The Prime Minister, John Curtin, gave assurance that the mobilization of women into industry was only 'for the duration', that he would prevent the erosion of men's jobs by the encroachment of 'cheap female labour' and that all women occupying what were traditionally 'men's jobs' would be replaced by men as soon as possible.

A Women's Employment Board was set up in April under the National Security Regulations and its job was to regulate the wages of women working in jobs previously undertaken by men, or jobs which had not been done before and for which there was no award wage. The mass movement of women into industry had created great confusion about what wages they should be paid: those working in traditionally female jobs, such as the clothing trade, still received the pre-war 54 per cent of the male basic wage, but unions feared the undermining of male wages if women in men's jobs received so little. Many unions pressed for equal pay in these industries in order to safeguard the jobs (and the higher wages) for men. The Women's

Employment Board's first judgment awarded women in some sections of the metal trades 60 per cent of the male rate for the first month and 90 per cent thereafter, and provided for juveniles to receive equal pay.[92]

But the Board's functioning was disrupted by the Opposition which used its majority in the Senate to disallow the regulations which established the Board; and by the Associated Chamber of Manufactures which refused to send a representative to the Board, claiming that it violated the principles of the Arbitration Court. After a protracted political struggle between these three bodies the Government threatened to dissolve both Houses of Parliament unless the Women's Employment Bill which reconstituted the Board was passed.[93] The Board eventually had jurisdiction over about seventy thousand women and most of them were awarded 90 per cent of the male rate in the occupation concerned, although in a few occupations – notably clerical work, tram conducting, car driving and certain retailing and manufacturing jobs – they received 100 per cent.[94]

Women were also induced to volunteer for the rural army. The Australian Women's Land Army, formed in October 1942, aimed at having 'a trained mobile force of 10,000 women rural workers'. The war in the Pacific and the arrival of American troops in Australia had led to shortages of food, especially of fruit, vegetables and beef. The Women's Land Army was employed in mixed farming, sheep, dairy and poultry work, growing asparagus, beet and other vegetables, on picking, pruning and spraying in orchards, in bee-keeping, flax- and tobacco-growing and driving tractors, trucks and other farm equipment. They were issued with uniforms, sent to a farm which was required to provide them with accommodation and they were subjected to discipline if they refused to accept a posting or went absent without leave.[95] The women were sent to do farmwork only but as they generally lived in with the farming family: '. . . it is often difficult for them to avoid doing part of the housework, which would not be expected of a man and which makes too great a burden.'[96]

As with World War One this war generated a large number of voluntary bodies in which women did unpaid work. This time, however, they were expected to do more than knit socks. Bodies like the Red Cross, the Country Women's Association, the Australian Comforts Fund and the Red Cross Letter Service may have continued the traditional forms of voluntary work, but other groups, such as the Women's Australian National Services, Women's Air Training Corps Air Raid Precautions, National Emergency Services and a host of others required women to acquire specific skills and to use them.

The Women's Australian National Services, for instance, had Aviation, Signalling, Civil and Quasi-Defence units; its members had to undergo training to reach the specified standards of their particular unit and once they qualified they were entitled to wear a uniform.

The extent and nature of women's participation in World War Two was radically different from anything which had been permitted to them before. By March 1944 there were 49,000 women in the Services and 3,000 in the Australian Women's Land Army.[97] The number of women in employment had risen by about 35 per cent from 644,000 in 1939 to 855,000 in 1944.[98] Just how many were engaged in voluntary work could probably not even be estimated. Women were doing men's jobs and were acquiring skills and earning high wages in a way that had never previously been open to them. Child-minding facilities were provided by specially trained corps from the Australian Women's National Service. Many women experienced a degree of freedom and mobility that was refreshingly new and even though it occurred within an overall atmosphere of anxiety and fear about those fighting overseas, and worry about how safe the country actually was from invasion, nevertheless those years gave a great many women a feeling of emancipation.

THE 'YANKEE INVASION'

Another factor contributing to this was the presence of large numbers of American servicemen in Australia. They were stationed, or sent on leave, to most cities and several large country towns. Their presence was referred to, often sarcastically or bitterly, as the 'Yankee invasion'. The Americans had plenty of money and access to a whole range of goods, such as cigarettes, chocolates, alcohol, nylon stockings and expensive and well-cut clothes, which the austerity measures imposed in Australia made scarce or impossible to obtain. Their free-spending meant that they received good service: taxis would ignore Australian servicemen if a bunch of Yanks hailed them, hotels would ensure a good table and the best food, they had their own all-night bars and clubs to which they could take guests, and even special brothels catering only for Americans. A great many Australian women, married and single, were literally swept off their feet by the Americans who treated them to dating and courtship rituals which were practically unheard of in Australia. The Americans could afford to, and did, buy the favour of Australian women with gifts of orchids, perfume, stockings, cigarettes and other rare commodities, but they also provided a style of entertainment and of flattering women which most Australian women had never before experienced. All this caused a great deal of bitterness and resentment amongst Australian men. Such gestures and compliments and protestations were regarded as unnecessary or even unmanly by most Australian men for whom the displaying of emotions was akin to running naked through the streets. Between ten and twelve thousand Australian women married American servicemen during the war[99] (compared with only about four thousand Australian servicemen who married while serving overseas), but a great many more had serious affairs or went along with them for 'a good time'.

Especially vulnerable to the charm and big-spending of the Yanks were young girls for whom the war did not mean emancipation but merely a form of slavery in factories. The Manpower Regulations empowered the Director General of Manpower to direct all unemployed persons to accept employment; and after the March 1942 nation-wide registration of all British subjects of both sexes over the age of sixteen, the Government had a record of all available persons in order to be able to determine the best deployment of workers. Later that year an order went out that all single women who were not gainfully employed and who refused to take jobs in essential industry or to enlist in the women's military or civilian services, were to be conscripted into essential employment.[100] In practice, the single girls most likely to be so conscripted were those poor or working-class girls who did not have fathers with the connections to get them an exemption. For the daughters of such influential men, the war years consisted of a whirl of parties with officers, with perhaps a few hours a week devoted to helping out at the Red Cross. But girls without such connections were subject to industrial conscription which meant being drafted into a form of work which had been impossible to fill with volunteers. Inevitably these were the dreariest of the traditional female jobs where the pay, especially for a juvenile, was a pittance, the hours were long and the work monotonous and enervating.

The Americans provided a wonderful opportunity to escape from all of this: a girl could shelter within the big-spending largesse, live from party to party and, especially if she was young and attractive, have no trouble in finding a bed to sleep in each night. Many girls engaged in a similar form of semi-prostitution to that which occurred, especially in Sydney, when the Americans came back during the Vietnam War. During the Second World War, however, there was the difference that Manpower authorities were on the alert for girls evading conscription and they were empowered to question girls seen with Americans, ask for their workcards and if these could not be produced, detain them. The girls were subjected to compulsory virginity and V.D. tests and if evidence was provided to suggest they had been prostituting themselves, they were sent to a reformatory. Kylie Tennant in her novel about war-time Sydney described the arrest of one such girl: 'She had had a wonderful life of orchids, expensive dresses, a fur coat, an engagement ring, presents and parties. Now it was reduced to "sexual intercourse", with a smell of pro-phylactics and clinics, blood-tests, talk of Wassermanns, slides and Sigh Phillis.'[101] The same situation occurred in *Come in Spinner* where it evinced an understanding response from an older woman: '. . . what do you expect a girl to do when she only gets a bit over a quid a week and pays ten bob for her room and can't even make a cuppa tea in it ?'[102]

HOW THE WAR AFFECTED WOMEN

Norman MacKenzie pointed out in 1962 that there had not been a comprehensive study of the contribution women made to the Australian war effort.[103] This is still so today. The information which does exist relates mainly to women in the services, especially those who performed work which was new to their sex or who endured internment or death while serving overseas.[104] There has been no detailed examination of the work and sufferings of women in civilian life; all that exists are cursory accounts of the number of women in industry, which are often accompanied by the implication that this experience changed their lives forever. Whether or not this was the case for a majority of women – it would certainly be true for some individuals – can only be guessed at. All we can do in the absence of more precise information is to examine some of the features of women's mobilization and the accompanying social, economic and cultural factors, and try to deduce their effect.

Of the 855,000 women in civilian employment, only about 70,000 were under the jurisdiction of the Women's Employment Board. This suggests that the vast majority of working women were employed in traditional female jobs (remembering the *raison d'être* of the Board) and would not therefore be earning a high wage. Nor would the work have been so exciting and stimulating as to enable them to see it as anything more than their war effort, certainly not something they would wish to continue after the war. One of the purposes of the Board was to replace women with male workers as soon as they became available, and so the more skilled and highly paid jobs which a lot of women had for four or five years could not be seen as permanent. Indeed it was a function of the Board to ensure that they were only temporary.

The birth-rate for both married and single women was only marginally higher during the war years than it had been during the 1930s. This is partly explicable by the fact that so many men were away and that many women would have been reluctant to bear babies during austere war-time conditions. But the low extra-nuptial birth-rate also suggests either that Australian women's dalliances with American servicemen were remarkably chaste or that contraceptive use and abortion were widespread. Norman Haire felt that in 1943 contraception was 'still regarded as something not quite respectable',[105] and that, to his knowledge, only two birth control clinics existed in the whole of the country. But, he said, 'abortion flourishes to a surprising and alarming extent.'[106] The war-time novels mentioned earlier were both written by women and both dealt with abortion, and it seems likely that Australian women resorted to abortion in large numbers in order to destroy the consequences of their war-time affairs.

As the war was ending, old ideas about what was appropriate for women began to be reasserted. In 1943 Curtin had said in the *Women's Weekly* in an interview about women's war-time role: 'The home remains her citadel, but the factory and the workshop have become her arena.'[107] He said that he expected that when the war was over 'most women will ultimately be absorbed into the home.'[108] The *Women's Weekly* itself began to prepare its readers (by now over half a million of them), for the post-war period when 'the normal way of life' would be resumed. In 1945 it expressed delight that the serviceman's 'riches are being restored to him – children's laughter and the sight of a small sleepy head upon a pillow – an armchair by the fire and clean sheets – tea in the kitchen and a woman's tenderness no longer edged by unspoken fears.'[109]

Women were being demobbed. Whether they wanted to or not, they were expected to return, not just to civilian life – for few had left it – but to the pre-war division of labour and status and power. Those women who tried to retain their war-time jobs, or to use the skills they had acquired in some related job, were expected to make way for returning ex-servicemen. A group of women in Melbourne who had been transport drivers during the war applied to the Melbourne City Council for licences to drive taxis but were refused on the grounds that all jobs were being made available to men who had served.[110] What women had done was not considered to be comparable. Many protested at being shunted back to the home but there was not sufficient organized resistance to reverse the process. To do so would have entailed a major restructuring of the economy and a direct challenge to the sex division of labour, for there were just not enough jobs to accommodate every person who had been mobilized during the war. But most women were as quiescent as they had always been. They were used to carrying out orders, to acting as deputies, and now that a new directive had come through, one that said 'populate or our nation will perish', most women obediently went back home and started having a baby.

The period between obtaining the vote and the end of World War Two had shown that women were active, resourceful and ingenious in a wide variety of occupations and situations. They could cope with economic depression and with war. Now they were being asked to cope with peace. That was proposed as being a return to 'normal'; but probably a great proportion of women, the younger ones especially, were uncertain what 'normal' was. Not knowing what was required of them, they had to seek guidance and there was no shortage of agencies willing to bombard them with prescriptive advice. The *Women's Weekly*, the Government, the churches, political parties, the returning soldiers, their own mothers – all dispensed guidance, and it all pointed in the one direction. Whether or not it could be reconciled with the hopes and dreams these women had acquired during the war became largely irrelevant for they were powerless to do any more than comply with this further prescription as to their roles.

NOTES

1. Carmel Shute, 'Heroines and Heroes: Sexual Mythology in Australia 1914–1918', *Hecate*, January 1975, p. 7.

2. cit. ibid., p. 9.

3. cit. ibid., p. 8.

4. cit. ibid., p. 12.

5. J. Harris, *The Bitter Fight*, University of Queensland Press, Brisbane, 1970, p. 236.

6. Shute, op. cit., p. 9.

7. Rachel Cookson, 'The Role of Certain Women and Women's Organizations in Politics in New South Wales and Victoria between 1900 and 1920', M.A. Thesis, University of Sydney, 1959, p. 41.

8. cit. Shute, p. 11.

9. Margaret Harland, *Woman's Place in Society*, Cheshire, Melbourne, 1947, p. 39.

10. Shute, op. cit., p. 14.
11. ibid.
12. ibid.
13. Ethel Turner and Bertram Stevens, eds, *The Australian Soldiers' Gift Book*, Voluntary Workers' Association, Sydney, n.d. (c. 1916), p. xiii.
14. Mrs Jamieson Williams and Mrs Andrew Holliday, eds, *Golden Records: Pathfinders of Women's Christian Temperance Union of N.S.W.*, John Sands, Sydney, 1926, p. 41.
15. This information was given to me by Dr Heather Radi, Department of History, University of Sydney.
16. The *Register*, (South Australia), 27 November 1928.
17. Norman MacKenzie, *Women in Australia*, Cheshire, Melbourne, 1962, p. 305. The following information about the CWA is all taken from this source.
18. Adapted from table compiled by Jean I. Martin and Catherine M. G. Richmond, 'Working Women in Australia' in *Anatomy of Australia*, H.R.H. The Duke of Edinburgh's Third Commonwealth Study Conference, Sun Books, Melbourne, 1968, p. 197.
19. Frances Fraser and Nettie Palmer, eds, *Centenary Gift Book*, Robertson & Mullens, Melbourne, 1934, p. 141.
20. Florence Gordon, 'Equal Pay for Equal Work: Effect on the Male Worker', The *Forum*, 19 December 1923, p. 4.
21. Peter F. McDonald, *Marriage in Australia: Age at first marriage and proportions marrying, 1860–1971*, Australian Family Formation Project, Monograph No. 2, Australian National University, Canberra, 1974, pp. 172, 184.
22. Racial Hygiene Association of Australia, *Minutes and Press-cuttings book*, 25 May 1926 – 31 October 1927. I would like to thank the Family Planning Association of New South Wales for kindly permitting me to examine these records.
23. ibid.
24. ibid.
25. ibid.
26. Constance M. D'Arcy, 'The Problem of Maternal Welfare', *Medical Journal of Australia*, 30 March 1935, p. 389. Regular Wassermann tests (to detect syphilis) were conducted on all parturient women at the Melbourne Women's Hospital, the Queen Victoria Hospital, Melbourne, and the Crown Street Women's Hospital, Sydney.
27. *Sydney Morning Herald*, 5 May 1927.
28. Maybanke Anderson, 'Women and the Drink Trade: In Favour of Prohibition', The *Forum*, 15 August 1923, p. 6.
29. *Official Year Book of the Commonwealth of Australia*, No. 29, 1938, p. 577.
30. ibid.
31. *Official Year Book of New South Wales 1927-28*, Sydney, 1929, p. 154.
32. ibid.

33. ibid., p. 155.

34. ibid., pp. 150–51.

35. *Official Year Book of the Commonwealth of Australia*, No. 26, 1933, p. 805.

36. *Official Year Book of the Commonwealth of Australia*, No. 58, 1972, p. 167.

37. Racial Hygiene Association of Australia, op. cit.

38. S. J. Marsden, *Parenthood Controlled: Methods of Birth Control Explained and Criticised*, Private circulation only, n.p., n.d., (Melbourne, 1923).

39. Adapted from Lincoln Day, 'Divorce' in A. F. Davies and S. Encel, eds, *Australian Society: A Sociological Introduction*, Cheshire, Melbourne, 1965, p. 171.

40. ibid., p. 170.

41. *Official Year Book of the Commonwealth of Australia*, No. 24, 1923, p. 948.

42. Don Aitken, Michael Kahan and Sue Barnes, 'What happened to the depression generation?' in Robert Cooksey, ed., *The Great Depression*, (*Labour History* No. 17), Australian Society for the Study of Labour History, Canberra, 1970, p. 179, original emphasis.

43. Robin Gollan, 'Some consequences of the Depression', in Cooksey, op. cit., p. 182.

44. Russel Ward, *Australia*, Ure Smith, Sydney, 1967, p. 139.

45. *Official Year Book of the Commonwealth of Australia*, No. 28, 1935, p. 550.

46. Victorian Census figures, taken from Muriel Heagney, *Are Women Taking Men's Jobs? A Survey of Women's Work in Victoria with special regard to Equal Status, Equal Pay and Equal Opportunity*, Milton and Veitch, Melbourne, 1935, p. 16.

47. *Official Year Book of the Commonwealth of Australia*, No. 28, 1935, p. 550.

48. ibid., p. 552.

49. Heagney, op. cit., pp. 34–5.

50. ibid., pp. 59–62. It is worth considering why the firm decided to employ girls in the first place. The employers contended that they intended to give the girls equal wages, as they expected production to increase with this changed employment policy. The work involved was extremely repetitive and boring, and boys previously engaged on the job had shown little interest in doing it: they were inattentive and uninterested and this led to a drop in production. The first female employees increased productivity by over 60 per cent by their application to the work. No doubt the high wage provided an incentive to work hard to keep the job, but it is probably also an early instance of the now common practice of employing women to do dreary and monotonous process work which men will not do.

51. ibid., p. 34.

52. ibid., p. 76.

53. F. A. Bland, 'A Note on Unemployment Relief in New South Wales', *Economic Record*, May 1932, p. 100.

54. Caddie, *Autobiography of a Sydney Barmaid*, Sun Books, Melbourne, 1966, p. 148.

55. Bruce Mitchell, 'The New South Wales Teachers' Federation', in Cooksey, op. cit., p. 68.

56. cit. Heagney, op. cit., p. 114.

57. Rosalie Stephenson, *Women in Australian Society*, Heinemann, Melbourne, 1970, p. 28.

58. cit. Heagney, op. cit., p. 115.

59. ibid., p. 110.

60. *Report on Relief of Unemployed Girls . . . August 1930 – July 1932*, incorporated in Heagney, op. cit., pp. 116–124.

61. ibid., p. 121.

62. cit. Heagney, p. 111.

63. ibid.

64. ibid.

65. ibid., p. 114.

66. ibid., p. 112.

67. Ruby Keating, 'A Note', *Golden Jubilee Souvenir of the Labor Women's Central Organizing Committee*, Sydney, 1954, p. 18.

68. McCarthy, op. cit., pp. 184–5.

69. John C. Caldwell et al., 'Australia: Knowledge, attitudes, and practice of family planning in Melbourne, 1971', *Studies in Family Planning*, March 1973, p. 54.

70. *Official Year Book of the Commonwealth of Australia*, No. 58, 1972, p. 167.

71. L. E. Goodisson, 'Sex Education: The Need for Racial Hygiene', The *Progressive Journal*, (Sydney), 1 August 1935, p. 32.

72. Norman Haire, *Sex Problems of Today*, Angus & Robertson, Sydney, 1943, p. 29.

73. ibid.

74. Goodisson, loc. cit.

75. D'Arcy, op. cit., p. 386.

76. Adapted from *Official Year Book of New South Wales*, No. 61, 1971, p. 321.

77. ibid.

78. ibid., p. 297.

79. Heagney, op. cit., p. 121.

80. cit. Judith Mackinolty, 'Sugar Bag Days – Sydney Workers and the Challenge of the 1930s Depression', M.A. thesis, Macquarie University, 1972, p. 56.

81. D'Arcy Niland, *Gold in the Streets*, Horwitz, Sydney, 1970, p. 43.

82. J. T. Lang, *The Turbulent Years*, Alpha Books, Sydney, 1970, p. 92.

83. *Australian Women's Weekly*, 23 September 1933, p. 2.

84. ibid., 6 October 1934, p. 10.

85. President's Message, The *Progressive Journal*, (Sydney), 5 April 1935.

86. Andree Wright, 'The Australian Women's Weekly: Depression and the War Years, Romance and Reality', *Refractory Girl*, No. 3, Winter 1973, p. 10.

87. Mollie Bayne, *Australian Women at War*, Left Book Club of Victoria, Melbourne, 1943, p. 14.

88. ibid., pp. 14-15.

89. ibid., p. 17.

90. Dymphna Cusack and Florence James, *Come in Spinner*, Heinemann, Melbourne, 1951, p. 207.

91. *Control of Manpower in Australia: a General Review of the Administration of the Manpower Directorate*, February 1942 – September 1944. Issued by W. C. Wurth, Director General of Manpower, Government Printer, Sydney, 1944, p. 20.

92. Bayne, op. cit., p. 29.

93. For details of this struggle see Bayne, op. cit., pp. 29–33; and S. Encel, N. MacKenzie and M. Tebbutt, *Women and Society: An Australian Study*, Cheshire, Melbourne, 1974, pp. 155–8.

94. MacKenzie, op. cit., p. 173.

95. Bayne, op. cit., p. 25.

96. ibid.

97. E. Ronald Walker, *The Australian Economy in War and Reconstruction*, Oxford University Press, New York, 1947.

98. MacKenzie, op. cit., p. 141.

99. McCarthy, op. cit., p. 189.

100. *Control of Manpower in Australia . . .* , op. cit., p. 95.

101. Kylie Tennant, *Tell Morning This*, Angus & Robertson, Sydney, 1947, p. 229.

102. Cusack and James, op. cit., p. 266.

103. MacKenzie, op. cit., p. 141.

104. For example, *They Wrote it Themselves: A Book of the W.R.A.A.F.*, Robertson & Mullens, Melbourne, 1946; and Jessie Elizabeth Simons, *While History Passed*, Heinemann, Melbourne, 1954, which is the story of the Australian nurses who were Japanese prisoners of war for three and a half years, and which describes the brutal Banka Island Beach massacre of twenty-one Australian nurses only one of whom, Sister Vivian Bullwinkel, survived to recount the horror.

105. Haire, op. cit., p. 29.

106. ibid., p. 42.

107. *Australian Women's Weekly*, 14 August 1943, p. 9.

108. ibid., p. 10.

109. ibid., 28 August 1945, p. 18.

110. Harland, op. cit., p. 18.

CHAPTER THIRTEEN

SUBURBAN NEUROTICS?

Now we see whole streets deserted in the day time, while mothers are forced to go out to work. I do not believe that all these women prefer monotonous jobs to the pleasure of being with their children and tending their home and gardens . . . Those of you who enjoy *Blue Hills* will know what I mean. It is fashionable to laugh at this delightful story, because it has continued for so many years; but that is the way families were intended to be. It is a story with great depth, wonderful characters and a fine example of family solidarity and warm affection.

Mrs DULCIE WILLACY, 'The Family in the Rural Crisis'
in *From a Woman's Point of View*, 1973

I firmly believe that a mother's first responsibility is to provide proper care for her children, especially up to the age of five. The woman who feels she will find her proper fulfilment in a career while someone else is minding her children is, in fact, depriving the children of their birthright. If a woman cannot find fulfilment in helping her children build the foundations of life in the stability and trust of those early years, then she will probably never find fulfilment. Fulfilment is found in relationships. And if she cannot find it in her own children, I wonder if she really deserves to find it elsewhere.

Dr FRANCIS MACNAB of the Cairnmillar Institute,
quoted in Patrick Tennison, *The Marriage Wilderness*, 1972

The previous three chapters have attempted to show that the sexist structure of Australian society has firm foundations and has proved able to persist even through changed social conditions. Apparent radical alterations to women's roles, such as occurred during World War Two, were temporary and of short duration, for the vast majority of women resumed their pre-war lives of full-time domesticity when their husbands, and other job-seeking men, returned from the war. As was suggested in the previous chapter not all women went quietly. *They* had begun to expand their self-definition and to realize that they had capabilities beyond those of mother and housewife. But they were still captives of their sex-role conditioning and the impulse to reaffirm traditional family relations after war-time separations was strong and was reinforced by a widespread reaffirmation of 'the family' ideology in the immediate post-war period. Men wanted to forget their war-time experiences by subsuming themselves in civilian work and family lives.

A decade or more of family consolidation took place. The birth-rate rose spectacularly in the late 1940s while large estates of new houses opened up to accommodate families seeking a privatized suburban life. Family life and suburban life quickly became synonymous and were idealized as the most desirable way to live and the best environment for raising children. With these certainties being so confidently asserted it became difficult for women to express whatever doubts they may have had about the restrictions suburban family life had for them. It would have entailed abrogating the security that comes from conforming to a socially approved lifestyle; they would have had to battle against incomprehension and hostility as well as their own self-doubts. 'There must be something wrong with *me*' was the usual reaction of these restless women: as suburban wives and mothers they were embodying the ideal female existence according to the prevailing ideology. Everyone else professed contentment and happiness so the sources of discontent were seen to be purely personal.

But by the early 1960s, this restlessness was becoming widespread and more women were starting to articulate it in various ways. As was shown in Chapter Four, the inbuilt contradictions of the wife/ mother role have caused uncertainty and unhappiness for large numbers of women and the manifestations of this misery have become so widespread that they have had to be publicly acknowledged. In recent years it has become almost a platitude that the suburbs are crammed with neurotic housewives who are searching for ways to inject meaning into their wasted lives.[1] If this *is* the case, and the evidence of discontent provided earlier would seem to mean that there is truth at least in the statement that many housewives are not happy, then it is necessary to look at possible reasons for this.

The immediate cause of housewives' dissatisfaction is the vast discrepancy between their socialized expectations that marriage and family will provide them with fulfilment, and the actual experience of being a wife and mother. Most women who are aged twenty and upwards today were socially conditioned to want and to expect to marry and bear children. Some might have been given encouragement to acquire some skills or training which they could use on the labour market but few women were given to expect that such skills were necessary except for filling in those few years between leaving school and marrying or having their first child. Yet the majority of women, while acquiring the expectation that many years of their lives would be devoted to full-time motherhood and wifedom, were not specifically prepared for it. The shape of their futures was definite but its actual details were hazy and undefined.

For many women, the extent of their preparation for the future was to engage in romantic fantasies about engagement rings and wedding days and perhaps to discuss with a female friend the respective merits of various house plans and interior decoration schemes. Never would it occur to a young woman that, after a few years of marriage, she could be isolated and marooned in a remote suburb in an under-furnished house with a couple of tiny children whose constant demands left her feeling continually tired and depressed. Her husband could be away for twelve or more hours a day if he had long distances to travel to work and also tried to fit in part-time study or a few beers with his friends at the end of the day. Far from feeling fulfilled, a young woman might start to feel cheated, to feel that she had been deceived about the romance of marriage and the rewards of motherhood, as she watched herself disintegrate from loneliness, overwork and boredom.

Yet children are still being inducted into these role expectations. Sex roles are so pervasive and so unquestioned, are so assumed to be the 'natural' order of things that the unhappy housewife seldom considers that this means of dividing people might provide a clue to her discontent. And so she does not refrain from instilling in her children traditional role behaviour and expectations. In this way 'the family' reproduces those very roles which are causing misery to its adult members.

Child-care centres still tend to reinforce a differentiation of the sexes which assures tiny girls that the dolls they play with will one day be replaced by living infants. Most girls still learn not only that maternity is their ultimate destiny but that they ought to tailor their entire lives towards preparation for it. Pre-schools today are less likely to encourage children into strictly defined sex-role behaviour, at least in games or other recreational activities. But the number of children who can attend pre-schools is still very small and, even where the children are thus privileged, their mothers are often horrified at the 'rough' behaviour of their daughters or the 'feminine' games of their sons.

No matter how 'progressive' the parents or teachers, a variety of factors conspire to ensure that no real subversion of this traditional idea occurs. A combination of 'progressive' parents and teachers is rare and so the prescriptions of one will often counteract the encouragement of the other. In any case, few children live in an isolated environment which prevents their being influenced by their playing companions, children's television and radio programmes, and the pervasive propaganda of newspapers, women's magazines, advertisements and virtually every other feature of the public world.

Feminists have pointed out that even what is considered to be an innovatory – in educational terms – children's television programme like 'Sesame Street' reinforces absolutely the idea that women are kitchen-creatures and child-raisers, and never portrays them in any other kind of role. The books most commonly read by pre-school children in Australia have been found to reflect overwhelmingly both the traditional sex division of labour and the differences in status which generally attend this division. A comprehensive survey of children's picture books conducted in Sydney in 1972 found that

The social attitude endorsed by these books is that domestic tasks are the province of the female. That this role is socially inferior to those adult male roles is described by the substitution of boys, undeniably social inferiors, in a number of all-male situations . . . The picture books examined include very few working women, and those few are treated unsympathetically, without exception. Small children will not, through these books, learn to accept their mother's desire for some fulfilment outside their home as legitimate, nor will those whose mothers do work be able to identify their mothers within these books.[2]

Nor will the young girls who read these books be encouraged to see for themselves any alternative or even an accompanying career to motherhood.

It is difficult to get an accurate picture of the life's ambitions of pre-school children as there has been no such survey done in Australia but just from observing the games and conversations of under-five-year-old girls and from talking with their parents the impression is gained that this generation has not internalized goals substantially different from their mothers' or even their grandmothers'. Some friends of mine recently found their four-year-old daughter (a renowned 'tomboy' who refuses to wear dresses and who shuns the company of other girls) in tears; when asked what the matter was she cried that she did not know how to cook and how was she going to look after her husband and children when she grew up.

Traditional sex-role attitudes and ambitions are still overwhelmingly present in young girls and boys today. R. W. Connell conducted a comprehensive survey of youth aged 12 to 20 in Sydney in 1969–70 which found that sex roles 'are already firmly established among 12-year-olds and are found at much the same strength at older ages, both in and out of school.' Moreover, he found the girls to be deeply imbued with those feelings of social responsibility which this book has identified as part of the God's Police stereotype:

A 'morality' inventory asking for opinions on issues of honesty, friendship, and personal responsibility found girls, on almost every item, more heavily endorsing the conventional view of strict morality. On social issues of personal freedom, boys are more libertarian and girls more restrictive. And a set of questions about sexual morality . . . showed the boys more permissive than girls on all issues but one (homosexuality). The pattern is clear, predictable, and almost completely consistent.[3]

There is plenty of evidence to suggest that on leaving school girls overwhelmingly expect that after a few short years at a job they will retire for life into connubial bliss and contented motherhood. Connell found that 9 per cent of his sample never expected to work, 72 per cent only until they had children, 14 per cent intended to work whether they had children or not and only a small 5 per cent said they did not intend to marry. I conducted a survey in 1970 which produced similar findings. I arranged for 118 fifteen-year-old girls at three schools to write essays which were designed to draw from them their expectations for adult life.[4] These expectations are set out in the table below. The figures refer to the percentage of girls in each group who made reference to their pursuing the four occupations listed.

Life Expectations of School-Age Girls

	Marriage	Children	Work Before Marriage	Work After Marriage
Private school	50%	39%	62%	12%
High school –				
'A' stream	84%	81%	77%	31%
Commercial stream	77%	77%	55%	13%
Technical school	91%	72%	63%	12%

The low percentage of girls from the private school who expected to marry can be accounted for by two factors. The essay topic which their teacher gave them was: 'It is 2036 and you are 70 years old – describe your life'. This future-oriented title evidently evoked visions of a catastrophe-wrought post-2000 world and 27 per cent of them devoted their entire essays to describing global havoc resulting from inter-continental wars, nuclear holocausts or widespread famine. Several girls related this to the futility, immorality even, of envisaging marriage and children although most were unable to place their personal futures into such a context and wrote fairly abstract, impersonal accounts of their projected future visions. Had the topic been the same as that given to the other groups it is probable that most of this 27 per cent would have been able to describe their personal expectations and that these would have corresponded with those of the majority of their classmates.

That marriage and family were talked about by these girls was evidenced in the additional 12 per cent who specifically argued against marriage, advocating free love. Several of them recounted that they had children by a variety of fathers. But what was most pertinent about this survey was the small number of girls who foresaw that they might work after marriage. Only one group – those from the 'A' stream at the high school – had expectations which in any way matched the current adult female workforce participation pattern. Particularly unrealistic were the expectations of the working-class girls. They appeared to be greater victims of the sex-role ideology than any other group since it was clear from their essays that the majority of them had working mothers but that they themselves still believed the myth that *they* would not have to work after marriage.

All of these schoolgirls, from the evidence in their essays, appeared to be totally unaware that most of them were likely, as well as marrying and having two or three children, to return to work, often even before their children had started school. That is, if present trends continue, their lives are likely to be even more irreconcilable with their socialized expectations than is the case with their mothers, the women who today are labelled 'suburban neurotics'.

In 1963 Betty Friedan drew attention to the vast gap between the expectations women had and the actual lives they led:

The problem lay buried, unspoken, for many years in the minds of American women. It was a strange stirring, a sense of dissatisfaction, a yearning that women suffered in the middle of the twentieth century in the United States. Each suburban wife struggled with it alone. As she made the beds, shopped for groceries, matched slipcover material, ate peanut butter sandwiches with her children, chauffeured Cub Scouts and Brownies, lay beside her husband at night, she was afraid to ask even of herself the silent question: 'Is this all?'[5]

A few years later, Australian women started to speak out about what it was like behind those suburban walls: 'I don't know who I am or what I'm supposed to be doing. I have two lovely little children, but I'm so bored I want to get back to work as soon as I can. I'll put them in pre-school kindergartens. But I feel very guilty about it. I feel I should be at home looking after them for a long time to come.'[6]

This woman is not alone in deciding that a paid job provides an attractive alternative to full-time domesticity. In the past decade the number of married women taking paid jobs has increased dramatically as the following table shows.

Married Women as a Proportion of the Labour Force, 1947–1973[7]

	Number ('000)	Percentage
Census June 1947	109.8	3.4
Census June 1954	258.2	7.0
Census June 1961	405.5	9.6
Census June 1966	686.3*	14.1*
Census June 1971	960.0	18.0
Feb. 1973	1,175.1	20.6
Feb. 1974†	1,249.4	n.a.
Feb. 1975†	1,285.0	n.a.

* This category is overstated compared to earlier Censuses because of a changed definition of the labour force in 1966.

† These figures are taken from The Labour Force, February 1975, Australian Bureau of Statistics, Canberra, July 1975, p. 6.

The labour force participation rate for all women has increased but it is the increase in the participation of married women which is most marked. In 1947 only 6.5 per cent of married women were in the workforce. This had increased to 17.3 per cent in 1961 and nearly doubled by 1971 to 32.8 per cent; in February 1973 it was estimated that 37.2 per cent of all married women were working, while by February 1975 this had risen to 39.7 per cent.[8] As Chapter Five suggested, it is probable that even more married women would seek jobs if suitable child-care facilities were available.

We now have the situation where over one million married women have extended their female roles to include a paid job outside the home. They have in effect negated one of the precepts of the God's Police ideology, that which stipulated full-time devotion to home and family was necessary to fulfil the role adequately. Altogether 29.2 per cent of women with children under 12 years are in the workforce.[9] But while these women are in practice defying the ideological prescription, society has not caught up with them and altered the ideology and so these women must continue to endure feelings of guilt about their defection.

This guilt generates anxiety and uncertainty especially as the God's Police ideology continues to be reinforced to adult women in a variety of forceful ways. It is still present in the publicly articulated policies of the churches and many political groups. It is present in the themes and assumptions of advertising directed towards women. It is present in the content of most women's magazines. And it is present in the theories of psychologists (and child psychologists), sociologists and many others who are either studying women or who have set themselves up to 'help' them. The ideology is still voiced in its purest form by right-wing political groups such as the Democratic Labour Party and the League of Rights. The DLP opposes married women working, favours a wage for housewives (to encourage them to stay at home) and wishes to perpetuate all policies which treat 'the family' as the basic unit of society and which therefore maintain the present sexist division of labour and society. Lady Phyllis Cilento expressed the traditional view of 'the family' and women's place within it, when she addressed the sixth annual seminar of the Australian League of Rights in 1972:

It is the women who make homes of houses; friendly fellowships of communities; enjoyable meals out of crude foodstuffs; who keep alive the spiritual side of life and religion in the home. It is they who give the intimate care and affection to babies, children of all ages and to their menfolk . . . I cannot but feel that 'the woman's point of view' is finally oriented to the welfare of her own family first, and her outgoing love embraces her community, her nation and indeed the whole family of man.[10]

The policy of the Federal Labor Government has been to facilitate women, especially married women, working. It has introduced maternity leave provisions for women in the Australian Public Service, has set up various inquiries into child-care (to recommend the most effective means of implementing a national child-care scheme and the forms the centres should take), and has begun to publicize and expand existing retraining schemes designed to enable women to return to the workforce with skills. This policy of encouraging women to work is an implicit denial of the former conception of women's familial role and by removing discriminatory features of the working conditions of women the Government is bringing some basic justice to the situation of working women, and is attempting to meet some of their special needs. But the relationship between legislative changes and long-held social ideas is a complicated one. No Act of Parliament can dissolve the accumulated cultural prescriptions which still play on women's psyches and which affect men's expectations of women.

This policy of government assistance is recent – since the change of government in 1972 – and so far has mainly benefited only women employed by the Australian Public Service. The flow-on to other women will be slow. In any case, we are immersed in a somewhat schizophrenic situation where alterations to the traditional female role are occurring, and are receiving some government support, but at the same time that role is being reinforced by other equally powerful forces in Australian society.

The churches still regard women as having to fulfil a discrete and traditional function. A Sydney theologian has criticized the attitude of the churches toward women:

The Christian Church in Australia, both Roman Catholic and Protestant, is one of the main agencies for reinforcing the low status of Australian women. At the most obvious level, it does this by discouraging them from positions of leadership or equality within its own ranks . . . The Australian mateship ethos, by which men only trust one another, has been transferred to Church life . . .[11]

All the churches argue for the retention of 'the family', and, like the DLP, thereby perpetuate sexist attitudes. An Anglican clergyman recently attacked the Government's proposed Human Rights Bill because it omitted the International Covenant on Civil and Political Rights definition of 'the family' as 'the natural and fundamental group unit of society which is entitled to protection by society and the State'[12] while the Catholic Archbishop of Sydney attacked the Government's Family Law Bill on similar grounds.[13]

The churches will seldom spell out in detail the precise form of family they want to have guaranteed by the State so it must be assumed they are arguing for the traditional form. They are thereby pleading for the retention of a sexual division of labour and the differences in opportunities and status this entails, the very situation which is causing women so much discontent.

But while the churches fear the erosion of what have traditionally been women's functions, other forces are busy refurbishing and maintaining them. Most advertising is directed at women. This fact, as well as the view that the producers of this advertising have of women is evidence enough of the assumptions they hold about the female role. The chairman and managing director of George Patterson Pty Ltd, Australia's biggest advertising agency, claimed in an interview that psychological research conducted by his staff '. . . tells us that instead of this shopping expedition to the supermarket [being] . . . a terrible thing . . . it is actually one of the great recreations during the week for the housewife, one of their great challenges during the week . . . '[14] This man heads the same agency which produced *The Patterson Report*, a book which purported to 'capture a little of the Australian scene as perceived by women in the 1970s'.[15] The Introduction claimed the book 'should be of paramount interest to everyone engaged in making or selling goods in the Australian market – in other words, everyone engaged in wooing the Australian woman.'

Advertisers operate on the assumption that women control family finances.[16] This assumption is used to attract other advertising as well as informing the contents of the actual advertisements. In 1972 the Sydney *Sun* advertised itself in a full-page of a national weekly newspaper in the following way:

The *Sun* woos and wins 403,000 [Sydney women] each day, the latest survey shows. That's 102,000 more women than the next on the list. And we've got more in every age group under 55 than any other daily. They also happen to be at the biggest-spending end of the population.[17]

If women *are* the big spenders this does not mean that women are wealthier than men. Chapter Five showed that women in Australia are, if not supported by a man, very likely to be in poverty. If women do spend the most it is because they have many people to buy for – husband, children and, if there is any money left, themselves. Shopping – which can include shopping for several people for food, clothes and other items – is just one more of a woman's many jobs, one that she must do even if she has a full-time paid job.

If psychologists have found that women enjoy the constant trips to the supermarket, arguing that it is a recreation and a challenge, there are several things they have not considered. It might be a challenge – to try and purchase family requirements when faced with constantly rising prices and a fairly static income, but it is hardly a challenge which is recreational. Rather, it is likely to produce greater worry and tension – 'how to make ends meet' – and if this recreation is engaged upon with a couple of young children who pull things off shelves, pile up their mother's trolley with items she does not want (or cannot afford) so that she must spend extra time replacing them on the shelves, then it is not going to prove very relaxing. Many women claim that such trips to the supermarket, including getting there (especially without a car) and carting heavy groceries home, are so exhausting that they need to rest afterwards.

Going to the supermarket might be a *change* from domestic routines and a superficial relief from the isolation and loneliness of being cooped up in a house with small children but it is hardly a recreation or a challenge. Such shopping trips can actually exacerbate a woman's isolation for although she will *see* lots of other people, her actual contact with them is likely to be limited. Unless she happens to meet other women she knows, her only conversations will be with shop assistants and be circumscribed by the conventions of such casual contact. Many of the large suburban shopping complexes, such as Roselands in Sydney, mount spectacular entertainments for shoppers, bringing well-known people from show business, sport etc. to 'meet the people'. These mass circuses may distract women shoppers from their personal problems but they are only momentary escapades, not real alternatives to the isolation of women in the suburbs from each other.

A further aspect of women spending money is exploited by advertisers. Quite often women will displace anxiety or depression by compulsive spending – the buying a new hat 'to cheer me up' syndrome – or by buying on impulse things they do not really need and maybe cannot afford. When this occurs, women's big spending is yet another measure of her oppression. Caught in a series of double-binds and conflicting desires about what she should do with her life, it is inevitable that many women will resort to that activity which is so assiduously encouraged in our market society – spending money. The advertisers are quick and cunning in their efforts to capitalize on a woman's anxieties and to woo money from her purse. Advertisements appeal to fears about being a good mother – 'your family needs product X' – and to anxieties about her appearance, her hair-style or colour, her body smells, her complexion, her clothes. They also appeal to women's anxieties about her family's status,[18] encouraging her to conformity in her purchasing: certain types of furniture, or cooking utensils or other items will show *you* are a discerning woman.

Advertising which employs these techniques still holds the assumption that it is women who are primarily responsible for the management of their family's lifestyle, that they do most of the buying and they decide what is to be bought. This assumption permeates the sales pitch, becoming yet one more pressure on women who are either confused about their roles or are trying to change them in some way. To be constantly cajoled that your family *needs* this product will create self-doubts in a woman in either position. Outwardly she may scoff at the advertisers' suggestions; inwardly her self-assurance is dented and the proscriptions and admonitions of the 'good mother' role will come flooding back into her confused consciousness. Often a woman who feels guilty about having a paid job will spend more, obediently complying with the advertisers' prescriptions in an effort to quell her self-doubts. She will compensate for her absence from full-time motherhood by plying her family with items it could not otherwise afford.

Affirmations of sexism are also explicitly propagated in all Australian women's magazines; their very existence assumes a society divided on sex lines. These magazines are an important feature of Australian life both for the ideas they contain and as mass vehicles for inducing women to spend money, and so their content and assumptions deserve some scrutiny. In 1971 women spent an average of $325,000 each week just on the three main weekly magazines (the *Australian Women's Weekly*, *Woman's Day*, *New Idea*[19]) while by mid-1975 Australians were spending $43 m. a year to buy 12,296,000 locally produced women's magazines.[20]

In 1972 the average issue readership for these magazines was as follows:

Average Readership Per Issue

Percentage of Persons 13 Years and Over[21]

	Women	Housewives
Australian Women's Weekly	47.5%	45.8%
Woman's Day	35.2%	33.5%
New Idea	27.8%	27.1%
Woman's World	11.0%	10.5%
Dolly	7.4%	4.7%
Pol	4.9%	3.6%
Belle	3.3%	2.1%

At the end of 1972 a new magazine, *Cleo*, appeared and mass promotion of the first few issues soon secured it record sales. A survey conducted after the first few issues found that single and married women aged 35 and under were the main readers of *Cleo*, and that of a readership potential of 1.3 million at the end of 1972, it had achieved a 9 per cent penetration into this market – 'far more than any other women's monthly'.[22] *Woman's World*, a weekly, started publication in 1972. Its promotion brochure claimed it was particularly effective in reaching housewives with children, notably those with large families who are heavy spenders on food and groceries, and that within six months it had achieved a higher proportion of its total readership in the 25- to 29-year 'home-making age brackets' than the three other weeklies.[23]

In her survey of the three existing women's weeklies in 1969, Madge Dawson concluded:

The women for whom our magazines seem to be writing typify long-standing concepts of the Australian woman. Her place is in the home; in her role of wife and mother she finds fulfilment; her role as worker or citizen, if any, is minor and subordinate. She is inward-turning – concerned only with things appropriate to her sex.[24]

Five years later the market is crammed with many new magazines (*Woman's World, Australian Family Circle, Dolly, Belle, Cleo, Cosmopolitan*) and the picture is rather more complex. Women's magazines now fall into two categories: the family-centred weeklies (*Australian Women's Weekly, Woman's Day, New Idea, Woman's World, Australian Family Circle*) and the woman-centred glossy monthlies (*Cleo, Dolly, Cosmopolitan, Vogue*), and the now quarterly, *POL* and *Belle*.

The oldest and still the most read women's magazine is the *Australian Women's Weekly*. In 1971 it had a circulation of 820,000 and reached over 50 per cent of the total population of women in Australia each week.[25] Every content analysis of this magazine has revealed it to propagate the idea that women are happiest as housewives. A recent study concluded, 'It's not that working women don't exist at all in the pages of the *Australian Women's Weekly*, but they exist ONLY as wives and mothers and housekeepers. They are not portrayed as active and independent units in an economic system, and so provide no choice of role models for young girls. The image of the role of women is of home duties as central.'[26]

The same study reported a survey which had found that 56 per cent of girls aged 12 to 17 years read this magazine weekly or nearly every week.[27] Large numbers of girls are thus still receiving a view of adult female life which not only contradicts *their* likely futures but which distorts the reality of the lives of their mothers.

All of the family-centred women's magazines present in their contents a society based on the traditional family and divided on lines of sex, in which the female's appearance, marital and maternal status and possession of numerous domestic skills are apparently her most appropriate attributes. They all extol escapism in the form of romantic fiction, features about Royalty or the international jet-set and numerous travelogues. They applaud traditional women's skills, such as cooking, knitting and other handicrafts, child-raising and home management and generally offer useful information or aids in the form of recipes, patterns and so on. But contemporary social and political issues of relevance to women – such as abortion law reform, equal pay, child-care, equality with men in the workforce and in society generally – are paid scant, if any, attention. Women's Liberation is treated as an interesting phenomenon, deserving of periodic feature articles, but the tendency is to separate it from the rest of the magazine's content by discussing the mere fact of existence of the Movement rather than what it aims for or what it has achieved. Some of the jargon of Women's Liberation, phrases such as 'male chauvinist pig', are used occasionally, with an amused editorial twitter, as if to highlight the differences the editors perceive between *their* readers and that bunch of crazy feminists.

The woman who has difficulty reconciling her socialization and her actual adult life will sometimes find a discursive 'commonsense philosophy' article on the break-up of the family, or new sexual standards, or some similar contemporary issue. But she will seldom be given concrete help with such dilemmas by articles which direct themselves to the roots of her problems. If practical advice is given to the working wife it will generally be in the form of recipes for quick-to-prepare meals. All this does is confirm that women must endure a double burden; there is no suggestion that the sexual division of labour itself, and the functions it serves for our society, should be examined. Thus these magazines, which profess a service function to women as their *raison d'être*, play a decisive role in actually defining the problems they consider it behoves a woman to have.

The economic function of the magazines is relevant to their editorial concerns. Editorial and advertising content merge into a single compelling whole and it is obviously necessary to distract women from basic problems of role conflict in order to keep them interested and receptive potential consumers. Hence the concentration on practical hints in domestic areas. Persuade a woman that she can expand her domestic competence and feed her with plenty of escapist or fantasy material to sustain her while she does it. In this way it just might be possible for women to remain permanently distracted, busy enough (especially if they have paid jobs as well as being house-wives) not to have time to think. In fact, this does not work for many women and these magazines are forced to acknowledge the existence of 'suburban neurosis', but they have to do so rather gingerly. They bravely suggest play-groups and other community activities to dissipate loneliness – seeing this as the major problem.

Woman's Day recently combined the usual woman's magazine obsession with diets and a recognition that many housewives are unhappy by publishing a 'High Energy Anti-depressant Diet'. The diet was introduced by a short article which discussed the problems many housewives have:

Do you frequently feel depressed, listless and lacking in vitality and energy? This condition is so prevalent nowadays that it has been labelled the 'housewife syndrome'. Many Australian women try to solve their problems by swallowing increasing amounts of tranquillisers, sedatives and anti-depressants. But drugs are not the answer. Physicians today say that sensible eating habits will correct this listless state.[28]

Women's magazines will consider physical or hormonal problems or lack of company to be causes of 'suburban neurosis' but never dare come to terms with the notion that the traditional roles for which they are catering are becoming increasingly anachronistic.

The glossy monthlies direct themselves to women as individuals and play down the family context. Even more blatantly than the weeklies, they exist because a market exists, not just a market for their magazines but for the products the advertisers, on whom they depend for existence, can promote through their pages. Unlike the weeklies, they do not assume heterogeneity of the female sex and cater for the swinging, with-it, Today Woman, whom they see as being discontented with the kind of images projected by the weeklies. The promotional brochures of these magazines define their purpose and their intent. 'Women ARE different . . . as different as DOLLY, BELLE and POL. That's why Sungravure now has three young women's magazines. Each has its own personality, each has its own thing to say . . . Yet they all have one aim in common – to entertain, to inform . . . to SELL to women – young women!' The chairman and managing director of *Vogue* explained his magazine's ethic: '*Vogue* does not appeal to age groups, but a standard of personal quality and a set of values . . . We therefore cater to an attitude in women who have this interest in improving the quality of their life and have the money to satisfy their aspirations.'[29]

Yet the 'liberated' image these monthlies project is as much a gloss as the coating on their pages. They do not reject the sexist division of society. They simply capitalize on it in different ways. *Belle* and *Dolly* hardly bother to differentiate themselves at all. *Dolly* concentrates on dolly-type clothes and endless articles on where and how to catch a man. Two feminists recently appraised the *Dolly* philosophy and wrote:

After having discussions with many regular readers it became clear to us that the girls, who were mainly between fourteen and sixteen, really felt that it did answer the right questions. For the real question is 'How do I get a man to love me?' There seems no point in plunging the girl into a worse dilemma by querying the values when the girl is well aware that in this society, without a man to love, cherish and provide for her, she will be doomed to loneliness, deprived of the only identity allowed a woman. *Dolly* provides very simple answers. The whole purpose of buying all the goodies advertised is to look good. This means assuming a particular appearance which is in keeping with current fashion. You will then feel good, all your nervousness will fade away. You will have become perfect 'manbait'! Consume in order that every man you meet will want to consume you![30]

The editor of *Belle* says her readers are

. . . proud of their role in an exciting, expanding feminine world, whether as career girl, young housewife or mother . . . The *Belle* woman wants to get the most living out of life she can. She knows a lot is expected of her. She's expected to create a home with that 'something special' look, to do wonders with menus, to serve wine knowledgeably, to wear the right clothes and, at the same time, to look beautiful, be desirable, and be informed. *Belle* will show her how to meet these needs.[31]

The *Belle* woman is in essence no different from the *Women's Weekly* woman: she has just incorporated a few modern trends into a traditional role. There is no recognition of the problems the young woman trying to be all these things might encounter; *Belle* defines the needs and then teaches women to fulfil them and portrays life as being much too breathless and interesting ever to be sullied with the slightest glimmer of self-doubt or conflict.

Cleo, Cosmopolitan and, in recent issues, *POL* are similarly motivated by market considerations but their content orientation is rather different. The *Cosmopolitan* credo, as outlined in a 1973 promotional brochure, sums up the ethos these magazines subscribe to:

WHO IS OUR GIRL ? SHE IS . . . Between the ages of 18 and 34. Loves men, may be married or single. Interested in sex but not preoccupied with it. Intelligent. Emotional . . . naturally. Chic . . . has class and money to spend on the products advertised (either her own or her husband's money). Probably has a job. If not, she is hip, lively, and interested in a lot of things. Not primarily house and home-oriented . . . May or may not have children. If she does, she loves them and is a good mother but she doesn't live through the children. She doesn't live through her husband either. She likes to do it herself.

These monthlies play it safe and never disavow the sexist division of society, and they readily assume that most – but not all – women will want to marry and have children, but they are more alive to the conflicts and problems experienced by young women today. They are heavily oriented towards sexual performance and problems (despite their statement that 'their girl' is not preoccupied with sex) and this is a definite change from the avoidance or euphemisms of other magazines and newspapers. They recognize female sexuality, and argue for a woman's right to sexual fulfilment. They also run features of practical help to women who want to, say, borrow money or buy a car without male assistance. They mouth support for feminist issues and many of their editorial pieces reinforce feminist ideas. *But* they are still caught within the contradiction of arguing against the superstructure of a sex role while wanting its foundations to remain intact. They argue for female independence without recognizing that this is impossible in the kind of sexist society Australia is. While their fashion pages and advertising continue to reinforce the idea that women should dress and make up to be alluring seductresses, that frippery is necessary to being female, in other words that women *should* accentuate their differences, then the cry for independence rings rather hollow.

The confusion for women created by these magazines is of a different order from the others. Their aura of 'liberation' appears to offer a way out of the old double-binds of the female role. But what they offer is an illusion, the myth that modernization is a substitute for the revolutionary changes that are necessary where organization along sex-role lines has led to a society in which women are ostracized from its culture, exploited economically and sexually and where women themselves constantly voice anger, frustration, annoyance or discontent at the roles they are expected to fulfil.

One of the major reasons for the gap between the expectations and the actual lives of most women is that there has been a shrinking of the traditional work performed by the housewife. Even though more women marry now than at any time in Australian history, the majority of married women have fewer children than their grandmothers and certainly their great-grandmothers had. Women who had completed their families at the time of the 1911 census had had around five children; this dropped to about four at the 1921 census and ever since has been less than three.[32] Factors such as early marriage, early child-bearing (and having fewer children) has restricted the effective period of reproductivity for Australian women to an average of eight years.[33] The median age for brides in Australia in 1971 was 21.39 years[34], and over half of all first births to married couples occur within the first two years of marriage.[35] Thus by age thirty a large proportion of married Australian women have completed their child-bearing and their eldest child will be half-way through primary school. By age thirty-five the youngest child will have commenced school and the time a woman can spend in actually supervising or tending her children has been considerably reduced. A woman who was born in Australia between 1946 and 1948 has a life-expectancy of 70.63 years[36] and so, with nearly half her life to go, a woman whose expectations of fulfilment have centred entirely around the idea that women should be wives and mothers is likely to discover that this is no longer possible.

She can of course expand these roles so that they occupy more time, by becoming a more fastidious cleaner, a more experimental cook, an inveterate redecorator of the family home. She can take up adult educational classes, or become involved in local politics. She can pursue hobbies or recreational activities which she previously had little time for. Various combinations of these 'solutions' are adopted by thousands of Australian women but they do little more than underscore the fact that in a sex-role divided society one sex's roles are no longer adequate to occupy their entire lives, that women have been deprived of a viable life-defining function.

Many men express resentment about the contrast between their own and their wives' working days. In reply to criticisms about the inferior status of women in this country they will often say that they would swap jobs with their wives, that they would prefer to have all day and nothing to do than to have to put in a work-filled day at office or factory. These are rarely serious suggestions of course for few men would be willing to forgo the monetary and status rewards which their jobs bestow. But even if they were, men would soon discover the enervating effects of having very little to do, particularly in a society which sneers at 'bludgers' and which sees industry as a virtue. For 'women's work' has not merely contracted, it has also lost most of the status which attended it until the last decade or so. As Chapters Ten and Eleven tried to show, early this century women had some success in obtaining for their work a respected status.

For about forty years, most particularly during the inter-war period, the housewife's role was a respected one. This was perhaps the major achievement of the first feminist movement. The respect the housewife role carried was contingent on accepting a sexual division of labour and the status of the housewife did not match that of most male occupations or recreations. But there did exist a separate sphere, a women's realm, within which women's competence went unchallenged, where her expertise was acknowledged and valued and which thereby provided most women with both status and function. It was possible for a woman to experience both pride and fulfilment in raising her children, caring for her husband and in keeping house.

An impressive repertoire of skills and accomplishments was necessary to be able to be an Australian Mum. She had to be an implacable creature, the mainstay of the home, the human bulwark against any forces (such as unemployment, death, family scandals) which might undermine family harmony and happiness. She had to clean houses that required seemingly miles of vacuuming or polishing and dusting, and to satisfy family appetites with a sparse available menu of acceptable foods (though the dull repetition of roasts, chops and steaks was compensated for by an apparently never-ending variety of cakes, puddings and biscuits). At the same time she had to demonstrate thrift by sewing children's clothes and soft furnishings, by preserving fruits and making jams and chutneys. She had to be tireless, able to be up at dawn to prepare breakfasts and school lunches and to be the last to bed, having put out the billy for milk and set the table for breakfast.

She had to be mother and lover, enduring in silence the ceaseless worry of an unplanned pregnancy – because contraception was never perfect and abortions hard to procure – for Such Things were not discussed even between husband and wife. All this as well as keeping up a lively interest in what the children were learning at school, how husband was getting on at work, corresponding with relatives interstate, organizing visits of reluctant children to ageing grandparents. The Australian Mum's work was seldom explicitly extolled, except in those women's magazines read only by Australian Mums. She could not expect constant praise. Her rewards were her family's appreciation, the annual tributes of Mother's Day and the occasional prose or verse outpourings by sentimental writers of either sex.

It was a more subtle form of oppression than exists today for it was cloaked in pious and sanctimonious attitudes which were not a just recompense for the labours performed by women. And women were more totally defined by their maternal responsibilities than is now the case. It was common for husbands to address their wives as 'Mum' rather than use their names and as mentioned earlier this practice still persists. Many women must have resented the fact that their individuality, their personalities, and their sexuality, had been engulfed by maternity. But it is probable that housewives during this period did not experience the widescale frustration and discontents of women today. This was mainly because it was a very busy occupation and one that was constantly punctuated by the demands or even just the presence of other people. Australian cities were smaller and, before the suburban sprawl began to dislodge people from the relatives, friends, clubs and so on which provided them with company, the loneliness of today's suburban housewife was something which only women in the bush would understand. Children arriving home from school would trail around the house after their mother, telling her of what they had done that day before they went off to play or to do their homework. There was no imperious television set demanding to be turned on as soon as school ended; if children listened to children's radio programmes it was very likely in the same room as their mother was preparing the evening meal and she could feel some involvement with their interests.

But also important was the way in which women reinforced each other, convinced themselves and their friends that their housewifely lives were busy and contented. This is not meant to imply that all Australian housewives were serenely happy in their roles; it is inconceivable that there were not many women who were restless with their domesticity, who longed to be more than somebody's Mum and who looked enviously at the rare women of those days who had careers. But the restlessness was nowhere as ubiquitous as it is today. The female role and the demands of society were attuned to each other, were in a kind of harmony. It was not economically necessary to family survival for many women, even working-class women, to work. The percentage of married women working rose only very slowly before the forced mobilization of the Second World War.

In 1933 5.4 per cent of married women had jobs outside the home compared with 4.4 per cent in 1921.[37]

Women were occupied within the home. There was little impetus for them to examine their roles critically. *That* came with the war-time mobilization and afterwards things could never be the same again. Even though the majority of women left their jobs and returned to their housewifely roles a major rupture had occurred. They now had some experience of a different kind of life. They had tasted a new kind of dignity, that which comes from performing a job which, no matter how menial it might have been, had the automatic status of a wage.

In the post-war period it became more and more impossible for the urban woman to be an Australian Mum. Those who bore children before 1950 could perhaps manage it for ten years but the shrinking of the tasks the housewife had to perform, along with other social factors, were irrevocably sabotaging housewifedom as an honoured profession. The balance which had existed before was never to be re-established once the Government realized that the country's women constituted a splendid labour reserve force. Henceforward the opening of jobs to married women, particularly in those areas of the economy which were low-paid and which men with a choice of jobs available were reluctant to undertake, was a foregone con-clusion. It was just a matter of time. And there was little question of having to coerce women out into these jobs. Australians in the early 1960s were acquiring consumer tastes which were beyond the family incomes of all but the upper strata of the middle-class. So for the family which wanted to purchase a new suburban brick veneer home and to fill it with the sparkling consumer durables that spilled out of department stores and, later in the sixties, discount houses, there was little alternative but for the wife to take a job. Australia was becoming a two-income society even though it still masked this with a one-income ideology.

Along with changes in the family already mentioned the workforce itself was changing as the demands of society became increasingly sophisticated and pluralistic. The service sector of the economy expanded rapidly as professional aid agencies opened and new avenues for consumer activity were created. Large numbers of women were needed to be social workers, health officers and office workers to support the activities of all these welfare agencies. Even larger numbers of women had to be employed in the multitudes of shops, theatres, recreation centres and so on which began to appear as evidence of the new diversity Australian society had acquired. If married women had not been prepared to juggle their roles a bit, and add working at paid jobs to their wife and mother roles, then the rapid expansion of these sectors of the economy would not have been possible.

Given the reality of so many married women working it could perhaps be said that the traditional role was disappearing, even if gradually, and that it was merely a matter of making the necessary adjustments to people's expectations. But as has been shown in this chapter there have been few signs of this happening. The traditional role is being performed full-time by fewer women but the ideology lingers on and seems as strong as ever. It has only been in the last two or three years that there has even been widespread public acknowledgement of what has been a reality for over a decade. Women, and men, are still inculcated with the idea that marriage and maternity are the primary routes to female fulfilment for women in Australia. This is evident not only in the 'positive' socializing agents already described but also in a host of 'negative' agents. These mainly take the form of social attitudes and as such are difficult to identify with precision but they are recognizable as part of a general currency of ideas and attitudes which can be gleaned from newspapers, from conversations with people and, less often, from books which claim to speak with some expertise. They are also sometimes confirmed by discriminatory treatment meted out to women who do not conform to these two great imperatives.

Marriage is still posed as desirable and necessary and women who spurn it are regarded as peculiar, eccentric, objects of pity or, if they have children, as immoral. The Whore stereotype is still strong even though, as will be discussed later, it has become less clear-cut as more women refuse to conform to some or all of the God's Police prescriptions. The middle-aged woman who has rejected marriage – or who perhaps did not have the opportunity for it, but the scorners seldom bother to inquire – is derisively referred to as a spinster and assumed to lead a dreary sexless unfulfilled life with only a caged canary and maybe a few bountiful (married) relatives for company. She is the object of cruel jokes about old maids and is generally excluded from most social gatherings except those ritualized family gatherings when her relatives feel obliged to invite her.

The younger single career woman is treated to a mixture of respect and awe – if she is successful – and pity. She might be able to have affairs now, they say, but who'll want her when she gets old. Such critics might be taken aback if it was suggested to them that sexual attraction is rarely a factor in cementing any marriage once the partners are middle-aged; their view of single women as being primarily sex objects precludes them from recognizing things like companionship, respect for a woman's intelligence and thus her conversation as being important.

If the critics are not harking on the joys a woman misses for not being married they will often voice the suspicion that she must be a lesbian. This prognosis is offered in whispers which manage to combine both prurience and horror with the implied view that she is a deviant and thus deserves to be either persecuted or pitied (depending on how liberal the critic is) or that, as an assumed man-hater, she is incapable of finding true feminine fulfilment anyway and so barely deserves inclusion in the female sex. Such is the view of practising clinical psychologist Ronald Conway who dismisses lesbians as 'psychic half-women'.[38] Most books about women in Australia do not mention lesbians at all; they and Conway make the same mistake of viewing lesbians purely as sexual categories and ignoring the fact that many lesbians are married – and have children. In terms of the prevailing sex-role ideology they *have* fulfilled themselves as women and so the intended slur is inaccurate as well as revealing a contempt (and a fear?) for women who professedly are not dependent on men for sexual or emotional fulfilment. This is an instance of the inappropriateness of sexist stereotypes and how their exclusive categories actually disguise the realities of many women's lives. In terms of the stereotypes a lesbian is by definition a whore since she lives outside the conventional family (even if she tries to emulate its sex roles in her relationships with women) and is viewed as being incapable of disseminating pro-family values. It is assumed that all married women and mothers are heterosexual and, in fact, heterosexuality would probably be a stipulated requirement of the God's Police role were the definers of the stereotype to suspect that their assumption is not always correct.

Socially, the single woman who has not been dismissed as a lesbian is assumed to be searching for a husband and so those people who will ask her to dinner or to parties will dredge up the weirdest assortment of men to be her partners. Their main distinguishing characteristic will be their unmarried status. It will be assumed that the older the single woman is, the more desperate and, therefore, the less discriminating she will be.

Single people of both sexes have to pay higher taxes, are denied the concession rates that families or married couples can obtain to many social functions or membership of political or other organizations[39], a rather hypocritical form of penalizing people society professes to pity because they are excluded from the joys of married life. But single women have to suffer further discrimination. Society's contempt for the single woman, especially the economically secure single woman, that most blatant contradiction to the idea that women ought to be married and dependent, is revealed in the ways it tries to remove that independence. It is difficult, and it used until about three years ago to be impossible for a woman of any income to borrow money without a male guarantor. This sometimes led to the ludicrous situation of a father guaranteeing a loan for a daughter who earned more than he did.

Single mothers elicit ambivalent attitudes from many people. Like lesbian mothers, they have conformed to part of the God's Police prescription by being mothers but they have transgressed another part of it by rejecting marriage. They are not regarded as being sinister in the way lesbian mothers often are. In the past, single mothers were also cast as whores but they were given means of redemption. Their 'sin' was not so much the extra-marital sex or the resultant pregnancy but the refusal to marry. 'Shot-gun' marriages have been an accepted, if concealed, part of Australian family custom for most of this century so this course of action has always been advised but if a woman refused this option she could show her remorse by hiding away during her pregnancy preferably in a religious home where she could do other people's washing without remuneration, and by giving up her child for adoption. The woman who did this would have to endure some whispering and moralizing but she was generally regarded as being deserving of 'a second chance' to prove her willingness to take the socially approved routes to female fulfilment.

Women were discouraged from keeping their children by the State making it virtually impossible for them to support them. In 1968 a single mother with one child in Queensland received $4.85 a week. The Victorian Government's policy of paying allowances only to the children, and not to the parent caring for them, meant in 1968 that a single mother with one child was paid $4.00 a week.[40] Other states paid varying amounts, the maximum being $17.00 a week in South Australia. The single mother in Victoria was in the worst position and it was not coincidental, as Sackville points out, that Victoria's rate of adoption of illegitimate children was very high compared with states offering greater assistance.[41] In 1968 the Commonwealth Government passed the States Grants (Deserted Wives) Act which was designed to create incentives for the states to provide more uniform levels of assistance for fatherless families[42] and single mothers were included in this scheme. But the average payment, of around $27 a week in 1968, an inadequate amount to house, feed and clothe two people, was a constant reminder of the low opinion society had for the husbandless mother.

There have been some changes since. The introduction of the Supporting Mothers' Benefit in 1973 brought all single, deserted and widowed mothers into one administrative category and paid them a uniform allowance six months after they became eligible for the benefit. As Chapter Five argued, the amounts paid are still inadequate but the Government is at least not discriminating against single mothers: all fatherless families receive the same amounts. The Government will also give paid maternity leave to single mothers employed by the Australian Public Service. With the changes of the past few years many more women have begun to keep their babies. Single mothers have banded together and formed organizations such as CHUMS (Care and Help for Unmarried Mothers) in New South Wales and the Council for the Single Mother and Her Child in Victoria in order to fight for State support for themselves and to give each other moral support against still-existing prejudices which they have to face.

The single mother is probably treated more kindly than most other categories of people who eschew marriage and it is certainly the case that social toleration of her existence has increased. But it is still other women who are her champions. A survey of attitudes conducted in Victoria in 1972 showed that 'men were more likely to disapprove of single mothers *in general* and gave proportionately more negative responses over all five attitude items than women. *Most of the women in the sample gave only positive responses, while most men gave at least one negative* or mildly negative response.'[43]

The sanctions applied to women who do not marry are accompanied by an even more coercive set against married women who will not have children or who wish to decide for themselves how many, and when. These sanctions were part of the now-declining view that Australia ought to populate or perish. While this notion was prevalent, and it dominated social welfare and much economic policy for over fifty years, often in obvious contradiction to the wishes of the majority of the population, women were viewed as breeders who were to be forcibly encouraged to bear as many little Australians as possible. The most obvious weapons the State wielded here were laws on abortion and contraception.

Abortion is a criminal offence in every Australian state except

South Australia where the law was liberalized in 1970 to enable medical practitioners to recommend and perform abortions *if two doctors concur that continuing a pregnancy would be a greater risk to a woman's life or would carry a greater risk to her physical or mental health than if the abortion were performed.* As in other states it is also possible to obtain an abortion if there is a substantial risk that the child of the pregnancy would suffer from such physical or mental abnormalities as to be seriously handicapped. Under this law it is virtually impossible for a married woman who is childless or who has only one or two children to procure a legal abortion except under the last provision. She will be forced to go interstate for an illegal termination unless there is a risk of physical or mental abnormality. In both New South Wales and Victoria abortion is still illegal but for the past three years the number of abortions being performed both in registered hospitals and in illegal clinics has steadily increased. Abortion referral centres operate openly in the large cities.

This quasi-legal situation is possible because of a combination of two lower court rulings and the exposures of police collaboration and paid protection of illegal clinics in both Melbourne and Sydney.[44] But until abortion is legalized by statute it remains expensive, and only available to women who are aware of the rather devious routes necessary to procure a termination. The existing situation means that poor women, women in other cities or in the country who have neither the money nor the time nor the knowledge to search out the illegal clinics, will be reduced to begging for a legal abortion from their local doctor or hospital. The woman in this situation will be subjected to the vagaries or the whims of those who can decide, for reasons of personal prejudice, distaste or religious conviction or because the 'abortion quota' for that month is already full, that she ought to take her pregnancy to term. And while abortion remains quasi-legal, being performed in defiance of still existing Crimes Act clauses, the attitude of the police can change at any time. So while at the present time many Australian women have access to abortions when they need them, the State has reserved its right to remove that access whenever it chooses.

The likelihood of a change of law appears remote after the pressure group campaign and the voting of Federal politicians during the Medical Practice Clarification Bill which came before the Australian Parliament in May 1973. The Bill as presented to Parliament proposed to allow abortion on request up to the twelfth week of pregnancy and to allow abortions after that point if two medical practitioners agreed that continuation of the pregnancy would seriously endanger the woman's physical or mental health. The Bill applied only to the Australian Capital Territory. A highly organized and obviously well-funded campaign by the Right to Life organization, based on horror colour photos, distortions of medical facts[45], appeals to sentimental attitudes about babies – which were equated with foetuses – and a massive letter-writing campaign to politicians and newspapers and revivalist-type public meetings totally dominated the proceedings. The Bill was rejected ninety-eight votes to twenty-three.[46]

These attitudes to abortion are even more barbaric in the context of State policies on contraception. The Labor Government has revoked the grossest aspects of these. It removed the $37\frac{1}{2}$ per cent tariff import tax which had previously been applied to all imported rubber contraceptives, and all female rubber contraceptives *were* imported, and has abolished the $27\frac{1}{2}$ per cent 'luxury' sales tax on all contraceptives. Oral contraceptives have been placed on the pharmaceutical benefits list, thereby reducing their cost to fifty cents a packet. Family planning clinics have at last been recognized as deserving of federal funds. These changes have all occurred since 1972 and are a catalogue of the various measures which were employed to make knowledge of contraception difficult for women to procure and to keep the contraceptives themselves very expensive. The advertising of contraceptives is still legally prohibited in most states and even though family planning clinics have been assured that they will not be prosecuted if they advertise their services 'tastefully', this concession hardly begins to meet the need to disseminate this information widely.

Women are still dependent on State paternalism and the medical profession's whims for controlling their fertility and while this situation persists the woman who lives her entire life without having to endure at least one unwanted pregnancy will be very lucky indeed. The coercion involved in this situation rather undermines the case of those who insist that it is 'natural' for women to want to bear children, as does the constant railing that those women who do not have them, or who delay having children for several years after marriage, are 'selfish'. This form of attack which has been used to induce guilt in women for the past fifty years is rather curious. It suggests uncertainty on the part of those arguing for childbearing; if the experience were as they extol it, surely those women who do not wish to have children need to have the joys they are missing pointed out to them. It can hardly be selfish to deprive yourself of something which you are convinced is nice. Self-sacrificing perhaps.

With such a range of negative sanctions in the form of attitudes and legal restrictions all reinforcing the idea that marriage and maternity are still necessary for female fulfilment – even if it is now being conceded that women may do other things *as well* – it is small wonder that many women find it difficult to reconcile their actual lives with their socialization. Women, especially those who are aged thirty and upwards now, are caught in an excruciating double-bind. Demographic and economic factors make it almost imperative that they take jobs outside the home, at least once their children are in school. But the sex-role ideology and the view that women can only fulfil themselves *as women* by being wives and mothers contradicts this.

Men learn that they can fulfil themselves as men through their jobs as well as through their sex roles and so they are not subject to the same double-bind. The male role does not have the same moral imperative attached to it, nor is it subjected to the same extensive examination and debate. Nor will men admit so readily to feeling insecure or unhappy with the demands of their sex roles. Men can be, and usually are, discussed outside the context of 'the family'. It is not considered necessary to know, say in a newspaper interview, whether or not a man is married and has children. It is possible to extract him and his job or hobby, or whatever it is that is of interest, from his family relations, whereas for women these are crucial. Women are still analysed and discussed as elements of a family and any extra achievements are things which are tacked on to that primary definition of their sex.

Much academic research on women perpetuates this tendency and the woman who feels the double-bind described above and who would like to be able to fashion some other means of self-definition will find little encouragement in the theories which emerge from institutions of research. For example, a much-quoted study of power relations within the family conducted by Dan Adler in 1957–58 concluded that 'the wife's leadership role in Australia compared with other Western cultures, is so prominent that it requires identification as the special social phenomenon which we call "matriduxy".'[47] He arrived at this conclusion by analysing who does what, who makes decisions and who carries them out within the family. After discovering that women both made more decisions and carry out more of them than their husbands he reached the amazing conclusion that this meant that women are more powerful than men within the family. This conclusion not only confuses activity with power, but, because it isolates the family group from its total economic and social context is completely unable to accommodate such factors as the husband's economic power, and, therefore, the wife's economic dependence.

Because the surveys were conducted amongst children – who were asked to list what their parents did – there were a further series of elements which were omitted from consideration. No account could be taken of sexual power, of the extent to which the wife can be forced into sexual activities against her will. In a society such as Australia where there is no legal recognition of rape within marriage, a husband immediately accrues an enormous armoury of oppressive mechanisms. He may not exercise them, but they are available to him. Further, the survey simply did not ask other pertinent questions. Maybe the wife decides many things but what else happens at home? Does the husband beat his wife or his children? The children were not asked this and the framework of the survey precluded them from volunteering such information. This survey obviously requires more detailed criticism than is possible here because its conclusions have been so widely disseminated and it has provided the justification for the conclusion that Australian women dominate their families to an even stronger degree than American 'Moms' are said to. It is obvious that when women are considered only in their family context then it will be found that, in comparison to men who have an entire working and recreational life outside 'the family', women are more active within that sphere, but this tells us nothing about the perceptions or the desires of the women. As has been pointed out before 'the family' is less and less able to provide for women the validation and fulfilment that it was once capable of doing. For women who are caught in this double-bind to be told that they are too powerful – for the finding is usually presented with a tinge of moral disapproval – is cold comfort indeed.

The second kind of thesis which is advanced about Australian housewives is that they are 'neurotic'. Such is the conclusion of Dr Francis Macnab of Melbourne's Cairnmillar Institute, a private consulting clinic which conducts therapy groups for unhappy women. Macnab believes that at least 70 per cent of women in Australia's urban communities are suffering emotional and, in some cases, physical hindrances through leading unfulfilled lives.[48] What he means by this is that many women find that they are discontented with their maternal and wifely roles and that this discontent is likely to become neurotic. In his view, women express this neuroticism by stating that they feel worthless, that their lives are empty and devoid of purpose and that they have little interest in their families. He finds these feelings incomprehensible and labels women who give voice to them as neurotic.

Macnab's views have been widely aired in newspapers and through the book *The Marriage Wilderness* which is a mouthpiece for Macnab's ideas and methods of treatment, and hundreds of women have been in therapy groups at the Institute. Yet the method of therapy adopted is a very restricted one because it is based on the assumption that the grievances aired by these women are personal rather than social problems. Although Macnab demonstrates compassion for the obviously unhappy women who seek his help, he sees the problems as personal ones which require personal solutions. He appears to have no understanding, or sympathy with, the kind of historical, demographic and economic explanations which have been advanced in this chapter to suggest why such feelings of self-abnegation are likely to be widespread amongst women. Rather than seeing these women as victims of social changes which have left them without life-fulfilling functions he instead blames women themselves – as the quotation at the beginning of this chapter suggests. Thus women who seek treatment for feeling guilty about their dissatisfaction are likely to have that guilt compounded when, acting on his advice, they try to find fulfilment in the traditional wife/mother role. That, I have attempted to show, is becoming increasingly difficult, if not totally impossible.

While it might still be possible for a woman to be completely happy and fulfilled for the first ten or even twenty years of marriage and motherhood, she is likely to find herself at middle age with her children grown up and left home, her husband devoting most of his waking hours to his work, and her previously busy life a dull and dispiriting void. We are confronted now with a situation which will not be alleviated simply by allowing that women can expand the traditional role slightly to incorporate paid work outside the home once the children have started school. As I have been arguing through-out this work, the whole notion of a sexual division of labour confined to a fairly rigid family structure is inherently oppressive. It is oppressive for both sexes but, as Chapters Four and Six argued, the results are more devastating for women. For long periods in our history this devastation was not evident simply because women were *busy* as wives and as mothers. But as women's familial work has contracted the oppressive nature of the structure is revealed and its limitations for providing self-fulfilment become more evident. Thus it is the *structure* of sexism and its supportive institution – 'the family'– which requires renovation and not the hapless women who are caught in its mesh. At present there is an overwhelming tendency to view this contradiction (or breakdown) of the traditional female role as being a problem for *women* and one that can be alleviated by women making enormous adjustments while the corresponding male roles remain static and unquestioned. At present women are being blamed for being unhappy about a life situation which they did not create and which they cannot control and they are then labelled as neurotic when they attempt to articulate the confused and directionless dimensions of that situation.

NOTES

1. For instance, Julie Rigg, ed., *In Her Own Right*, Nelson, Melbourne, 1969. Chapters 9 and 10; Graham Williams, 'Loneliness of the long enduring housewives', *Sunday Australian*, 22 August 1971, as well as many articles in the women's pages of newspapers over the past three years.

2. Denise Bradley and Mary Mortimer, 'Sex Role Stereotyping in Children's Picture Books', *Refractory Girl*, No. 1, Summer 1972–3, p. 14.

3. R. W. Connell, '*You Can't Tell Them Apart Nowadays – Can You?*' *Search*, July 1974, p. 283.

4. Students were instructed to write an essay entitled 'Reflections on My Life'. No guidance was provided as to how far into the future they were to project since I wanted to try and elicit from them how far their expectations extended. Four groups of girls from three schools were tested: (1) an exclusive private girls' school, (2) a high-school in a lower middle-class suburb; an 'A' stream and a commercial stream were tested, (3) a technical high school in a working-class suburb. Thus it was hoped to cover a wide spectrum of class and educational differences.

5. Betty Friedan, *The Feminine Mystique*, Penguin Books, 1968, p. 13.

6. Graham Williams, 'Loneliness of the long enduring housewife'.

7. Taken from *Facts and Figures*, Women and Work, No. 11. Women's Bureau, Department of Labour, Melbourne, September 1973, p. 5.

8. ibid. p. 13; *The Labour Force, February 1975*, Australian Bureau of Census and Statistics, 1975, p. 6.

9. ibid., p. 16.

10. *Ladies Line*, Vol. 6, No. 12, 10 June 1972, p. 50.

11. Barbara Thiering, *Created Second?* Family Life Movement of Australia, Sydney, 1973, pp. 19–20.

12. Reported in the *Australian*, 26 December 1973.

13. Reported in the *Australian*, 15 January 1974.

14. 'Australian wives smarter than their husbands?', Interview in the *National Times*, 8–13 May 1972.

15. *The Patterson Report or 'Wooing the Australian Woman'*, George Patterson Ltd, Sydney, 1972. Introduction.

16. 'It is an article of faith among the Australian market executives I talked to that women make 90 per cent of consumer decisions for the family; an academic survey suggests that they control at least two-thirds of family expenditure and that their influence may be pervasive in decisions about the other third. Even in those families where women have challenged the traditional division of roles, seeking to enter the world of ideas, sharing the task of providing or demanding the assistance of their men in tending home and family, the wife's role as chief consumer appears to prevail.' Julie Rigg ed., *In Her Own Right*, op. cit., p. 136. The same proposition is maintained by Janet Wolff, *What Makes Women Buy?* McGraw-Hill, New York, 1958, p. 280.

17. *National Times*, 15–20 May 1972.

18. A study of prestige and status awareness in Australia found women to be more sensitive to status differences in residential suburbs and occupations than men: women over-rated high prestige jobs and suburbs while giving very low ratings to lower prestige ones. Men's assessments were closer to the rank objectively assigned to the job or suburb. A. A. Congalton, *Status and Prestige in Australia*, Cheshire, Melbourne, 1969, pp. 31–2, 71–3.

19. Glennys Bell, 'Australian women love their magazines, and both are changing', *National Times*, 29 November – 4 December 1971.

20. Dennis Minogue, 'A war for women', The *Age*, 31 May 1975.

21. McNair Print Readership Survey, *National Magazine Readership Survey*, Sydney, Melbourne, Brisbane, Adelaide, Perth, 1972.

22. *Newagents' News*, No. 140, March 1973.

23. *Australian Financial Review*, 15 January 1973.

24. Madge Dawson, *The Australian Woman as Portrayed in Women's Magazines*, Paper delivered to A.N.Z.A.A.S., Adelaide, 1969.

25. Shirley Sampson, 'The Australian Women's Weekly Today', *Refractory Girl*, No. 3, Winter 1973, p. 14.

26. ibid., p. 17.

27. ibid., p. 15.

28. *Woman's Day*, 22 April 1974.

29. *Australian Financial Review*, October 1973.

30. Fay Chambers and Marthe Scott, 'Dolly is a girl like you', *Dissent*, No. 28, Winter 1972, p. 20.

31. *Australian Financial Review*, 9 December 1971.

32. W. D. Borrie, 'Recent Trends and Patterns in Fertility in Australia', *Journal of Biosocial Science*, Vol. 1, No. 1, January 1969, p. 65.

33. ibid., p. 67.

34. *Official Year Book of the Commonwealth of Australia*, No. 58, 1972, p. 164.

35. ibid., p. 174.

36. ibid., p. 178.

37. Jean I. Martin and Catherine M. G. Richmond, 'Working Women in Australia' in *Anatomy of Australia*, Sun Books, Melbourne 1968, p. 197.

38. Ronald Conway, *The Great Australian Stupor*, Sun Books, Melbourne 1971, p. 135.

39. The Communist Party of Australia which professes to oppose the institution of the family reinforces it in practice by offering lower admission prices for married couples to its social functions, that is, treating a married couple as a unit rather than as two individuals. This is without enquiring whether or not the wife has an income of her own.

40. Ronald Sackville, *Social Welfare for Fatherless Families in Australia: Some Legal Issues*, Australian Council of Social Service, 1972, p. 21.

41. ibid., p. 22.

42. ibid.

43. Rosemary Kiely, 'Social Attitudes to Single Mothers: a pilot study', *Melbourne Journal of Politics*, No. 5, 1972, p. 89. Emphasis added.

44. See Tony McMichael, ed., *Abortion: the Unenforceable Law*, Abortion Law Reform Association of Victoria, 1972, for several articles concerning the legal position in New South Wales and Victoria.

45. See Anne Summers, 'No Holds Barred as Battle Rages', The *Bulletin*, 12 May 1973 for an account of some of the distortions of medical facts used by Right to Life propaganda.

46. *Hansard, House of Representatives*, 10 May 1973, p. 2001.

47. Dan L. Adler, 'Matriduxy in the Australian Family' in A. F. Davies and S. Encel, eds, *Australian Society*, Cheshire, Melbourne, 1965, p. 155.

48. Patrick Tennison, *The Marriage Wilderness*, Angus & Robertson, Sydney, 1972, p. 6.

LETTER TO THE
NEXT GENERATION

FEAR OF FEMINISM

It is now more than twenty years since the modern women's movement began its profound social revolution, and we pioneers of that movement are now a generation older and starting to ask ourselves, What comes next? While we were immersed in the activism of the 1970s we rarely stopped to wonder about the future, or to ruminate on who would fill our shoes when the time came. Since we were so sure that the changes we had set in motion would endure, even if they took years to complete, I suppose we just assumed that the next generation of women, when they reached young adulthood, would stand alongside us and keep the movement, and the fight, alive.

So I was at first horrified, and then mortified, to encounter during the 1980s young women who regarded we feminists of the 1960s and 1970s as being utterly remote from them and *their* lives and ambitions. We were, after all, a mere generation apart. No chasm of history separated us and distorted who we were the way earlier groups of feminists were disconnected from us. So why did they look at us through such unsympathetic eyes? Was it us, or was it them? Was this just a generation gap – or something more profound?

When I first heard young women expounding their unflattering opinions of the women's movement, I largely ignored what they were saying. Or, as I had mostly *read* their remarks, I blamed the messenger, assuming the media had either misrepresented these young women or else sought out for interview people who were predisposed to be hostile. So what, I thought, if these young puppies want to call me angry, bitter, aggressive or manhating! It's not true, just as bra-burning was never true. Along with most of my contemporaries I was absolutely comfortable with my feminism, and no amount of name-calling was able to unsettle my convictions.

Nor could I imagine any young woman who wanted to do something with her life not being able to make the connection between the great array of choices now available to her and the battles we had fought. Wouldn't she acknowledge this? Wouldn't she feel something – gratitude? a debt? a responsibility to keep widening those choices for herself and her generation? To me, it seemed inconceivable that young women in their early twenties would not feel as drawn to the movement to increase women's opportunities as I had been when I was their age.

But, increasingly, I had to acknowledge, at least to myself, that this was not the way most young women saw it. As the evidence to the contrary piled up, I realised that my generation had a problem that we had to confront. The evidence revealed itself in various ways. Conversations with young women, listening to women talk about their lives during the market research conducted by the Office of the Status of Women in 1992, even my experiences with younger staff members when I was Editor-in-Chief of *Ms.* magazine all convinced me that feminists of my generation could no longer pretend – as so many still do – that we have successfully presented our case to young women today. The problem was eloquently articulated by a young American woman in an article that appeared in 1991:

Although feminism is, by definition, the theory of the political, economic and social equality of the sexes, the word has become abused and distorted. Fearing that feminism means becoming unfeminine, anti-men and ultimately alone, many women have distanced themselves from it. Feminism seems to present a social equivalent of Sophie's choice: which of our children will we let die – our heart or our mind, our attractiveness or our independence?[1]

Her words recalled for me an uncomfortable encounter during my time at *Ms.* when I had asked the younger staff members to come up with some story ideas for the magazine that reflected their interests and the issues they thought young women would respond to. These young women editors were, naturally enough, all feminists (why else would they be working at *Ms.*?) but I sensed they felt the magazine offered them little that was personally useful. Nevertheless I was unprepared for their response.

Instead of a list of story ideas, they came up with a critique of *us*, the senior editors. The message was very clear: they did not want to be us! They wanted the magazine to show them how they could avoid our fate which, they judged, was having had to sacrifice our personal lives on the altar of the women's movement. These young women knew us too well to adopt the conventional wisdom and see any of us as bitter or angry or man-hating but, what was worse, they felt sorry for us! Most of them wanted to marry, or at least find partners, and to have children and they were having trouble identifying with a women's movement, and a magazine, whose veterans' own lives seemed to imply this was impossible.

It was then that I understood how little we have left for those who follow – how we have failed to explain ourselves, what we did and why, the choices we made, the consequences we accepted (or at least became reconciled to). I realized that we must write our history, record who we were and what moved us. I had looked around at my colleagues at *Ms.* and seen a group of strong, independent women, with great jobs, in control of their lives and who I assumed considered themselves far better off then any previous generation of women; that was how I felt about myself, at any rate. *They* had looked at us and seen a bunch of sad and lonely people who lived only for their jobs and their politics and they had pitied us. I knew then that I had to address the fact that so many women, including young feminists, feel alienated both from the women's movement of my generation and from we women who have made it our lives.

So let me begin.

Anyone can read this letter but it is addressed especially to women who were born after 1968, to you who are the daughters of the feminist revolution. The world began changing for women as you were being born, and as you have grown, so too have women's expectations and opportunities. By the time you came of age, the changes were so great that the world was almost unrecognizable to women like myself who had come of age as you were being born. There have been few periods in the past when women's prospects have expanded so dramatically in such a short time and even though they so far have fallen short of what we wanted, we could judge it a good beginning. We could feel some satisfaction that you, the daughters of our revolution, would find the world a more hospitable place for women than we had.

Some of you may be pleased with this inheritance, others may regard it with scepticism; most of you probably just accept without reflection the world as you find it. Whichever way you feel, you are, like it or not, the custodians of the future and I urge you to become acquainted with your recent past so you can gain some perspective on your lives today. You may not be able to imagine a world where married women were not allowed to be permanently employed teachers (or any other professional on the government payroll), where pregnant women could be fired, where you could be refused a job or a course of study because you were female, where abortion was illegal and dangerous, where it was the law of the land to pay women only 75 per cent of the male wage, but this was the world into which *I* came of age in the mid-1960s. Then, women Members of Parliament were rare (and the handful who were there mostly occupied seats left vacant by the deaths of their husbands or fathers); the only women we saw on news and current affairs television were the 'weather girls'; it was virtually unheard of for women to be managers or bosses, except of other women, and only then in what were considered women's occupations, like nursing where they still had to defer to the male doctors and administrators; women were starting to go to university in large numbers but more often to find a husband than to acquire career training, and the thought that a woman would retain her own last name after marriage was considered a dangerous and rebellious act. Not that it happened often.

One of the reasons I decided to add to, rather than rewrite and update this entire book was because I felt strongly we need to preserve a picture of our recent past. With the exception of the historical chapters, most of this book stands as a snapshot of how it was for women, and men, in the mid-1970s when it was first published. If the portrait of Australian society it presents seems unbearably quaint and old-fashioned, I hope it can thus serve as a measure of how much has changed in less than twenty years. If you contrast your life today with the description of how life used to be, you will have some idea of what we have won – and what you must never lose.

Past waves of feminism seldom lasted more than a generation, so there was rarely an opportunity for the old to speak directly to the new. There was little possibility of passing the torch. Today there is some connection. Even where it is marked by misunderstanding or even repudiation, our generations are contiguous and we can, if we choose, talk to each other. I am optimistic enough to believe that many of you want to maintain the momentum and keep pushing forward. Some of you even seek guidance or inspiration from us; in doing so, you are more embracing than we were.

As we young women began our rebellion I was struck by the way the earlier generation of feminists reached out to *us*. They were excited about us, so glad that their movement was reviving, and they wanted to know all about us. One evening, during a women's liberation meeting in the inner Sydney suburb of Glebe, an elderly neighbourhood woman stormed through the doors and exclaimed to the startled group inside, 'I've been waiting for you women all of my life!' But Bessie Guthrie was an exception with her uncritical enthusiasm; the gulf between us and them was enormous – far greater than that which separates us from you. Most of these women were our grandmothers' age and they could not understand, or approve, the way we dressed, the crudity of our language or our obsession with sexual issues. We, in turn, felt no connection to them. We did not even call ourselves feminists, a word we judged to be old-fashioned. Feminists, we thought, were quaint relics with their fixations on peace, abstinence from alcohol, and an obscure concept called rights. We weren't for women's rights, an old-fashioned notion I associated with fighting for the right to vote and other long-past issues; we were women's liberationists! Quite a different thing altogether. Oddly, at the time most of us did not see ourselves as part of the peace movement; we were anti-war, the Vietnam War in this case, which we took to be a more aggressive and radical stance than the passive protests of the peace movement. It was some years before we realized they were two sides of the same coin.

Yet we were flattered by the attention of these older women and their efforts to understand us. The first time it happened was on International Women's Day 1969 when I was invited by the Adelaide branch of the Women's International League for Peace and Freedom to come to their celebrations and tell them about this new group of angry young women. I was not the key speaker; that honour rested with the distinguished jurist Roma Mitchell, the first Australian woman Queen's Counsel and, subsequently, Supreme Court judge, later a Dame of the British Empire and the nation's first woman governor. After speaking for only a few minutes, I was astonished to hear Dame Roma say, 'I'm going to stop now because we all want to hear about this new women's liberation' and suddenly the spotlight was on me, a 24-year-old student facing a roomful of women in their fifties and sixties, trying to find the words to tell them that a revolution was underway.

A few years later, this time in Sydney, a friend and I received an invitation, conveyed by a quavering voice over the telephone, to have afternoon tea with Ruby Rich. By then, I had begun researching this book and was becoming familiar with the names of early Australian feminists, so I knew about Ruby Rich. Almost fifty years earlier she had founded a society in Sydney to disseminate sex education literature (see pages 436-37), a radical act in those days, and she had fought all her life for women. She was now in her late nineties, frail but alert, and eager to give us advice. It was not an easy meeting. My friend and I had made concessions (we were respectful and we wore dresses instead of our usual jeans) but the more than seventy years that separated us was simply too great; it became easier to ask her about the past than to explain what we were all about.

It is almost the opposite today. Now it is the older women who are impatient with the young, unable to understand why so few of you are embracing the women's movement, why you seem to reject us and all we stand for when you mouth that anthem of the 1980s, 'I'm not a feminist, but . . .' Yet I am not as dispirited as some of my contemporaries. I think you are there but, like us, you will do it in your own time and in your own way. I also recognize that for many of you, being the daughters of a revolution is far more difficult than was being on the front-lines of the battle for change. I hear this in conversations with women who are exhausted with the effort of trying to 'have it all' and wonder why equality and opportunity have to be such hard work. I watch women all around me trying to come to terms with a world which is still confusing, contradictory and often so combative as to make you sometimes wonder how much things really have changed.

I don't want to wait until I am ninety-eight to try and explain to a 25-year-old what moved me and so many of my generation to activism and revolt. I want, while there is still some chance of communicating, to tell you the story of the modern women's movement. I want you to know how it started, what we did, and what it did to us. In hearing our story, I hope you will also learn something about yourselves, about where you stand in this great movement of change, and that it might just move some of you to reach out for the torch. It is time for it to be passed.

OUR STORY

It is astonishing that the group which learned the hard way that history belongs to those who write it has not yet written its story. We had to delve through dusty library shelves to get just the bones of the story of the women who preceded *us* fifty or so years earlier, and one of our demands soon became that women's history be taught in schools and universities so that the circumstances and accomplishments of our gender were no longer 'hidden from history'.[2] Because our history was rarely written, or failed to be absorbed into the mainstream of the story of our civilization, each new wave of activists has almost always had to begin all over again: making the case for women's rights, arguing against those who would deny us equality, reaching back into the past for reassurance that others have been there too. I remember my excitement at discovering the battles waged to win votes for women by *fin de siècle* English and Australian suffragettes. It was chastening to realize these women of my grandmother's generation were far more militant than we young women's liberationists of the 1970s – they horsewhipped Cabinet Ministers, they chained themselves to public buildings, they went to prison and, once there, went on hunger strikes and were forcibly fed by barbaric methods which often ruined their health and shortened their lives. I found it astonishing that I had completed a high school education without even hearing about these women warriors.

Yet we soon became so engrossed in discovering the past, and so absorbed in redefining the present, that we neglected to record the evolution of our own movement and our struggle in any permanent and continuingly accessible form. The history of the modern women's movement in Australia remains to be written.[3] There have been two or three engrossing histories of the early days of the American movement[4] but there is nothing to match the literature other contemporary revolutions, like the civil rights movement, have spawned. We told our story as it happened, in pamphlets and small-circulation newspapers, in now out-of-print anthologies or hastily published books. It still exists, difficult or impossible to retrieve unless you know exactly what you are looking for[5] but no one has yet drawn on this material to produce a book or movie or television programme which could become a more enduring record of what it was like to be there, on the crest of an exhilarating wave of radical social change.

They were intensely exciting times. The first subversive thoughts of women's liberation trickled in from the United States when I was in my early twenties and still at university (I was a late starter!), and my friends and I embraced them hungrily. Here were notions that made so much sense. It was *true*, we realized with that flash of empathy that forever changes one's life, that while we were all passionately espousing the cause of liberation for oppressed peoples everywhere (people of colour, Third World people, students, workers, and so on) oppression stalked our own daily lives. It had not even occurred to the radical groups of the 1960s which boldly demanded the transformation of the state, the military, the corporation and the classroom, to question the inequality which governed relations between women and men. Once we women began to apply the language of liberation to ourselves, and to insist that *we* be part of this radical restructuring of society, there was no looking back.

Everything was suddenly open to question; not just why women should have to resign from permanent employment in government jobs upon marriage, but also why women were waiting hand and foot (making coffee, cranking mimeograph machines, performing sexual favours) on the male radicals of the anti-Vietnam War movement. Not

just why abortion was illegal, obliging women with unwanted pregnancies to resort to dangerous and expensive back-yard operators, but why there was no child-care despite the increasing numbers of women in the work-force. Not just why women received on average 60 per cent of men's wages even when they were doing the same work, but why university text-books in literature, history, politics (you name it) contained virtually no references to women. Not just why victims of rape could not press charges unless there were collaborating witnesses, but why advertisers persisted in using women as sex kittens to sell products as diverse as automobiles and lawn-mowers. Why? Why? Why? we asked, and of course asking the question was the first step to finding its answer.

The ideas, the theories, the speculations came tumbling out, as if they had simply been damned up inside the collective unconscious of women for decades; as of course they had. We soon discovered that Simone de Beauvoir had said most of it back in 1949 in her landmark work *The Second Sex*, that Betty Friedan had documented contemporary suburban women's relegation to child-like second class status in *The Feminine Mystique* in 1963, and that for hundreds of years women had been writing passionate tracts about the unequal treatment of their sex. Names like Aphra Behn, Mary Wollstonecraft, Harriet Martineau, Charlotte Perkins Gilman, Christabel Pankhurst and Vida Goldstein soon became familiar as we dug up our past. In no time at all, a contemporary lexicon of new words was invented to name the problem – male chauvinism, patriarchy, sexism – and women's liberation and, ultimately, feminism to describe the solution.

Because the late 1980s and early 1990s have been such depressed and gloomy times, characterized at national levels by economic scarcity and political inertia, it is difficult to recall, let alone relive, the optimism and exuberance of twenty years ago. Then, we had immense faith that we really could change the world. Even when the obstacles appeared overwhelming – and several thousand years of patriarchy was no small stumbling block – we fervently believed reform, if not revolution, was achievable. It was partly because we lived in an era when immense change was taking place (civil rights legislation had been passed in the United States, the tiny nation of North Vietnam was staving off the military might of America, student protests on campuses around the world had produced unprecedented changes in university structure and curriculum). From the perspective of today, an era that has seen the collapse of communism in Eastern Europe and the dissolution of the Soviet Union, these might not appear very significant. Historical hindsight might produce the judgement that these victories were transient or hollow: the civil rights legislation was systematically reversed by the United States Supreme Court, the North Vietnamese victory produced a dictatorship which drove thousands of their people away in boats, and campus reform in many places evolved into an often tyrannical stranglehold on universities by mediocrities who proclaim their ideological soundness to dictate intellectual endeavour. But no retrospective recantation can steal the faith we felt then that change would happen because it was necessary, and it was right.

It might at first seem paradoxical that we women who were young as the 1970s dawned should be so receptive to feminism. We were the first generation of women to have opportunity and choice; we had known neither war nor economic depression; many of us, like me, were the first members of their family ever to attend university; we had the contraceptive pill and could be sexually active without paying the price of an unwanted pregnancy; we expected to have jobs, if not careers, and to be economically independent. If anyone had told me as I entered my twenties that I should be fighting for women's rights, I would have laughed and said, We have everything we want. And so it seemed. Except there were inconsistencies and contradictions, even if at first we did not pay them much attention. If we took note of the fact that all our university teachers were men, with the occasional exception of a lowly tutor, we thought nothing of it; it certainly did not occur to us that we could not aspire to be university lecturers. If we even noticed that the politicians who governed our country were all men, it did not concern us because we were not interested in politics.

We were, in fact, conditioned to accept the invisibility of our sex. Nor did we realize it then, but we had also been conditioned to accept limitations on our ambitions; *because* we seemed to have an array of options denied to our mothers or grandmothers, and because we had not yet really begun to test ourselves against a wider world so had not encountered outright discrimination, we were scarcely aware it was there. The things we *did* notice, like the way men felt they could patronize us or expect us to wait on them even though we were, as students, supposedly their equals, were irritants but we did not immediately see what we could do about them.

My first glimmering that I was too accepting of an order of things that was inherently unjust to my sex came in 1966 when I read a long article entitled 'Women: The longest revolution' by the British writer Juliet Mitchell.[6] Mitchell selected four areas for analysis: production, reproduction, socialization and sexuality – and with the kind of Marxian precision that was so fashionable back then produced a compelling argument that, despite our supposed advances, women were still second-class citizens who were not treated equally in any of the worlds to which we thought we belonged. I did not need to be told twice! When I compared my life with her exposé, I could see the truth of what she was portraying. Sure, I was able to attend university but I was studying arts; it had never occurred to me, and no one had ever suggested that I consider law, or medicine or engineering. Sure, I could choose whom to marry and we could expect an equal relationship but once there were children, there was no question as to whose responsibility those children were even if it meant setting aside my career aspirations.

These were provocative thoughts and I shared them with my women friends. We started to look at the world differently, we began to notice things, and to be angry about what we had previously taken for granted. Why, we asked, should we have to settle for second best? It was *because* the door had opened partially for us, because our expectations had been raised, that we could not settle for anything less than everything.

So when a year or two later we heard the first whispers of women's liberation we were ready. Juliet Mitchell had provided us with the cool logic, the rational underpinnings of the case for women to be up in arms; now the American women injected passion, anger, irreverence and wit. They named things in ways which instantly and gratifyingly changed the way we saw things. Yes! cock rock was the perfect description of the all-male world of rock'n'roll. Yes! A woman's place *is* in the House – and the Senate! Yes! Male chauvinism did describe the arrogance and domination of the men in the anti-war movement (and the rest of the world too). The American women talked about equal pay, and child-care, and equal education and all the serious issues, but they also brilliantly honed in on the culture of degradation and exploitation. They staged protests at beauty pageants, they attacked advertising which belittled women, they dumped their bras in garbage bins. We were delighted - and certainly not too proud to imitate their actions. We revelled in the serious fun of it all. We learned that even our orgasms weren't equal! When I saw the expressions of outrage and anger on the faces of the engineering students at Adelaide University the day a couple of us budding women's liberationists tacked onto trees outside the student library posters advertising our latest American import, a pamphlet called 'The Myth of the Vaginal Orgasm', I knew we had really started something!

The American women also devised the emblem which instantly became the logo for women's liberation worldwide: the clenched fist inside the biological symbol for women. They reached into the past to retrieve the colours used by the suffragettes, purple for valour and white for purity, and these became our colours (although we sexually adventurous young women could not really emphathize with the purity part, we quickly adjusted its meaning to refer to our political goals). Soon the purple and white women's liberation badges were part of our daily uniform; for special occasions, like an International Women's Day march, we sported T-shirts with the same proud, defiant symbol emblazoned across our breasts.

Women learned, too, to have faith in each other. At first it seemed odd to attend meetings of only women – and we found ourselves justifying and defending it in the face of wails of criticism from those who were excluded – but we gained an unaccustomed strength in speaking our minds in this new, non-judgemental setting. We also discovered what it meant to share our common experiences as women, to 'raise our consciousness' about the many ways we felt put down and put upon because of our sex.

Armed with this invigorating confidence, a product of our new consciousness, we exploded into political action. We held demonstrations outside beauty contests, we handed provocative pamphlets to startled people on city streets, we published newspapers and magazines. It all happened very quickly; within a few months of attending my first women's liberation meeting with a handful of other students in Adelaide in 1969, I was off to Melbourne and to Sydney for the first national conferences. Within a year we numbered ourselves in the hundreds and not long after that we were suddenly so large that we began to have factions, to split into radical and reformist wings and to begin an argument which persists to this day as to the most effective ways to get what we want.

Australian feminists were, in my belief, fortunate to have burst onto the political scene just as Australian politics was emerging from the long conservative hibernation of the Menzies years. In late 1972 the Whitlam Government was elected, the first Labor government for a generation, with a mandate for reform which included a commitment to women's issues. By contrast, in the United States, the Nixon Administration coincided with those years when the women's movement was at its most energetic and most enthusiastic. There was no interest in a feminist agenda on the part of that Administration; indeed Richard Nixon vetoed a comprehensive child-care Bill in 1971, the same year his conservative Australian counterpart Sir William McMahon in the dying days of his government committed federal money to a small child-care initiative which would be built upon by successive administrations in Canberra. The Whitlam Government's promises to women were the result of pressure from the women's movement, especially the Women's Electoral Lobby (WEL), which polled all candidates in the 1972 elections for their attitudes on a range of women's policies, but the presence of this reformist government in turn created a pressure on *us* to engage with it. The distinctive pragmatism of the Australian women's movement was born in those years. Unlike the American movement which, after two decades of political disappointments[7] and something of a retreat into personal and cultural issues, was in the early 1990s having to re-learn electoral politics, Australian feminists quickly learned to grapple with the intricacies of the government submission and the techniques of lobbying politicians and bureaucrats.

The results were astonishing. A flurry of reforms at both State and federal level quickly altered the legal landscape, and before the untimely demise of the Whitlam Government (after only two and a half years in office), funding for women's refuges, rape crisis centres and other women's services had been put in place. It soon became a logical consequence for feminists themselves to start entering government and become advisors on women's policies or, in some cases, administrators of the policies they had stomped the streets to achieve. By the mid-1970s, that other distinctively Australian feminist accomplishment, the femocrat, or feminist bureaucrat, was born and as we entered the 1990s these women could be found working at various levels throughout the commonwealth and State public services.[8]

Although feminism very quickly became an international phenomenon, at least in the industrialized world, distinctly national styles of feminism simultaneously evolved. Australia was no exception. Australian feminists certainly drew on the thinking and the agendas of women in the United States and, to a lesser extent, Britain but it was not long before we grew impatient with being mere imitators and began to fashion our own programmes, deciding what were the priorities for Australian women, and developing our own strategies for addressing these.

A good example of this was the way we tackled the terrible problem of violence against women. At first we just discussed the issue. Although we had our theories about why men were violent towards women we did not immediately see what we could do about it, then several searing experiences made a number of us determined to do something concrete and practical. The first such experience was a personal one.

Late one evening, at home with the two friends with whom I shared a house in inner-city Sydney, we heard a pounding on our back door. We were startled, and a little frightened, because our back-yard was inaccessible except through the house. We rushed through the kitchen and found a young woman with a baby standing at our door. She was in a state of complete terror and begged us to take her in; once inside she told us her husband had been beating her and to escape she had clambered over the 8-foot high fence which separated our back yards. I could scarcely believe how she had managed such a feat, let alone with a baby in her arms, and I suddenly understood the desperation of a woman who fears for her life at the hands of a violent husband. I knew then that the women's movement had to do something immediate and concrete to help women escape permanently from such violent situations. Within a week a small group of us began meeting to decide what to do.

We knew of Erin Pizzey who had started a refuge for battered women somewhere in the north of England and we decided to do the same. I phoned Erin to talk to her about how she had got started. It was not an especially satisfying conversation as she was obviously stressed, babies were screaming in the background and there was not a lot of relevant advice she could provide. Just do it, she said, and that was really all we needed.⁹ We began looking for a house.

At first, I thought we could persuade someone to give us one. I approached a number of Sydney property developers and explained what we wanted, and tried to make the idea attractive to them by pointing out the favourable publicity such a gesture would bring. (At the time, developers were getting a very bad press for the heedless manner in which they were tearing down historic inner-city houses and replacing them with ugly high rises.) Only one responded and the house he offered us was not suitable because, apart from being totally derelict, it was on a very busy street and we thought it would be neither restful for women seeking refuge nor safe for their children. Then I remembered a recent ABC television documentary which had exposed the role of the Church of England as a slum landlord in the inner-city suburbs of Sydney; the programme had revealed that as properties became vacant they were being warehoused in the hope they could be sold to the federal government for its proposed new public housing scheme.

I began a systematic survey of all vacant Church of England-owned houses and I knew I had struck gold when I found myself standing outside a pair of tiny semi-detached cottages in Westmoreland Street, Glebe. They appeared to be in reasonable condition, and seemed to have working plumbing, they were in a quiet tree-lined street in a neighbourhood that probably had a higher density of feminists than any other part of Sydney – and they were unoccupied. One of the houses even had a woman's name: Elsie.

All this happened in February 1974. Early in March, to mark International Women's Day, a huge two-day speak-out on violence was held at the Teachers' Federation auditorium in Sussex Street. It was an emotionally wrenching experience to listen as woman after woman stood up and told her story. We heard women tell of being raped, of being beaten, of being intimidated, of living in fear. Many of these women were telling their stories for the first time, finally able to reveal what had seemed a shameful secret. By the end of the first day, there was not a woman present who was not weeping in empathy and seething with rage: we had to *do* something. The next afternoon I rose to speak. Mine was not a personal story, I said. My purpose was to tell everyone about the plans a small group of us had to establish a refuge for women wanting to escape from violence – and to invite them to join in. The next Thursday, at our final planning meeting before seizing Elsie, more than 100 women turned up. We explained that we intended to break into the house we had found, change the locks and thereby establish legal tenancy, and then try to shame the Church of England into letting us remain there rent-free until we could approach the federal government for funds to run the refuge. Security was paramount, we warned, because we did not want the police to be there to prevent us gaining entry. We did not disclose the address but asked everyone to meet us on Saturday morning in a nearby street from where we would march to our destination.

It was accomplished with utter ease. Once we had taken possession of the two houses, we rang all the television networks and announced to the world that Australia's first women's refuge was now open for business. We organized ourselves into rosters to ensure Elsie was open 24 hours a day – and waited for our first woman to show up. She came three days later, a Scottish woman with two small boys who had been beaten by her husband for years but because she had no family in Australia had nowhere to go to escape him. She had seen us on television, and found her way in from Sydney's outer-western suburbs to our front door. Within a week the two houses were crammed full with women and children – and a new movement was born.

It was very quickly apparent that two little houses could not begin to meet the demand for refuge. Other groups began planning to establish new refuges in other locations and soon there were three, then thirty, in every city and every State. Within five years there were more than

100 refuges, all of them receiving at least some government funds. A great many of them, in tribute to the first, have women's names. The refuges established by the women's movement differed from traditional shelters run by religious or charitable organizations in several important ways. When members of our group had visited some of these places we found that women could not stay there during the day, nor could they leave their children while they travelled into the city to apply for emergency relief money. This meant that women had to find somewhere for themselves and their kids to spend more than eight hours each day, not an easy task in any city, and an almost impossible one for someone who is traumatized, often injured, and usually has no money. We resolved that *our* refuges (and we chose that name deliberately to differentiate them from the shelters run by these organizations) would provide women with total psychological, physical and economic support. 'The Refuge would be a living and working community based on autonomy and self-management, in which we would put into practice the Women's Movement's organizational principle of collectivity,' explained Vivien Johnson in her account of the Marrickville Women's Refuge, which opened its doors in April 1976.[10]

Australian feminism thus began a unique pattern of directly providing services to women in need. In doing so, we soon learned that we also had to become skilled in the art of supplicating governments because it cost money to provide for the women who came to us. Elsie existed for nine months on donated food, furniture, clothing and labour but it was a hard, hand-to-mouth existence and sometimes we felt guilty that the women who came to us had to live in such squalid conditions. We were accused by other feminists of being reckless with these women's emotional lives by failing to provide them with privacy and stability. Most of the other refuges waited until they got government money before they opened. But if our way of doing it was foolhardy, it was undeniable that there was a desperate need for the service, a need which sadly to this day continues to grow. In 1990, 265 women's refuges received government funding.[11] We also learned that it was impractical and even dangerous to lump all victims of violence together. Women who had been raped could not be catered for by the refuge, and soon another group spun itself off and established the Sydney Rape Crisis Centre, a 24-hour telephone advice and referral service. I happened to be on duty late one night during our first few months when we received a call from a man who said he needed help: a woman friend of his had been raped by more than a dozen men after leaving a Balmain hotel the night before.

These experiences of direct contact with women who had suffered violence at the hands of men had two important and enduring influences on the direction of Australian feminism. They not only toughened us up, moved us quickly from being mere theorists to being providers of practical services, but they required us to become very pragmatic. This, I think, is one of the hallmarks of Australian feminism and one of its most attractive qualities. Although there has always been a great deal of internal debate within the movement about the extent to which our provision of services both absolves governments and other agencies from responsibility and props up rather than radically reforms an oppressive system, at the end of the day most Australian feminists would rather act than talk. Our commitment to improving women's lives is real, tangible and enduring. It is a tradition of which we can be proud, and a legacy I hope you will embrace.

The past twenty years have not been without their set-backs. Governments have either reduced spending on programmes which fund services like refuges or have failed to allow them to grow in real terms. Many women were especially hard hit by the economic recessions of the early 1980s and 1990s, and their real levels of unemployment failed to be accurately recorded in official statistics. In many areas of employment, the initial rush of progress seems to have stalled and women complain that their prospects for promotion and higher earnings, especially in the corporate sector, seem as remote as ever.

But in surveying more than twenty years of accomplishment, the women's movement is entitled to feel some satisfaction, and to recognise that far more has been won than has been lost. For instance the commitment to meet total demand for child-care, especially, and its announcement as part of a general economic statement rather than in the women's package during the 1993 election campaign, represents a quantum leap forward, an acknowledgement that women's claims are integral to the political process. So, why don't more feminists, especially those of my generation, feel more of a sense of pride? Why is there widespread despondency, paranoia even, and a tendency to downgrade our achievements, dispute their legitimacy, even their existence, and to concentrate on negatives, on what hasn't changed at the expense of what has?

I think we are actually more pleased with ourselves than many of us are prepared to let on; no one who grew up in the 1940s or 1950s, or even the 1960s, can seriously claim that women's choices and opportunities are not immensely greater than they were then. But it is not really in the makeup of rebels to rest on their laurels, or to announce that the war is over; there is always another issue, a fresh outrage, a dire cause to command our attention and keep us battle-ready. It is our continual pointing out of what remains wrong which I think causes many younger women to be wary of us, to consider us as too negative (read: anti-men), too pessimistic, too depressing, and not therefore adherents of a movement they would want to join. Who wants to be constantly portrayed as a victim? To have only the down-side pointed out without the balancing reminders that life is not all unremitting gloom? We have too frequently lapsed into a kind of ghetto mentality, and have been too inclined to point out continually how women are put upon, forgetting that most women are happy enough just to try and get on with their lives. This tendency has made the movement unalluring to women who want to feel (and who indeed are) confident and assertive and ready to deal with the world on their terms.

Did we pay a price? Most of us did. Very few marriages or relationships were able to survive the first ferocious years of feminism. Then, as now, women were the prime instigators in ending relationships that no longer suited them. Most of us felt unable to continue in arrangements that had been contracted on the old, unequal terms, and many men retreated bruised and puzzled at their misfortune at having their wife or girlfriend fall under the sway of these radical new ideas. It was not uncommon when this book was first published for men I did not know to approach me and blame me for the breakup of their marriage! Many of us went for years unable to find a relationship that satisfied both our emotional and our political needs. Many women today still can't, because most men have still not been able to adapt to the new realities of women's lives. This has been pointed out by social researcher Hugh Mackay who has described 'the widespread failure of Australian men to adapt their behaviour to match the redefinition of gender roles which has taken place in the minds of women'.[12] Many women have preferred to live alone rather than endure the never-ending battle. Many feminists of my generation are childless, a fact that worries some young women today. Do we have to choose between independence and our desire to have children? they ask. The answer is, No it should no longer be necessary. But a generation ago it was a tougher choice and many of us opted for independence at whatever price. (Many women had last-minute regrets about this and as my contemporaries neared the age of 40, there was a surge of single motherhood amongst those who decided they did not want to miss out on being a mother just because they did not have a husband or a partner. Not only has this trend continued, and been made famous by the United States television sitcom *Murphy Brown*, but changed social attitudes towards single mothers means that the kind of stigma that was still there even in the 1970s is no longer an obstacle.)

Younger women complain, too, that it is not easy to find men who understand that women today are different – and who approve of the changes. Younger men should be different too; after all they grew up to a changed world, and many of them have been raised by feminist mothers. Yet why are so many of them resistant? Why can't they see that a relationship between equals is more pleasurable and more satisfying than the traditional inequalities? It remains a sad fact that it is not just women of my age who are confronted with these hard choices; most of us will be, one way or another, until the human species completes its evolution towards true equality. We can take comfort from the fact that the choices are there for us; previous generations of women seldom had any choice but to comply meekly with the wishes of father and husband.

Not all the feminists of my generation have remained activist in the sense of belonging to groups and continuing to agitate for further change, but I can think of no one who has repudiated her feminism. Our lives, and our way of looking at the world, were so utterly transformed that the possibility of going back simply does not exist. Feminism became the filter through which we measured *everything*: books and movies, newspaper articles and politicians' pronouncements, day-to-day encounters and everyday speech. It is simply impossible for us not to flinch when we see or hear examples of sexism, it is likewise difficult for us to ignore them; even women who have retreated from organized activities are still in the trenches when it comes to contending with daily life. Those people who find this behaviour atavistic, who tell us that this kind of constant vigilance is now tedious, that we need to lighten up, simply can't comprehend the impossibility of what they ask.

There have been times, I admit, when my feminist filter has seemed like a burden, when I have become weary of always being the one to object to a remark, of being the spoiler or, worse, when people adjust their behaviour around me and, if they allow an ill-judged comment to slip out, apologize as if it were only my presence, rather than the inherent offensiveness of what was said, that was the inhibitor. I don't want to be anyone's moral guardian, a modern-day God's Police. A conversation or a comment which demeans women is obnoxious, not because I or another card-carrying feminist happened to overhear it, but because it relies on sexual stereotypes or reduces women to sexual functions. The only consolation I take from such situations is that by exhibiting some shame the apologist is at least acknowledging the extent to which attitudes have changed. Twenty years ago, when we first began to protest the everyday depictions of women as chicks or even cunts (to name just a couple of the labels we endured then), we were scoffed at: Waddya mean that's sexist? Back then, that was life. Today, at least defensiveness and squirming have replaced bafflement and bluff, and young women who have grown up in this somewhat improved environment would have to go back to old (say, 1950s or 1960s) movies and magazines to get some idea of how bad it used to be.

Similarly, when we survey our unfinished agenda it is easy to be overwhelmed by what lies ahead, and to discount what we have already accomplished, rather than take heart from a record in which progress has outpaced setbacks. The strong streak of negativism which has always characterized the women's movement could be seen as part of its Australianness (since Australians are generally prone to negative thinking) were it not for the fact that a similar attitude seems to pervade feminism in all developed countries.

No doubt because the odds were so enormous when we confronted centuries of patriarchal society, we girded ourselves with a protective armour of pessimism and paranoia but sometimes I think we forget how joyful and optimistic we were when we began. As our movement matured, and our programme for change became more complicated (especially as we developed internal disagreements about both substance and priorities), the early exuberance waned. Today, I think we understand that it is going to be decades before we see the final shape of the profound social revolution we unleashed; that recognition is profoundly depressing – particularly to those who fear that you, the women who are young today, are not ready to pick up the cudgels and continue the fight. We worry that our wins might be whittled away. That had begun to happen in the United States during the Reagan and Bush years where the legal right to abortion was under siege, a setback that thankfully was reversed after the election of President Clinton. We also wonder what will happen to the momentum for change if new energies and fresh visions are not brought to the task. Will women continue to improve their position in the work-place, and to increase their earnings relative to men, if pressure from the women's movement wanes? Will apathy replace activism and seem to signal that, once again, women are content with what they already have?

AN AGENDA FOR THE REST OF OUR LIVES

What disturbs me most is the prospect of a generation gap emerging in our agenda. As I have already explained, we pioneers will not let go, we cannot let go, but our focus is already beginning to change as we take on issues that are newly relevant to us as we become older. As we pursue these, we will have less time for matters that are no longer so pressing on us. When we launched ourselves into political action, we weren't doing it for posterity. We wanted a better world for ourselves. We still do. As we age, our issues are changing and so will our priorities. We are coming to the end of our reproductive years and are having to confront the condition of being no longer capable of maternity in a society which still overemphasizes women's maternal status. We are beginning to discover a whole new set of medical problems and social stigma associated with the onset of menopause. It is logical, I suppose, that the generation which launched the movement will have to see it through, and that new issues will emerge according to where we are in our life-cycle. (Twenty years ago we used to joke about setting up feminist retirement communities for when we got old; suddenly it is no longer a joke and we are starting to wonder, and to worry, about how to deal with being a physically frail and economically weak elderly woman after a life-time of being strong and self-sufficient.) What this means for you is that we will not always be there to fight for the things you need. You are the ones who will have to remain vigilant.

What will your issues be? You will have to decide, but I think it is likely that, as happened with us, you won't choose them – they will choose you. You will act if you find obstacles standing between you and what you want, or if an entitlement you assumed was yours forever looks like being taken away. The threat to legal abortion in the United States introduced to political action thousands of previously apathetic young women (and men). I hope Australian women will not have to contend with an emergency of this magnitude, but I do expect that you will at various times in your lives be drawn into action simply because there is still so much unfinished business.

You are able to have it all, in the sense that you are not forced by law or convention, as earlier generations of women were, to choose between marriage and family or a career. But simply being able to do it does not make it easy. It is often exhausting and debilitating, especially for those women in their thirties who are having babies just at the time their careers are at their most demanding. I know many young professional women who after struggling for a year or so to juggle this double-burden, take the reluctant decision to leave their jobs for a while, or to work part-time, because they can no longer endure the constant tiredness, the nagging feelings of guilt that they are short-changing their children during those early formative years, the never having any time to themselves. But this choice is often not guilt-free either. Many women feel they should be able to manage, and have to deal with feelings of inadequacy when they finally admit to themselves that they cannot. But it is not these women who should torture themselves with the thought they have failed. It is the individual employer, the industry, and the society as a whole which has failed them. We are not providing women with real choices if the price exacted from them is so steep; nor is this option open to every harassed working mother, since many families cannot survive without the woman's earnings.

We still have a long way to go in reconciling the demands of home and work. We have to make the work-place, and work schedules, more accommodating to the needs of working women, especially those with young children. We also have to stop seeing this as just an individual problem, or a women's problem. Men are involved too, as fathers, as employers, as co-workers. So is society at large: we all must share the responsibility for perpetuating our civilization whether we as individuals are parents or not. There is some recognition of this in the laws that now provide for maternity and parental leave, in government funds allocated to child-care, and in trade union and other campaigns to heighten awareness of the issues. But these gestures have barely begun to make an impact in individual work-places, and on the lives of most working parents. It is going to be a continuing battle, and one that will involve many of you in the most intimate way.

The other, even more intimate battleground is your love life. You will also be challenged to find new and more satisfying ways of reconciling love and independence. We all need both, but many women in previous generations had to choose. The terms of marriage, or a long-standing relationship, are inherently unequal when one partner is economically or emotionally entrapped, and for most of recorded history most women had no choice but to surrender their independence in return for economic support. We no longer need do that, but we have barely begun to learn how to relate to our lovers under our new circumstances. Everything now is open to question and negotiation, not just the mundane (like sharing housework) but the really important – Will our relationship be exclusive and committed? If one of us gets an exciting job offer in another city, will we both move? Will we have kids? If so, when and how many? Whose job is set aside if that becomes necessary while the kids are young? And so on.

Most of these subjects simply did not arise under the old, unequal terms of relationships. It was an uncontested assumption of marriage that where sacrifices had to be made, the woman would make them. If you no longer see it that way, it is a sign of how far things have changed. But the pace of change has been uneven and erratic, and I think it is fair to say that most men have not changed as quickly or as profoundly as most women have. Indeed a great many men saw no need for change – why, indeed, when the cards were stacked in their favour! – and continue to resist it. For many women of my generation, the battle was simply too wearisome, and they walked away from it, some of them into the arms of other women, or to a life of solitary freedom. Some of you may make similar choices, but most of you will want to love and live with men, and there is no escaping your need to have that love coexist comfortably with the other parts of your life. Today, too, we live in a world which is terrifyingly more risky than when I was young, and where trust between women and men has never counted for more. We can no longer be cavalier about sexual freedom when the price might be a sexually transmitted disease which, like AIDS, is fatal, or like chlamydia can lead to infertility. We are still groping towards understanding the consequences of these new perils for our love lives. It is widely predicted that we will become more conservative, that sexual fidelity will once more become cherished and as imperative as it was before effective methods of birth control. This perhaps is already happening, but we need to be wary that fear of the sexual jungle beyond our sexually safe little world does not become a new form of involuntary dependency, as constricting as economic dependence once was for women.

These are all difficult issues but they are in a sense the price of our success. They need to be worked out, and they will be, however slowly and painfully, and we will all be better off as a result. But we must not forget, you especially must not forget, that there are two even more fundamental freedoms without which everything else is merely academic. If you cannot control your fertility, and you have no means of economic sustenance, you can control nothing else in your life. You only start to have choices about your lives once you control these essentials. It might sound so elementary as to be barely worth saying, but I have to remind you because for most women these are very recent accomplishments, and for still too many women, they have yet to be won. If you are not in control of when and if you become pregnant, either by contraception, abstinence, or abortion if birth control fails, you are not in control of your life. An unintended pregnancy can end, or at least interrupt, your education, derail your job or career and, if you proceed with the pregnancy, burden you with a whole set of unavoidable responsibilities which will alter your life forever.

Similarly, if you are not economically self-sufficient, if you are financially dependent on another person, your ability to make decisions about your life is likely to be restricted. I saw this time and again with the women who came to Elsie. They had had no choice but to stay with violent husbands until the women's refuge movement offered them an alternative. A woman who has an income, even if it is a moderate income, can walk away from an intolerable situation; a woman who is dependent is destitute. It is obviously no simple matter for women to achieve economic self-sufficiency, especially when we still mostly do not receive equal pay, but it has to be part of the life goals of any young woman who wants to be in control of her life to try to get as much education and training as she can to allow her to earn sufficient income to be in charge of her life.

There are many other matters I could raise. I am all too aware that we still have to contend with ubiquitous sexism (in conversations, in advertising, in the media, in the arts and in most areas of our lives); violence against women, including sexual abuse of little girls (and boys), seems to be increasing; employment discrimination, including sexual harassment, persists despite laws intended to prevent it; women are still a tiny minority in most areas of public and corporate life. I could go on. But I decided to concentrate on what I see as the fundamentals because I want to urge you never to lose sight of them. We have to be clear-headed about what is important – and what is essential. Once we understand that we must grasp the essentials and never let them go, the rest will eventually follow. I hope it will still happen in my life-time, but I know it will happen in yours.

NOTES

1. Susan Jane Gilman, 'Why the Fear of Feminism?', *New York Times*, 2 September, 1991.

2. This phrase became the title of a book by the British feminist Sheila Rowbotham published first by Pluto Press in 1973.

3. There have been some excellent books published which deal with segments of the movement, for instance, Marian Sawer, *Sisters in Suits: Women and Public Policy in Australia*, Allen & Unwin, Sydney, 1990, and Jocelyn Clark and Kate White, *Women in Australian Politics*, Fontana, Sydney, 1983. Others have recorded the contemporary stories or sentiments of activists, for instance, Ann Curthoys, *For and Against Feminism: A Personal Journey into Feminist Theory and History*, Allen & Unwin, Sydney, 1988, and Jocelynne A. Scutt (ed.), *Different Lives: Reflections on the women's movement and visions of its future*, Penguin, Ringwood, 1987. But there is no comprehensive history of the movement as such, its origins and diversity, its successes and setbacks. I was pleased to learn in late 1991 that

several such projects were, at last, in progress. I look forward to their publication.

4. See, for instance, Marcia Cohen, *The Sisterhood: The Inside Story of the Women's Movement and the Leaders Who Made it Happen*, Ballantine, New York, 1989, and Alice Echols, *Daring to be Bad: Radical Feminism in America 1967–1975*, University of Minnesota Press, Minneapolis, 1989.

5. Australian libraries, by and large, have done a good job in collecting the raw material as it was created. The Australian National Library, in particular, has an excellent collection of leaflets, small-circulation newsletters and magazines and even badges and T-shirts, as well as published books on the new feminism. The material is there, just waiting to be read.

6. See 'Women: the Longest Revolution', *New Left Review* No. 44, 1966; it was also published in greatly expanded form as *Women's Estate*, Penguin, Harmondsworth, 1971.

7. The failure to ratify the Equal Rights Amendment (ERA) to the constitution was a huge political and psychological defeat; its passage had seemed so certain as 30 of the 38 States needed for ratification had signed on in the first year (1973), but the momentum faltered and by 1977, when the deadline expired, only 35 States had ratified. Even though Congress in an unprecedented action allowed a three-year extension, by that time the anti-ERA forces had succeeded, through a hysterical and mostly inaccurate campaign of denigration, in turning public opinion against the ERA, leaving American women without constitutional guarantees of equality. During the 1980s, a similar campaign by anti-abortion forces succeeded in having the United States Supreme Court whittle away at women's constitutional right to legal abortion, guaranteed by the 1973 court decision *Roe v. Wade*. In 1986 *Webster's* decision weakened the federal ruling by allowing the States to regulate access to abortion and at the time of writing (early 1992), the Supreme Court was scheduled to review State laws which had the potential to be the occasion to reverse *Roe v. Wade* totally. The result would be that each State would regulate as to the legality of abortion and, given the anti-abortion composition of so many State Houses, the likelihood was that at least one-third of America's fifty States would make abortion illegal. No issue has galvanised the American women's movement more in recent times than this threat to abortion rights, and there has been a resurgence of energy directed at trying to elect women candidates who, in addition to being pro-abortion, would be supportive of other women's issues such as child-care and parental leave. In 1993 President Clinton promised legislation to protect women's right to abortion.

8. See Hester Eisenstein, *Gender Shock: Practising Feminism on Two Continents*, Allen & Unwin, Sydney, 1991, for an appreciation of the Australian femocracy by an American feminist who spent eight years living in Sydney and working as (what else) a femocrat. See also Sawer, op. cit.

9. See Erin Pizzey, *Scream quietly or the neighbours will hear*, Penguin, Harmondsworth, 1974, for her account of how she founded the first refuge for battered women in England.

10. Vivien Johnson (comp.), *The Last Resort: A Women's Refuge*, Penguin, Ringwood, 1981, p. 3.

11. See 'Women's Budget Statement 1990–91', AGPS, Canberra, 1990, p. 110.

12. Extract from Hugh Mackay, *Reinventing Australia, Australian*, 1 February 1993.